Income Distribution and Growth in the Less-Developed Countries

Charles R. Frank, Jr., and Richard C. Webb
Editors

THE BROOKINGS INSTITUTION / WASHINGTON, D.C.

THE BROOKINGS INSTITUTION is an independent organization devoted to nonpartisan research, education, and publication in economics, government, foreign policy, and the social sciences generally. Its principal purposes are to aid in the development of sound public policies and to promote public understanding of issues of national importance.

The Institution was founded on December 8, 1927, to merge the activities of the Institute for Government Research, founded in 1916, the Institute of Economics, founded in 1922, and the Robert Brookings Graduate School of Economics and Government, founded in 1924.

The Board of Trustees is responsible for the general administration of the Institution, while the immediate direction of the policies, program, and staff is vested in the President, assisted by an advisory committee of the officers and staff. The by-laws of the Institution state: "It is the function of the Trustees to make possible the conduct of scientific research, and publication, under the most favorable conditions, and to safeguard the independence of the research staff in the pursuit of their studies and in the publication of the results of such studies. It is not a part of their function to determine, control, or influence the conduct of particular investigations or the conclusions reached."

The President bears final responsibility for the decision to publish a manuscript as a Brookings book. In reaching his judgment on the competence, accuracy, and objectivity of each study, the President is advised by the director of the appropriate research program and weighs the views of a panel of expert outside readers who report to him in confidence on the quality of the work. Publication of a work signifies that it is deemed a competent treatment worthy of public consideration but does not imply endorsement of conclusions or recommendations.

The Institution maintains its position of neutrality on issues of public policy in order to safeguard the intellectual freedom of the staff. Hence interpretations or conclusions in Brookings publications should be understood to be solely those of the authors and should not be attributed to the Institution, to its trustees, officers, or other staff members, or to the organizations that support its research.

FOREWORD

During the 1960s, the less-developed countries were generally successful in attaining the economic growth objectives they had set for themselves. But they and such donor organizations as the World Bank and the U.S. Agency for International Development became increasingly aware that even rapid and large-scale economic growth may improve living standards of the poorest segments of the population little or not at all, owing to patterns of income distribution that restrict the extent to which the benefits of national economic growth are shared. In some instances, improvement in general economic welfare has even been accompanied by deterioration in the living standards of the poor.

This book represents part of the results of a project that was undertaken to promote better understanding of the relation between income distribution and economic growth in the developing countries. The project, financed by the U.S. Agency for International Development and carried out jointly by the Brookings Institution and the Woodrow Wilson School of Public and International Affairs at Princeton University, included a number of studies that sought to explain how government policies in various economic and social sectors of a given economy affect the distribution of income in the economy as a whole. The authors of the sectoral studies were asked to examine with particular care policies that might be effective in altering the distribution of income. They were also encouraged to collaborate with colleagues in other disciplines and to concern themselves with political, economic, and social influences on the desirability and practicality of policies designed to achieve income distribution objectives.

The project necessitated extensive statistical and data-processing activities. Sherman Robinson of Princeton and Richard J. Szal of Brookings collaborated in work on the theory of measurement of income distribution. Mr. Szal supervised a series of data surveys in six groups of countries in the developing world that, although not presented in this volume, were made available as working papers by the Princeton Research Program in Development Studies. Another activity of the project was the preparation of an extensive annotated bibliography on income distribution in the developing world by Gerald Epstein and Jean-Louis Terrier, portions of which appear at the end of this volume.

The book is organized in three parts. The first (chapters I and II) presents an overview of the broad theory and framework for analyzing income distribution policy. The second part (chapters III-XI) consists of the individual sectoral papers. The third (appendixes I-III) presents a statistical paper and two papers that apply mathematical techniques to the analysis of some of the issues. The authors presented and discussed their contributions to this volume at a series of workshops at Princeton Unviersity, culminating in a conference at Princeton in September 1974.

The editors of this volume, Charles R. Frank, Jr., and Richard C. Webb, were also the project coordinators. Throughout most of the project, Frank was a senior fellow in the Brookings Foreign Policy Studies program and Webb was associated with the Princeton Research Program in Development Studies. When they left their respective institutions as the project drew to a close, their coordinating responsibilities were assumed by Professor John P. Lewis of Princeton and Richard J. Szal, a Brookings research associate. All four project coordinators gratefully acknowledge the assistance of the staff of the Woodrow Wilson School, and especially that of the Research Program in Development Studies. Doris Garvey and Dorothy Reiger were particularly helpful. At Brookings, Mary Baird, Gerald Epstein, and Jean-Louis Terrier were indispensable in helping to administer the project and in bibliographical work.

The U.S. Agency for International Development not only provided financial assistance but also made available the helpful advice of Robert J. Muscat, Edward Cohn, and their colleagues in the agency's Bureau of Program and Policy Coordination.

Social scientists in developing countries took part in the project at various points. Especially worthy of note was a group of ten scholars who participated in a six-week seminar connected with the project that was held at Princeton in the fall of 1973. The group consisted of Drs. Hak-chung Choo (South Korea), A. O. Phillips (Nigeria), Indira Rajaraman and Kanta R. Ranadive (India), Oey A. Meesook (Thailand), Miguel Urrutia (Colombia), Carlos Geraldo Langoni and Maria Da Concepção Tavares (Brazil), Leoncio Durandeau (Mexico), and Alper Orhon (Turkey).

The project coordinators are also grateful to the sizable number of social scientists working in the United States who participated in meetings in 1973 and 1974 devoted to the preparation and review of the studies presented here. The involvement of Henry Bienen of Princeton and other political scientists was particularly useful. Finally, the editors are indebted to the three readers who served as reviewers and whose comments led to many improvements.

The views expressed in this volume are solely those of the contributors, and should not be ascribed to the Agency for International Development or to the officers, trustees, or staff members of the Brookings Institution.

BRUCE K. MAC LAURY

President

August 1977
Washington, D.C.

CONTENTS

LIST OF TABLES

INTRODUCTION

The Second Development Decade of the sixties witnessed unprecedented rates
of economic growth in many developing countries. Questions have been
raised, however, regarding the extent to which the fruits of this growth
have reached all segments of the population of those countries. Have the
hoped for spillover effects occurred, or have the benefits accrued primarily to those who control economic resources and/or political power? As
one response to these questions, increased concern is being shown in
developing countries because egalitarian goals are being neglected in
development plans.

In analyzing problems of developing countries, economists have generally tended to emphasize growth rather than distributive goals. Some
have suggested that these two ends are contradictory and that a redistribution of income would lead to lowered savings as a proportion of income,
and thus to a smaller growth rate of income, whereas if growth were given
primary emphasis, enlarging the pie, there would be ample benefits for
all. Others have pointed to recent empirical evidence which seems to
indicate that the effect of income redistribution on savings is minimal
and that other factors, such as the propensity of the poor to consume a
larger proportion of labor-intensive goods, can more than offset the negative impact of reduced savings on aggregate economic growth.

This volume is based on the findings of the Princeton-Brookings
research project on income distribution, growth, and public policy in
developing countries. The principal focus of the project is the question:
What can be done to reduce income inequality in developing countries?

A great deal of information relevant to this question had been accumulated by persons working in the development field. This information, the
result of both research and personal experience, had not been directed
toward a systematic evaluation of alternative income distribution policies
in a variety of country and policy settings. The present project was
therefore designed to meet the need for such an evaluation.

The main features of the project were, first, that it addressed itself to a broad range of policy areas, since all forms of economic policy have some potential distributive impact. Second, it focused on political and administrative as well as economic issues. In particular, the question of political feasibility was a central issue. A third and related feature was the stress on defining goals when considering the problem of income distribution. For example, Is the goal of redistributive policies to be the elimination of poverty, an increase in labor's share of national income, or a reduction in the inequality of the size distribution of income? Finally, the analysis of distributive impact covered both the direct effects, or "reach," of specific instruments and their indirect effects, chiefly on product and factor markets. Many of the distributive problems associated with specific policies arose precisely in the form of negative, or "backlash," indirect effects.

A special feature of the project was the diversity of people involved, either as authors of papers or as active participants in the discussions in an initial six-week workshop in the fall of 1973 and in several subsequent meetings, including a final conference in September 1974.[1] Included were specialists in the income distribution field from many developing countries, political scientists, many students with work experience in developing countries, officials from aid-giving institutions, and specialists in particular policy areas. The resulting broad range of views and experiences led to an emphasis in the project on the importance of specific settings; one of our main conclusions is that income distribution effects cannot be judged in general terms, since both the direction and size of those effects vary a great deal according to the economic, social, or political setting.

Of the many papers and studies prepared for the Princeton-Brookings project, the editors, also the directors of the project, selected eleven broad policy papers for inclusion as chapters in this volume. The first of these chapters, An Overview of Income Distribution in Less Developed Countries: Policy Alternatives and Design, by Charles R. Frank, Jr., and Richard Webb, attempts an overview of the lessons learned in the project—not only from papers prepared for the project (some not published here) but also from discussions in the related workshops, seminars, and conferences.

The second chapter, also by Frank and Webb, assesses the theories in literature on development and on income distribution in developing countries and the relation between these theories and policy choices having an impact on income distribution. This chapter sets the stage for a series of nine chapters that follow, each dealing with a specific policy field and the potential for using policy tools in different fields to influence income distribution. Each of the authors of these chapters was asked to answer the following questions:

(i) What is known about the effects of policies in a particular field on income distribution?

(ii) What definition of income distribution, or income distribution goal, is most likely to be affected by policies in the particular field?

(iii) What scope is there for policy change in this field? Specifically, what are the administrative and political factors involved in the change and implementation of policy?

Although the authors were urged to answer each of these questions in some detail, the resultant focus of each author was somewhat different. Depending on the author's individual tastes, state of knowledge in the field, and the difficulties of addressing each of the above questions, the chapters sometimes stress one of the questions and sometimes another.

Henry Bruton's study, Industrialization Policy and Income Distribution, argues that a more outward-looking, small-scale, and nonurban industrial policy, with fewer capital and labor pricing distortions, would generate both faster growth and a faster increase in low-end incomes, though a rising profit share must be accepted as a necessary cost of such a strategy.

Frederick Harbison's chapter, The Education-Income Connection, stresses the differences between formal schooling, organized nonformal education, and work-related skill generation, and uses international data to reveal the unequal allocation of formal education within most developing countries.

Bryan Boulier's analysis, Population Policy and Income Distribution, evaluates alternative instruments for improving the coverage of low-income groups by family planning programs.

Richard Webb's chapter, Wage Policy and Income Distribution in Developing Countries, notes the limited and usually negative income distribution effects of government attempts to raise wages and argues that upward wage pressures in modern sectors generally exist despite any government preferences to the contrary.

Arnold Harberger examines the potential redistributive impact of tax policy as a whole in Fiscal Policy and Income Redistribution, and concludes that possible tax levels are severely constrained, particularly by the high mobility of capital and skilled labor.

William Cline's chapter, Policy Instruments for Rural Income Redistribution, reviews findings on the income and employment effects of the principal instruments for raising the productivity of small farms. The chapter makes a strong plea for land reform, arguing that compensation to landowners can increase political feasibility without eliminating the favorable equity effects of reform.

John Lewis focuses on the rural poor in his chapter on Designing the Public-Works Mode of Anti-Poverty Policy. He examines the political and administrative issues which determine the feasibility, as well as the relative desirability, of large-scale public works programs as a mode of raising rural incomes.

James Levinson and Olav Oftedal contribute a survey, Equity and Income Effects of Nutrition and Health Care, noting the limitations of most traditional approaches to these programs.

Some issues of urban poverty are examined by Rakesh Mohan whose study, Urban Land Policy, Income Distribution, and the Urban Poor, finds that land policies are relatively ineffective instruments for reaching the urban poor.

Appendixes to this volume contain three technical papers written in connection with the project. The first, Measuring Income Inequality by Richard Szal and Sherman Robinson, contains an analytical review of the various ways to measure income inequality and makes a new contribution by suggesting a measure of income distribution that stresses the degree of individual mobility within a given income distribution.

Jorge Cauas and Marcelo Selowsky, in Potential Distributive Effects of Nationalization Policies: The Economic Aspects, stress the potential constraints on the degree of redistribution that can be effected through the nationalization of part of the corporate sector. Those potential limitations depend on how nationalization affects investment behavior, and on who benefits from the expropriation.

The short paper by Frank and Bruton, Mathematical Appendix, lays out the mathematical derivation of the labor absorption equation used in two of the policy papers in the volume: the Frank-Webb study on a theoretical framework, and the Bruton chapter on trade and industrialization policy.

Introduction

NOTES

1. Research Program in Economic Development. "Summary of Proceedings" (final conference). Mimeographed. Princeton University, Woodrow
Wilson School of Public and International Affairs, 19–21 September 1974.

CHAPTER I

AN OVERVIEW OF INCOME DISTRIBUTION IN LESS DEVELOPED COUNTRIES: POLICY ALTERNATIVES AND DESIGN

Charles R. Frank, Jr., and Richard Webb

This chapter attempts to provide an overview of the various papers and proceedings of meetings associated with the Princeton-Brookings project on income distribution in developing countries. Despite the paucity of data, especially on some of the most crucial aspects of income inequality--extreme poverty and extreme wealth[1]--a number of generalizations are possible.

First, improvement for the poor is possible, and not only in the wake of political revolution. Many factors appear to be raising the absolute incomes and improving the welfare of broad segments of the poor in countries with very different political settings. Despite a widespread pessimism, there does appear to be scope for policy.

Second, and paradoxically, both market forces and public policies are, by and large, working in the direction of increasing relative inequality. The following sections review some evidence on these generalizations.

A. Factors that are raising incomes of the poor

The cross-country evidence on income trends of the poor has been compiled by Ahluwalia, and by Adelman and Morris.[2] A few more recent studies[3] have added to those collections. Though the data sources for these income trend estimates are tenuous, the compilations present a picture of rising absolute incomes in a broad variety of economic and

---

NOTES:

    (i) The authors wish to acknowledge the helpful comments and suggestions of Edwin Cohn of the Agency for International Development.

    (ii) Footnotes appear at the end of each chapter.

political settings, usually, though not always, accompanied by increasing relative inequality. The most striking cases of reduction of poverty are under the socialist economies and in countries with rapid growth rates such as South Korea and Taiwan.

There are some reasons for the good performance on poverty in these latter countries.

(i) First, social services such as education, population control, medical care, sanitation and water supplies, are sometimes widely available for the poor as well as the rich. For example, Oftedal and Levinson in chapter 10 point out that some socialist countries, such as the Peoples Republic of China, Cuba, North Vietnam, and Tanzania, have a paramedical approach to health care, emphasizing inexpensive and widespread treatment. By contrast, conventional health programs involve highly trained doctors and expensive care in narrowly distributed services. There are also examples of wide distribution of social services in nonsocialist countries. For example, Taiwan emphasizes services for the rural poor, partly for historical reasons. The Japanese administration contributed public health campaigns, expanded education, railroad, road, and other infrastructure development, and scientific agronomy. When the Nationalist Chinese came from the mainland, they assumed complete political control. The wealthy entrepreneurs and elites of the island generally were native Taiwanese, while a majority of the immigrant Chinese became small farmers. The government, therefore, paid considerably more attention to the needs of the rural population--both the immigrant Chinese and the original Taiwanese peasants--than to those of the more urbanized, native Taiwanese.

(ii) A second factor favoring widespread distribution of income in some countries is cultural homogeneity among the population. This, for example, seems to be a significant factor in Korea. The reasons are discussed later in this book.

(iii) Third, in those countries where society places a high value on education, such as Korea and China, the population quickly becomes highly literate and well educated, even at low levels of development. Widespread educational attainment prevents the emergence of large wage and salary differentials based on acute shortages of skilled and educated manpower.

(iv) Fourth, in countries with good transportation and communication facilities, regional disparities in income are less marked. Capital, labor, and product markets are more highly integrated. Growth, which begins in one region, can spread more quickly to others. In contrast, countries with relatively poor transport and communication facilities suffer from increasing regional disparities which exacerbate the national distribution of income.

(v) Fifth, another important reason for the even distribution of income is the equal distribution of land, such as occurs in many African and Asian countries. In large parts of Africa the size of a man's holding is often the maximum he can farm with traditional methods. In revolutionary socialist countries such as Cuba, North Vietnam, and North Korea, land is equally distributed because of radical land reform. Land reform has also been successful in nonsocialist countries. In South Korea and Taiwan, land reform occurred when a new regime came into power, representing ethnic groups different from those of the large landholders.

(vi) Finally, trade and industrialization policies seem to be involved in the more satisfactory experience of some countries. As Bruton argues strongly in chapter 3, an inward-looking, import-substitution strategy often involves protection for the urbanized, modern sector of the economy at the expense of the urban and rural poor. Controls and quotas on imports and investments create monopoly rents which accrue to the wealthy. Protective tariffs and import controls enable techniques to be used which are highly capital-intensive but inefficient and much higher wages to be paid to the highly organized elites in the modern sector. In India, such effects have been reinforced by government policies that have kept the prices of energy, raw materials, and refined metals charged by both public- and private-sector producers comparatively low, in effect subsidizing the modern-sector industrialists.

When tariffs are moderate and not highly variable from sector to sector, and export incentives are generally low and used at most to compensate for moderate levels of protection to import-substitution industries, wage rates in the modern sector are not significantly different from those in the urban traditional sectors. The distinction between modern and traditional sectors becomes blurred as their respective labor and capital markets are more integrated. Bruton points out that in countries with moderate and equable protection, profit rates tend to be high but reinvestment is also high, growth is rapid, and the absorption of under-utilized labor into high-productivity jobs reduces absolute poverty more rapidly.

Some of the causes of relative equality in the distribution of income, such as cultural and geographical homogeneity, are difficult to promote by deliberate policy changes. Land reform, distribution of social services, building of transportation and communication networks, and setting rules of protection and subsidy, however, are government actions that can have great influence on the distribution of income over a period of time far less than a generation.

B. How policies reinforce inequality

In chapter 2 Frank and Webb discuss the hypothesis that a developing economy will first experience a worsening and then an improvement in the distribution of income. They attribute this pattern, sometimes called the U-shaped effect, to the mechanics of absorption of workers from the traditional sector into the modern sector. A conclusion that can be drawn from many of the policy papers, however, is that this natural effect, caused by redistribution of population between the two major sectors of the economy, is reinforced by government policies. For example, medical facilities tend to be built in the major urban centers. In the initial stages of development, when the degree of urbanization is low, very few segments of the population have access to medical services. Furthermore, since incomes tend to be higher in the urban areas and the political and economic elites are usually located there, the provision of medical services worsens the distribution of income in the early stages of development. Later on, as medical facilities spread into rural areas, medical help becomes available to wider segments of the population. Furthermore, as the proportion of the population living in cities increases, more people have access to medical facilities.

Education also tends to exacerbate income differentials in the early stages of development. Initial government efforts involve expansion of secondary schools and university education. In Africa, for instance, the departure of former colonial powers left a great need for Africanization of the elite ranks of the civil service and of major firms in the private sector, requiring a large expansion in higher education. In such cases, the provision of educational facilities initially widens disparities because of unequal opportunities for educational advancement. In most countries, however, the urban population has successfully pressed for rapid expansion in secondary and university education irrespective of the degree of social need. As development has taken place, universal primary education has become a more feasible goal and gradually more education is provided on a universal basis.

Population policy also reinforces the U-shaped effect. Initial demographic changes in a less developed country bring a lowering of the death rate, usually most markedly among the poor. The poor also tend to have higher birth rates. Overall, birth rates tend to fall much more slowly than death rates and only after initial reductions in mortality. Thus poor families tend to have a very much larger family size in the initial stages of the demographic transition. Conversely, the decline in the birth rate seems to occur first among higher income and urbanized segments of the population. For one thing, the desire to limit family size occurs most often among wealthier, urban, more educated population groups. Thus their demand for population-control services is greater. Moreover, the distribution networks for such services are usually weak in the initial stages of a program and those who have access tend to be the more educated and urbanized. On both counts, therefore, government efforts to promote population control are apt initially to be skewed toward more educated urban and higher-income groups. Thus wealthier families tend to have much smaller families than poor families in the early stages of the demographic transition. The result is that the per capita distribution of income tends to worsen relative to a given distribution of income by family or by wage earner. Only in the latter stages of the program are techniques devised for distribution of population-control devices and information to the rural poor scattered throughout the countryside. At this stage, the earlier tendency is reversed.

As Mohan points out in chapter 11, public housing projects tend also to go, not to the poorest groups in the population, but to the middle- and upper-income groups. First of all, housing programs tend to be concentrated in urban rather than in rural areas. Second, even within the urban areas, the poorest groups are rarely helped. Benefiting relatively poor groups often requires site and service projects which involve the laying out of streets and sewer lines and provision of some basic minimum services while allowing squatters to construct their own housing on land prepared by government. Even if the resources needed to carry out such projects

can be mobilized, there is no way of assuring that access to the facilities
is limited to the very poorest segments of the population, who often lack
the knowledge and skills to become eligible for inclusion.

C.   Goals for redistributive policies

Past discussions of redistributive policy have been clouded by a
failure to recognize that redistribution means different things to
different people. "Social justice" is in reality an ethical compound
made up of several separable goals, such as the desire to alleviate
extreme poverty, to increase mobility, to remove excessively high incomes, and to reduce income dispersion per se. For many people, some
sources of inequality are more acceptable than others. And, obviously,
ideas differ regarding the tolerable or optimum degree of inequality.

Distributive policy-making has been confused by treating these
separate social goals as a single norm, while the practice of measuring
and discussing income distribution as a single number has reinforced
that confusion. The chapters in this book seek, with varying degrees
of success, to open up the discussion of redistributive impact in
terms of these alternative goals. In an appendix to this book, Robinson
and Szal also stress the many different goals that can be set for redistributive policy, and they analyze the usually implicit value assumptions
that underlie different statistical measures of inequality.

The disaggregation of redistributive goals helps to overcome some of
the conceptual and practical difficulties attending the presumed tradeoff between growth and equality. Earlier arguments that stressed a conflict between these goals (e.g., because work and mobility incentives had
to be rewarded and because capitalists save more) as well as more recent
counterarguments that claim complementarities (e.g., because large farms
are inefficiently managed and the rich consume capital- and import-
intensive goods) can be unhelpful overgeneralizations once the policy
issues are phrased in terms of specific target groups and specific tools
of redistribution. Disaggregation permits a more constructive approach
that involves searching for particular combinations of policies and target groups that will make best use of potential complementarities, or at
least, minimize trade-offs.

Disaggregation also brings out into the open what is surely the
principal conflict in the design of distributive strategy--that between

most aid-givers and non-LDC observers, who emphasize the alleviation of extreme poverty, and governments of most developing countries, which favor urban and labor groups that fall outside most definitions of extreme poverty.

Both A.I.D. and the World Bank, for instance, define target groups in terms of poverty levels alone. As outsiders, they can more easily assume a position of statistical impersonality, detached from the particular social groups that dominate the distributive discussion in each country. The compelling economic justice of this approach is matched by its apparent maximization of financial feasibility, since it generates the greatest additional welfare for any given amount extracted from the rich.[4] Simple calculation shows that relatively small transfers make relatively large improvements possible for the very poor, thanks to the leverage provided by extreme inequalities. There remain, of course, the enormous and to some intractable problems of delivering that income, and those problems have been discussed in detail throughout this volume. But such problems have not deflected the primary emphasis placed on the elimination of extreme poverty by most aid-givers and non-LDC observers, and to a lesser extent, by some members of LDC elites.

Within developing countries, on the other hand, economic justice covers a host of distributive goals among which the attack on extreme poverty has, with few exceptions, been least important. The principal thrust of redistribution has been an attack on extreme wealth, with a redistribution in favor of organized and urban labor groups that are usually in the top quartile or third of the income distribution. This pattern has generally accompanied the transfer of power to middle-class reformist elites. In some countries, e.g., Nigeria and Brazil, rapid growth and/or social mobility has had the self-justifying effect of elevating economic mobility within the hierarchy of social goals, at least in the eyes of the elites. Finally, regional and communal income differences are in center stage in distributive battles in almost all countries. As a result of all these factors, the almost exclusive concern with extreme poverty among aid-givers today is rejected as a foreign conception by the elites in most LDCs--despite constitutional requirements of living wages, despite the official attention placed on extreme poverty by a few countries such as India, and even despite the new egalitarian current that has flowed from Cuba and China.

The logic of the antipoverty goal misses the strong roots that justice has among LDC elites in the notion of desert, i.e., that what people have a right to depends on what they have done or on who they are. The particular choice of redistributive targets by LDCs is thus strongly shaped by these conceptions of socially deserved or justified distribution. Social justification, for instance, explains the much stronger attacks on the "unearned" income and usually inherited property of landowners than on the often self-made and seemingly more growth-relevant wealth of industrialists. It helps to explain the much greater strength of demands for redistribution via wage increases and agrarian reform than for the less visibly legitimized sharing associated with fiscal transfers from the richer modern sector as a whole to the rest of the economy. The notion of desert is also a major force underlying the distaste, by LDC policy makers as well as aid donors, for current-income transfers to the poor, except through slow-acting "job-creating" and "productivity-raising" programs. Even the extremely poor must be seen to "earn" their incomes.

Those who deplore the neglect of the very poor by most developing countries rightly note that much of the attention given to competing moral claims is window dressing for political aims; that clumsy policy design and implementation account for some of the neglect, as when regional income differences are used as proxy indicators of poverty; and finally, that much of the current design of redistributive programs—for instance, attacks on the wealthy, and the preoccupation with the highly visible urban poor—reflects the preferences of elites, and not of the poorer majorities. These arguments, however, do not remove the dilemma faced by foreigners offering policy advice or aid to developing countries: To what extent should they accept the distributive goals of LDC governments or to what extent should the "true" (as assumed by the foreigner) distributive preferences of the poor be respected? This dilemma is most evident, of course, with regard to the desired degree of redistribution.

In most of the chapters in the book the policy emphasis is on extreme poverty. There is little discussion of the problem of foreign dominance or of ostentatious consumption by the rich and powerful. In the chapter by John Lewis on public works programs, it is explicit that the programs are to be designed with the rural poor as a target group. Rakesh Mohan, in writing on urban land policy, is concerned principally about the urban poor. In the chapter on health and nutrition by Levinson and Oftedal and in the chapter on education by Harbison, it is clear that the main concern is for the poorest segments of the population.

Bruton, in his discussion on industrialization, points out that there is a conflict between the goal of poverty reduction and the distaste for high profits. He argues that the rapid absorption of labor into high-paying, modern-sector jobs requires an increase in the profit share rather than a decrease since, when the profit share is large, the rate of investment tends to be higher, thus accelerating the rate of growth of output and the rate of labor absorption into high-productivity jobs.

D. The scope for policy

One view of the scope for redistributive policies is that the existing distribution of income (including government benefits) is closely determined by the distribution of political power: There exists what could be described as a "tight fit" between economic and political power. By this view it is academic to discuss policies that would alter the current situation to the disadvantage of the powerful. The repeated frustrations of reformers, who often fail to put across even minor and seemingly almost costless changes, appear to bear out this pessimistic assessment. The implication is, of course, that radical political change must precede any significant improvement in the lot of the poor.

Our view is that, despite the weight of existing power and wealth, the relationship between power and income is more complex and fluid than implied by the "tight fit" argument. A better knowledge of the various factors affecting that relationship should, therefore, provide a basis for assessing the opportunities for, and limits to, possible reform.

1. Political factors

There is not a strong correlation between the political difficulty of making a given income transfer and the amount involved. The acceptability of any transfer depends also on the mode and purpose of the transfer. This is partly a matter of visibility and partly one of moral legitimacy. It is usually more difficult to extract incomes already received, via direct taxes for instance, than to spirit them away, en route to the recipient, through a market-price adjustment such as a tariff, a differential exchange rate, or an excise tax.

Perhaps more important is the role of moral legitimacy, particularly in relation to the purpose of a transfer. In general, transfers are more acceptable when destined to raise productivity than to subsidize current consumption. Education has a particularly high degree of legitimacy, perhaps largely because it is associated with productivity, though the right to education seems to have an independent status not enjoyed by any other benefit provided to the poor.

The greater moral acceptability of productive transfers to the poor may be hard to distinguish from self-interest on the part of business elites, who benefit from more productive workers and from larger consumer markets. The nationalist motives of elites, particularly the military, also favor resource transfers to the poor. National strength is built up through the cultural and territorial integration of poor regions (which are often border areas), by upgrading a nation's human resources, and by reducing income disparities that may become a source of internal friction and instability.

The political process can generate more power for the poor than that provided by their scanty command over economic resources. This can result from competition among elites, chiefly in democratic or quasi-democratic systems where electoral body-counts matter. And it can result from erratic discontinuities and interruptions that upset a class-based political order. The best examples of the latter are military coups and the granting of independence to former colonies. Some of these sources of divergence between economic and political power are discussed below.

If there is a fluid, competitive, pluralistic political regime, for instance, the disadvantaged can be helped by coalitions with middle- or upper-income subgroups who identify or share interests with the poor. For example, Lewis suggests that rural public works programs can be de-signed so that benefits can be obtained by both local elites and the rural poor. Not all interests are class based. Thus, ethnic or regional interest may cut across class. Patron-client networks and personal fac-tions exist too. Thus, there may be more fluidity in a political system than a class analysis would allow. Coalitions can be made by varied groups, which link different income levels.

In some countries there have been conspicuous divergences between economic and political power. For example, in Taiwan the Nationalist Chinese had overwhelming political power, yet the native Taiwanese had much greater economic resources. The Chinese political elites used the system of government to increase their income and access to public services.

In East Africa, economic power was largely in the hands of foreign firms and local Asian groups. Yet with independence in the early sixties, indigenous Africans used their new political power to economic advantage-- and that was turned in the service of tribal and other indigenous rivalries. Foreign firms, foreign executives of local firms, and highly paid foreign civil servants gradually were squeezed out. Asians were progressively circumscribed and forced to provide more opportunities for indigenous Africans in their enterprises. In Uganda, the Asians were expelled massively.

The latitude for policy change can increase if political power, like income, spreads out and eventually trickles down to the very poor and disenfranchised. This can happen, for instance, when elite groups look for allies among middle-class and poorer income groups. There are also class renegades, and institutional groups like the military, who look for allies outside the elite.[5]

Frequently, the pattern of change in the configuration of political power has involved the following steps: first, control lies in the hands of a few landed oligarchs, foreign executives of large foreign enter-prises, indigenous business elites, or some combination of these. In the next stage, a reform regime emerges which represents new interest groups in the middle- and upper-middle-income brackets. Finally, power is seized by organized labor, government civil servants, or military officers. This pattern is evidenced in the rise to power of Bhutto in Pakistan, the formation of an RPP government in Turkey in 1973, and in the developments that culminated in a military takeover in Peru.

Although the rhetoric of reform seems to be responsive to the needs of the poor, often the policies that are followed help not the poorest groups but the middle-income groups that provide the political backing for the regime. For example, it is widely recognized that the Chilean and Peruvian land reforms mostly benefited workers on large

estate farms.[6] Small subsistence farmers and landless laborers tended to
be hurt by adverse price policies.

In the case of Turkey, the first moves of the new RPP reform regime
were to raise minimum wages by eighty percent and to increase farm price
supports substantially. The former was a way of redistributing income in
urban areas, the latter an attempt to help farmers. But increases in
minimum wages and salaries for organized labor and civil servants increased
demands for food and other consumer goods to the detriment of the very
poor self-employed tradesmen or casual workers and of the rural poor without enough land for their own food needs. Increases in price supports
helped the large landholders most. The urban poor, landless laborers,
and small landholders were hurt, but one compensating factor for the rural
poor was that demand for labor on the larger farms was increased through
the higher price supports.

Although the initial efforts of a reform regime may not be to help
the very poor, the loss of power by the wealthy may be a necessary first
step toward the eventual total restructuring of political power. As the
middle-class groups gain power, they will in turn come under pressure
from poorer groups who begin to organize or be organized and to articulate
their needs more effectively.

One possible explanation of political trickle-down is a ratchet-
effect: many social gains are easier to achieve than to reverse. Once
income taxes have been legislated, schools built, unions allowed to
operate and land redistributed, beneficiaries become more conscious of
their benefits and more easily mobilized in the defense of those benefits.
As a result, successive and perhaps only occasional leftward swings of
the political pendulum cause a gradual leftward drift in the political
center of gravity. The historical trend in labor legislation is a good
illustration of this process, as argued by Webb in chapter 6 on wage
policy. The process can be reversed by forceful repression and, perhaps,
by using time to erode gains that even a strong rightist government cannot afford to attack frontally. The current regimes in Brazil and Chile
are examples of these means of reversing previous reforms.

Under some political, cultural, or historical circumstances the
process of political trickle-down can be bypassed or foreshortened. In
Tanzania, for example, the power and prestige of a highly purposed leader,
Julius Nyerere, has resulted in programs which help the very poor. Nyerere

has suppressed organized labor in urban areas and made conscious attempts to organize a power base among the rural poor. Some compromises had to be made with powerful civil servants, but there was no revolution. Unlike Turkey, Peru, and Chile, organized labor never was an important force in Tanzania. More generally, the survival of the regime seems not to have depended so urgently as in Turkey and Chile on the delivery of quick redistributive benefits to already organized groups. In the latter two countries reform regimes were extremely precarious. They depended on coalition partners of dubious loyalty and indifferent commitment to the needs of the low-end poor. Increases in minimum wages and agricultural price supports were highly visible redistributive measures that played to the self-interest of the more active constituencies of the regimes.

If there are so many potential sources of slippages between political and economic power, and, consequently, of possible gains by the poor, why are incomes distributed so unequally? Why is there so much absolute poverty? The preceding discussion has been deliberately biased toward stressing the possible sources of reform.[7] It is meant to suggest where to look for opportunities for change. The political constraints are more obvious. But the above reasoning also points to an additional conclusion. The constraints on redistribution are not wholly political, and perhaps not even primarily political. The degree of inequality, for instance, and the extent of absolute poverty are not radically less in most countries usually described as socialist or more egalitarian (though they do appear to be radically less in the Communist regimes of Cuba, China, North Korea, and North Vietnam). Part of the explanation of this paradox lies in economic factors that also determine the scope for redistribution.

2. Economic factors

Redistribution is easier the more concentrated are (i) the sources of income or, what often comes to the same thing, the greater the rent component in income, and (ii) the target group.

(i) Most redistributive instruments involve some form of continuous market interference. Such is the case, for instance, in respect to taxes, price controls, and wage setting. Even once-over transfers, such as property redistribution, create temporary market repercussions. When policy makers decide to interfere in a market for redistributive purposes, they must assess the extent of the resultant market disequilibrium. The greater the disequilibrium or "market tension," the greater will be the demand for political and administrative resources to implement or enforce that distortion. Since political and administrative resources are limited, the nature of markets must be an important consideration in the choice of redistributive instruments and targets. In general, low elasticities of supply or demand imply smaller disequilibria and, therefore, easier implementation.

This point is best illustrated by considering two extreme cases. A tax on domestic oil production is extremely easy to administer, and it has minimal market repercussions. Such a tax need entail no sharp fall in supply of the sort that would upset consumers. Nor is it likely to cause quick unemployment of oil industry workers. In short, political costs are low. At the other extreme, a minimum wage for domestic servants is almost impossible to administer; furthermore, if it were implemented, many servants would become unemployed. Competitive markets, with large numbers of dispersed buyers and sellers, are a powerful defense against attempts to divert or appropriate income flows originating in those markets. By contrast, it is easier to interfere in markets where production is geographically concentrated, or carried out by few firms and a small number of workers, or in which the rent (natural resource) or quasi-rent (long-lived capital investment) is high. An important additional consideration is that international trade creates a powerful mechanism for taxation by concentrating the flow of products through a few transit points.

The nature of markets is thus a powerful determinant of how much redistribution occurs and whom it affects. In a country such as India, with an economy that is predominantly agricultural and oriented to internal markets, there is much less room for political influence on income flows; the income distribution is primarily market determined. The major exception to this is the possibility of land redistribution, which is constrained more by political than by market problems. By contrast, political control has been a major determinant of income distribution in the oil- and mineral-producing countries, as well as in such agricultural exporting countries as Ghana, Nigeria, Argentina, and Uruguay, where export taxes, tariffs, and exchange rate policy have been used by urban groups to appropriate a large share of the income originating in agriculture.

The contrast between market types is perhaps more important within than between countries. The socialist and egalitarian leanings of so many developing countries have been powerfully constrained by the dispersed, atomistic nature of their rural and traditional sectors. Socialism in most of these countries is limited to the modern sector. Massive administrative and political resources are required to extend political control to traditional-sector labor, capital, and product markets. The principal exceptions occur when agricultural exports or concentrated land ownership provide opportunities for economically easier income redistribution in the traditional sector.

(ii) The economic feasibility of redistribution is also determined by the degree of concentration or fragmentation of target groups by regions, occupations, productive sectors, and other groupings that are relevant to the normal coverage of redistributive instruments.

Most transfers, be they services such as schools and health or resources such as roads and credit, usually benefit groups rather than individuals. A group can be a village, a district, an occupational class, farmers producing a particular crop, or the consumers of a particular product. The target efficiency of a transfer, i.e., the proportion of the transfer that actually reaches the target group, depends both on the discriminatory ability of the transfer mechanism and on the degree of concentration of the target group.

In the simplest and cheapest case, the poor will be concentrated in one region; they will specialize in one occupation and productive activity; and no rich, or nontarget, individuals will live in that region or be dedicated to that activity. However, if there are some poor in most villages, in most regions, and in most occupations and activities, it will be far more expensive to make any given income transfer. The income available for transfer will be diluted, either because many nonpoor will also benefit (e.g., the rich members of a village to which a road has been built) or because it is administratively expensive to discriminate and ensure that only the poor benefit. The clumsiness of most distributive instruments and the relatively dispersed nature of the poor in most countries can greatly magnify the cost of achieving any given increase in welfare for the poor. Policy makers should therefore become acquainted with the coverage of different policy instruments and with the location, sources of income, consumption habits, and other features of the poor.

3. The scope for policy: a summary

We have argued that opportunities for redistribution are not necessarily tightly constrained by the balance of power and that, by contrast, they are strongly influenced by structural characteristics of the economy. A general implication is that it is misleading to consider the scope for redistribution in the singular. Given the variety of distributive goals, of sources of slippage between economic and political power, and of structural features of the economy, it is hard to conceive a situation in which all of these elements are so aligned that they preclude any possibility of improvement.

E. Policy design

Effective policy design requires three elements. First, account must be taken of the broader economic and social policy context, particularly of the way in which nondistributive targets, such as growth and stability, are being pursued. Second, policies must make economic sense. Taken together, the important direct and indirect economic effects must have a net favorable effect on the poor. Third, political and administrative elements will be critical to the implementation of policies. Commitments to reduce inequality, taken at the highest level of government, may make unrealistic demands on administrative capacities, or they may be subverted because they run counter to the interests and attitudes of bureaucrats, or they may be weakened through the pressure of interest groups working on the bureaucracy.

1. The policy context

Redistribution is rarely an overriding policy concern. Even the more socialist countries are strongly committed to economic growth and stability. Redistribution often becomes paramount immediately after a sharp leftward shift in government. The period of intense commitment to reforms, generally involving wage increases, nationalization, and a start toward land reform, is usually followed by a return to the growth objective and often to some retrenchment made necessary by the stabilization and growth problems that result from redistributive "excess."[8] Most of

the time, and across most of the political spectrum, there is little scope
for policies which appear to conflict with growth.

Planning for redistribution, therefore, has much to gain from a joint
examination of growth, stability, and distribution policies. Since a
large part of the total policy impact on income distribution will usually
consist of byproduct effects of policies aimed at growth and stability,
much of the opportunity for achieving a better income distribution will
consist of improvements in the design of policies that are not primarily
aimed at distribution. Also, the sensible objective is to attain some
degree of net redistribution, not to ensure the maximum progressive impact of each policy instrument. Finally, if the principal distributive
goal is to reduce absolute poverty rather than to narrow income differentials, then growth, as long as it entails some spillover to the poor, is
not an alternative objective; it is itself an instrument, along with
redistribution, for reducing poverty.

2. Indirect economic effects

In designing redistribution policies, full account should be taken
of the indirect as well as the direct effects. Often policies meant to
redistribute income toward the poor do just the reverse because of un-
anticipated indirect effects. There can be economic backlash. It may
be partial, or it may completely reverse the intended direction of the
policy effort.

Often unintended backlash occurs because of a simple failure to
understand the proper relationships of supply and demand. When prices
are controlled at low levels, for example, quantities supplied are
reduced. If the price of food is kept low through concern for the poor,
less food may be available. The poor end up suffering because little
food is sold at controlled prices, and they may have to supplement purchases at controlled prices with purchases at high prices in the black
market. Cline points out that credit policies which encourage low
interest rates for small farmers do not provide sufficient returns for
lenders to cover their costs. The result is a reduction in the credit
available to small farmers and much of the limited institutional credit
which is available flows to large farmers.

Another kind of economic backlash occurs whenever quantities are
controlled. For example, import controls, whether on such luxury goods

as refrigerators and cars or on such essentials as tractors, force up prices. Windfall gains accrue to existing owners and to those lucky enough to obtain import licenses, thus redistributing income toward unintended groups.

A third form of economic backlash can occur because of a failure to consider the external sector of the economy. Harberger argues in chapter 7 that high levels of taxation on incomes encourage emigration by professional people--doctors, engineers, and university professors--who have significant opportunities to practice outside the country. Likewise, stiff taxes on profits, interest, and other returns to capital may encourage capital to leave the country, both legally and illegally.

Fourth, backlash can occur because the long-run effects counteract the favorable short-run effects. In chapter 9, John Lewis points out that, although the initial effect of public works projects may be to help the rural poor, particularly by providing employment and raising unskilled wages, the eventual beneficiaries of public works projects may be the large landholders, whose incomes rise in response to the building of new access roads and better irrigation facilities.

Fifth, economic backlash can occur because the aggregate effects of a policy differ from the micro effects--the famous fallacy of composition. For example, one small farmer may benefit from rural education and extension programs, cheap capital, and subsidized farm inputs. If the program is expanded on a large scale, however, the resulting decrease in farm prices may be so great that it reduces the income of small farmers.

Sixth, backlash can occur because government activities in one sector of the economy affect expectations and business behavior in other sectors. This is the major theme of Jorge Cauas and Marcelo Selowsky on nationalization in an appendix to this book. Partial nationalization may affect the expectations of entrepreneurs in the private sector so adversely that investment and profits decline and government resources available for redistributive purposes are reduced.

Finally, backlash may occur because of general equilibrium effects. For example, this chapter suggests, as does Henry Bruton in chapter 3, that increases in the wages of civil servants and modern-sector laborers can have a depressive effect on traditional-sector incomes. Not only is labor absorption from the traditional to the modern sector reduced, but induced migration from rural to urban areas adds to the labor supply in the urban traditional sector, further adding to downward pressure on wages. Moreover, Cline suggests that the Green Revolution has in many cases hurt rather than helped the poor. Rising land rents and induced mechanization have often reduced job opportunities for landless laborers and resulted in the eviction of small tenant farmers from land.

There are political backlash effects too. If a decision is made to grow now and redistribute later, disadvantaged groups may not wait patiently. Meantime, growing concentration of income and wealth may make future redistribution politically more difficult. Resources may have to go into the instruments of coercion. Similarly, a government may have to face the negative reactions of those whose oxen are being gored if redistribution means taking from some to give to others. The costs of implementing such a policy may turn out to be greater than anticipated.

The authors of the policy papers suggest a number of approaches to avoid the pitfalls of backlash. For example, in chapter 7 Harberger suggests that a progressive expenditure tax will mitigate the capital flight caused by steeply progressive income taxes since savings would be exempted from taxation. Harberger also advocates a self-assessment approach to land taxation to avoid the incentive to corruption and cheating. (Under a self-assessment scheme, property owners would be subject to forced sale at the self-assessed value declared for tax purposes.) Harbison suggests in chapter 4 that charging students for higher education will improve the allocation of public funding for education and reduce the problem of underemployment of educated people.

In some cases, total rather than partial approaches have to be followed to eliminate adverse side effects. Partial nationalization and partial land reform often do not work because of the adverse effects on sectors that have not been expropriated.

Sometimes governments can intervene in markets in a useful way to help the poor. For example, Mohan suggests in chapter 11 that the government might usefully enter the market for land to counter activities of speculators, improve the supply of developed land, and keep prices of land from rising too rapidly. John Lewis is concerned in chapter 9 with the effect of public works on increasing employment and raising wage rates paid to unskilled labor. The potential long-run adverse impacts can be avoided by careful planning and design so that, for example, feeder roads are built into areas in which small farmers predominate, small-scale

irrigation works are provided for peasant farmers, or cooperatives are
formed to take advantage of capital improvements, such as tubewells,
which may normally be available only to large farmers.

3.   Policy implementation: political and administrative factors

John D. Montgomery[9] has made the point that most of the income-
equalizing forms of public intervention are not policies but programs.
Once programs are the subject of concentration, questions must be asked
about administrative factors. It has already been pointed out that it
is important to understand the organizations and preferences of administrative personnel. Administrative personnel have their own class-based
or ethnic-based predilections. They have professional commitments; and
they have constituencies that they service and that pressure them.
Thus, for example, some health ministries have been very resistant to
paramedical training and development programs. Administrative structures
have preferences for different kinds of technological or delivery systems,
as well as preferences for substantive goals.

There are often conflicts between different central ministries.
There can also be conflict between general and specialized administrators
and between agents of central ministries in the field and personnel working at ministerial headquarters. There can be conflicts between agents
of local or regional governments and central government agents. The
outcome of the interactions between levels and types of bureaucracies cannot be a matter of indifference to those concerned with redistributive
policies. The ways that taxes are collected, if they are collected, may
depend very much on the agent or extractive channels employed in tax
collection. What standards will govern the administrative agents? How
can they be held accountable and to whom? Which policies will be administered faithfully and which will simply be avoided or bent to the "private-
regarding" interests of bureaucracies?[10] The first question that a policy
maker designing a tax structure might ask in a developing country is not:
Will it play in Peoria? but, Will it go down among the people who are
supposed to administer the program?[11]

As noted, credit and agricultural extension policies often have benefited rural elites. This may only partially be a function of the political power of better-off farmers. Administrators may prefer to deal with
people more like themselves in terms of values or education. Or they

may respond to those who can write or otherwise make their voices heard. Or they may have more of a professional interest in agricultural innovation and growth than in rural poverty.

It has been widely observed that processes of planning and budgeting tend to yield only incremental changes because of the balancing of forces between bureaucracies and within them. Accordingly, it has been urged repeatedly that developing country bureaucrats be trained in "development administration" rather than in "public administration."[12] But, as Bernard Schaffer has said, it is one thing to give people technical knowledge and another to succeed in changing their practice, giving them new or different skills, and making them want to use them.[13]

Thus, it has to be asked: What levers exist for bending administrative structures in new ways? Obviously the strength of structures other than those of civil service matters here. Thus the relationship of party and/or army to civil service will be critical. If economic and political fits are important, so are administrative and political ones. The supply of administrative or potential administrative personnel will be important too. And just as we noted that splits within a political elite give leverage to reform-minded actors, so do splits within and between bureaucracies. It may be possible to appeal to people on a rank and age basis, although this may disrupt lines of command within the civil service. It may be possible to appeal to administrators to support redistributive programs on professional grounds, that is, on efficiency terms.

In the end, however, it may be necessary to circumvent the formal administrative structure. This is easier to do when the intended social changes can be brought about quickly, as in land seizure or nationalizations, than when redistributions are sought over lengthy periods of time. Indeed, one of the attractions of nonreformist or radical redistribution policies has been that they might be applied not by the normal administrative agents of control but by special ones, e.g., the military in Peru, peasant committees for land reform in various countries, or shock troop industrial workers brought to the countryside to help collectivize in the Soviet Union. The dangers of these policies are obvious: deflection from other duties of the agents used; disruption of the functioning of the regular bureaucracy; and turmoil and inefficiency.

F.   The prospects for better policies

Any redistributive strategy will address three separate problems:
how to take from the rich, how to give to the poor, and how to reduce the
need for redistribution by improving the market as a distributive mechanism. The relative stress placed on each will depend on the social priorities in the country and on the inequalities of its market distribution of
income. The political and technical feasibility of attaining each of
these objectives may differ considerably within and between countries.
The present discussion draws on the later chapters of this book to note
the policy prospects for each.

1.   Taking from the rich

There is a tendency to equate the problem of taking from the rich with
the problem of political feasibility. This equation errs on two counts:
first, as the Harberger and Cauas-Selowsky papers point out, there are
economic as well as political problems involved in extracting from the
rich; second, political feasibility, defined broadly to include attitudes
and degrees of acceptability, is relevant to the design of policies for
reaching the poor and for changing market structures.

The chief alternative means of reducing high incomes are closely
identified with different political arrangements and possible degrees of
redistribution. Weaker governments generally attempt to raise wages;
stronger regimes are better able to enforce income and wealth taxes; radical governments redistribute property. Most of the economic problems
arise under the first two approaches--wages and taxation--though property
transfers also have negative economic side effects.

Unfortunately, wage increases are at once the most politically
attractive mode of extracting from the rich (short of radical socialization) and the most problematic in the eyes of the economist. Sharing high
productivity with workers has a high degree of legitimacy, generally favors
a clearly identified and vocal set of beneficiaries, and seems easy to
implement since no government financial intermediation is involved. But,
as Webb's chapter on wage policy points out, a limited degree of redistribution via wage increases is possible only for a minority, and usually
an already relatively better-off minority, of the labor force. Outside this
sector, market forces are exceedingly powerful constraints on wage policy.

Furthermore, wage increases will almost always hurt the very poor by slowing modern-sector growth and employment expansion.

Income and wealth taxes also strike opposite chords with politicians and economists. Their unpopularity with politicians has been matched by their appeal to economists. Redistribution through taxes can minimize distortions and maximize fairness in both taking and giving. Perhaps to balance the traditional enthusiasm of economists, Harberger in chapter 7 has chosen to point out the market constraints on the use of taxes to redistribute wealth. The principal constraint noted is the possibility of migration abroad. This point reinforces earlier arguments against high taxes on capital income which stressed the reduction of both the incentive and the capacity to invest.

Chapter 7 is a useful corrective to the idea that one can use taxes to make major inroads into concentrations of income and wealth. Given the even greater limitations of wage policy, there seems no way short of radical property redistribution to achieve a significant reduction in very high incomes. This argument, however, must be qualified on two counts. First, there are surprising differences among less developed countries in the extent of income and wealth taxation, differences that are not explained away by degrees of development or by the size of the foreign sector. Such differences (e.g., between Brazil, where taxes recently equalled 21.4% of the GNP, and Colombia and Mexico, where they equalled 10.9% and 9.9%, respectively) suggest more room for maneuver than is implied by the economic constraints. Second, the fact that taxes cannot make major reductions at the top of the distribution does not imply that they cannot make a large impact at the bottom; small percentages of GNP can make enormous relative improvement if transferred (efficiently) to the very poor.

The third way to attack high incomes is via the redistribution of capital. This book does not address itself to the issue of the socialist alternative, which entails massive redistribution of property income. Partial redistribution of property, however, is a common feature of market and mixed economies, and the chapter by Cline and appendix 2 of Cauas and Selowsky examine the principal forms of such redistribution: agrarian reform and partial nationalization of business enterprises.

Their attitudes are in strong contrast. Cline sees land reform as one of the most promising approaches to redistribution. He argues that political resistance can be overcome through compensation, that the positive production effects of land reform can be sufficiently great that considerable benefits are left to peasants even after compensation, and that care in land allocation can avoid an inequitable pattern of allocation.

The success of land reform efforts depends more, however, on the configuration of political power than on monetary compensation. Most successful cases of land reform have taken place following sharp political change. In Kenya and Algeria, it occurred after a loss of power by foreign groups, who had become major landholders. In Egypt, Ethiopia, Mexico, and Bolivia, it followed a sudden political upheaval. In South Korea, the Japanese had acquired large landholdings during their occupation from 1910 to 1945. Under the impetus of the post-World War II American military government, the Korean regime which took over in 1948 expropriated the Japanese landholders and redistributed the land to Korean smallholders. In Taiwan, the Nationalist Chinese expropriated the native Taiwanese in favor of immigrants from the mainland. After the partition of the Indian subcontinent, an effective land reform was mounted in Muslim-run East Pakistan, where much of the best and largest landholdings were in Hundu hands. In contrast, in West Pakistan, Muslim landholders predominated and effective land reform did not occur.

There are, however, other contexts in which land reform might be successful. In Chile, Peru, and Venezuela, for instance, the wealthy landed class had undergone progressive political decline with the rise of reform-minded governments. The shift of economic activity from agriculture to the cities also led to a decline in the economic importance of these classes. A similar erosion of the power of landlords can be expected to occur in other countries as development proceeds, and as those countries shift from a predominantly agrarian structure to a more industrial one. As the political and economic power of landed elites declines, land expropriation becomes a more feasible policy. Ironically, however, as the feasibility of land reform is enhanced, its relevance as a means of redistributing income declines because the bulk of income is by then generated in the cities.

The allocative problems are also probably greater than is suggested by Cline. The disproportional grants of land, for example, to already better-off peasants or farm workers on the coast of Peru and on larger

Chilean farms, as well as the exclusion of most landless from the benefits of land reform in Iran, Egypt, and Algeria reflect more than policy mistakes. The spatial distributions of good land and of peasants rarely overlap closely, and moving peasants is a complicated social and technological task. On the other hand, difficulties of this sort rarely add up to a case against land reform; rather, they qualify the expected benefits both with respect to the number of potential beneficiaries and to the size of income gains.

Cauas and Selowsky concentrate on the possible negative side-effects of partial nationalization, chiefly through loss of confidence by investors and loss of tax revenues. They also argue that the beneficiaries of nationalization generally are not the extremely poor, since that result requires that the nationalized surplus be appropriated by the general budget and spent on the very poor; more likely, beneficiaries are clients of the nationalized firm (often, the rich owners of firms that are not nationalized) or workers in the affected firm. These arguments do not negate the potential of partial nationalization as a means of reducing high incomes if a government attaches enough weight to that objective to ignore its possible adverse side-effects.

In summary, short of substantial socialization, there are major economic as well as political constraints on attempts to reduce high incomes substantially, though such constraints are not usually tight enough to prevent the acquisition of the resources required to make a large impact on low incomes.

2. Reaching the very poor--and improving "delivery" in a market context

There has been a gradual change, amounting almost to a reversal, in the conventional wisdom regarding the redistributive problem. Until recently, the difficulty was thought to consist primarily in extracting income from the rich, and this, in turn, was closely identified with the need for major political change. Today, there is a much greater awareness of the difficulties involved in giving to the poor. This "delivery" problem is less a matter of basic power structures or regime types; instead it involves attitudes, perceptions, secondary political structures, administrative behavior, and market complications--distortions and backlash effects that are the inevitable results of attempts to modify market outcomes within a market economy. In most countries, redistribution is still difficult on both counts but, also in most, the chief barriers now seem to be on the delivery side.

This awareness of implementation and delivery problems is reflected in much of this volume, particularly in the chapters dealing with transfers of welfare and capital to the poor. This lesson has been learned the hard way, through the disappointing experience of numerous reformist and radical governments and the frustrated reform efforts of the aid agencies, over at least the last two decades. Regimes of all types seem to stumble over the same set of delivery problems. The most powerful evidence of such problems is provided by the comparatively feeble rural development programs of such oil- or mineral-rich countries as Iran, Zaire, and Ecuador. And it is evident in the contrast between egalitarian rhetoric and rural neglect in such radical regimes as Algeria, Egypt, and Peru.

Efforts to understand and explain delivery problems have been rudimentary. One reason is that awareness of such problems has been largely limited to persons involved in actual implementation, who usually attribute the specific difficulties they encounter to human failings, e.g., ignorance of supply and demand laws, wrong motivations, or insufficient entrepreneurial capacity. Most radicals, in turn, see such failures as proof of the need for major change in power structures, thus implying that there is some minimum critical redistribution of power—not achieved by "reformist" governments—that is a prerequisite for takeoff into an egalitarian society. The recurring and universal nature of most delivery problems suggests that more useful systematic explanations could be found by examining patterns in (i) the nature of extreme poverty, and (ii) the nature of reformist responses.

Many delivery failures can be traced to ignorance regarding who are the very poor. Such ignorance not only misleads sincere attempts to reach the poor but also facilitates hypocrisy regarding intended beneficiaries. Examples range from the gross, such as "low-cost" housing programs that benefit the top quartile and even top decile families, to the less obvious, such as land reforms that give least or nothing to peasants living in areas of marginal farmland where there is no good land to redistribute. Much of the policy literature underestimates the degree of variety among the poor and between and within countries—with respect, for instance, to the role of landlessness, unemployment, the health-productivity connection, social discrimination, urban or rural residence, backward regions, and lack of education and skills. The fact that the very poor in each country cut across multiple categories, in proportions that may differ considerably among countries, complicates the job of designing the right policy mix; the scarcity of studies on who are the poor has made it easy for poverty features noted in a particular country or region to be falsely generalized.

The lack of understanding of market mechanisms outside the modern sector has also hampered many delivery efforts. It has been learned, for instance, that land consolidation and crop diversification programs must allow for the risk-averting advantages of traditional arrangements, that rural credit cooperatives must compete with the flexibility and the marketing and other services provided by traditional moneylenders, that urban job expansion may increase the absolute number of urban poor, and that, as Levinson notes, school lunch programs may produce no net increase in nutritional intake by children. Other types of error resulting from a failure to predict market responses were cited above under the category of "backlash" effects.

What has reached the poor? It has been stated that the broad picture is not one of complete stagnation; indeed, for many of the poor, income growth has been rapid. General economic growth and deliberate policy efforts have interacted to produce some development for the poor. Different types of policy efforts are contributing to this development.

One category consists of small-scale, high-quality, and well-targeted programs. They tend to be run by highly motivated and talented individuals; many are sponsored by religious, private, and foreign sources. The programs cover many fields; some specialize in informal training, others in health services, others in agricultural extension, and yet others in urban housing. For both philosophical and budgetary reasons, the programs stress self-help and strive to develop motivation and entrepreneurial capacity. For the same reasons, principally limited budgets, they are oriented more to human resource development and do little in the way of infrastructure. Their prevalence varies widely: Latin America has been particularly open to such efforts; in Africa they have been curtailed by nationalism; while their largely Western cultural origin has greatly restricted their freedom to operate in the Middle East and in many Asian countries.

Some examples of successful programs of this type are the low-cost housing program, Hogar de Cristo, initiated by a Jesuit priest in Chile over 12 years ago, which has become a large-scale, well-organized institution that builds homes that are cheaper than those of official housing programs and yet are highly marketable. Private and Christian Democratic groups in Honduras are responsible for an extensive system of radio-schools providing adult literacy and technical training to a broad audience in remote communities scarcely touched by government rural development efforts. And in Guatemala there is a U.S. doctor who gave up his practice in the United States to start a small clinic and to train paramedics in a neglected rural district; his system of training villagers with scarcely two or three years of schooling to act as village health practitioners (selling their services) led to improved health conditions in a broad rural area outside the range of official health services. As is common with programs of such types, these cases have succeeded despite an often hostile government attitude.

The critical questions regarding such programs are, how replicable are they and are they suitable models for larger scale, more bureau-cratically managed programs? Many of these efforts have high hidden costs in the form of high-quality managerial inputs; in those programs where managerial costs are not subsidized, costs tend to be very high, as in the case of many programs staffed by UNDP, UNESCO, and other inter-national agency personnel. Their multiplicity and individualism also raise a question regarding replication: Which of the many programs are appropriate models for standardization on a mass scale? The missionary qualities which underlie their success unfortunately also lend themselves to strongly held diverse formulas of techniques for development. Despite a common stress on motivation and a grass-roots approach, they often point to a different cultural, political, or economic variable as the key that will turn vicious circles of poverty into beneficial circles of development.

A second source of benefits to the poor, at the opposite extreme, are the large-scale, usually low-quality and poorly targeted government programs—chiefly schooling, health services, farm extension and credit, and community infrastructure projects. The content of what is delivered through these programs tends to be poor and is at times dreadful, be it overly academic authoritarian-values oriented schooling, health services

designed to provide curative medicine for local elites rather than preventive public health to rural inhabitants, or services of agricultural
extension agents who are scarcely familiar with the ecology or culture
of their assigned regions.

On the other hand, a program which is ninety percent waste may be
better than none at all. Few would argue against mass primary schooling
even in an ineffective form.[14] And there is certainly a plausible argument, based on both a priori considerations and on circumstantial evidence, that mass primary schooling can promote broad economic and social
change. There is a strong correlation, for instance, between countries
with high human resource expenditures and more equality;[15] many would
relate the advanced social policies of the state of Kerala in India to its
early commitment to mass literacy. And there surely has been some sense
to the traditional opposition by landlords and local elites to educating
the peasants; although ninety-nine of every hundred students return to
plough the soil with nothing gained, the community as a whole may gain
one literate leader.[16]

Though reformists continually shy away from the seemingly hopeless
task of improving these bureaucracies, preferring instead to set up parallel small-scale model programs aimed at inspiring (but usually fated to
antagonize) the establishment, the fact remains that the sheer size of
these bureaucracies provides enormous leverage to even the smallest improvement. Judged by cost-benefit standards, they are grossly inefficient, but since their absolute benefits are probably not negative, they
must be considered as at least one approach to reducing absolute poverty.

A third source of benefits to the poor is the spillover or leakage
from programs and projects aimed either at better-off groups or at overall
economic growth with no deliberate distributive targeting. Major infrastructure projects fall into this category: a major road linking two
industrial centers cannot help but provide access to a large number of
rural inhabitants in between. Service innovations, such as government
institutions to develop marketing channels for new farm exports, become
available to small as well as to large farmers.

There is a widespread tendency to downgrade the potential for
income improvement via spillover or trickle-down. This view, supported
both by wide evidence of growing dualism and slow employment growth and
by a belief in the power of exploitative arrangements, has served to

underwrite the more powerful reformist attacks on the rich. If the
potential gains from spillover are large, however, then the additional
efforts on behalf of the poor by radical regimes may be more than offset
by the loss of modern-sector growth that results from attempts to
squeeze, rather than substitute for, the capitalist sector. Such potential spillover consists not only of modern-sector employment expansion
but also of both the additional demand for small-scale service jobs in
cities and the leakage of benefits from capital and innovations intended
for the modern sector, such as highways and new marketing arrangements.
Bruton's chapter stresses the potential employment benefits of rapid
modern-sector growth. There can be no a priori answer to what is the
best mix of growth and redistribution for the poor. The degree of spillover will depend both on market features and on policy design, and the
same is true of how redistribution affects growth. The basic point, however, is that both growth and redistribution are tools for raising low-end
incomes and that a best policy mix for reaching the poor must consider the
probable effect of each.

Three broad areas of policy effort have been discussed, each making
some contribution to raising low-end incomes. They should clearly be seen
as complementary rather than as alternatives, despite possible variations
in the stress placed on each. A good strategy would attack the problem of
absolute poverty along all three lines, partly because none is highly
promising in itself and partly because they serve different functions and
also reinforce each other.

Small-scale efforts, for instance, have the advantage that they reach
down to some of the very poorest groups—groups that are usually bypassed
by the larger official programs and by market spillovers. Such efforts
also contain innovations and continually challenge the musty procedures
of bureaucracies; and they are usually subversive, working at the community level and injecting an attitutde of self-reliance and an aggressive,
demanding posture before the authorities, in contrast to the authoritarian
and paternalistic attitudes that characterize bureaucracies.

The larger government programs, in turn, help through sheer volume;
their existence makes it easier for poor communities to perceive wants
and formulate demands (e.g., upgrade a village school or add an extra
nurse to the local health center), and they provide a channel for the
gradual introduction or filtering-down of new ideas and techniques

regarding both content and method of delivery. Some pilot programs and experimental approaches have excellent potential for growing into highly promising large-scale programs. Two have been discussed in detail: various types of family planning schemes reviewed by Boulier in chapter 5 and large-scale public works programs proposed by Lewis in chapter 9. The adult literacy program in Brazil (MOBRAL) seems to be an example of a large-scale official effort that has retained the entrepreneurial dynamism of smaller programs.

Finally, growth-oriented efforts make an additional contribution to raising low-end incomes, in part by direct market spillovers and in part because market-generated increases in income are necessary to other efforts to improve health and nutrition, to lower population growth, and to increase human capital. Levinson makes this point very explicitly "...it is unlikely that nutrition policies alone will provide viable long-term benefits to the lowest income groups in the absence of related socio-economic improvements. The two are complementary and must be addressed in tandem if desirable results are to be achieved."[17]

In the end, however, reaching the poor may be as difficult and as much a "structural" problem as that of extracting from the rich. Past experience indicates that severe constraints are imposed by working within a society whose institutions and values must be primarily geared to the dominant sources of income. In this sense the radical thesis may be right, that profound structural change is a prerequisite to any transfers to the poor beyond the current trickle, though not because of the greediness and power of the capitalist rich. In fact, although socialization of all modern-sector property might provide the financial base for redistribution, it does little to solve the delivery problem if the institutions and administrative attitudes are biased toward large-scale and capital-intensive activities unsuited to the needs of traditional-sector producers.

Thus the socialization of the modern sector is probably not the principal, perhaps not even an appropriate, answer to the problem of effecting a substantial increase in income and capital transfers to the poor. The answers needed are more particularistic and subtle. They are more complex. But they are no less difficult and radical.

3.   Improving the market as a distributive mechanism

The two elements of a redistributive strategy examined thus far--taking from the rich and giving to the poor--both entail considerable economic and political difficulties. One way to lighten the burden on these forms of redistributive intervention is to adapt the market to produce a more equitable distribution in the first place. In developing countries, this could be done largely by redistributing the ownership of physical capital and by reducing dualism in the productive structure. To what extent are such policies feasible? To what extent are they compatible with growth?

The issue of property redistribution was discussed above under the heading of "taking from the rich." It was argued that there is a substantial difference between the redistribution of land and of other physical property. Land reform has by far a greater redistributive potential for several reasons: it is likely to have broader political and social effects within the countryside that favor the poor; it is a way of reaching very poor groups directly; and often it is complementary (and perhaps a prerequisite) to other policies needed to raise low-end incomes in the rural sector (chiefly measures to raise the productivity of small farms). By contrast, although nonagricultural business property can be nationalized, there is no straightforward way of transferring that property income to the very poor. The poorer rural multitudes cannot be made shareholders or owners of urban property in any meaningful sense, i.e., with some ability to control its management. The only political arrangement that is likely to ensure the transfer of that property income to the very poor is a socialist government with the power to prevent workers in the nationalized firms, and other middle and urban groups, from appropriating that income. The expropriation of the rich could eventually have favorable political results for the poor, but such effects are less certain and would follow less directly than those to be expected from land reform.

The second way to reduce market inequalities is to reduce dualism in the productive structure, i.e., to reduce the differences between productivity levels in the modern and traditional sectors. Some of the effects of dualism on income distribution are discussed in this chapter. This strategy is often called "employment creation," since it consists largely of making the modern sector more labor-intensive and thus of employing more people in the modern sector with a given stock of capital. This strategy is recommended by Bruton in chapter 3.

Reducing dualism in the productive structure should generate a better income distribution for several reasons. First, wage differentials between the modern and traditional sectors will be smaller for either or both of the following reasons: capital-intensive firms require more skilled and educated labor; and they facilitate unionization and wage pressures. Second, capital ownership is likely to be more evenly spread when firms are labor-intensive because such firms have fewer economies of scale and thus lend themselves to easier entry and to smaller scale production by many firms. Third, to the extent that dualism is _caused_ by market distortions, and also, to the extent that dualism--whatever the cause--has _generated_ wage distortions, reducing dualism should increase efficiency and growth, and thus enhance market spillover to the traditional sector. Finally, there is the broader argument that income is more easily redistributed within than between productive (modern and traditional) sectors:[18] groups that are in some way involved in the production or control of modern-sector output--chiefly capitalists, modern-sector workers, and the civilian and military bureaucrats--are favored both by tactical advantage and a sense of legitimacy in pressing their claims for a share of that sector's output.

The potential for reducing productivity differentials naturally varies enormously between countries; dualism has become extreme in the oil- and mineral-rich countries. Also, since the distributive effects of dualism create vested interests, it is politically more difficult to undo these effects than to prevent them.

One major source of dualism consists of factor price distortions, and strong arguments have been advanced by economists[19] that better pricing and allocation policies are likely to produce major long-run benefits in the form of faster growth and lesser inequality. If the short-run effects of such policy corrections on existing vested interest groups can be minimized, e.g., by heavily subsidizing labor-intensive investments (through tax breaks and export bonuses for instance), a "distributive swindle" becomes possible: Large distributive improvements can be brought about over the long run at the price of small, regressive government favors today.

Less commonly noted, however, is a second major source of dualism:
the growth of socialism or state capitalism. This is partly an ideological trend and partly "an act of God": Oil and mineral riches are thrust-
ing socialism on many countries. The enormous revenues from such sources
are necessaily appropriated by the public sector. Governments are strongly
biased toward uses of those resources that are highly capital-intensive.

The good, and perhaps most powerful, reason for that bias is the
scarcity of entrepreneurial talent in government; and large-scale,
capital-intensive investments are far cheaper in terms of managerial
resources per dollar invested than a multitude of small-scale and region-
ally dispersed investments in labor-intensive enterprises. The bad
reasons include corruption, which thrives with the purchase of large-scale
capital goods, and the technocratic biases of bureaucrats. These factors
help to explain the paradox of regimes with strong socialist and egalitarian leanings, such as those in Algeria and Peru, which channel the
bulk of their investible resources into projects that are highly capital-
intensive rather than into the traditional sector.

The prospects for reducing dualism are therefore highly variable
between countries. Where the prospects are good, a potential exists for
long-run improvements in income distribution or, at least, for avoiding
growing inequality. Even in the best of cases, however, it is an indirect (and slow) tool for attacking low-end poverty, particularly in such
largely agrarian countries as India and Indonesia, and should thus be
considered a complement to more direct policies aimed at reducing poverty.

G.   Conclusions

The chapters in this book are more detailed in pointing out difficulties and negative effects than in indicating positive opportunities. This
bias is a reflection of actual situations, in the sense that there are
more failures and problems to record than successes, and of the feeling
that many of the related problems have resulted from naive and careless
policy-making and that a review of common errors is therefore constructive.

Even so, very few generalizations can be drawn from so broad a review,
and on so disparate a data base. The variety of distributive ends, policy
means, and economic and political circumstances imply that policy opportunities and best options must be discovered case by case. The following
are guides to the evaluation of distributive possibilities in particular case

Regime type, particularly the degree of "leftness," is less of a critical determinant than is often thought. The particular mix of policy opportunities, however, will nonetheless be related to regime types: In less redistributive-minded regimes the best feasible strategy will be one that is less overtly redistributive and more opportunistic in designing policies aimed at other goals that have favorable redistributive effects as well. The strategy should also search for those types of measures favoring the poor that have a particularly high degree of legitimacy or elite support, whether for reasons of morality or self-interest.

In most settings, the best strategy will be one that is highly mixed and integrated with policies aimed at nondistributive goals. None of the policy approaches reviewed in this book will carry distribution far on its own. A wide variety of approaches must be pursued simultaneously for the total effect to be meaningful.

Growth must be an integral part of redistributive strategy because growth is a direct tool for raising low-end incomes, via the spillover of demand for labor and rural output and the leakages from growth-oriented investment projects, and because the growth target will co-opt or limit many of the available policy instruments so that redistributive possibilities must be framed within the context of a growth strategy.

There seems to be no easy solution to improving equity. Even socialism may not carry redistribution far, particularly poverty reduction, unless it involves a strong egalitarian intent and a heavy political and administrative control of the rural sector. Markets as well as politics impose constraints on the extent and form of feasible redistribution. A greater awareness of those limitations and of the need for a multiple approach to achieving more equity will provide a better basis for future identification and design of more promising redistributive strategies.

Finally, a critical prerequisite to success will be seriousness of purpose. Improvement is most likely to follow from partial advances along many different fronts, from a constant bearing in mind of distributive aspects when considering growth and other policy objectives, and from more attention to minor design aspects and to the manner and degree of implementation. These are qualities of policy-making that can be found in regimes with very different political orientations. In the end, therefore, much will turn on human qualities, particularly on a sincere

intent and dedication in searching for and following up the many opportunities for change.

Chapter 1

NOTES

1. See Richard J. Szal, "A Methodology for Evaluating Income Distribution Data," Discussion Paper 54, Research Program in Economic Development, Woodrow Wilson School, Princeton University.

2. Montek S. Ahluwalia, "Income Inequality: Some Dimensions of the
Problem," ed., H. Chenery et al., Redistribution With Growth (London:
Oxford University Press, 1974), pp. 3-37; and Irma Adelman and C. T.
Morris, Economic Growth and Social Equity in Developing Countries
(Stanford University Press, 1973). Most of the trend evidence in these
compilations is based on the comparison of percentile shares in income
shown in sample surveys taken in different years. Differences in coverage, concepts, and sampling procedures make such comparisons extremely
risky.

3. See Albert Berry, "Changing Income Distribution Under Develop-
ment: Colombia," Review of Income and Wealth, ser. 20 (September 1974);
I. Rajaraman, "Poverty, Inequality and Economic Growth: Rural Punjab
1960-61 - 1970-71," Discussion Paper 45, Research Program in Economic
Development, Woodrow Wilson School, Princeton University, 1974; and,
Webb, "Trends in Real Income in Peru, 1950-1966," Discussion Paper 41,
Research Program in Economic Development, Woodrow Wilson School, Prince-
ton University, 1974.

4. On the assumption of declining marginal utility of income, i.e.,
an extra dollar means more to a man who has $100 a year than to a man who
has $10,000 a year.

5. Military coups, for instance, caused sharp leftward movements in
Peru, Ethiopia, and Portugal.

6. See discussion of evidence by Cline in chapter 8.

7. Excellent discussions of political constraints and reform possibilities may be found in Albert O. Hirschman, Journeys Toward Progress:
Studies of Economic Policy Making in Latin America (Twentieth Century Fund,
1963); and Clive L. G. Bell, "The Political Framework," ed., Hollis Chenery
et al., Redistribution with Growth.

8. See Arthur Lewis' comment cited by Webb in chapter 6. Stabilization problems in 1952 forced Peron to reverse some of his earlier wage
increases. The military regime in Peru has also followed this pattern.

9. John D. Montgomery, Professor at the J.F.K. School of Government of Harvard University, participated in a number of the seminar and conference meetings held during the project, and provided a written commentary, "Fiscal Policy and Social Equity," on A. Harberger's "Fiscal Policy and Income Distribution," which is printed as chapter 7 in this book.

10. There is a wide literature on the private-regarding behavior of civil servants. See for example, Bert F. Hoselitz, "Levels of Economic Performance and Bureaucratic Structures," ed., Joseph La Palombara, Bureaucracy and Political Development (Princeton University Press, 1963), pp. 168-198; Arnold Heidenheimer, Political Corruption (New York: Holt, Reinhart, and Winston, 1970).

11. See, for example, Ralph Braibanti et al., Political and Administrative Development (Durham: Duke University Press, 1969).

12. See, for example, Irving Swerdlow, ed., Development Administration (Syracuse University Press, 1963). Also see Hyden Jackson and Okumu, Development Administration: The Kenyan Experience (Nairobi: Oxford University Press, 1971).

13. Bernard Schaffer, ed., Administrative Training and Development: A Comparative Study of East Africa, Zambia, Pakistan and India (New York: Praeger, 1974).

14. Harbison is skeptical in chapter 4 about the value of crash programs in achieving universal primary education but does not suggest the curtailment of existing expenditure on primary schools, which often amounts to between ten and twenty percent of government budgets, and would even accept increased levels of expenditure in regions where growth is being stimulated in other ways.

15. Irma Adelman and C. T. Morris, Economic Growth and Social Equity; also Ahluwalia, "Income Inequality: Some Dimensions of the Problem," p. 29.

16. A more realistic result may be that fifty return to their farms, forty-nine migrate to towns, and one remains as a better potential leader.

17. Levinson and Oftedal, chapter 10 of this book. Harbison also stresses in chapter 4 the complementarity between human resource improvement and programs that promote general economic development.

18. This argument is developed in R. Webb, Government Policy and the Distribution of Income in Peru 1963-1973. (Cambridge, Mass.: Harvard University Press), 1977.

19. For example, Bruton in chapter 3 of this book; and Gustav Ranis, "Industrial-Sector Labor Absorption," Economic Development and Cultural Change, vol. 21, no. 3 (April 1973), pp. 387-408.

CAUSES OF INCOME DISTRIBUTION AND GROWTH IN LESS DEVELOPED COUNTRIES:
SOME REFLECTIONS ON THE RELATION BETWEEN THEORY AND POLICY

Charles R. Frank, Jr., and Richard Webb

Policies which affect income distribution are the main focus of this book. There are two theoretical questions, however, which ought to receive attention before launching into a discussion of policy. The first is a positive question; the second a normative one.

The positive question that must be asked is: What is the nature of the economic mechanism which generates a distribution of income? The nature of this mechanism affects very much how various policies might work and, most importantly, what might be the secondary, or unintended, effects of a particular policy action. If market imperfections are a main source of variations in income and wealth among individuals, then policies designed to break those imperfections may be the most efficacious.

The normative question that must be asked is: What are the goals of policy? Should policy be designed to alleviate the grinding poverty of the very poorest segments of the population? Should it attack the incomes of the very richest? Or should the focus be not on income distribution per se but on increasing the mobility of individuals within a particular distribution of income?

The theoretical basis for review of the second or normative question is the subject of an appendix to this book by Richard Szal and Sherman Robinson. The first question, about the mechanism that generates the distribution of income and changes in that distribution as development takes place, is discussed from a theoretical standpoint in this chapter.

NOTE:

The authors thank Gerald Epstein who served not only as a research assistant but also as a perceptive critic.

A.   Introduction

The standard approach in the literature on the economics of income
distribution is to analyze the receipt of income in terms of returns to
the factors of production--land, labor, and capital.   The starting point
is usually marginal productivity theory.[1]   Modifications are often made
to the theory to take into account market imperfections.   The theory of
income distribution is not well developed for analysis of policies for
altering the size distribution of income among individuals or families,
which is the principal focus of this chapter.

It is not surprising that there is no well-unified theory of income
distribution.   There are many factors which affect the distribution of
income and many conceivable policies which could alter income distribution.   It is foolish to think that any one theory can provide a model for
analyzing all of these factors and policies.   Theoretical models must be
designed with a specific and limited purpose in mind.   Otherwise, the number of variables and the inter-relationships among them become so complicated that analysis is impossible.

In section B of this chapter, some simple theoretical models of
income distribution and growth in less developed countries are first
considered, with emphasis on the distinction between the traditional (or
informal) sector and the modern sector.   In section C, there is a discussion of the case of extreme dualism in which incomes in the modern and traditional sectors diverge very significantly, and the divergence seems to
grow.

In sections D and E, respectively, the income distribution implications of the distribution of human capital assets and of private physical
assets among the population are analyzed.   Section F discusses how government expenditure and taxation policies can modify the distribution of
income.   Section G considers size distribution of income over time.

In section H there is a consideration of the various policy options
available which might alter the distribution of income and the theoretical
constructs useful in the analysis of these policies.   Four distinct sets
of policies are identified: (i) market interventions, (ii) confiscatory
policies, (iii) redirection of public services, and (iv) government
policies that are expenditure oriented.   Each of these policy sets is
analyzed in a different manner, from the standpoint of theory and relevant

literature. This will provide a solid basis for more detailed analysis
of these policy issues in later chapters.

B. <u>Simple models of the relationship between income distribution and
    growth</u>

The basic model chosen for use in analyzing the relationship between
income and growth is the dualistic model in which there are two main sectors, modern and traditional, or more appropriately, modern and informal.
At times, there may be a need to distinguish between urban and rural
subsectors of the informal and modern sectors.

Workers in the traditional sector have much lower average levels of
productivity and also lower wages than those in the modern sector. Capital
accumulation in the modern sector is more rapid than that in the traditional sector, and workers are transferred from the traditional sector into
the modern sector as development proceeds. As in the usual labor surplus
model of growth, the supply of labor from the traditional sector to the
modern sector is infinitely elastic.[2]

Growth in the dualistic context is in part a consequence of being a
late-comer: Resources are suddenly switched from very traditional technologies to the best-method techniques of today. In these labor surplus
models, growth takes place more by the large, discrete jump in the productivity of factors reallocated from informal to modern activities than
by a widespread and gradual increase in the productivity of all factors.

In the initial stages of dualistic development the distribution of
income worsens, first because the growth in total income makes greater
inequality possible[3] and second, because dualistic growth in a labor
surplus context implies that most of the growth in output and incomes
will accrue to owners of capital and to the minority of workers who make
the transition from the informal to the modern sector. This model also
implies that the trend toward increasing inequality will slow down, and
that it may reverse. Once a majority of labor is incorporated into the
high-productivity, high-wage sector, further transfers of workers actually
improve the distribution of labor income. Also, eventually labor in the
informal sector is no longer in excess supply, so further modern sector
absorption of labor will tend to raise traditional-sector incomes.
Whether the overall distribution of income actually begins to improve,
however, will depend on changes in the share and degree of concentration

of property income, and these changes cannot be predicted from this model.[4]

Several statistical studies tend to corroborate the predicted relationship between growth and inequality. The best known is the observed association by Kuznets of inequality and levels of development.[5] Measures of GNP per capita and inequality compiled by Kuznets fell into a pattern that is now commonly referred to as the Kuznets, or U-shaped, hypothesis: Inequality first rises and later falls as an economy progresses from very low to high levels of development. This pattern was borne out by both the cross-section and the time-series data examined by Kuznets, who outlines various mechanisms to explain this pattern, particularly the earlier trend of increasing inequality. His explanations are plausible but, to the extent that they go beyond the mechanics of the labor-surplus model, they are more suggestive than rigorous. Other studies which support the U-shaped hypothesis include those of Adelman and Morris, Weiskoff, and Paukert.[6]

The dualistic model of development implies a somewhat fatalistic approach to income distribution in developing countries. In the initial stages of development, the size distribution of income is certain to become worse. The modern sector is dynamic and is the source of profits and savings from profits. What little surplus emerges in the traditional sector often accrues to a rentier class which, in the best of circumstances, transfers the surplus into modern-sector investments or, at worst, dissipates the surplus in high living. In the long run, however, the degree of inequality is certain to diminish—but the distribution of income must first get worse before it gets better.

This basically pessimistic conclusion is reinforced by the usual presumption that it is the rich households that save and the poor households that consume. It is often argued that any attempt to redistribute income from the rich to the poor will reduce total savings and investment and thus reduce the rate of growth. The validity of these arguments, however, depends on fairly large differences in _marginal_ (rather than average) savings rates between the rich and the poor. Recent empirical work indicates that such large differences do not seem to exist and that the tradeoff between more equal income distribution and savings rates is very small, if it exists at all.[7]

Furthermore, there is little in the way of recent historical experience of developing countries to indicate that the relationship between growth and the distribution of income is a very simple one. A study by Ahluwalia suggests that the fastest growing less developed countries have less rather than more inequality.[8] In some rapidly developing countries, inequality has been decreasing (e.g., Taiwan), in others, it has neither increased nor decreased (e.g., Korea), while in still others, the distribution of income is rapidly becoming more unequal (e.g., Mexico and Brazil). Although the Ahluwalia study lends some credence to the Kuznets, U-shaped hypothesis, the relationship is weak and there are many countries which deviate substantially from the Kuznets norm. The levels of inequality vary substantially among poor countries and among rich countries. There is considerable overlap in the degree of inequality among countries at all levels of development.

The empirical evidence suggests that there are many factors which operate on the distribution of income and that these factors may change over time within any one country. It also suggests that there is considerable scope for policies to alter the distribution of income.

A more complicated theory of growth and distribution is required to explain the empirical findings. One way to approach such a theory is to assume that the overall distribution of income can be decomposed into two parts: (i) that due to variations of income within the modern and traditional sectors (or within the urban and rural subsectors), and (ii) that due to variations in income between sectors. The overall level of inequality is a function, then, of the two sources of variation, that within and that between sectors, and also of the relative size of the various sectors.

C. Isolation of the modern sector: dualism run rampant

In order to analyze further the relationship between distribution and growth, let us contrast two extremes in terms of initial conditions. At one extreme, the modern and informal sectors are highly differentiated, with large differences in productivity and wage structure between the sectors. The modern sector, with its relatively high wage rates, is highly capital-intensive, enjoys high levels of import protection, and uses relatively sophisticated technology. At the other extreme, the differences between the sectors are minimal. Wage rates are similar for similar jobs, and the markets for labor and capital are highly competitive, with relatively few imperfections.

In an economy with highly differentiated sectors, high profits are maintained by protection from imports, subsidized interest rates, modest taxes on corporations, and an overvalued domestic currency, combined with an exchange control system which encourages imports of low-cost capital goods.[9] In an economy which is not highly dualistic, high profits arise because of modest real wages in the modern sector, rather than because of capital subsidies. If profits in both types of economy are relatively the same, the overall distribution of income in the highly dualistic economy will be much more uneven than in the relatively homogeneous economy.[10] The reason, of course, is the difference in income between modern-sector workers and workers in the informal sector.

A simple way to represent the link between dualism and income distribution is shown in figure 1.[11] The curve PP' describes the distribution

Figure 1

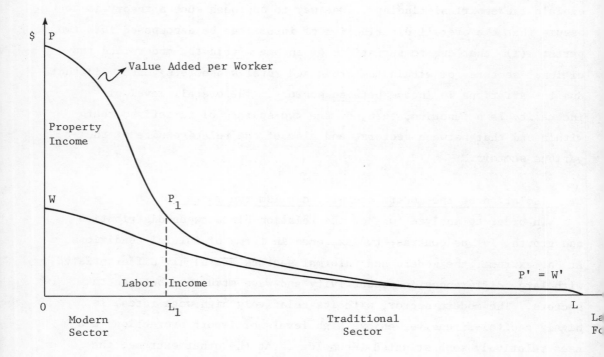

of labor productivity in a dualistic economy: a small number of workers (OL_1) working with large amounts of machinery, equipment, and natural resources, and using modern technology have high levels of productivity (value added per worker); scarce resources and traditional technologies generate much lower levels of productivity for the labor force in the "traditional sector" (L_1L). The latter sector generally has both urban and rural components, while the modern sector is largely urban in most countries but can have a large modern farming or plantation component in some countries.

The income distribution is described in figure 1, first, by the shape of WW', which represents the income received by each worker, be it a wage or a mixed entrepreneurial and labor income, if he is self-employed. The area under WW' is the share of labor in national income; the area above is the share of property income not accruing to self-employed persons, i.e., it is the share accruing to "capitalists."

A pattern of growth now common to many developing countries involves increasing dualism: output per worker grows faster in the modern than in the traditional sector, and at the same time, the modern sector does not grow significantly as a proportion of the labor force. This growth pattern, described by P_1P' in figure 2 is contrary to the horizontal, labor-absorbing growth path predicted by the labor-surplus model (PP_2P').

Increasing dualism in the structure of production is accompanied by increasing income disparities between sectors. Differences in income between modern and traditional sectors become far more important in explaining income inequality than variations of income within sectors.

The key mechanism in this growing concentration of income is the growth of wages in the modern sector.[12] Wage increases in this sector can come about because of increased unionization and the political strength of labor groups. Another reason why wages in the modern sector might be pushed up and relatively few workers employed in the modern sector is an increase in the supply of skilled and educated labor. This results in employment of more high-level manpower and possibly considerable substitution of high-level manpower for unskilled workers, especially if the elasticity of substitution between skilled and unskilled workers is high.

High wages and low levels of employment in the modern sector may also be a function of imported technology, particularly that embodied in imported capital equipment. If imported equipment is skilled-labor using

Figure 2

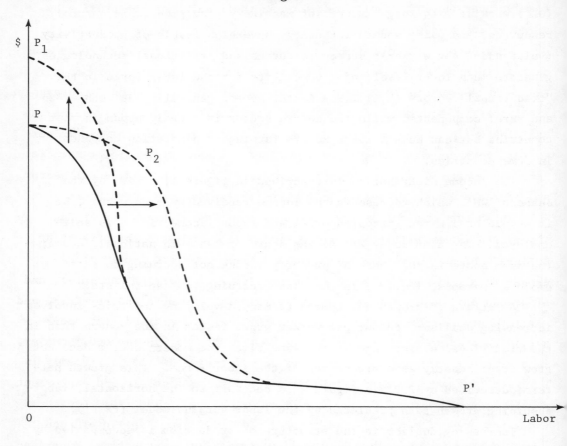

and unskilled-labor saving, the demand for skilled workers will increase
relative to the demand for unskilled workers. The wages and employment
of skilled workers relative to unskilled workers will increase, driving
up average wages in the modern sector. Alternatively, the capital
equipment used in the modern sector may require workers to be trained on
the job to very high levels of skill and productivity. If these skills
are transferable from one firm or factory to another, at least part of
the increased productivity due to on-the-job training will accrue to the
individual worker in the form of higher wages.

A final type of mechanism involves government policies, such as subsidized credit and an overvalued currency, which encourage capital-
intensive modes of production in the modern sector. Entrepreneurs, basing
their investment decisions on current wage rates and subsidized capital,
may install plant and equipment which locks them into a high capital-labor
ratio. Under these circumstances, the level of profits per worker may be

quite high. Ex-post, organized labor groups within a highly capitalized firm may see the opportunity to increase their share of the profits by pressing for higher wages.

With such factors operating, there is a tendency for high wages and capital intensity to interact. High wages relative to the cost of capital induce entrepreneurs to invest in a capital-intensive fashion. Conversely, highly capital-intensive firms provide opportunities for: (i) on-the-job training which increases productivity and (ii) high levels of profit per worker, both of which lead to higher wages. These interacting tendencies make the modern sector more and more distinct from the traditional sector and increase income disparities between the two sectors through time.

The above view exaggerates the degree of "bottling-up" of productivity and income within the modern sector. It neglects the offsetting influence of smaller-scale technological changes within the informal sector (e.g., new seeds, bicycles, power tools, and sewing machines), and of demand spillovers for both urban traditional products and services, and for farm goods. The first is a relatively autonomous trend, not necessarily related to developments in the modern sector. The second, however, is a direct function of the growth of modern-sector income, especially in the case of the urban traditional sector where total income and employment depend largely on total income in the modern sector. The rapid growth of the urban traditional sector is a major form of income "spillover" and thus, a major qualification to the simple dualistic growth model described above.

The existence of these various offsetting influences to increasing dualism is evident in the income growth experience of broad groups of informal-sector workers in countries such as Colombia,[13] Mexico,[14] and Peru.[15] At the same time, the existence of some trickle-down amounts to a qualification but not a substantial modification of the picture of growing dualism and inequality described in figure 2.

By way of contrast, in the homogeneous economy, since there is no factor price distinction between modern and informal sectors, as development proceeds, the increased demand for labor tends to raise real wage rates uniformly throughout the economy. Whether income inequality increases or decreases depends, in part at least, on the elasticity of substitution between labor and capital.

D. Returns to human capital assets

In section C the role of wage rates in influencing the distribution of income was emphasized. In this and the next section, rates of return to privately owned assets, both human capital assets and physical assets, and the distribution of those assets among the population are emphasized. An unequal distribution of wealth in the form of physical or human capital assets can make the distribution of income vary considerably both within sectors and between sectors.

The returns to human capital assets in the form of wage and salary payments differ considerably from individual to individual and from country to country. Generally, in less developed countries disparities in wages among different skill levels tend to be very great. For example, in a less developed country a common laborer might make $1.00 per day, a skilled craftsman $7.00 per day, and an office manager $25.00 per day. In a developed country, however, the ratio instead of being 1 to 7 to 25 might be 1 to 2 to 2.5 for the three different classes of workers.

One explanation for wage and salary differentials is marginal productivity theory.[16] According to the theory, each individual is paid his marginal product. Marginal products differ because of differences in both acquired and innate skills. The differences are particularly acute at low levels of development since persons with a high level of acquired skills are in short supply relative to the supply of unskilled labor. Those individuals in possession of scarce skills receive quasi-rents. As skills are acquired through education and training, wage and salary differentials should narrow and the quasi-rents accruing to individuals with scarce skills should disappear. Differences in wages and salaries remain because of differences in innate abilities and differences in motivation and attitudes which lead to productive efficiency.

One of the corollaries of the marginal productivity theory is that it would be inefficient to attempt to equalize wages and salaries. Without these differences there would be no incentive to improve skills through education and training, no reward for motivation and effort, no premium for the use of imagination and innovational abilities. Even innate skills would not be used unless some differential were paid to elicit their use. Wage and salary equality can be bought only at the expense of inefficiency and stagnation. This is particularly true in less developed countries where equalization of wages and salaries would induce skilled individuals to emigrate to other countries where their skills are rewarded differentially.

This corollary, however, carries little force if there are significant market imperfections or skills are acquired on the job rather than through education or prior training. For example, the tradeoff between equality and efficiency might not be as great as the marginal productivity theory suggests if there is not equal access to education and training for the acquisition of skills. Only children of rich families can afford to forego income during the period of education and training. In theory, a poor family could borrow to educate its children and the return in the future would more than enable the loan to be repaid. Capital markets, however, are imperfect, so that borrowing for such a long-term and uncertain return is not usually feasible for the poor family. The answer by the marginal productivity theorist to this criticism is usually that the solution lies not in attempts to equalize wages and salaries but in attempts to improve the functioning of capital markets by some form of government intervention.

Another type of market imperfection occurs when monopoly power is exercised by various segments of the work force. The basic techniques used are the restriction of entry into specific jobs or professions which forces up the market price of the workers or professional services among the members of a trade, profession, or industrial union. Sometimes entry into a trade or profession is restricted by numerical quotas, as is done by some skilled trade unions. At other times, entry may be restricted by professional opposition to an expansion in training facilities, as the medical profession in the United States has been accused of doing. Some professional groups, such as certified public accountants and insurance actuaries, have a very stiff series of examinations which must be taken over an extended period of time and which serve effectively as a barrier to entry for many people aspiring to these professions. Entry into professions is often restricted by customs which discriminate against minority groups, blacks, ethnic groups, or foreigners, or discriminate on the basis of class or caste, political affiliation, sex, and so on.

Examples of the use of bargaining or political power to set fees or prices for services also abound. Real estate (and in some countries, stock) brokers operate on the basis of fixed commission schedules. Labor unions bargain for higher wages. The more powerful unions or those led by more skillful bargainers reap the largest gains in wages and fringe benefits. Those not represented by powerful unions suffer relatively. This is particularly a problem in less developed countries, in which the modern urban sector is relatively small. Workers in that sector are often the only ones represented by strong unions or they are able to exercise political power directly through demonstrations and general strikes. The great mass of workers operating in the traditional sectors do not have such power.

Another reason for the lack of tradeoff between equity and efficiency is that skills may be very job specific and acquired only by training on the job. An individual may be selected for a particular job only by chance. If he is lucky enough to be selected for a job which requires a high degree of training, his wage or salary will grow as he acquires skills, and eventually will reach a high level. His employer has an incentive to pay him well since the employee, unless he is under a long-term contract, can move to another employer for whom his skills are transferable. Alternatively, an individual may be selected for a particular job on the basis of caste or class, ethnic background, regional origin, or on the basis of some other social or cultural distinction not necessarily related to abilities or skill. A person from a particular class or ethnic background or region may obtain preferred access to jobs which involve a high level of skills acquired through on-the-job training. This gives him preferred access then to a high income.

Education may also be used as a filtering device to determine access to high-skill, high-paying jobs. This theory in its extreme form involves the assumption that education has nothing to do with the acquisition of skills. Educational qualifications are merely used as a means of restricting access to jobs. Desirable jobs have high education qualifications attached to them as a means of eliminating the number of applicants who have to be considered by an employer for a particular job. As average educational attainment increases, educational qualifications for various jobs are elevated. According to this theory, any other filtering device might do just as well as education.

A variant of this theory is that education imparts no skills at all but merely provides a series of barriers at each level of education over which only the more able and industrious are able to hurdle. Real skills are acquired on the job, but educational attainment is related to the ability to absorb training and acquire skills rapidly since education is an indicator of intelligence and diligence.[17]

The theory that skills and earning capacity are acquired on the job and are very job-specific leads to different conclusions with regard to the effects of artificially imposed wage equality. Under this theory, wage and salary differentials arise because skills are embodied in workers through the process of on-the-job training. If wages were made more equal, employers would still have incentive to train their workers and increase productivity. Wage and salary differentials are not needed to give incentive to workers to increase their education and training prior to their entry into the job market.

E. Factors affecting the distribution of income from private assets

Although there may be a host of factors operating to determine income from wages and salaries, the main difference between the very rich and the poor is not wages and salaries but income accruing from privately held assets.[18] In many less developed countries, particularly in Latin America, large fortunes are made from holdings of large tracts of land. As industrialization takes hold, some people become very rich through the accumulation of industrial assets.

As in the case of returns to labor, the most well-developed economic theory of the distribution of income from assets is the marginal productivity theory. The return from the use of a physical asset is its marginal productivity.

According to the marginal productivity theory, assets are accumulated through time by individuals with a low rate of time discount.[19] People with a low rate of time discount save and invest and in this manner accumulate assets. Differences that arise in the rate of accumulation of assets also arise because of differences in risk aversion. Since some investments are risky while others are not, and some investors have an aversion to risk, the investor who is willing to take extra risks can expect a higher average return on his assets, and thus on the average, investors who are willing to accept risks will accumulate assets more rapidly.

If the rate of return on assets were eliminated or forced to a low level, there would be no incentives to accumulate assets, either by improving land or investing in buildings, equipment, or machinery, and no incentive to take risks. Some returns, which are in the form of pure

rents, accruing to ownership of land and natural resources, could be confiscated without any adverse effect on incentives and efficiency. It
might be difficult, however, to determine the pure rental element of an
asset's value, and any attempt to confiscate the pure rental element
may in fact also reduce the incentive aspect.

The marginal productivity theory is criticized by those who see
little justification for interest income. A problem arises in trying to
explain the rate of interest; marginal productivity theorists would say
that the rate of interest is the marginal productivity of capital (or
capital goods in general). Critics of the marginal productivity theory,
however, have shown that this assertion is inconsistent with the notion
of a declining marginal productivity of capital.[20]

The difficulty with the marginal productivity theory is not the
conceptual problems involved but the fact that it is an equilibrium
theory in which returns to assets should be equalized from industry to
industry and owner to owner. In fact, returns vary significantly among
different industries and owners of assets, and exogenous shocks constantly
give rise to disequilibrium situations and substantial windfall gains. In
this kind of economy, fortunes, large and small, are often made in a very
short period of time, much less than a generation, through a combination
of luck, skill, and imagination starting with only a small amount of
capital. Very often luck is the only factor involved. The owner of a
piece of land on which someone else discovers oil, the commodity trader or
stock broker who buys on margin or sells short and catches a few price
swings going in the right direction, or the owner of a shop on a country
road which is converted into a major highway may be nothing more than
lucky, totally lacking in skill, imagination, or willingness to take
large risks. Windfall gains of this sort occur frequently; sometimes
they are taken in the form of capital gains, sometimes in the form of
increasing earnings over the lifetime of an asset.

Luck is one factor involved in the returns from physical assets.
Another factor is pure rent obtained from assets which are in fixed supply. Ownership of land and other natural resources in fixed supply
confers a rental value. Natural rents are unearned in the sense that
they represent a surplus over marginal productivity. In theory, if they
are taxed or confiscated, there will be no adverse effects on efficiency.
In fact, few natural resources are in truly fixed supply,[21] so that it is

not easy to determine what part of a payment for an asset represents pure rent.

Another factor is monopoly rents. The return to assets is a function of market power and the way in which market power is used to increase the return.

Entrepreneurial and management skills are another factor. Although the extra return to assets obtained by skillful management might be thought of as a return to human assets, in fact these skills often cannot be exercised or developed unless one is an owner of substantial assets.

Market imperfections caused by restrictive government policies can also substantially alter the return to assets. By placing import restrictions on certain items, the owners of import licenses and domestic producers of restricted items may receive a much better return on their assets. A rental value is created for their assets by a government-imposed scarcity. Investment controls, price controls, and foreign exchange controls all create distortions in prices and values which confer extra returns to owners of some assets and reduce the return to owners of other assets.[22]

Market imperfections may be caused by a host of other factors in such a way that returns to assets are distorted. For example, cultural differences often reduce opportunities to earn returns on assets for some cultural and ethnic groups and enhance opportunities for others. The distinction between Chinese and Malay in Malaysia,[23] Indian and Ladino in Guatemala, black and white in the United States, and European, Asian, and African tribes in East Africa are some examples. Class distinctions reinforced by school identification, manners, and speech often mark people for the kind of opportunities to which they are likely to have access. Class and ethnic distinctions often determine who has access to information about particular investment opportunities, who receives bank credit when loans are difficult to obtain, and who has introductions to people who can be helpful in making a sale or taking advantage of other limited opportunities. Class and ethnic distinctions are particularly pernicious in that they are reinforcing over time. The more advantaged groups prefer doing business among themselves and essentially restrict entry into more lucrative professions or other lines of business.

F.   Government taxation and expenditure

Government taxation and expenditure policies can play a major role
in determining the distribution of income. Government taxes can be
progressive, when the rich are taxed relatively more than the poor, or
regressive, when the rich benefit at the expense of the poor. A major
problem in determining the net effect of government taxation in altering the distribution of income is the question of incidence. The
analysis of incidence of direct taxes on income received is usually
straightforward. The more difficult problem arises in determining the
incidence of indirect taxes. Is the burden of an excise tax on a commodity, for example, carried by those who purchase the commodity, by
the wholesale and retail outlets that sell the commodity, by the firm
that produces the commodity, or by the workers of the firm that produces the commodity?[24]

Although the difficulties of determining the incidence of taxation
are great, they are surpassed by those of determining the incidence of
government expenditures. There are many relevant aspects of government
expenditures to take into account.[25]

One important distinction is between government investment expenditures and government current account expenditures. Current account
expenditures involve either general administration of the government
bureaucracy or the provision of services to the public, such as defense,
police protection, libraries, parks, hospitals, public health measures,
public utilities, and education. Investment expenditures are those
relating to the construction of roads, government buildings, schools,
public housing, hospitals, reservoirs and dams, irrigation systems, electricity generating stations, and public water supplies, sewage systems,
and street lighting. Once the assets created by these investments are in
place, they generally provide a stream of public services, usually in
conjunction with current expenditures of one sort or another, such as
expenditures on teachers, books, and supplies in the case of school
buildings, or maintenance in the case of roads.

A major question, then, is who benefits from the services provided
by a government, either directly through current expenditures or indirectly through services provided by public assets. Some services are
usually regarded as being generally available to the public. These
include defense, diplomatic representations, and general administration.

Other services, however, are thought to benefit only those who avail themselves of the services, such as those who attend school, use roads, stay in a hospital, or use electricity. It is difficult to assess benefits to users in most cases. The value placed by an individual on a particular government service, theoretically, could be measured by his consumer surplus but in practice is usually measured on a cost basis. Individuals or groups of individuals are assigned a certain percentage of total use of a service and the benefits are measured by applying this percentage to the total cost of providing the service and subtracting the user charges. User charges include school fees, tolls on roads, electricity tariffs, rents on public housing, and hospital charges. Problems abound:

(i) How does one assign percentage use to an individual or group? For example, who uses a monument or who benefits from a city park?

(ii) How are joint costs allocated?

(iii) Investment costs, as well as current costs, should be included. How does one allocate investment costs?

(iv) How does one determine user costs paid by particular individuals and groups?

In addition to benefit incidence, another important concept is expenditure incidence. Government expenditures involve the hiring of people at government wage scales. If the government tends to pay higher wages than the private sector, or if there is significant unemployment, government expenditures confer benefits on those who are employed. Even under less than full employment circumstances, the government often exercises such a large influence on labor markets that wages are raised by the government's labor demand.

Government may also be a mechanism for effecting direct transfer payments. For example, social security and workmen's compensation programs involve direct monetary transfers. School feeding and other food distribution programs are very much like transfer payments in kind. The analysis of the income distribution effect of government transfers is more straightforward than that of other kinds of government expenditures.

In this section, benefit and expenditure incidence of government activities have been discussed in the context of traditional types of public service activities. Government-owned productive enterprises can be treated much like private enterprises in analyzing their impact on

income distribution. Government ownership of productive enterprises may
be an efficient means of capturing nonlabor incomes, the surplus of
those enterprises, for social purposes. Government-owned enterprises
may also set policies toward their employees which influence general
wage levels and fringe benefits for workers.

G.   Size distribution of income over time

The size distribution of income by household is a combination of
income from human capital assets, physical assets, and government taxation and expenditure. Income from assets may either be in the usual
form of income, i.e., interest, rents, or profits, or in the form of
capital gains. Capital gains income is not usually included in most
national accounts definitions of income. Yet some of the highest levels
of consumption are financed from capital gains.

The stream of income derived from human and physical assets may vary
considerably over time for any individual household. Income will exhibit
a life cycle, as well as random variations from year to year. Thus, at
any point in time, an examination of the distribution of income will show
a wide dispersion, even if total lifetime income of households is evenly
distributed.

The distribution of household income and income accruing to individuals may be quite different. If large households are also low-income
households, the distribution of individual income may be even more skewed
than that of household income.

The size distribution of income, by family or by household, is
affected over the long run by the way in which both human resources and
physical assets are passed on from one generation to another. Inheritance
customs and inheritance taxes affect the way in which transfers between
generations occur. The factors which influence income over the average
human lifetime, however, may be so strong that inheritance customs and
laws have relatively little influence except for a very few of the
wealthiest individuals in the population.

H.   Policy options

Four main policy approaches toward making the distribution of income
more equal are distinguished: (i) direct market interventions by government in favor of the poor, (ii) confiscation of income or wealth by

government, (iii) provision of public services for the poor, and (iv) government policies that are expenditure oriented. A direct market intervention is any attempt by government to control prices and quantities of goods which are available in private markets. Confiscation can take the form of either fiscal expropriation of income or wealth through progressive tax measures or physical confiscation through land reform or nationalization of industry. The third approach involves the provision of services such as housing, health, education, and water and electricity supplies directly to the poor. Finally, government-expenditure policies are those designed to affect factor prices indirectly, particularly wages paid to the poor, unskilled workers, through government expenditure patterns.

1. Market intervention

The first approach involves operating on prices or quantities of goods and services available in private markets. Within this general approach, however, there are four different ways to attempt to have the desired effect: (i) through price controls, (ii) quantity controls, (iii) tax or subsidy incentives, and (iv) direct measures to remove market imperfections. Minimum wage legislation, food price controls, and interest rate ceilings are all examples of direct price controls which affect the distribution of income.

Direct quantitative controls are most often used with respect to imports. Imports of luxury goods can be restricted while imports of basic necessities are allowed in freely.

Tax incentives can take many forms. Accelerated depreciation rules and investment allowances affect the private cost of capital; payroll taxes can affect the cost of labor. Fertilizers, water, and insecticides may be subsidized for the farmer. The prices of crops may be affected by government purchases and stockpiling or by government marketing boards which either run surpluses (thus taxing the farmers and lowering the price which he receives) or deficits (thus subsidizing the farmer and raising the price). Tariffs and excise taxes are other examples of the use of taxes to alter prices.

The fourth method of affecting markets is to attempt to break market imperfections. Equal opportunity legislation, enhanced educational opportunities for disadvantaged groups, antitrust enforcement, and efforts to break restrictive practices among tradesmen and professionals are some of the techniques used.

Extreme examples of market intervention to improve income distribution include a freeze on upper-end wages and salaries. This has occurred in the civil service in Tanzania. In Cuba, most salaries are subjected to a very modest upper limit which prevents large disparities in wage and salary income.

Another approach aimed at alleviating poverty is to provide for each individual, as a matter of right, a basket (canasta) of basic necessities. The theory is that no individual need be deprived of necessities because of inability to pay market prices.

Economists who believe in the utility of using markets usually advise against the use of direct price or quantity controls and in favor of using tax and subsidy measures, or the use of efforts to reduce market imperfections as a tool to modify income distribution. The use of direct price and quantity controls usually can be shown to be inefficient and the same objectives can be accomplished more efficiently by tax and subsidy measures or a reduction in market imperfections.

Income inequalities often arise because of attempts to control prices and quantities directly for reasons other than income distribution objectives. Some inequalities may be reduced by eliminating the controls. A control regime which attempts to keep prices down on mass consumption goods may in fact have adverse income distribution implications because of the effects on supply of these goods and the emergence of black markets. In fact, then, less of controlled commodities at a higher average price may be consumed by the poor, particularly if they have limited access to markets in which prices are effectively controlled and must make more of their purchases in black markets than do middle and upper income groups. The same type of problem also arises in connection with controlled credit. Controlled interest rates and allocation of credit result in less credit at higher interest rates for small borrowers, since the latter must often go into gray or black markets for credit.

The effect of market intervention policies which influence the price of labor and capital can be analyzed through a version of the surplus-labor model discussed earlier in this chapter. Let us assume that there are three sectors rather than just two, informal and modern. In particular, let us assume the existence of a modern sector, an informal urban sector, and an informal rural sector. There are four different classes of people: (i) modern-sector capitalists, (ii) modern-sector workers, (iii) urban, informal-sector workers, and (iv) rural, informal-sector workers.

Assume that the production function for the modern sector exhibits constant returns to scale, and labor-augmenting and capital-augmenting technical change. It is possible to show (see appendix 3) that the rate of growth r_L of the modern-sector labor force is given by

$$(1) \qquad r_L = r_K + r_a - r_b[(1 - \mu - \sigma)/(1 - \mu)] - \sigma r_W/(1 - \mu) ,$$

where r_K is the rate of growth of the modern-sector capital stock, r_a is the rate of capital-augmenting technological change, r_b is the rate of labor-augmenting technological change, σ is the elasticity of substitution between capital and labor, μ is the share of labor in total output, and r_W is the rate of growth of the real wage.

The important thing to note in equation (1) is that increases in the real wage reduce the rate of labor absorption into the modern sector. The amount of this reduction is directly related to the elasticity of substitution between labor and capital, and to the labor share in total output. The last term in (1), however, captures only the direct effect of wage increases in the modern sector on labor absorption. To the extent that wage increases reduce profits and profits are the major source of savings and reinvestment, increases in modern-sector wages reduce profits and the rate of capital accumulation r_K in equation (1). Thus, there is a deceleration effect due to wage increases in the modern sector.

The effect of a wage increase in the modern sector is to increase the incomes of the workers in that sector, the second of our four groups of people with whom we are concerned. The per capita income of entrepreneurs in the modern sector, however, is reduced. Workers in the rural, traditional sector may be adversely affected, although they might become slightly better off because of increased migration from the countryside due to the attraction of higher modern-sector wages.[26] The migration from the land may increase the marginal and average productivity of rural workers, thus increasing wages and rents accruing to rural, traditional-sector workers.

The sector which tends to bear the brunt of any reductions in per capita income is the urban, traditional sector. Because of the reduction in the rate of labor absorption, fewer workers in this sector are absorbed into high-paying jobs in the modern sector. The increase in wage rates also reduces total output and, thus, total income in the modern sector. To the extent that demand for urban, traditional output is a derived demand dependent on modern-sector activity, the increase in wages in the modern sector exerts a depressing influence on urban, traditional-sector output. Finally, increased migration from the rural sector to the urban areas may swell the total urban labor force, thus exerting further downward pressure on wages and per capita incomes in the traditional sector.

One can show that the reduction in per capita income of the urban traditional sector (see appendix) is directly related to the elasticity of traditional-sector output with respect to modern-sector output, the share of labor in total output of the modern sector, the importance of the modern sector relative to the urban traditional sector, the decrease in the rate of labor absorption into the modern sector, and the elasticity of labor migration from the rural to the urban areas.

When modern-sector wages increase, the change in the degree of inequality is quite ambiguous—some groups gain, while others lose. The urban poor, in particular, tend to be much worse off. Although those remaining in the countryside may be slightly better off, those who migrate to urban areas may be better off or worse off, depending on whether or not they get high-paying jobs. It is certain that the degree of underemployment and unemployment in the urban areas tends to increase. In an economy characterized by the model described here, the poorest segments of the population are not helped by wage increases in the modern sector. The lot of the urban poor is made worse and low productivity and poverty in the countryside are transformed into urban poverty and unemployment through migration.

An analysis of those market interventions which affect the price of capital can be made in a similar fashion. In order to determine the effect of a reduction in the cost of capital, let us assume that the cost of capital affects only the capital-intensity of new investment. Once an investment is made, the cost of capital becomes a fixed cost and is not a factor in determining the capital-labor ratio. Ex-ante, however, for a constant elasticity of substitution (CES) production function, the optimal incremental capital-labor ratio is given by

(2) $\qquad \dfrac{dL}{dK} = \left[\dfrac{\delta}{(1 - \delta)} \dfrac{P_K}{W} \right]^{\sigma} ,$

where δ and σ are the distribution and substitution elasticity parameters, respectively, of a CES production function and P_K is the price of capital, interpreted here to mean the price of capital goods.

Suppose that the rate of capital accumulation in money terms is a linear function of profits (π) on existing capital stock. Then, the real rate of capital accumulation is given by

(3) $\qquad dK = (a + b\pi)/P_K .$

If we substitute (3) into (2) and differentiate, we obtain

(4) $\qquad \dfrac{d(dL)}{dL} = (\sigma - 1) \dfrac{dP_K}{P_K} .$

That is, the percentage change in labor absorption of new investment relative to the percentage change in the price of capital depends on the elasticity of substitution.

There are two effects to take into account. First, the reduction of the price of capital results in a substitution of capital for labor, which reduces labor absorption. At the same time, a lower price on capital goods makes for more rapid capital accumulation in real terms, which increases labor absorption. If the elasticity of substitution is greater than unity, the first effect outweighs the second and labor absorption is reduced when the price of capital goods is decreased.

The effect of a reduction in the price of capital can then be analyzed in terms of the four groups of people. Total modern-sector output and profits increase so that modern-sector entrepreneurs benefit from a reduction in the price of capital. Labor absorption into the modern sector may either increase or decrease, depending on the elasticity of substitution--thus, neither traditional sector can expect to gain much by the opening up of more modern-sector, high-paying jobs. The urban, informal sector may gain somewhat through increased derived demand resulting from increased modern-sector output. The rural traditional-sector and modern-sector wage-earners are unlikely to be much affected at all.

None of this takes into account the fact that the capital subsidies require either increased taxation or inflation in order to effect the implied real resource transfers to capitalists. If these are taken into account, the rural, traditional-sector and modern-sector wage earners are likely to be worse off. The small spillover gains made by the urban, traditional sector may be completely vitiated. The big gainers are the modern-sector entrepreneurs.

Manipulation of modern-sector wage rates or subsidization of the cost of capital to modern-sector entrepreneurs are unlikely, then, to make much of a difference in the overall variability of income. Some relatively poor groups gain while other lose, due to secondary effects. In particular, the poorest groups, workers in the traditional sectors, are the greatest losers under policies designed to raise modern-sector wages or reduce the cost of capital to modern-sector entrepreneurs.

2.   Confiscatory policies

Confiscatory policies include taxation, land reform, and nationalization of industry. Progressive taxation is not always very effective. In a poor country only certain segments of the population are likely to be affected by taxation; in particular, government workers and wage and salary earners in the modern sector. Accurate records of wages and salaries are kept regarding these workers, and many less developed countries have instituted a pay-as-you-earn system of wage and salary tax deductions. It is much more difficult to tax non-export agricultural incomes and incomes in the urban traditional sector. It is also difficult to tax most forms of unearned income. This is especially serious if a major cause of inequality derives from an unequal asset distribution. Unearned incomes are difficult to assess and may easily be hidden enterprise costs in the form of expense allowances, company housing, and company transport.

A more radical approach to income redistribution involves the redistribution of directly productive assets rather than fiscal redistribution. In predominantly agricultural less-developed countries, land redistribution might be the most effective instrument in reducing income disparities. The historical record, however, has not been good. Political opposition in many countries has effectively stalled or severely diluted plans for

drastic land reform. Land reform seems to be carried out most often in
the wake of major social upheavals, such as the Communist revolutions in
Russia and China, the South in the United States after the Civil War,
the takeover in Japan and Korea by the United States after the Japanese
defeat in World War II, the Nationalist takeover of Taiwan after their
expulsion from the mainland, the revolutions in Mexico, Cuba, and Bolivia,
and the socialist election victory in Chile.

Nationalization as a policy has some of the same drawbacks as land
reform. Politically, it is difficult to achieve. Although nationalization may decrease the income of the wealthiest groups, it may increase
the disparity in incomes between the modern and traditional sectors if
it leads to higher wages and a slower rate of labor absorption by the
nationalized industries.

A major problem of both land reform and nationalization is that
they often do little to help the small peasant, the landless, rural
laborer or the urban traditional worker. Land reform benefits often
accrue to wage laborers on large-scale farms who gain land or are able
to increase their share of the surplus, or industrial, modern-sector
workers who are able to capture an increased share of industrial profits.
Thus, land reform and nationalization chiefly redistribute income from
upper- to lower- and middle-income groups within a sector.

Redistribution of assets, if it is to be effective in assisting the
lowest-income groups, must be horizontal across sectors rather than
vertical within the modern sector. Horizontal transfer policies, however,
have played a smaller role and indeed have often been regressive, even in
relatively distribution-oriented regimes. Thus, it is not uncommon that
countries with very "advanced" labor legislation--which in practice favors
modern-sector workers only--have regressive or neutral fiscal systems.
Only the more ambitiously egalitarian regimes, such as those of Cuba,
Tanzania, and China, have created major systems of horizontal redistribution.

Why has redistribution been so much limited to vertical transfers
despite the strongly egalitarian principles of many developing countries?
One obvious cause is the self-reinforcing political strength of the
modern sector--particularly, of bureaucratic and labor groups. Administrative factors are also involved, since horizontal transfers need more
intermediation.

A less obvious but also relevant cause is that vertical transfers enjoy a moral support that is not associated with horizontal redistribution. This moral support is expressed, for instance, in the labor theory of value. It is rooted in those notions of justice that link rights to the creation of something of value, rather than to its use in "historical" as against "pattern" or "end-state" principles of justice.[27] In discussions of the right to property income, the argument often centers on the question of who really produced that income. Both parties are implicitly accepting the distributive claim arising out of the act of production.

By contrast, the ideal of income equality, which is required to sustain policies of horizontal redistribution and more generally to separate distribution from production, is a weaker moral precept. Horizontal transfers are more commonly supported by feelings of charity than of justice, and charity is much the weaker of those sentiments. The Communist precept--to each according to his needs--remains an ideal for a society of "new men," not a banner for political action today. Most of the indignation provoked by "inequality" is satisfied by removing the extremes in income levels; in poor countries it amounts to a feeling of scandal at the existence of a few rich among the many poor, and leveling down these extremes of wealth can be achieved without horizontal redistribution. The nature of moral feelings thus reinforces the natural, political, and administrative difficulties of achieving horizontal redistribution. (Theoretical models for purposes of analyzing income distribution, land reform, and nationalization are developed in some detail in papers by Cline, and Selowsky and Cauas in this volume.)

3. Provision of public services

A third major set of policies to redress income imbalances involves the provision of government services for poor groups. These include such things as (i) investment in feeder roads and in village electric and water supplies in poor rural areas; (ii) broadening access to education and expenditures on public health and nutrition; (iii) site and service projects in urban areas; (iv) birth control information and subsidization of contraceptives for the poor; (v) farmer extension services and subsidized seed; (vi) fertilizers and pesticides for small farmers; and (vii) agricultural and industrial research aimed at improving the productivity of the small farmer or entrepreneur. Public works projects are classified as an expenditure-oriented policy in so far as the public works affect employment and wage rates, but the capital assets which result from these projects may provide services for the poor segments of the population.

Two problems arise with respect to public services for the poor. One is that of access. Access to a road, a hospital, a school, or a public park, for example, may be limited because of location factors.

A related problem is that of complementarity. Access to public facilities may be limited because of lack of complementary assets. For example, roads are best used by those who have automobiles; hospitals, schools, and parks by those who have a means of transport; farmer extension services, rural feeder roads, input and price subsidies, and irrigation facilities by those who have land. Because of the complementary problem, provision of public services may do nothing more than reinforce existing income disparities. This suggests that redistribution of privately held wealth may be a necessary precondition for other redistribution policies to have the desired effect.[28]

Alternatively, the state may want to restrict access to public goods. The use of a hospital, for example, may be restricted to low-income families. Access to irrigation water may be granted only to small farmers. Use of public housing or site and service projects may be restricted to low-income groups. In some cases, it is extremely difficult to identify the poor and to ensure that only they have access. In other cases, custom, tradition, or social policy dictate that access not be restricted--public schools and roads are usually available to anyone who is able to use them.

Access to public services may be modified by user charges. Often user charges do not cover the full cost of providing an asset. Thus, the user charges have an element of subsidy. Even when user charges cover full costs, there may be an element of subsidy to the user if the service would not be available at any cost unless the government provided it. The existence of user charges, however, may restrict access by low-income groups who cannot afford even modest user charges. User charges may be determined in a discriminatory fashion as a means of overcoming this problem. Lower-income classes may be charged less. This may be possible in some cases, such as for medical care or schools, but not in others, such as for road tolls.

4. Expenditure-oriented policies

Finally, government may try to increase incomes of the poorest groups by engaging in heavily labor-intensive public works projects. Projects of this sort have two basic goals. The first is to absorb unemployment, particularly seasonal unemployment. The second is to raise wage levels for the poorest, least skilled workers.

To the extent that public works projects utilize unemployed workers, they both increase economic efficiency and redistribute income. The increased efficiency makes it possible for the poor to receive more at a relatively modest cost to the rich over the long run because of increased productivity.

Public works may be associated with a rural development program which aims at increasing small farmer productivity. Thus, the program may have both an expenditure effect on wages and employment and a benefit effect. All too often, however, the benefits go, not to the smallest farmers or the landless, but rather to the larger farmers.

Alternatively, public works programs may have an urban focus—such as the building of low-cost public housing. Like rural public works, the projects may provide substantial benefits to the poorest groups as well as expenditure effects. The key to expenditure-oriented policies, however, is that they focus on labor-intensive, construction activities.

A related policy is one in which the government serves as an employer of last resort. With this kind of policy, the government offers to hire anyone for some specified minimum wage below the going market wage. One need not be very concerned about the quality or amount of work performed. In this way the poorest members of the potential work force can receive some minimum level of income. Furthermore, this policy has the advantage of providing a test of how much and how severe is the problem of unemployment by assessing the number of people who offer their services at the government minimum wage.

I. Conclusions

The various policy alternatives discussed here from a theoretical standpoint are dealt with at much greater length from a policy standpoint in other chapters of this volume. The analysis of the efficacy of these policies, however, depends greatly on the use of an appropriate model of the inter-relationship between growth and income. The model may vary from country to country.   In a highly dualistic economy, policies ought to be aimed at reducing discrepancies between traditional and modern sectors.   If windfall gains are a major explanation of the distribution of income, then confiscatory policies might be more effective.   Appropriate policies and policy mixes will be summarized and examined in the last chapter of this volume with these kinds of relationships in mind.

Chapter 2

NOTES

1. For a comprehensive discussion of marginal productivity theory as it relates to income distribution, see Martin Brofenbrenner, Income Distribution Theory (Aldine-Atherton, 1971).

2. See W. Arthur Lewis, "Development with Unlimited Supplies of Labour," Manchester School of Economics and Social Studies (May 1954), pp. 139-192; and John C. Fei and Gustav Ranis, Development of the Labor Surplus Economy--Theory and Policy (Irwin, 1964).

3. Inequality cannot be great in a largely subsistence economy; see Melvin W. Reder, "A Partial Survey of the Theory of Income Size Distribution," ed., Lee Soltow, Six Papers on the Size Distribution of Wealth and Income (Columbia University Press, 1965).

4. For a good discussion of these relationships, see R. Albert Berry, "Income and Wealth Distribution in the Development Process and Their Relationship to Output Growth," Yale Economic Growth Center, Discussion Paper 89 (July 1970).

5. Simon Kuznets, "Economic Growth and Income Inequality," American Economic Review, vol. 45 (March 1955), pp. 291-303.

6. Irma Adelman and Cynthia Taft Morris, Economic Growth and Social Equity in Developing Countries, chap. 5 (Stanford University Press, 1973); Richard Weiskoff, "Income Distribution and Economic Growth in Puerto Rico, Argentina and Mexico," Review of Income and Wealth, ser. 16 (December 1970), Felix Paukert, "Income Distribution at Different Levels of Development: A Survey of Evidence," International Labour Review, vol. 108 (August-September 1973), pp. 97-125.

7. See, for example, William R. Cline, Potential Effects of Income Redistribution on Economic Growth: Latin American Cases (New York: Praeger, 1972); and Clark Reynolds, "The Recent Evolution of Savings and the Financial System in Mexico in Relation to the Distribution of Income and Wealth," paper presented at the Workshop on Income Distribution and Its Role in Development, Program of Development Studies, Rice University, 25 April 1974. In the same context should be mentioned efforts by James Land and Ronald Soligo to analyze the relationship between income redistribution and growth: "Income Distribution and Employment in Labor Redundant Economies," and, "Models of Development Incorporating Distribution Aspects," respectively, Program of Development Studies Discussion Papers nos. 9 and 22, Rice University (1971 and 1972). Their basic

hypothesis is that income redistribution results in more demand for labor-intensive commodities and less demand for import-intensive commodities because of differing expenditure patterns among the rich and the poor. Thus, income redistribution might result in more efficient production and stimulate rather than retard growth. Empirical tests of these hypotheses, however, have been inconclusive. See Land and Soligo, "Consumption Patterns, Factor Usage, and the Distribution of Income: A Review of Some Findings," paper presented at the Workshop on Income Distribution and Its Role in Development, Program of Development Studies, Rice University, 25 April 1974; Gregory J. Ballantine and Ronald Soligo, "Consumption and Earnings Patterns and Income Redistribution," and Donald L. Huddle, "Inflation, Government Financing of Industrialization and the Gains from Development in Brazil," paper presented at the same workshop. Finally, see Ronald Soligo, "Factor Intensity of Consumption Patterns, Income Distribution and Employment Growth in Pakistan," and Tuncay M. Sunman, "Short-Run Effects of Income Distribution on Some Macro Economic Variables: The Case of Turkey," respectively, Program of Development Studies Discussion Papers nos. 44 and 46, Rice University (1973).

8. Montek Ahluwalia, "Income Inequality: Some Dimensions of the Problem," ed., Hollis Chenery et al., Redistribution with Growth, chap. 2 (London: Oxford University Press, 1974).

9. For a good theoretical and empirical survey of these issues, see Ian M. D. Little, Tibor Scitovsky, and Maurice Scott, Industry and Trade in Some Developing Countries: A Comparative Study (London: Oxford University Press, 1970).

10. Adelman and Morris found that income inequality was highly associated with dualism in their forty-four country sample, Economic Growth and Social Equity.

11. For a more detailed exposition of this model, see R. Webb, Government Policy and the Distribution of Income in Peru, 1963-1973, chap. 5 (Cambridge, Mass: Harvard University Press, 1977).

12. For a detailed theoretical and empirical survey of these issues, see Little, Scitovsky, and Scott, Industry and Trade in Developing Countries; and David Turnham with Ingelies Jaeger, The Employment Problem in Less Developed Countries: A Review of Evidence (Paris: OECD Development Center, 1971).

13. See Albert R. Berry and Miguel Urrutia, Income Distribution and Government Policy in Colombia (Yale University Press, forthcoming).

14. See I. Navarrette, "La Distribucion del Ingreso en Mexico," El Perfil de Mexico en 1980 (Mexico: Siglo XXI, 1970), pp. 15-61.

15. See Webb, The Distribution of Income.

16. As supplements to the comprehensive review of marginal productivity theory in Bronfenbrenner, Income Distribution Theory, see Reder, "A Partial Survey"; and Jacob Mincer, "The Distribution of Labor Incomes: A Survey," Journal of Economic Literature, vol. 8 (March 1970).

17. A similar model in which skills are imparted on the job, not in school, is the "job competition" model of Lester Thurow and Robert Lucas, The American Distribution of Income: A Structural Problem (U. S. Congress, Joint Economic Committee, 1972).

18. Though property income explains the very high income of a few, the fact that most families own little or no property, plus the existence of large wage and salary differentials makes differences in labor income the main source of total inequality in at least some countries. See, for instance, The Distribution of Income, Webb, chap. 3.

19. The most thorough discussion of determinants of the distribution of private wealth is in James Meade, Efficiency, Equality, and the Ownership of Property (Harvard University Press, 1965).

20. In fact, there can be re-switching between capital- and labor-intensive techniques; see Joan Robinson who initiated a long series of attacks on the marginal productivity theory of distribution, "The Production Function and the Theory of Capital," Review of Economic Studies, vol. 21 (1953-54), pp. 81-106. For a few of the more important critiques, see N. Kaldor, "Alternative Theories of Distribution," Review of Economic Studies, vol. 23 (1955-56), pp. 83-100; and, Piero Sraffa, Production of Commodities by Means of Commodities--Prelude to a Critique of Economic Theory (Cambridge University Press, 1960). For a good survey of the recent controversy on marginal productivity theories of distribution and other related issues, see G. C. Harcourt, "Some Cambridge Controversies in the Theory of Capital." Journal of Economic Literature, vol. 7 (June 1969).

21. Land can be reclaimed from the forest, the desert, or even the sea, and mineral resources continue to be discovered.

22. Monopoly profits created by foreign exchange controls are discussed by Gordon Winston, "Overinvoicing Underutilization and Distorted Industrial Growth," Pakistan Development Review, vol. 10 (Winter 1970), pp. 405-21; and Anne O. Krueger, "The Political Economy of the Rent-Seeking Society," American Economic Review, vol. 61 (June 1974), pp. 291-303.

23. Donald Snodgrass discusses the relation between ethnic groups and income inequality in Malaysia, The Fiscal System as an Income Redistribution in West Malaysia, Economic Development Report 276, Development Research Group (Harvard University Press).

24. For classic discussions of tax incidence, see Richard A. Musgrave, The Theory of Public Finance: A Study in Public Economy, chap. 10 (McGraw-Hill, 1959); and Earl R. Rolph, The Theory of Fiscal Economics, chap. 6 (University of California Press, 1954). For a more recent study, see Richard A. Musgrave and Peggy B. Musgrave, Public Finance in Theory and Practice (McGraw-Hill, 1973), pp. 354-77.

25. For a summary of the literature and issues as they relate to less developed countries, see L. DeWulf, "Fiscal Incidence Studies in Developing Countries: Survey and Critique," mimeographed, International Monetary Fund (1974); and Charles E. McClure, "On the Theory and Methodology of Estimating Benefit and Expenditure Incidence," paper presented at the workshop on Income Distribution and Its Role in Development, Program of Development Studies, Rice University, 26 April 1974. The best known expenditure study is, Irwin W. Gillespie, "Effect of Public Expenditures on the Distribution of Income," ed., Richard A. Musgrave, Essays in Fiscal Federalism (Brookings Institution, 1965).

26. See Michael P. Todaro, "A Model of Labor Migration and Urban Unemployment in Less Developed Countries," American Economic Review, vol. 59 (March 1969), pp. 138-48; and John R. Harris and M. P. Todaro, "Immigration, Unemployment and Development--A Two-Sector Analysis," American Economic Review, vol. 60 (March 1970), pp. 126-42.

27. This distinction is developed by Robert Nozick, "Distributive Justice," Philosophy and Public Affairs, vol. 3 (Fall 1972), pp. 45-126.

28. Vito Tanzi maintains that redistribution through government expenditures on public services at best transfers income from the richest to the upper middle class because of limitations of access and complementarity, "Redistributing Income Through the Budget in Latin America."

CHAPTER III

INDUSTRIALIZATION POLICY AND INCOME DISTRIBUTION

Henry J. Bruton

A. Introduction

The purpose of this chapter is to study the relationship between
industrialization and foreign trade policies and income distribution,
particularly their effect on poverty and employment. More specifically,
the objective is to examine the way in which measures that affect access to
and price of factors of production, particularly foreign exchange and
imports, act on the distribution of income. Attention is given to the
effect of policies with respect to exchange rates, tariffs, licensing and
other direct controls, and subsidy systems. Related policy measures have
been largely aimed at fostering industrialization in the developing
countries, and how they have affected the distribution of income is
examined below.

There are six substantive sections in this chapter. In section A
some general notions are discussed. These are definitions and the statement of some of the obiter dicta that provide the point of departure of the
chapter. Section B discusses the role of industry in the overall income
distribution picture and describes a general model that identifies the
principal determinants of income distribution over time in the industrial
sector. These include rates of return on investment, wage rates, productivity growth, the composition of demand, foreign trade, and rural industrial activity. Each of these is discussed in the following sections of
the paper. The last, section G, is a summary and a brief review of the
policy implications of the various arguments.

In this section, some general notions are outlined in an effort to
make clear what is being talked about, and why, in the rest of the chapter.

NOTE:

This paper was completed in the Fall of 1974.

(i) It is necessary to begin with an observation or two on distribution itself. Economic welfare is generally more directly related to
size distribution than to functional distribution. Size distribution is
not, however, unrelated to functional distribution, and one of the tasks
of the chapter will be to examine how policies that have a direct effect
on functional distribution also have an impact on size.

Conventional measures of size distribution usually encompass the
entire economy. The Gini Coefficient, the Kuznets Ratio, the Pareto
Coefficient are all indicators of the extent to which a given proportion
of national income accrues to a given percentage of the population. These
are useful measures but, for most developing countries at the present time,
the most pressing social problem seems to be the existence of widespread
severe poverty. It would appear then that a more specific guide to policy
than any of the less relevant general measures is the extent to which the
very poor are helped by the policy. For example, a poverty line may be
defined, and the measure of effectiveness of a policy may be determined
by the rate of reduction in the percentage of the population whose income
is below this poverty line. "Improved" income distribution would then
refer to an increase in real income for that part of the population whose
present income is below the defined level. The source of increase may be
reduced income of the richer groups but may also be increased total output
that raises both the income of the low-end poverty groups and that of the
richer groups by as much or more.

This criterion is meant to represent an empirical judgment, not a
value judgment. It is assumed that the very poor are mainly interested
in having more absolutely, not simply more in relation to some other group.
"Mainly interested" means that the low-end poverty groups have, at the
present time, a welfare function whose arguments are absolute levels of
income, not relative levels. Evidently such a function may change as a
country grows richer, but that is a later story. In the language of
Albert Hirschman's tunnel metaphor,[1] the interest is in getting the
stationary lane moving and not in what happens to the other lane--except
in those instances where the speed of the fast-moving lane is responsible
for the nonmovement of the poverty lane. As will be argued just below,
the attack on high-end riches is best undertaken by direct taxation.

(ii) The second general point has to do with some of the notions
that underlie the approach taken in subsequent sections of this chapter.

Various broad-based studies of income distribution in developing countries
have appeared recently which have identified a fairly common list of factors
accounting for inequality in general and for the failure of those whose
income is very low to experience much of a rise over the past two decades.[2]
Such a list includes a great variety of factors: extent of dualism in
the system, size of the government-controlled sector, extent of dependence
of the economy on raw materials or agriculture, structure of foreign
trade, and so on. These studies demonstrate the fact that income distribution, as is characteristic of all economics, depends on everything else.
The studies have been helpful in outlining the various factors that affect
income distribution. Some few hypotheses specific enough to be tested
have emerged, but in general they are of such a broad, historical nature
that they lead to few policy conclusions. It is, however, important to
appreciate the point that the existing accumulated inequalities are the
result of the way the economies of countries have developed over the past
rather than of peculiarities in one sector or another. The fact that many
countries have experienced essentially the same distribution pattern suggests that the problem is not a matter of size of country, form of government, availability of natural resources, or other country-specific characteristics. It also appears generally correct to say that governments
only rarely seek explicitly to hold down the growth of income of the very
poor. Rather it seems that the problem emerges from, or at least is
accentuated by, the policies that have been followed in the search for
development and from the kinds of institutions and power structures that
have evolved as these policies have been pursued. The fact that it is
now necessary to attack the problem in the face of the existing set of
policies, institutions, and power bases that have brought about the
problem complicates matters. It not only makes the implementation of
any new policy much more difficult than it would have been twenty years
ago but also makes the design of the policy itself a more complicated
matter.

There is one further observation suggested by the preceding paragraph.
A common practice of recent years has been to downgrade the importance of
rates of growth of GDP as a measure of the success of a policy. Such a
downgrading is somewhat misleading. The problem would appear to be with
our understanding and practice of the development process, not with the
objective of increased output of goods and services. It seems clear,

however, that to attack the income distribution problem (as defined above)
simply by seeking higher rates of growth of output by the same methods as
those widely used during the 1960s will not succeed in producing continued
growth or in helping the very poor. What does seem to be the case is that
a development policy built on a more effective use of domestically available resources can produce a growth rate and a distribution of the
rewards of that growth that are more compatible with general notions of
equity and social and political stability than has been the case in the
recent past. To argue in this way implies considerable confidence that
major effects can be accomplished by specific policy measures of the conventional sort, i.e., policy toward exchange rates, wage rates, credit,
and so on. And, as will be argued explicitly later, getting conventional
policy right--or at least working in the right direction--is necessary
before one proceeds into the more intractable areas of institutional
change and revolution.

(iii) Specific references to taxes and transfers as a policy instrument to help relieve low-end poverty should be noted. This is the subject
of another chapter in this volume and need not be elaborated here. At
several points in later discussions, however, the key role of taxation
will emerge. It is especially relevant in efforts to reduce extreme
wealth and to break the power hold of dominant groups.

(iv) The specific economic characteristics that seem to account for
the low-end poverty are also explored in another paper. Data are not
very plentiful, but three such characteristics are fairly firmly established and are of special significance in the set of issues examined
below. They may be summarized as follows:[3]

(a) The poor are engaged in very low productivity activities.
In some instances they have no job at all, but literal open unemployment
is a luxury the poor can rarely afford.

(b) The poor have little human capital and are not in a position to accumulate it, either through formal training or job experience.

(c) The poor own little physical capital or land and, of course,
have little capacity to acquire it.

Such characteristics follow almost from the definition of poverty,
but they do help to isolate a bit more the nature of the problem. The
question of the present chapter may now be phrased: How do the several

aspects of trade and industrialization policy affect these three major characteristics of the low-end poor?

B.   Role of manufacturers

This section discusses the role that manufacturing can play in the attack on low-end poverty. Given this role, two variations of a model are presented that provide the basic framework for the analysis of the remaining topics in the chapter.

Manufacturing accounts for a modest portion of GDP in most developing countries and offers employment to an even smaller proportion of the labor force. (In modern-sector manufacturing, productivity per worker and wage income are generally much higher than in other sectors of the economy.) Despite its small size, modern-sector manufacturing occupies an important position in the efforts to alleviate low-end poverty.[4] The early versions of the labor-surplus, dual-economy model of development imply that a high rate of growth of the modern sector (dominated by manufacturing) would produce a rate of growth of demand for relatively unskilled labor such that the employment and poverty problem would be solved in an acceptably short period of time. The resolution of the problem would work in two directions. The modern sector itself would absorb increasingly large numbers of workers and thereby reduce the numbers who remained in traditional, low-productivity activities. Reductions in the numbers remaining in traditional activities would result in a rise in the quantity of goods available per capita in that sector and, more importantly, facilitate a rationalization of techniques and practices there that would in turn produce an increased rate of growth of productivity. The origin, the prime mover, of the process in the model is, however, investment in the modern sector. This location of the prime mover is important in the story as it has a significant impact on the policy followed, and on policy changes to be suggested below.

If the level and structure of wage rates do not change over time; if the price of capital remains unchanged; if there is no change in productivity due to technological improvements, to learning, or to increased human capital; if there are constant returns to scale; and if there are no major changes in the composition of output, then output and employment in the modern sector must grow at the same percentage rate. If wage rates (and productivity) in the modern sector are higher than in

the traditional sector and than in the economy as a whole, the growth of
the modern sector in excess of the labor force will result in a shift of
labor from lower to higher productivity activities. The more rapid the
growth of investment and output in the modern sector, the more rapid
will this shift be. In this context then, growth of the manufacturing
sector offers a major focus for the alleviation of low-end poverty.

This way of thinking contributed to the establishment of a series
of policies aimed primarily at generating as rapid a rate of growth of
capital and output in the modern sector as possible. These policies (to
be examined below) did in fact produce the high rate of capital accumulation, especially in the period of the early 1950s to the mid-1960s,
but the expected corresponding growth of employment did not follow. In
the following subsections, a model is established that helps to pinpoint
the variables that are relevant in explaining this pattern of development.

1. First model variant

Consider first a model in which productivity-increasing technical
progress embodied in physical capital plays an important role.[5] Figure 1
will serve as the basis around which to build the discussion and
illustrate the arguments. The vertical axis of the diagram measures the
average product of labor. The horizontal axis is divided into units of
a given capital-labor ratio. To simplify the initial discussion, it is
assumed that the same amount of investment (in real terms) is achieved
every year, and that this investment creates the same number of new jobs.
However, the productivity of the newly created capital and the newly
employed labor in year t is $(1 + a)$ times that of year $t - 1$. Thus the
productivity of both capital and labor are assumed to rise at a constant
annual percentage rate equal to a. The slope of the line FAB is therefore equal to a, as the line itself is the locus of points of labor productivity. These assumptions mean that the source of the higher productivity is incorporated in the newly created capital or the newly hired
labor or both, and once incorporated cannot be modified. This assumption
makes considerably more sense for physical capital than it does for
labor but, as is discussed later, has some merit for labor as well.

This set of assumptions seems especially useful in the context of
the industrializing developing countries. New forms of physical capital
are being made available year after year which for the most part embody

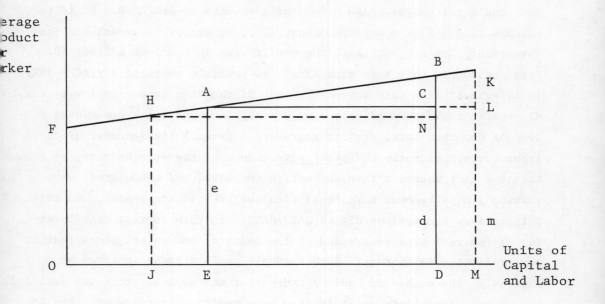

Figure 1

a technology that existing capital cannot use. Most of the economies of
these countries are now adding to capital rather than replacing old capital, so that to a greater degree than in richer countries capital of
varying productivity is observed. Similarly new managers and workers
entering the labor force may be more productive due to better training,
better infrastructure, and more efficient distribution arrangements. It
perhaps should be noted that rising productivity of the already employed
labor force due to learning-by-doing cannot be shown on figure 1. What
then does this set of assumptions teach us about distribution as industrialization gets under way?

In figure 1 the newest unit of capital and labor is that marked d.
It is this unit that yields the highest labor (and capital) productivity.
With a wage rate equal to AE, the least productive capital labor unit
that is profitable to use is that identified as e. With capital labor
unit e the wage paid absorbs the entire output and no profit at all is
realized. The capital to the left of e is so unproductive that, at a
wage AE, labor costs would not be covered and profits would be negative.
With the most productive capital, d, profits per capita are equal to BC.

Total employment equals ED, the total wage bill is EACD, total profits
ABC, and total output, EABD. So profit's share is ABC/EABD. If it is
assumed that FAB is a straight line, i.e., productivity growth and the
investment rate are constant, the profit area is equal to 1/2(BC)·AC.
Total output is this area plus AE·AC, so profit's share is BC/(BC + 2AE).
It is evident from this expression that if the wage rate were lower, e.g.,
HJ, profit's share would necessarily rise, as would total employment.
Suppose now that total profits accrue to a (small) fixed number of the
labor force, evidently the per capita income of the wage earners; at
the same time income within the entire (employed and unemployed) wage
earning groups becomes more equal with the rise in employment, and total
output rises proportionately to HAEJ/ABDE. In this context, the lowering of the real wage rate added to the quantity of capital stock that it
was profitable to operate. Such a result could also be achieved by
increasing the number of hours per day that the capital stock was utilized.

A more important--or at least a more empirically relevant--case is
what happens as new capital-labor units are formed with still higher productivity while wage rates remain at AE. The new unit, m, is more productive than the d unit, and if wage rates remain constant, profit's
share is greater with m than with d, and therefore profit's share of total
output must be greater now than was the case before m was created. Here
again total output rises, and the total output accruing to labor also
rises. Therefore, with the added employment (equal to DM), income distribution among wage earners becomes still more equal, low-end poverty
is reduced, and output available to the nonprofit receivers rises. The
increased output is due to the higher productivity of the new capital-
labor units and to the added employment. On the other hand, if wage
rates rise with the productivity growth, profit's share would remain
unchanged as would labor's. In this event, output will rise only by the
annual increase in productivity, and the total output accruing to labor
will be less than if wages remained constant. Of course the employed
workers have higher pay, but if it is they who support the unemployed
then evidently they too would benefit more from constant wage rates
than from rising wage rates.

Under present assumptions, the profit rate is also rising over time
as new units of capital labor are created.[6] This process continues (in
the model) until full employment is reached, i.e., until all workers in

the economy are receiving a wage at least equal to AE. After this point, wage rates would (in the model) begin to rise along with productivity, and shares would remain constant. When this point is reached, then the assumption of a given capital labor unit becomes open to question even more than before. Presumably as wages rise, the capital-labor ratio will also begin to rise and possibly incentives may emerge that result in the situation where productivity growth does not affect both inputs equally. More on all of this later.

In this argument, enlargement of profit's share is a consequence of the raising of per capita incomes of the labor groups, i.e., it is a consequence of creating employment in those sections of the economy where productivity is higher. (This is not the same thing as arguing that high profits are necessary to produce the saving that will permit a satisfactory rate of capital formation.) It is also evident from figure 1 that with a more rapid increase in productivity--a greater slope of FAB--profit's share and the profit rate rise more rapidly, as the relationship between BD and AE governs the relative shares. At the same time the higher rate of productivity growth generates investment opportunities and thereby should contribute to a more rapid eastward movement along the horizontal axis. Finally, the diagram shows that technological depreciation penalizes the movement toward effective utilization of labor and the levelling off of relative shares. That is, if physical capital falls apart, then this fact reduces the rate of increase in profit's share and employment growth and thereby increases the time required to reach the full employment point.

This form of the vintage model assumes no substitution between capital and labor after construction of the physical capital. Prior to construction there is substitutability, but the capital-labor ratio remains unchanged because real wage rates and capital costs are assumed constant and productivity growth is assumed to act on both inputs equally. If some ex post increase in productivity is technically possible, the diagram becomes more complicated, but the general argument remains relatively the same. If it is assumed that a remains positive and constant and some increase in productivity growth can occur ex post, then FAB itself shifts upward with the same slope. This upward shift in FAB would also contribute to a rising profit's share and a rising profit rate.

As this happens, the wage rate AE (figure 2) falls below the level
of productivity of labor with unit e. If there exists unutilized physical
capital to the left of e, the producer now has an inducement to bring
these machines into use. In figure 2 employment will rise by EH, the wage
bill by G'AEH, and total profits by G'A'A. Profit's share of the new output (G'B'DH) will also be greater than it was before the upward shift in
FAB. In the event that there are no unutilized capital units available,
then evidently this source of increased employment is impossible. If, in
addition, there is zero ex post substitution between capital and labor,
then a rise in wage rates from AE to A'E will not penalize employment
growth and will contribute to increasing per capita income of labor.
Such a rise in wage rates will also reduce the growth of profit's share
and the rise in the profit rate. These consequences may also reduce the
rate of eastward movement on the horizontal axis, but this cannot be told
without further assumptions.

On the other hand, if there is positive ex post substitutability
between capital and labor (and no previously idle machines), the increase
in labor productivity to A'E with wages remaining at AE will induce an
increase in employment relative to capital. In this case employment will

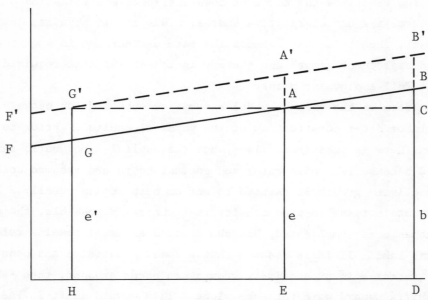

Figure 2

rise relative to capital until Q/L is equal to AE again. How much increase
this amounts to depends on the elasticity of substitution. The greater it
is, the greater will be the increase. If this happens, then the effect
on relative shares depends also on the value of the elasticity of substitution. The outcome of this argument cannot be shown on the diagram as it
involves a change in the unit of measurement along the horizontal axis.
Further implications of a changing K/L are examined in the following section. It is, however, clear what the consequences of rising wages are in
this circumstance.[7]

To summarize briefly: The modified vintage model described above
brings out the impact of productivity growth, wage rates, profits, investment, and output growth on employment, profit's share, and labor's per
capita income. It shows that a rising profit's share with constant wage
rates is a necessary consequence of increasing employment and increasing
the per capita income of labor, employed plus unemployed. If government
owns the plants, profits accrue to the government, but that does not modify the argument. Rising wage rates will prevent the share of profits
from rising but will then create intra-labor inequality, and penalize employment growth. It is likely that there is more sharing within labor
than between labor and profit receivers, but it is not likely that there
is enough sharing within labor to justify seeking simply to maximize labor's
share. (This is not, to repeat, the same thing as arguing that a rising
profit's share is necessary in order to achieve an adequate saving rate.
Nor is a trickle-down notion involved here.) Profit's share will continue
to rise until "full employment." Profit's share rises faster as does the
profit rate, the more rapid is embodied productivity growth, given constant
real wages and the longer the physical life of the capital. So too does the
rate of growth of employment and income accruing to the labor sector. In
the context of the industrialization effort of less developed countries the
conclusion would seem to be that rapid rates of growth of productivity,
output, and investment with constant real wages in the modern sector
will in fact produce a rising profit's share, but the same process generates the most rapid growth of employment and labor incomes possible with
a given rate of capital formation. In particular it is clear that rising
real wages, though holding down the growth of profit's share, will penalize the growth of employment and labor's income. The only instance where
rising wage rates do not penalize employment and labor's income is in the

case where there is a disembodied increase in productivity <u>and</u> there is zero substitutability between capital and labor. In the case where productivity grows as a consequence of accumulated experience, increased wage rates will add to intra-labor inequality while holding back the growth of profit's share.

2. Second model variant

The argument is neater if it can be assumed that none of the increased productivity is embodied, i.e., that it occurs irrespective of the level of investment.[8]

Suppose that all firms hire labor until the marginal product of labor equals an exogenously given wage rate. Suppose further that capital formation is determined autonomously, and that the following production function describes the modern manufacturing sector:

(1) $Y(t) = F(a(t)K(t), \quad b(t)L(t))$,

where Y = output,

    a = the index of capital-augmenting productivity growth,

    b = the index of labor-augmenting productivity growth,

    L = labor,

    K = capital, and

    t = time period.

Assume this production function has constant returns to scale. Then as is shown in appendix 3, the proportionate rate of growth of the demand for labor is

(2) $r_L = r_K + r_a - r_b + \dfrac{\sigma Y}{Y - wL} (r_b - r_w)$,

where the r's identify proportionate rates of growth, e.g., $\dfrac{dL}{dt}\dfrac{1}{dL}$, and so on, w is the wage rate, and σ is the elasticity of substitution. Evidently, employment grows with capital formation and capital-augmenting productivity growth, and falls with labor-augmenting productivity growth. The most interesting component is the last, which tells us that labor-augmenting productivity growth, not matched by wage increases, will produce employment growth if the elasticity of substitution exceeds zero. If $\sigma Y/(Y - wL)$

exceeds one and r_w is zero, the net effect on employment growth of labor-augmenting productivity growth is positive. A "low" capital share also facilitates employment growth.

There are three points in particular to note about (2). First, if $r_a = r_b$ then employment will grow faster than r_K if $r_b > r_w$ and $\sigma > 0$. In this event the greater are σ and r_b (relative to r_w), the greater will be r_L. If r_w is zero, the capital labor will rise only if $r_b[\sigma Y/(Y - w_L) - 1]$ is negative and absolutely larger than r_a. This suggests that considerations with respect to r_b, r_a, and σ are relevant in the income distribution problem. It may be noted in passing that in almost all developing countries, capital's share is larger than in the more developed countries. Therefore with a given elasticity of substitution and a given difference between r_b and r_w, employment will expand more rapidly in the latter than in the former countries.

Secondly, if $r_b = 0$, then $r_L > r_k$ if $r_a > r_w[\sigma Y/(Y - w_L)]$. If $r_b = r_w = 0$, then $r_L - r_K = r_a$. In either case if $r_b = 0$, employment will grow more rapidly, the higher is r_a and the lower is r_w.

Third, the rate of growth of labor's share (with product prices assumed constant) (LS), can be shown to be[9]

(3) $\qquad r_{LS} = (\sigma - 1)(r_b - r_w)$.

Labor's share will rise if r_b exceeds r_w and the elasticity of substitution exceeds unity. If wage rates were constant, and $\sigma > 1$, then labor's share will rise over time in this model. Earlier it was shown that employment will grow more rapidly, the greater is r_b relative to r_w and the greater is σ. Now from (3) it is evident that if σ exceeds unity, the greater it and r_b are, the more rapidly will labor's share rise. With r_w equal to zero, the increase in labor's share is due entirely to increasing employment. In this event employment grows more rapidly than output, and observed labor productivity falls. These circumstances would appear to produce the most favorable effect on low-end poverty as well as on the overall size distribution of income. If $\sigma > 1$, rising wage rates actually reduce the rate of growth of labor's share by putting a penalty on employment growth. It is also evident that if $r_w > r_b$, then a σ less than unity will produce a rising labor share, at the expense of a slow growth of employment.[10]

C. <u>Role of industrialization policies</u>

The models just considered place a heavy role on investment in modern manufacturing activities, but that investment must take place in a manner consistent with the resource endowment of the economy. The investment must "fit" the economy if it is to serve the income distribution objectives very effectively. In this section, some aspects of the role that industrialization policies seem to have on the rate and the form of investment are reviewed. The first subsection considers formal investment incentives; the second considers the profit rate and its relationship to the rate and composition of investment.

1. Investment and incentives

Almost all developing countries have a variety of regulations intended to encourage investment in manufacturing. There are a great variety of such regulations, but some common characteristics do obtain, and some general observations appear legitimate. In almost all instances the incentives are in terms of exemptions from company taxes or from customs duties and include measures that may reduce the level of taxable income (at least for a time), e.g., accelerated depreciation and investment allowances. The latter are less frequently found and result essentially in deductions of part of the cost of investment from taxable income. Outright grants for investment are very rare. The range of variations and modifications within these categories is great indeed. Tax holidays vary widely in the length of time that they are applicable, may apply to the entire income or to some part only, may or may not apply only to pioneering enterprises, may or may not apply to a firm's expansion, or to its location, and so on. Exemptions of customs duties are here and there dependent on available domestic supplies, type of commodity, sometimes apply to raw materials and sometimes not, and on and on. In many instances the advantages increase as the absolute size of the investment increases, and some indeed have a minimum-size investment requirement. In most countries the vast majority of investment projects in terms of number are not affected at all by the incentive system, but in terms of money value of investment the proportion affected is much higher.[11]

It is correct to say, as many have, that almost all incentive systems favor the use of capital at the expense of labor. There is little empirical evidence on the extent to which the incentives themselves contribute to the observed rising capital-labor ratios or result in a choice of activities that have a higher capital-labor ratio than would have been the case in their absence. If one believes that these particular incentives are necessary to produce the investment, then of course employment growth is greater with them than it would be without them. Again efforts to measure the effect on the rate of investment of incentive systems have not been successful, but qualitative evidence is leading an increasing number of economists to conclude that any such effect is minor. This evidence is largely from reports on interviews with producers and from studies in developed countries of the determinants of investment. Answers to questionnaires on this kind of issue are not completely reliable, but the consistency with which tax advantages are downgraded appears convincing. These questionnaires usually consist of a set of questions about the factors that led to the decision to invest. Tax advantages rarely appeared high on such lists and were frequently not mentioned at all. In particular countries at particular times, tax incentives may be crucial, but it now seems safe to conclude that the case should be proved, and where there is no evidence to the contrary, the best assumption is that tax advantages have little impact on the rate of investment.

From the standpoint of employment growth and allocative decisions, the worst of all worlds is the situation where the rate of investment is not affected, but the choice of techniques and choice of sector are affected in a manner that penalizes employment growth of unskilled workers, discourages the use of domestically produced inputs, and discriminates relatively against small-scale operations. This in fact seems to be the case in many countries at the present time. There are other consequences more directly related to the distribution of income that may be worth discussing in the present context.

Any incentive that is built around relief from profit taxes evidently depends on the earning of profits. If profits are not earned early in the life of the firm, or if they are not expected to be earned, then tax forgiveness cannot have any effect on investment decisions. Tax holidays increase the variability in profits relative to that which would obtain in their absence. Thus the rich firms get richer, and the firms that may have a hope if they can survive for a few years get no help. Evidently where the extra profits (profits that would otherwise be taxed) are paid out in dividends, the size distribution of income in favor of the higher income groups is enhanced.

A second aspect of investment incentives relevant to the employment and income distribution follows from the fact that in many countries the incentives apply only to certain types of activities, otherwise additional government authorizations are necessary. For example, imports of capital goods may be exempted from duty, but an import license must be obtained. The retaining of considerable discretionary power requires consideration of criteria for deciding which activities or imports to allow. One such criterion that has found favor in a number of countries is whether or not there is "room" for an additional producer. This usually means that the decision-making authority asks itself what would happen to product prices and to the utilization rates of existing capacity if new capacity were to become available. (If such consequences appear undesirable from the standpoint of the existing producers, new applications are rejected.) Under this arrangement the new industry is offered not only protection from imports but also protection from future domestic competition. As is discussed more fully below, this kind of protection has especially adverse effects on the kinds of productivity and employment growth that help reduce the proportion of the labor force left beyond the reach of the modern sector. It is evident that such an incentive provides more or less guaranteed profits without any inducements to find and install cost-reduction measures. Evidence seems completely lacking on this point, but it may well be that removal of guarantees of protection of this kind would have marked negative effects on the rate of investment in some countries, especially in those activities where exporting potential is assumed to be slight.

A third point having to do with incentive systems is their cost in terms of government projects foregone because of lacks of funds. It has often been noted that if tax relief has zero effect on the rate of investment, then the producers profit and the government foregoes tax revenues. The amounts involved may not be large but in many cases are large enough to matter, especially if foregone customs receipts are included. Lent estimates that revenue foregone (on the assumption that the incentives have no effect on the level of investment) ranges between two and thirteen percent of total government revenues.[12] For countries at the upper end of this range, foregone receipts can clearly matter. They matter even more if the government seeks to obtain revenue through other taxes, e.g., payroll taxes, that unambiguously penalize employment growth. The consequence of this on the objectives of income distribution and employment depends of course on what each government and industry does with resources available to it. The situation undoubtedly varies from country to country, but in many countries evidence would seem to suggest that government projects could be devised that would contribute more to these objectives than is likely to be the case with untaxed profits. In particular, government expenditures that facilitate the growth of small-scale industry, and still more particularly that facilitate new activities in nonurban areas, are more likely to contribute to these objectives than private expenditures for the same purpose.

A final general point is this: The investment-incentive packages almost always refer (in fact or in law or both) to modern enterprises of larger scale. In some countries the packages are more often aimed at foreign rather than at domestic investors. This often means that the government officials neglect or actually discourage smaller undertakings and those employing the more traditional methods. This in turn has two general effects on low-end poverty and income distribution. Indigenous activities that fit the economy are rarely helped and are sometimes destroyed by the (unnecessarily) subsidized new firms, and thereby opportunities for income-earning activities that can reach a significant segment of the labor force are lessened. More generally, however, is the fact that the investment climate that is created militates against indigenous activities and the evolution of those kinds of activities that best fit the system. This notion is at once vague and important. Discussions with industrial policy officials in many parts of the world confirm this attitude. It is an attitude based partly on an implicit assumption that the only hopeful long-run prospect is rapid growth of large-scale, modern factories. More generally it seems to be based on the notion that policies cannot be designed that will help the truly indigenous enterprises. This latter notion, like export pessimism and variable coefficient pessimism, can only be eroded away, if at all, by success stories.

To summarize briefly: Most developing countries have investment incentives that usually involve tax advantages to the investor. Although empirical evidence is slim, several reports of interviews and questionnaires indicate that these incentives are not especially important in generating investment. They do have other effects, however, most of which dampen employment growth and contribute to increased inequality of earnings among producers and among recipients of firm income. Guaranteed protection from foreign and domestic competition does appear to be important and has adverse effects on productivity growth. These incentives are generally relevant, and in some cases only applicable, to modern-sector activities of larger scale. As such they direct attention and energy away from small-scale indigenous operations that fit the economy better and that are more likely to generate employment for the low-end poor.

2. Profit rates

In any discussion of income distribution, the rate of return on physical capital in manufacturing enters in a variety of ways. (The return on human capital is discussed in the section on wage rates.) On the one hand, of course, is the presumption that high rates of return on physical capital induce the further accumulation of more capital, and the further presumption that variation in profit rates affects the allocation of capital among manufacturing sectors. On the other hand, as noted above, profits go (or are assumed to go) to the rich at the expense of the poor, thereby exacerbating the distribution problem. More revealing is the effort to distinguish between useful profits and useless profits. Useful profits are those profits that induce investment and that measure the social contribution of investment, and the latter are those that result only in income inequality. The point here is not just that high profits may be saved or may be consumed but to understand their impact on the rate and allocation of investment.

The models in section B of this chapter show that if a large part of productivity growth is of the embodied type, then it is expected that profit's share and the profit rate will rise over time if the maximum contribution to relieving low-end poverty and to preventing growing intra-labor inequality is to be made. If these high and rising profit rates are legitimate signals and if they induce a high rate of investment, then movement toward the elimination of low-end poverty is accelerated. If, however, the high profits come from excessive protection, from inappropriate incentives, from penalizing productivity growth, and so on, the result will simply be inequality of income distribution. While data do not permit a very inclusive analysis, there are several general pieces of evidence and a couple of case studies that are helpful in understanding the problem.

First, all available data show that total value added less the wage bill is a much larger share of value added in almost all less developed countries than it is in the richer countries. This suggests that profit rates in developing countries are relatively higher.

Second, there are also a few efforts at a direct estimation of the rate of return. These estimated rates are usually quite high. For example, Bent Hansen and Girgis A. Marzouk[13] estimate a before-tax profit rate of 17 to 13 percent of capital replacement costs for total industry in Egypt for 1960. A detailed study of Argentinian profit rates over the years 1961-67 has been made by A.H. Petrei.[14] His calculations show rates (before taxes) ranging from a low of 10 percent in 1962 to a high of 25 percent in 1965.

The effect of high or rising profit rates on income distribution and the alleviation of low-end poverty depends on the extent to which they induce capital formation in an economic environment in which the distortions are relatively modest. The models of section B suggest that a rising profit share and profit rate can often be expected if the maximum contribution to the relief of low-end poverty is to be made. But the more rapid is the rate of capital formation, the sooner will a situation be reached in which wage rates can begin to rise without penalizing employment growth.

Most observers would probably agree that investment rates in manufacturing have been reasonably satisfactory over the past fifteen to twenty years. The precarious conclusion just reached that profit rates have been "high" does not necessarily mean that the latter induced the former. At the same time, it seems reasonably safe to argue that the attractive profit rates were a necessary condition for the high investment rates. It has also been argued that the various tax-incentive arrangements were rarely very important to the investment decision. What does seem unambiguously important in many instances was protection from imports, and probably (implied or explicit) protection from domestic competition. The distortion created by the tax-incentive arrangements can be removed therefore without penalizing investment. Lewis's analysis of Pakistan in the 1950s suggests that a relatively undifferentiated import policy and high rates of investment can co-exist, and the high

rates of profits can be reduced over time by high rates of capital formation. Studies of recent Brazilian experiences, though much less complete
than Lewis on Pakistan, suggest a similar conclusion.[15]

Can then protection schemes be designed that afford the necessary
time and encouragement for industrial development without so imposing
distortions that the investment generated does little toward absorbing
unskilled labor? Along with foreign trade policy, two other general
categories of policy appear particularly strategic, wage rates and technology. These three components of policy--foreign trade, wage rates,
and technological development--must be consistent with and contribute to
a high rate of capital formation if the manufacturing sector is to play
a very strong role in effecting a more acceptable sharing of the rewards
of development. In addition, ways must be found to generate productive
manufacturing activities in essentially rural areas and small towns. The
following parts of this paper consider some of the aspects of these
several issues. Before that, however, a brief comment is made on the
rationale and origin of direct controls and the role of the market.

3. Wage rates

In the models in section B, a constant wage rate was found to be
necessary if the maximum contribution to employment growth and to the
elimination of low-end poverty were to be achieved from a given rate of
investment. Richard Webb considers the general question of wage rates
in chapter 6, and it is possible to limit the discussion here to specific
issues connecting wage rates and industrialization policy. There are
many sides to any answer to this question, and some sides apply to some
countries and others to other countries. One point, however, is general
enough for special attention. The system of protection and exchange-rate
policies generally penalizes all exports. The traditional sectors, where
wage rates have not risen or have risen only moderately or foreign demand
is quite inelastic, can export to the extent necessary to keep the balance
of payments afloat (with protection, licenses, and so on). Foreign aid
and private capital inflows also help. The protection of the domestic
manufacturing activity eliminates foreign competition, and traditional
exports (with protection, aid, capital inflows) maintain the balance of
payments. The new manufacturing sector has then a captive market, and

nothing happens to penalize the existing activities in this sector as wage rates rise.

To dramatize this argument consider an example suggested by John Power.[16] Suppose that almost all of Philippine industry were located in Manila. And then suppose Manila seceded from the rest of the Philippines. The rest of the Philippines would no longer be forced to buy Manila's high-cost manufactures but could buy from cheaper sources in other parts of the world. The new Manila industry could not continue (in the absence of large capital inflows) its practice of paying high wage rates, since its balance of payments would collapse if it did so. Wage rates and prices would necessarily fall or there would be a devaluation that has the same effect. Evidently then the rising wage rates could not take place without the captive market, i.e., without the marked inequality in wage rates (and presumably income) between the manufacturing enclave and the rest of the economy. Evident also is the fact that new manufacturers in city states such as Hong Kong and Singapore cannot indulge themselves with high wage rates as the cities have no captive markets and no traditional sector to maintain their balance of payments.[17]

In this argument, emphasis is placed on the protection of the manufacturing sector from foreign competition. Modern-sector activities gain at the expense of the traditional activities, as the latter support the balance of payments and are forced to buy the high-cost domestically produced manufactures. It may also be noted that income distribution could shift in favor of the workers and owners of the newly created manufacturing activities with very strong balance of payments pressure and even stronger upward pressure on manufacturing wage rates. In this event, the nonmodern sectors are penalized (as modern sector wages rise) because of balance of payments pressures. Something like this may happen in most developed countries.[18] In this case, wage (and other) income in some sectors is forced down by happenings on the balance of payments front, made necessary by the (autonomously, e.g., union-induced) rising wage rates in manufacturing. For the developing economies, to which the argument applies, the milieu in which modern-sector wages rise is less definable, less able to be pinpointed than strong labor union pressures. And the role of protection from foreign and domestic competition is crucial.

The extent of the applicability of the above arguments varies from country to country. In some countries, e.g., the Central American countries (possibly), the observed rate of increase in wage rates is probably due to more conventional supply and demand matters. More complete country studies are necessary, of course, but there seems ample reason to believe that the kind of argument sketched here is applicable to a substantial number of countries.

This argument suggests that the protection system is a significant source of intra-labor inequality. This same system also helps to keep any excess supply of labor from impeding the upward push of wage rates. In this case therefore it is not only profits that are protected, it is the workers employed in the modern industrial sectors as well. The strategic policy instrument in this situation appears to be the exchange rate, to be discussed in the next section.

It seems clear enough that the same set of industrialization policies that have produced distortions and bottlenecks as well as "excess" profits have also produced--or at least, allowed--rising wage rates. A case can be made that, in some instances, such wage increases are necessary to induce the acquisition of a necessary skill or as the outcome of a bargaining exercise following a productivity-increasing experience. These instances appear relatively rare, and there is a general presumption that rising wage rates are unnecessary and penalize the employment and income distribution objectives. It is a particularly relevant part of the present argument--and hence worth repeating--that the industrialization policies that have been so frequently condemned for creating unnecessarily high profits have also created high and rising wage rates, thereby exacerbating the distribution problem. The firmness and severity of this conclusion depends in part on the extent of substitutability between labor and other inputs as modified by capital's share. (See equation (2) in section B of this chapter.) Even so, however, the conclusion appears defensible in light of the empirical evidence on the extent of that substitutability.

D.   Nature and sources of productivity growth

In the models of section B, productivity growth entered in a crucial way in the explanation of both employment growth (and the consequent reduction of low-end poverty) and the functional and size distribution of income. The task of section D is to examine the nature and sources of productivity growth in some further detail. The first subsection considers a number of general points associated with this issue and then develops a rather specific model of productivity growth. The second subsection considers what kind of policies and economic environment facilitate the appropriate kind of productivity growth.

1. Role of technology

There are assumptions that will result in the domination by technology of the entire process. If one assumes that the production coefficients are fixed by engineering considerations, that the composition of output is also given, and that there is no productivity growth, then the growth rate of employment is set by the growth rate of capital formation. The wage rate is determined by institutional factors of a social and political nature, but has no effect on the choice of technique used or on the choice of product to be produced. In terms of equation (2) of section B, all of this adds up to assuming $r_a = r_b = \sigma = 0$. The picture can be further darkened and the role of policy further downgraded by assuming that engineering considerations produce over time an r_b in excess of zero while leaving r_a about zero. This alone would explain the observed excess of output and capital growth over employment growth. More discouragement can be generated, however, by assuming that changes in the composition of demand result in demand for products that "require" increasing capital-intensity (both physical and human) in their production. This assumption too adds to the probability that employment will lag behind capital formation and output growth, and that a privileged (and small) group of workers and owners is an inevitable part of the development of an industrial complex. The income distribution problem is worsened by the fact that the technology used often imposes heavy demands not only for physical capital but for human capital as well. The requirement for high skills on the part of labor adds to the cost of creating the productive unit and increases intra-labor inequality because the skilled workers must be paid at least enough to induce the acquisition of a skill.

The technology that produces these results is imported from the rich countries and is modified only slightly, if at all, in the course of its use in the developing countries. Productivity per worker is high and rising, but employment growth is low. The policy implication

of this way of thinking is unambiguous: Do everything possible to achieve
a rapid rate of capital formation. "Everything possible" includes heavy
subsidies to capital formation because such subsidies cannot penalize
employment growth or labor's share because both of these are determined
by technological and institutional factors that are not affected by the
subsidies that favor the use and accumulation of capital.

The preceding summary of an argument underlies many of the approaches
to development found around the world and, as noted earlier, is a major
part of the rationale justifying the development strategy pursued. It is
not a nonsense strategy and, if population growth in developing countries
since 1950 had been one percent rather than about three, it might have
worked. However, to achieve a capital-labor ratio in the developing
countries equal to that in Western Europe or Japan at the same time that
the labor force is growing at a rate of three percent imposes what is
surely an impossible task.

A more important reason why the above described strategy has accentuated the distribution and low-end poverty problem is simply that its
basic assumptions now appear quite inappropriate. As producing units
responded to the incentives and to the investment environment there
emerged the rising capital-labor ratios, a constant or only slightly
falling proportion of low-end poor, and the appearance of bottlenecks
that brought the growth process to a slowdown or halt. Thus, it seems
that policy measures do affect what is done and how it is done and that
technology need not be, in all instances, so dominant.

2. An approach to the creation of an appropriate indigenous
   technology

How can a strategy be devised by which a process of technological
change can emerge that makes increasing use of the most abundant resources? First, one must understand the process by which technological
innovation takes place. Consider an example. A new plant is built by
foreign or domestic entrepreneurs which incorporates a fairly modern
technique. It will probably not incorporate the most modern technique,
especially if it is a foreign-owned firm. Foreign-owned firms tend to
install a technique from which all bugs have been removed. This is
done to reduce the probability of breakdowns, the need for an inventory
of spare parts, and the necessity of keeping or bringing into the country
highly skilled repair people. The choice of initial technique or process

in terms of labor-intensity or capital-intensity is not as crucial as other matters to be described below. Evidently the more labor used in this initial version the better, but the choice of the initial technique from the "shelf" of techniques is not the crucial issue. The plant operates and the workers and managers gain experience. They learn more about what the supply problems and possibilities are, about alternative sources of inputs, about marketing opportunities. As a consequence of this learning process, adjustments are made. It becomes crucial, therefore, for the economic environment to be such as to lead this learning process into channels that exploit the economy to the greatest extent. Industrialization strategy has great relevance in making clear what in fact it is that the economy has to offer.

An illustration or two may help. At the outset of operations the new plant uses an imported input. This it does partly because a foreign source has supplied this particular input to other producers around the world, and partly because of unfamiliarity on the part of management with possible alternative domestic sources of supply. If the exchange rate undervalues foreign currency and if import policies permit the item to be imported easily, there is little inducement to look toward internal sources. On the other hand, suppose the undervaluation of foreign currency is eliminated, and the imported input becomes very costly. The firm then is pressed to find a domestically available replacement. It may do this by search by its own people or it may do so by asking specific help from a research organization. The latter has apparently happened with Korean manufacturers and the Korean Institute of Scientific Development.

A second example is more general. Some recent studies have shown that producers may use a technique that is less appropriate than the prevailing technology and factor prices would allow. In other words, even granted that factor price distortions exist, observed techniques are still less suitable than would obtain if these prices were dominant in the choice of technique. Two explanations are suggested to account for this.[19] One is that engineers are more potent in deciding what is done than economic advisors or business executives. Engineers, it is assumed, are more interested in using machines than in using labor. The second is that managers and foremen accept at the outset the decisions made by engineers but then adapt and adjust as they learn more about the economic environment in which they operate. The policy objective then is to create inducements to move from a situation in which the employed factor combinations are inappropriate to the employment and income distribution objectives (either because engineers dominate or because an examination of alternative techniques is not feasible) to one where the combination used is more appropriate to these ends (as alternative techniques are examined and managers learn how to exploit the advantages the economy offers). The literature often distinguishes between ex ante and ex post substitutability of factors, and the former is assumed to be greater than the latter, i.e., that initially construction or purchase options exist, but afterward few changes can be made in response to changing conditions. Such arguments always assume that the initial choice is the optimum for prevailing factor and product prices. The argument here is that ex post substitutability is greater (or that it rises over time) as managers learn and as new techniques are sought out. The common practice of requiring by edict that a firm use an increasing number of domestically produced inputs is an attempt to achieve a similar end. Such edicts, however, do more to penalize productivity growth than to enhance it and, more importantly, tend to reduce search for and efforts to create more flexibility. When the pricing signals are right it can be expected that the productivity increases that occur after plant and equipment are initially installed will be those which facilitate the use of the most abundant resources of the economy. Howard Pack, for example, observed in Kenya instances where a simple change in the position of two processes within a plant increased output.[20] Perhaps the most obvious kind of change that facilitates the increased use of labor is that which results in the utilization of physical capital a larger and larger proportion of the time.[21] Moving to arrangements that are more consistent with factor endowments aids productivity in other ways. Evidence on some Latin American countries during World War II indicates that when these countries were forced back on their own resources, because no imports were possible, they were remarkably effective in finding ways to use their own resources. In this process, productivity (r_a and r_b) grew more rapidly than it did later when these countries began their big push toward industrialization through import substitution.[22]

Emphasis is placed in this argument on the role of managers and foremen, and on the existence of inducements and signals and information that push the managers and foremen to adjust in the "right" direction. As noted above, most evidence is consistent with the assumption that

workers' skills are so rarely a bottleneck that, except in specific
instances, they can be ignored. The "supply" problem then is managers
and foremen, and one important reason why the evidence often indicates
that foreign-owned and -run firms use more labor-intensive techniques
than locally owned ones is that the former have better managers than
the latter.

The question of direct relevance to this paper that emerges, however,
is what the impact of industrialization strategies is on this mechanism.
A general statement is virtually self-evident: Any policy that protects
or results in the creation of misinformation impedes this substituting,
productivity-increasing process. For example, the correction of the undervaluation of foreign currency can set in motion a search process to find
domestic sources of supply of certain inputs. Investment incentives that
reward on the basis of employment per dollar of investment could have a
similar effect. There are few examples of investment incentives built
around employment, and even fewer that are based on investment-employment
ratios. Policies that point out, that bring into unmistakable relief, the
direction in which the technology (and other) search efforts should move,
appear necessary in most developing countries. This would seem to indicate that the principal policy approach is that of creating a set of
inducements to search and incentives to reward the successful search.

There is one important additional consideration that has to do with
small, indigenous industries. These industries, almost by definition,
fit the economy much better than do most modern-sector manufactures.
These small-scale industries have many analogies in agriculture.[23]
There are many units, geographically dispersed, operating in a variety of
types of markets. Also, as in the case in agriculture, they are generally unable to provide their own technical needs. A case can be made
therefore for more centralized research and extension services along the
lines of agricultural research and diffusion. Of course, agriculture
research has had its problems but also some considerable successes. Much
work has been done on helping small industries, but it is not easy to
find specific formulas that have helped much. This subject is returned
to in section F.

To summarize: Technical choices enter directly and significantly into
the determination of the rate of reduction in low-end poverty and in the
reduction of inequality in the size distribution of income. The nearly

exclusive reliance on imported technology (in collaboration with the investment incentives described earlier) has tended to defeat the contributions that appropriate technology could make to these objectives. In terms of the models of section B, such reliance has produced low elasticities of substitution, high rates of growth of r_b (labor-augmenting) relative to r_a (capital-augmenting), some relative increase in high skill requirements, and upward pressure on wage rates. All of these effects, as shown in section B, handicap efforts to increase employment growth and develop an industrial sector suitable--that fits--the resources of the community.

Efforts to meet this problem by establishing a variety of formal research institutions have not been very effective. Arguments have been suggested to the effect that an approach that relies more heavily on individual firm search activity, search for new processes, techniques, and products, puts more of the burden on managers and foremen than on engineers and scientists, and the former group has a much closer working knowledge of the firm's needs than does the latter. It also puts a burden on the policy maker to see that incentives and other rewards are such as to force this search into directions consistent with the achievement of the objectives. This approach may be less effective for the small, indigenous manufacturers who also play a strategic role in the argument, and this question is considered in section F.

E.   Trade policy issues

Foreign trade is perhaps the most fertile area of policy for affecting industrialization. Almost all countries have in one way or another used trade policy to try to step up their industrialization efforts. Such policies have had effects on wage rates and technology which, as has been seen, act directly on the income distribution and employment activities. Trade policy also affects the quantity supplied and the price of consumption commodities, and in that way too affects income distribution. This section begins with a brief discussion of the general question of outward- and inward-looking strategies, and then proceeds to examine a range of more specific issues of trade policy.

Although much attention has been given to the role of trade policies, it should be noted at once that trade policies may be a consequence of other decisions, rather than the initiating force. Thus a development

corporation or ministry of industry may decide to build a particular kind
of factory, and then trade policy is arranged to accommodate that decision.
This is one reason why changing and designing trade policy is so difficult.
In many instances efforts to change trade policy must include references
to investment decisions by the government and the private sector.

1. Inward- and outward-looking policies

The many critical examinations of the import-substitution strategy
of development in the 1960s produced the widespread opinion that the opening
up of the economies was essential if the problems of employment and income
distribution were not to worsen, and if distortions were not to become so
severe that sustained growth would be impossible. The general policy objective advocated was that of trade liberalization, more or less equalization of tariff rates, elimination of discriminatory exchange rates as well
as the employment of more realistic exchange rates, and possibly the
introduction of specific export and employment incentives. Studies show
that effective protection often results in the lowest income groups
(peasant farmers) paying more for many of their consumption items and
receiving less for their output. That plus empirical estimates of such
protection added to the urgency of change that many expressed. At best,
it was argued by a few that import substitution was a necessary phase
for a country before it made economic sense for movement toward a more
outward-looking strategy. Even this final defense did not last long and
has been pretty thoroughly demolished.

Recently, however, a backlash has set in, not so much in support of
the import-substitution strategy itself as in support of encouraging
trade among developing countries and strongly discouraging it between
developed and less developed countries. The central theme of the argument is that openness and outward-looking strategies reduce the incentives and capacity to develop indigenous processes and products suitable
for the low-income, labor-plentiful economy. Thus, economic contact
with the rich countries is self-defeating. It necessarily results in the
reproduction of rich country techniques of production and in rich country
products in an economic environment in which their use is possible, if at
all, only in a small enclave. By isolating an economy--or at least minimizing the contact it has with rich countries--techniques, processes, and
products that are consistent with its environment are much more likely to

emerge. The idea is not to protect infant industry, provide learning time, or create investment incentives. Rather the idea is to protect the society itself from a contact that necessarily leads to wants, practices, and to products that are not appropriate. By development in virtual isolation, employment and income distribution problems are solved because the development fits the economy so well. China is frequently cited as an example of success with this kind of an approach, just as Taiwan is usually cited as an example of a successful outward-looking strategy.[24]

Those who thus attack openness and liberalization seek the same objective as those whose position is being attacked. The latter have emphasized the role of price distortions, misleading signals, indiscriminate adoption of rich country technologies in the emergence of an industrial structure that exacerbates, rather than resolves, the distribution problem. To correct this, they suggest opening the system to competitive pressure, removing sources of distortions, providing accurate price signals, and bringing the entrepreneurs into contact with new ideas. Supporters of the alternate strategy say that the same result can be reached only by internalizing effort. The advocates of the inward-looking approach have not spelled out a mechanism or process by which their result is to be achieved; and until this is done, appraisal will be difficult. Study of China's recent development may bring out what this process is.[25] Clearly mere isolation is not enough. There must be something more, and what this "something" more is can be crucial. It also seems probable that a large country is better able to proceed in this way than a small country. The argument, therefore, is interesting, but not because it reveals new mechanisms or processes of development, nor because it suggests a new idea, since autarchy is as old as economics. Rather it is interesting because it reveals another way of saying what is surely valid and important and has been emphasized before, namely, that a pattern of economic development that fits the society is more likely to succeed than one that does not.

2. Protection

There is much reason to believe that the major source of the distortion that produces low employment growth and continuing inequality in income distribution is the very high and uneven level of protection that characterizes so many countries. The major problems are not with protection as such but rather with its level, permanence, and unevenness. The type of protection that has been emphasized most frequently has been a low duty on capital goods (plus the usual ease of getting an import license on capital goods). This means not only that capital-intensity is encouraged but that domestic production of capital goods is discouraged, and that of previously imported consumer goods is encouraged.

This kind of protection dampens employment growth in a rather obvious way. More importantly, the imported consumer goods were generally products consumed only by the rich. Thus a productive capacity is encouraged whose use requires--as noted above--inequality of income. This process has created a small group of industrialists and workers in many countries whose private productivity is very much higher than the average productivity of the society. In this way, then, the protection of the manufacture of consumer goods aggravates and requires inequality. It is also evident that this chain would, or at least could, be broken if the goods produced could be exported. But the very nature of protection makes exporting difficult.

Protection affects distribution in another, sharper way. In most developing countries manufactured goods have been imported and agricultural products exported. Keeping out low-cost foreign manufactures means that farmers must then buy from the high-cost domestic producers. The penalty for this can be severe. S.R. Lewis' data show that for Pakistan over most of the 1950s, farmers received less than one-half of the value that their produce would have brought at world prices, and in some years it was less than one-third.[26] Pakistan's tariff has been studied most completely, but a similar result applies to many other countries. The basic rationale of such a policy is, of course, an infant industry argument. If productivity in the new industries rises rapidly enough and if prices follow productivity, then the original shift in income distribution can be reveresed. The costs of a number of new manufactured goods in Pakistan did fall significantly during the 1950s.[27] The great questions then are the productivity growth question, already considered, and the pricing question. If productivity rises and prices do not fall, then the income distribution effect is more severe and continues longer. A protective policy that continues more or less indefinitely, therefore, creates an indefinitely long change in the domestic terms of trade. Protection from foreign and domestic competitors tends, almost inevitably, to have this effect.

In many countries studies show that domestic prices often exceed the imported c.i.f. price plus the tariff. This kind of evidence is pretty convincing about the existence of monopoly profits. And again one concludes that the protection system is not just providing a time for learning but really a time for reaping unnecessary profits at the expense of the agricultural consumer. Agricultural products are the principal wage good of the manufacturing worker, and the earlier labor-surplus models emphasized the importance of keeping food prices low to avoid the upward push of urban wage rates. This, however, is a different situation from that in which the agricultural sector pays not only the necessary cost of the beginnings of the industrialization effort but also is forced to continue to pay monopoly (i.e., unnecessary) profits to the industrialists and their workers.

Efforts to define and measure effective protection showed that relevant tariffs were in fact usually much higher than nominal tariffs would indicate. The penalty on those who must buy domestically produced items rather than imported ones may be very great. While reliable estimates have been made in only a few countries, the presumption is strong that the penalties have been great. More important is the fact that the penalty, once created, seems to decline only in isolated instances.

The failure of the domestic price to fall is, as just noted, partly a matter of technology and partly a matter of price. The failure of prices to fall with productivity can be the result of a number of things, of course, but the two most important are the behaviors of wage rates and quasi-rents, discussed in section C.

The problem is further complicated because tariffs (along with exchange rates) rarely limit imports enough to protect the balance of payments. There must then be other controls to hurdle before importing is possible. In a number of instances the tariff may in fact be relatively unimportant in determining what is imported and who imports it. Where actual imports depend heavily on specific decisions of a government official, the effects of the tariff level and structure are difficult to pin down. As already noted, however, there is little evidence that licenses and other specific import controls do much to counteract the direction in which the tariffs work. In those cases where imports of inputs are essential if existing capacity is to be utilized, the non-tariff system of rationing imports can be an important element in preventing monopoly rents from being "competed" away. This has surely happened in many developing countries over the

1960s. Also there appears considerable evidence that direct control systems almost invariably favor the large, established firm. This favoring is due in part to the requirements for preparation of documentation and for negotiation with government officials. Small firms (and especially new ones) find these activities difficult. Government officials seem to find it easier and safer to deal with an established producer. This effect is strengthened if, as is often the case, retail importers of capital goods are less favored than direct users. Small manufacturers who use the retail importer are, therefore, handicapped. These two situations, (i) allowing monopoly rents and monopoly wage rates to come into existence and to continue indefinitely and (ii) the relative penalty against small and new firms, are perhaps the major ones in the effect of non-tariff trade controls on manufacturing employment and income distribution in developing countries.

There is one important qualification to all of this insofar as it bears on the income distribution issue. Consider as an extreme example that only the already rich have been importing consumer goods. Suppose further that these same goods are now heavily protected and that, as high-cost domestic production comes into being, the rich continue to buy. If the poor had not previously been buying the cheap imports, they are not now penalized by the protection. Suppose again that as a consequence of the protection, domestic entrepreneurs are induced into action and learn by experience. In this case, it is the rich who are paying for the entrepreneurial learning. If this learning results in increased productivity, falling relative prices, and more effective use of domestic resources, then the distribution effect can be toward greater equality, and the rich have paid for it. This pure case is hardly realistic, but it is not completely unrealistic in many instances. The fact that manufacturing prices rise relative to agricultural prices is not sufficient evidence that the poor peasants are paying for the industrialization; though, of course, it is a necessary condition for that result. This example brings out once again the crucial role of learning, productivity growth, and the elimination of monopoly rents. That these should all be accomplished is, in fact, more important than the initial situation created by the protection system. The extent to which response to inequalities occurs is central as well as is the question of who pays the cost of learning. Little research has been done in these areas.

3.   Exchange rates

Part of the industrialization package usually includes an exchange rate that undervalues foreign exchange. There are two questions that bear on income distribution: one has to do with what the appropriate exchange rate is in the context of an industrialization program and the other with what impact changes in the exchange rate have on many of the variables that act on income distribution.

What is the appropriate exchange rate? To say that an exchange rate undervalues foreign exchange usually means that, with existing tariff rates and other impediments to trade, the prevailing exchange rate does not protect the balance of payments. Consequently, as just discussed, some kind of licensing or other rationing device is often necessary. Suppose, however, that the exchange rate does in fact maintain an acceptable balance of payments position, would this then be the "right" rate from the standpoint of an industrialization strategy that seeks to make the greatest contribution to employment growth and reduced inequality?

Of course, with tariffs or other impediments to imports, the exchange rate that maintains the balance of payments values foreign currency below that value that would prevail with free trade. It is in this sense that any form of protection necessarily penalizes exports. But most developing countries have significant inflows of foreign capital and aid that further bolster the balance of payments. Also many countries have a small number of raw material or mineral export items that have few linkages with the rest of the economy but that do produce foreign exchange. All of these factors strengthen the balance of payments and hence permit a still lower valuation of foreign exchange. This means that an exchange rate policy in the context of development (with tariff protection, aid and other capital inflows, and export enclaves) that seeks simply to maintain a stable balance of payments will also be one that makes it very difficult for new manufactures to enter export markets.[28]

Devaluation, however, in this context could well reduce foreign exchange earnings, even if manufactured exports shoot up, if foreign demand for the major foreign exchange earners is quite inelastic. A subsidy to manufactured exports with no devaluation or a devaluation and a tax on the major traditional exports would overcome the impediment to the exportation of new manufactures without reduction in foreign exchange earnings. Subsidies are difficult to administer, and the devaluation makes more profitable

the use of domestically produced raw materials and other inputs, i.e., provides further inducement to replace other than consumer good imports. In
either case foreign exchange earnings should tend to rise, and this in turn
should permit a stepped-up rate of investment. In this case the higher
value of foreign exchange represents a more accurate picture of the resource
endowment of the economy and leads to more satisfactory allocation of
resources. In more extreme language, one might say that the source of the
increased growth and employment following devaluation is not more foreign
exchange as such but rather an allocation of resources that makes more
effective use of domestically available resources.

To illustrate this last point, consider the following argument. After
a new manufacturing activity is created, a rapid increase in productivity
is expected, indeed it is sought.[29] This increased productivity occurs as
the activity expands its output rapidly to supply the domestic market.
When it has more or less usurped all of the domestic market, its growth
rate must fall as further increases in demand now depend primarily on the
growth rate of total income. This slowdown in the growth of demand at the
same time that productivity rises (at given capital-labor ratios) will
mean that employment growth must fall or even that the absolute level of
employment must decline. On the other hand, if the activity can begin to
export, its rate of growth is not so limited, and the advantageous effect
of productivity growth on employment, previously outlined, can obtain.
Furthermore, the capacity to export avoids the kind of premature widening
of the industrial sector that has characterized so many countries and
that represents the use of resources in increasingly less suitable
activities.

This discussion of exchange-rate policy is built around the assumption that to export manufactured goods is of great importance, and that
the exchange-rate policy is an essential part of any export strategy.
The principal reason for exporting is that described in the previous
paragraph. There are others. Exports must in general meet world competition and in that respect producers are pushed toward the search and
adaptation process described above. Exports, of course, can be pushed
by policies that in effect protect them from world competition, but this
is much less common.[30]

An exchange rate favorable to the export of manufactured goods is
also helpful in inducing producers to think in terms of exporting and to

search for export markets. In many ways an extra favorable exchange rate
is necessary in the same way that an incentive system that rewards rapid
rates of growth of employment is necessary. It tends to emphasize, to
call attention to the advantages of, exporting. The impossibility of
exporting is referred to frequently (just as is the necessity for growing
capital-intensity), and a favorable exchange rate is often necessary to
overcome this attitude. This argument is an argument for exporting, not
for dismantling direct controls. Evidence from the Republic of Korea,
Brazil, Colombia, and Taiwan suggests that exchange-rate manipulation
can be instrumental in inducing exports. Carlos Diaz-Alejandro suggests
that a least-risk approach is to get exports growing rapidly, then initiate
the liberalization efforts.[31] The exact implication of this point is not
clear, but it does suggest that an export-oriented policy breaks--or prevents from appearing--bottlenecks that so penalize many import-substituting
economies. It is doubtful that the export orientation does this merely
by making more foreign exchange available than otherwise would be the case.
If this were the case, then one would expect that foreign aid, private
capital inflows, large autonomous exports of minerals or raw materials
would have an impact similar to that of increased exports. This is
decidedly not the case. The mechanism then appears to be that export
inducement policies (just as employment inducement measures) result in a
structure of industrial activity that "fits" the economy better, and it
is this better fit that prevents the bottlenecks and allows a more sustained growth. The very fact that bottlenecks stop the economy less
frequently implies that the growth process is one that takes more effective advantage of the country's endowment.

This discussion of exchange rates puts into clearer relief a central
point of the underlying theme of this chapter and (what is believed to be)
a significant difference between current and earlier thinking about
development policy. The argument here gives prime place to the creation
of an environment in which inducements and incentives exist to make maximum use of available resources in the solution of all micro problems.
Were this done then the aggregate problems would be solved more simply
and easily. The alternative arguments seem to be that if it is possible
to achieve high rates of growth of key aggregates (especially capital formation), then the micro problems would be swamped. Experience has surely
shown this to be false. Joan Robinson is reported to have said that

growth is the result of rational policy, not its objective.[32] When it is
said that it is not that "more foreign exchange is earned" as a consequence
of devaluation that is most relevant but rather the establishment of a
better-fitting manufacturing sector, then a notion similar to that of
Professor Robinson's is implied.

An extra favorable exchange rate may also mean an extra high price
for consumer goods imports, some of which may be consumed by the very
poor, e.g., certain basic food stuffs such as rice and wheat. In this
event a devaluation to encourage manufactured exports will penalize the
poor and help the rich. Where these consumer goods are few in number,
subsidies are a reasonable means of meeting this problem. The more
important point, however, is that if a devaluation induces the kind of
adjustment described above, the cost may be rapidly reduced by increased
employment. This is not to say, of course, that the poor _should_ bear
the burden. It is to argue, as before, that a measure that rationalizes
the industrial growth can contribute, in the manner described above, to
an effective reduction in low-end poverty. To put the point a bit differently: If devaluation is necessary in order to produce a good "fit,"
then not to devalue in order to keep certain consumer prices low is to
choose to live with the source of the problem rather than to attack
that source. It may also be noted that just as a tariff policy can be
thwarted by licenses or other direct controls, so too can the effect of
devaluation. This fact qualifies Diaz-Alejandro's point, noted above,
that liberalization may (and possibly should) come after devaluation and
stepped-up export growth. This argument presumes that the effects of
devaluation not be countered by other measures. Indeed one of the more
important aspects of liberalization as such is that it does clear the
deck for the indirect measures, such as exchange rate adjustment, to
work themselves out.

To summarize, industrial activity needs protection, needs learning
time. It is industrial activity that needs learning time, not simply
domestic activity. But it is not protection from incentives and inducements to search for increased productivity and increased use of domestic
resources that are required. Indeed the central problem of protection
is how to protect from that foreign (and domestic) competition that
destroys local industry without protecting from the pressures that induce
entrepreneurs to seek increasingly effective utilization of domestic

resources. It has been argued above that tariff policy as such, plus the
direct controls that further limit imports, plus the exchange rate policy
that often undervalues foreign exchange, creates an economic environment
in which there is not only protection from destruction but also from the
pressures to reduce costs, to seek out export markets, and to learn.
There are several implications of this for the employment and income
distribution issue. It has helped produce permanent monopoly rents, to
dampen productivity growth, to discourage the use of domestic resources,
to encourage overinvoicing (and underinvoicing), to produce bottlenecks
that stop or slow down the system, and to produce an enclave of alien
economic activity. How important quantitatively these matters are is not
known, and it is always possible to cite counterarguments. At the same
time, it is difficult not to be convinced that more suitable foreign
trade policies are possible, and that their use would make a significant
difference. The recent experience of Brazil is perhaps the strongest bit
of evidence, although this period is not yet very well documented.
Studies of the Republic of Korea, Taiwan, Mexico, and Colombia relative
to Argentina, India, and for a brief period for Pakistan, all are consistent with the view that the arguments summarized in this section do
matter significantly.[33]

F.   Small-scale indigenous activities

It was argued earlier that an essential ingredient of an industrial
policy package is the encouragement of small-scale, nonurban, nonagricultural activities. In this section, a few arguments on this issue are
outlined. It should be noted that small-scale, informal operations in
the urban areas are also important. In previous pages it has been argued
in several places that many industrialization measures that governments
adopt have helped only large-scale projects and have often even penalized
small, indigenous efforts. This is especially the case in urban areas.
The withering of such activities adds to the employment problem of course,
and to the low-end poverty group. The more general problem, however, is
the distinctly lower incomes in rural areas than in urban areas.[34]   If it
is completely unrealistic to assume that modern, urban industry can grow
at a rate and in a manner sufficient to eliminate low-end poverty and
rich enclaves, then evidently ways must be found to provide more

productive employment opportunities in nonurban areas. The main site of the task is in agriculture, but industry has a role as well.

The most interesting success stories in this regard are China and Taiwan. Keith Griffin notes that in Taiwan the categories rural and urban do not correspond very closely to agriculture and industry.[35] The policy to disperse industrial activity over the land has been exceptionally successful in the northern and central areas. Textiles, food processing, and construction materials appear in all parts of the island. These rural industries have, in particular, provided seasonal employment opportunities for agricultural workers. In the north and central areas over sixty percent of income in rural areas has been earned from non-farm sources, and in the south, over forty percent. Income in the rural areas of Taiwan is therefore much nearer the income of urban industrial workers than is the case in almost any other less developed country. Of more importance in the long run is the emergence of close links between rural industry and agriculture. Some peasants have become and others are becoming small businessmen and entrepreneurs and others are becoming more dependent on employment as industrial wage earners. Along with fuller employment and rising income (absolutely, and relative to urban workers) has come a greater heterogeneity and social differentiation that is conducive to further change and growth and to further use of domestic resources.

The evidence on China is less complete, but several observers have emphasized that rural industries play an important role in providing employment at levels of productivity not nearly so dissimilar to those in urban centers as in most countries. Production in these rural areas involves the use of a more primitive, more indigenous technology than that in the big cities.[36]

Most of the output of these industries is used in agriculture, directly or indirectly, and is aimed at increasing agricultural output. This increased output in turn provides raw materials and markets for the local industries. There is some handing-down of machinery from the modern, urban sector to rural activities. In some instances there are regulations which restrict production of certain commodities to the smaller units of individual countries. This is to prevent the larger (more socially efficient?) units from gobbling up these enterprises. There is little evidence, however, to indicate whether or not these small, indigenous units are in fact more suitable than the larger, modern plant. This "walking on two feet" notion does, of course, require firmly enforced controls, and it implies something of a holding action in the rural areas. Comparisons with most other countries is useful. Most other countries have used agriculture as a reservoir to hold workers (in poverty) until (hopefully) modern-sector activities could absorb them. China on the other hand seems to be earmarking certain industries for the rural areas to help raise incomes and provide employment until the modern-sector manufacturing and agriculture can absorb enough people to solve the problem. Wage income is lower in the rural activities than it is in the modern sector. Almost all observers comment on the complete absence of the more unrelenting, damaging forms of poverty.

The exact policy mechanism by which the dispersion in Taiwan occurs is not completely clear. It is not due to offering a tax exemption for one more year to investors choosing rural sites. More generally it would appear that the absence of the kind of tariff and exchange rate and control policies discussed above that provide such misleading signals vis-a-vis the use of domestic resources is important. Perphaps the key piece of evidence on this point is the share of wages in value added. This share ranges from eighty to forty percent—in the various manufacturing activities.[37] As noted above almost all developing countries show a very low labor share (twenty to thirty-five percent). The wage share in Taiwan declined over the 1953-69 period, but since then it has been rising due mainly to high rates of employment growth. Also the Taiwan government has long been aware of the advantages of dispersing and was successful in providing the kind of infrastructure and lending facilities that lead entrepreneurs to invest outside Taipei.[38]

As far as can be ascertained, the Chinese policy is largely a matter of directives, but the fact that (apparently) successful efforts are being made to provide the kind of opportunities that would help induce similar action voluntarily eases the implementation of the directives. Controls on the movement of labor from rural to urban areas appear especially important.

In both these countries attention is focused on the local level, and there is little in the way of big aggregative plans. Local initiative and local problem solving are relied upon heavily. In doing this it can be expected that the use of local resources and local expertise will be much more extensive than where central planning (or at least the writing of a central plan) occupies a primary place in economic policy-making. It is also to be expected that out of this kind of approach a more indigenously oriented industrialization process will emerge. Finally, it may be worth reiterating that Taiwan has achieved its development by heavy use of price signals, while China has apparently not relied on such signals. In both countries there is a close link between the rural industries and agriculture. This adds to the extent to which such industrial activities serve the community; it also brings out the importance of rural development in contrast to increased agricultural output as such as part of the way to meet the distribution objective.

A number of economists have pointed to the importance of the link between industrial development and the use of the new seeds having high yield. The use of these seeds requires more care and work on the part of the cultivator than do the older varieties. They, therefore, have the potential of creating more jobs and more productive jobs in agriculture. Whether or not this happens depends largely on the kind of technology available, and that in turn depends in part on what is happening in industry in general and to rural industry in particular.[39]

Pakistan in the 1960s illustrates the nature of the problem. Fertilizer was imported and sold well below landed cost, agricultural machinery was freely imported and also sold to farmers below landed cost, and the Pakistan rupee was clearly overvalued. Taxes on agricultural income and on land were virtually nonexistent. Since it is the large-scale, advanced farmer who has access to funds to buy tractors and to the bureaucracy to clear imports, it is he who enjoys these advantages. This kind of a policy package means that it is virtually certain that excessive use of tractors will accompany the use of the new seeds. The absence of such contrary policies does not automatically insure that local industrial activities will appear that provide the kinds of machinery that effectively exploit the available labor supply.[40] It is clear, however, that with such policies, none will. It is also clear that a rural strategy that includes industrial activities would at least wrestle with the problem. The little evidence from a few countries suggests that there is room for some optimism that in a situation where the rewards of new suitable instruments are high (because of the productivity of new seeds when properly cultivated), new industries will emerge. The nurture of such industries may require some inducements--credit subsidies, some technical extension service, and so on--and these things are difficult to provide to small, rural activities. But all this says is that because the wrong thing is easy to do is not a reason for doing it. This issue links up with the technology discussion, but the emphasis here is placed on the need to develop an industrial capacity in nonurban areas that meshes with agricultural developments and serves other possibilities as well.

In this area perhaps more than in any other, case studies are needed as bases for isolation of general policy principles. But studies of this type appear rarely. Further research on Taiwan and China would help. Some things that are wrong are known, but what specific things work is much less clear.

G. Policy implications

The manufacturing sector alone cannot solve the low-end poverty and income distribution problem. In most developing countries it can do more than it has done over the preceding two decades. In section B of this chapter models were developed that showed why and how rapid rates of investment and high rates of growth of productivity would produce rising capital's share, rising profit rates, and greater overall size inequality at the same time that it produces the highest rate of absorption of labor into the more productive sectors of the economy. The working of the model depends mainly on the rate of investment, the rate of growth of labor-augmenting and capital-augmenting productivity, changes in wage rates, and the extent of the substitutability of labor for capital. Development policies have concentrated heavily on achieving a high rate of capital accumulation and, in so doing, have penalized the other variables in the argument The basic point of this paper is that a high rate of capital formation, without penalizing the other variables, is essential (and is possible) if the manufacturing sector is to do its share.

Attention has been given to the kinds of inducements that would produce a high rate and suitable composition of investment. A general target of constant wage rates in the manufacturing sector is a major aspect of the policy package. So too is an economic environment in which producers have major incentives to search out new technologies and to price products in accordance with productivity growth. Perhaps the most important policy area is that affecting foreign trade. The general policy aim is to offer protection that provides learning time without eliminating the incentives to learn. Finally, there must be a sizable nonurban centered manufacturing effort. This cannot be accomplished by present tax holiday arrangements but calls for a different kind of policy approach.

Chapter 3

NOTES

1. Albert O. Hirschman, "The Changing Tolerance for Income Inequality in the Course of Economic Development," Quarterly Journal of Economics, vol. 87 (November 1973), pp. 544-66.

2. See especially Irma Adelman and Cynthia Taft Morris, "Who Benefits from Economic Development?" International Meeting of Directors of Development Research and Training Institutes (August 1972), mimeographed; and Richard Webb, Government Policy and the Distribution of Income in Peru, 1963-1973 (Harvard University Press, 1977).

3. For a general discussion of profiles of the very poor, see Economic Commission for Latin America, Income Distribution in Latin America (New York: United Nations, 1971).

4. Some small developing countries are essentially manufacturing economies, e.g., Singapore and Hong Kong, and some large ones, e.g., Brazil and India, have large (absolutely) manufacturing sectors, but the text statement stands as a reasonable generalization. The argument in this section is limited to manufacturing. The modern sector includes service activities (especially government and retail and wholesale distribution) and social overhead facilities. A more complete analysis would include these sectors and thereby include a larger proportion of total employment. To extend the analysis in this way, however, is beyond the scope of the paper.

5. The model developed here is built from the arguments and models found in W.E.G. Salter, Productivity and Technical Change (Cambridge University Press, 1960); Robert M. Solow, Capital Theory and the Rate of Return (Amsterdam: North-Holland, 1963); Richard Nelson, Paul Schultz and Robert Slighton, Structural Change in a Developing Economy (Princeton University Press, 1971); W.A. Eltis, Growth and Distribution (Macmillan, 1973); Henry J. Bruton, Principles of Development Economics (Prentice Hall, 1965). Figure 1 is adapted from W.A. Eltis, Growth and Distribution, p. 45.

6. This follows from the fact that profit's share is increasing and the capital-output ratio is falling as one moves east on the diagram.

7. There are some complications for wage policy arising from particular sources of increased productivity. Some of these are discussed in section D of this chapter.

8. The argument presented here follows that in Henry J. Bruton, _Employment, Productivity, and Import Substitution_, Center for Development Economics Research Memorandum 44 (Williams College, 1972). This more complete version owes much to the help of my colleague, Thomas O. McCoy.

9. It is evident that this expression is consistent with the well-known conclusion that labor's share rises with a fall in wages if the elasticity of substitution exceeds unity.

10. If labor's share is rising, capital's share is falling, and the rate of return on capital will decline unless the capital-output ratio is falling at the same percentage rate. Presumably if a given rate of return is sought by investors, the rate of capital formation will in fact tend toward this rate. Let r_L be the rate of growth of labor services (i.e., $r_I + r_b$), and LS and KS be shares, respectively, of capital and labor. Then if $r_K = r_L + \frac{KS}{LS} r_a - (\sigma - 1) (r_b - r_w)$, the capital-output ratio will fall at the same rate as capital's share, and the profit rate therefore remains constant.

11. For rather complete surveys of tax incentives in developing countries, see Georges Lent, "Tax Incentives for Investment in Developing Countries," _International Monetary Fund Staff Papers_ (1967), pp. 249-323, and "Tax Incentives for the Promotion of Industrial Employment in Developing Countries," _International Monetary Fund Staff Papers_ (1971), pp. 399-419. See also Jack Heller and Kenneth Kauffman, _Tax Incentives for Industry in Less Developed Countries_ (Law School of Harvard University, 1963).

12. Lent, "Tax Incentives for the Promotion," p. 409.

13. Bent Hansen and Girgis Marzouk, _Development and Economic Policy in the UAR (Egypt)_ (Amsterdam: North-Holland, 1965).

14. Amalio Humberto Petrei, "Rates of Returns on Physical Capital in Manufacturing Industries in Argentina," _Oxford Economic Papers_ (November 1973), pp. 378-404.

15. Charles R. Frank and his associates have completed a thorough study of the effects of trade policy on economic growth, income distribution, and employment in Korea. The evidence that Frank offers in the study is broadly consistent with the argument in the text.

16. John Power and Geraldo Sicat, _The Philippines Industrialization and Trade Policies_ (Oxford University Press, 1971).

17. Interviews with managers of "footloose" industries in Singapore and Hong Kong indicate that they would move their factories to lower wage areas (e.g., Indonesia) at the drop of a welcome mat.

18. E.H. Phelps-Brown and P.E. Hart argue in this way from the historical evidence on Great Britain, "The Share of Wages in National Income," _Economic Journal_, vol. 62 (June 1952), pp. 253-77.

19. This argument is developed more fully and supporting evidence cited in James Pickett, D. Forsyth, and N. McBain, "The Choice of Technology, Economic Efficiency and Employment in Developing Countries," World Development, vol. 2 (March 1974).

20. Howard Pack, "Employment and Productivity in Kenya Manufacturing," Eastern Africa Economic Review (December 1972), p. 35.

21. The very low rates of utilization of capital observed in most developing countries provides evidence of the failure to exploit all available resources (even those in "short" supply) and provides virtually costless opportunities to increase output and employment. Gordon C. Winston has a long series of papers on these issues; see Gordon Winston, "The Theory of Capital Utilization and Idleness," Journal of Economic Literature, forthcoming.

22. See Henry J. Bruton, "Productivity Growth in Latin America," American Economic Review, vol. 57 (December 1967), pp. 1099–117.

23. See John W. Mellor, Developing Science and Technology Systems – Experience and Lessons from Agriculture, Department of Agricultural Economics Occasional Papers 63 (Cornell University, 1973).

24. This argument is developed in various forms in a variety of places. See especially the papers of Frances Stewart, "Technology and Employment in LDC's," World Development (March 1976), pp. 17–46 and Paul Streeten, ed., Trade Strategies for Development (London: Macmillan, 1973). See also, John Friedmann and Flora Sullivan, "The Labor Absorption in the Urban Economy: the Case of Developing Countries," Economic Development and Cultural Change, vol. 22 (April 1976), pp. 385–413; Donald B. Keesing, "Income Distribution from Inward Looking Development Policies," mimeographed (Williams College, 1976); and Jon Sigurdson, "Technology and Employment in China," World Development, vol. 2 (March 1976), pp. 75–85.

25. See for example, Dwight H. Perkins,"Growth and Changing Structures of China's Twentieth Century Economy," Institute of Economic Research, Discussion Paper 339 (Harvard University, 1974).

26. Stephen R. Lewis, Economic Policy, op cit.

27. Stephen R. Lewis, Economic Policy, op cit.

28. This type of situation may now be becoming more common and more severe as prices of many traditional exports from less developed countries continue to rise markedly.

29. Both r_a and r_b of equation (2) in section B of this chapter.

30. The pervasive tendency to undervalue foreign currencies is difficult to explain. In part it is probably part of the general policy to keep capital prices low and thereby encourage investment. Devaluations have also been discouraged by elasticity pessimisms and fears that they breed inflation. These fears incidentally are generally unfounded. See Richard N. Cooper, Currency Devaluation in Developing Countries, Essays in International Finance (Princeton University, 1971). Finally, part of the

suspicion, noted in section C, that frequently attaches to the use of prices as policy instruments, applies to reliance on exchange rates to ration foreign exchange even where extensive and high tariffs prevail.

31. Carlos Diaz-Alejandro, "Trade Policies and Economic Development," Economic Growth Center Discussion Paper 180 (Yale University, 1973).

32. Professor Joan Robinson is so quoted by Paul Streeten, ed., Trade Strategies.

33. For a number of detailed country reports, see Bela Balassa, ed., The Structure of Protection in Developing Countries (Johns Hopkins Press, 1971); Ian Little, Tibor Scitovsky, and Maurice Scott, Industry and Trade in Some Developing Countries (London: Oxford University Press, 1970); and Santiago Macario, "Protectionism and Industrialization in Latin America," Economic Bulletin for Latin America, vol. 9 (March 1964), pp. 61-103.

34. A useful discussion on informal activities in urban centers may be seen in, "A Strategy for Increasing Productive Employment in Kenya," International Labour Office, Employment Incomes and Equality, chap. 22 (Geneva: I.L.O., 1972).

35. This paragraph is based largely on Keith Griffin, "An Assessment of Development in Taiwan," World Development, vol. 1 (June 1973), pp. 31-43.

36. See J. Sigurdson, "Technology and Employment in China," World Development, vol. 3 (March 1974); and Christopher Howe, Employment and Economic Growth in Urban China (Harvard University Press, 1971).

37. Hoing Mo-Huan, Taiwan Industrialization and Trade Policies (Oxford University Press, 1971).

38. Keith Griffin, "An Assessment of Development in Taiwan."

39. Good general discussion of these issues may be found in Walter P. Falcon, "Agriculture Employment in Less Developed Countries: General Situation, Research Approaches, and Policy Palliatives," Economic Staff Working Paper 113 (International Bank for Reconstruction and Development, April 1971). See also Montague Yudelman, Gavan Butler, and Ranadev Banerji, Technological Change in Agriculture and Employment in Developing Countries (Paris: OECD, 1971).

40. It can even be doubted that the kind of tractors imported increased yields per hectare by more than they would have been increased by using more labor with the new seeds and traditional implements.

CHAPTER IV

THE EDUCATION - INCOME CONNECTION

Frederick H. Harbison

A.   Education: a nationwide learning system

A very broad definition of education is used in this chapter. It
has three major components: first, formal education at primary, secondary, and higher levels consisting for the most part of age-specific,
graded, pre-employment schooling; second, nonformal education consisting
mainly of organized out-of-school education and training programs; and
third, work-related skill and knowledge generation consisting mainly of
on-the-job training, which is an integral component of all working environments. Thus education, as conceived in this chapter, encompasses a
broad range of learning opportunities and programs. In this context, an
education system is more aptly called a "nationwide learning system."

Formal education performs many functions. It enriches human life;
it builds consensus on values which condition attitudes toward work,
cooperation, and nationhood; and it can become an instrument of indoctri-
nation. Its main economic functions are to develop the skills, knowledge,
and capacities of people for participation in the labor force and to serve
as a selection system. Formal education thus is a means of human capital
formation and at the same time acts as a giant sorting machine which
determines access to positions of status, wealth, and power. In all
developing countries, formal education is a big industry; it employs more
people than other government services and consumes a very large proportion of public expenditures. The administration and control of formal
schooling is usually lodged in a single ministry of education.

Nonformal education is more difficult to define. It consists of a
heterogeneous conglomeration of seemingly unrelated learning programs with
a wide variety of objectives. It is not the responsibility of any single
ministry; administration and control of its programs are widely diffused

throughout both the public and private sectors. In this chapter only a few of the better known out-of-school programs which provide important productive learning opportunities are dealt with. These are agricultural extension, rural multiple-purpose training centers, work-oriented literacy programs, urban trade training and testing centers, training organizations and nutrition-health information programs supported by payroll taxes.

These six nonformal programs have several common denominators: first, they are organized activities for which funds are allocated to develop specific skills; second, they lie outside of the control of ministries of education; and, third, in some respects they provide unique learning opportunities, but in others they also provide alternatives to and/or extensions of formal education. Many other important learning services (such as radio, television and other mass media, activities of churches, village polytechnics, and community development projects) could be included in this analysis if time and space permitted.

The third broad category of learning activities is work-oriented skill and knowledge development. This takes place routinely and often unconsciously through learning-by-doing, instruction or inspiration from others, association with peers or fellow workers, or simply through participation in a working environment. Here the process of human capital formation is for the most part inseparable from the process of production of goods and services. Most work-related learning is a response to practical needs. As a rule, working environments develop the skills and knowledge that they require. In primitive subsistence agriculture, for example, simple skills are handed down from father to son. In modern-sector agriculture, farmers and workers receive specific instruction and supervision (training) in the use of fertilizers, insecticides, and water, and in planting, cultivating, and handling of crops. In a modern-sector factory, specific on-the-job training is given to operators, and most skilled craftsmen learn their trades on the job. Automobile mechanics in Nigeria and other African countries learn their trade in small garages or in the larger service shops of the automobile distributors. Most of this learning takes place automatically without specific allocations of resources.

The nationwide learning system thus is a mixture of formal schooling, nonformal education, and work-related skill acquisition. These three kinds of learning opportunity have an impact on income distribution. More specifically, they may increase the mobility of individuals from lower- to higher-income groups; they may alleviate or aggravate low-end poverty; and they may increase or decrease disparities in income between the rich and the poor.

B. Formal education and income distribution

Formal education encompasses the complex of primary, secondary, and vocational schools as well as technical institutions, colleges, and universities. It connotes age-specific, full-time classroom attendance in a linear graded system geared to certificates, diplomas, degrees, and other recognizable credentials. It is associated mostly with "the school-age population," and it concentrates on pre-employment preparation of future members of the labor force. In most developing countries the orientation of formal education is toward more education. Success at each level is measured by passing tests and gaining access to the next level. Since the university is at the apex of the formal education system, entry into and completion of higher education are the supreme goals dominating the entire system. The university thus casts its shadow over every branch and level of education. Those who "make it" through the university hold the required entry passes for admission to the more prestigious positions in the modern-sector enclaves, and those who "don't make it" are, in varying degrees, selected out as failures along the way by this educational screening process.[1]

Without any question, formal education is an avenue through which some members of low-income groups gain access to the higher-income occupations. The son of a subsistence farmer may reach the higher levels of a government bureaucracy if he is fortunate enough to have had the right levels of schooling. Poor parents in developing countries often invest their meager resources in the education of one of their children who appears most likely to successfully climb the schooling ladder. Even in the most remote rural areas, the aspiration of poor families is to have their offspring "get book" (primary education) or "big book" (higher education) so that they may escape a life sentence in traditional agriculture. And in many countries, government aid is available for a small number of poor students up to and including full support in high-quality universities. In short, a few fortunate children of the poor have risen to riches, and more may do so as educational opportunities are expanded.

However, in many of the less developed countries, large numbers of children have no access at all to primary schooling. In some countries this is the plight of the majority of the school-age population; in many more, well over a quarter have no access to schooling. And if we look at the disparities within particular countries, the situation is even more distressing. In Colombia, for example, which is one of the more advanced of the less developed countries, nearly sixty percent of the rural schools offer no more than the first two grades of primary school; only six percent have facilities to offer a four-year primary sequence.[2] In Kenya about eighty to eighty-five percent of the relevant-age children in the more advanced Central Province attend primary school; but in several other districts and provinces, the rate may be as low as thirty-five percent.[3] In Mexico the percentage of the population that has completed four or more years of schooling is strikingly higher in the Federal District (Mexico City)--60.6--than in the rural states such as, for example, Chiapas (11.3), Guerrero (9.8), and Oaxaca (11.9).[4]

Thus, in the developing countries there are millions of children of elementary school age who are not currently in school; there will be millions more yet unborn who may never gain access even to the most elementary formal schooling. The avenues of upward mobility provided by formal schooling are effectively closed to vast numbers of children; these avenues become progressively narrower as one climbs the academic ladder; and thus the opportunities for movement into good occupations in the modern sector are sharply limited. In this respect, children in the rural subsistence sector are much worse off than those in the urban traditional sector who at least are located near the centers of schooling. Nevertheless, the tremendous pressure for universal primary education, a goal not likely to be attained by many developing countries in this century, is grounded in the belief that schooling can and will provide every child with some opportunity to move out of poverty into the better life in the modern sectors.

It is doubtful whether formal education can do much to alleviate low-end poverty. The major objective of primary schooling is to prepare pupils to qualify for higher levels of education. It does not claim to generate specific skills for the labor market. In the poorer areas, parents, students, and teachers think of education as a route of escape from the local environment rather than as a means of making that environment more productive. Thus, a massive drive to extend primary school to traditional rural areas might simply raise levels of frustration rather than levels of living, unless it were accompanied by other measures to provide opportunities for raising the income levels of the poor. And experience has also demonstrated that literacy, although helpful, is by no means a prerequisite for generation of skills required to take advantage of such opportunities.

The question of whether formal schooling increases or decreases income gaps between individuals and groups is more complex. Here it is necessary to look at the pattern of expenditures on formal eduction, the allocation of educational opportunity, and the ways in which formal education is financed.

Fortunately, in many countries there are some data on public outlays, enrollments, and per-student expenditures on formal education. The following statistics are based on a sample of 30 countries--10 more advanced countries and 20 less developed--which were selected on the basis of their representative nature as well as on the availability of data.

(i) Most developing countries devote a substantial proportion of GNP to education. Although there is a wide variation between individual countries, the less developed of them appear to spend on education a somewhat smaller proportion of GNP than do the more advanced. The medians and ranges of public recurrent expenditures on education as a percentage of GNP in the two groups are (see appendix table 1):

	median	range
More advanced	4.5	1.4-7.9
Less developed	3.6	1.3-5.6

In most countries the proportion of the GNP going to education has been increasing in the past decade.[5] In this sample, it has been true of seven out of ten more advanced countries and fifteen out of eighteen of those less developed.

(ii) The less developed countries, in contrast to those more advanced, appear to allocate greater proportions of total public expenditures to higher education (see appendix table 2):

	3rd level education	
	median	range
More advanced	15.5	6.6–30.2
Less developed	18.5	1.8–54.5

(iii) The proportion of students in secondary and particularly in higher education is much smaller in the less developed than in the more advanced countries (see appendix table 2):

	2nd level education		3rd level education	
	median	range	median	range
More advanced	29.4	13.5–47.5	6.0	3.0–12.7
Less developed	15.0	4.5–28.5	1.7	0– 3.8

(iv) The ratio of the percentage of total public expenditures on higher education to the percentage of students at that level is much higher in the less developed than in the more advanced countries (see appendix table 2):

	3rd level education	
	median	range
More advanced	2.7	1.10– 4.3
Less developed	11.6	3.50–76.7

In African countries, this ratio seems to be exceptionally high. In Ghana, for example, it is 83.7 and in Ethiopia, it is 61.7.

(v) In the less developed countries the annual per-student expenditures on secondary and particularly on higher education are proportionately much higher than in the more advanced countries. Using primary education as a base index of one, the medians and ranges for secondary and higher education are given (see appendix table 4):

	2nd level education		3rd level education	
	median	range	median	range
More advanced	1.7	1.03– 3.1	5.7	2.1– 9.8
Less developed	3.5	1.04–12.2	18.6	7.2–155.6

Thus, in the developing countries students in higher education receive relatively high benefits in the form of public recurrent expenditures on education. To a somewhat lesser extent, those in secondary education also receive very high benefits. The same conclusion would also hold if public capital expenditures were also included. The extent to which their benefits[6] exceed student contributions or those of their parents is more difficult to estimate. It is probable that students in higher education tend to come from the richer families, because the prerequisite secondary education often involves expenses in the form of fees and foregone earnings. It is possible also that their parents contribute considerable amounts to their education, and thus may pay for a substantial proportion of it. But, it is clear that the students in higher education receive the lion's share of public expenditures as well. Their critical advantage, however, is that their education provides them with entry passes into the higher-paying occupations, and in this respect widens the ultimate income gap between them and the less educated masses.

Up to now this discussion has been concerned primarily with the allocation of opportunities for schooling. The disparities appear to be enormous. But, to determine the total impact on income distribution it is also necessary to examine how education and other learning services are financed. In developing countries, unfortunately, it is extremely difficult to get hard facts on the incidence of taxation, fees paid by students for education, and sources of funding for private schooling. With perhaps only one exception (which is discussed below), estimates of the distribution of the burden for financing learning services are a matter of guesswork in nearly all developing countries.

It is probably reasonable to conclude that the greater part of support for formal education comes from public sources. Yet, the proportion supplied from private sources may be larger than is generally recognized. In many countries parents pay some fees for primary education. In a few, secondary education may be provided largely by fee-charging private schools. Although most higher education is public, there are some private universities which charge tuition. And missionary organizations, foundations, and private businesses contribute to the support of educational institutions in many developing countries. Finally, in theory at least, foregone earnings of students in school should be counted as part of the cost of education. Indeed, in higher education, such opportunity costs usually exceed the direct costs of schooling, and thus persons who are studying full-time instead of working are in effect paying for much of their education.

Jean-Pierre Jallade of IBRD has made a pioneering and exhaustive study of public expenditures for formal education and their impact on income distribution in Colombia, and his work may be a model for further research in this area.[7] He concludes that the public financing of primary education actually redistributes income from the thirteen percent richer families to the eighty-seven percent poorer families, and that the redistributive effect is particularly beneficial to the forty percent poorest families, most of whom live in rural areas. In the case of secondary education, the main beneficiaries are middle-income groups comprising a little less than fifty percent of all families. As he points out, "The public financing of secondary education redistributes income from both the forty percent poorest and the thirteen percent richest families to a sort of lower middle class, eighty percent of whom are living in urban areas..." The situation for higher education is much the same except that the middle-income groups subsidized both by the poor and by the rich are higher up on the income scale and are almost exclusively urban dwellers. All in all, he concludes that aggregate public expenditures for education in Colombia have the effect of distributing income from the rich to the poorer classes, but most of this is attributable to the financing of primary education.

It would be dangerous, however, to generalize from Jallade's analysis of Colombia. In the first place, Colombia spends a smaller proportion of its public funds on higher education than other countries, for instance Brazil and Chile. If Colombia spent more, Jallade's conclusions might be quite different--showing relatively greater benefits for the rich. Second, the larger part of secondary education in Colombia is provided by private, fee-charging schools. This is not the case in most developing countries. Thus, we have a rather unique situation in Colombia where those who are relatively rich pay an unusually high proportion of the costs of education for their children. Third, Jallade's analysis concentrates on benefits received by those having some access to formal schooling; it does not take into consideration the non-benefits of those who never enter a classroom. Thus, studies in other countries, taking these factors into consideration, might reach quite different conclusions.

A major difficulty in all attempts to study the education-income connection is the estimation of the benefits of schooling. One method is to measure the value of schooling in terms of expenditures per student or total expenditures for schooling for a certain income group or class. Then the net benefit is calculated as the total expenditure per individual or group minus contributions in the form of taxes or payment of fees. This is the method used by Jallade in his study of Colombia. Most economists would argue, however, that, if appropriate data are available, benefits should be calculated on the basis of returns to investment in schooling as well as access to employment opportunities.

Using a somewhat different approach from Jallade, Bhagwati reaches quite different conclusions in a recent study based upon Indian data.[8] His major hypothesis is the following:

> For each class of education, the state (in capitalist LDCs) will subsidize the cost of education; the benefits of these subsidies will accrue disproportionately less to the poorer groups at each level of education; the higher the educational level being considered, the higher will be the average income level of the groups to which students belong; and the rate of governmental subsidization to higher education will be greater than that to primary education.[9]

Thus, Bhagwati suggests that for all levels of education the richer classes receive greater benefits in the form of educational subsidies than do the poorer classes. He claims, moreover, that for primary education the opportunity costs for the lowest income groups are greater than those for the highest income groups; the benefits to the former are lower and thus the private rate of return to them on primary education is lower; and the cost of capital, to which the rate of return must be compared, is higher than for the higher-income groups. The same is true for secondary and higher education, except that the relative benefits to high-income groups are much higher.

Bhagwati supports his argument as follows:

> These hypotheses are based on the following assumptions about the lower-income groups:
> (i) The opportunity cost of labour, resulting from the fact that children of primary-school age cannot work during the time that they attend school, is higher because typically these groups can and do use children of this age in gainful work, whereas this is not possible (or allowed) with the other, higher-income groups.

    (ii) The benefits from primary education are lower for these groups again because (a) the probability of finding rural jobs such as primary school teaching and post office and such other jobs requiring primary (and secondary) education is lower for these groups; (b) if higher returns accrue through increased productivity on the farm, it is unlikely to accrue in full to the educated but low-income landless labourer, whereas these returns would accrue fully to the educated but richer landholding farmer; and (c) insofar as the higher returns accrue through higher mobility to the urban sector where jobs requiring primary education (e.g., watchmen in Delhi colleges) are relatively less scarce, the lower-income groups with less urban contacts and generally lower mobility would correspondingly have less access to such returns from primary education.

    (iii) At the same time, clearly, in a world where many of the members of the lower-income groups, especially in the rural areas, have indebtedness at high rates of interest, their opportunity cost of capital is greater than that of the middle- and upper-income groups in general; this asymmetry is further reinforced by the general banking and lending practice of charging higher interests rates to the smaller borrowers.[10]

Bhagwati supports these proportions by evidence from Indian experience. And he observes that the higher-income groups are likely to get away with this as long as the education system, by enabling some lower-income groups to educate their children and gain access to better paid jobs, gives the appearance of providing mobility and greater equality of opportunity than might otherwise obtain in a capitalist society. In a capitalist society, Bhagwati would advocate that the higher-income groups pay the full cost of education of their children.

    In conclusion, knowledge about the incidence of costs and benefits of formal education in developing countries is meager. But some tentative generalizations seem plausible: The provision and financing of formal education is regressive, with the burdens falling more heavily on the lower-income groups and the benefits accruing largely to the upper-income classes. But such disparities tend to decrease as countries advance. In most cases the higher-income groups clearly receive the lion's share of benefits of education, whether in the form of acquired skills and knowledge or simply as entry passes into the higher-paid occupations to which access is limited by arbitrary educational requirements. It may also be true in some developing countries that, while receiving the larger share of benefits of public educational expenditures, the rich may at the same time be investing substantial private resources of their own in the education of their children. In looking at the impact on income distribution, therefore, it is important to determine how important these private contributions are in comparison with the benefits from public expenditures. And, it is likewise essential to evaluate the importance of the "barrier effect" which excludes the uneducated from access to the more lucrative occupations. The need for more research in these areas is obvious.[11]

C. Nonformal education and income distribution[12]

As stated earlier, nonformal education is a kind of shorthand designation for a heterogeneous conglomeration of organized education and training programs which are not connected with the formal schooling system. A brief description of the six major nonformal education programs examined in this paper follows.

Agricultural extension services of some kind are available in nearly all developing countries. Their function is to extend knowledge of agricultural processes and animal husbandry to farmers, to help the farmers to improve output, to teach them new technologies, and to assist in solving production problems. Sometimes agricultural extension services also provide assistance in the purchasing, credit, and marketing areas. Typically, the services are financed and managed by ministries of agriculture.

Rural multi-purpose training centers provide a variety of learning opportunities for rural dwellers. The centers may include programs in agricultural technology, home economics, rural crafts, elementary farm management, and various kinds of literacy projects. In some cases they also serve as bases for agricultural extension work. In theory, at least, they may provide a wide variety of learning opportunities through short-term residence programs, and they have the potential for coordination of many different services designed for the rural population. They may be financed and managed by different government ministries, and sometimes as joint projects of several ministries.

Work-oriented literacy programs, though still largely in the experimental stage, have great potential for improving skills and knowledge of adults and younger persons who have not had access to primary education. The theory of these programs is that literacy can and should be developed through the process of learning more productive ways to grow crops or perform industrial work, and that learning useful skills should be a byproduct of literacy training programs. This dual objective approach is alleged to be a faster and more practical way to develop literacy and a more efficient way to develop productive skills.

Urban training and testing centers are designed to upgrade the skills of persons already employed. They are usually geared to the specific needs of particular plants and industries. In most countries they are much more effective in skill generation than are formal vocational schools, and they can reach far larger numbers of learners.

A more elaborate system for specific skill development of both employed and pre-employed members of the labor force are the training and apprenticeship training pools financed by payroll taxes; these pools are commonly found in many Latin American countries. A good example is SENA in Colombia.[13] This organization operates a vast array of training service for employers and workers (both within plants and in training centers) in commerce, industry, agriculture, and animal husbandry. It draws its financial support from a tax of two percent on salaries and wages levied on both public and private enterprises. It is a semiautonomous organization within the Ministry of Labor, but it controls its own resources and plans its own operations in close contact with participating employers in both the public and private sectors. By any measure, SENA is a big operation in Colombia. In 1971, for example, its total expenditures were equivalent to about one-eighth of total public expenditures on education. And since its revenues are geared to payrolls, it is virtually assured of a continuous and growing source of funds.

Finally, nutrition and health information and training services are included in this analysis. To be sure, improvements in health and nutrition may not show up immediately in national or personal income statistics. But they can improve the levels of living of the poor and in the long run raise the vitality and mental development of future generations, which can be a potent factor in increasing productivity.

In recent years it has been fashionable to downgrade the contributions of formal schooling to development and to extol the virtues of nonformal eduation programs. The shortcomings of formal schooling are, of course, well documented; sharply rising costs, inflexibility, lack of relevancy, top-heavy administration, unequal access by rural and urban dwellers, and poorly trained teachers. Many people contend that nonformal education programs _potentially_ can be much more productive. They may be less costly, more flexible and innovative, more relevant to practical needs, more decentralized in administration, more readily available to rural dwellers, and less dependent upon trained teachers. Nevertheless, in general there is almost no concrete evidence to prove this contention. Cost-benefit and cost-effectiveness studies are virtually nonexistent. Indeed, no country has yet even attempted to make a complete inventory of its non-formal education programs or to estimate total resources allocated to them.[14] It is thus very difficult to assess the probable impact of non-formal education programs on income distribution, but a few rather plausible hypotheses are suggested.

First, in comparison with formal schooling, nonformal education pro-grams provide fewer avenues for upward mobility. They rarely offer degrees, certificates, or other credentials essential for passage through the gate to positions of status, power, and wealth. Participation in an agricultural extension project, farmer training center, or literacy class is not likely to provide poor rural dwellers with an "escape from bush" into the modern-sector enclaves. Unlike a diploma from a secondary school or a degree from a university, completion of most nonformal education pro-grams carries no great prestige or rights to high pay. Indeed, the objec-tive of most nonformal programs is to make people more effective at what they are presently doing rather than to move them upward in the hierarchy of the labor force.

Second, there is little evidence to indicate that nonformal programs have in practice done much to alleviate low-end poverty. In the develop-ing countries nonformal education services are mostly utilized by the richer and better-educated elements of the population. The larger and better-off farmers are usually the principal beneficiaries of agricul-tural extension; the apprenticeship programs of SENA are open only to those with previous formal schooling; and even most literacy programs are confined to the urban areas. As a general rule, the lowest-income groups are seldom the major beneficiaries of most public services, and nonformal education activities are no exception.

Finally, as with formal schooling, nonformal education programs probably increase the disparities between the rich and the poor. A relatively small proportion of the population has access to them; expenditures per person served may be quite high; and the well-to-do usually receive the larger share of the benefits. But, in contrast with formal schooling, nonformal education programs are less likely to become selection devices. Completion of a nonformal program does not bring the same kind of high status and pay as a diploma or a university degree. Thus it is probable that nonformal programs are not as strong a force in widening income gaps as is formal schooling.

It is probably true, however, that nonformal education could be beamed at different target groups. Agricultural extension could be directed to subsistence farmers as well to those who are more prosperous. Training centers, apprenticeship programs, literacy classes, and nutrition programs could concentrate on the underemployed and the undereducated. In most countries this might involve rather fundamental changes in the goals of strategies of national development.

D. Work-related skill and knowledge generation and income distribution

Learning on the job is the most universal of all processes of learning Working environments and institutions of employment, whether primitive or modern, produce most of the skills that they require almost automatically without the conscious attention of planners, bureaucrats, or educators. This kind of human capital formation is a constant albeit largely unnoticed process. And, it is virtually impossible to separate out the costs of this kind of skill development.

Of the three kinds of learning processes, work-related skill and knowledge generation probably offers the fewest opportunities for upward mobility. One could not argue that, in itself, it widens or narrows the gap between the rich and the poor. For most of the low-income groups, it is the only available means of skill and knowledge acquisition. However, if working environments could be improved, these groups might be the main beneficiaries. In short, the best means of attacking low-end poverty could be to reorganize agricultural production, to improve transportation and communication, and to disseminate better technologies as widely as possible But this requires the creation of a new organizational architecture, the

motivation and training of new leadership, and, most important, the adoption of new priorities in the modernization process.

Thus the improvement of working environments and the skill and
knowledge generating capacity inherent in them requires other human
inputs, and here both formal and organized nonformal educational activities may play critical roles. Organization builders, technologists, and
skilled cadres are needed to transform working environments, and their
effectiveness may be directly related to their prior participation in
both formal and nonformal education activities.

E.   Summary: learning programs and income distribution

To summarize, different learning opportunities can have different
effects on income distribution. Formal education may provide limited
opportunity for some low-income persons to move upward in the labor force
hierarchy, but it is not apt to alleviate low-end poverty and it tends to
widen the gap between the rich and the poor. Organized nonformal education programs offer very little upward mobility, and in practice they too
may increase income disparities and do little to help the very poor. However, nonformal programs could be redesigned to raise living standards of
the less affluent elements of the population. Work-related learning is
the only widely available opportunity for most low-income groups to
acquire productive skills and knowledge, but it provides little or no
upward mobility. Improving the skill and knowledge generation capacity
of working environments, particularly in rural areas, appears to be the
most effective means of raising living standards of the masses and thus
alleviating low-end poverty. But this requires inputs of organizational
and technical manpower to lead the march of modernization which in turn
makes demands upon both formal and nonformal education.

It would be unwise to make sweeping generalizations about the connection between learning opportunities and income distribution for all developing countries. One must examine separately the learning systems of individual countries, and even here hard data are generally unavailable.
However, it is possible to specify the processes for analysis of the
national learning system in individual countries and to examine as well
the probable outcomes of pursuing different development goals.

F.   The processes of analysis of learning systems

In some respects, a nationwide learning system (including its three constituent elements) can be thought of as a sector of the economy. Thus some of the techniques of sector analysis which are useful in analyzing other sectors such as agriculture or manufacturing may be appropriate. Yet, in other respects learning is an integral element of all productive activities. And this is particularly true in the case of work-oriented skill and knowledge generation. For this reason, the methodology for analysis of education and learning services is somewhat unique; the simple calculation of benefit-cost ratios is of only limited usefulness; and inputs and outputs are often impossible to measure in tangible quantitative terms. At least for the present, analysis of learning systems must be based more upon rational judgment than on hard quantifiable data.

The first step in the analysis of a learning system is to look at the generation of skills and knowledge in the various working environments. This is called the manpower-training assessment and calls for examination of employment and skill acquisition processes in all rural and urban activities. More specifically the following questions need to be explored:

(i)   Access to working environments

What is the aggregate employment in the modern traditional and intermediate sectors of the economy?

For each sector and major activity, what are the principal "ports of entry" into employment?

In each sector and major activity, what pre-employment education or skills are required for entry?

(ii)   Learning process

In each sector and major activity, how do people learn to perform their tasks?

What kinds of organized training are provided by the larger employing institutions?

What kinds of skills cannot be developed practically "on-the-job," i.e., in what critical areas is there a need for persons with specific kinds of formal or non-formal education?

(iii)   Constraints

What are the practical limits of work-related skill and knowledge generation in each sector and major activity?

What measures, if any, would be effective in improving the skill generation capacity of various working environments?

What are the essential inputs of educated manpower—organizational and technical human resources—required to take appropriate measures to improve working environments?

At best, answers to questions such as those posed above will be rough estimates, and where hard data are unavailable, answers may have to be based upon informal judgments. Nevertheless, a careful assessment of the employment and skill-generating potential of working environments should be the starting point for a rational analysis of a nationwide learning system.

The next step is to examine the formal education system. Developing countries have a good deal of experience in making formal education reviews. Typically they include estimates of enrollments, outputs, and drop-outs at various levels; enrollment ratios by major areas or regions; pupil-teacher ratios; the need for teacher training; unit costs for various levels and kinds of schooling; and the appropriateness of the orientation and curriculum of education at all levels. In some cases, the formal education review is related to a survey of "needs" for medium- and high-level manpower in the modern sectors. But rarely, if ever, has it been based upon a comprehensive prior analysis of the work-oriented learning process as described above. The important questions for consideration are these:

(i) Access to formal education

At each level, who gains access to formal schooling, and more important, what groups are denied access and for what reasons?

What are the differential rates of access between modern, intermediate, and traditional sectors (rural and urban)?

(ii) Orientation of formal education

What are the major objectives of various levels and types of schooling?

Is formal education at various levels effectively geared to the requirements for educated manpower in working environments?

(iii) Constraints

What are the limits, financial and human, to expansion and improvement of education?

How rapidly can access be extended to presently excluded groups?

How can the financial burdens of education best be shared?

Education planners are familiar with all of these questions, and reasonably good quantitative data are available in many countries.

The third step, assessment of organized nonformal education, is more difficult. Nonformal education activities are operated by a wide variety of ministries and private organizations. Except perhaps in the case of agricultural extension services, there is very little coordination of programs and no single locus of planning. Information on enrollments and outputs is scarce, and data on costs and benefits are almost nonexistent. The best that can be expected is a general estimate of access, enrollments, outputs, orientation, and constraints of major programs such as those mentioned earlier in this chapter.

The fourth and most critical step in analysis of learning systems is the assessment of possible alternative combinations of available or potential learning opportunities. In short, how can one determine the most appropriate mix of programs, the highest quality and lowest cost combinations, and, thus the most effective strategy for the overall development of the nationwide learning system? Here one must start by classifying learning opportunities.

Each of the three categories of learning programs performs some unique service. For example, formal education has a comparative advantage in developing quantitative skills; nonformal education may be necessary to develop specialized skills; and work-oriented learning may be the only practical way to develop most lower-level skills. In other cases, different learning processes may be complementary. For example, some kinds of trade training may require completion of primary education; or the on-the-job training of agricultural assistants may be dependent on some prior formal technical education. Thus, the complementarities between learning programs must be specified with as much precision as possible.

Finally, some programs are substitutable. Here there are critical choices to be made both within each of the three basic learning categories as well as between them. In this case, comparative cost-benefit studies may be useful.

The choices within the formal schooling system are perhaps the most widely recognized. For example, In expanding access to first-level education, is it better to provide a minimal program of four to five years for a larger number of children than perhaps six to eight years for a smaller number? Is it better to opt for large numbers of teachers with little formal education (perhaps eight or nine years) or to rely on higher-paid teachers with longer pre-employment training? In allocating

related resources, what are the appropriate shares that should go to
primary, secondary, and higher education? For example, an Ethiopian
Education Sector review (1972) faces such questions squarely. It projects overall availability of resources based upon expected growth in
GNP and government revenues; it then subtracts fixed amounts for secondary
and higher education; and it allocates the remainder to first-level primary schooling and specified nonformal education programs. It opts for
a four-year basic primary school with minimally trained teachers and adult
education programs to provide learning opportunities for those who have
never had access to formal schooling. In effect, from a social objectives
perspective, it places the goal of providing a universal learning opportunity before that of universal primary education for children.[15]

Another series of alternatives faces the rural development planner.
Given finite amounts of resources, what emphasis should be given to agricultural extension, farmer training classes, or multiple-purpose rural
training centers that may provide combined programs in nutrition, health,
homemaking, rural crafts, and functional literacy in addition to farming
techniques? And within the vast array of other nonformal education activities, what are the best choices between radio and television programs,
traditional literacy classes, and functionally oriented community development projects? In many countries it may be possible to estimate the costs
of these various programs; studies of their relative effectiveness are at
least in the beginning stages. The most perplexing problem in all cases,
however, is the difficulty of evaluating outputs. Here simple quantitative measures may be meaningless, and qualitative differences must be
distinguished largely by informed judgment.

There are also critical choices in improving the learning services
of the employing institutions. Will taxes or subsidies induce large
employers to offer better training opportunities? Are "training pools,"
such as the payroll-tax-financed training provided by SENA or comparable
Latin American institutions, the most feasible method of extending
services to small- and medium-sized enterprises? Will technical assistances
to small proprietors improve the operation of indigenous apprenticeship
systems, or would they do just as well if left alone?

The choices between the three broad categories of learning services,
however, are more difficult yet often more fundamental than the choices
within them. Some examples follow.

Skilled craftsmen such as electricians, carpenters, masons, fitters, and automobile mechanics may be trained in employment either through apprenticeship arrangements or by the less formal means of gaining experience on the job. But the craftsmen may also learn their trade in formal vocational schools. Take automobile mechanics as a case in point. In the developing countries most young people learn this trade as apprentices in small garages and shops. This indigenous training system might be improved by organizing extension services for the garage owners, or by off-duty training classes in the principal towns and cities. Another alternative might be to induce the major distributors of cars and trucks, which usually have the best facilities for producing mechanics, to train a surplus beyond their own needs. Pre-employment formal training in vocational schools is the other alternative, but probably in most cases it is the most expensive and least effective. A good sector review should weigh carefully the alternative processes of training such skilled craftsmen and suggest those combinations most likely to develop the quality of craftsmen needed in the shortest period of time and at the least expense. In many cases, the logical choice might be to rely heavily on employing institutions, to subsidize on-the-job training programs, and to de-emphasize if not forego completely the formal vocational schools.

The training of senior technicians is another area for serious consideration. Technicians are persons whose skills are highly specialized for particular working environments. Most of their training must be in employment. Often a technician must be sent abroad for short periods to learn the technology of a particular industry, process, or complex of equipment. It is ridiculous to assume that a formal school or institute can produce a full-blown standardized technician for "industry" in the developing countries. In most cases, technical trainees in the poly-technic institutions must be sponsored by particular employers, and courses of instruction must be specialized to meet the requirements of the particular sponsoring organization. Here again a proper assessment would evaluate carefully the capacity of employers to train technicians and the extent to which pre-employment education in formal schools is either required or relevant.

The training of nurses and medical technicians is another example where attention must be directed first to the role of employing institutions. For the most part, paramedical personnel are trained in hospitals or clinics rather than in school classrooms. Another related question is whether physicians must get their clinical training in expensive teaching hospitals associated with the universities or in rural hospitals and medical stations.

Finally, there is the crucial question of developing managers and administrators. Such persons certainly cannot be prefabricated in schools of business or university courses in public administration. They can get a good deal of relevant education before employment, but then leadership and mangerial skills are developed in the crucible of practical experience. Staff training courses for those already employed are useful as stimulants to learning and as refresher courses in relevant engineering and scientific fields. Here again it is argued that skill and knowledge generation in the modern sectors of developing countries is not a matter of educating a predetermined number of persons to fill an estimated number of occupational slots, but rather it is a continuous process of human resource development centering upon the dynamic imperatives of employing institutions.

Many more examples of critical choices of alternatives could be presented. In any developing country, the range of such choices is wide, and the logical selection of the best alternatives is the key to effective human resource development planning.

Information on which to calculate relative costs and benefits of alternative learning programs is disappointing. Few attempts have been made to assess costs and benefits of organized nonformal eduction, and practically none, for on-the-job training. The most ambitious attempt is a recent one by Zymelman for the IBRD. It includes an exhaustive review of the literature which relates for the most part only to relatively advanced countries. The comparisons of training costs and benefits, moreover, are available only for a rather narrow range of modern-sector industrial occupations. And from these it is impossible to make generalizations for the developing countries with respect to relative cost-effectiveness of formal schooling, nonformal education, and work-related learning.[16] In conclusion, it is unrealistic to expect that reliable quantitative cost-effectiveness studies of different kinds of learning programs can be made in developing countries in the near future.

G.   The selection of goals

The processes of analysis of learning systems are important, and the need for much more reliable quantitative data is clear. However, even more critical is the selection of development goals. In short, the objectives of the overall strategy of modernization are in the end the most crucial determinants of the education-income connection in the developing countries. For example, a strategy designed primarily to maximize opportunities for employment will require a different mix of learning programs from a strategy aimed primarily at maximization of the GNP. Although both might provide the same amount of growth, the patterns of income distribution and the allocation of learning opportunities could be quite different.

The full-employment objective, or human resource approach, holds that human resources, not material wealth as such, form the ultimate basis of the wealth of nations. Thus, the major goals of development are maximum activity and the maximum possible development of their relevant skills and knowledge. Economic growth as expressed by the increase in GNP then becomes the logical consequence of effective utilization and development of manpower. This approach stresses the importance of utilizing all human resources in productive activity and developing the skills, knowledge, and capacities of the entire labor force. In this perpsective, the development effort should not be concentrated solely or even mainly on a few leading sectors. Small per capita improvement in earnings of the masses is considered to be just as important for aggregate growth as spectacular advances in the modern-sector enclaves. Thus, the human resources approach emphasizes growth with greater income equality.[17] In most countries it would stress more learning opportunities of all kinds for the rural populations, even at the expense of curtailing expenditures on formal education in the modern-sector enclaves. It would give high priority to improvement of working environments in the agricultural sector and place less emphasis on technical education for urban industrial development.

In contrast, a development strategy aimed at maximization of GNP as such might concentrate on rapid modern-sector growth, emphasizing capital-intensive industrialization, exploitation of mineral resources (i.e., iron or petroleum, if available), and large plantation agriculture. In this case the small minority of the population in the modern-sector enclaves would reap the rewards of progress while the rural economy would remain stagnant. Indeed, many of the developing countries have had this kind of dualistic growth characterized by ever-widening disparities in income distribution. A learning system geared to this kind of economy would give high priority to formal education in the urban areas, and particularly to proliferation of vocational schools, technical institutes, and large-scale universities, all of which would result in further widening of the income gap between the rich and the poor.

Clearly, the overall design of the strategy for development will be the major force determining labor force mobility, alleviation of low-end poverty, and narrowing of income variances. Education and learning programs have only minor impacts. A country's learning system is logically derived from an overall development strategy based upon explicit or implied goals; it is seldom the initiating force in the building of such a strategy.

H. Conclusions

The argument presented in this chapter may be summarized briefly: Formal schooling, organized nonformal education, and work-related skill and knowledge generation are the principal components of a country's learning system. All three may have differing effects on upward mobility, low-end poverty, and income variances between groups and individuals. To estimate these effects it is necessary to analyze the operation of learning systems in individual countries. In order to change the education-income connection in a particular country, one must first examine carefully the comparative advantages of each of the components of the learning system as well as the consequences of substitution of one component for another. This is presently very difficult because of the dearth of quantitative and qualitative data, particularly with respect to nonformal education activities and work-related learning. The most crucial considerations, however, are the broad goals of development in each country and the strategy employed to achieve them. These shape the patterns of income distribution, and they also determine the parameters of the nationwide learning system. One is not likely to change the economic, social, or political philosophy of a nation and its leaders by simply tinkering with the education and learning system.

Sweeping generalizations about the education-income connection in developing countries are not in order. Yet, a few observations, which

might better be presented as hypotheses, are permissible. The following
are posed for consideration:

(i) In most developing countries, it might be advantageous to cur-
tail the outlays for higher education, or at least to keep them from rising.
This does not necessarily imply a lessening of total expenditures for
higher education. It means simply that a greater proportion of costs could
be assumed by the beneficiaries, by their parents, and to some extent by
the larger private enterprises. Educational institutions could charge fees
to cover a greater proportion of instruction costs and offer loans repayable
by the beneficiaries from future earnings at a later time. At the same
time, bursaries could be given to students of the poorer families. Although
this approach would encounter formidable administrative and political
resistance, the principle is sound. In developing countries individual
returns to investment in higher education are higher than social returns.
Little is to be gained by subsidizing students of the richer families.
Also, an often neglected source of support is the provision by private
enterprises of sponsored scholarships in fields of study where there is a
critical demand for certain strategic skills. Engineering, scientific,
and business education are cases in point.

The increase in private funding for higher education would have these
positive advantages: First, more public funds would be available for other
important learning services which have higher priority for expansion;
second, some of the artificial demand for higher education stemming from
substantial public subsidies would be curtailed, and this might help solve
the ever-rising problem of underemployment of educated people; and finally,
there might be a greater incentive to gear higher education more closely
to the effective demand for high-level manpower. Private funding of
higher education most certainly would work in the direction of decreasing
income inequalities.

(ii) The allocation of greater proportions of public expenditures
to primary education might be appropriate, but only under rather limited
circumstances. That millions of children may be denied access to formal
primary education for several decades has already been noted. But a
crash effort to achieve universal primary education, in itself, might do
little to promote either growth or greater income equality.

In the first place, there is little advantage in making people
literate if there is nothing for them to read. Particularly in rural

areas reading materials are scarce. Thus, the provision of primary school-ing in stagnant rural areas might do little more than encourage young school leavers to migrate to the urban areas in search of nonexistent jobs. Schooling, as such, is not likely to induce growth, but it can contribute to a growth process which is already underway. Thus, priority should be given to expansion of formal education in those areas where concerted efforts are already being made to bring about broadly based rural development, and where progress is being made in raising agricultural incomes, expanding small-scale industry and commerce, and improving the infrastructure of roads and communications.

There are also other critical questions in allocating additional resources for primary education. There is the tradeoff between numbers and quality; there are choices in use of educational technology; there is the problem of relevancy of the curriculum; and there are the questions related to self-help contributions of local communities and the require-ments for financing from provisional or central governments.

Thus, one should be wary of the advice of some economists who, on the basis of superficial rate-of-return analysis, would advocate more across-the-board allocations for primary education. Investment in more schooling can be wasteful as well as beneficial; in most of today's devel-oping countries, the allocation of additional resources to provide "more of the same" kind of schooling might be tragically unproductive.

(iii) The allocation of a larger proportion of resources to non-formal education probably could have a significant positive effect on income distribution. As a practical matter, the developing countries would have to concentrate resources on a relatively small number of clearly productive educative services which promise the highest payoffs. The fol-lowing are probably among the best candidates: agricultural extension, rural multiple-purpose training centers, work-oriented literacy programs, urban trade training and testing centers for employed workers, and nutrition-health training programs.

At this point, however, a word of caution is injected. Access to the various kinds of nonformal training services described above may be just as unequal as access to formal schooling. The high-income groups may be the principal beneficiaries of these learning opportunities, and they may share a relatively small proportion of the costs. In some cases, as with SNA in Colombia, unit-costs of out-of-school training may be quite high compared with those of formal schooling.[18] And some training programs may be ineffective in attaining their objectives. Nonformal education activities, therefore, warrant much more study, critical evaluation, and careful planning. And particular attention must be focused on the integration of formal and nonformal education programs. In some cases, nonformal training may be a substitute for formal schooling; in others, some formal education may be a prerequisite for winning effective benefits from nonformal training. In other words, one must consider the costs, financing, and benefits of "packages" of learning opportunities as well as isolated programs.

(iv) As stressed earlier, developing countries have much to gain by placing greater responsibility for skill training on employers. Particularly in the modern sector, large expatriate firms, automobile distributors, petroleum companies, and most kinds of manufacturing enterprises have tremendous capacity for training workers. In most cases they do very well in training their own employees. With appropriate incentives they might train a surplus for employment in the smaller enterprises. And, organizations for pooled training financed by payroll taxes have proven to be highly successful throughout Latin America, and the idea is catching on in other areas as well.[19] Shifting more of the burden of training to employers is likely to have a positive impact on income distribution; at the same time, it may be a more efficient means of skill development than further investment in pre-employment vocational trade training.

(v) Any efforts to equalize and improve learning opportunities should be integrated with and not separated from other fundamental measures for promoting growth with greater equality of incomes. Learning, although desirable as an end in itself, does not necessarily initiate economic development. It is more likely to contribute to growth already in progress. Both formal education and out-of-school learning activities work best when earning opportunities are expanding; they may be quite useless in stagnant economies. Thus, other programs for rural and industrial development may have to reach a takeoff stage before additional investments in learning services can effectively contribute to growth.

I. Research priorities

In a field where knowledge is so underdeveloped, it is appropriate
to specify research priorities. A few are suggested below:

(i) The outcomes of formal schooling at all levels need a great
deal more study. Here the project undertaken by the Public Service Labora-
tory of Georgetown University for the U.S. Agency for International Development is making a substantial contribution. The several papers it has
commissioned may provide a summary of available knowledge and identify
many of the more important areas for further research. Hopefully, attention will be given to relating outcomes such as examination scores, tests
of cognitive skills, and motivation measurements to subsequent incomes in
the work world. Data, of course, are a major problem. In the less developed countries there is very little information about earnings, education,
and age and training of those who leave school; even where it exists,
information is generally based only upon one or at most two census
enumerations.

(ii) Knowledge about the effectiveness, costs, and income impacts
of nonformal education programs is even more meager. Here research on
rural extension services is perhaps of highest priority. Recent experience with "the green revolution" suggests that the larger and more prosperous farmers are the principal beneficiaries of the new technology,
thereby increasing income disparities between the rich and the poor in
rural areas. Efforts should now be made to assess the costs and consequence of providing more extensive services to the smaller and poorer
farming units. Other critical nonformal education programs need similar
exploration. Fortunately, interest in this area is growing. Studies of
out-of-school education are in progress in many universities; pilot
projects are mushrooming; and some economists are attempting cost-
effectiveness analyses of a few programs.[20] A focal point of future
research effort should be on tradeoffs between formal and nonformal edu-
education, the linkages between the two, and the possibilities of a combination of both in national learning systems.

(iii) The study of the potentialities of "the employer-as-trainer"
is next on our high priority list. Despite the shortcomings of formal
education, vocational schools, literacy and technical education, employers
in the modern sectors of developing countries have successfully trained
even the highest-level manpower for their operations. One might even say

that they have been trained effective labor forces in spite of rather than because of formal education. It is relatively easy to staff and operate a steel mill, a petroleum refinery, or a large manufacturing complex in a developing country. The job requirements are known, the training techniques are available, strategic personnel may be imported, and technical assistance is available from suppliers of equipment. Automobile distributors can service and repair their own vehicles; hotels can train their own personnel; and government bureaucracies are quite able to teach their functionaries how to produce mountains of memos! The amount of training, both good and bad, which takes place routinely on the job is enormous; the improvements which could be made by better management and more deliberate efforts at training may be infinite. And the potential does not end here. Small garages train mechanics in apprenticeship; the "market ladies" in Ghana teach their children, relatives, and husbands the essentials of business administration; the model farmer is often more knowledgeable about growing crops than is the university-trained extension officer. The challenge for research is simple. Why not study, appraise, and evaluate the potential of this vast mechanism for human resource development, and explore the ways and means to improve its operation?

(iv) More case studies such as Jallade's analysis of expenditures on education and income distribution in Colombia would be very valuable. However, they should be extended to nonformal as well as formal education. And, where possible, they should attempt to measure the benefits of education to individuals and groups in broader terms than in those of the present expenditures on schooling minus payments in taxes. Data problems, again, are the major obstacles for at least the near future.

(v) More longitudinal or "tracer studies" are needed to relate schooling and organized training to experience in the workplace. Admittedly, such follow-up studies are difficult and expensive, but the returns, in terms of project evaluation and feedback to skill and knowledge generating institutions, could be very great.

(vi) Finally, the most critical need of all is for research on the organization, leadership requirements, and skill generation processes for rural development.

Today, the leadership of many developing countries is aware that a rural transformation in which the masses share some of the fruits of progress is one of the imperatives for an industrial revolution. In many countries there are experimental pilot projects in rural development, some fairly successful and others with quite mixed results.[21] These should be studied carefully, for they may suggest some solutions to the problems of rural development which presently seem intractable to modern man.

Chapter 4

NOTES

1. For a further analysis of formal education, see Frederick H.
Harbison, Human Resources as the Wealth of Nations, chap. 3 (New York:
Oxford University Press, 1973).

2. International Labour Office, Towards Full Employment, A Programme for Colombia (Geneva: 1970), p. 219.

3. ---. Employment, Incomes, and Equality, A Strategy for Increasing Productive Employment in Kenya (Geneva: 1972), p. 511.

4. Harbison, Frederick H. et al., Quantitative Analyses of Modernization and Development, appendix VIII.B (Industrial Relations Section,
Princeton University, 1970).

5. Ibid, chapter 7.

6. As expressed in public monies spent on students' education.

7. Jean-Pierre Jallade, Public Expenditure on Education and Income
Distribution in Colombia (IBRD Education Dept., Central Projects
Staff, April 1973), mimeographed.

8. Jagdish Bhagwati, "Education, Class Structure and Income
Equality," World Development, vol. 1 (May 1973).

9. Ibid, p. 24.

10. Ibid, p. 25.

11. Definitive studies of the connection between formal education and
income distribution are virtually nonexistent, but some scholars apparently
are initiating new theoretical and empirical investigations. One example
is a draft paper by Asim K. Dasgupta for the World Bank entitled "Income
Distribution, Education and Capital Accumulation." The author reviews the
human capital doctrine, constructs an econometric model, and gives some
conclusions from empirical applications in India and Colombia. He concluded
that investments in education in both countries tend to disequalize incomes.
In India, during recent years, government policy has tended to support and
reinforce the forces of the private sector which tend to increase income
disparities. In Colombia, on the other hand, government policy appears to
have worked toward equalization, although its effect has been minor. See
Asim K. Dasgupta, "Income Distribution, Education and Capital

Accumulation," paper prepared for the Development Economics Department of IBRD (May 1974), mimeographed.

12.   Much of the material in this chapter is based upon an analysis of the literature on nonformal education made by my colleague, Francisco Swett, during the summer of 1974. Francisco Swett, "Formal and Nonformal Education in Educational Development: A Review and a Critique of the Literature," Discussion Paper 48, Woodrow Wilson School, Princeton University (1974), mimeographed.

13.   For a brief description, see Harbison, Human Resources, pp. 85–89.

14.   Within the past three years, several organizations have concentrated on research on nonformal education. Particularly noteworthy are the studies of the International Committee for Educational Development, Essex, Connecticut, under the direction of Philip Coombs which were made for UNICEF and the IBRD, and the extensive studies made and in progress by the Institute for International Studies in Education at Michigan State University, under the leadership of Cole Brembeck. None, however, have as yet issued traditional cost-benefit analyses of specific programs mainly because of unavailability of adequate quantitative data. However, they do provide a wealth of case studies on a wide range of nonformal education programs in many different countries, and they attempt to assess the effectiveness of these programs in terms of their stated goals. See in particular, Philip H. Coombs and Manzoor Ahmed, Attacking Rural Poverty – How Nonformal Education Can Help (Johns Hopkins Press, 1974); and Richard Niehoff and Bernard Wilder, Program of Studies in Nonformal Education (Michigan State University), mimeographed.

15.   Ministry of Education, Education Sector Review (Ethiopia, 1972), mimeographed. For an analysis of this review, see Richard Niehoff and Bernard Wilder, "Nonformal Education in Ethiopia," in Russell Kleis et al. Study Team Reports (Program of Studies in Nonformal Education, Michigan State University), mimeographed.

16.   Manuel Zymelman, Cost Effectiveness of Alternate Learning Technologies in Industrial Training (IBRD, Staff Working Paper 169).

17.   For further elaboration of this approach, see Harbison, Human Resources, chap. 6. This approach is quite similar also to that used in the recent ILO country studies of employment generation. International Labour Organization, Employment, Incomes and Equality: A Strategy for Increasing Productive Employment in Kenya (Geneva: 1972); Employment and Income Policies for Iran (Geneva: 1973); Matching Employment Opportunities and Expectations: A Programme of Action for Ceylon (2 vols.) (Geneva: 1971); Towards Full Employment: A Programme for Colombia (Geneva: 1970).

18.   Harbison, Human Resources, pp. 85–89.

19.   Ibid.

20.   International Council for Educational Development, Nonformal Education for Rural Development (Committee for Educational Development, 1973), 2 vols.

21. <u>Study Team Reports</u> by Russell Kleis et al., describe some educational programs as related to rural development. Also in the same Reports by Niehoff and Wilder there are excellent evaluations of rural programs in Ethiopia, "Nonformal Education in Ethiopia."

CHAPTER V

POPULATION POLICY AND INCOME DISTRIBUTION

Bryan L. Boulier

This paper analyzes ways in which population policies can and do
affect income distribution in less developed countries. Population
policies are designed to influence one or more demographic processes:
fertility, nuptiality, mortality, and migration. Policies to influence
fertility are stressed, although relationships between mortality and
fertility are examined. The paper is divided into the following sections:

    A. Demographic characteristics of less developed countries

    B. Population change and income distribution in the absence
        of policy

    C. Welfare analysis of fertility reduction programs

    D. Categories of population policy

    E. Population policy and income distribution

    F. Politics of population policy

    G. Summary

A.   <u>Demographic characteristics of less developed countries</u>

    As can be seen from table 1, demographic parameters vary considerably
across countries. For instance, the expectation of life at birth is an
average of about 45 years in Africa but is over 60 years in many Latin
American countries. The average number of children ever born to a woman
through the child-bearing ages varies from less than four to more than
eight. Customs and practices affecting fertility and knowledge, attitudes,
and practices of contraception differ among societies. The rates of
growth of populations are on average 2.0 to 2.5 percent per annum, although they exceed 3.5 percent in some countries. The consequence of
high fertility is a very young age distribution with as much as 45 to 50
percent of the population less than age 15.

Table 1. Demographic Characteristics of Selected
Less Developed Countries

	Date	Crude Birth Rate[a]	Crude Death Rate[a]	Growth Rate[a]	Date	Expectation of Life
Africa						
Total	1965–71	47	21	26	1965–71	43
Algeria	1965–70	49	17	32	1965–70	51
Cameroon	1971	50	26	24	1965–70	41
Ghana	1965–70	47	18	29	1965–70	41
Kenya	1971	50	17	33	1969	49
Nigeria	1971	55	25	30	1965–66	37
United Arab Republic	1971	35	13	22	1961	54
Asia						
Total	1965–71	38	11	27	1965–71	50
India	1965–70	43	17	26	1951–60	41
Iran	1971	48	16	32	1965–70	52
Korea (South)	1971	31	9	22	1965–70	62
Philippines	1971	47	16	31		
Singapore	1972	23	5	18	1965–70	68
Taiwan	1971	24	5	19	1965–70	68
Thailand	1971	41	11	30	1960	55
Latin America						
Total	1965–71	38	10	28	1965–71	60
Brazil	1971	41	11	30	1965–70	61
Chile	1971	27	9	18	1969–70	63
Colombia	1971	43	11	32	1969–70	63
Costa Rica	1972	32	6	26	1962–64	63
Mexico	1971	44	11	33	1965–70	62
Peru	1971	44	15	29	1965–70	54

[a]Measured as births, deaths, and natural increase per 1,000 population.

SOURCES: Dorothy Nortman, "Population and Family Planning Programs: A Factbook," Reports on Population/Family Planning, 5th ed., 2 (September 1973), pp. 13, 22–31.

United Nations, Demographic Year Book 1972 (New York: United Nations Department of Economic and Social Affairs, Statistical Office, 1973).

Besides variations in demographic parameters among countries, there are also differentials in mortality and fertility within countries. In general, fertility is higher in rural areas and is inversely correlated with the income and education of parents. For instance, in Thailand in 1969-70 the number of children ever born per ever-married woman aged 40-44 was 6.89 in rural areas, 5.82 in provincial urban areas, and 5.32 in Bangkok-Thonburi. The reported numbers of living children for the three groups were 5.63, 5.21, and 4.95, respectively. In urban areas, ever-married women aged 35-44 with no schooling had 5.88 children ever born; with one to three years of schooling, 5.36 children ever born; with four years, 4.89; five to nine years, 4.52; and with ten or more years, only 3.03.[1] Persons who come from low-income families are also exposed to higher levels of mortality.

The discussion in this chapter refers primarily to countries which have achieved some measure of mortality decline, have high fertility, and display rapid rates of population growth. It should be remembered that not all countries or groups within countries have these character-istics, and that population policies need to be tailored to the parti-cular country.

B. Population change and income distribution in the absence of policy

In this section, the effects of population parameters on income distribution are examined on the assumption that there is no active popu-lation policy. Subsection 1 explores population change and the functional distribution of income and subsection 2 outlines the effects of differer.-tial fertility and mortality on the size distribution of income.

1. Population growth and the functional distribution of income

Economists have long been concerned with the relationship of popu-lation growth to the functional distribution of income. Malthus and Ricardo, for instance, argued that increases in population raised the share of rent in national income. The analysis of the effects of population change on functional shares is necessarily complex since it depends inter alia on the effect of population growth on the rates of growth of other factors of production and the composition of final de-mand, the substitutability of factors for one another in production, the pricing mechanism, and the openness of the economy to international trade. A full analysis of this complex of factors cannot be undertaken in this chapter. Only the most important relationships will be reviewed.

Numerous studies have explored the effects of population growth on capital accumulation. Early studies argued that rapid rates of population growth reduce the ratio of private savings to income by increasing the ratio of dependents to adult members of the labor force and, thereby, the ratio of consumption to income.[2] More recent work has suggested that the magnitude of the dependency effect is less than might be supposed. Dependents are born into a family group so that an additional child's consumption is met partially by a reduction in the consumption of other family consumption not just savings. If incomes are so low that there are no savings, increased numbers of dependents can have little impact on household savings. Additional children may also induce other members to increase their work effort and to augment family income.[3]

Another criticism of the dependency burden approach is that it is really a model of household savings, and household savings comprise only 30 to 40 percent of total savings. Other important sources are business and government savings. The impact of population growth on these sectors has not been much explored. Bilsborrow suggests that an increase in the number of dependents may marginally reduce business and government savings.[4] In his macroeconomic model, an increase in the number of dependents reduces household expenditure on nonagricultural goods, diminishing business profits and savings and indirect taxes on business receipts. Government savings are also affected if government expenditures are sensitive to population growth. If educational expenditures or health expenditures per child are fixed, decreases in population growth rates would permit increases in government savings. It may, however, be the case that reductions in expenditures would result only in increased expenditures on other services.[5] Indeed, a benefit of reduced growth is that for the same volume of expenditures, a greater fraction of children could be educated or investments with more immediate returns could be undertaken.

Empirical work on the effect of the dependency burden is hampered by inadequate data.[6] In a cross-national study, Leff has shown that youth dependency depresses the ratio of savings to income,[7] although Gupta shows that the relationship does not hold for countries with extremely low per capita incomes.[8] Kelley analyzes the empirical relationship in

greater detail.[9] On balance it would appear from available evidence that
population growth does reduce savings. Empirical estimates of the magnitude of the effect are not very precise.

Thus far it has been seen that population growth undoubtedly raises
the ratio of labor to capital and of labor to land and reduces the ratio
of capital to land. But as has been noted, the connection between these
factor changes and income distribution is complex and can be examined
fully only in the context of a general equilibrium model. Several models
have been applied to the Mexican economy by John Isbister.[10] Isbister
compares the growth path of the Mexican economy under two alternative
population projections: (i) no change in fertility and (ii) a decline
in the general fertility ratio (the ratio of births to women 15-44) from
.22 in 1970 to .10 in the year 2000.[11] His models are of the Lewis-
Ranis-Fei type with three sectors (manufacturing, urban-traditional, and
agriculture), with all savings from profits, and no investment in agriculture. When the economy is closed and the urban wage is a fixed multiple of the agricultural wage, reduced population growth lowers the relative
price of food and money wages in the manufacturing sector, thereby stimulating increases in manufacturing employment, output, profits, and savings.
In the longer run, the low fertility population has a smaller labor force
and rural average earnings, and the supply price of urban labor rises,
with a tendency for profits and savings to decline.

Isbister finds that by the year 2015, the high fertility population
numbers about 295 million and the low fertility, only 170 million; the
rates of growth are 3.95 percent per year and 1.88 percent, respectively.
The ratio of profits to GNP is 45 percent in the low fertility projection compared to 42 percent in the high projection, but the ratio of
profits to GNP has begun to decline because of upward pressure of wage
rates. In this simulation at least, the effect of lower fertility is
to increase profit's share in GNP for at least a generation and to decrease the share of wages plus rent. However, per capita income in the
low fertility population is 70 percent higher than in the high fertility population, and food production per agricultural worker is 49 percent higher with low fertility.

To return to the classical question about the consequences of population growth, it would appear that reductions in population growth rates
are likely to reduce the share of rent in national income. First, smaller

populations need not resort to inferior land to supply additional agricultural output. Second, with diminished population growth greater capital accumulation permits substitution of capital for land. Third, as a result of increased per capita income, the consumption bundle is less land-intensive.

To sum up this section, all that can be said is that the relationships between population change and functional income distribution are complex and that there are no general findings.

2.   Demographic parameters and the size distribution of income

It is generally the case within LDCs that fertility is inversely related to family income and the education of the parents.[12] While the effects of differential mortality partially offset higher fertility to reduce the differentials in the number of surviving children per family, it is still generally the case that the number of surviving children per family is larger for low-income and low-education households.[13] This pattern of differential fertility affects both the current distribution of consumption and the future distribution of income.

a)   Current distribution of income

For a given size distribution of income among individuals, the distribution among families will be less unequal, since low-income individuals belong to larger family units.[14] However, the size distribution of consumption will be more unequal than the distribution of family incomes since the number of persons per family is larger in low-income families. For instance in Puerto Rico in 1953, the lower 60% of families received 30.3% of income and the upper 5% received 23.4% of income. A crude adjustment of data for family size by reestimating ordinal shares for individuals yields a share of only 26.8% for the lowest 60% of individuals and a share of 26.8% for the top 5%.[15]

Equalizing tendencies include economies of scale in consumption, the possibility that additional dependents stimulate additional work effort on the part of parents, and contributions by older children in excess of their consumption requirements. There is no evidence for economies of scale in consumption in LDCs, although Espenshade has shown in the United States that the marginal cost of a child declines as the number of children increases.[16] There is no reason to suspect that this might not also be true for LDCs. There is also no evidence from LDCs that children stimulate increased work effort on the part of the parents. Indeed, additional children may reduce the labor supply of the wife.[17] In any case, the marginal returns of additional effort are likely to be small and there is a decrease in utility from a reduction in leisure. Children may, however, add to family incomes, particularly in rural areas. In some LDCs as many as 20% of children less than 15 are in the labor force. In India in 1961, 11.1% of the rural and 5.3% of the urban male labor force consisted of children aged 7 to 15.[18] Whether they contributed income beyond their own consumption is unknown. To the extent that additional children force their older siblings into the labor force it may be at the cost of educational investment, depending upon the extent to which education is financed by the family and there is overlap of the employment period with school.

While there have been no studies of the individual connections between family size and consumption, the net effect has been examined. In a study of preschool children in Candelaria, Colombia, in 1963 it was found that malnourishment increased with the number of living children. For families of women 30 or more years old, 48.7% of children from families with six or more living children were malnourished compared with only 35.2% of children from families with four or less.[19] The relationship also holds when the literacy of the mother is held constant. Among lower classes in Great Britain, the height that children attain is inversely correlated with the number of siblings.[20] And, holding constant the social class, there is a decrease in IQ of about 1.8 points for each additional sibling.[21] There is also substantial evidence to show that:

    (i) The incidence of contagious diseases increases with family size;

    (ii) Maternal mortality and complications of pregnancy increase with parity;

    (iii) Maternal mortality and complications of pregnancy are inversely related to birth intervals; and

    (iv) Infant mortality, morbidity, and malnutrition are inversely related to birth intervals.[22]

In short, the bulk of the evidence suggests that differential fertility can contribute to a distribution of consumption worse than is implied by data on the distribution of family income.

b)   Future distribution of income

Besides influencing the current distribution of consumption and income, differential fertility may have adverse consequences for the long-run distribution of income. First, the consumption effects of differential fertility reduce the future income of children in large families by reducing investment in such children and lowering the productivity of investment.[23] Second, children born into large families receive a smaller share of an already small inheritance. Inheritance may be quite an important factor in the distribution of agricultural holdings over time. While a detailed analysis of inheritance and the long-run distribution is too complex for this chapter, it is easily seen that the role of inheritance is dependent inter alia on the following factors:

(i)   The initial distributions of property and the returns to property;

(ii)   The distribution of earned income;

(iii)   The determinants of wealth accumulation, including what part of income is consumed and what part is transmitted to heirs;

(iv)   Taxation of inheritance;

(v)   Inheritance patterns (e.g., primogeniture or equal division);

(vi)   Marriage patterns (e.g., no marriage between income classes or equal probability of marriage between classes);

(vii)   The level of, and differentials in, fertility, and

(viii)   The level of, and differentials in, mortality.[24]

Demographic factors play the following fairly obvious roles. The smaller the degree of intermarriage between income classes, the greater is long-run inequality. Since low-income families have larger family size, they accumulate less wealth and their wealth is split into more fragments. The mean length of generations of low-income families is shorter, so that initial property is split more often.[25] Furthermore, given the level of mortality, the higher is the level of fertility the more rapid is the rate of growth of population. As discussed above, this depresses the rate of growth of capital, raises the rates of labor to capital, raises the returns per unit of capital, and lowers the returns per unit of labor. If capital and the returns per unit of capital are more unequally distributed than labor earnings, the variance in the distribution of income will be larger.

The influence of the level of, and differentials in, mortality on income distribution is complex. Given the level of fertility, the lower is mortality the higher is the growth rate. And as has been argued, rapid growth may lead to greater income inequality. However, there is evidence that levels of fertility and mortality are not independent, since high mortality may encourage high fertility.[26] In most LDCs, children are sources of old-age security and provide income when parents are unable to work because of illness. If children are subject to a high risk of dying, parents must have larger numbers of children to insure an adequate number of survivors. Moreover, since high mortality reduces the returns to, and raises the riskiness of, investment in human capital,[27] parents are encouraged to substitute numbers of children for increased expenditures per child under conditions of high mortality. Thus, reductions in mortality may lead to lower fertility. The net effect of a reduction in mortality is probably to increase the growth rate since the demand for surviving children is probably not perfectly inelastic.[28] To some extent mortality differentials by income class offset some of the effects of differential fertility outlined in the previous paragraph. Three other effects of mortality should also be noted. First, mortality influences the age at which property is transferred. Second, high mortality may encourage consumption rather than savings by raising the subjective discount rate for prospective investments,[29] so that if low-income persons face higher mortality their accumulation of property is further depressed. Third, mortality and morbidity are associated. Improvements in health which increase life expectancy for the poor are also likely to reduce the incidence of morbidity and raise their productivity.[30]

It is likely that high fertility and high mortality and fertility and mortality differentials within countries imply a long-run worsening of the income distribution. Quantifying the various connections has not been attempted, but it appears that they are significant. If that is the case, programs to reduce fertility where mortality has begun to decline and to reduce fertility differentials may have great impact on the long-run distribution of income while at the same time improving the current distribution of consumption.

C.   Welfare analysis of fertility reduction programs

Numerous studies have indicated that reductions in fertility would yield substantial increases in per capita income or per capita consumption.   For instance, in the Isbister article cited earlier the reduction in fertility yielded a per capita income 70 percent higher than simulations without a reduction in fertility.[31]   Total GNP may also be higher with a reduction in fertility depending upon the productivity of labor and the extent of increased capital accumulation with lower fertility.[32]   These figures suggest that a fertility reduction would be desirable if it occurred spontaneously.   A more difficult problem is to evaluate the benefits and costs of projects to encourage a fertility reduction.   Approaches to these problems are reviewed in this section.

1.   Costs

Conceptually, calculating the costs of averting births in conventional family planning programs is relatively straightforward.   In practice, insufficient data have precluded accurate estimation.   Several estimates are discussed below.

Table 2 gives estimates of program costs per birth averted and costs per contraceptive acceptor for various programs.   There is insufficient information about the cost data and the procedures for calculating births averted to compare the costs of the various programs.   Estimates of the cost per birth averted from acceptor data are quite sensitive to the procedure used in deriving births averted.[33]   Births averted per acceptor depend upon the fertility of acceptors in the absence of the program and their fertility subsequent to acceptance.   For instance, if acceptors are merely substituting publicly provided supplies for private supplies of similar contraceptive efficiency, the program has no effect on fertility. If program supplies do increase contraceptive usage, then births subsequent to acceptance depend upon the method chosen, the effectiveness with which it is used, and the age and fecundity of the acceptor.[34]   For example, a tubal ligation of a 25-year-old woman will prevent more births than the sterilization of a 40-year-old woman.

The rank order of cost per birth averted by method in Singapore need not apply to other countries since it depends upon the cost of distributing supplies and the characteristics of acceptors by method, which may vary considerably between countries.

Table 2. Costs per Birth Averted and Costs per Contraceptive
Acceptor in Various Family Planning Programs

India (1969-70):

    Average cost per birth averted (in Rs.), all states: 153.66
        Range: 83.55-288

Philippines (1967-71):

    Cost per acceptor (in US$)   9.55
    Cost per birth averted (in US$)   7.72

Singapore (1971):

    Recurrent cost per birth averted (in 1971 US$):

Oral	37.23
Condom	14.70
IUD	17.64
Other	22.86
All	29.72

Cost per acceptor, various countries (in 1970 US$):

Korea (1961)	6.70
Singapore (1963)	3.61
Taiwan (1963)	4.00
Mauritius (1969)	20.47
Hong Kong (1950)	8.47
Iran (1967)	5.93
Thailand (1968)	10.60
Colombia (1968)	12.70
Tunisia (1969)	39.00
Ceylon (1966)	10.15
Philippines (1970)	14.50

Cost per acceptor (in 1969 US$):

Korea (1969)	8.25
Taiwan (1969)	5.00

Costs of incentive programs to avert births are more difficult to
ascertain since any large incentive program could require tax increases
sufficient to reduce the supply of effort or redistribute sufficient income
to families with lower savings propensities to affect savings measurably,
so that current and future output may be affected by the program.

2.   Benefits

Calculations of the benefits of averting births is conceptually
more difficult. A varity of methods have been suggested. In an analysis
of a reduction in fertility in India, Julian Simon using Coale and
Hoover's projections calculated the benefits of averting a birth by
discounting the difference in GNP over a 25-year period attributable
to fertility reduction by the discounted births averted.[35] The welfare
comparison assumed that India is at least as well off without the program
as it is with the project if GNP is at least as great with the program.
At a 15% discount rate it was calculated that the economy as a whole
would benefit up to Rs. 570 or $114 per birth averted in 1952-53
prices. That is, the low fertility population could afford to transfer
up to $114 per birth averted and still be as well off as the high fertility
population.

There are three important shortcomings of the Simon procedure. First,
it concentrates only on changes in aggregate income, while per capita income may be a more relevant economic variable. Second, the real resource
costs of the transfer payments are ignored. Third, the Simon procedure
ignores some of the distributional aspects of population policy. The
second point was discussed under the costs subsection. The first and
third points are now discussed.

In the Coale-Hoover model, the marginal product of labor is zero.
If the marginal product of labor is not zero, aggregate GNP may well
be larger in the long run with higher fertility. Unlike most investment
projects which affect only aggregate output, population projects are
fundamentally different in that they alter the size of the population
receiving the product. Application of the Simon technique might not
yield a very large payment per birth averted in the Isbister model since
aggregate GNP is at most 3% higher with low fertility and is 2%
lower at the end of 45 years, even though income per capita is 70%
higher with low fertility. Demeny[36] examines, for instance, the maximum
amount of real resources which could be invested in a population program
and leave the lower fertility population at least as well off in terms of
per capita income. Needless to say, this approach yields a larger amount
which could be invested per birth averted. If population projects are to
be compared with other investment projects and per capita income is the
decision criterion, then returns to alternative projects should be

deflated by population. This procedure ignores the utility of children, however.

An alternative way of approaching the problem of fertility reduction projects is through conventional welfare analysis. If couples made their decisions about additional births by weighing the benefits and costs of those births, and there were no externalities or market imperfections (including information), and individuals' preferences were to be counted in evaluating population programs, there would be no a priori reason for government intervention in the fertility decision-making process. Clearly, however, couples make fertility decisions in the absence of information about fertility control, and there are important externalities.

a) Information

There is considerable evidence that couples in LDCs are unaware of contraceptive alternatives, with the result that they choose suboptimal contraceptive methods and have higher fertility than they might other- wise choose.[37] Direct questionnaires indicate that couples in many LDCs have little information about efficient contraceptive methods. Contraceptive information is inversely correlated with education and income. Numerous studies have also indicated that couples are unable to restrict fertility to desired levels.[38] The high incidence of abortion in some countries may also be an indicator of less than optimal fertility control.

Lack of knowledge about the benefits and costs of children may also be a source of nonoptimal fertility decisions. Publicity to inform couples about the costs and benefits of children may be desirable. Where mortality has been reduced, campaigns to acquaint prospective parents about the higher probability of child survival may be relevant, since part of the decision to have an additional birth is motivated by the actuarial decision to ensure a sufficient number of surviving children. On the other hand, Schultz's results for Taiwan and the results of Nerlove and Schultz for Puerto Rico[39] indicate that the lag between reduced mortality and reduced fertility may be as little as three years.

Finally, couples may falsely assume that society expects them to follow high fertility norms. Psychic costs to defying these norms may be reduced with propaganda promoting low fertility.[40]

b)   Externalities

A second important reason why private decisions about fertility may
be socially nonoptimal is a divergence between private and social costs
of children. If parents do not bear the full costs of child-bearing, it
may be presumed that fertility will be higher than is socially optimal.
In this section, four types of externalities are considered: (i) intra-
family externalities, (ii) public consumption externalities, (iii) long-
run externalities, and (iv) political externalities.

(1)   Intra-family externalities

There are intra-family externalities if members of a family unit
are affected by the decision to have an additional child but are not
compensated for the losses they suffer. The most important externality
is probably that existing children suffer diminished consumption, investment, and inheritance when a sibling is added.[41] While the family unit
may be thought to be an ideal unit to internalize these externalities,
children do not have very great bargaining rights in these matters.

A similar intra-family externality occurs in extended families. If
the present value of the marginal product of a birth is less than the
present value of its share of income, others suffer a net loss.

(2)   Public consumption externalities

Public consumption externalities refer to consumption of publicly
provided goods or transfer payments. If the present value of taxes paid
by an additional child is less than the present value of public expenditures on the child, there is a net loss to the rest of society.[42] True
public goods, where the marginal costs of extending the service to an
additional person are zero, are not relevant. Education and health
expenditures are probably the most important sources of externalities in
less developed countries. An evaluation of the costs and benefits of a
post-partum family planning program in Jamaica yielded a benefit-cost
ratio of 4.5 to 1, where costs included the capital and operating costs
of the facility discounted at 10% and the benefits were the discounted
private cost-savings by the avoided costs of child-rearing and government savings in expenditures on health and education.[43] If private
resource savings are excluded from the calculation and tax payments
are ignored, the benefit-cost ratio falls to 2.3 to 1. In general

it may be expected that the present value of tax payments is low or even
zero if there are tax deductions for children or the marginal product of
labor is low.[44]

(3) Long-run externalities

Long-run externalities refer to the costs imposed on others when
the child enters the labor force. Suppose that labor markets were
perfectly competitive, with each person receiving his marginal product.
An additional member of the labor force reduces the marginal product of
labor and thus the wage rate. Recipients of labor income suffer a
decline in income; owners of property receive increased income. If the
marginal utility of income of wage earners is greater than that of
property owners, there is a negative externality. Needless to say, the
magnitude of this externality is not easily quantified, especially since
it depends upon the weights of the various members of society in the
social welfare function.

(4) Political externalities

Political externalities refer to the proposition that political
groups receive political power in proportion to their numbers. While
all may benefit if fertility is generally lowered, it is not in the
interest of any single group to do so.[45] Achievement of low fertility
is afflicted with all the problems of public goods.[46] The failure of
Lebanon to take a census in recent years is attributable to the fear of
upsetting a delicate balance of power between Christians and Moslems,
which was established when there were more Christians than Moslems.
Higher Moslem fertility has presumably reversed the size ordering.
Lincoln Day (1967) has shown that, ceteris paribus, the fertility of
Catholics is inversely related to their population proportion.[47] Opposition to family planning programs in the United States by some black
leaders is also a reflection of this political externality. For further
examples, see Weiner.[48]

c) Social and private risk

A final market imperfection leading to nonoptimal fertility is a
divergence between private and social risk. An important motive for having children is old age insurance.[49,50] When mortality is high, each

couple must have a large number of children to ensure a reasonable probability of having support from their children when they are old. Assuming
that couples continue to have children until they have had enough to
assure a .95 probability of having a son when the father reaches age 65,
each woman surviving through the child-bearing ages must have 4.96 births
when the expectation of life at birth is 50 years. The intrinsic rate of
natural increase for a population with these characteristics is .025 per
annum.[51]

A substantial amount of evidence has been accumulated that suggests
that fertility is a function of mortality.[52] It is also clear that the
expected rate of return on births for old-age support is quite small,
since the costs begin immediately and the returns, which must be discounted by the probability of parent and child survival, are received at
a much later date. On the other hand, in the absence of alternative
arrangements for old-age security, they may be the best available
alternative.

Given that old-age security is an important motive for fertility, it
is at once apparent that the level of fertility privately chosen is
greater than the optimal number, since private and social risks diverge.
The social risk of having an inadequate number of the next generation
for parental support is zero, while the risk to a low fertility family
facing a high mortality schedule is large. The implication of this point
is that policies to provide families with social security may be important
in reducing fertility. Varying the level of social security payments with
the level of fertility attained may be desirable.[53] Such policies are
examined in the policy section of this chapter.

3. Summary

One may conclude from the evidence presented in sections B and C that
reductions in fertility and in fertility differentials are likely to yield
less unequal distributions of current and future income, and that the returns to investments in programs to reduce fertility are quite large even
with fairly conservative criteria, so that such investments are justifiable
on efficiency grounds. In the next two sections, specific policies and
their distributional consequences are examined.

D.   Categories of population policy

Policies to influence fertility may be divided into three basic categories: persuasion, alterations of relative prices, and coercion.[54] Persuasive policies attempt to affect preferences for children. Policies using the price system alter the direct and opportunity costs of, or returns to, fertility. Antinatal coercive policies provide legal sanctions against fertility or nuptiality; pronatal coercion includes legal restrictions on the purchase or sale of methods of fertility limitation. Table 3 lists examples of the different policies. The examples are primarily antinatal policies, but they could be used to promote fertility. For instance, a tax on births is an antinatal policy. The pronatal analogue is a birth subsidy.

Table 3. Population Policies

Persuasive policies

> Propaganda to encourage couples to reduce fertility to promote the ideal of a small family.
>
> Promotion of labor force participation by females.
>
> Encouragement of breast-feeding.

Price policies

> Provision of contraceptive information.
>
> Subsidies for contraceptive devices, sterilization, or abortion.
>
> Payments for the practice of contraception (e.g., vasectomy bonuses).
>
> Payments for periods of nonpregnancy or for child-spacing.
>
> Withdrawal of maternity benefits after N children.
>
> Withdrawal of family allowances after N children.
>
> Taxes on births or removal of tax deductions for children.
>
> Provision of only N years of free schooling to each nuclear family.
>
> Contributions to pensions varying inversely with family size.

Coercive policies

> Minimum legal age for marriage.
>
> Required abortion for illegitimate pregnancies.
>
> Legal sanctions against abortion, sale of contraceptive devices, or provision of contraceptive information.
>
> Restrictions on the import of contraceptive materials.

---

1.   Persuasion

It is difficult for economists to evaluate the role of persuasion or propaganda in a population program, accustomed as they are to assuming preferences as "given." Rationales for persuasive policies usually presume that the government or state should play a paternal role for its citizens and is in a superior position to determine what is best for the nation viewed as a whole. From that position it is easily argued that the state should take an advocacy position to counter institutional control over reproduction, which amounts to "coercive pronatalist policy."[55] A campaign slogan saying "Two is Best" is a logical slogan in that framework. If, on the other hand, the state is viewed as a collection of individuals, each of whom is capable of evaluating his own welfare given sufficient information, the arguments for persuasive policies have little basis for support. Rather, provision of information, not exhortation, is a proper role of policy. "Children are Costly" is a logical slogan.

While some population programs have attempted to persuade couples that fewer than three or fewer than four children are ideal family sizes, little is known about the effectiveness of purely persuasive policies in reducing fertility, although it is fairly certain that pronatal persuasive policies in developed countries have had small impact on behavior.

2.   Price policies

In section C, it was shown that market imperfections and externalities yield private decisions about fertility which are socially nonoptimal. Raising the private direct or opportunity costs of births, reducing the money and psychic costs of birth prevention, and correcting for divergence between private and social risk can be accomplished by altering prices. The effectiveness of such policies and their effects on income distribution will be examined in considerable detail in section E.

It should be noted that a variety of government policies, particularly policies that are intended to redistribute income, could have pronatal consequences, although their impact may be small. Free education, maternal and child welfare care benefits, and provisions for public housing based on family size fall into this category. Analysis of European family allowances indicates that they have had little impact on fertility.[56]

3. Coercive policies

Coercive policies consist of laws prohibiting individuals from undertaking certain activities. Penalties may be imposed for breaking the law. In some ways, coercive policies are analogous to price policies in that they have price effects. For instance, a law prohibiting marriage of women below age 15, if enforced, raises the price of legal marriages for 14-year olds to infinity. The relative price of consensual marriages falls. The average price of marrying for 14-year olds increases, thereby diminishing the quantity demanded, although there is substitutability of extra-legal for legal marriage. Laws penalizing abortions raise the money price and psychic costs of abortions, thereby discouraging their purchase and sale. The extent to which the number of abortions decreases is a function of the price increase (itself a function of law enforcement) and the price elasticity of demand.

The use of coercive policies depends upon the seriousness with which population problems are viewed, the population's approval of the policy, and the administrative expense of enforcing the policy. For instance, required abortions for illegitimate pregnancies or pregnancies after the Nth live birth would find little support in any nation and would (partially for that reason) be expensive to administer.

The examples of laws affecting requirements for entry into marriage and abortion were not chosen capriciously. Policies to reduce the rate of population growth by raising the age of marriage or otherwise reducing marriage rates have been proposed by some authors as has liberalization of abortion laws.[57] In this section, these two policy measures are discussed briefly.

Lestaeghe has demonstrated that changing patterns of marriage could have significant impact on the rate of growth of populations in less developed countries.[58] In a simulation analysis of Middle Eastern countries, he showed that the gradual acceptance of a European pattern of marriage[59] over a thirty-year transitional period would reduce the crude birth rate from 46 per thousand to about 34 per thousand at the end of 75 years, assuming no change in age-specific marital fertility rates. A reduction of age-specific fertility rates of about 40 percent over a transitional period of 40 years was required to yield a similar reduction in crude birth rates, assuming no change in age patterns of marriage.[60] Unfortunately there are only a few examples of the application of nuptiality policies which might serve as guides to the formulation of a marriage policy. Three examples which have been studied are the People's Republic of China, India, and Bavaria in the nineteenth century.

Shortly after coming to power in China, the Communists set the minimum legal age of marriage at 18 for women and 20 for men. Attempts to raise the minimum age have been defeated, but the "optimal age" was set at 30 for men and 22 for women by the Party in 1963. The government has used administrative powers to enforce the optimal age by restricting access to education and assigning "noncompliants to unpromising jobs or to inhospitable frontiers or rural areas."[61] Chen suggests that the sanctions primarily affect urban educated youth and are not applied in rural areas. There are no data to evaluate the effects of the policies on the age at marriage or in turn on fertility.

In India, where the average age of marriage for women is perhaps the lowest in the world, laws setting the minimum legal age of marriage for women at 14 were passed in 1929 and the age was raised to 16 in 1956. While the laws appear to have had some effect in raising the age at marriage, there is considerable controversy over the effects on fertility. First, there is a delay between marriage and consummation (or "return marriage"). This period is inversely related to the age at marriage. For instance for marriages from 1930 to 1939, the delay averaged 27.6 months for women married below age 15 but only 3.2 months for those married at age 15 or older.[62] Second, pregnancy at very young ages may result in later subfecundity.

The final example of limits on marriage were restrictive laws passed in German provinces in the 1830s. Knodel has concluded that increased illegitimacy offset between 50 and 90 percent of the legitimate births prevented by the legislation.[63]

The second example of coercive policy is prohibition of abortion. Very few less developed countries permit abortion on request of a woman or a woman and her spouse.[64] While data on abortions are unreliable, given social and legal sanctions against abortions, induced abortion rates in many less developed countries appear to be quite high.[65] Indeed, high abortion rates have been partly responsible for the adoption of family planning programs in countries such as Chile and Mexico.

Aside from the lack of reliable data on the extent of illegal abortion in less developed countries, very little is known about the costs of incorporating abortion in a family planning program or the costs of restrictive abortion laws. Costs of incorporating abortion in a family planning program in a less developed country have not been estimated.[66] Data from countries that have liberalized abortion laws should permit calculation of these costs. The costs of restrictive abortion laws are associated with increased birth rates and increased maternal morbidity and mortality. Table 4 gives illustrative annual rates of pregnancies and deaths associated with pregnancy, contraception, and induced abortion in developed countries. No estimates for less developed countries are available. The costs associated with treating illegal abortions may also be quite large. An interview study of women in three Latin American cities estimated that 26.7 to 40 percent of induced abortions resulted in hospitalization. Armijo and Monreal in 1965, and Omran in 1971, estimated that each hospitalized post-abortion case in Chile required 3.21 bed days.[67]

Table 4. Hypothetical Annual Rates of Pregnancy and Death Risks with Contraception and Legal Abortion per 100,000 Women of Reproductive Age in Fertile Unions[a]

	Pregnancies	Deaths
No contraception, no abortion	40,000–60,000	8–12
No contraception, all pregnancies aborted	100,000	3
Highly effective contraception, no abortion	100	3
Moderately effective contraception, no abortion	11,800–13,000	2.5
Moderately effective contraception, all pregnancies aborted	14,300	0.4

[a]Assumes low maternal mortality.

SOURCE: Christopher Tietze and Deborah Davison, "Induced Abortion: A Factbook," Reports in Population/Family Planning 14 (December 1973), p. 47.

Little is known about the income distribution impact of including abortion in family planning programs. Table 5 shows percentage estimates of the number of induced and spontaneous abortions by socio-economic class for

Table 5. Percentage of Women Who Have Had One or More
Abortions, by Socio-Economic Status

Country or Sub-National Area	Year of Survey	Socio-Economic Indicator	% Women With Abortion Experience	
Chile: Santiago, Quinta Normal district[a]	1962-63	Education:		
		Illiterate	27	
		Intermediate level	33	
		Intermediate level	41	
		Intermediate level	24	
		4 years secondary or more	26	
Korea, Republic of: Seoul, Sung Dong Gu[b]	1963	Education:		
		No school	17	(16)*
		Intermediate level	23	(31)*
		Intermediate level	30	(39)*
		Intermediate level	35	(60)*
		College or more	37	(80)*
Korea, Republic of: Yongi Gun (rural)[c]	1965	Education:		
		No school	4	
		Intermediate level	6	
		Middle school or more	8	
Peru: Lima[d]	1964	Class:		
		Lower	45	
		Intermediate level	33	
		Upper	35	
Taiwan[e]	1966	Education:		
		Low	9	
		Intermediate level	14	
		High	18	
Taiwan: Taichung[f]	1962-63	Education:		
		No school	8	
		–	17	
		–	18	
		–	17	
		Graduate senior high school or more	28	

[a]448 working-class women of fertile age.
[b]3,204 currently married women, 20-44.
[c]2,084 currently married women aged 20-44; random sample.
[d]500 Peruvian-born upper-class women; area cluster sample.
[e]4,989 married women, 20-44; random probability sample.
[f]2,432 women, 35-39.
*By completion of child-bearing, aged 40-44.

SOURCE: Emily Campbell Cavar, International Inventory of Information on Induced Abortion (New York: International Institute for the Study of Human Reproduction, Columbia University, 1974), pp. 387-89.

several countries. The two types of abortions cannot be separated. It is likely that larger proportions of women from lower socio-economic classes have had spontaneous abortions since they have higher fertility, poorer nutrition, and less access to medical care. Thus, higher income classes may well have greater demand for induced abortion. In addition, if provision for abortion is tied to the existing distribution of medical manpower and institutions (see below), resources used for abortion will be positively related to income class. Study of Tunisian data should permit further examination of this point.

Although legal restrictions on abortion result in higher birth rates and maternal mortality, the decision about legalizing abortion involves complex ethical issues. However, since some countries have liberalized abortion laws or are contemplating liberalization, further research on the role of abortion in family planning programs is desirable. Finally, if less developed countries do choose to include abortion in their program mix, restrictions on aid programs which prohibit funding of such activities seem unwarranted.

E.   Population policy and income distribution

In sections B and C, it was shown that in the long run, reductions in population growth may yield considerable improvements in per capita income and in the real standard of living of workers. The interactions between income distribution and fertility reductions in the absence of policy were also outlined in those sections. In this portion, concern is with the distributional consequences of specific population programs. In particular, who have been the beneficiaries of conventional family planning programs? What change in programs would spread benefits more widely? What are the distributional consequences of tax and incentive schemes?

Traditional family planning programs are examined in the next subsection. Levels of expenditures by source of funds are examined first. Then the distribution of direct services among users is presented. Subsection E,2 evaluates the likely success and distribution consequences of tax and incentive programs.

1.   Family planning programs

Traditional family planning programs have concentrated on providing information about contraception and supplying contraception services including sterilization at or below market cost. The information aspects of such programs are undoubtedly redistribution to middle- and low-income groups since high-income groups already possess such knowledge. The provision of subsidized services involves some direct redistribution of income. The amount of redistribution depends upon the sources of program finance and the characteristics of users.

a)   Expenditures and sources of funds

The sources of funds for family planning programs include foreign aid, domestic taxes, and user fees. Table 6 shows a breakdown of total and per capita funds for major family planning programs for several LDCs for the most recent year for which data are available. As can be seen from the table, expenditures per capita and sources of funds vary considerably among countries. Generalizations are:

(i)   Foreign contributions to program expenditures are large relative to other government programs. International funding for population research and program funding increased from $2 million in 1960 to $124 million in 1970 and perhaps $250 million in 1972.[68] In 1971, official population assistance by Western countries was less than 2% of official development assistance. In that year, about 2.9% of U.S. development assistance ($96 million) was allocated for population activities.[69]

(ii)   Government expenditures on family planning expenditures are ordinarily less than 0.2% of total government expenditures. Exceptions are: Fiji (0.27% in 1972), India (3.7% in FY 1972),[70] Indonesia (0.6% in FY 1971), Mauritius (1.1% in FY 1972), and the Philippines (0.63% in 1972).

(iii)   Government family planning expenditures are generally less than 5.0% of expenditures on health. Exceptions are: Indonesia (24.2% in FY 1972), Iran (5.2% in FY 1971), South Korea (12% in 1972), Mauritius (9.1% in FY 1972), Philippines (10.5% in 1972), and Taiwan (9.3% in FY 1973).[71]

Table 6. Total and Per Capita Funds for Family Planning
Programs by Major Source of Funds

Country and Year	Total Funds (in US $1,000)					Annual Per Capita Budget (in US cents)	
	Government	International Agency	Foreign Government	Private Organization	All Sources	Government	All Sources
Bangladesh (FY 1972)	3,200	800	0	0	4,000	4	5
Dominican Republic (1972)	80	u	24.6	74	178	1.9	4.1
Fiji (1971)	157	u	u	u	157	29	29
Ghana (FY 1972)	391	6	u	165	562	4	7
Guatemala (1973)	34	517	0	105	656	0.60	12
Hong Kong (1972)	249	133	u	73	455	6.0	11.1
India (FY 1972)	86,590	u	u	u	u	15.3	u
Indonesia (FY 1972)	5,663	4,000[a]	-[a]	u	9,663	4.6	7.9
Iran (1972)	9,000	1,600	u	96	10,696	29	35
Jamaica (FY 1971)	1,090	u	u	u	u	56	u
Korea, South (1972)	3,470	550	1,112	450	5,582	10.4	16.7
Laos (1972)	u	6	500	28	534	u	17
Malaysia, West (1973)	1,060	u	u	u	u	11.1	u
Mauritius (FY 1972)	673	215[a]	-[a]	0	888	81	107
Morocco (1972)	347	u	u	u	u	2.2	u
Nepal (1970)	85	u	305	u	390	1.8	2.6
Pakistan[b] (FY 1969)	u	u	u	u	22,405	u	17.2
Philippines (1972)	1,331	0	4,500	160	5,991	3.4	15.6
Taiwan (1973)	1,012	0	0	225	1,237	6.6	8.1
Thailand (1973)[c]	1,900	1,400	1,000	700	5,000	4.8	14.0
Tunisia (1973)	278[d]	819	543	u	1,640	5.2	30
Turkey (1972)	u	u	u	u	1,797	u	4.8

[a]Any foreign government allocation is included under international agencies.
[b]Prior to the independence of Bangladesh.
[c]Includes an estimate of contributions of personnel and facilities of the
health network to the family planning program.
[d]Includes only the direct monetary costs of the program. Does not include
contributions of any health program into which the family planning program is integrated.
[u]Unavailable.

SOURCE: Dorothy Nortman, "Population and Family Planning Programs: A
Factbook," Reports on Population/Family Planning, 5th ed., 2
(September 1973), pp. 89-91.

(iv) Expenditures per capita are small. In only one country (Mauritius) are expenditures of funds from all sources as great as $1.00 per capita.

There are no data to show the extent of private payments for contraceptive services and supplies. Fees for services are common, especially for oral contraceptives, condoms, and diaphragms, although in the majority of countries fees are reduced or waived for those unable to pay.[72] When incentives are offered on a large scale, payments are made only for male or female sterilization, except for India where a payment for IUD insertion is given in some states. Cash payments as large as $8.00 have been offered at some vasectomy camps, and $2.00 has been paid for female sterilization. In Pakistan (1972), there were payments of $1.50 for male sterilization and $2.00 for female sterilization. An indirect incentive also exists in countries where health care may be provided free with visits to family planning clinics. Experimental incentive programs will be discussed in the next section.

Besides government programs and expenditures for fertility reduction, there is a considerable private market for contraceptive services. As much as 40% of total expenditures for contraceptive supplies consists of private expenditures.[73] Table 7 shows the percent of women using public and privately provided contraceptive supplies, for various countries. There are practically no data to show the use of privately marketed supplies by income class, although some evidence in the next section indicates that high-income couples use private-sector supplies even when family planning clinics are available, and current or ever use of contraception varies positively with education in countries with no programs.

b) Distribution of benefits

Traditional family planning programs provide information and services. In this section, data on the distribution of benefits of family planning programs are analyzed. The evidence supports the conclusion that on balance the benefits are larger the lower is income, except that the very lowest income and education groups are under-represented among users. Two reasons for the under-representation are lack of demand for services and the tendency for program facilities to be located in urban and higher-income areas.

Table 7. Users of Family Planning Services by Source of Supplies[a]

Country and Year	All Sources		Program Supplies and Services		Private Sector Supplies and Services	
	Number of Users (1,000s)	Users as a Percent of Married Women Aged 15-44	Number of Users (1,000s)	Users as a Percent of Married Women Aged 15-44	Number of Users (1,000s)	Users as a Percent of Married Women Aged 15-44
Egypt (1973)	1,015	20.7	776	15.8	239	4.9
Fiji (1973)	26.8	33.4	23.2	28.9	3.6	4.4
Guatemala (1973)	44	3.8	31.9	2.7	12	1
Hong Kong (1973)	235	52	113	25.2	122	27.1
India (1973)	u	u	13,861	13.6	u	u
Indonesia (1972)	u	u	850	3.3	u	u
Iran (1971)[b]	>403	>9.3	328	7.6	u	u
Kenya (1971)	45.4	2.2	45.4	2.2	u	u
Malaysia, West (1973)	u	u	123.5	9.3	u	u
Mauritius (1972)	24.6	21.2	19.5	16.8	5.0	4.3
Mexico (1973)	910	13.1	66.5	1.0	843.5	12.2
Morocco (1973)	126.5	5.6	48.0	2.1	78.5	3.5
Nepal (1971)	u	u	59.9	2.5	u	u
Pakistan (1971)[c]	2,600	12	2,600	12	u	u
Philippines (1973)[d]	563	11	563	11	u	u
Singapore (1973)[e]	49.9	18.3	49.9	18.3	0.0	0.0
Taiwan (1973)	1,120	58	530	27	590	30
Thailand (1973)	1,284	25.7	883	17.7	401	8.0
Tunisia (1973)	u	u	45	6.4	u	u
Turkey (1973)	u	u	160	2.5	u	u

[a]Includes sterilization.
[b]Includes only IUDs and oral pills.
[c]Prior to the independence of Bangladesh.
[d]Most private supplies and services are provided by clinics that receive financial support from the government, and acceptors at these clinics are reported in the program data. Private use through other channels is considered too low to affect the total.
[e]Includes only oral pills and sterilization.
[u]Information unavailable.

SOURCE: Dorothy Nortman, "Population and Family Planning Programs."

Information. A priori, one expects the information benefits to be
progressive, since high-income and -education groups already possess
relatively more contraceptive information. There have been some attempts
to measure increases in knowledge as a result of information campaigns.
In West Bengal, following an intensive campaign of newspaper advertise-
ments, radio broadcasts, slides and films, exhibitions and street
posters, the greatest gains in knowledge of at least one contraceptive
method "were among women with primary school or lower education and among
the lowest income groups."[74] On the other hand, following a radio campaign in Cali, Colombia, "increases in knowledge of where to go for service
were greater among the better educated than among the less educated."[75]
It would appear that increases in knowledge of contraception depends upon
where and by what means communications are made.[76] Finders fees and user
incentives can have considerable impact on the diffusion of contraceptive
information.[77]

Finally, it should be remembered that the goal of an information campaign is not just to provide family planning information but to stimulate
contraceptive use. If higher-income groups are more responsive to marginal information than are low-income groups, it is possible that purely
informational campaigns could yield greater benefits to the rich.

Use. The more important question of the use of program services is
now discussed. There are only a few studies that compare the population
of acceptors with the population at risk. Table 8 summarizes five studies
from various parts of the world. The Philippines study compares users
with the national population; the Indian study compares users with eli-
gibles in Howrah district; and the Nigerian study is only for Lagos.
Excepting Nigeria, it appears that users of services are drawn predominantly from the middle- and lower-middle-education groups, with the
highest-income and -education groups under-represented. The highest-
income groups are under-represented because they rely on privately provided services. In the Philippines the lowest-education groups are
under-represented because the clinic-population ratio falls off in rural
areas. Location of clinics may also partially explain the Nigerian findings, although it would also appear that the underlying demand for
services by low-income groups is also small. The Costa Rica example
compares users with the populations served by six clinics scattered over

Table 8. Distribution of Benefits of Family Planning Programs

Philippines (Jan.-June 1970):

Education	Acceptors	Married Women, 15-44
None	1.4%	13.2%
Grades 1-4	17.0	32.0
Grades 5-7	36.8	32.6
High school 1+	26.8	14.7
College 1+	18.0	7.5
Occupation of Husband		
White collar	18.9	14.8
Blue collar	50.2	12.5
Farmer-fisherman	24.6	60.9
Other	6.3	11.8

Lagos, Nigeria (1971)

	Education		
	No Formal	Primary Only	Secondary and More
Acceptors	38.7%	37.6%	23.7%
KAP Survey	56.9	28.5	14.6

Howrah District, India (1968-70):

	Area					
	Urban		Slum		Rural	
Education	Clinic	Eligible	Clinic	Eligible	Clinic	Eligible
Illiterate	23.9%	41.0%	68.3%	46.4%	59.7%	70.4%
Literate but below primary	32.4	11.7	10.5	14.6	19.9	8.8
Primary	26.7	30.8	11.3	18.6	14.7	15.7
Middle+	16.4	16.4	9.9	20.4	5.9	5.0

Costa Rica (1970):

Annual Income (1970 colones)	Attended Clinic	Did Not Attend Clinic
<100	65.8%	34.2%
100-399	65.4	34.6
400-699	53.7	46.3
700-999	48.1	51.9
1000+	35.1	62.5

SOURCES: Philippines--J.E. Laing, "The Philippines: Family Planning Acceptors, January-June 1970," Studies in Family Planning, vol. 2, no.
5 (May 1971), pp. 113-19.

Nigeria--Robert W. Morgan, "Family Planning Acceptors in Lagos,
Nigeria," Studies in Family Planning, vol. 3, no. 9 (September
1972), pp. 221-26.

India--Murari Majumdar et al., "Use of Oral Contraceptives in
Urban, Rural, and Slum Areas," Studies in Family Planning, vol.
3, no. 9 (September 1972), pp. 227-32.

Costa Rica--R. Michielutte et al., "Factors Associated with
Utilization of Family Planning Clinics in Costa Rica," Social
Biology, vol. 20, no. 2 (July 1973), pp. 160-72.

the country.   The lowest-income groups are as likely (or more likely) to use the clinic services.

The evidence of these studies suggests that the benefits of family planning programs typically are received by middle- and lower-middle-income and -education segments of the population, but that in many populations the lowest-income and -education groups would participate more heavily in programs if clinics and service dispensaries were dispersed more widely.   Part of the reason why programs have been concentrated in urban rather than in rural areas is that programs have restricted the dispensing of IUDs and oral pills to physicians, who tend to be located in urban areas.   While access to medical care is desirable in the event of complications, there is no reason why dispensing these contraceptives requires a physician.   Several programs have trained and employed para-medical personnel, including midwives, to distribute IUDs and orals.

(i)   In 1966 Pakistan began training local family planning visitors.   By 1969, paramedical personnel were performing 70 to 80 percent of all IUD insertions.[78]

(ii)   Fifteen percent of all IUD first insertions (6 percent urban and 20 percent rural) in South Korea in 1968 were performed by midwives, nurses, and family planning workers.[79]

(iii)   In Barbados, starting in 1965, nurse-midwives were used as primary insertors of IUDs.[80]

(iv)   In Malaysia over 90 percent of acceptors use orals and the majority of prescriptions are given by lay personnel.

(v)   And in Thailand, permitting midwives to dispense orals in mid-1970 increased the number of health clinics with family planning services from 300 to 3,000.   Whereas there were only 26,000 acceptors in rural health centers in 1968, there were 137,000 acceptors in 1970. In 1970, there were 133,000 pill users, and in 1971 there were 294,000 users.[81,82]

Studies in Pakistan, India, South Korea, Barbados, and Nigeria indicate that there is little difference between IUD insertions by physicians or paramedical personnel in terms of complications or continuance rates.[83]   And Rosenfield has found that paramedics do a satisfactory job of screening potential pill acceptors in Malaysia and Thailand.[84]   The International Planned Parenthood Central Medical Committee has concluded with respect to orals that "the health benefits almost certainly outweigh the risks of use in almost all cases....(and that)...(it has been found that the complications that do occur are difficult to predict by examination prior to use, but that access to follow-up facilities can be important, especially in enhancing continuation....(whoever normally meets the health needs of the community, whether doctor, nurse, traditional midwife, pharmacist, or storekeeper, can be an appropriate person to distribute oral contraceptives."[85] Research on nonmedical distribution of orals should be undertaken. An important part of any such program should be provision of access to trained medical personnel for women who have complications or who require assurance.[86] While taking orals appears to be much safer than risks imposed by the probability of additional pregnancies (see table 9), unsatisfactory experiences by women taking the pill may reduce acceptance by others.[87]

Increased emphasis should be placed upon commercial distribution of condoms and other conventional contraceptives. The Indian Nirodh program (launched in September 1968), which uses the distribution network of the six largest consumer goods marketing companies and makes condoms available to consumers at less than 20 percent of the usual market price, seems to have considerable success in increasing the use of condoms and in widening the distribution to smaller towns. Estimated monthly purchases of Nirodh condoms were 1,585 thousand in June 1969 and 5,494 thousand in the period April 1971 to March 1972; monthly purchases of other brands declined from 705,000 to 509,000 over the same period. Twenty percent of Nirodh condoms were sold in towns of less than 20,000 population, compared to only six percent of other brands.[88] Indian data also indicate, however, that condoms are more likely to be used by couples of higher socio-economic status than users of terminal methods of contraception (i.e., sterilization).[89] Whether the same pattern would be found in other countries is open to question since the Indian family planning program has concentrated primarily on terminal methods, so that the observed structure of methods in use does not necessarily represent the underlying preference structure.

In any case, it is important to stress that family planning programs should not concentrate solely on a single method. First, discontinuation rates of methods such as the pill and the IUD are often quite high. Evidence from Taiwan and Korea shows that a high proportion of those who discontinue one method do switch to other methods if they are available. Second, couples differ in their preferences among contraceptive

Table 9. Contraception and Maternal Mortality per
1,000,000 at Risk, by Level of Health Care

	No Contraception[a]	Condom/ Diaphragm	IUD	Oral Contraception
Maternal mortality of 250 per 1,000,000 births				
Pregnancies in any year	600,000	150,000	35,000	20,000
Deaths				
Due to pregnancy	150	38	9	5
Due to method	0	0	10[c]	30[c]
Total deaths	150	38	19	35

	No Contraception[a]	Other Methods[b]	IUD	Oral Contraception
Maternal mortality of 5,000 per 1,000,000 births				
Pregnancies in any year	400,000	112,000	22,000	26,000
Deaths				
Due to pregnancy	2,000	560	110	130
Due to method	0	0	10[c]	30[c]
Total deaths	2,000	560	120	160

[a]Pregnancy rates with no contraception assume prolonged breast-feeding in countries with maternal mortality of 5,000 per 1,000,000 births.
[b]"Other methods" include condom (70 percent), spermicides, diaphragms, and a small number of Depo-Provera acceptors.
[c]These figures are approximations and the differences between IUDs and oral contraceptives are not of statistical significance.

SOURCE: Linda Atkinson, et al., "Oral Contraceptives: Considerations of Safety in Nonclinical Distribution," Studies in Family Planning, vol. 5, no. 8 (August 1974), p. 244.

alternatives. For instance, couples desiring to space children would find sterilization unacceptable. Expanding the alternatives may well increase demand.

c) Distributional consequences of family planning

Examining only the distribution of expenditures, one may conclude that middle- and lower-middle-income and -educational groups have benefitted most from conventional family planning programs, with high-income groups consuming private-sector services and the location of facilities and in some cases lack of demand inhibiting distribution of services to the very lowest income groups. Ways have been discussed in which programs can be modified to distribute benefits more widely. How successful they will be depends in part upon the demand for services by low-income groups. In the next section, tax and incentive schemes which are designed to encourage reduced fertility are discussed.

2.   Tax and incentive schemes

Recognition of the benefits of reduced fertility for achievement of increases in per capita income and dissatisfaction with the response of fertility to family planning programs have prompted some to advocate tax and incentive policies to penalize high fertility or reward low fertility. And, since externalities are associated with births, tax or subsidy programs to internalize the external costs of fertility appear economically justifiable.

This section is divided into three parts. The first part examines the success of programs that have attempted to use tax and incentive schemes. The second and third parts examine the distributional consequences of such programs.

a)   Evaluation of the success of tax and incentive schemes

Table 10 gives examples of programs that have moved "beyond family planning."[90] The actions taken in Singapore and the Philippines are too recent for any evaluation of their effects on fertility. It is also too soon to evaluate the short-term effects of the Taiwanese educational scheme on fertility, although 67% of eligible couples joined the plan, and a recent survey has shown some increase in contraceptive use.[91]

The Gujarat and Ernakulem campaigns were exceedingly successful. The Ernakulem campaign (1971) paid Rs. 114 in cash and in kind to vasectomy patients and Rs. 135 for female sterilization. With the bonuses, there were 63,418 vasectomy acceptors compared to 10,662 in 1968-69 and 15,005 in November and December 1971.[92] The reported median age of the wives of acceptors was 30.8 years, and the mean number of children ever-born was 4.1 compared to an average of 4.2 in the district. The crude birth rate was estimated to have dropped three points as a result of the campaign. The Gujarat campaign paid Rs. 65-75 per vasectomy acceptor, and 232,000 vasectomies were performed in a two-month period. Sixty-five

Table 10. Tax and Incentive Programs

Singapore: elimination of priority for large families in the allocation of subsidized housing; limitation of paid maternity leave to that for two children; scaling of delivery fee by parity; a reduction of income tax relief from five to three children; lower priority for choice of primary school admission for children of fourth birth order or higher; and waiver of delivery fees if the husband or wife elects sterilization after the last birth. (August 1973)

Philippines: tax relief for dependents restricted to four persons (March 1972); paid maternity leave which employers must grant to women employed for more than one-half year is limited to the first four deliveries. (March 1973)

Taiwan: experimental program in one township establishing free bank deposits earmarked for redeemable education certificates. Enrolled women with no more than three living children receive annual deposits to the account. Entries plus interest can total $385 after 14 years for couples with two or fewer children or $192 for couples with three children. Couples with four children are dropped from the plan. (September 1971)

India: vasectomy and female sterilization bonuses in sterilization campaigns in Gujarat and Ernakulem; payment of vasectomy bonus to workers in Tata industrial firms (September 1967-March 1970); and an experiment on a tea estate with payments into individual savings accounts for periods of nonpregnancy, to be paid out when the woman reaches age 50. The payment is viewed as a form of social security in place of children.

---

percent of the acceptors were illiterate.[93] No comparison with the population at risk has been made. The success of these two campaigns has sometimes been attibuted to the incentive payments. Lack of an experimental design makes quantitative evaluation difficult.

In the Tata experiment two groups of firms were chosen to examine the effects of vasectomy bonuses. Starting in September 1967, a total of 3,988 workers in four factories were offered incentives of Rs. 210-220 (about $27 U.S.). A total of 3,872 workers in five other nearby firms (presumably the two sets of factories were chosen randomly from the same set) were offered Rs. 10-20 (three factories) and Rs. 35-55 (two factories). For the lowest paid Tata workers, the incentive of Rs. 210-220 represented well more than a month's pay.[94] In the first six months, 2.58% of workers in the high-incentive factories adopted sterilization and 0.71% in the low-incentive factories. By March 1970, the cumulative percentage of adopters was 8.99% and 5.84% in high- and low-incentive factories, respectively.[95] Table 11 indicates that

Table 11. The Tata Incentive Program

Monthly Income (Rupees)	Percent of Factory Workers Adopting Sterilization	
	High-Incentive (3,988 workers)	Low-Incentive (3,872 workers)
Less than 200	10.6%	3.3%
201–500	9.3	6.2
501–1,000	6.4	7.6
More than 1,000	4.0	5.9

low-income workers were more likely to adopt sterilization when the large incentive was paid.

The final incentive experiment has been carried out on ten estates in India. This experiment has been financed by the estates. For each month of nonpregnancy, each woman receives Rs. 10 per month deposited in a blocked savings account. The woman is to receive the accumulated savings at age 50. For each birth occurring to a woman who has zero, one, or two children, no payments are made for one year. For a woman who has three or more children, an additional birth results in a loss of payments for one year and a deduction of up to Rs. 880 from the account. The firm pays maternity costs and hospital care and contributes approximately Rs. 100 per year for food, schooling, and clothing for children less than age 12 and approximately Rs. 15 for medical care for children ages 13 to 17. Discounting costs at .065 per year yields a present value of Rs. 1,000 per child. Ten Rs. per month for 13 years discounted at the same rate, yields Rs. 1,000. Since, however, two, three, or four births would be averted, the firm gains substantially if the program is successful but suffers no losses if it is not successful. The program had no difficulty in gaining acceptance by workers and appears to be successful in reducing fertility.

Too few data exist at present to evaluate the success of incentive schemes, although the tea estate plan shows considerable promise. More experimentation should be undertaken to evaluate the costs of such schemes. It should be noted that the payments made in schemes have thus far been far smaller than the value per birth averted, as estimated in various macro-models.

b)   Distribution of consequences of tax and penalty programs

Taxes on births, withdrawal of family allowances or maternity benefits, or limiting tax deductions to <u>N</u> children raise the cost of children.
There are several difficulties with such programs. Taxes on births or
limitations on tax deductions could not be applied in some countries
because only a small part of the population is subject to the income
tax. Birth taxes would be difficult to administer in any case. Withdrawal of family allowances or maternity benefits could only have a large
impact on fertility in countries where such benefits are paid to more
than a small part of the population.

In countries where such policies could be pursued, they are likely
to have adverse distributional consequences. Taxes on children or births
are likely to be regressive since low-income families have higher fertility, although taxes varying with income could be devised. In addition,
taxes, reduced allowances, or limits on the amount of education available to each nuclear family further reduce the welfare of children who
already suffer with the addition of a sibling. No tax or negative
incentive can surmount this obstacle.

3.   Distributional consequences of incentives

In this section, incentives are defined as positive payments in money
or in kind to couples for avoidance of births, for periods of nonpregnancy,
or for contraceptive acceptance. Incentive payments to persons who find
clients or payments to suppliers of contraceptive services are not discussed, although they have played an important role in many programs.[96]

The effects of taxation or penalty shemes and positive incentive
schemes are related, since both transfer income from those who have high
fertility to those who achieve low fertility. There is some presumption
therefore that positive incentive schemes may well worsen income distribution. Whether this is so depends upon the incidence of taxes to finance
the scheme, the nature of the incentive, and the characteristics of those
who receive the incentive. For example, if taxes are progressive and lower
income couples are more responsive to the incentive scheme, there may be
some redistribution to lower-income groups. The Tata industrial program
is an example where low-income workers accepted vasectomies at higher
rates.

There are numerous variations in incentive schemes.[97] Payments can
be made for contraceptive acceptance, periods of nonpregnancy, or varying
social security benefits with numbers of children ever-born. Payment for
contraceptive acceptance is probably only feasible for sterilization,
since other forms of contraception are subject to "non-use." Payments can
also vary with the age of the acceptor (for sterilization) or perhaps
parity. Payments can be made concurrent with either sterilization or a
period of nonpregnancy or can be postponed to the end of the child-bearing
period or retirement. They might also have an annuity feature.

Payments for periods of nonpregnancy are likely to be expensive to
administer since they require periodic examinations (say two per year)
and are subject to the difficulty that couples can receive benefits for
several years, stop, have a child, and then resume receiving payments.
Varying payments with the length of period since the time of last pregnancy may be devised to lengthen the interval between births. Longer
intervals, even if children ever-born per woman does not change, increase
the mean length of generation and reduce the growth rate. Large payments
for four or five years with reduced payments thereafter may increase
intervals between births, although payments which are reduced significantly may induce couples to have an additional birth so as to begin
receiving the large payments again. Large payments immediately after
birth also contain a significant amount of rent since fecundability is
lower in the first year (or more with breast feeding) after the last
birth.

Varying social security payments with the number of children ever-
born presents administrative difficulties in phasing in each generation
and is subject to abuse when there is inadequate birth registration. In
addition, such schemes do not have the immediacy that payments earlier in
life would have.

Payments for sterilization would seem to be a possible complement
to existing family planning programs in countries where sterilization is
acceptable. Ethical acceptance can be gained by presenting a payment at
the time of sterilization as a compensation for the time and inconvenience
involved and an additional deferred payment as old-age security compensation for not having children for old-age support.[98] Ridker (1969) has
worked out various schemes for India involving payments of a Rs. 1,000

bond for sterilization after three children and Rs. 1,500 for sterilization after two children.

Assume that India's birth rate drops only to 31.2 by 1991 without the
scheme. The population size of India would be 953 million at that date.
If 50% of the women accept the three-child scheme, the birth rate would
drop to 25.3 by 1991, and the population would be only 836 million at
that date. If payments of Rs. 50 are made at the time of sterilization,
the cost of the program would have been Rs. 94 million in 1966 and would
be less than Rs. 150 million by 1981. When significant numbers of women
reach the age of 50, the current outlay increases to about Rs. 2,000
million per year in 1986. One-hundred percent acceptance of the three-
child scheme would reduce the birth rate to 17.5 per thousand by 1991,
yielding a population of 720 million at that time.

All things considered, incentive schemes deserve consideration as
adjuncts to family planning programs. By compensating individuals for
having smaller families (if children have positive present values), incentives stimulate demand for contraception and may have positive effects
on income distribution. Only by experimenting with alternative schemes
will the effects on income distribution, fertility, and the costs of
alternative programs be known.

F. Politics of population policy

In recent years there has been a significant expansion in the number
of countries with official policies to reduce population growth rates or
support family planning activities for other than demographic reasons.
Table 12 shows positions taken by governments of developing countries by
region. Part of the increase in interest in population policy may be the
result of increased funds available for population programs and of pressure
by aid donors. For the most part, however, the adoption of policies has
come about for more fundamental reasons:

(i) New estimates of exceedingly high rates of population growth;

(ii) Surveys showing that substantial numbers of women (and men)
want more information about controlling fertility and want to limit their
family size;

(iii) High abortion rates;

(iv) Increased awareness that development plans have been frustrated
by rapid rates of population growth; and

Table 12. Number of Countries and Distribution of the Population in the
Major Regions of the Developing World, by Government Position on
Population Growth and Family Planning Activities: 1972

Government position[a]	All developing countries	Africa	Latin America[b]	Asia and Oceania[c]
	Number of countries			
All positions	118	47	29	42
Official policy to reduce the population growth rate	31	7	6	18
Official support of family planning activities for other than demographic reasons	28	9	14	5
Balance: no policy to reduce the growth rate and no support of family planning activities	59	31	9	19
	1972 population (in millions)			
All positions	2,678	363	273	2,042
Official policy to reduce the population growth rate	1,970	79	34	1,857
Offical support of family planning activities for other than demographic reasons	341	146	121	74
Balance: no policy to reduce the growth rate and no support of family planning activities	367	138	118	111
	Percent distribution of population			
All positions	100	100	100	100
Official policy to reduce the population growth rate	74	22	12	91
Official support of family planning activities for other than demographic reasons	13	40	44	4
Balance: no policy to reduce the growth rate and no support of family planning activities	13	38	44	5

[a]Government positions are based on the latest information available, and
population data are estimates for 1972. For a full description of the
criteria used to classify government positions and the problems encountered, see Nortman (1973).

[b]Includes the Caribbean area plus Central and South America but excludes
Argentina (24 million) and Uruguay (3 million), both of which have low
fertility.

[c]Excludes Japan (106 million) and Israel (3 million), which have low fertility. Includes Melanesia, Polynesia, and Micronesia in Oceania (4
million).

SOURCE: Dorothy Nortman, "Population and Family Planning Programs: A
Factbook," Reports on Population/Family Planning, 5th ed., 2
(September 1973), p. 21.

(v) Demonstration effects of adoption of population programs by other countries.

There are still countries without policies, and in countries with policies the level of resources devoted to population programs is less than might be desirable. Opposition to, or lack of support for, population policies arises from many motives. Among them are:

(i) Equation of population size with power;

(ii) A belief in some countries that uninhabited areas "offer limitless opportunities for colonization--and that one of the major obstacles to taking advantage of these conditions is the shortage of people."[99]

(iii) A belief that development will induce reductions in population growth;

(iv) Religious conviction that fertility control is immoral;

(v) Fear of charges of genocide by internal opposition;

(vi) Nationalism; and

(vii) Ideology.

Nationalism as a source of opposition to population limitation assumes many forms. First, in some countries there is concern with populating boundary areas against encroachment by neighbors.[100] Second, some individuals are persuaded that the concern in developed countries, particularly in the United States, about the population growth of LDCs reflects an attempt on the part of the former to preserve the LDC natural resources for use by the developed countries. And in Latin American countries, some "do not want to believe that they have a population problem precisely because the United States is foremost in insisting that they have one."[101]

There is also ideological opposition from the left. Some contend, as did Marx, that concern with population is merely a ploy to disguise the true sources of underdevelopment and social ills. Others believe that a revolutionary transformation of society is a prerequisite for development and that population pressure will hasten the revolution.

Given the sensitivity to population questions in some countries, donors should beware of overselling population policy. For the same reason, it is probably desirable to funnel aid for population policy through multilateral agencies. Involvement of personnel from LDCs with active population policies is also desirable. Where there is opposition to family planning programs, donors might concentrate aid in the infra-structure which might be used for population programs, especially those pertaining to maternal and child health. Assessing demographic parameters and training indigenous demographic researchers is also part of long-run formulation and promotion of population policy.

G.   Summary

This paper has attempted to summarize existing knowledge on the relationships between population policy and income distribution. It has been argued that high rates of fertility and patterns of differential fertility prevalent in LDCs tend to lead to less equal size distributions of current and future incomes. Rapid rates of population growth also impede the attainment of higher levels of per capita (and perhaps aggregate) income and frustrate the accomplishment of almost all other goals, such as improvements in nutrition, education, and health of the population.

Examination of the benefits and costs of fertility limitation programs indicates that benefits significantly exceed costs when income distribution aspects of such programs are ignored. Analysis of traditional family planning programs supports the conclusion that on balance the benefits are larger the lower is income, except that groups with the very lowest income and education are under-represented among consumers of family planning services. Two reasons for the under-representation are lack of demand by low-income groups and the tendencies for program facilities to be located in urban and higher-income areas. Greater use of paramedical personnel in programs and more reliance on commercial channels may widen the population served by family planning programs. As a possible alternative, tax and positive incentive schemes have been examined. Although only limited evidence is available for positive incentive schemes, it appears that they may be successful in inducing increased demand for fertility limitation by low-income groups and in distributing income toward them. Tax schemes or negative incentives are likely to be difficult to administer and may have adverse distributional consequences.

Although this chapter has concentrated on programs immediately directed toward fertility limitation, it must not be forgotten that determinants of fertility involve a whole complex of factors not included in family planning or incentive programs. Education, health care, female employment, and social insurance are also important. While there is no catalogue of necessary and sufficient conditions for fertility decline, all of these factors are to some degree related to fertility and are important in attaining a sustained fertility decline. In short, a population program is no substitute for development, but it should be an important component of a development program.

Chapter 5

NOTES

1.   John Knodel and Pichit Pitaktepsombati, "Thailand: Fertility and Family Planning among Rural and Urban Women," Studies in Family Planning, vol. 4, no. 9 (September 1973), pp. 235, 238.

2.   Robin Barlow, "The Economic Effects of Malaria Eradication," American Economic Review, vol. 57 (May 1967, pp. 130–48; Ansley J. Coale and Edgar M. Hoover, Population Growth and Economic Development in Low Income Countries (Princeton: Princeton University Press, 1958); S. Enke, "Economic Aspects of Slowing Population Growth," Economic Journal, vol. 76, no. 30 (March 1966), pp. 95–110.

3.   Kelley concludes that additional children do stimulate work effort in a 1972 analysis of an 1889 survey of workers in the United States, but Bilsborrow concludes from a study of cross-country data that higher dependency rates have negative effects on female labor force participation. Richard Bilsborrow, "Effects of Economic Dependency on Labor Force Participation Rates in Less Developed Countries," unpublished manuscript (February 1974); Allen C. Kelley, "Demographic Changes and American Economic Development: Past, Present, and Future," U.S. Population Commission Reports, vol. II, Economic Aspects of Population Change (Washington, D.C.: U.S. Government Printing Office, 1972).

4.   Richard Bilsborrow, "Fertility, Savings Rates, and Economic Development in Less Developed Countries," in International Union for the Scientific Study of Population, International Population Conference, vol. I (Liege 1973), pp. 445–62.

5.   R.H. Cassen, "Population Growth and Public Expenditure in Developing Countries," in International Union for the Scientific Study of Population, International Population Conference, vol. I (Liege, 1973), pp. 333–50.

6.   For a review of empirical work on determinants of aggregate savings in LDCs, see Raymond F. Mikesell and James E. Zinser, "The Nature of the Savings Function in Developing Countries: A Survey of the Theoretical and Empirical Literature," Journal of Economic Literature, vol. XI, no. 1 (March 1973).

7.   N. Leff, "Dependency Rates and Savings Rates," American Economic Review, vol. 59 (December 1969), pp. 886–96.

8.   Kanhaya L. Gupta, "Dependency Rates and Savings Rates: A Comment," American Economic Review, vol. 61, no. 3, pt. I (June 1971), pp. 469–71.

9. A.C. Kelley, Savings, Demographic Change and Investment, MSS (June 1973).

10. John Isbister, "Birth Control, Income Redistribution, and Saving," Demography, vol. 10, no. 1 (February 1973), pp. 85–98.

11. In both projections, the expectation of life is assumed to increase from 63.1 years in 1970 to 68.0 years in 1980.

12. Exceptions can occur if income levels are so low as to reduce food consumption to the point where fecundity is impaired. R. Frisch and J. MacArthur, "Menstrual Cycles: Fatness as a Determinant of Minimum Height and Weight Necessary for their Maintenance or Onset," Science (13 September 1974). High mortality and rules restricting widow remarriage may lower fertility by reducing the period of exposure to intercourse. Jeanne Clare Ridley et al., "The Effects of Changing Mortality on Natality: Some Estimates from a Simulation Model," Milbank Memorial Fund Quarterly, vol. 45, no. 1, pt. 1 (January 1967). In some developed countries, a U-shaped pattern has emerged, so that the highest and lowest income classes have the highest levels of fertility. Eva M. Bernhardt, "Fertility and Economic Status--Some Recent Findings on Differentials in Sweden," Population Studies, vol. 26, no. 2 (July 1972), pp. 175–84.

13. This is not always the case. For instance, in Sierra Leone a 1969–70 survey revealed the following data for women aged 40–44:

	Live Births	No. of Survivors	% Surviving
Freetown	5.8	4.1	71
Towns	5.2	3.5	67
Villages	8.3	3.9	47

SOURCE: Thomas E. Dow, Jr., "Fertility and Family Planning in Sierra Leone," Studies in Family Planning, vol. 2, no. 8 (August 1971), pp. 153–65.

It should be noted that these data compare urban-rural differences in fertility and not, strictly speaking, differences by income class. In addition, the observed differences in percent surviving reflect differences not only in mortality but in the timing of births. To the extent that village women had births at earlier ages, their children had on average longer exposure to the risks of dying. On the other hand, to the extent that village women had larger numbers of births past age 35, their children have had less exposure to mortality. There are no data to indicate the duration and the extent of bias in the percent-surviving figures.

14. Simon Kuznets, "Quantitative Aspects of the Economic Growth of Nations: VIII, Distribution of Income by Size," Economic Development and Cultural Change, vol. XI, no. 2, pt. 2 (January 1963).

15. The distribution of lifetime income is likely to be somewhat worse than is implied by this crude adjustment. If income increases with age and then begins to decline at some more advanced age, then the lowest income group in a cross-section includes young persons who have not yet experienced fertility and retired persons whose children have left. The former group is larger the more rapid is the rate of increase of the population. Kuznets, "Quantitative Aspects of the Economic Growth," pp. 32-33.

16. T.J. Espenshade, Estimating the Costs of Children and Some Results from Urban United States (Berkeley, Calif.: International Population and Urban Research Center, Univ. of California at Berkeley, 1973).

17. Bilsborrow, "Effects of Economic Dependency on Labor Force."

18. Jan L. Sadie, "Demographic Aspects of Labour Supply and Employment," background paper presented at the World Population Conference (Belgrade, 1965).

19. Joe D. Wray, "Population Pressure on Families: Family Size and Child-Spacing," in National Academy of Sciences, Rapid Population Growth, vol. II (Baltimore: Johns Hopkins Press, 1971), pp. 403-61.

20. Ibid, p. 419.

21. Calculated from Wray, "Popular Pressure on Families," p. 425.

22. See Wray, "Popular Pressure on Families," p. 441, for an evaluation of evidence on these points. The word "Kwashkior" is an African tribal term meaning "the disease of the deposed baby when the next one is born."

23. For a study of the effects of malnutrition on income, see Marcelo Selowsky, "An Attempt to Estimate Rates of Return to Investment in Infant Nutrition Programs," paper presented at the International Conference on Nutrition, Development, and Planning, Massachusetts Institute of Technology, 19-21 October 1971.

24. For analyses of (iii), see Stiglitz and Meade. For models with no differential fertility and an application to the United States, see Blinder. Pryor examines the first seven factors in the context of a simulation model. His analysis may understate the consequences of differential fertility since the level of a couple's fertility in his simulation depends upon relative rather than absolute income.

Allen S. Blinder, "A Model of Inherited Wealth," Quarterly Journal of Economics, vol. 87, no. 4 (November 1973), pp. 608-26.

J.E. Meade, "Life Cycle Savings, Inheritance and Economic Growth," Review of Economic Studies (January 1966).

F.L. Pryor, "Simulation of the Impact of Social and Economic Institutions on the Size Distribution of Income and Wealth," American Economic Review, vol. 63, no. 1 (March 1973), pp. 50-72.

J.E. Stiglitz, "Distribution of Income and Wealth Among Individuals," Econometrica, vol. 37, no. 3 (July 1969), pp. 382-87.

25. Simulation analyses have overlooked the differential age patterns of fertility and nuptiality.

26. T. Paul Schultz, "Determinants of Fertility: A Microeconomic Model of Choice," ed., E.A.G. Robinson, Economic Factors in Population Growth (London: Macmillan, 1975), forthcoming.

27. For an analysis of the effects of mortality on investment in human capital, see Bryan Boulier, "Mortality and the Returns to Investment in Human Capital," 1974, unpublished manuscript. Increased mortality reduces the average returns to investment in human capital and increases the risk or variance of returns.

28. T. Paul Schultz, "Explanation of Birth Rate Changes over Space and Time: A Study of Taiwan," Journal of Political Economy, vol. 82, no. 2, pt. II (March/April 1973), pp. S238-74.

29. Boulier, "Mortality and the Returns to Investment."

30. Barlow, "Economic Effects of Malaria Eradication."

31. Isbister, "Birth Control, Income Redistribution, and Saving."

32. In the short run (up to 15 years), the size of the labor force is essentially unaffected by the reduction in fertility. It may be slightly higher if female labor force participation increases. After 15 years, the size of the labor force is smaller with low fertility. In Isbister's simulation, GNP is the same or slightly higher with low fertility until the year 2010. Thereafter, total GNP is smaller in the low fertility population. In the year 2015, the labor force in the low fertility population is only 76% of the labor force in the high fertility population.

33. For discussions of procedures to calculate births averted by family planning programs, see: Alice S. Clague and Jeanne Clare Ridley, "The Assessment of Three Methods of Estimating Births Averted," ed., Bennett Dyke and Jean Walters MacClure, Computer Simulation in Human Population Studies (New York: Academic Press, Inc., 1974), pp. 329-82; William J. Kelly, A Cost-Effectiveness Study of Clinical Methods of Birth Control: With Special Reference to Puerto Rico (New York: Praeger, 1971); B.M. Lee and J. Isbister, "The Impact of Birth Control Programs on Fertility," ed., B. Berelson et al., Family Planning and Population (Chicago: University of Chicago Press, 1966), pp. 744-47; Robert G. Potter, Jr., "Estimating Births Averted in a Family Planning Program," ed., S.J. Behrman et al., Fertility and Family Planning (Ann Arbor: University of Michigan Press, 1969), pp. 413-34; John A. Ross and J.E. Forrest, "Program Effects Upon Fertility," to appear in Nathan Keyfitz, ed., Statistical Problems in Population; George B. Simmons, The Indian Investment in Family Planning (New York: The Population Council, 1971); D. Wolfers, "The Demographic Effects of a Contraceptive Programme," Population Studies, vol. 23 (1969), pp. 111-40.

34. Calculations are made more difficult for methods other than sterilization by the fact that users of one method may switch to other methods or other sources of supply with the passage of time.

35. Julian L. Simon, "The Value of Avoided Births to Underdeveloped Countries," Population Studies, vol. 23, no. 1 (March 1969), pp. 61-68. Births are discounted since the bonuses paid to avert births would occur in the future. Discounting the number of births is equivalent to discounting the bonus payments.

36. Paul Demeny, "Investment Allocation and Population Growth," Demography, vol. 2 (1965), pp. 203-32.

37. Coition and births are joint products. Contraceptive methods with lower psychic costs reduce the opportunity costs of birth prevention.

38. Comparisons of actual and desired family sizes are difficult to interpret. See Ronald Ridker, "Desired Family Size and Efficiency of Family Planning Programmes," Population Studies, vol. 23, no. 2 (July 1969), pp. 279-84.

Several surveys have shown that the percent of women (and men) who have three or four living children and want no more children is often quite high and is larger than the number who are able to achieve that size. The following tabulation from the KAP Surveys shows the percentage of people in various countries who do not want any more children.

Country, sex	Year	Number of Living Children		Percentage, All Respondents
		3	4	
South Korea, female	1968	54	74	52
Mexico, female (Mexico City)	1963	49	65	65
Niger, female	1970			
Urban		7	11	7
Rural		9	15	9
Philippines, female	1963	56	68	50
Taiwan, female	1962-63	36	63	60
	1970	68	84	63
Thailand, rural	1969-70			
Female		65	75	62
Male		65	76	68

SOURCE: Dorothy Nortman, "Population and Family Planning Programs: A Factbook," Reports on Population/Family Planning, no. 2, 5th ed. (September 1973), pp. 82-83.

39. Marc Nerlove and T. Paul Schultz. Love and Life Between the Censuses: A Model of Family Decision Making in Puerto Rico, 1950-1960, RM-6322-AID, Rand (September 1970); T. Paul Schultz, "Explanation of Birth Rate Changes."

40. Paul Demeny, "The Economics of Population Control," in National Academy of Sciences, Rapid Population Growth, vol. II (Baltimore: Johns Hopkins Press, 1971), pp. 199-221.

41. Ibid. On the other hand, their share of old-age support for their parents is probably reduced.

42. This assumes, of course, that the size of one's family does not enter into the utility function of others.

43. As King notes, this procedure is conservative in the sense that it ignores the fact that the population size changes. Timothy King, "Jamaica Population Project: An Economic Analysis," Seminar paper presented at Princeton University (19 April 1971).

44. If family consumption is switched from nonagricultural goods to agricultural goods as a result of high fertility, and there are indirect business taxes on corporate profits, taxes may be further diminished. See Bilsborrow, "Fertility, Savings Rates, and Economic Development."

45. It should be kept in mind that the argument is not as strong if political power depends upon factors other than sheer numbers. See Eva Mueller, "Economic Motives for Family Limitation," Population Studies, vol. 26, no. 2 (November 1972), pp. 383-403.

46. Demeny, "Economics of Population Control."

47. L. Day, "Natality and Ethnocentrism: Some Relationships Suggested by an Analysis of Catholic-Protestant Differentials," Population Studies, vol. 22, no. 1 (March 1968), pp. 27-50.

48. Myron Weiner, "Political Demography: An Inquiry into the Political Consequences of Population Change," in National Academy of Sciences, Rapid Population Growth, vol. II (Baltimore: Johns Hopkins Press, 1971), pp. 567-617.

49. See Mueller, "Economic Motives for Family Limitation."

50. Insurance of an adequate supply of family labor when morbidity is high is a related motive for having children. This point has been suggested by Mark Perlman.

51. These data are taken from David M. Heer and Dean O. Smith, "Mortality Level, Desired Family Size: Further Variations on a Basic Model," Demography, vol. 6 (1969), pp. 141-49. Assumption of more complex behavior, namely that parents adjust their fertility in response to survival of children already born reduces total fertility and the rate increase. See Stephen Enke and Richard A. Brown, "Old Age Security with Fewer Children," Studies in Family Planning (October 1972); Donald J. O'Hara, "Mortality Risks, Sequential Decisions on Births, and Population Growth," Demography, vol. 9, no. 3 (August 1972), pp. 485-98.

52. See Schultz, "Determinants of Fertility," for a review of the literature.

53. It is plausible to argue that such schemes are essentially a procedure to cope with intra-family externalities, since social security is a bribe by the younger generation to induce the older generation to reduce the number of siblings with whom they must share income and inheritance. For an elaboration of this point, see Richard Blandy, "The Welfare Analysis of Fertility Reduction," Economic Journal, vol. 84, no. 333 (March 1974), pp. 109-29.

54. This division is taken from Demeny, "Economics of Population Control" and also "Welfare Considerations in U.S. Population Policy," in U.S. Commission on Population Growth and the American Future, Aspects of Population Growth Policy, vol. VI of Commission research reports (Washington, D.C.: U.S. Government Printing Office, 1972).

55. Judith Blake, "Coercive Pronatalism and American Population Policy," U.S. Commission on Population Growth and the American Future, Aspects of Population Growth Policy, vol. VI of Commission research reports (Washington, D.C.: U.S. Government Printing Office, 1972).

56. Bernard Berelson, "An Evaluation of the Effects of Population Control Programs," Studies in Family Planning, vol. 5, no. 1 (January 1974), pp. 2-12.

57. For a discussion, see Bernard Berelson, "Beyond Family Planning," Studies in Family Planning, no. 39 (Supplement) (March 1969), pp. 354-85; and Kingsley Davis, "Population Policy: Will Current Programs Succeed?" Science, vol. 158 (10 November 1967), pp. 730-39.

58. R. Lestaeghe, "Nuptiality and Population Growth," Population Studies, vol. 25, no. 3 (November 1971), pp. 415-32.

59. The French schedule for 1966 was assumed.

60. The reduction in nuptiality had a slight advantage in that birth rates declined at a somewhat faster pace.

61. Pi Chao Chen, "China's Birth Control Action Programme, 1956-1964," Population Studies, vol. 24, no. 2 (July 1970), pp. 141-50.

62. Murari Majumdar and Ajit Das Gupta, "Marriage Trends and Their Demographic Implications," Sankhya, ser. B, vol. 31, pt. 3 and 4 (December 1969), pp. 491-500.

63. John Knodel, "Law, Marriage, and Illegitimacy in Nineteenth-Century Germany," Population Studies, vol. 20, no. 3 (March 1967), pp. 279-94.

64. Liberal abortion laws have been passed in the following countries: India (1971), Korea (1973), People's Republic of China (1957), Singapore (1969), Tunisia (1965, 1973), Turkey (1965), and Zambia (1972). For the provisions of the laws of these and other countries, see the excellent survey by Emily Campbell Moore-Cavar, International Inventory of Information on Induced Abortion (New York: International Institute for the Study of Human Reproduction, Columbia University, 1974). The Iranian Parliament also passed a declaration in 1973 permitting abortion for social as well

as medical reasons. Carolyn E. Dean and P.T. Piotrow, "Law and Policy," Population Report, ser. E, no. 1 (George Washington Medical Center, July 1974).

65. See Moore-Cavar, International Inventory on Induced Abortion, for a compilation of data and a discussion of the difficulties of estimating induced abortion.

66. Trussell has estimated for Great Britain that the discounted costs of providing a woman with abortion services over a 15-year period in a family planning clinic are similar to costs of providing the patient with condoms, diaphragms, or orals (about Ł25 in 1972 prices at a discount rate of 15 percent); are cheaper than spermicides (Ł40); and are more expensive than an IUD (Ł13) or a vasectomy for her husband (Ł11). He calculates that the minimum monetary cost of achieving any desired level of effectiveness includes a combination of coitus interruption and abortion. T. James Trussell, "Cost versus Effectiveness of Different Birth Control Methods," Population Studies, vol. 28, no. 1 (March 1974), pp. 85-106.

67. Rolando Armijo and T. Monreal, "The Problem of Induced Abortion in Chile," Milbank Memorial Fund Quarterly, vol. 43, no. 4, pt. 2 (October 1965), pp. 263-80; and Abdel R. Omran, "Abortion in the Demographic Transition," in National Academy of Sciences, Rapid Population Growth, vol. II (Baltimore: Johns Hopkins Press, 1971), p. 506.

68. Bernard Berelson, "World Population: Status Report 1974," Reports on Population/Family Planning, no. 15 (January 1974), p. 40.

69. Ibid, p. 41.

70. The figures cited for India in the text appear to be federal-level expenditures.

71. For India, the figure is 156%. This figure refers to federal-level expenditures, and many health programs are carried out at the state level.

72. Dorothy Nortman, "Population and Family Planning Program," pp. 55-57.

73. Alfred D. Sollins and Raymond L. Belsky, "Commercial Production and Distribution of Contraceptives," Reports on Population/Family Planning, no. 4 (June 1970).

74. T.R. Balakrishnan and R.J. Matthai, "India: Evaluation of Publicity Program on Family Planning," Studies in Family Planning, vol. 12, no. 12 (December 1971) pp. 241-48.

75. J.A. Ross et al., "Findings From Family Planning Research," Reports on Population/Family Planning, no. 12 (October 1972), p. 22.

76. For a bibliography and summary of family planning communications impacts, see Ross et al., "Findings From Family Planning Research," pp. 17-23, 43-44.

77.   E.M. Rogers,"Incentives in the Diffusion of Family Planning Innovations," Studies in Family Planning, vol. 2, no. 12 (December 1971), pp. 241-48.

78.   Ross et al., "Findings From Family Planning Research," p. 26.

79.   Ibid.

80.   Ibid.

81.   A.G. Rosenfield et al., "Thailand: Family Planning Activities 1968-1970," Studies in Family Planning, vol. 2, no. 9 (September 1971), pp. 181-92.

82.   C. Hemachudha et al., Studies in Family Planning, vol. 3, no. 7 (July 1972), pp. 151-56.

83.   Ross et al., "Findings From Family Planning Research," pp. 26-27.

84.   Ibid.

85.   Text of IPPF Central Medical Committee (April 1973) reprinted in T.T. Piotrow and C.M. Lee, "Oral Contraceptives," Population Report, ser. A, no. 1 (April 1974).

86.   Ibid.

87.   At present, in 45 less developed countries responding to a postal survey, no prescription for orals was required in 19 countries. The survey also revealed that "even in countries without a prescription law, commercial pill distribution is still largely confined to licensed pharmacies." Timothy R.L. Black, "Oral Contraceptive Prescription Requirements and Commercial Availability in 45 Countries," Studies in Family Planning, vol. 5, no. 8 (August 1974), pp. 251,253. Given the number and distribution of licensed pharmacies in less developed countries, the distribution network for orals is severely limited.

88.   Anrudh Jain, "Marketing Research in the Nirodh Program," Studies in Family Planning, vol. 4, no. 7 (July 1973), p. 187.

89.   Indian data from the 1971 All-India Survey of Family Planning Practices show the following percentage distribution of condom users and users of terminal methods:

	Current Users		
	Terminal Methods	Condoms	All Couples
Wife's education			
Illiterate	66	40	79
Primary	16	19	11
Secondary	17	35	9
College	1	6	1
Family income (rupees)			
Below 100	32	11	39
101-200	31	29	36
201-500	26	38	19
501-1000	8	14	4
1,000 or more	3	8	2

SOURCE: Jain, "Marketing Research in the Nirodh Program," table 7, p. 189.

90. This phrase is due to Berelson in "Beyond Family Planning."

91. C.N. Wang and S.Y. Chen, "Evaluation of the First Year of the Educational Savings Program," Studies in Family Planning, vol. 4, no. 7 (July 1973), pp. 157-67. Social and economic variables were not predictors enrollment.

92. Total costs per acceptor (including incentives) were estimated to be Rs. 145 per vasectomy and Rs. 166 per female sterilized. Benefits were estimated at Rs. 950 per birth averted, and a benefit-cost ratio of 9 to 1 has been cited for the project. There are insufficient data to evaluate these estimates.

93. The reported income distribution of acceptors was:

(Rupees)	%
Less than 500	14.8
500-999	30.0
1,000-1,499	19.7
1,500-1,999	15.4
2,000-2,499	10.2
More than 2,500	10.8
Not available	.1

94. Julian Simon, The Effects of Income on Fertility (Chapel Hill, N. Car." Carolina Population Center, 1974).

95. Ibid, p. 102.

96. Rogers, 1971; Ross et al., "Findings From Family Planning Researc

97. This section draws heavily from Ridker, "Proposal for a Family Planning Bond."

98. The choice between current and deferred payment depends upon the confidence which couples have that they will be paid in the future. Large current payments are "more costly, open to misuse, and open to the charge that it smacks of bribery." Ridker, "Proposal for a Family Planning Bond," p. 14.

99. R.L. Clinton, "Opposition to Population Limitation in Latin America: Some Implications for U.S. Policy," ed., R.L. Clinton and R.K. Godwin, Research in the Politics of Population (Lexington, Mass.: Lexington Books, 1972), pp. 95-112.

100. Ibid, p. 100.

101. Ibid.

Chapter 5

BIBLIOGRAPHY

Agarawala, S.N. Age at Marriage in India. Allhabad: Kital Mihab
   Private, Ltd.

Arriage, Eduardo. "The Effect of a Decline in Mortality on the Gross
   Reproduction Rate." Milbank Memorial Fund Quarterly 45:3:1
   (July 1967): 333-52.

Berg, Alan. The Nutrition Factor: Its Role in National Development.
   Washington, D.C.: The Brookings Institution, 1973.

Bogue, Donald J. "Population Perspectives: Some Views from a Sociolo-
   gist." Population Dynamics Quarterly 2:2 (Spring 1974): 2,20.

Boserup, E. The Conditions of Agricultural Growth. Chicago: Aldine,
   1965.

Châu, Ta Ngoc. Population Growth and Costs of Education in Developing
   Countries. Paris: UNESCO, Institute for Educational Planning, 1972.

Clark, Colin. Population Growth and Land Use. New York: St. Martin's
   Press, 1967.

Corsa, Leslie, Jr., and Oakley, Deborah. "Consequences of Population
   Growth for Health Services in Less Developed Countries - An Initial
   Appraisal." In National Academy of Sciences, Rapid Population Growth II
   Baltimore: Johns Hopkins Press, 1971: 362-403.

Davidson, M. "A Comparative Study of Fertility in Mexico City and
   Caracas." Social Biology 20:4 (December 1973): 460-72.

Dipti Das, Kum. "Inter-State Variations in the Cost-Effectiveness of
   Family Planning During 1969-1970." Journal of Family Welfare 18:2
   (December 1971): 55-69.

Ebanks, G.E. "Social and Demographic Characteristics of Family Planning
   Clients in Barbados." Social and Economic Studies 18:4 (December 1969):
   391-401.

Finningan, Oliver D., and Sun, T.H. "Planning, Starting, and Operating
   an Educational Incentives Project." Studies in Family Planning 3:1
   (January 1972):1-7.

Hickman, Bryan D. Economic Incentives: A Strategy for Family Planning
   Programs. Santa Barbara, Calif.: General Electric Company - TEMPO
   (October 1972).

Jones, Gavin W. "Effect of Population Change on the Attainment of Educational Goals in the Developing Countries." In National Academy of
   Sciences, Rapid Population Growth II. Baltimore, Johns Hopkins Press:
   1971: 315-67.

Kee, Wan Fook and Tee, Quah Siam. "Singapore: A Cost-Effect Analysis of a Family Planning Program." Studies in Family Planning, 3:1 (January 1972): 8-11.

Keeny, S.M., ed. "East Asia Review, 1973." Studies in Family Planning 5:5 (May 1974).

King, Timothy. "Budgetary Aspects of Population Policy: The Role of Benefit-Cost Analysis," In International Union for the Scientific Study of Population, International Population Conference 1 (Liege, 1973): 365-76.

Krishnakumar, S. "Ernakulem's Third Vasectomy Campaign Using the Camp Approach." Studies in Family Planning 5:2 (February 1974): 58-61.

Marckwardt, Alan. "Findings from Family Planning Research: Latin American Supplement." Reports on Population/Family Planning 12 (Supplement), (June 1973).

Ohlin, Goran. "Population and Alternative Investments." In International Union for the Scientific Study of Population, International Population Conference, London 1969 (Liege, 1971): 1703-28.

Osteria, Trinidad S. "A Cost-Effectiveness Analysis of Family Planning Programs in the Philippines." Studies in Family Planning 4:7 (July 1973): 191-95.

Piotrow, Phyllis. World Population Crisis-the United States Response. New York: Praeger, 1973.

Requena, M., and Monreal, T. "Evaluation of Induced Abortion Control and Family Planning Programs in Chile." Milbank Memorial Fund Quarterly 46:3:2 (July 1968): 191-222.

Robinson, W.C., and Horlacher, D.E. "Population Growth and Economic Welfare." Reports on Population/Family Planning 6 (February 1971).

Rutstein, Shea Oscar. "The Infuence of Child Mortality on Fertility in Taiwan." Studies in Family Planning 5:6 (June 1974): 182-88.

Yaukey, David. Marriage Reduction and Fertility. Lexington, Mass.: D.C. Heath and Company, 1973.

CHAPTER VI

WAGE POLICY AND INCOME DISTRIBUTION IN DEVELOPING COUNTRIES

Richard Webb

In the House of Commons on Thursday, Mr. Moore on presenting a petition
from the ribbon and silk weavers of Coventry, moved for leave to bring in
a Bill for increasing the present low prices of manufacture. Mr. Moore
stated that workmen were divided into five classes, all working 16 hours
a day, or 96 hours a week. The first class did not earn more than 10s.
a week, being about 2-1/2d. for every two hours of the hardest kind of
labor; the second class earned 5s.6d. a week; the third 3s.9d.; the fourth
2s.; the fifth 18d. or about 3d. for 12 hour's labor. The motion being
generally opposed, Mr. Moore withdrew it. (From The Observer, Monday,
17 May 1819.)[1]

The Child Care Center will give free attention to maternity cases
and to babies, for employees up to class 40 on the attached table, as
well as their respective dependents. (Clause 16 of the 1959 Collective
Agreement with Workers' Union at the Volta Redonda Steel Works in Brazil.)[2]

A. Introduction

The stark contrast between the world of the Coventry ribbon weaver in

1819 and that of the Volta Redonda Steel worker in 1959 cannot be attributed

to general economic development in Brazil; in 1959 about half of the Bra-

zilian population lived on annual incomes of between U.S.$50 and $100.[3]

Nor can it be imputed solely to an improvement in labor and welfare legis-

lation. At the San Pedro sugar plantation in Northeast Brazil, for instance,

"Two-thirds of the heads of households made less than the legally established

minimum daily wage ... which was then approximately U.S.$0.90. ... Three-

NOTE: I am particularly grateful to Charles Frank, Jr., with whom I jointly
developed the outline and main ideas for this chapter. Helpful comments
and suggestions were also provided by John Eriksson, Arnold Harberger,
Peter Thormann, Henry Bruton, and Richard Sandbrook. I received considerable research assistance from Carl Dahlman, Doris Garvey and Louka
Papaefstratiou. The views expressed in this chapter are my own and should
not be ascribed to the World Bank or to its affiliated institutions.

quarters of the heads of families were illiterates; 83 percent of the children of school age were not going to school."[4] Yet, 80 percent of the heads of households were union members.[5] Despite minimum wage laws, an officially recognized union, and a relatively large firm (about 2,000 workers), the average income of farm workers at San Pedro was $0.50 a day.[6]

These contrasts--both over time, and within one poor country--raise questions regarding the actual and the desirable contribution of wage policy. Clearly these contrasts are the joint result of greatly changed labor policies (along with underlying attitudes--in part, a demonstration effect of developed countries) and of a different, much more dualistic structure of economic growth.

On first examination, wage policy appears central to any redistributive program. Most inequality in poor countries can be broken down into that between capitalists and workers, and that within labor--the labor "elite" versus the rest of the labor force. The obvious redistributive approach is to level wages, and raise them at the expense of capital income. Also, since many of the rural poor are part- or full-time wage earners, any attack on rural poverty will eventually mean raising rural wage levels. Thus, it is hardly surprising that wage increases are the most familiar feature of redistributive political programs.

Yet there is a broad consensus among economists that wage increases are, by and large, "the easy solution" but a "most unfortunate"[7] approach to income redistribution in LDCs. This generally negative attitude toward wage increases is supported by three different arguments: such pressure is held to be (i) futile, because for most of the labor force, and in the long run, market forces will dominate; (ii) inequitable, because it benefits a relatively small "middle-income" group rather than the mass of the poor; and (iii) harmful, because it reduces employment by increasing capital-intensity in the modern sector and slows growth by reducing savings. There is, of course, an inconsistency between the futility and the bad-effects arguments, but each may be valid in different situations.

This chapter is a review of the arguments and the evidence regarding the impact of wage policy on income distribution in LDCs. Following this introduction, the impact of wage policy on income distribution will be traced by examining policy formulation (section B); policy implementation, particularly as it is constrained by market structures (section C); and the direct impact of policy on the wage levels of target groups (section D).

Direct effects on current wage levels are only half the story of wage policy. Wage changes have indirect consequences throughout the economic system. The most important of those repercussions are those which affect factor choice and employment absorption in the modern sector, and those which affect growth. These repercussions have distributive effects which, in the long run, may be more significant than the current redistributive potential of wage policies. This chapter, however, deals only with direct impact; the indirect impact is discussed in both the income distribution model contained in chapter 2 by Frank and Webb, and in Bruton's analysis of trade and industrialization policies in chapter 3. Also, rural wage policy is not dealt with here. Though the principal target group for distributive policy is the rural poor, many of whom are chiefly wage earners, most wage policy, in practice, is directed at urban and modern-sector workers. This omission is compensated to some extent by the discussion of farm productivity strategies and of rural employment creation through public works in chapters 8 and 9 by Cline and Lewis, respectively.

Wage policy is defined here as being aimed at either (i) raising, (ii) maintaining, or (iii) lowering the market wage that would obtain in the absence of government wage measures. In this sense, policies can be described as being pro-labor, neutral, or pro-capital.[8] "Government measures" referred to here primarily mean current measures, since today's "market" wage is obviously partly determined by the history of government acts that have helped to shape the institutional setting of today's market structures. Second, "wage measures" are defined here more broadly than is usual in that they include direct wage-setting, institutional or legal changes (such as strike laws) that indirectly affect wage outcomes, and administrative partiality in the application of rules that affect collective bargaining outcomes. Other aspects of labor policy, such as social security laws and the effects of job security laws on the choice of technologies, are discussed only briefly here. Finally, policy refers to intent rather than outcome.

B. Policy formulation

1. Variables

The choice of wage policy is complicated by the variety of (i) policy objectives, (ii) target groups, and (iii) policy instruments involved.

Wage policy is relevant to at least four separate political and economic goals: equity, growth, price stability, and political stability.
This chapter is concerned with the first, but wage policies are in practice
formulated with these several ends in mind. Furthermore, each of these
objectives may require wages to rise or to fall in different circumstances.
Two basic target groups will be studied: modern- and traditional-sector[9]
wage earners, since policy must allow for the very different market characteristics and usually different income situations of each. Finally, a
major concern of wage policy is with differentials between various categories of workers such as skilled and unskilled, white- and blue-collar,
and with regional and racial categories; again, wage policy may seek to
increase or reduce those differentials.

Wage policy is implemented through a particularly broad and varied set
of instruments. These operate on two levels. The first involves intervention, both administrative and legal, in the current wage-determination
process. It includes the normal decisions regarding government employee
pay scales and the occasional direct wage-setting for the private sector,
particularly during rapid inflation. It includes the greater or lesser
government participation in the setting of minimum wages, and in collective
bargaining, usually through tripartite boards. Finally, it includes the
administrative and judicial implementation of labor and price legislation.

Wage policy also operates at a second level by modifying the wage-
determination environment, namely the institutional and legal framework,
and the economic structure of labor markets. The most obvious of such
changes consists of legislation regulating union activity--the legal status
of unions, whether and when strikes are allowed, whether and how union
funds can be collected, job security for union leaders and strikers, and
so on. Less obviously, government can affect market outcomes by changing
the structural characteristics of the market in ways that affect the degree
of competition. Tariff protection, for instance, creates monopoly rents
that invite wage increases. Conversely, export-promoting policies will
make the business sector more cost conscious; exporters are less able to
pass on wage increases by raising prices.

One effect of this two-tiered influence on wages is that it makes wage
policy more flexible. A government that is sympathetic to labor, for instan
can make basic changes in the rules of collective bargaining to favor labor
in future negotiations and simultaneously hold down wages to meet immediate

stabilization or growth targets. Second, it becomes more difficult to know what a government is actually doing--whether its actions are biased toward raising or lowering wages--since it can be moving in different directions at these two levels. Third, changes in the institutional and economic environment of collective bargaining tend to outlast the particular bias of the regime or regime period. The history of labor policy in most countries records a series of legislative advances in favor of labor. Such advances have tended to cumulate with a ratchet effect despite political vicissitudes, because legislative reversals have required major political shifts against labor.

2. Policy choice

Wage policies seem to cluster around three main approaches which can be described respectively as (i) the low-wage policy, (ii) the industrial consensus approach, and (iii) the pro-modern-sector labor approach aimed at evolutionary political radicalization. Contrary to most preconceptions, high-wage policies aimed primarily at redistribution are the exception. Each of these approaches is consistent with particular economic settings and political priorities. Elements of each may be found at any one time in a given country. The combination of a pluralist government with a policy that can be implemented through several instruments lends itself to confused political sharing, where each view regarding that policy can appear to be satisfied to some extent--like a boat with several rudders being steered simultaneously by several captains. Policy intent is easier to define when only one major instrument is available. Thus, there is no such easy way of appearing to satisfy opposite views on the relative priority of mass rural schooling; the schools are either built or not.

The ambiguity of labor policy results from the variety of instruments that are relevant to wage levels and that may easily operate in conflicting directions. Ambiguity also results from the <u>continuous</u> nature of labor policy-making: wage levels are being decided continuously by the joint influence of market and government forces so that governments can easily modify, and even reverse over short periods, the intensity and direction of their intervention, especially, of course, in inflationary environments. Finally, complications arise from the dual function of wages--they are simultaneously a distributive objective and a key instrument for other objectives such as stability and overall growth.

Despite such identification difficulties, it is possible to find cases where policy appears to be dominated by a stress on low wages, or on collective bargaining (consensus), or on the institutional reinforcement of organized (and "organizable") labor. There is surely a correlation between the political strength of a regime and the choice between these wage policy alternatives.

The low-wage approach is the orthodox policy preference of economists. It aims principally at keeping modern-sector wages low but is not inconsistent with (low) minimum wages that would prevent "exploitation" and provide a welfare floor to the very poor. It is advocated on grounds of both growth and equity. Most economists would still subscribe to the argument that savings are likely to be higher in a low-wage, high-profits economy either because of the nature of savings propensities of workers and capitalists or because profit income is easier to tax. This traditional argument for low wages is now reinforced by the employment and equity case against "high-wage islands."[10] On the other hand, this line of economic reasoning, i.e., low wages to encourage rapid, labor-absorbing modern-sector growth, leads to acceptance of skill, occupational, and even regional wage differentials required to draw labor into high-productivity activities.[11] Acceptance of such differentials, which may at times be large and growing,[12] weakens the short-run equity case for this approach but it can be argued that the more important result for the poor is that employment absorption into the modern sector is accelerated and, therefore, that poverty is reduced more rapidly.

It seems obvious, however, that only strong governments can adopt a low-wage policy. Such a policy seems to require more than government neutrality; it usually involves active suppression. Part of the reason lies in the well-known organizational and tactical resources of modern-sector labor, and part of the reason has to do with legitimacy. Of all redistributive claims, wage demands surely have the highest degree of moral legitimacy. For most people "justice" is primarily "desert," or receiving what one has produced. The notion of equal sharing, or sharing based on need, is a more abstract and less powerful mover of men. Because wage demands are a claim to the fruits of one's own labor, they have a degree of legitimacy that is not enjoyed, for instance, by the appeal for higher agricultural prices, or for larger public expenditures in rural areas.[13] Strong alternative moral claims can be used to offset wage demands

Such claims are provided, for instance, by the highly egalitarian content of
Cuban and Chinese policies, and by the Arusha Declaration that provided the
basis for the 1967 reversal of wage policy in Tanzania. National emergen-
cies, such as those created by war or risk of war, can be another substitute.
They surely gave some legitimacy to anti-union policies in South Korea and
Taiwan, thus easing somewhat the degree of repression applied in these
countries. Failing such powerful moral substitutes, however, low-wage
policies generally require considerable repression of the natural political
power of modern-sector labor.

The industrial consensus approach is most identified with collective
bargaining, which minimizes government participation, but it includes the
corporate approach to wage determination where government comes close to
direct wage-setting. The common element is a largely politically motivated
stress on consensus, on industrial peace. The guiding economic principle
for wage settlements of this approach is capacity to pay.

The collective bargaining approach has been the standard policy
prescription of the ILO and of many labor economists.[14] It places priority
on the development of a balanced, smooth-running, industrial relations
machinery with the double objective of minimizing government "interference"
in labor markets and either minimizing or institutionalizing industrial
conflict. The wage outcome is given less importance than the procedure;
or else, it is argued or presumed that an efficient labor market will generate the "best" wage outcome. Because balanced bargaining forces are an
essential ingredient in this approach, and because labor has traditionally
been organizationally weaker than business, the collective bargaining
approach has generally stressed the institutional reinforcement of labor.
Perhaps more important than the wage outcome, however, is the political
attractiveness of a wage-determination process that minimizes both labor
conflict and government input.

Though the preference for collective bargaining is largely independent
of any desired wage outcome, in practice it is commonly associated with
what is close to a golden rule for wage determination: wages should rise
in line with productivity. There is a presumption that "balanced" collective bargaining will tend to produce this outcome, and that such an outcome
is socially just and efficient.

Liberal and anti-communist ideologies have also contributed to the widespread avowal, if not adoption, of collective bargaining as a wage-determination process. The ILO, AID, and AIFLD[15] have reinforced these ideologies through recommendations, training programs, and financial support for non-communist unions.[16] These ideologies have generated support for pro-labor policies that consist of institutional reinforcement, but they have inhibited wage planning and direct wage determination by government.

Few governments do not officially subscribe to the principle of collective bargaining as the desirable mode of wage-determination. In practice, however, a stress on collective bargaining remains a model or ideal for most LDCs. The rule is greater or lesser government involvement ranging from unagressive participation in tripartite wage boards to almost direct wage-setting through highly detailed regulations of most working conditions and strong pressures to force settlements and accept government mediation.

The former pattern, or less government participation, is likely to characterize weaker governments, while the latter pattern is found in countries with strong corporatist, nationalist ideologies. In weaker governments it is often harder to identify any dominant wage policy approach at all because competing groups simultaneously pursue different policies, most notoriously in inflationary settings: pro-labor factions obtain large wage increases while pro-business groups block price and profit controls. Government implementation of labor market rules and mediation in disputes may be highly erratic and inconsistent with regard to its bias. A natural political defense in such settings is to proclaim the ideological virtues of collective bargaining, and to allow the stronger market forces, by and large, to win out, despite the existence of official wage targets for stabilization and growth purposes.

A strong preference for political stability, and therefore for industrial peace, has characterized governments with corporatist and national ideologies. The populist ideology of Kemal Ataturk, for instance, stressing absolute unity of the Turkish people, was accompanied by a rejection of class conflict and class-based organizations. His prohibition of unions and stress on public arbitration may be interpreted as a low-wage, rather than neutral, collective bargaining attitude, but the intention seems to have been strongly oriented toward ensuring consensus rather than imposing a pro-business wage policy.[17]

Mexican wage policy during most of the period since 1910 has been similarly concerned with avoiding the political instability created by class conflict,[18] via the incorporation of labor into the ruling party power structure and through a wage policy strongly guided by the ability-to-pay criterion.[19] A striking example of a corporatist attempt to eliminate class conflict through legislation on profit sharing and wage-determination is provided by the recent Industrial and Social Property Laws of Peru. Publication of these laws was accompanied by explicit reference to the expected elimination of class conflict.[20]

The third policy approach, favoring modern-sector labor organization, is a straightforward political strategy. This does not refer simply to vote-buying wage increases but to the longer-run strategy aiming at eventual transfer of power to labor as a whole, a strategy which accepts the necessity and feasibility of beginning with the more easily organized and potentially powerful modern-sector workers. The underlying presumption is that strengthening the political power of modern-sector labor will indeed make possible a next step involving transfer of power to traditional-sector workers.

A paradoxical result is that political groups on the left, who are presumably most concerned with equity, find themselves defending measures that favor modern-sector workers and which are likely to hurt the very poor, at least pending the day that a revolutionary transfer of power becomes possible. Another implication of this approach is that, if successful, it is self-liquidating: once a socialist regime has been established, the goals of equity and rapid growth take precedence, and they necessarily require the retraction of privileges previously given to modern-sector labor.

A common pattern in many developing countries has consisted of a switch from an early, largely politically motivated support for labor to greater emphasis on an incomes policy and on wage restraint. This was noted, for instance, by Arthur Lewis, who wrote: "Recognition of the connection between wages and employment has opened up a gulf between trade-union leaders and political leaders in new states, especially where government is the chief employer of labor, or is concerned about the adverse effects of high wages on exports, import-substitution and employment, or even prefers high profits to high wages because it can tax profits more easily than wages. Governments have therefore begun to think in terms of an incomes policy."[21]

The above discussion has treated wage policy formulation as if it were guided solely by long-run economic and political objectives. To a considerable extent, however, wage policy has been the product of short-run stabilization needs. Continuing instability has converted successive short-run wage targets into the ex post long-run wage policy. The standard wage prescriptions of stabilization programs are wage restraint and the golden rule, i.e., wage gains limited to productivity increases. Stabilization goals of themselves, however, have rarely been the basis for the imposition of a long-run low-wage policy. For one thing, the belt-tightening required by stabilization programs is generally sold by alleging a relatively balanced or equitable contraction of incomes; this opens the way to prompt readjustments when wages fall too far behind other incomes. Also, the recessions that often accompany stabilization efforts create an incentive to raise wages as a quick way to increase aggregate demand. In Chile and Argentina, such readjustments have accompanied the continuing and cyclical course of inflation over the last two to three decades. In the second place, stabilization targets commonly enshrine the "wage increase equal to productivity gains" rule which runs counter to the stricter rules of a low-wage policy. Stabilization income targets therefore tend to produce long-run wage outcomes similar to those of a smooth-running collective bargaining machinery, despite sharp, short-run fluctuations in real wages.

The basic wage policy alternatives described above are complicated in practice by other considerations. The standard growth and employment argument for low wages, for example, has at times been challenged by the "need for a large internal market" argument. One form of this argument is that which asserts that consumption by profit recipients has a higher import and capital content and, therefore, that a redistribution of income to wage earners will lessen pressure of the foreign exchange and capital constraints, thereby permitting faster growth.[22] This view reinforced the redistributive intent of wage and price policies of the Allende regime during 1970-71. So drastic a redistribution would not have been attempted on political or equity grounds alone: they were supported by a conviction that wage gains would accelerate industrial growth.[23] The internal market argument, along with preventive politics, has also been cited as a factor in the switch in South African wage policy for Black wage earners. After a deliberate policy decision in 1957, the Wage Board began to enforce wage readjustments that led to an average two to three percent annual increase in real wages between 1957-58 to 1966, though wages for Whites have been rising even faster.[24] A similar mix of preventive political relaxation, with a concern for an adequate domestic market, may have contributed to the relaxation of the severe low-wage policy followed in Brazil between 1965 and 1968-69.

Another basic element in the choice of wage policies concerns minimum wages. The general acceptance of non-intervention in labor markets is reversed with reference to minimum wages: the state is commonly expected, and often constitutionally required,[25] to ensure that its citizens at least survive. Over the last two decades minimum-wage legislation has become generalized, though only recently in many countries. Thus, the first national minimum wage laws in Peru were legislated during 1964-65; in Honduras a general system of minimum wages was established only this year. The issue regarding minimum wages has become less their existence than their level and, particularly, the extent of adaptation to existing regional-sectoral wage differentials. Considerable adaptation, which amounts to acceptance of a capacity-to-pay criterion, is the rule; less frequent is imposition of uniform rates based on "need," either nationally or for broadly defined regions. In India, for instance, despite an egalitarian orientation and the constitutional requirement of a "living wage," the Supreme Court has repeatedly upheld the principle of regional-sectoral differentials in minimum wage rates, and the resulting differentials appear to exceed regional cost of living variations.[26]

Immediate distributive considerations are necessarily in the forefront of day-to-day decisions regarding wage claims. Governments directly affect the income distribution each time they legislate or decree wage rates or benefits, or mediate in disputes, or refuse to mediate. Yet the choice between the major alternative wage policies that underlie daily decisions appears to be much less a statement of distributive preference than a response to other, often more pressing economic and political goals. Since growth is the primary concern of many, if not most, of those governments (on both the left and the right) that are not entirely absorbed in day-to-day political survival, it seems fortunate that a low-wage policy appears to be best for both growth and poverty reduction. However, where equity is not a major objective of the low-wage policy, other necessary conditions for achieving both rapid and labor-absorbing growth such as the underpricing of capital to large enterprises and policy biases in favor of

the capital-intensive heavy industries, may not be met.[27] Where this
happens, low wages may hurt the poor in both the short and long run.

Likewise, redistribution is not the primary consideration leading
governments to stress collective bargaining as a wage policy, or even to
adopt pro-labor policies when those measures are limited to modern-sector
wage earners. In both cases, the objectives are more immediate and are
primarily political. Moreover, in practice, both discriminate in favor
of modern-sector labor, either deliberately, or indirectly by rigging the
market in such a way that wage rates are strongly influenced by capacity
to pay. These implications of wage policy choices are developed in the
sections on policy implementation and policy impact.

C.   Policy implementation and market structures

The distributive impact of wage policy depends as much on the manner in
which it is implemented as on the basic direction of policy. Furthermore,
policy acts on, and through, an economic structure. This section will discuss some characteristics, first, of wage policy implementation and second,
of labor markets, that have a bearing on how policies affect wages.

1.   Policy implementation

The distance between laws and implementation is often great.[28] However, this gap is not necessarily a measure of frustration. In the first
place, ambitious legal targets are commonly in advance of expected and
even intended short- and medium-run implementation. "The function of the
written law in some of the Latin American countries is sometimes more
educational than normative..."[29] More importantly, legal comprehensiveness
and complexity combined with traditions of weak judiciaries and of greater
state involvement in wage-determination give executives more opportunity
for discriminatory application of the law. "Labor law in (Latin America)
is extremely complex and regulates virtually every aspect of worker
activity. For administrative and political reasons, its provisions are
often selectively or arbitrarily applied."[30] The institutional and legal
frameworks inherited by a particular regime (be they defensive or suppres-
sive of labor) are only a partial constraint on current preferences. An
illustration of the strength of administrative action vis-a-vis the law
is seen in the growth of the labor movement in Colombia under President
Alfonso Lopez (1934-38). "The growth of unionism after 1931...is not the

result of legislative recognition of the right of laborers to organize
Colombia. Rather, the development of the labor movement in this period
can be accredited, in large measure, to the informal support which the
executive branch of the government gave unionism and to the manner in which
that executive interpreted the law....For example, the government mediation
of labor-management disputes often consisted of executive pressure on
companies to bargain and give concessions, and the initiative for the
creation of unions often came directly from the labor office."[31]

The effect of inflation on the flexibility of wage policy is hard to
evaluate. Certainly real wages often move sharply over short periods.
Even in Chile, with its long experience of continuous inflation, annual
growth in real wages between 1960 and 1970 ranged from -8.7% (1962-63)
to +15.5% (1966-67).[32] This is not proof that _permanent_ wage adjustments
are more easily made under inflation, but it suggests, at least, that
inflation makes it easier to put a foot in the door when a permanent redistribution is intended, as in Brazil after 1964. A contrary argument,
however, is that inflation raises awareness of distributive gains and
losses caused by price and wage movements, and increases pressure on the
state to intervene in defense of group interests. As a result, the government may lose some of its power to pursue either a given wage target or a
collective bargaining "hands off" wage strategy.

A second characteristic of policy implementation concerns coverage.
This point ties in closely with the dual nature of labor markets, discussed below, and it may be considered a special case of the point made
above concerning laws versus practice. It is well-known that the degree
of enforcement of labor laws is much higher in large firms, and in urban
areas. This is true over and above the frequent explicit legal discrimination between large and small firms: thus unionization is usually restricted
to firms having a certain number of employees.[33] Labor inspectorates
appear to be administrative Cinderellas relegated by both low-wage and pro-
labor regimes, since the latter concentrate on either major wage agreements
or on the creation of new unions rather than on policing existing legislation. Despite its advanced labor legislation, the Chilean Labor Inspection
Department in 1966 had only one vehicle, and a staff that could scarcely
cope with routine inspections.[34] And despite the authoritarian regime of
Guatemala, it is widely believed in that country that labor inspectors can
venture into many rural areas only at the risk of their lives. Two possible

measures of the degree of discrimination in the enforcement of wage laws against workers in small firms, and against farmworkers in general, would be first, the number of small-firm workers receiving less than the minimum wage, and second, the proportion of the rural labor force that legally could be, but is not, unionized.

The substantial discrimination that generally characterizes enforcement of labor laws cannot be attributed entirely to the nature of implementation. Discriminatory enforcement has two components. One is indeed a departure from the announced or legislated policy intent that can be explained partly as an administrative failure but mostly as an accommodation to differential feasibility of enforcement, since laws and administrative systems rarely admit or provide for the differential costs of enforcement. A second and perhaps major component of discriminatory enforcement, however, cannot really be called a "slippage" at the level of implementation but is rather a deliberate administrative expression of a wage policy that wishes to give due allowance to the capacity to pay. In other words, to a large extent, enforcement is not intended for much of the small-scale and rural sector, despite the all-embracing language of legislation. This blurs the distinction between policy choice and its implementation, but there is surely an element of both administrative bias or slippage in enforcement and unwritten discriminatory intent in policy as it is implemented

This distinction is not academic. To the extent that discriminatory enforcement is really unwritten policy (i.e., there is a majority consensus within government on its desirability or necessity, given market or administrative constraints) then a change in policy output, e.g., more widespread enforcement of minimum wage laws, would require more than reprimands and/or additional budgetary support for labor inspectors. It requires a change in policy. One of the first acts of President Lopez Michelson of Colombia, for instance, was to suspend a majority of the government's labor inspectors on the grounds that the widespread payment of wages below the legal minimum was prima facie evidence of supervisory failure.[36] To have imposed a radically tighter supervision, however, would have amounted to a change in policy and would have required substantial support within the Lopez government, rather than a simple administrative improvement. Of course, such a change in policy requires also that broader supervision is not offset by a more disciminatory evolution of the structure of minimum rates, i.e., by the extent to which the previously unwritten law becomes written law.

2.   Market structure,

Market structures in developing countries impose two substantial constraints on wage policies: first, they severely limit the reach of such policies; and, second, they create upward wage pressures within modern sectors.

a)   Coverage of wage policies

The redistributive potential of wage policies is limited first by the relatively large self-employed component of the labor force. Table 1 shows that in most developing countries the self-employed make up about half or more of the active population. The share of employees in the total labor force is lower in the poorer countries and tends to rise as countries develop. Wage policies can obviously benefit or hurt the self-employed indirectly, chiefly through modern-sector employment and growth effects,[37] but the potential redistributive impact of wage policies on the self-employed is comparatively slow, small, and one-sided in that the policies more easily hurt than help the self-employed.

In practice, however, the relevant limitation on coverage is the size of the urban and modern component of the wage-earning sector, i.e., firms where wages and working conditions can in fact be controlled. The enforceability of pro-labor policies declines rapidly with the size of firm and is lower in rural than in urban areas. In agriculture, the size-threshold of enforceability is a much larger firm than in the urban sector and is enormously complicated by the prevalence of seasonal employment, "piece rates," particularly in harvesting, and pay in kind. The threshold of enforceability will vary with the government's administrative effectiveness and with the particular instrument involved, e.g., minimum wages are more broadly enforced than are compulsory pension schemes. Finally, the degree of unionization, and particularly the strength of industrial or occupational rather than enterprise unions, will also affect the margin of enforcement. Nevertheless, the major determinants of enforceability are size and urban presence.

For the bulk of that large class of employees working in small, labor-intensive and more mobile establishments, a majority of whom live in small towns or rural areas, pro-labor wage policies are not enforced. The illusion of enforcement is often created by minimum-wage systems that discriminate by industry and region and that in practice essentially ratify

Table 1. Structure of Labor Force[a] in Some Developing Countries
(percentage of total labor force)

Country	(1) Census Year[b,c]	(2) Total Employees	(3) Nonfarm Employees	(4) Modern-Sector Employees[d]
Argentina	1960	70	61	na
Uruguay	1963	71	61	na
Chile	1970 (1960)	70 (73)	57 (54)	(27)
Venezuela	1961	61	50	28
China (Taiwan)	1966 (1956)	53 (37)	50 (31)	na
Brazil	1970	55	43	na
Mexico	1970 (1960)	62 (64)	43 (35)	na
Panama	1960	48	40	21
Costa Rica	1963	66	40	na
Colombia	1964	57	37	18
Iran	1966	48	37	16
Ceylon	1963	65	36	na
Egypt	1966 (1960)	54 (49)	34 (30)	(20)
Algeria	1966	68	33	na
Peru	1961	48	32	18
Iran	1956	46	30	na
W. Malaysia	1957	56	30	na
Korea	1966 (1960)	32 (22)	27 (18)	16
Ecuador	1962	47	26	na
Morocco	1960	38	25	na
Philippines	1960	29	22	na
Indonesia	1971	32	17	na
Ghana	1960	21	15	8
India	1971 (1961)	17 (30)[e]	16 (12)	(6)
Turkey	1960	19	14	6
Thailand	1970 (1960)	13 (12)	11 (9)	(5)
Pakistan	1961	20	10	6[f]
Nepal	1961	16	3	

[a]Unemployed and persons seeking first employment were subtracted from labor force totals in most countries.

[b]Bracketed figures correspond to the earlier census.

c
Data on government and domestic employees were directly from the
census of the respective countries except for Egypt where an estimate
made by Doctor and Gallis, "Size Characteristics of Wage Employment in
Africa: Some Statistical Estimates," International Labour Review, vol. 93,
no. 2 (February 1966), p. 170 was used.

d
The basic criterion for "modern-sector" status was size of firm.
Since size was not known in many cases, common sense approximations were
used. Thus, nonagricultural employees from column 3 were broken down by
broad industrial category (ISIC 1-9). The employees in each category were
then classified as modern or traditional using the following methodology-
ISIC 1: mining: all modern; ISIC 2-3: manufacturing: modern = employees
in enterprises above a given size (this was usually 5 or 10 workers, but
for India it was 20 for industries not using power, for Ghana it was 30,
and for Venezuela it was the reporting firms); ISIC 4: construction: all
traditional; ISIC 5: electricity, gas, water and sanitary services: all
modern; ISIC 6: commerce: 20% modern, 80% traditional; ISIC 7: transport,
storage, and communication: 80% modern, 20% traditional; ISIC 8: services:
government = all modern, domestic servants = all traditional, the remaining
portion of services was then distributed 1/3 modern, 2/3 traditional;
ISIC 9: activities not adequately described: 50% modern, 50% traditional.
In addition, persons in ISCO major groups 0-2 (professional, technical and
related workers, administrative, executive and managerial workers, and
clerical workers) who were classified as employees, own account, family
workers, or others (i.e., the nonsalaried or wage-earner status category)
were added to the wage earners since they were considered modern sector.
In most countries this increased the modern-sector size by 1 or 2 percentage
points.

Construction workers are not easy to classify: most are low skilled;
many are workers in large firms or projects but have high turnover. In some
countries (e.g., Peru), however, they have as much political and union clout
as factory workers, perhaps because the practice of cost-plus contracting in
public construction projects made government interventions in wage-setting an
early necessity. Once identified as the direct wage-setter, the government
is politically more vulnerable to wage demands; and "minimum profitability"
cannot be used as a defense against large-wage demands. This also applies
where cost-plus pricing is common in much of private-sector construction.

e
The number in parentheses is the percentage share of employees in
the EAP if 31 million persons classified as agricultural laborers in the
status "other" and "unknown" are added to the 2 million agricultural workers
classified as wage earners.

f
Source: Government of Pakistan, Ministry of Labor, Report of the Study
Group on Employment (Islamabad: 1971). Modern-sector defined as all
all enterprises employing at least 10 persons.

SOURCES: Columns (1) - (3): International Labour Organization Yearbook
of Labour Statistics, 1966, 1971, and 1972. (IL): Geneva).

Column (4): Data on employees in manufacturing by size of firm were
from U.N. Statistical Office, The Growth of World Industry 1970 Edition:
Vol. I: General Industrial Statistics, (New York: U.N. 1972), except for
Venezuela which was from Venezuela, Direccion General de Estadistics y Censos,
Anuario Estadistico 1971 (Caracas: 1973).

market wages. Minimum-wage systems, or other pro-labor laws that attempt
significant departures from market wages, can usually be enforced only in
the modern sector. As may be seen from data provided in table 1, attempts
to redistribute via wage policies will, therefore, usually reach no more
than 10 to 20 percent of the labor force.[38] Furthermore, the redistributive potential of labor policies also depends on the size of the "surplus,"
or non-labor income share. Since surplus per worker is larger in urban-
and modern-sector firms, capacity to pay is closely correlated with enforce
ability. Thus, the enforcement of wage increases in most rural or urban
traditional-sector firms would not only be costly in administrative terms,
it would also have a smaller redistributive impact given the lower surplus
per worker and the fact that many employers in those sectors are themselves
poor.

b) Links between implementation and market structure

The link between enforceability and market structure has two component
The more obvious component was referred to above; it amounts largely to
visibility and accessibility--features inherent in modern-sector firms
which tend to be large, to locate in cities or along major transport
facilities, and (every cloud has a silver lining) to advertise blatantly.

The second link, however, is of a more general nature and is less
obviously related to the modern-traditional sector dichotomy. Any policy
attempt to distort a market outcome will create some degree of disequilibri
or "tension." The amount of tension is determined by market conditions, an
is itself a determinant of the degree of political and administrative effor
required for implementation.

More specifically, the degree of market tension will be a function of
the supply and demand elasticities in each labor market: the greater the
elasticities, the larger will be the disequilibrium resulting from a given
departure from a market wage, and, hence, the stronger the market forces
working against government policy. Thus, if labor supply is highly elastic
any wage above the free-market level will generate a large number of job
seekers; and any wage below could be implemented only by somehow forcing a
large number of potential job leavers to remain at work. If the demand for
labor is elastic, a wage above the free-market level will cause a large reduction in employment and a greater disruption or readjustment in the struc
ture of production.

Tension also results when government attempts to change the underlying supply and demand conditions of markets. A major part of wage policy, for instance, is directed at either increasing or reducing the competitiveness of labor supply, chiefly by measures that weaken or strengthen unions. The amount of effort required to implement such measures will depend on the structural characteristics that underlie market supply conditions, such as the skill homogeneity of the labor force, its regional concentration or dispersion, its education, and other social characteristics that affect both market knowledge and ease of organization.

As a general rule, the tension created by a given policy-distortion of wage levels is smaller in the modern than in the traditional sector. This is because the elasticity of demand for labor tends to be lower, and because labor supply conditions are more easily affected in the modern sector, e.g., unionization is easier, and job stability laws are more easily enforced. These arguments imply that wage policy is more easily implemented in the modern sector for two kinds of reasons--the greater visibility and accessibility of modern-sector firms, and the lesser tension created by market distortions in that sector.

c)   The law of rising (modern-sector) wages

One of the most frequently repeated empirical generalizations regarding developing countries is that modern-sector real wages are rising more rapidly than (i) traditional-sector incomes, and (ii) in most cases, than GDP per capita. This phenomenon flies in the face of the orthodox conception of the underdeveloped country as the labor surplus economy with relatively competitive labor markets. The contradiction is most often attributed to unionization and political power of modern-sector labor.[39] An alternative and complementary explanation involves the skill requirements of modern-sector activities and the consequent skill upgrading of the modern labor force.[40] The search for a theory of rising modern-sector wages is relevant to wage policy first, because a "competitive market" explanation (e.g., rising human capital) implies the absence of distortion. If skills largely explain high wages in the modern sector, there is no need to lower wages for efficiency purposes, while the reverse implication follows from the "market distortion" explanation.

Second, such a theory would reflect on the feasibility of wage policy, particularly of a low-wage policy: the ease of policy corrections will depend on the nature of the "distortions" or market forces involved.

In this chapter, a preferred point of departure is the generalization that upward wage pressures are created by features inherent to modern-sector technology and market structure. This appears obvious with respect to the higher skill requirements of this sector. But it is also true of wage increases resulting from unionization and direct political power. The principal features of modern sectors are capital-intensity, large-scale units, urban presence, and rapid output growth.[41]

The skill effect on wage levels is the combined result of the need for new skills plus a structural constraint on the supply of those skills. Because such skills are largely learned on the job, their supply tends to lag behind the creation of new job positions. This kind of scarcity, and the resulting wage pressure, will be very sensitive to (i) the rate of growth, since slow expansion will allow skill supply to grow through some job turnover and deliberate on-the-job training of extra men; and (ii) the degree of structural change in sectoral output, since the expansion of the same activity will create a pool of each new skill and reduce the monopoly power of individual workers; and (iii) the absolute size of the market, since a large market will also tend to create pools of workers with the required or closely related modern-sector skills that diminish the bargaining edge of each individual. Skill premiums of this type could be reduced by institutional arrangements that forced or induced firms to generate a larger supply of on-the-job trainees.

Wage differentials may also result because the high fixed costs created by capital-intensity put a premium on low worker turnover and on dependability. Capital-intensity firms therefore pay higher wages to reduce turnover, to be more discriminating in their search for workers who rank high in personal characteristics associated with carefulness and dependability, and to elicit responsibility through good will. Such wage premiums, however, will only generate a rising relative wage in the modern sector if employment in the more capital-intensive component is growing as a proportion of total modern-sector employment.

Modern sectors are also conducive to wage gains through unionization and direct political pressure. The opportunity for such gains is created by the high productivity and inelastic demand for labor, both of which are due largely to capital-intensity. Elasticity of labor demand varies directly with the share of labor in total cost.[42] Also, capital-intensity usually implies a large rent or quasi-rent component in the return to property, partly because large-scale capital assets tend to be long lived, and partly because modern-sector assets in LDCs are often complementary with natural resources. Quasi-rent also arises from the monopoly element that is present in much LDC manufacturing and other activities as a result of tariffs, licenses, and other such privileges.[43]

Modern-sector characteristics, at the same time, facilitate the exploitation of such opportunities by labor: unions in LDCs usually originate in, and are often limited to, modern-sector establishments. Such firms tend to hire more experienced and better-schooled workers, concentrate them geogrphically--in a small number of establishments and in one city or in a few cities--and provide them with an external environment of discipline and organization. Modern-sector firms, in short, are natural breeding grounds for unions. This impact of modern, industrial forms of production on worker consciousness and organization was the basis of Marx's class analysis.[44] The same features of modern-sector activity create direct political power, namely, urban presence, susceptibility to organization, and disruptive potential.

The processes underlying white-collar salary trends are somewhat different, on both supply and demand sides. As distinct from the largely market-determined supply of manual workers (which is either unskilled and highly elastic, or skilled and subject to supply-creation by the modern-sector itself), the supply of white-collar labor is mostly a function of schooling, particularly secondary school output, and is, therefore, a direct result of policy. On the demand side, the market for white-collar employees is complicated by the existence of a massive single employer in the public sector--whose wage policy cannot be separated from consideration of other policy goals, principally in the area of fiscal policy, and of the major political force represented by public employees. Changes on the supply side, however, are likely to cause a cycle in salary trends: secondary schooling output is almost universally growing faster than are modern-sector employment opportunities and is likely, therefore, to slow the growth of white-collar salary levels.

One major policy implication of these varied forces tending to raise modern-sector wages is that a low-wage policy probably requires much more than a neutral attitude to competing income groups; it would seem to require active suppression of the natural political power and ease of unionization of modern-sector labor, as well as an aggressive training and educational policy aimed at enlarging the supply of both on-the-job trainees and of those leaving secondary schools. A second implication is that the capacity-to-pay criterion, which implicitly underlies the collective bargaining approach to wage policy, tends to sanction and reinforce the dualism and income differentials between modern and traditional sectors.

D.   Policy impact

1.   Some issues

The following is a not untypical evaluation of the impact of wage policy in developing countries: "The reasons for the existence of wage levels, especially for unskilled labor, which are 'too high' are mainly institutional. In some countries, and at certain periods, trade unions play some role. But the major factor is government policy, and the ideological or political ideas which guide it. Government is a major influence on wage levels and structure in most LDCs, by its wage decisions with respect to government employees, and in its role as regulator through minimum wage policies, wage boards, Industrial Courts, etc."[45] In my opinion, wage policy is more diverse in intent, more indirect in form, and more constrained in practice than is suggested by that evaluation.

It is both statistically and conceptually difficult to separate the contributions of policy, unions, and market structure. Today's market structure and union strength are both partly the product of yesterday's policies. In this broader sense, much more can be attributed to policy. But today's wage decisions and mediation in wage disputes only rarely push wages very far above, or below, their market- (including union) determined level. This suggests that a policy reversal will be a slow and complex process because it must, in turn, unwind the fabric of protective labor and business laws that are now part of the market environment in most LDCs, and that largely explains wages that are "too high."[46]

Furthermore, though it is natural for an economist to treat policy as an exogenous variable, the resulting analytical procedure misses the interrelation that exists between policy choice and economic structure and is consequently unable to assess either the political feasibility or the mix of political and economic changes required to implement a different policy Once a protected sector of labor and business groups exists, how feasible is a policy of wage restraint? And how feasible is a policy that not

merely restrains wages but carries out other policies required for employment creation such as the dismantling of many forms of capital subsidy in
the modern sector and the transfer of income out of the modern sector to
create capital and employment in the traditional sector?[47]

2. Policy versus market forces

The literature on LDC wage policies contains some attempts to assess
the separate contribution of government intervention on wage levels, chiefly
in the modern sector. Berg,[48] Turner and Jackson,[49] and Frank,[50] for
instance, have stressed the role of active or permissive government wage
and unionization policies in explaining sharp wage increases in the
modern sectors of various African countries. On the other hand, Ramos[51]
and Isbister[52] argue that in Mexico and other Latin American countries,
market forces are responsible for most of the recent trend in modern-
sector wages. Isbister explains wage increases in Mexico by a growing
traditional-sector productivity; Ramos argues that rising skill levels
explain wage trends in Latin America. Ridker[53] also suggests that high
modern-sector wage levels are to a large extent caused by market rather
than policy forces.

The source of modern-sector wage increases was also discussed by
Tidrick[54] and Eriksson,[55] who measured the effect of these wage increases
on employment in Jamaica and Latin America, respectively. Both authors
begin by assuming autonomous wage increases and then study the wage effect
on productivity and employment. Tidrick then argues that the reverse
causation is possible but unlikely, given some features of his data.
Eriksson is more agnostic, admitting that causation may run either way.

One attempt at a systematic measurement of the separate contribution
of market and policy forces was made by Ramos, but his argument consists
largely of providing detailed measures of labor quality, which, according
to his figures, has been rising.[56] Though he considers these data sufficient to explain the observed wage increases, this does not rule out a
parallel and significant contribution by government policy.

This issue was also dealt with, at some length, in a controversy
following an article by Kilby,[57] who attributed wage increases in Nigeria
to the political power of unions. Weeks, for example, argued that "wage
levels in Nigeria have been basically determined by economic conditions,
though superficially through political mechanisms."[58] Kilby's argument

was supported by Warren[59] who stressed the political rather than the direct collective bargaining power of unions, even though the resulting pro-labor policy was implemented through a "concessionary" attitude in wage negotiations. Knight makes a similar point regarding urban labor in Uganda.[60] This controversy suggests the awkwardness and perhaps irrelevance of the original question ("market versus policy?") since, like the scissors analogy for supply and demand, "the source" of the wage increase is clearly an interaction.

Some other aspects of this discussion concern effectiveness of policy in raising wages through (i) welfare and supplementary benefits legislation, (ii) minimum wage laws, and (iii) wage leadership. Thus a common theme in discussions of wage policy is that legislation regarding social security and supplementary benefits is a source of additional upward pressure on real wage levels.[61] Such benefits often add as much as 50% or more to the wage bill. It is plausible, however, that part if not all of such benefits are eventually offset by smaller future increments in basic wages, though there does not appear to be any study that examines this question.

The impact of minimum wages has been discussed more often in the context of the more backward African economies where unskilled and less-organized workers make up a larger proportion of the wage-earning labor force, and consequently where minimum rates are both directly applicable to more workers and are a powerful lever on the whole structure of rates. Several authors have cited minimum wages (along with government pay scales) as a main source of the substantial increases in modern-sector wage levels in these countries.[62] The impact of minimum wages in the more developed and differentiated labor markets of Latin America is probably less pronounced and limited to a small number of workers on the fringe of the modern sector According to Berg, the minimum rate is the effective rate for about half the workers in some African countries.[63] But, survey evidence for Peru,[64] for Mexico,[65] and the recent statement by the President of Colombia suggest that a large proportion of wage earners in those countries receive less than the minimum wage and most receive wages that are either higher than or below the minimum. On the other hand, Puerto Rico seems to have been a special case of considerable upward pressure on wages exerted through the minimum rates; wage policy thus dominated and overrode the potential contributions of either unions or rising skills.[66]

Existing labor force surveys for many countries could be used for a
fuller study of the impact of minimum wages. A first set of questions
would relate to coverage. What proportion of the labor force is in fact
paid the minimum? How many, and who, fall below? What are the political,
market, or administrative constraints that impede full coverage? A second
set concerns the leverage effect of minimum rates, i.e., the extent to
which increases in minimum rates also raise wages of higher-paid workers
because wage differentials must be maintained for market reasons, or to
satisfy union requirements. Presumably, leverage is proportional to the
number of workers actually paid the minimum, which in turn is a function
of the degree of skill differentiation, and of unionization.

The demonstration or pull-effect of wage increases by "leading"
sectors--chiefly the public sector or large foreign firms--on the other
modern-sector wages has been cited as a key wage increase mechanism,[67]
and one that presumably is particularly easy to reverse. As with minimum
wages, the argument has been applied most particularly, and plausibly, to
the smaller and less differentiated modern sectors of some African nations.
If wage leadership is to explain rising real wages, however, it must explain who loses from the wage increase: the additional wage income may come
out of modern-sector profits, or taxes, or the traditional sector through
relative price changes. All of these mechanisms are plausible, but an
adequate explanation of the leadership mechanism must explain the particular mechanism by which real income is transferred and, therefore, why the
wage increases do not simply result in general inflation.

3. Wage trends and policy

This section asks whether wage trends are indicative of the direction
or bias of wage policy. The policy literature frequently assumes that
rising or falling real wages can, in fact, be attributed to wage policy.
This assumption is tested by examining the relationship between wage
behavior and the apparent wage policy in some selected countries.

A meaningful comparison between wage trends and policy, however,
should adjust for the effect of market forces. A crude but simple measure
of the overall growth in demand for labor is the rate of growth of gross
domestic product. Rapid growth in output will tend to pull wages up to
meet the need for rapid migration and skill acquisition, despite wage-
restraining policies. Conversely, it is difficult to raise wages in the

context of a stagnant economy. A better index of the effect of policy, therefore, is a wage trend adjusted for the rate of growth in aggregate output. In the following discussion, wage policy is related to both the absolute growth in wages and to a wage trend adjusted simply by subtracting the rate of growth of GDP.

The wage data used for this comparison are real wage trends in the manufacturing sector over a period of approximately sixteen years. This should be a sufficiently long period to net out the effect of year-to-year fluctuations in political and stabilization goals. The data are summarized in table 2, and more detailed statistics, broken down into four-year periods from 1956 to 1972, are presented in appendix tables 1 to 3.

Some general features of these statistics deserve comment. First, they bear out the expectation of a broad correlation between the growth of wages and GDP per capita. Second, the diversity of wage behavior, including long-run trends, conflicts with the common impression that manufacturing wages are rising in a more uniform manner, and generally exceeding GDP growth.[68] In a surprisingly large number of countries (half the sample), wages have grown more slowly than GDP per capita.

The following subsections will briefly examine wage policies in the categories of "high-wage" and "low-wage" trends, as suggested by the differences between wage and GDP trends shown in table 2. The general question posed here--whether wage trends are indicative of policy bias--cannot be answered without a more thorough analysis of both policy and market variables in each country, but the following brief review of policies suggests that patterns of policy bias can be distinguished, and can be related to wage behavior, if one makes allowance for the independent influence of rate of growth in the demand for labor--measured here by the growth of GDP per capita.

   a)   Cases of "low-wage trends"

It is not surprising that most of the countries in the category of "low-wage trend" (GDP growth exceeds wage increase), such as South Korea, Thailand, Taiwan, Guatemala, Pakistan, and Brazil (since 1964), had long periods of authoritarian and anti-union policies.

In other respects there is a diversity of policies and market structure Brazil and the South Korea - Taiwan duo, for instance, are opposite paradigm Brazil of dualistic growth, where capital subsidy and sectoral allocation

Table 2. Trends in Manufacturing Wages and GDP Per Capita
(annual average changes, in percentages)

Country	(1) Real Wage (1956–72)	(2) GDP per capita (1959–71)	(3) Difference (1) – (2)
Tanzania	9.4	2.2	7.0
Nicaragua	7.1	3.5	3.6
Zambia	6.5	3.1	3.4
Colombia	4.7	1.9	2.8
Dominican Republic	3.6	1.0	2.6
Chile	4.6	2.1	2.5
Jamaica	(5.6)	(3.1)	(2.5)
Peru	4.1	1.8	2.3
Ecuador	4.1	1.8	2.3
Venezuela	(2.7)	(0.6)	(2.1)
Ghana	1.4	−0.1	1.5
Ceylon	3.1	2.1	1.0
Panama	5.5	4.7	0.8
Egypt	(1.2)	(1.1)	(−0.1)
Mexico	3.8	3.9	−0.1
Turkey	(3.5)	(4.0)	(−0.5)
Brazil	2.3	3.1	−0.8
Pakistan	1.0	2.2	−1.2
Guatemala	1.8	2.1	−1.5
Burma	(0.4)	(2.0)	(−1.6)
Costa Rica	(0.5)	(2.2)	(−1.7)
Argentina	0.5	2.6	−2.1
Taiwan	3.2	5.7	−2.5
Korea	4.2	6.7	−2.5
India	−1.3	1.5	−2.8
Philippines	−1.4	1.6	(−3.0)
Thailand	(−2.6)	(5.3)	(−7.9)

NOTES: Brackets indicate cases where data were available for short subperiods only; the periods covered are given in notes to appendix table 2.

The dates shown in column headings indicate maximum period covered; in some cases (see appendix table 2), the periods are shorter.

The maximum periods for columns (1) and (2) do not match fully, but they overlap sufficiently to indicate the approximate relationship between manufacturing wages and GDP per capita.

SOURCES: Column (1): From appendix table 1; Column (2): OECD, Latest

policies reduce the potential employment and distributive effects of rapid growth, Taiwan and South Korea of balanced urban-rural, evenly distributed growth.   Indeed, in Taiwan and South Korea the task of wage restraint was facilitated by a lesser degree of dualism: output is much less concentrated in a few large urban high-productivity firms. Their governments had to contend with weaker market and organizational forces. Much of this, of course, is circular: lesser dualism is to some extent (some argue, primarily) a result of wage restraint.

Wage repression in other countries, even when applied over relatively long periods, has been paralleled by capital-pricing, licensing, and other policies that both subsidised capitalists, particularly in manufacturing, and contributed to more dualistic growth patterns. This policy mix has been most evident in Brazil,[69] but it also characterized the Philippines as well as Pakistan during the decade of the sixties. In Guatemala and Thailand, wage repression seems to have been the complement primarily of pro-landlord, rather than pro-urban capitalist policies, though tariffs and capital subsidies have also been favorable to the urban wealthy.

Other countries seem to be in the "low-wage" group for different reasons: India, in particular, is a major political exception. The strongly egalitarian intent of the Indian Constitution certainly provides a basis for a tight rein on manufacturing wages, yet there is much in the institutions and principles of wage-determination in India that would lead one to expect wage trends strongly guided by capacity to pay, particularly the acceptance of collective bargaining or tripartism, the rejection of direct government intervention, and the approval of industry-cum-regional differentiation in minimum wage rates. Moreover, India is supposedly a "soft state" and has relatively strong regional governments which participate in wage-determination. Despite these characteristics, which preserve more democratic appearances, the wage-determination machinery in fact has managed to establish principles of strong central control, of wage restraint and egalitarian wage criteria.[70] Along with general wage restraint, there has been a sharp reduction in skill differentials. Some of the instruments that have achieved these results, for instance, are the centralization of the Labor Appellate Tribunals, the establishment of the industry-region rather than individual firm as the basis for determining the ceiling capacity to pay, and the involvement of independents in the Wage Boards, persons who generally lean conservatively toward consumers' and community interests.[71]

Argentina appears to have switched from being a classic case of
redistributive pro-labor policies, under Peron, into the category of low-
wage countries. Though the overall trend from 1954 to 1972 is a lag in
manufacturing wages behind GDP per capita (0.5% versus 2.6%), the story of
wage policy over this period is complicated by numerous regime changes, by
an overriding concern with stabilization problems, and by the powerful
effect of external terms of trade on the internal distribution of income
between urban wage earners and farmers. The principal tools used to affect
wage outcomes involved direct price-setting on a highly aggregate scale--
broad wage readjustments, exchange rate policy, and the rate of inflation;
few changes were made in labor legislation, and the solid organization of
labor unions was not challenged. The net effect of these broad and continually shifting policy interventions was a sharp initial post-Peron reduction in the wage share in national income from 46% in 1954 to 38% in 1959.
followed by a burst of rapid wage growth, as real wages grew 8.4% per
annum from 1959 to 1965 while GDP per capita grew only 2.4%. The 1965
military coup then initiated a long stagnation and even slight decline as
real wages fell 0.6% per annum between 1964 and 1972 despite an annual
growth of 3.2% in GDP per capita. The overall picture shows some correlation between wage trends and basic regime attitudes, but the extreme
annual fluctuations of key variables, the major impact of external price
developments--chiefly of wheat and beef--and the relative weakness of all
governments during this period suggest that any conclusion regarding
policy impact is somewhat speculative.

    b)   Cases of "high-wage trends"
    As was suggested in the analysis in earlier subsections, countries
with high rates of wage increase relative to GDP tend to be less authoritarian and to have relatively dualistic economies. These are the political
and economic conditions that, on the one hand, motivate collective bargaining, "capacity to pay" types of wage policies, and on the other hand,
provide the market structures where such policies can be used to good
effect.
    If manufacturing wage earners gained from policy in these countries,
who lost? In countries with small modern sectors (e.g., Tanzania,
Nicaragua, and Zambia), there was more leverage to finance wage increases
by redistributing income from the traditional sector, via relative prices,

or agricultural export taxes for instance. Yet in many of the high-wage trend countries, such as Colombia, Peru, and Chile, the traditional sectors were too small (e.g., under one-third of value added) to support, via such transfers, the large wage increases in the modern sector. Instead, wage gains must have been financed largely from capital income, or foregone taxes; where wage gains resulted chiefly from capacity-to-pay policies, there would have been little perception of "loss"--the wage gains would have appeared as a natural sharing in productivity increases.

Of the high-wage trend countries shown in table 2--those for instance where real wage growth exceeded GDP per capita growth by over 2.0% per annum--only Tanzania could be described as a case of deliberately redistributive pro-modern-sector wage policy. High-wage trends in the other countries seem to be associated instead with consensus-type wage policies.

These countries have had alternating periods of rapid and of slow wage change, often as a result of fluctuating inflation rates and stabilization programs. The capacity-to-pay orientation lends itself to flexibility of this type. Also, shifts in the political balance of power cause fluctuations around the basic permissive trend made possible by governments too weak to suppress unions, and by dualistic productivity differentials that are to some extent self-reinforcing because rising wage costs induce greater capital intensity. In Peru, for instance, wage policy became markedly permissive--favoring the stronger organized sectors, such as miners--during the first two or three years following the 1968 military coup; the result was a marked acceleration in the growth of real wages. These increases were achieved directly through the government's participation in tripartite wage boards. At the same time, the government began a continuing effort to weaken union organization. These policies contrasted with the labor policies of the Belaunde government (1963-68). Belaunde's policies also involved a pro-labor influence in mediating disputes and enforcing labor legislation, but this influence was less pronounced than in the early years of the Velasco government; instead, Belaunde followed a mix of consensus and pro-labor organizational policies that permitted both steady differential wage increases in modern firms and greatly expanded the extent of unionization, chiefly in modern agriculture.

A more dramatic case of deliberately redistributive wage policy was Chile's attempt at massive redistribution to labor under the Allende regime particularly during 1971 when an exceptionally powerful attempt was

made to raise wage levels and wage shares. The policy involved sharp
increases in minimum wages, price controls, and easy access to credit to
smaller and medium-sized firms financially affected by the cost-price
squeeze. Furthermore, acquiescence to wage increases was facilitated by
the legally sanctioned threat of government "intervention" (i.e., takover)
in firms that failed to resolve labor disputes. The combined effect of
these measures was a massive transfer of modern-sector property income to
labor during 1971: real wages that year rose 26%! The financial and productive implications of these measures, however, were untenable, and much
of the redistribution was reversed, in part as deliberate policy, through
the inflation of 1972-73. This rather erratic instance of an extreme pro-
labor policy, like the longer-lived Peron experiment, is revealing of the
mechanisms involved in implementation, of market responses, and of the
ultimate difficulty of achieving a permanent redistribution through such
means.

An important feature of both the more aggressively pro-labor and the
consensus wage policies is the way in which labor policy has accommodated
to the existence of large differences in productivity levels and to differences in political vlnerability, chiefly between foreign-owned and
national firms. Governments have accommodated to this differentiation by
allowing company unions to become the principal negotiating units: industry-
wide bargaining is the exception in most LDCs. The history and role of
company unions in Colombia is stressed, for instance, by Urrutia.[72]
Gregory[73] cites the role of plant unions in Chile; he argues that such
unions weakened the labor movement, but this broad political result is
not inconsistent with the achievement of differential wage gains correlated
with productivity levels and changes between firms. Bargaining by company
unions results in price discrimination by labor in the sense that firms
with less elastic demand for labor curves can be forced to pay higher wages.

Price discrimination by labor also helps to explain the wide dispersion
of wage rates within LDC modern sectors, over and above the differentials
between modern and traditional sector firms. Since productivity is
closely correlated with capital-intensity, there is a correspondingly
close relationship between wage levels and capital-labor ratios in firms.
Gregory cites this correlation for Chile, and evidence for Peru and Colombia
is given by Webb,[74] and Nelson, Schultz. and Slighton,[75] respectively. A
striking example of correlation between wage and productivity differences,

explainable largely in terms of price discrimination, is provided by eight
large sugar estates in Peru. Data for 1968 show a similar <u>structure</u> of
wages <u>within</u> and large differences <u>between</u> each estate (reflecting differences in average productivity). Thus the average annual wage ranged from
U.S.$713 to $1,643.[76]

E. Conclusions

The "high-wage policy" that allegedly characterizes LDCs, and that is
routinely attacked in discussions of employment and equity, is a misrepresentation of wage policy in LDCs. Cases of straightforward redistributive
pro-labor policies, such as the post-independence experience of several
African countries and the Peron period in Argentina, have been the exception not the rule. Wage restraint and industrial consensus policies are
the more common LDC attitudes toward modern-sector labor. Modern-sector
wages have risen more often <u>despite</u> primarily repressive or neutral wage
policies. Those increases are caused by an interaction of economic structures and political aims that favor modern-sector labor. Those natural
advantages must either be actively checked, through repression, or by the
substitution of moral incentives; or they must be accommodated through
consensus politics.

Perhaps the most frequent policy outcome is one which favors discriminatory wage increases that match differences in productivity growth. The
"capacity-to-pay" criterion is a hardy plant, fed by political convenience,
by the marketplace ideology, by notions of fairness, and by the economic
opportunities of dualistic economies. This is a pessimistic conclusion
with respect to the prospects for more equitable and employment-creating
wage policies. The argument of this paper implies that calling for wage
restraint is preaching to the converted, at least in most LDCs, and that
modern-sector wage restraint is an option open only to authoritarian
governments.

APPENDIX

Appendix Table 1.   Trends in Real Wages, 1956–72
(average annual changes, in percentages)

	(1) 1956–1960	(2) 1960–1964	(3) 1964–1968	(4) 1968–1972
Argentina	-2.5	5.5	-1.2	-0.1
Brazil	0.3	2.5	0.5	7.6
Chile	–	1.6	9.2	5.5
Colombia	9.9	4.9	1.9	-0.4
Dominican Republic	4.4	13.5	-6.4	3.3
Ecuador	0.0	1.7	2.0	6.7
Egypt	0.3	5.4	0.6	0.0
Ghana	5.1	-1.7	2.0	0.7
Guatemala	2.6	1.2	3.2	-0.1
India	-0.9	-2.6	-0.4	0.8
Korea	4.4	-3.7	10.1	6.6
Mexico	2.4	8.6	2.3	1.6
Nicaragua	2.4	3.1	9.7	–
Pakistan	-0.9	5.3	-3.7	4.9
Panama	9.0	6.0	2.9	5.6
Peru	2.9	0.7	-1.9	5.5
Philippines	0.5	-4.5	0.3	-1.7
Puerto Rico	6.6	4.0	3.7	3.1
El Salvador	5.6	0.2	2.9	1.5
Sri Lanka	9.9	-0.8	1.4	1.4
Syria	–	–	-0.9	-0.8
Tanzania	6.8	18.2	4.9	4.0
Thailand	–	–	-3.9	-0.3
Turkey	1.6	1.6	5.7	2.5
Venezuela	–	–	3.7	1.8
Zambia	3.1	13.5	3.1	6.2

NOTES:

Actual periods covered are as follows:

Col. (1):   Ecuador, 1957–60
Peru, 1957–60
El Salvador, 1956–59

Appendix Table 1.   (continued)

NOTES (continued)

Col. (2):   El Salvador, 1961-64

Col. (3):   Brazil, 1966-68
            Korea, 1965-68
            Nicaragua, 1964-67
            Tanzania, 1965-68
            Turkey, 1964-67

Col. (4):   Brazil, 1968-70
            Colombia 1968-70
            Dominican Republic, 1968-70
            Egypt, 1968-70
            Ghana, 1968-71
            India, 1968-70
            Korea, 1969-72
            Pakistan, 1968-70
            Panama, 1968-71
            Philippines, 1968-71
            Tanzania, 1968-70
            Thailand, 1968-70

SOURCES:

   For years 1956-64:   Smith, Anthony D., ed., Wage Policy Issues in
Economic Development (London: Macmillan, 1969), table 2, p. 47; and
International Labour Organization, Yearbook of Labor Statistics, 1966 editic

   For years 1964-72:   I.L.O., Yearbook of Labor Statistics, 1973 edition.

Appendix Table 2. Trends in Real GDP Per Capita, 1956–72
(average annual changes, in percentages)

	(1) 1956–1960	(2) 1960–1964	(3) 1964–1968	(4) 1968–1972
Argentina	1.6	1.7	2.7	3.7
Brazil	3.3	2.1	2.6	6.1
Chile	0.3	2.3	1.9	2.9
Colombia	0.1	1.8	1.4	3.0
Dominican Republic	0.8	3.7	−2.2	7.4
Ecuador	1.6	1.2	–	–
Egypt	–	–	−0.2	3.9
Ghana	–	0.1	−1.5	1.6
Guatemala	1.2	2.4	2.5	2.8
India	1.7	2.5	−0.5	3.3
Korea	2.3	3.6	6.8	8.9
Mexico	2.3	3.8	3.3	3.6
Nicaragua	0.0	7.3	1.1	1.3
Pakistan	0.7	1.5	1.9	−1.5
Panama	–	4.7	5.0	4.8
Peru	3.8	1.6	0.9	2.2
Philippines	0.5	1.3	1.0	2.8
Puerto Rico	6.4	6.2	5.6	5.0
El Salvador	–	3.3	1.6	−0.3
Sri Lanka	2.0	−0.5	2.6	2.9
Syria	−5.0	7.0	−0.9	6.0
Tanzania	–	1.2	3.5	1.7
Thailand	4.7	7.2	9.0	5.9
Turkey	0.2	1.9	3.7	3.8
Venezuela	–	4.1	0.9	1.3
Zambia	–	0.4	7.3	1.3

NOTES:

Actual periods covered are as follows:

Col. (4): Argentina, 1968–71
Brazil, 1968–70
Chile, 1968–71
Dominican Republic, 1968–71
Egypt, 1968–70

Appendix Table 2. (continued)

NOTES (continued)

        Ghana, 1968-70
        India, 1968-70
        Pakistan, 1969-71 (excluding Bangladesh)
        Panama, 1968-71
        Philippines, 1968-70
        El Salvador, 1968-71
        Sri Lanka, 1968-71
        Zambia, 1968-70

SOURCES:

For years 1956-60; U.N., <u>Statistical Yearbook</u>, 1966 edition, pp. 546-

For years 1960-72; Ibid., 1973 edition, pp. 549-52.

Appendix Table 3. Difference in Trends in Manufacturing
Wages and GDP Per Capita
(average annual changes, in percentages)

(Table 1 - Table 2)

	(1) 1956–1960	(2) 1960–1964	(3) 1964–1968	(4) 1968–1972
Argentina	-4.1	3.8	-3.9	-3.8
Brazil	-3.0	0.4	-2.1	1.5
Chile	-	-0.7	7.3	2.6
Colombia	9.8	3.1	0.5	-3.4
Dominican Republic	3.6	9.8	-4.2	-4.1
Ecuador	-1.6	0.5	-	-
Egypt	-	-	0.8	-3.9
Ghana	-	-1.8	3.5	-0.9
Guatemala	1.4	-1.2	0.7	-2.9
India	-2.6	-5.1	0.1	-2.5
Korea	2.1	-7.3	3.3	-2.3
Mexico	0.1	4.8	-1.0	-2.0
Nicaragua	2.4	-4.2	8.6	-
Pakistan	-1.6	3.8	-5.6	6.4
Panama	-	1.3	-2.1	0.8
Peru	-0.9	-0.9	-2.8	3.3
Philippines	0.0	-5.8	-0.7	-4.5
Puerto Rico	0.2	-2.2	-1.9	-1.9
El Salvador	-	-3.1	1.3	1.8
Sri Lanka	7.9	-0.3	-1.2	-1.5
Syria	-	-	0.0	-6.8
Tanzania	-	17.0	1.4	2.3
Thailand	-	-	-12.9	-6.2
Turkey	1.4	-0.3	2.0	-1.3
Venezuela	-	-	2.8	0.5
Zambia	-	13.1	-4.2	4.9

NOTES: The dates shown in column headings indicate maximum period covered:
in some cases (see notes, appendix tables 1 & 2), the periods are shorter.

The maximum periods from appendix tables 1 & 2 do not match fully, but
they overlap sufficiently to indicate the approximate relationship between
manufacturing wages and GDP per capita.

SOURCES: Tables 1 and 2.

Chapter 6

NOTES

1. From "150 Years Ago," a column in The Observer, a London newspaper, cited in the edition of 17 May 1969.

2. Cited by James O. Morris in "Latin American Collective Bargaining Agreement: An Illustration," Stanley M. Davis and Louis Wolf Goodman, ed., Workers and Managers in Latin America (D.C. Heath & Co., 1972), p. 211.

3. See Albert Fishlow, "Brazilian Size Distribution of Income," American Economic Review LXII 2 (May 1972), table 1, p. 392.

4. Emanuel de Kadt, Catholic Radicals in Brazil (London: Oxford University Press, 1970), p. 177. Data refer to 1965.

5. de Kadt, Catholic Radicals, p. 177.

6. de Kadt, Catholic Radicals, p. 185.

7. Stephan R. Lewis, Jr., "Notes on Indistrialization and Income Distribution in Pakistan," Research Memorandum no. 37, Center for Development Economics (Williams College, September 1970), p. 15.

8. In this special sense, socialist and other leftist regimes could be described as pro-capital; in fact, socialist governments generally are pro-capital. This classification is modified below to acknowledge the distinction between policies aimed at raising wages in either the modern or the tradition sectors.

9. "Modern" and "traditional" are considered here as having high or low labor productivity. Perhaps the latter terms could have been used to avoid confusion but the former concepts are more generalized and mean roughly the same. High labor productivity correlates well with size of firm (excluding farms), with the "organized" sector, with what could be called the "formal" sector, and with the "enumerated" sector. For distributive analysis, however, the most useful criterion is productivity since it identifies where income originates and where it goes. Enumeration and size of firm, however, are useful statistical approximations or proxies for the high-productivity sector.

10. The growth and employment case for low modern-sector wages is put forward in chapter 3 by Henry Bruton, "Industrialization Policy and Income Distribution" in this volume. See also Gustav Ranis, "Industrial Sector Labor Absorption," Economic Development and Cultural Change, vol. 21, no. 3 (April 1973), pp. 387-408.

11. Bruton, in an unpublished discussion of wage policy, states that "The general outcome of [on-the-job skill accumulation plus job mobility] is quite likely to be some increase in wage rates due to accumulated experience. It is difficult to be alarmed about these increases. They do not penalize employment and they do not result from exercise of any monopoly or discriminatory power."

12. The widening of the wage and salary structure in Brazil over the last decade, for instance, has been explained as a necessary consequence of rapid growth. (See Carlos G. Langoni, "Distribucao da rende e des envolvimiento economico do Brazil," Estudios Economicos, vol. 2, no. 5 (October 1972), pp. 1-88.) Also, the rapid increase in white-collar incomes in Africa immediately after independence has been attributed to the greatly expanded personnel demands of the public sector.

13. This argument is developed in R. Webb, "Government Policy and the Distribution of Income in Peru, 1963-1973." Discussion paper no. 39, Research Program in Economic Development (Princeton University, March 1974), pp. 28-29.

14. See E.A. Landy, in International Labour Review, vol. 101, no. 6 (June 1970); p. 555; and James O. Morris, who equates a "more advanced" industrial relations process with one that places greater reliance on collective bargaining, Morris, "Latin American Collective Bargaining," p.209.

15. These include AID and AFL-CIO-supported labor institutes in each of the three major world regions (the AIFLD [The American Institute for Free Labor Development] is for Latin America), devoted largely to the support of non-communist labor organizations in developing countries.

16. D. Jackson, "The Political Economy of Collective Bargaining—The Case of Turkey," British Journal of Industrial Relations, vol. IX, no. 1 (March 1971), for instance, discusses the substantial budgetary support and training assistance provided to the anti-communist Turkish labor federation Turk-Is.

17. Jackson, "Political Economy of Collective Bargaining," p. 69 Ataturk's labor policy, embodied in the Labor Act of 1936, was reversed after the 1960 revolution.

18. See Roger D. Hansen, The Politics of Mexican Development (Baltimore: Johns Hopkins Press, 1971), especially pp. 113-16. The main exception was the Aleman administration (1946-52) which followed a deliberate low-wage policy.

19. Hansen, p. 92. This policy was made explicit by President Cardenas (1934-40). See Joe C. Ashby, Organized Labor and the Mexican Revolution under Lazaro Cardenas (Chapel Hill: University of North Carolina Press, 1963).

20. See President Velasco's Message to the Nation of 28 July 1971.

21. Arthur Lewis, "A Review of Economic Development," American Economic Review, vol. IV, no. 2 (May 1965), p. 15.

22. See Celso Furtado, Subdesenvolvimiento e Estagnacao Na America Lat
(Rio de Janeiro: Editora Saga, 1968), p. 81. Furtado's argument culled fr
several publications, is favorably reviewed by Werner Baer, "Furtado on
Development: A Review Essay," Journal of Developing Areas (January 1969),
pp. 270-80. This argument also underlies several empirical studies under-
taken as part of the Rice University Program of Development Studies project
on income distribution. See James Land and Ronald Soligo, "Models of
Development Incorporating Distribution Aspects," paper no. 22, Program of
Development Studies, Rice University. See also the International Labour
Organization report on Colombia, Towards Full Employment (Geneva: ILO, 197(

23. See, for instance, Plan Anual 1971, ODEPLAN (Santiago, 1970), p. 1
"La concepcion general del Plan...se expresa en lo immediato en una fuerte
redistribucion de ingresos a favor de los asalariados....Esta redistribucio
de ingreso se traducira en un sustancial aumento de la demanda y, por ende,
en un fuerte estimulo al aparato productivo, hasta ahora muy deprimido y
subutilizado. Por este mismo hecho, se cuenta con la necesaria capacidad d
respuesta a las nuevos condiciones, asi como tambien existe un vasto
contingente de fuerza de trabajo susceptible de ser empleados productivamen

This expression of faith in the short-run elasticity of aggregate
supply is supported by a broader argument that inequality is a growth bottl
neck, expounded for instance in Pedro Vuskovic, "Distribucion del Ingreso
y opciones de desarrollo," Cuadernos de la Realidad Nacional, no. 5
(September 1970), pp. 41-60. Vuskovic was Allende's first Minister of
Economy (1970 to mid-1972) and is considered the chief architect of
Allende's economic policy.

24. D. Pursell, "Bantu Real Wages and Employment Opportunities,"
South African Journal of Economics (June 1968), pp. 87-103. Arnt Spandau
later questioned Pursell's interpretation of Bantu wage policy but did not
deny, or provide alternative explanations of, the wage increases cited by
Pursell. A. Spandau, "South African Wage Board Policy: An Alternative
Interpretation," South African Journal of Economics, vol. 40, no. 4
(December 1972), pp. 377-87.

25. Cf. the Indian Constitution cited in C.K. Johri, Issues in Indian
Labour Policy, Shri Ram Center for Industrial Relations (New Delhi: New
India Press, 1969), p. 42. Article 43 of the Directive Principles of the
Constitution requires the state to secure a living wage to workers (my
italics).

26. Johri, Issues in Indian Labour, p. 15.

27. It can be argued, for instance, that Brazilian-style growth,
combining low wages with capital-cheapening policies, is not the best
distributive alternative. The ILO argues that this has been the case in
the Philippines.

28. "The desire for legal perfection which is so strong in Latin
America sometimes leads to a situation where the law is in advance of the
real economic and social situation...," International Labour Review (Octobe
1961), pp. 269-91.

29. International Labour Review (October 1961), 269-91.

30. Kenneth P. Erickson, Patrick Peppe, Hobart Spalding, "Research on the Urban Working Class and Organized Labor in Argentina, Brazil and Chile: What is Left to be Done?" Latin American Research Review, vol. IX, no. 2 (Summer 1974), p. 127.

31. Miguel Urrutia, The Development of the Colombian Labor Movement (New Haven: Yale University Press, 1969), pp. 118-19.

32. Ricardo Ffrench-Davis, Politicas Economicas en Chile (Santiago: Ediciones Nueva Universidad, Universidad Catolico de Chile, 1973), 345.

33. In Peru in 1970, for instance, the minimum-size firm for creation of a plant union was one with 20 employees.

34. Alan Angell, Politics and the Labor Movement in Chile (London: Oxford University Press, 1972), p. 80.

35. The Indian Fourth National Seminar on Industrial Relations in a Developing Economy, when grappling with the problem of minimum-wage fixing for the unorganized sector, recorded a unanimous objection to the use of the capacity-to-pay criterion, "Industries that could not afford to pay the minimum wages had no right to exist." (Johri, Issues in Indian Labour Policy, p. 44.) At the same time, though, the Seminar endorsed discrimination on a broader scale by favoring differential rates on an industry-cum-region basis. Also, the differential enforcement within the traditional sector of Factories Act provisions was accepted as inevitable: some argued for more uniform implementation while others for separate legislation. (Johri, p. 16).

36. Reported in Latin America, a weekly newsletter published in London, vol. VIII, no. 35 (August 1974).

37. See chapters by Henry Bruton, and Charles Frank and Richard Webb in this volume.

38. From the sample of twelve countries for which estimates were made of the size of the modern-sector labor force, a rule of thumb can be formulated that modern-sector employees will equal about half of total nonfarm employees. For all but one of the countries (Egypt), the proportion was between 43 and 59 percent.

39. Thus, some discussions of wage differentials in urban markets distinguish principally between the "organized" and "unorganized" sectors, thereby defining the wage differentials in terms of degree of unionization.

40. This view, stressing the role of skills, is argued by J. Ramos in Labor and Development in Latin America (New York: Columbia University Press, 1970), see especially pp. 174-78.

41. A similar model of interaction of economic and political determinants of modern-sector wage gains is suggested by H. A. Turner and D. A. S. Jackson, "In the model that best fits the data of this study, the major immediate determinant is institutional behavior--the behavior of employing and workers' organizations, and to some degree that of governments. On the other hand, the model is conditioned by certain characteristics of the

economic system, and particularly by different rates of productivity
growth between the economy's branches—which appear both as a factor
facilitating wage inflation and as indicating a certain restraint upon
it. So that here, economic and noneconomic factors interact, rather
than oppose each other," in "On the Determination of the General Wage
Level: A World Analysis; or Unlimited Labour Forever," Economic Journal, vol. 80, no. 320, (December 1970), p. 846.

42. When wages rise, the demand for labor falls partly because capital
and other factors are substituted for labor and partly because costs rise
and output falls. The negative output effect however is proportionate
to the share of labor in total cost.

43. Cf. R. Slighton, in "Perspective on Economic Policy-making," ed.,
Luigi Einaudi, Latin America in the 1970's, Rand R-1067-DOS (December 1972),
pp. 121-22. "Monopoly or partial monopoly positions in production arising
from tariff protection and import controls create opportunities for labor
to exact monopoly rents, and unions have not been backward in exploiting thi
opportunity."

44. "...with all the miseries it imposes upon (the workers), the preser
system simultaneously engenders the material conditions and the social
forms necessary for an economical reconstruction of society." From Karl
Marx, "Value, Price and Profit," in Karl Marx and Frederick Engel, vol. I
(Moscow: Foreign Publishing House, 1962), p. 446.

45. Elliot Berg, "Wages, Policy and Employment in Less Developed
Countries," paper presented to Conference on Prospects for Employment
Opportunities in the Nineteen Seventies (University of Cambridge, 1970),
p. 5.

46. Berg, "Wages, Policy," defines "too high" as (i) higher than the
wage needed to recruit new workers, (ii) higher than the general level
of incomes in the economy, and (iii) higher than the marginal social
opportunity cost of labor.

47. The special problems with each "horizontal" or inter-sectoral
transfer are discussed in Webb, "Government Policy and the Distribution of
Income in Peru," pp. 73-76.

48. Berg, "Wages, Policy," p. 5.

49. Turner and Jackson, "On the Determination of the General Wage
Level," pp. 827-49.

50. Charles Frank, Jr., "Urban Unemployment and Economic Growth in
Africa," paper no. 120, Economic Growth Center (New Haven: Yale University
1968), pp. 262-65.

51. Ramos, Labor and Development in Latin America.

52. John Isbister, "Urban Wages and Employment in a Developing Economy
The Case of Mexico," Economic Development and Cultural Change (October 1971
pp. 24-46.

53. Ronald Ridker and Harold Lubell, Employment and Unemployment Problems of the Near East and the South East (Delhi, Bombay: Vikas, 1971).

54. Gene Tidrick, "Wage Spillover and Unemployment in a Wage Gap Economy: The Jamaican Case," research memo 47 (Williams College, 1972).

55. John Eriksson, "Wage Change and Employment Growth in Latin American Industry," research memo 36 (Williams College, June 1970).

56. Ramos, Labor and Development in Latin America.

57. Peter Kilby, "Industrial Relations and Wage Determination: Failure of the Anglo-Saxon Model," Journal of Developing Areas, vol. 1 (July 1967), pp. 489-520.

58. John F. Weeks, "Further Comment on the Kilby/Weeks Debate: An Empirical Rejoinder," Journal of Developing Areas, vol. 5, no 2 (January 1971), pp. 165-74.

59. W.M. Warren, "Urban Real Wages and the Nigerian Trade Union Movement, 1939-1960," Economic Development and Cultural Change, vol. 1, no. 1 (October 1966), pp. 21-36.

60. J. B. Knight, "The Determination of Wages and Salaries in Uganda," Bulletin of Oxford Institute of Economics and Statistics, vol. 19 (October 1967), p. 250.

61. Efren Cordova, "Labor Legislation and Latin American Development: A Preliminary Review," International Labour Review, vol. 106, no. 5 (November 1972).

62. For example, E. Berg, "Wage Structures in Less-Developed Countries," ed., A.D. Smith, Wage Policy Issues in Economic Development (London: Macmillan, 1969), and Frank, "Urban Employment."

63. Berg, "Wage Structures."

64. Unpublished tabulations of 1969 national sample survey.

65. W. Paul Strassman, Technological Change and Economic Development (Ithaca: Cornell University Press, 1968).

66. Lloyd Reynolds, "Wages and Employment in a Labor-Surplus Economy," American Economic Review, vol. 55 (March 1965).

67. Berg, "Wages, Policy," p. 6; Knight, "Determination of Wages and Salaries in Uganda."

68. Data presented by H.A. Turner and D.A.S. Jackson, for instance, in "On the Determination of the General Wage Level" suggest such uniformity. This implication was criticized by J.B. Knight and Robert Mabro in "On the Determination ...: A Comment," Economic Journal, vol. 82, no. 326 (June 1972), pp. 677-86.

69. Cf. "...policy as practiced became one of maximum wage containment," Albert Fishlow, "Some Reflections on Post-1964 Brazilian Economic Policy." ed., H. Jon Rosenbaum and William G. Tyler, Contemporary Brazil: Issues in Economic and Political Development (New York: Praeger, 1972) p. 86

70. See D. Jackson, "Wage Policy and Industrial Relations in India," Economic Journal, vol. 82, no. 325 (March 1972), pp. 183-94; and Myron Weiner, The Politics of Scarcity: Public Pressure and Political Response in India (U. of Chicago, 1962).

71. B.N. Datar and S. Mongia, "Industrial Awards in India," Indian Economic Review, 1954, p. 65.

72. M. Urrutia, Development of Colombian Labor Movement.

73. Peter Gregory, Industrial Wages in Chile. (Ithaca, New York: State School of Industrial Relations, 1967).

74. Webb, "Government Policy and the Distribution of Income in Peru."

75. Richard Nelson, T.P. Schultz, and R. Slighton, Structural Change in a Developing Economy (Princeton: Princeton University Press, 1971).

76. Santiago Roca, La Distribucion del Ingreso en las Cooperativas Azucareras del Peru, 1968-1972 (Lima: ESAN, 1973).

CHAPTER VII

FISCAL POLICY AND INCOME REDISTRIBUTION

Arnold C. Harberger

The main objective of this chapter is to put into perspective the possibilities for poor countries to use their fiscal systems for redistributive purposes. Most of the discussion will be centered on the taxation side of the fiscal equation. The conclusions emerging from it will probably be disheartening to those who believe that a major assault on the problem of inequality can be effected by fiscal means. But this does not mean that tax policy is of no help in promoting greater equity. Indeed, though its limitations are severe when judged against the goal of a major improvement in the overall distribution of income, the possibilities for significant achievements look far brighter when viewed in terms of the more limited objective of bringing about a more equitable distribution of the fiscal burden itself. In fact, if there is any single message to emerge from this chapter, it is that when we look at a tax system with the distribution issue in mind, we are far better advised to think in terms of bringing about a fairer distribution of the tax burden than in terms of having a major impact on the overall distribution of income in the society in question.

A.   The main constraints on tax policy

Frequently, when the income distribution problem in LDCs is discussed, statements like the following emerge: "The top quintile of the income distribution now gets half of the existing total after-tax income, while the bottom quintile gets only 5 percent. Thus if only an additional tenth of the top group's share were taken away and given to the bottom group, the latter's share could be doubled." This kind of arithmetic makes good fodder for seminars but does not do much for policy, as it papers over all of the problems involved in effecting the sort of change it contemplates.

Basically, these problems fall into five classes:

    (i) The affected factors of production may leave the country.

    (ii) The affected factors of production may shift to other activities (in which lower taxes are paid) within the country.

    (iii) The taxes in question may be evaded.

    (iv) The taxes in question may not be levied in the first place.

    (v) The taxes may be levied but not have the desired effect.

There follow some brief comments on each of these items.

1.   On factors of production leaving the country

This may at first glance appear to be a point of little practical importance, given the constraints that exist in today's world with respect to international migration. Nonetheless, I think such a judgment is unwarranted, especially in the context of redistributive fiscal policy measures. The facts, I believe, are that the strongest barriers to international migration bear against the poorest strata of the income distribution in LDCs, while the possibilities for migration by the upper strata are quite real.[1]

A factor of much more importance than labor migration, however, is that of capital. There can be little doubt that most wealthy people, in any less-developed country in the world, can and do find ways of having bank accounts and securities portfolios abroad. In many cases, the capital-market movements involved are perfectly legal; in others, the black market is used as a vehicle for transferring funds. But in any event the funds do get abroad, where they earn incomes which rarely pay any tax to the treasury of the country of origin. I believe that we can and should take as a datum that wealthy people in most LDCs earn yield on their foreign holdings equal to the nominal yields on those investments minus whatever taxes may be withheld at the source by the host country. These are the yields which they compare with what they can earn at home.[2] If the economic return to capital becomes more unfavorable for home-country investment, this will carry as a consequence a greater flow of funds overseas, where it will be beyond the effective reach of the LDC tax net. Any discussion of redistribution by fiscal means which does not recognize the existence and importance of this avenue of escape from local taxation must be characterized as hopelessly unrealistic.

2.   Tax "shelters" within the country,

Realism also dictates that one recognize the existence (and probable inevitability) of areas within most LDC economies where factor incomes are taxed at effectively lower rates than in other areas. As far as capital is concerned, there is usually a relatively high rate of taxation of corporate profits, a lower rate of tax applying to many noncorporate activities (e.g., farming, retailing), and probably no tax at all on the imputed income from owner-occupied housing. In addition there are often special tax-incentive schemes aimed at attracting funds to backward regions (e.g., Northeast Brazil) or to specified activities (e.g., low-income rental housing).

With respect to labor income, such special provisions are far less common, but substantial differences in the effective burden of taxation arise through differential evasion. Heavy taxation, at the source, of salary incomes thus gives rise to professional services being carried on under special contracts outside the formal salary structure of the firm. Similarly, heavy taxes on wage incomes lead to the subcontracting of simple manufacturing processes to small supplier firms which are in a better position than large companies to avoid or evade such taxes. Even where direct subcontracting is not undertaken, it appears that the relatively heavy taxation of wage and salary incomes in "organized" industry (e.g., modern textile firms, supermarkets, department stores, and so on) is a key factor in the survival of competitive activities (e.g., handicraft textiles, small retail shops) in the "unorganized" sector.

3.   Tax evasion

Tax evasion clearly plays a role in the processes discussed under sections 1 and 2 above. It merits a separate heading mainly to underline its ubiquity and inevitability. This is not to say that efforts to attack tax evasion are in vain--quite the contrary, such efforts are utterly essential for any reasonable degree of equity in taxation. But I do feel that a frank recognition of the phenomenon of evasion is required for the design of an equitable tax system. To pretend that farmers, shopkeepers, and independent professionals pay income taxes with anything like the same fidelity as wage and salary workers subject to withholding only leads to an exaggerated reliance being placed on personal income taxation as a revenue source, and to a consequently greater degree of horizontal inequity between those who cannot evade the legally applicable tax and the other groups with easier access to evasion routes. The course of wisdom for most LDCs is to combine a diversified tax portfolio (so that those groups that can evade a particular tax are at least picked up on other taxes in the package) with moderate rate structures (to limit the incentive to evade) and energetic enforcement (to limit the degree of response to whatever incentive exists). There can be no doubt, however, that this strategy has the effect of blunting the apparent possibilities for strongly redistributive taxation—a conclusion which, in my view, should be taken as a fact of life.

4. Political constraints

This is probably the best term under which to summarize the reasons why strongly redistributive taxes may not be levied in the first place. The United States is able to have marginal income tax rates of 50 percent on personal incomes of, say, 8 times the per capita GNP. Such rates are evaded to some extent and by some groups, but they are paid in full by salaried workers subject to withholding and by others. But what can be taxed in the United States out of incomes of $50,000 per year and more, cannot be done in India on incomes of $800 per year and up, or in Central America on incomes in excess of $4,000 or $5,000. Part of the reason why it cannot be done lies in real factors like those mentioned under sections 1 and 2 above. But a very important part lies directly in political factors. Put very simply, heavy taxation of incomes above the indicated figures would directly hit the very civil servants who design and administer the tax structure, and also the legislators who put it into law. In spite of the fact that their incomes put them in the top percentile or two of the income distribution, these groups, by and large, do not consider themselves as rich but rather as part of a struggling middle class. Their tastes and consumption habits are not extravagant by international standards, or even in terms of the traditions of the elite in their own countries. The fact that these people are demonstrably a part of the very upper stratum of society in their own impoverished nations does not make them any more eager or willing to impose new, heavy tax burdens on themselves. As long as this attitude prevails, and as long as the groups in question have the political clout to make it stick, even U.S.-style

progressivity in income taxation will remain out of the range of possibility for the LDCs in question.

5. Incidence

The incidence question is in a sense simply the reflection of the
forces referred to above. In very broad terms it can be summarized with
the comment that tax structures are likely in fact to be a lot less progressive than they look. If, for example, the owners of capital in an LDC
have access to outlets for their funds in the world capital market at
yields of 8 percent, efforts to tax the use of those funds at home will
have the effect of a further capital outflow. In all likelihood, the
final result will be that capital invested at home will still have an
after-tax yield of 8 percent (or whatever is judged by the investors to
be reasonably comparable with the yields obtainable on the international
market). If the taxation of income from capital at home is light, lots
of funds will stay at home and will produce a before-tax yield of, say,
10 percent. If the relevant taxation is heavy, more capital will flow
abroad, and that which stays at home may end up with a before-tax yield
of, say, 16 percent. In both of these cases the LDC owners of capital are
really in the same income position--earning 8 percent after taxes on their
investments. But in the first case they appear to be bearing low taxes
and in the second, to be bearing high taxes. In fact, as the example was
framed, the burden of taxation on income from capital is in both cases
passed on in the form of higher real product prices or lower real wages
or both. Its ultimate incidence will depend on the distribution among
income groups of the consumption of the affected products, and on the
degree of substitutability of labor for capital in the affected activities.
But reasonable values for the relevant parameters covering these aspects
of incidence would surely lead to a tax which is effectively more like a
consumption tax and/or a general wage tax than a tax which truly reduces
the real income of capital owners by the amounts collected.

The incidence effects of taxes work similarly when labor migration is
involved. If some members of the affected group move out of the country
as a consequence of the tax structure, the before-tax rewards of those who
remain are increased, so that patients, for example, end up paying part of
the tax burden which nominally falls on doctors.

Where the reallocations induced by the tax system take place within the economy (i.e., by a reshuffling of factors from activities with heavier taxes to those with lighter taxes) rather than by a net out-migration of labor or capital, the situation is somewhat different. Here the most directly traceable effect of heavier taxation of a factor in some activities is to lower the real rewards earned by the same factor in activities with lighter taxes. Thus, for example, the heavier taxation of corporate earnings, in the absence of out-migration of capital from the country, operates to drive down the rewards earned by capital in noncorporate uses. Similarly, the heavier taxation of the earnings of salaried professionals works in the direction of lowering those of professionals in independent practice. Under certain circumstances,[3] this process simply works as a tax-spreading device--the tax on the income of corporate capital falls in the final analysis on the income of all (i.e., corporate plus noncorporate) capital, and the tax on the earnings of salaried accountants is spread ultimately among all (i.e., salaried plus self-employed) accountants.

This "tax-spreading" effect--which means that when a particular factor is subject to higher taxation in some activities than in others, the effect of this higher taxation is felt by similar factors in all activities[4]--is the clearest implication of incidence theory when out-migration is not a significant element in the picture. But there may be other effects as well--causing impacts on consumers as a group or on the real earnings of other productive factors. I shall not go into those effects here, however, since one cannot generalize even about their direction without knowledge of the particulars of the case at hand.

B.   Some redistributional fiscal policy exercises

The discussion of the preceding section can best be viewed as a spring board for the analysis about to be presented. It is a springboard in the sense that, to pass from the previous section to the exercises we are about to engage in, a certain leap is involved--the exercises are not the logical consequence of what went before but are, I hope, motivated and made plausible by it.

The particular meat that I would like to extract from the previous section for use in what is to follow is the judgment that there are strong grounds for caution and deliberation in the design of tax structures. In particular, crude arithmetical exercises purporting to show the redistributive potential of the tax system should be viewed with skepticism. I hope that enough skepticism has been implanted in the minds of my readers that they will be willing to accept the following self-imposed rules for judging what can plausibly be done by progressive taxation in an LDC context.

(i) We will consider progressive taxation to begin at a level equal to the average per-family (or per-earner) income of the country.

(ii) We still consider applying only moderate rates of tax (say 10 to 25 percent) to incomes immediately in excess of the average described in (i). Thus, earnings in excess of the average but less than 1 1/2 times the average would be taxed at rates no greater than, say, 10 percent; and earnings between 1 1/2 and 2 1/2 times the average would be taxed at rates no greater than, say, 20 percent.

(iii) For incomes substantially in excess of the average, higher rates can be applied, but they should only gradually approach a limit of, say, 40 percent, and this limit should come into play at incomes in excess of, say, five or six times the average as defined in (i).

These rules are in fact quite "optimistic" ones when it comes to assessing the redistributive potential of taxes in an LDC environment. Pechman and Okner, in a recent monograph, have analyzed the entire U.S. tax system (federal, state, and local) under eight different sets (variants) of incidence assumptions. Under none of these sets does the average rate of tax of the 95th percentile of the income distribution exceed 25 percent, or that of the 99th percentile exceed 30 percent, or that of the top percentile exceed 40 percent.[5] Our "simulations" for LDCs, we shall see, come quite close to these figures when combined with a "base" of proportional taxation (such as might be provided by sales or value-added taxation) which strikes all income groups at a rate of around 10 percent.

We start with a hypothetical LDC income distribution which is, in relative terms, a bit more equal than that reported by Pechman and Okner for the United States.[6] Columns (1) and (2) of table 1 present this distribution. In Column (3) the average income of each fractile, relative to the overall national average, is calculated. Where this relation exceeds unity, the excess over one represents what rule (i) would permit to be tapped for progressive taxation. This excess is shown in Column (4). Column (5) gives the marginal tax rates which were applied to each group's income, in accordance with rules (ii) and (iii).

Table 1.

Hypothetical Pattern of Income Distribution With Progressive Taxes
(U.S.-Type Distribution)

(1)	(2)	(3)	(4)	(5)	(6)	(7)	(8)
Fractile of Income Distribution	Percentage Share of Total Income Received	Average Income in Fractile, As % of National Average Income [=(2)÷(1)]	Excess Fractile Average Income Over National Average	Marginal Tax Rate Applied	Calculated Tax Per Unit in Fractile	Average Rate of Tax in Fractile [=(6)÷(3)]	Total Tax in Fractile, As % of Total Income [=(7)x(2)]
Lowest quintile (20)	5	.25	--				
Second quintile (20)	10	.50	--				
Third quintile (20)	15	.75	--				
Fourth quintile (20)	25	1.25	0.25	.10	.025	.02	.500
Ninth decile (10)	15	1.50	0.50	.16	.065	.043	.645
91st-95th percentile (5)	10	2.00	1.00	.20	.165	.083	.830
96th-99th percentile (4)	12	3.00	2.00	.30	.465	.155	1.860
Top percentile (1)	8	8.00	7.00	.40	2.465	.308	2.465
Total	100						6.300

The derivation of the average tax per unit in the fractile group, presented in Column (6), was done as follows: for the fourth quintile, the rate of 10 percent was applied to the tax base of 0.25 "average incomes," shown in Column (4). For the ninth decile, with a taxable income of 0.50 [from Column (4)], the first 0.25 was taken to be taxed at the rate of 10 percent, and the second 0.25 was assumed to be taxed at a rate of 16 percent, the total resulting tax being .065[7] "average incomes." The rest of Column (6) is built up in the same way. For the 91st to 95th decile, "taxable income" is 1.00 "average incomes." The first 0.50 of this would carry a tax of .065 (as calculated above), to which would be added a tax of 20% on the second 0.50, yielding a total tax of .165 "average incomes."

In Column (7) the average tax rate for each group is found by dividing the calculated tax [Column (6)] by the average income of the group [Column (3)]. Finally, in Column (8), the total tax of each group is calculated, as a percent of total income, by multiplying the average rates of tax from Column (7) by the percentage shares [from Column (2)] of each group in total income.

The global total of tax collections under the hypothetical setup depicted in table 1 is 6.3 percent of the total income of all groups taken together. This is a sizeable sum, viewed in fiscal policy terms. And it is to be emphasized that the tax system in question, viewed as the progressive component to be added to some proportional base, is significantly more progressive than is the U.S. tax system under any of the incidence variants explored by Pechman and Okner. It is thus probably quite unrealistic to expect so strong a tax performance from a typical LDC. But we shall explore its consequences nonetheless, with the aim of setting outside limits on what can reasonably be expected.

Needless to say, the tax side of the fiscal equation does not by itself effect a full redistribution. For this the expenditure side must also be taken into account. This is done in table 2, where the assumption is made that the benefits associated with the expenditure side are distributed among groups in proportion to their incomes. The net gains and losses accruing to the different income groups under these assumptions are shown in Column (5) of table 2. The most notable feature of this table is the relatively small degree of benefit received by the lower income groups, in spite of the quite progressive tax structure.

Table 2.

Group Gains and Costs of Progressive Taxes
Cum Proportional Expenditures

(1)	(2)	(3)	(4)	(5)
Fractile of Income Distribution	Percentage Share of Total Income Received	Costs of Progressive Taxes (From Table 1, Col. 8)	Gains From Proportional Expenditures	Net Gains (+) or Costs (−)
Lowest quintile (20)	5	--	+ .315	+ .315
Second quintile (20)	10	--	+ .630	+ .630
Third quintile (20)	15	--	+ .945	+ .945
Fourth quintile (20)	25	− .500	+1.575	+1.075
Ninth decile (10)	15	− .645	+ .945	+ .300
91st–95th percentile (5)	10	− .830	+ .630	− .200
96th–99th percentile (4)	12	−1.860	+ .759	−1.101
Top percentile (1)	8	−2.465	+ .501	−1.964

This draws attention to the obvious point that the expenditure side has a very important influence on the ultimate redistributive properties of the fiscal system. Unfortunately, our capacity for quantifying incidence by income group is even more limited on the expenditure than on the tax side, so I shall only make a few general statements here. A great many government outlays go for general purposes (administration, police, the courts, national defense) whose assignment as benefits to particular income groups is necessarily quite arbitrary. The notion that these benefits are roughly proportional to income and/or wealth, however, seems at least to be a plausible approximation. Allocation in accordance with income also seems to be a sensible basis for government expenditures on such items as highways and other infra-structure investments, insofar as their costs are not covered by direct user charges, which for present purposes should not be counted as taxes. When one asks what are the expenditures that can reasonably be allocated on a per-capita or per-family-unit basis, they turn out to be relatively few: primary education, publicly dispensed medical services, and family allowances[8] seem to be the best candidates here. Expenditures that are truly concentrated toward the bottom end of the income distribution are even harder to find. This category could include welfare payments in developed countries, but few LDCs have direct welfare programs. Within the LDCs only a few cases can be found in which the benefits of government outlays accrue predominantly to the poor.[9]

Thus I believe that the type of redistribution implied by table 2 can probably be taken as an optimistic assessment of what fiscal policy is likely to be able to do for income distribution in most LDCs. The effect is certainly small, if one starts with grandiose hopes of a major impact. The Gini coefficient for the distribution of income represented by Columns (1) and (2) of table 1 is .402. That result when Column (2) is adjusted for the transfers shown in Column (5) of table 2 is .372--only a modest change.

If the above gives a realistic picture of the possibilities of fiscal policy, based on the assumption that expenditure incidence is proportional, one may perhaps inquire as to what would happen if the moneys raised from taxation were spent much more equally. An attempt in this direction is reflected in table 3, where the assumption is made that the same amount of revenue as is involved in the tax explored in table 1 is instead raised by proportional taxation but spent in such a way that each unit (individual or family, as the case may be) benefits equally. This last is an absurdly optimistic assumption, from the point of view of redistribution, but we explore its consequences nonetheless. Its implied effect on income distribution is given in Column (5) of table 3. Here it is seen, as should be expected, that the lowest income strata are more strongly benefited than is the case with the implicit transfer explored in table 2. But nonetheless the overall change in income distribution is again modest, with the Gini coefficient being reduced from .402 to .377.

Tables 4, 5, and 6 are patterned after the corresponding tables 1, 2, and 3, the only difference being that the assumed income distribution is more unequal, more closely approximating present-day reality in most LDCs. Together with the stretching of the upper tail of the income distribution, there is a corresponding stretching of the range over which the assumed tax rates apply, but the general pattern of rise of marginal rates from 10 percent to 40 percent is similar to that in table 1. The shift in assumptions between the first three tables and those of tables 4 through 6 has very

Table 3.

Group Gains and Costs of Proportional Taxes
Cum Equal Expenditures Per Unit

(1)	(2)	(3)	(4)	(5)
Fractile of Income Distribution	Percentage Share of Total Income Received	Costs of Proportional Taxes	Gains from Equal Outlay Per Unit	Net Gains (+) or Costs (−)
Lowest quintile (20)	5	− .315	+1.260	+ .945
Second quintile (20)	10	− .630	+1.260	+ .630
Third quintile (20)	15	− .945	+1.260	+ .315
Fourth quintile (20)	25	−1.575	+1.260	− .315
Ninth decile (10)	15	− .945	+ .630	− .315
91st–95th percentile (5)	10	− .630	+ .315	− .315
96th–99th percentile (4)	12	− .759	+ .263	− .496
Top percentile (1)	8	− .501	+ .052	− .449

little effect on the overall conclusions to be drawn from the exercise.
With the more unequal distribution of tables 4 through 6, a somewhat larger
fraction (8.5 versus 6.3 percent) of total income is raised by the assumed
progressive tax pattern. The net redistribution revealed in table 5, where
the progressive tax is joined to a proportional expenditure pattern, is also
somewhat larger than that emerging from table 2, but the basic picture of a
very modest impact on the lowest quintiles of the distribution remains.
The Gini coefficient falls from .498 to .462 as the distribution of Column (2) of table 4 is modified by the transfers shown in Column (5) of
table 5.

The distributional shift entailed in shifting from outlays proportional
to income to equal outlays per unit is (as should be expected) more marked
when the underlying distribution of income is more unequal. The transfers
shown in Column (5) of table 6 reveal this, but the Gini coefficient is
still only reduced from .498 to .456. And the significance of even this

Table 4.

Hypothetical Pattern of Income Distribution With Progressive Taxes
(LDC-Type Distribution)

(1) Fractile of Income Distribution	(2) Percentage Share of Total Income Received	(3) Average Income in Fractile, As % of National Average Income [=(2)÷(1)]	(4) Excess of Fractile Average Income Over National Average	(5) Marginal Tax Rate Applied	(6) Calculated Tax Per Unit in Fractile	(7) Average Rate of Tax in Fractile [=(6)÷(3)]	(8) Total Tax in Frac- tile, As % of Total Income [=(7)x(2)]
Lowest quintile (20)	4	.20	--				
Second quintile (20)	8	.40	--				
Third quintile (20)	12	.60	--				
Fourth quintile (20)	20	1.00	--				
Ninth decile (10)	16	1.60	0.60	.10	.06	.038	.608
91st-95th percentile (5)	12.5	2.50	1.50	.20	.24	.096	1.200
96th-99th percentile (4)	16	4.00	3.00	.33	.74	.185	2.960
Top percentile (1)	11.5	11.50	10.50	.40	3.74	.325	3.738
Total	100						8.506

Table 5.

Group Gains and Costs of Progressive Taxes

Cum Proportional Expenditures

(LDC-Type Distribution)

(1)	(2)	(3)	(4)	(5)
Fractile of Income Distribution	Percentage Share of Total Income Received	Costs of Redistributive Taxes	Gains from Proportional Expenditure	Net Gains (+ or Costs (−)
Lowest quintile (20)	4	--	.340	+ .340
Second quintile (20)	8	--	.680	+ .680
Third quintile (20)	12	--	1.021	+1.021
Fourth quintile (20)	20	--	1.701	+1.701
Ninth decile (10)	16	− .608	1.361	+ .753
91st–95th per-centile (5)	12.5	−1.200	1.063	− .137
96th–99th per-centile (4)	16	−2.960	1.361	−1.599
Top percentile (1)	11.5	−3.738	.978	−2.760
			8.505	

modest fall must be tempered by the realization that the assumption of equal per-unit expenditure incidence (for a significant fraction of total public outlays) is distinctly extreme.

When this paper was initially presented at a preliminary conference of authors and discussants,[10] the principal suggestion made was that the analysis underlying tables 2, 3, 5, and 6 be extended to cover cases built on the assumption that moneys raised by progressive taxation would be spent in an egalitarian way (i.e., equal outlays per taxpaying unit). This is done in tables 7 and 8, and the effects of various combinations of poli-cies on the Gini coefficient are summarized in table 9.

Table 6.

Group Gains and Costs of Proportional Taxes
Cum Equal Expenditures Per Unit
(LDC-Type Distribution)

(1) Fractile of Income Distribution	(2) Percentage Share of Total Income Received	(3) Costs of Proportional Taxes	(4) Gains from Equal Outlay Per Unit	(5) Net Gains (+) or Costs (−)
Lowest quintile (20)	4	− .340	+1.701	+1.361
Second quintile (20)	8	− .680	+1.701	+1.021
Third quintile (20)	12	−1.021	+1.701	+ .680
Fourth quintile (20)	20	−1.701	+1.701	−−
Ninth decile (10)	16	−1.361	+ .851	− .510
91st−95th per- centile (5)	12.5	−1.063	+ .426	− .637
96th−99th per- centile (4)	16	−1.361	+ .340	−1.021
Top percentile (1)	11.5	− .978	+ .085	− .893

As shown in table 9, one gets almost identical Gini coefficients for the Progressive Tax, Proportional Expenditure Package as for the Proportional Tax, Egalitarian Expenditure Package—under either assumption concerning the basic distribution of income.

Not surprisingly, the combination of progressive taxes with egalitarian expenditure produces about twice the reduction in the Gini coefficient as either of the intermediate packages. However, I would like to emphasize the gross unrealism of this combination as a practical target for a major fiscal reform. It is certainly possible to find incremental expenditures which indeed are distributed in an egalitarian way, and to finance them by incremental taxes that are raised in a progressive fashion. But that is a far cry from reorganizing the whole of a country's governmental expenditures so that they are egalitarian in their incidence, and reordering its entire tax system in order to be as progressive as our numerical examples

Table 7.

Group Gains and Costs of Progressive Taxes

Cum Equal Expenditures Per Unit

(1)	(2)	(3)	(4)	(5)
Fractile of Income Distribution	Percentage Share of Total Income Received	Costs of Progressive Taxes (From Table 1 Col. 8)	Gains from Equal Outlay Per Unit	Net Gains or Costs (-
Lowest quintile (20)	5	--	+1.260	+1.260
Second quintile (20)	10	--	+1.260	+1.260
Third quintile (20)	15	--	+1.260	+1.260
Fourth quintile (20)	25	- .500	+1.260	+ .760
Ninth decile (10)	15	- .645	+ .630	- .015
91st-95th per-centile (5)	10	- .830	+ .315	- .515
96th-99th per-centile (4)	12	-1.860	+ .263	-1.597
Top percentile (1)	8	-2.465	+ .052	-2.413

assume. Yet this type of major—indeed revolutionary—sort of change is what would be required to produce the Gini coefficients of the last row of table 9. Hence my classification of them as unrealistic.

C. Observations on the struggle for greater equality

The main lesson emerging from the preceding sections is that those wh are striving to improve the distribution of income in LDCs should be prepa for a long, arduous, demanding, and often frustrating struggle. The reali ties of unequal income distributions are stark, but the limitations and constraints that stand in the way of improvement are equally strong and real. There is no simple trick or touchstone, short of totally uprooting the existing economic, social, and political structure, that will with one or two or three strokes substantially alter the distributional picture tha we now observe. The challenge is one of mustering the forces for an es-sentially permanent struggle, with many battles that are purely defensive,

Table 8

Group Gains and Costs of Progressive Taxes

Cum Equal Expenditures Per Unit

(1)	(2)	(3)	(4)	(5)
Fractile of Income Distribution	Percentage Share of Total Income Received	Costs of Progressive Taxes (From Table 4 Col. 8)	Gains from Equal Outlay Per Unit	Net Gains (+) or Costs (−)
Lowest quintile (20)	4	--	+1.701	+1.701
Second quintile (20)	8	--	+1.701	+1.701
Third quintile (20)	12	--	+1.701	+1.701
Fourth quintile (20)	20	--	+1.701	+1.701
Ninth decile (10)	16	− .608	+ .851	+ .243
91st-95th percentile (5)	12.5	−1.200	+ .426	− .774
96th-99th percentile (4)	16	−2.960	+ .340	−2.620
Top percentile (1)	11.5	−3.738	+ .085	−3.653

and others that gain ground bit by bit as a result of hard and continuous effort.

To give a sense of the directions that such a struggle might take, I present below an illustrative listing of some possible measures to improve the distribution picture:

(i) Eliminate the income-tax exemption of imputed rent on owner-occupied dwellings. There is probably no single fiscal area in which the cause of equality could be more directly and surely promoted than this one. Countries in which the very poor sleep in the streets are nonetheless implicitly subsidizing the housing of the wealthy to the tune of their marginal income-tax rates times the implicit rental in their dwellings (often two or three per family). This fact is clear, yet the political resistance to this particular reform is incredibly strong, and comes from homeowners of all income levels, and even from those who, though they do not now own houses, hope and plan some day to do so.

Table 9.

Gini Coefficients for Alternative Tax-Expenditure Packages

	Basic Distribution of Income	
Policy Package	U.S. Type	LDC Type
None	.402 (1)[a]	.498 (4)[a]
Progressive Tax, Proportional Expenditure	.372 (2)	.562 (5)
Proportional Tax, Egalitarian Expenditure	.377 (3)	.456 (6)
Progressive Tax, Egalitarian Expenditure	.347 (7)	.419 (8)

[a]Figures in parentheses give the table number in this chapter from which each Gini coefficient was derived. Gini coefficients calculated under the policy package labeled "None" are obtained from the unadjusted income distributions given in Column (2) of tables 1 and 2, respectively. Other Gini coefficients are based on these initial distributions, modified by the net gains and costs shown in the tables indicated.

(ii) Shift part of the weight of progressive taxation from the in-come tax to a progressive consumption-expenditure tax.[11] This, to my knowledge, is the best way to induce the repatriation of capital held abroad by nationals of the country in question, to deter further capital outflow, and to capture within the local tax net the expenditures made by nationals traveling abroad.[12]

(iii) Improve assessment procedures for property tax purposes, prefer-ably by shifting to a self-assessment scheme. The property tax, as pres-ently administered, is shot through with inequities. Assessed values differ from market values in grossly different degrees on different properties; in-flation tends to be reflected in assessments only after incredibly long lags; and corruption is rife in the assessment process in many countries. self-assessment scheme (particularly the market-enforced variety) would go far to rectify all these deficiencies.[13]

(iv) <u>Categorically eliminate subsidized housing for those above</u> <u>the median income</u>. It is my general impression that most beneficiaries of public housing in LDCs are in fact in the upper half of the income distribution.

(v) <u>Institute electricity rate structures that reflect the true</u> <u>economic cost of power generation</u>. There can be little doubt that the cross-sectional demand for electric power is income elastic, yet this is one of the most ubiquitously subsidized public services.

(vi) <u>Institute substantial tuition charges for public higher edu-</u> <u>cation, with special provision for the financing of the education of poorer</u> <u>students (preferably via loans)</u>. This is of particular importance in LDCs where free or nearly free university education is given predominantly to the children of the rich.

(vii) <u>Where unemployment and underemployment are serious problems,</u> <u>institute programs in which the government serves as an "employer of last</u> <u>resort."</u> The government, in such cases, can perform a truly positive function by being a "bad" employer, i.e., by standing ready to employ those who would otherwise be destitute, on terms and conditions such that no se- rious competition with "regular" employments is involved. Such programs have great potential for ensuring some opportunity to the very worst-off segments of society (at least those who are able-bodied), and they can also serve a useful informative function in giving direct information on the na- ture and extent of the poverty problem.

(viii) <u>The government should avoid, in its own employment practices</u> <u>and in its legislation and regulations covering private-sector employment,</u> <u>the creation or perpetuation of "labor elites."</u> Labor elites are generated when wages and conditions in certain protected segments of the labor market are very substantially superior to those in the market at large. The syn- drome of the government as a "model employer," paying not only greater-than- market wages but also throwing in a variety of ample fringe benefits[14] should be shunned. The money spent in providing amenities to the labor elite is better spent on activities that truly help the really poor.

(ix) <u>Tax incentives to industry should be viewed with great suspi-</u> <u>cion</u>. While no categorical case can be made against tax incentives which are properly designed to compensate for market imperfections or weaknesses, the fact remains that most tax incentive schemes actually adopted in LDCs have artificially encouraged the use of capital-intensive methods of production, and many have in addition resulted in the transfer of substantial sums from the public treasury into pure "producer surplus" in the hands of the owners of the affected enterprises.

The above listing could readily be extended, but I believe it is sufficient to support my main conclusions. They are:

(i) The attack on the income distribution problem should be multifaceted, operating on many different fronts at once.

(ii) There is no particularly close connection between the various facets of this attack. The battles can, by and large, be waged independently. All do not have to be fought or won simultaneously, and gains can be had by winning something along any given front.

(iii) Serious political resistance is to be expected along any relevant front. Almost by its nature, redistribution is a game in which there must be losers as well as winners. And the losers, being those who already gain from the status quo, are likely to have substantial entrenched power in the existing setup.

(iv) Struggle is the key word where income redistribution is concerned. Mere lip-service to the cause will do no good.

Chapter 7

NOTES

1. For example, the large fractions of the output of doctors by Philippine and Colombian medical schools that have ended up practicing in the United States; and the large numbers of Indian social scientists in the U.S., Canadian, and British universities.

2. It should be noted that the use of the black market as a vehicle for the transfer of funds does not in itself lower the yield perceived by the LDC investor. For example, if the official exchange rate is Rs.7.5 to the dollar, and the black market rate Rs.11.25, it is true that it takes 50 percent more rupees to buy a black market dollar than an official one, but if the black market dollar is invested abroad at a yield of 8 percent, and if the proceeds of the investment are then transferred back to the country of origin at the black market rate, the yield in rupees is also 8 percent. Black market transactions run risks of detection (though in fact the likelihood is small) and of changes in the relevant exchange rate between the time of initial investment and the time that funds are repatriated, but the investment yield itself is unaffected by the use of the black market to transfer funds.

3. The so-called Cobb-Douglas case is the best example.

4. Even those subject to little or no taxation.

5. See Joseph A. Pechman and Benjamin A. Okner, Who Bears The Tax Burden? (Brookings Institution, 1974), table 4-4, p. 51. Some readers might wonder why this study of the U.S. tax system is introduced into a paper dealing with income redistribution in the LDCs. The answer is that the Pechman-Okner study is unique. It is the only study that so thoroughly covers the incidence of a complete tax system in such detail. It should also be noted that none of the conclusions of the present paper is derived from Pechman-Okner's results. I have really used their study only to convey an idea of how taxes affected income distribution in an important developed country with a good record of tax compliance and administration. My belief is that one cannot reasonably expect a much better "performance" than this in an LDC.

6. Pechman and Okner, table 4-2, p. 46.

7. $.065 = (.25) \times (.1) + (.25) \times (.16)$.

8. Actually, many family allowance setups apply only to certain categories of workers, which exclude the very poor; and public secondary and higher education has benefits which at least in LDCs are concentrated disproportionately among the well-to-do.

9. Such as India's famine relief and rural works programs.

10. Workshop on Income Distribution in Less Developed Countries, Brookings Institution/Princeton University, Princeton, September 1974.

11. For elaboration on the following points, see A. Harberger, "The Panamanian Income Tax System, A Heterodox View," mineographed (June 1973).

12. This is an important category of luxury spending in nearly all countries, but particularly for the smaller ones.

13. For more on self-assessment, see "Issues of Tax Reform for Latin America," ed. A. Harberger, Taxation and Welfare (Boston: Little Brown and Co., 1970).

CHAPTER VIII

POLICY INSTRUMENTS FOR RURAL INCOME REDISTRIBUTION

William R. Cline

A.   Introduction

This chapter surveys the recent literature regarding redistributive effects of principal policy instruments affecting the agricultural sector in
developing countries, updating a smilar evaluation prepared in an earlier
study on the relationship between agricultural strategy and income distribution.[1]   In addition, specific attention is given to a model of land reform
with compensation to owners, in view of the special importance of land redistribution as an instrument for improving rural income distribution. The other
policy instruments examined include land taxation, policy on sharecropping,
new technology, farm mechanization, and channeled credit. Other instruments
are touched on but not examined in detail, including price support programs,
minimum wages, colonization, irrigation, rural education, and farm extension.

The interaction between rural equity and agricultural production is
not explored in this chapter. Some instruments for improving equity should
clearly increase production (e.g., land redistribution where large estates
with idle land are predominant). For other instruments it might be argued
that policies seemingly inequitable in direct terms (e.g., mechanization
on large farms) are indirectly equity oriented because they stimulate food
production, thus lowering food prices and improving real income relatively
more for the lower classes (urban and rural) than for upper income groups.
The burden of proof lies with the advocates of such arguments, since equal
or greater production impact should be available through instruments having
favorable direct impact on equity as well.

B.   Land reform

1.   Recent literature

The single most powerful policy instrument for the combined objectives
of rural equity and output growth is land reform. The theoretical reasons

why land redistribution should increase output as well as improve rural equity are considered at length in an earlier study by the author.[2] The central thrust of the arguments is that large estates underutilize their available land resources while at the same time the latifundio-minifundio landholding structure compresses excess labor into the very small properties (minifundia) and into an underemployed landless labor force. Poor utilization of land on large farms results from various factors: "labor market dualism" in which the effective price is higher for hired labor on large farms than for family labor on small farms; land monopoly and monopsony over labor in larger estates;[3] the holding of land as a portfolio asset rather than for production; and the fact that production partly for own consumption provides small farms with greater market certainty than large estates. The resulting misallocation of resources within agriculture means that output could rise from the combination of underutilized labor on small farms and in the landless labor force with underutilized land on large farms. Production function analysis using Brazilian farm survey data indicates that the creation of family farms would incur no loss in potential efficiency since returns to scale are constant, and simulations of the production impact of redistribution of land into family farms of equal size suggest production gains for Brazil of 25% overall.[4] Numerous other studies, particularly those concerning Latin America, reach similar conclusions, and they need not be recounted here. It is worth noting, however, that these conditions are not limited to Latin America alone. Even in the Asian context of a modest spectrum of farm sizes, the pattern of an inverse relationship between output per farm area and total farm size is well documented (see for example Bardhan regarding India,[5] and Dorner and Kanel[6] for data demonstrating the relationship for India, Taiwan, and the Philippines as well as Brazil, Colombia, Mexico, and Guatemala).

Recent literature on land reform includes caveats about its distributional effects (Berry,[7] Sinha,[8] and Minhas,[9] and useful reports by Barraclough and Fernandez[10] on recent land reform in Chile, and by Horton,[1] in Peru. Berry makes the point that if in actual execution a land reform distributes land of large estates to a relatively limited class of former small farmers (or, the logic of the analysis would require, to a favored subset of landless workers), then there may be a perverse distributional effect concerning income distribution among landless workers and small farmers. While the latter may gain at the expense of former landlords (equalizing distribution at the upper end of the income scale), they may begin to employ family labor for tasks that formerly were performed on the large estates by landless workers, thereby reducing the total demand for labor from the landless work force (and, possibly, the rural wage).

The warning raised by Berry is particularly important. Any land reform which excludes the majority of rural labor from direct benefits will, as a minimum, fail to achieve its full potential for increasing equity, and may also reduce the demand for hired labor. Nevertheless, Berry's analysis does not appear to give sufficient weight to the output effect of land reform on labor demand. The increase of land cultivation and production which should follow from redistribution of land should increase labor demand, and by an amount more than proportionate to the output increase since it will be accompanied by a shift toward labor intensity in the overall factor combinations within agriculture, given the relatively low utilization of labor relative to land and capital on pre-reform large farms.[12]

Another current of thought on the limitations of land reform for rural redistributions is represented in an essay by Sinha.[13] Referring to the Asian context of dense population (rather than to the Latin American case), the author argues that there is so much rural labor and so little land that equal division of land would create a structure of hopelessly small inefficient farms. In particular, Sinha assumes an "optimal" farm size which maximizes farm output given available agricultural land; a farm structure with smaller farms would generate less total output despite its absorption of more labor, according to the author. Aware that this proposition is inconsistent with past evidence showing systematically higher output per farm area on smaller farms, Sinha maintains that this old pattern no longer holds thanks to the Green Revolution and its relative increase in land productivity of larger farms, and he cites fragmentary evidence for support.[14] Based on the underlying assumption of an optimal farm size exceeding that which would absorb all rural families in an equalizing reform, the author then maintains that the best strategy for rural equity would be to limit land redistribution to a subset of the rural population (i.e., a number consistent with optimal farm size) while absorbing the remainder in rural public works. This scenario would take advantage of the greater marketable surplus the author believes would be forthcoming from the somewhat larger land reform parcels operated on a "commercial" rather than "subsistence" basis to finance the public works and, similarly, would permit the bureaucracy to focus its limited administrative resources on such programs rather than have these resources bogged down in assisting the countless subsistence farms which would result from fully equalizing land redistribution.

The difficulty with this analysis is its presumption of an optimal farm size and the notion that smaller size with more labor retained in agriculture would actually reduce potential output. While the idea of an optimal farm size is extremely popular, it is simply inconsistent with the vast bulk of empirical analysis, which shows constant returns to scale considering inputs actually used as well as greater utilization of available land as farm size diminishes. The author's argument of change in this pattern due to new technology is unconvincing, especially when the potential for small-scale labor-intensive use of new varieties and fertilizer is considered; temporary advantage on larger farms no doubt may be observed but it reflects the S-curve sequence of adoption in which the larger farms adopt new techniques first but may be soon followed by the smaller. The most serious difficulty with the approach is its assumption that ongoing employment can be generated in nonagricultural pursuits for the excess labor left out of a land reform. Yet public works by their nature create current employment but not necesarily the capital requirements for permanent jobs. Moreover, from the standpoint of income distribution it should be noted that the public works carried out by the excess labor would enhance the profitability of agriculture for those fortunate enough to remain in a reformed agricultural structure, conferring additional benefits on them.

In sum, the appropriate farm size for an equalizing land redistribution into family farms is merely the available land divided by the number of agricultural families net of those which can realistically be expected to be absorbed into nonagricultural activities. Given growing population as well as very limited industrial employment growth, it seems reasonable that this formulation will normally involve absorption of the total agricultural population into the reformed structure. Whether a substantial portion instead can be siphoned off into rural public works with permanent employment prospects in socially efficient work is a matter for careful empirical analysis which should neither be ruled out as a possibility nor counted upon as an article of faith.

Minhas[15] presents a viewpoint similar to that of Sinha, arguing that
land redistribution to the full rural population in Indian conditions
would leave a structure of rural population mostly below the "poverty
line," so that instead fewer rural families should be included in reform,
much more attention should be given to the integration of currently
splintered (i.e., physically separated) parcels under operation by single
farm units, and unabsorbed rural labor should be attended to through
public works. The same difficulties cited above apply to this approach,
in addition to the point that any arbitrary "poverty line" constitutes
precarious basis for policy-making as it is more likely to reflect aspiration than realistic potential.

The cases of Chile and Peru represent important recent experiences in
the area of land reform in developing countries. Barraclough and Fernandez
have compiled a description and analysis of the Chilean reform through
mid-1972.[16] Under the Frei government land reform had reached a total of
approximately 14% of productive land; the Allende regime by mid-1972 had
extended the total area expropriated to 35% of the country's total land
(where it apparently remained at the time of the coup against Allende).
The reform sector included practically all land formerly in estates larger
than 80 irrigated hectares equivalent (HRB) as well as land from poorly utilized farms from 40 to 80 HRB. The reform units remained undivided in As-
sentamientos, Centers of Agrarian Reform (CERAs), or Centers of Production
(CPs), all essentially cooperative farms. These units were dualistic: they
contained areas of collective operation (on the basis of wages to members
and outside workers) as well as plots cultivated by individual members for
their own account (goces and talajes). Barraclough and Fernandez emphasize
that this structure led to poor utilization of the collective resources
within the reform units: members tended to concentrate their working time,
as well as some of the inputs belonging to the cooperative, on their own individual plots, leaving larger collective areas inadequately worked.

Despite its impressive speed and extent, the Chilean land reform benefited directly only approximately one-tenth of the rural labor force. Thus,
while 75,000 workers became members of reform units on the large farms where
they previously worked, another 700,000 rural workers remained outside the
reform sector.

The reform units did increase their employment of labor by 25% above
pre-reform levels. Nevertheless, the low labor-intensity on former large

estates continued to dominate the agrarian structure, and the reform sector absorbed only 18% of total agricultural labor, despite its possession of 35% of the land (adjusted for quality). Output in the reform sector did rise, despite the decapitalization accompanying reform, as expropriated owners withdrew capital onto the "reverse" farm areas they were permitted to retain. However, the bulk of the output increase appears to have been in the individual plots (goces) of the reform unit members rather than on the more extensive collective areas (with approximately 13% of reform unit area but 33% of its output represented by the individual plots). The marked difference in labor/land ratios among sectors persisted after the reform: on minifundios (under 5 HRB), labor per area remained ten times as high as on the new reform units, and even the medium-farm sector retained a slightly higher labor/land density than the reform units.

At the time of the study, Barraclough and Fernandez emphasized the importance of the medium-size farm sector to the supply of marketed surplus and therefore to the future of the Allende regime. A mushrooming of monetary income of lower classes had provoked an enormous increase in demand for food, only partially met by increased imports. Despite the fact that aggregate agricultural production rose 6% by 1972 compared with 1970, demand grew much faster and, in the face of official food price controls, queues and black markets developed. The medium-farm sector (20 to 80 HRB) supplied 45% of output but perhaps as much as 60% of marketed output, and its continued production growth was crucial to food supply. The authors noted the very strong performance of the sector but cautioned that much clearer government plans would have to be announced before sufficient certainty would exist to encourage continued investment and output growth in the sector, in view of the threat of reduction of the permissible private farm size ceiling below the 80 HRB limit.

The Barraclough-Fernandez report implies several important points. (i) The difficulties of agricultural supply resulted not from production declines attending land reform but from price controls on food in the face of rapid expansion of money incomes of the urban poor; actual quantities supplied rose but inconsistent policies led to apparent shortages. (ii) Despite its substantial territorial penetration the land reform reached only a minority of the rural poor. This pattern appears to have resulted from the turning over of land to pre-existing workers on large estates. Although some partial increase in labor use followed, the increase was inadequate to redress the dramatic underutilization of labor on this land previously characterizing the private estates. As a result the pre-existing workers received a windfall gain and became an elite rural "middle" class. (iii) The failure to divide reform units into individual family parcels created a clash of ideals with reality: the ideal of collective production collided with the reality of past tradition of access to individual plots; and the reality of much more direct reward to the worker for effort expended on his individual plot conflicted with appropriate allocation of resources within the reform sector.[17]

To the present author, there are important lessons from this experience. First, land expropriated should not be considered the preserve of its former workers alone but should incorporate an appropriate additional portion of the landless labor force.[18] Second, the ideological pursuit of large collective farms may lead to an inefficient reform unit; division into family farms would generally appear preferable from the efficiency standpoint unless vigorous planning efforts are successful in duplicating the resource allocation patterns which would be generated spontaneously under a small family farm structure. (The role of ideology is evident in the prologue to the study by Fernandez, who asserts that "the small family farm is a stagnant production form," a viewpoint perhaps echoing that of some Chilean land reform planners.) Fernandez and Barraclough frequently cite the existence of economies of scale in support of nondivision of the estates; however, the large body of empirical production function estimates available shows constant returns to scale. Third, as the authors of the report suggest, certainty for the nonreform sector is crucial to continued aggregate agricultural supply.

Horton has conducted a field investigation of 27 new reform enterprises as the basis for an evaluation of recent land reform experience in Peru.[19] After a long history of pressure for land reform, including especially a land reform law in 1964 which went unenforced and, according to the author, discouraged investment and increased peasant pressure for land redistribution, the military government in 1969 decreed a new land reform law and began energetic implementation. Expropriating land primarily with compensation in long-term agrarian bonds, the government first took over 12 large coastal sugar plantations and a limited number of extremely large livestock ranches in the highland. Subsequently regional units of the national Land Reform Agency expropriated additional units. Reform units became "Agrarian Production Cooperatives" (CAPs), with collective ownership of resources in large-scale units, or "Agrarian Social Interest Societies" (SAIS), primarily cooperatives maintaining the physical unity of large-scale livestock units while distributing their profits to neighboring peasant communities. In addition expropriated land went to peasant communities or individuals.

Horton reports that government plans called for the redistribution, by 1976, of 9 million hectares of farmland among 340,000 beneficiaries, with 80% of the land in CAPs and SAIS; 16% for peasant communities, and 4% for individuals. These changes in agrarian structure would then leave 43% of Peru's land in private farms, 32% in the possession of peasant communities, 13% in CAPs, and 12% in SAIS. In terms of resources this target profile for agrarian structure would leave only a small portion of the country's livestock in the CAPs and SAIS, but close to half of foodstuff production. Only one-third of the rural population would benefit directly from the land redistribution after fulfillment of the complete plans for 1976.

Production characteristics have changed very little as a result of reform, according to Horton. The principal difference is worker ownership of former private estates. Where profits were previously ample, there is thus scope for increased wages; Horton found that real wages had remained constant on the coast, risen one-fourth on interior livestock enterprises, and more than tripled on interior crop enterprises. An important structural difference between the Peruvian reform units and those of Chile is that the CAP in Peru prohibits the use of resources for individual production. Production is collective, with worker management, and profits are distributed among members in proportion to the number of days worked by each. This system appears to avoid the serious problem of diversion of effort to individual plots to the detriment of the collective area encountered in the Chilean cooperatives.

The economic impact of the land reform to date is unclear. Horton reports that although production data are generally unreliable, land reform has not caused major disruptions in agricultural production. At the same time, the study relates that the reform has induced substantial slaughter of cattle, leading to a subsequent meat shortage. Employment effects have been a major area of disappointment, according to the author. Land reform has neither increased nor decreased employment. Officials seeking to increase the employment impact have forced cooperatives to grant membership to a "few previously part-time workers"; otherwise, reform enterprise members are apparently not hiring additional labor or expanding membership, in order to protect their profits.

Finally, the study describes the strong ideological commitment of the government to collective, large-scale production. This orientation succeeded in the coastal sugar estates, but elsewhere (particularly in the highlands) authorities met strong opposition in the attempt to collectivize individual production by tenants and sharecroppers on former private estates. In these areas cooperative members were subsequently allowed to keep their individual livestock and small plots of land. The determination of the government to establish large collective units derives in part from the notion that reform units will as a result be self-contained and constitute less of an administrative burden than would a complex of numerous small farms.

In summary, the Chilean and Peruvian experiences appear to represent redistribution of rural income away from the former landholding class to the former workers on expropriated estates. As such, they constitute improvements in rural distribution, but they not only fail to take the opportunity to make the income equalization as thoroughgoing as it could be through more equal distribution of land among the entire rural work force[20] but also fail to realize the full output-increasing potential of reform.

A broader question raised by the experiences of Chile and Peru is the relationship between post-reform structure and potential output gain provided by land reform. Indeed, an important area for research is the identification of probable output (and equity) effects of land reform when the change is from pre-reform structures of alternative types, to post-reform structures of various types. A catalogue of pre-reform types would include: (i) the Latin American latifundio-minifundio complex; (ii) a structure of relatively equal sized tenant farms with little landless labor; (iii) a modest span of farm sizes but intense population pressure and sizeable land-less labor force (e.g., the Indian case); (iv) capitalized plantation agriculture; (v) communal landownership; and so forth. Alternative post-reform types would include: (i) family farms of modest size, absorbing the entire rural labor force; (ii) state farms; (iii) large cooperatives; and so forth. There would be major variants within each category (pre- and post-reform). There exists little analysis of production and distributional effects of transition from structure "i" to reformed structure "j." The author's predilection is that the maximum output gain occurs in moving from pre-reform type "i" to post-reform type "j," but this is a complex issue warranting theoretical and empirical examination.

2.   Land reform with compensation to landowners

While properly executed land reform constitutes a powerful instrument for rural income equalization and output growth, it is frequently ruled out as politically infeasible. Yet sweeping land redistribution with little real compensation to owners may be out of the question politically in circumstances where more limited land redistribution with full payment to owners is a realistic policy option. Landowner opposition is certain to be mitigated when the prospects for compensation are good. Moreover, if the reform process is gradual rather than complete in a single sweeping stroke, ground rules of full compensation will contribute to the mainte-nance of investment incentives in agriculture outside the reform sector, since remaining producers will not fear total loss of the value of their investments from subsequent reform. The maintenance of incentives in the non-reform sector in turn is essential if short-run disruption of produc-tion is to be minimized in a land reform.

The potential for raising output through land redistribution provides the opportunity for a "capitalist land reform" which would improve worker income while fully compensating former owners. Such a reform would con-stitute a classical "Pareto optimal" redistribution: one in which some individuals are made better off while the rest are made no worse off than before. Indeed, consideration of reasonable magnitudes of the relevant effects suggests that there would be quite ample room for improvement in income levels for the rural poor even with full compensation paid to owners in a land reform.

The appendix presents a model which permits an evaluation of income increases for workers in a "capitalistic land reform." The central elements in the analysis are the following: (i) Potential income growth for the workers is "leveraged" because they only receive a portion of output before reform (the labor share), so that even a modest rise in output can confer a sizeable percentage rise in labor income after reform; (ii) The market interest rate for financial debt instruments is typically lower than the discount rate used by entrepreneurs to assess an income-earning asset

with risk involved (for example, 6% versus 15% per annum, respectively).
Therefore, if the recipients of land reform parcels repay the land's market
value under loans with financial market interest rates, there will be an
additional portion of output left over for their net income improvement--
equal to that portion of the former landlord's profit share representing
the amount by which the financial interest rate falls short of the capitalist discount rate.[21]

Computing these effects under reasonable ranges of output gains (25%
to 50%), interest rate (6%), and capitalist discount rate (10% to 15%),
the model in the appendix finds very substantial scope for worker income
improvement under land reform with full compensation to owners. Labor
income net of interest payments rises by between 90% and 200%; and if
amortization of loans is deducted as well (since it represents income constrained to forced savings), net worker income still rises by between
60% and 140%.

In sum, "capitalistic" land reform may hold promise for substantially
increasing income of the rural poor while at the same time being more
feasible politically than land redistribution without compensation. In
addition it should be noted that to enhance receptivity of landlords to
the program, they might be paid in bonds which are more favorable (e.g.,
redeemable at earlier date) if the proceeds are put into selected development programs by the landlord recipients. Such a mechanism has been
employed in the Peruvian land reform, in which long term bonds given for
compensation to expropriated landlords were made eligible for immediate
use if invested in industrial projects (with the degree of discount applied
for such purposes related to the priority assigned by the government to the
project).

Finally, it is important to consider whether land reform based on
full compensation is feasible from the standpoint of financial requirements.
Actual experience is one guide to answering this question. In the case of
Peru, reliable sources indicate that the government anticipated a total
cost of approximately $850 million for acquisition of land, capital, and
livestock assets on the full target reform area of 9 million hectares.
This cost amounted to approximately 10% of GNP and was considered fully
manageable given payment over time (terminating in 20 years). In the case
of Brazil, there is also evidence that financing for "capitalist land
reform" is available. The government earmarked more than $1 billion for

a "Program of Land Redistribution" in the Northeast over five years beginning in 1971. At market land prices as of 1973, this funding would have
been adequate to purchase 8 million hectares of land, practically one-
fifth of the entire land area of the region. Instead, the funds have
been used almost completely for credit to the existing agricultural
structure.

In more general terms, it seems likely that the total value of land
and capital in the agricultural sector of the developing country is approximately equal to one year's GNP.[22] Full compensation for an instantaneous
complete expropriation would be out of the question. On the other hand,
a program expropriating one-tenth of agricultural land annually over five
years (for example) would involve government borrowing or extra tax revenue
equal to 1/10 of GNP in the first year and less thereafter as peasant re-
payments accrued. Such a magnitude would amount to perhaps a one-third
increase in the government spending in many countries, a very large effort
indeed but one not impossible and a reasonable one in view of the radical
transformation of agricultural production and equity which could be obtained.

C.   Land taxation

An instrument sometimes considered an alternative to land reform is
land taxation. Berry has considered the effects of a "presumptive income
tax on land" for the case of Colombia.[23] In his formulation, imputed income
based on a standard rate applied to land value would be added on to the
income reported for income tax purposes. The author first examines the
effects of such a tax in the context of perfect markets. Berry concludes
that in this case the tax would reduce land prices (by lowering net return
to land) and could have positive, neutral, or negative investment and
agricultural output effects "depending on relative present future wealth
elasticities of consumption."[24] In a context of unequal farm sizes, still
with perfect markets, there would also be an effect of land sales by richer
farmers to poorer, smaller farmers because the standard presumptive
income inputed would be taxed at a higher rate for the higher income
farmers, given a progressive income tax.

Turning to the Colombian case, Berry modifies the analysis to take
into account the serious market imperfections which generate a pronounced
pattern of higher value added and higher labor input per unit of constant
quality land on smaller farms than on large. In this context, the

presumptive tax would almost certainly have a positive effect on output (as long as the tax is levied on raw land, not on improvements) because it would include the sale or rental of land from large farms to smaller units where it would be more fully exploited. The income distributional effect would be positive, although if the fragmentation of large farms led to creation of very small family farms, the hired labor force might suffer a loss of employment (whereas it would gain jobs if the transition were to a structure of medium-sized farms using hired rather than family labor).[25] Finally, Berry judges that the political prospects of a presumptive income tax on land have improved in Colombia and notes that farm groups consider-ing themselves progressive have advocated such a tax, feeling they would escape the burden due to their high productivity.

One difficulty with the analysis appears to be that it specifies an imputed income per land value which is added onto actual income regardless of the level of the latter. One would have thought that a presumptive tax would instead specify a minimum income per hectare (or per land value); farmers actually producing more than this minimum would be unaffected by the tax.[26] With this "tax on minimum imputed income" approach, most of the analysis would require revision; most importantly, the effects would be even more equalizing than those assessed by Berry since small farmers with high income per land value would pay no additional tax while large owners with very low income per land value would have to pay much more in taxes than before. Another aspect requiring additional attention is the market for land purchase credit. In the absence of efforts to provide long-term credit for land purchase, a presumptive income tax on land would probably fall far short of its potential for fragmenting large estates into small family properties; instead, rental of formerly unused land would be the likely result.

Lewis similarly argues that a progressive land tax (by farm size) or a tax on potential rather than actual farm income can help reform the agrarian structure.[27] He notes (as have others) the influence of portfolio asset decision-making in land use: land may be held for capital gains purposes without productive utilization, and more progressive capital gains or land taxation will make such holding more costly, pressuring owners to use the land more fully themselves or to rent or sell it. He adds that the land tax may have been a major factor in bringing about the important con-tribution of agriculture to development in Japan.[28]

An opposing line of argumentation is presented by Sazama and Davis,[29] who examine the influence of land tax on land use in Colombia, Chile, and Brazil. The authors maintain that land tax has erroneously been seen as a substitute for land reform; in actuality, they argue, land tax is inadequate for this purpose, and the tax should be viewed as a potential instrument for revenue (which in turn can be used to good purpose) rather than as an instrument for structural reform. The authors begin with the postulate that since a tax on unimproved land value falls on economic rent, it will have no influence on production or land redistribution. They then soften the stand to allow for possible increases in production as owners attempt to recover the wealth loss from a new land tax.

The authors' argument that land is a fixed asset and taxation of its rent will influence nothing appears quite shaky. In the Latin American context (and in underdeveloped areas generally), output and labor inputs per unit of land available are systematically higher on smaller than on larger farms. The effect of a tax on land must therefore be more onerous to large landowners than to small. In effect, a tax on unimproved land should raise its relative price as a productive input, causing those farms (the large estates) using it heavily in combination with little labor and capital[30] to shift factor combinations, to employ more capital and labor per hectare, and to raise "land utilization." Moreover, the cost of holding the land idle for portfolio purposes rises, as mentioned above. In short, it appears theoretically inadequate to assert that a tax on land does not affect output decisions and factor combinations, on the grounds that land is a fixed asset.[31]

The authors seem on more solid ground in their empirical analysis. Data for two counties in Colombia indicate no difference in land utilization between the two, although in one the land tax burden was double that of the other due to a recent reassessment. In Chile, a variety of "performance" indicators fail to show strong relationships to the land tax burden over time,[32] despite a substantial rise in tax rates after 1962 and despite interview material suggesting farmers do take land tax into account in their decisions. Finally, one county in Brazil resembled its neighbor in land utilization although its land tax rate was seven times as high.

The evidence presented by Sazama and Davis supports the contention that, as practiced in Latin America, land taxation has been a poor

instrument for structural reform and has had little influence on land use.
However, in all of the cases they considered, the basic tax rate was minimal,
and it was usually applied to a nominal value radically eroded by inflation.
There is therefore no basis on the evidence for concluding that a higher
tax rate applied to realistically updated land values would be ineffectual
in terms of structural reform. There is, however, the political difficulty
of instituting such rates, and Sazama and Davis maintain that if the political context is ripe for meaningful land taxation it is also ripe for land
reform. Berry's view is the opposite.

On balance, land taxation as an instrument for rural equalization
deserves continued attention. If land tax rates can be raised to levels
sufficiently high to influence land use (by means of "presumptive income"
measures or otherwise, and with the necessary corrections for inflation),
then the instrument may have a sharper cutting edge than is usually admitted.
However, it is certainly true that policy makers will be practicing decep-
tion (possibly including self-deception) if they eschew land reform under
the justification that taxation can accomplish the same structural reform,
and then proceed to institute trivial tax levels.[33]

D. Tenancy conditions

Revision of sharecropping and rental conditions is a policy measure
frequently recommended as a partial substitute for redistribution of
landownership. Indeed, it is often argued that transfer of landownership
to current tenant workers is a "safe" form of land reform because worker
incentive will increase while all else--physical production units and
patterns--will remain undisturbed, circumventing output declines in a
transitional phase of reorganization.[34]

In a highly unequal landownership structure, agrarian reform based on
conversion of tenants to owners is likely to suffer from the same inefficiencies as conversion of wage earners to owners on large estates without
absorption of additional workers onto the properties: labor density per
farm area will be less than optimal from the standpoint of agriculture as
a whole. In other words, large owners placing their land in sharecropping
or renting it out are not likely to have higher labor density per area
(and higher land utilization) than large owners utilizing wage labor.
Therefore, conversion of tenants to owners without absorption of additional
labor onto tenant-farmed area should be viewed with suspicion.[35]

But what about reform of "tenancy conditions?" One tenancy form in particular has been a popular candidate for reform among economists: sharecropping. The traditional argument has been that sharecropping causes inefficient factor allocation: the tenant will apply inputs, including his own labor, only to the point where his <u>share</u> of their marginal product equals their full marginal cost, violating marginal cost equal to marginal product conditions for efficiency and leading to under-utilization of land.

Cheung has challenged this view.[36] He argues that its proponents have erroneously assumed that the landlord's share is "mysteriously" fixed exogenously. According to Cheung, once it is recognized that both (i) the share, and (ii) the amount of land allocated to each sharecropper are endogenous variables resulting from landowner wealth maximization, the normal efficient, neoclassical allocation of resources can be seen to result even from sharecropping. The author employs Lagrangian multiplier analysis to demonstrate the point, but his argument condenses to the following: (i) The landlord will maximize output subject to the constraint that what he pays to labor has to equal what it can earn elsewhere, equal to the wage rate. (ii) As a result, sharecropping is nothing more than a masquerade leading to the same results as profit maximization with wage labor; the landlord is smart enough to juggle both his "share" and the amount of land he places at the disposal of each tenant to ensure this result. In the process, it turns out that landlord share is nothing other than the familiar elasticity of output with respect to land; and marginal products of land and labor equal the rental rate per land area and the going wage--all neoclassically reassuring.

The weak spot in Cheung's analysis is that he replaces rigid landlord share <u>cum</u> tenant maximization with rigid (or "passive") tenant labor behavior <u>cum</u> landlord maximization. By assuming that the landlord can set a fixed amount of land to which the tenant will then apply his full labor availability, Cheung robs the tenant of his decision making; yet the tenant's decision-making process is precisely where inefficiency enters according to the traditional analysis, since the tenant will always, at the margin, ask why he should devote ΔNw worth of extra work to the plot (as opposed to outside work) when the result for him will be $(1-r)\Delta Nw$ extra income.[37] In short, it appears unsatisfactory to conclude with Cheung that all's for the best in the best of all sharecropping worlds under the notion that landlord share and land allocation per worker will settle down to an equilibrium which imitates the standard entrepreneurial wage-labor equilibrium.

Bardhan and Srinivasan[38] were quick to notice the problem in Cheung's analysis and proposed an alternative model introducing maximization on the land-demand side from the tenant's standpoint to complement maximization on the supply side by the landlord. Despite adroit mathematical features, the Bardhan-Srinivasan model has its serious shortcomings: early in the model the unacceptable assumption is made that the marginal product of land is zero.[39] This feature results from the assumption that share-croppers will "demand" land until it no longer produces anything extra for them (i.e., their share times the marginal product of land falls to zero; hence, the marginal product of land equals zero since the tenant's share doesn't). Yet this requirement of the model invalidates it for meaningful application to land-scarce, surplus-labor countries where the marginal product of land is anything but zero.[40,41]

In pragmatic terms the problems of sharecropping become evident when considering adoption of new technological packages. If the sharecropper receives only half (say) of the benefits of extra output, and if further-more even this half should exceed the cost to the sharecropper of the package to allow margin for risk of failure, then the package must be highly productive indeed to warrant adoption by the sharecropper. More-over, even if the landowner agrees to pay a share of the cost of the package equal to his share in output, the "real" cost share of the tenant will still exceed the tenant's output share if application of the package requires the devotion of extra days of labor at the peak season when the tenant could out-hire his labor. Hence, the landowner's share of new technology package costs may have to exceed his share in output in order to keep the tenant's "real" share of costs including foregone extra earnings equal to the tenants' share in output, if such technology is to be adopted.

For policy purposes the implications of the debate on the efficiency of sharecropping depend on the realistic options under consideration. If redistribution of landownership from large estates to sharecroppers cur-rently working the land is a serious option, then there is reason to expect current inefficiencies under sharecropping to represent potential for improved production after such a redistribution (in addition to the potential for improvement generally associated with the dichotomy between small and

large farms in incentives for land utilization, as discussed in section B
above). However, if land redistribution is ruled out, the only option to
current sharecropping arrangements may be governmental prohibition of
sharecropping and insistence on the use of cash rental payments in all land
rentals. It would be ill advised to interpret the sharecropping literature
as supporting this type of prohibition, if for no other reason than the
central fact that sharecropping does provide a vehicle for risk reduction
for the tenant, who would probably not be prepared to hire as much land
and produce as much output if his rental payment were a fixed cash sum
(which a poor crop might not cover) rather than a share of his actual produc

E. New technology: improved seeds and fertilizer

A representative assessment of distributional effects of the new
high-yielding varieties (HYV) is reported by Ahmad.[42] After documenting
the rapid growth of HYV wheat (from 4% of crop area to 40% in India and
from 2% to 46% in Pakistan between 1967 and 1970) and rice (2.8% of crop
area to 12%, India; 0 to 6.7%, Pakistan; 6% to 40%, Philippines, for the
same period), Ahmad's review finds that the potential for distributional
equity inherent in the scale neutrality of new seeds and fertilizer has
not been realized in practice. Instead, greater capacity of larger farmers
for installing complementary tubewell irrigation, easier meeting of high
credit requirements by the larger farmers, discouragement of adoption of
HYV among sharecroppers due to sharing distortions to incentives, have
all concentrated HYV gains in the larger farm sector. Moreover, pressures
for land reform have abated as the result of the new belief that income
gains through technical improvements offer the land-poor an alternative
to increased access to land through land redistribution, and because a
new class of "progressive farmers from nonagricultural sectors" (Ricardo's
capitalists) has emerged which is welcome to output-conscious governments
and which possesses political clout.

Ahmad's survey points out the conflicting evidence on whether labor
has gained or lost from the HYV. In India, the demand for hired labor
may have risen by as much as one million man-years for rice and wheat
converted to HYV in India.[43] This gain would constitute less than 1% of
the rural labor force. At the same time, there is evidence of substantial
labor displacement through mechanization (discussed below) and eviction of
tenants or raising of rental charges. Ahmad also emphasizes the difference

between irrigated and rain-fed areas, noting that the greatest potential
for increased labor demand is in the irrigated areas suited to double cropping. These, according to an Asian Development Bank survey cited by the
author, amount to less than 10% of the rice and wheat area for Asia as a
whole. Finally, Ahmad presents data showing a mixed pattern of real rural
wages in India; of ten states, real wages rose in six but fell in four in
the 1960s.

Bartsch has assembled from a variety of sources data concerning the
impact of new varieties and mechanization on the demand for labor in Asia.[44]
Distinguishing among three levels of "technology" ("traditional"; "improved,"
with one or more of the following--improved seeds, irrigation, chemical
fertilizers; and "modern"--with a complete package of HYV seeds, fertilizers,
and assured irrigation), and three "techniques" (traditional, intermediate,
and mechanized), the author defines nine possible production modes for each
crop. Based on selected data for rice and wheat in regions of India,
Pakistan, the Philippines, Sri Lanka, and Thailand, Bartsch reaches the
following conclusions: (i) Holding technology constant, a shift toward
mechanized technique unequivocally reduces labor demand. (ii) Holding
technique constant, a shift toward HYV technology unequivocally raises
demand for labor per unit of cropped area (as more labor is required to
prepare the seed bed, apply cultural treatments and, especially, harvest).
(iii) A combined shift toward mechanization and HYV technology is ambiguous
in its effects on labor: the result is usually a decline in labor requirements per unit of cropped area, which may or may not be fully offset by a
rise in the incidence of multiple cropping. (iv) Modernization, either of
technique or technology, reduces labor requirement per unit of output,
raising ominous implications for labor demand unless the product has highly
elastic demand due to potential for import substitution (or, the reader
infers, in a small country export context). Indirect demand for industrial
labor is quite limited for agrochemicals and is much higher for "partial
mechanization" involving modest improvements in implements than for a high
degree of mechanization requiring large sophisticated equipment produced
on a capital-intensive basis.

While these conclusions are not new, and while the study pleads
insufficient evidence on the crucial question of the net impact on labor
of mechanization and HYVs with increased double cropping, the study is
particularly useful in placing quantitative estimates on the various
labor-demand effects by synthesizing a number of isolated empirical studies.

Bell has examined the distributional impact of the new technology.[45]
Following a semantic bout differentiating "technique" from "technology,"
the study raises familiar observations: the HYV is intrinsically scale
neutral, but better access to credit due to better collateral and privileged
social status (in addition to the desire of official agencies to maximize
impact by focussing on "the stronger farms"), as well as greater margin
for risk-taking, permits the larger farmer to exploit the new technology
more fully than the small farmer. This tendency is reinforced by tractor
and tubewell indivisibilities.

The empirical evidence presented in the study indicates the surprising
result that, for wheat in the Bihar region of India, shifting to HYVs
raises wage labor participation in value added. The data appear to represent the "constant technique, improved technology" category in Bartsch's
taxonomy, so that increased labor requirements for cultural practices are
not swamped by mechanization. Even so, it is surprising that yield-
multiplying innovation would increase labor costs by a greater proportion
than value added;[46] and Bell warns that the conclusion must be treated
with caution (adding that his data on labor are merely "notional").

A particularly interesting phenomenon which Bell mentions in passing
is that the fertilizer dose applied to HYV wheat has fallen progressively
since the first year of widespread utilization of the seeds (1967/1968).
High yields with the recommended dose were followed by lower yields the
second year despite application of the same fertilization; the third year,
farmers reduced fertilizer application, prompting a further decline in
yields, and so forth, until low-level equilibrium seemed to have been
reached. Bell interprets the development as evidence of peasant cunning in
the face of extension agents' horror. More recently, a renewed decline in
the use of fertilizers must certainly have been stimulated by energy-crisis
fertilizer price increases. Since a crucial attribute of the HYVs is their
ability to respond to increased fertilization, the likely decline in fertilizer use would seem to bode ill indeed for the production gains of the
Green Revolution.

Bieri, de Janvrey, and Schmitz emphasize the sociological relationship
between income distributional impact of technological change and the generation of that change.[47] The authors first characterize labor and machinery
as close substitutes, land and chemicals as close substitutes, and postulate little substitutability between these two subsets of factors. They

then conclude that mechanization confers gains on landowners, whose land values rise from the resulting reduction in cost at constant output. In contrast, innovations using chemicals raise total output (by extending the constant quality equivalent land endowment), conferring benefits on consumers in the closed economy (as price declines), upon both producers and consumers in the open economy (as export and import increases spur welfare gains through trade specialization), or upon producers alone in a support-price context. The authors maintain that once market imperfections, input producers, and consumers are considered, the income distributional effects of technological change cannot be foreseen simply (e.g., in a dichotomy naming mechanization as unequalizing and seeds-fertilizers as equalizing), but that one can be certain that the nature of the inventions will be swayed by the landlords who lobby for mechanical innovations and by the "agribusinesses" which push innovations in order to sell inputs.

One of the more rigorous examinations of distributional effects of the Green Revolution is provided by Srivasta and Heady.[48] The authors used farm-level data for two states in India referring to pre- and post-technological change periods to estimate CES production functions. The results indicate that technical change was labor saving, since the parameter determining labor's marginal productivity relative to that of capital declined.[49] Moreover, the production functions indicate that the elasticity of substitution between capital and labor increased. The effect of the increase was unfavorable to labor's share, because during the period the price of labor rose relative to that of capital.

Labor's actual share declined in the two states, consistent with the production function estimates. Srivasta and Heady note that despite the decline, both the absolute number of wage workers and the agricultural wage rose. The authors attribute the rise in wage to a sharp increase in the demand for peak-season labor, unaccompanied by a similar increase in demand for off-season labor.

The study may be misleading in that it employs only capital and labor as inputs in the production function. The land input is subsumed into capital value, thereby forcing land to be a perfect substitute for machinery (precisely the opposite of the approach taken by Bieri, de Janvrey, and Schmitz in "Agricultural Technology and Distribution of Welfare Gains"; and intermediate inputs of seeds and fertilizers are absent from the production function altogether. Moreover, the analysis does not clothe the particular empirical results in substantive detail indicating why one would have expected the technical change to have been labor saving (and, in particular, differentiating the potential factor "bias" of HYV--which is probably neutral--from the ex post realized bias in view of simultaneous mechanization).

Gotsch has explored the influence of rural institutions on the distributional impact of new technology.[50] First he issues a caveat that evaluation of the distributional effect of a particular technology requires detailed microanalysis. As examples, he notes that despite the frequent classification of biological-chemical innovations as labor-using and mechanical innovations as labor-saving, herbicides are highly labor-saving and tubewells can be labor-using in their impact (as can tractors, where essential for multiple cropping). The author then discusses the relationship of the organization of input markets to the social structure, emphasizing the difficulty of creating institutions that deliver services to the small farmer.

The case of tubewell innovation in Pakistan is contrasted with that in Bangladesh to illustrate the crucial role of rural institutions as opposed to the technology itself. Comilla District in Bangladesh has a small farm structure with relatively equal land distribution; the Sahiwal District in Pakistan has a much larger median size of holdings and more unequal distribution. Since one tubewell irrigates from 50 to 80 acres, the small (1- to 2.5-acre) Comilla farms perforce banded together in cooperative organization to install tubewells, while in Pakistan the larger 50% of owners installed tubewells individually. Subsidized official credit assisted the large farmers in this effort. The distributional result (at least as mapped by programming models) will be that tubewell adoption aggravates inequality in Pakistan while spreading benefits relatively equally in Comilla District. Gotsch does note, however, that the extent of tubewell adoption has been much greater in the Pakistan district than in Comilla.

There also has been feedback reinforcing the divergence between distributional effects in the two cases. According to Gotsch, tubewells strengthened the hand of large landlords heading political factions, making it more difficult for sharecroppers and other workers dependent on them to form horizontal groups to break the power of the vertical political factions. (Indeed, the main new political lobby was that of large commercial farmers opposing land reform and taxes and advocating support prices.) In contrast, the tubewell strengthened community organization among middle and small peasant classes in Comilla.

Concerning receptiveness to technical change, Gotsch reports that several studies indicate smaller farmers in the Asian context adopt new varieties practically as completely as larger farmers, although perhaps with a one- or two-year lag and utilizing less than optimal fertilizer inputs.

Dalrymple and Jones have drawn interesting parallels between the Mexican experience with high-yielding varieties and current experience in Asia.[51] Noting the S-curve relating the fraction of area in new varieties to time, they emphasize that the HYV cycle is still in its early phase in Asia. They find it not surprising that the initial wave of adoption was concentrated on larger farms, given their greater access to credit and greater ability to take risks; yet it would be misleading to conclude from this pattern that the HYV will have inequitable distributional effects over the long run, because eventually adoption is likely to spread to all farm sizes.[52] In Mexico, where the "cycle" began with the first family of new varieties in 1948, improved wheat varieties are now used on virtually all farm sizes, and more than 40% of wheatland is in _ejido_ farms (according to the 1960 census).

The authors also note the trade implications of the variety adoption cycle. In the case of Mexican wheat, an early phase of rapid import substitution was followed (after complete replacement of imports) by a temporary effort at exportation subsidization, then reversion to supply for domestic demand alone. The import substitution phase has particularly important implications for labor demands: by providing infinitely elastic product demand over an initial range of output, import substitution circumvents the negative impact on demand for labor which is inherent in an inelastic product demand situation--given the decrease in labor input per unit of output (as opposed to labor demand per cultivated area) associated with introduction of HYV (as noted in Cline, "Interrelationships Between Agricultural Strategy and Rural Income.").

Considering the implications of the Green Revolution for Latin America, Thiesenhusen[53] has argued that in the absence of land reform the result of the new technology will be a deterioration in the already unequal income distribution. Influences causing unequal benefits from the

supposedly scale-neutral HYV are the same as in Asia only worse (given
Latin America's more extreme inequality of land distribution). The
credit and technical assistance institutions are "usually designed to help
the large-scale farmer." Compounding the distributional problem is labor's
displacement from rapid mechanization in the hemisphere, stimulated by
favorable exchange rates and cheap credit. Not only will small owners fall
behind, Thiesenhusen notes, but renters and sharecroppers will be displaced
as landowners become more determined to avoid all claims against their
appreciating land.

Thiesenhusen then cites the success of yield-raising varietal adoption
in small farm areas of southern Brazil. He reports the favorable experience of credit agencies in Venezuela (CIARA) and Mexico (Puebla Project)
in improving technology on small-farm, post-reform sectors (noting that
in the Venezuelan case credit has been refused to farmers unwilling to
follow the proposed crop scheme with new varieties). The author concludes
that it is quite possible to achieve production gains from small farmers
if an appropriate technological package and credit are available, and that
while similar gains may occur on large estates in the absence of land reform
the resulting distributional effect will be seriously detrimental.

The above references represent recent views in the literature on the
Green Revolution's income distributional effects. In summary, three basic
questions are involved: (i) the distribution of HYV technology across
farm sizes; (ii) the effect of the new technology on labor demand and
functional income shares; and (iii) the price elasticity of demand for
domestically produced agricultural goods. With regard to distribution
across farm size, the evidence indicates that the small farms are receptive
to adopting new varieties, and that where in practice the large farmers
have been the principal adopters the reason is usually better access to
credit and inputs, due in large part to institutional structure in which
the sources of these prerequisites cater to the large farmers. This assessment has optimistic policy implications since it indicates that where
policy makers vigorously attempt to channel improved inputs to small farmers
they should meet with a receptive response. Channeled credit and inputs
should be an effective instrument for rural equalization (as discussed
further below). This optimism receives additional support if past experience with the S-curve for the varietal cycle is an indication of the
pattern of future adoption by small farms.

The issue of functional distribution hinges on the final balance between the positive influence of increased demand for labor for new cultural practices and extra harvesting, and the negative influence of mechanization and decreased labor requirements per unit of output. Even without mechanization there is a strong likelihood that the HYV will reduce labor's share. The more productive technology raises labor productivity, so the percentage rise in labor-demand falls short of the percentage rise in gross output. Intermediate costs rise greatly (from a very low base), so that value added also rises less than proportionately with gross output. The behavior of labor's share in value added thus depends on whether the proportionate rise in labor-demand exceeds or falls short of the proportionate increase in value added (as long as wage is constant, reasonable in a surplus-labor context).

To demonstrate the point, it is useful to consider some definitional relationships along with some "stylized" data. Where:

V = Value added, Q = gross output;

λ_o = initial ratio of value added to gross output;

N = labor;

I = intermediate input cost; and

ρ = proportional rise in output per worker.

Using a dot to indicate proportional changes, we have:

$$(1) \quad \dot{N} = \frac{\dot{Q} - \rho}{1 + \rho},$$

$$(2) \quad \dot{V} = \frac{\dot{Q} - \dot{I} + \lambda_o \dot{I}}{\lambda_o}.$$

Equations (1) and (2) follow from the definitions, as may be shown easily. Consider the following "stylized" parameters: (i) ρ = .33 (from Bartsch[54] for HYV rice and wheat, India and Pakistan); (ii) $\dot{Q}$ = .75 (Bartsch);[55] (iii) λ_o = .9 (from Bell);[56] (iv) $\dot{I}$ = 2 (that is, expenditure on seeds and fertilizer triples). Then from (1) and (2), $\dot{N}$ = .32 and $\dot{V}$ = .61. The shift to HYV even without mechanization raises output 75% and value added by 61% but raises labor demand by only 32%. As long as wage remains constant, labor's share must fall in this "typical" case because labor-demand increases less than proportionately with value added. Increased labor productivity swamps increased intermediate input cost.

In view of these relationships, planners should not be surprised if the new seed-fertilizer technology shifts the income distribution away from labor, and the likelihood of the result is reinforced if the new inputs are coupled with mechanization and if the country's demand for the grains in question is inelastic. Limited prospects for labor's share make land reform all the more important, since in a small family farm structure the worker receives land and capital shares as well as the labor share.

The third major issue concerns demand elasticity. If agricultural demand is inelastic, then rising labor productivity due to the new technology can reduce the absolute demand for labor as well as labor's relative share. In this crucial dimension the recent literature is probably already outdated. The literature does not deal with what may be a new medium- or long-term agricultural scarcity associated with the entry of socialist countries into the world grain market, prolonged drought (especially in Africa's Sahel), decreased real volumes of food aid, and increased costs for petroleum-derivative agricultural inputs. The "new scarcity" would appear to guarantee "brighter" prospects for elastic demand for agricultural goods produced within the developing countries, ameliorating the potential income distributional problem involved in rapidly rising agricultural labor productivity.

Finally, an important distributional aspect of the Green Revolution mentioned by several authors is the expulsion of former tenants by landowners desiring to operate the land themselves in view of the new profitability of production with improved inputs. With land value enhanced by increased profitability, the owner can no longer afford the chance that tenants will acquire legal claim to it, and at the same time the owner is prepared to incur risks associated with production expenses that formerly were unattractive compared to the simpler option of permitting operation by sharecroppers.

F.   Mechanization

Another instrument affecting rural income distribution is policy toward farm mechanization. National governments and foreign aid agencies in the past have stimulated farm mechanization in the general belief that "modern" agriculture is necessary for development, or in the more specific desire to achieve impressive production gains through combining mechanizati

with varietal and chemical innovations of the Green Revolution. The
reaction of many economists has been dismay, under the presumption that
agricultural mechanization would displace abundant labor and use scarce
capital in the one sector where there appeared to be ample scope for substitution between the two factors. A debate has ensued which to date has
failed to reach definite conclusions on the merits of farm mechanization
but which on balance leaves to its advocates the burden of proof in establishing the special circumstances justifying mechanization on a case-by-
case basis.

Singh and Billings conducted early work on the implications of
agricultural mechanization in India.[57] They acknowledged the caveat that
mechanization could be inappropriate due to excess labor but maintained
that by speeding up operations at peak seasons mechanization could increase
double cropping and thus increase total labor-demand although reducing it
for a single operation or crop. Their projections for the states of Punjab
and Maharashtra concluded that within two decades extensive mechanization
(tractors, pumpsets, threshers) would decrease demand for labor substantially (by 17% for Punjab) but that extension of the use of high-yielding
varieties and increased crop area would more than offset this labor displacement (although the resulting net growth of employment in Maharashtra
would be insufficient to absorb the expected increase in the labor force).
The overall approach of the authors was that output gains justified
mechanization.

Inukai presented a similarly favorable view for the case of Thailand.[58]
Challenging the conventional opinion that mechanization was inappropriate
due to labor abundance, the author maintained that plowing with tractors
rather than bullocks permitted earlier preparation of the soil (which
otherwise was too hard to work prior to monsoon rains), thereby spreading
out labor requirements from their previous peak period when labor was a
constraint. The result was to permit expansion of cultivated rice area
which, added to a switching from "broadcasting" to transplanting in the
planting process, increased total labor demand despite the tractor mechanization. In addition the author estimated regressions of yield on an index
of mechanization and concluded that mechanization raised yields per acre
(although these tests were undoubtedly biased due to the omission of
variables for fertilizer use and seed variety).

Lawrence reached similar conclusions for irrigated areas in West Pakistan.[59] Based on the assumption that tractor mechanization permitted more timely plowing and therefore increased double cropping as well as improved yields, Lawrence calculated that tractors were socially profitable, although similar analysis revealed them to be socially unprofitable in East Pakistan where there was a lower sensitivity of rice yield to planting time

In contrast, other studies appearing at approximately the same time roundly condemned farm mechanization policies. Kaneda disputed the notion that mechanization raised yields per acre and attributed rapid mechanizatio in Pakistan to overvalued exchange rates and tariff exemptions which, together with high wheat price supports, stimulated farm machinery imports. Bose and Clark rejected the "timing" argument on grounds that improved implements could speed up bullock plowing.[61] They maintained that the case for tractors hinged on whether their opportunity cost exceeded that of the irrigated area which could be released from production of fodder for bulloc replaced by machines. Making such an evaluation, Bose and Clark concluded that tractor mechanization was socially unprofitable though privately profitable (due primarily to high crop price supports).

Yudelman, Butler, and Banerji concluded, from evidence on several developing countries, that large-scale farm mechanization was often profitable in private terms but unprofitable at social costs.[62] The authors identified the "managerial and technical difficulty of employing a large labor force" as one important factor stimulating mechanization on large farms. Noting that a wide variety of evidence indicated that large-scale mechanization reduced demand for labor (ceteris paribus) by 16% to 27%,[63] the authors called for "pre-emptive" institutional change such as land reform or formation of cooperatives to stave off the likely transition of developing-country agriculture toward patterns of Western agriculture but with a much larger proportion of rural households "disenfranchised." The study did advocate "selective" mechanization, which the authors believed capable of increasing output without reducing labor-demand (for example, through reducing seasonal labor shortages). Turning to case studies, the authors identified Taiwan and Japan as instances of technique choice appropriate to factor endowment, and cited Mexico as a case of inappropriat mechanization in view of labor abundance.

More recent literature has produced certain recurrent themes:
(i) farm mechanization has been excessively stimulated by subsidized credit

(often from international aid entities) and favorable access to foreign exchange at overvalued exchange rates; (ii) there can be certain types of machinery and certain production conditions for which mechanization is appropriate; (iii) in practice radical reductions of labor demand have not been observed along with mechanization due to concomitant innovations in varieties and chemical inputs; (iv) nevertheless, at the most general level farm mechanization tends to be socially unprofitable; (v) farm size and institutional structure are crucial determinants of the course of mechanization.

Concerning mechanization's influence on yields, I have estimated regressions relating rice yields to tractor and fertilizer use for a southern state in Brazil, and have found the net influence of tractor mechanization on yields to be negligible.[64] Gotsch has argued that there probably are such yield effects due to the possibility of planting at the optimal time with mechanization, but apparently he assigns little weight to the effect since he explicitly omits it in subsequent empirical esti- mates of rates of return to mechanization.[65] The same study by Gotsch makes an overall assessment of mechanization for the case of Pakistan. He notes that the divergent earlier conclusions of Bose and Clark on the one hand and Lawrence on the other stemmed from their different assumptions about yield and double-cropping effects of mechanization. Judging that the availability of irrigation water in Pakistan is insufficient to permit the radical increase in double cropping assumed by Lawrence, and noting that price declines should be incorporated into such analysis presuming output growth, Gotsch concludes that net social benefits are negative for current patterns of farm mechanization in Pakistan (because irrigation is inadequate to provide sufficient output gains on land liberated from fodder production as bullock requirements decline).

Gotsch then presents results of linear programming exercises evaluating the profitability of farm mechanization (with and without tubewells). He differentiates between the "capitalist" and "landlord" cases, with the latter including effects from the eviction of tenants as well as substitution of mechanical for animal power. The results indicate high rates of return for mechanization (especially when combined with the tubewell) at private costs. Even after adjusting foreign exchange and interest rates to "scarcity" costs, the author finds high rates of return to mechanization. The "social" rate of return adjusting for opportunity cost of labor is not calculated, yet the author considers social return to be negative (based, apparently, on the bullock fodder opportunity cost argument). Accordingly, he recommends not only the termination of official subsidization of mechanization through low exchange rates, cheap credit, and artificially high crop prices,[66] but also imposition of taxes on tractors (although the author admits limited political feasibility of this measure).

As noted above, a recent study by Bartsch synthesizes data from several Asian countries to identify the separate influences of mechanization (technique) and varietal and chemical inputs (technology) on labor requirements. With traditional "technology," shifting from traditional to mechanized techniques reduces labor-demand per cropped area by 24% for Punjab wheat and by 50% for rice (India, transplant method). With improved varieties and fertilizer, the corresponding labor reductions due to mechanization are 78% and 59%. Once double cropping is accounted for, changes in labor requirements per cultivated area are more ambiguous. Bartsch appears to attribute increased scope for double cropping to varietal changes (shorter growing seasons) rather than mechanization, so that one could argue the negative partial impact of mechanization is even greater after considering double cropping. What tends to occur in practice is the simultaneous shift toward modern varietal and fertilizer inputs, greater mechanization, and greater double cropping. The study's summary evaluation of this joint movement is that its effects on labor requirements per cultivated area are unclear (although the effect on labor per unit of output is clearly a reduction).

In a study of mechanization in the Philippines, Barker, Meyers, Crisostomo, and Duff reach a similarly ambiguous conclusion.[68] They find that government-stimulated mechanization in the rice sector has not resulted in major labor displacement and that reduced labor requirements for land preparation have been offset by increased labor requirements for weeding, harvesting, and threshing. It appears that the latter increases are attributable to the concurrent introduction of high-yielding varieties, however, suggesting that labor requirements would have risen in the absence of mechanization. The study contains a useful demonstration of the response of mechanization to factor prices, showing that the variations in mechanical horsepower per agricultural worker in Thailand, Taiwan, the Philippines, and Japan are related to the ratio of the price of horsepower to farm wages. The authors also emphasize the institutional influences on mechanization: they indicate that credit at favorable interest rates stimulated tractor imports during 1966 to 1969, while the floating of the exchange rate in 1970 discouraged them. The influence of fluctuating official policies was much stronger than inherent technological characteristics in determining the pace of mechanization, according to the authors. Despite the absence of a clear trend in demand for labor per cultivated area, the study notes the unfavorable long-run income distribution implications of the decline in labor requirement per unit of output.

A study of farm mechanization in India and Sri Lanka by Raj is even more cautious in its conclusion that available information on mechanization is "not adequate to determine precisely how and to what extent it has been responsible for suboptimal use of the available resources."[69] Raj points out that tubewell "mechanization" almost certainly increased employment. Even tractor mechanization may have done so in selected cases, as in certain districts of Sri Lanka where tractors substitute for irrigation by permitting the tillage of soil while it is dry and hard. In other cases, according to Raj, there is strong evidence that large landowners mechanized merely to reduce dependence on tenants or hired labor.

Raj presents interesting data showing the concentration of tractors in the Indian states of Punjab and Uttar Pradesh, in contrast to the low share of these two states in other types of machinery (diesel engines, electric pumps). He suggests that advance tractor mechanization in the Punjab is explained by the large size of farms characterizing the region. This evidence lends support to his proposition that agrarian structure may be more important than the underpricing of capital and foreign exchange in leading to inappropriate mechanization.

Clayton has examined the course of farm mechanization in East Africa.[70] His study is particularly informative from the standpoint of illuminating the partial influence of institutional bias toward equity versus inequity. In contrast to most Latin American and Asian countries, Kenya, Uganda, and Tanzania appear to represent cases where government agencies have biased their assistance toward the small farmers. Clayton reports that the government of Uganda attempted to provide tractor hire services to small farmers, but that the system required heavy subsidies and eventually failed. In Kenya, private mechanization proceeded rapidly on the large units replacing former European plantations, but subsidized government sales of tractors to smallholders proved to be a failure (due to the farmers' lack of experience with the equipment and its maintenance requirements, according to Clayton). Subsequently the Kenyan government instituted a limited tractor hire service at commercial rates, which met with more success. In Tanzania, while mechanization has been profitable in the plantation sector, various government attempts to supply tractor services to the small-farm sector experienced poor results, and the five-year plan beginning in 1969 specifically downgraded mechanization plans.

The repeating patterns of failure of government tractor schemes for small farms in the face of strong private mechanization trends in the plantation sector in East Africa suggest that the pattern of large-farm mechanization in other areas is not attributable alone to institutional favoritism to the large-farm sector. The implication is that economic forces play a crucial role in large-farm mechanization. Specifically, the need to simplify supervision of a large labor force and a higher relative price of labor to capital (even in the absence of subsidized official credit) lead to mechanization on large farms, while a low effective price of family labor plus the frictions involved in using machinery commanding an area in excess of the property unit (through hiring tractor services, cooperative ownership, and so on) discourages machinery use on small farms. If the shadow price of capital is high and that of labor low, then these structural forces point to greater social efficiency of the small-farm sector and the existence of socially inefficient technique choice on the large-farm sector even in the absence of access to subsidized capital from the government.

Abercrombie has recently examined farm mechanization and employment in Latin America.[71] Although mechanization has penetrated only large farms in the region, it has been quite rapid (11% annual growth in the 1950s and 7% in the 1960s) and has extended much further than in other developing regions(reaching by 1968 a regional average of 220 hectares of cultivated land per tractor compared with 440 hectares in the Near East, 560 in Africa, 1,540 in the Far East, 40 in the United States, and 25 in Europe). Abercrombie catalogues the government measures typically stimulating large-farm mechanization in the region: tariff and tax concessions for machinery, cheap credit (often with negative real interest rates), overvalued exchange rates, and minimum wage and social security costs which raise the relative price of labor. Social unrest in the labor force has been an additional impetus to mechanization.

Very rapid mechanization of sugar cane in Cuba constitutes one phonomenon of particular interest in view of the interaction of institution

and technology. It would be highly interesting to analyze whether this
development represented socially inefficient use of capital-intensive means
due to ideological commitment to mechanized state farming, an efficient
strategy due to a truly increased opportunity cost of labor resulting from
provision of productive employment alternatives, a technological necessity
to overcome harvest bottlenecks, or some other dominant influence. Another
specific feature of the region's mechanization is its geographical concentration. The author reports that 70 percent of Brazil's tractors are in
the state of São Paulo; 70 percent of Argentina's farm machinery is in the
pampas; and that machinery has comparable geographical concentration in
Mexico and Uruguay. The spatial concentration is similar to that in India's
Punjab. It undoubtedly reflects physical phenomena (e.g., flat land suitable for mechanization) as well as farm-size structure and the relative
scarcity of labor.

Abercrombie presents estimates of labor requirements per hectare with
and without mechanization, on the basis of which he estimates that one
tractor replaces from 4 workers in Chile to 7 in Guatemala; the author adds
an approximate estimate of 2.5 million jobs as the magnitude of direct
labor displacement throughout Latin America by the more than 500,000 tractors
existing in the region. The indirect employment gains from industrial manufacture of farm machinery are very limited, according to the author, although
the indirect gains due to the increased area cultivated may be as great as
one-third of the direct labor displacement effect.[72]

The study concludes with recommendations for "selective mechanization"
where required for output increases (e.g., mechanized soil preparation where
necessary to expand cultivated area, or mechanization to overcome seasonal
labor bottlenecks where multiple cropping is possible) but the exclusion
of mechanization which merely saves labor. The author notes that such
proposals have been elaborated within the Colombian Ministry of Agriculture
(which favored mechanization of soil preparation and rice harvesting, the
latter to permit double cropping on irrigated areas, but opposed other
mechanization such as post-planting operations and harvesting). He cites
government credit as the most powerful instrument for selective mechanization, while admitting the difficulty of limiting credit for mechanization
to specific operations (as opposed to crops or regions). As a minimum,
governments should remove the windfall gain to machinery purchasers due to
low interest rates in the face of inflation.

Finally, it is useful to note the results of a simulation study by
Thirsk examining the effects of farm machinery subsidization in Colombia.[73]
The approach taken by Thirsk is completely different from that of the other
studies reported here. The author does not examine the issue so central
to many of the other studies--whether machinery merely replaces labor or
instead makes possible increased output. Rather, Thirsk assumes mechanization essentially replaces labor, but he explores the various general equilibrium effects accompanying mechanization. According to the analysis, subsidized mechanization on large farms in Colombia (i) increased employment
on large farms (as they expanded output); (ii) decreased effective employment by an even greater amount in the small-farm sector (in response to
the decreasing agricultural price resulting from increased output in the
large-farm sector); (iii) increased industrial employment per unit of output (as the industrial wage cost declined due to shifting terms of trade
against agriculture); (iv) increased employment and output to some extent
as extensively used cattle lands were converted to large-farm crop production; (v) in the aggregate, reduced economic growth below what could have
been achieved by allocating excessive capital to agriculture and thereby
taking it away from industry where its return was higher; and (vi) redistributed income away from labor and small farmers toward capital owners.
The analysis is particularly thorough, although specific results hinge on
a myriad of parameters (such as elasticities of substitution among factors
in supply and among products in demand), the empirical estimation of which
(on the basis of numerous other studies) can yield widely differing results.
Furthermore, a crucial thrust of the analysis concerns terms of trade
between agriculture and nonagriculture; yet it is not clear that "optimal"
terms of trade and sectoral allocation would have obtained in the absence
of farm machinery subsidization, given the likely bias favoring industry
in other policies (e.g., tariff protection).

In summary, the studies surveyed here repeatedly emphasize the need
to remove artificial incentives to the replacement of labor by farm
machinery (cheap credit, tariff exemption, overvalued exchange rate);
they suggest that, other things being equal, a large-farm-size structure,
abetted by government institutions biased in favor of large farms, stimu-
lates excessive mechanization; they admit the existence of cases in
which mechanization increases output rather than merely replacing labor;
they indicate that while the partial influence of mechanization is

almost always to displace labor, the joint effects of mechanization, new
varieties and fertilizer, and increased double cropping tend to leave
little net increase or decrease in labor use (although reducing it per
unit of output), and they point to policies of "selective" mechanization
although the operational characteristics of such policies remain vague.

G.   Channeled credit

Farm credit is a particularly important policy instrument in terms of
distributional impact. In the past it has usually benefitted the large-
farm sector disproportionately (as in the pattern of subsidized credit for
mechanization discussed above). However, it should be possible to employ
credit in an equity-oriented manner. Two principal modes for this objective
should be considered: (i) the supplying of credit specifically to small
farms; and (ii) the linkage of credit access to number of workers employed.

At the outset, it should be noted that the viewpoint currently predominant is that small-farm credit faces many difficulties. Practitioners
and academics participating in the Agency for International Development's
"Spring Review of Small Farmer Credit" drew a bleak picture of the instrument. They found the conditions for its successful application typically
absent; in particular, technology available was insufficiently attractive
to warrant borrowing (after considering risk), and market conditions were
frequently unfavorable (both regarding price and infra-structure). Where
credit inputs were justified by technological and market circumstances,
existing private facilities (including the traditional moneylender) were
usually adequate to supply the credit. Improved inputs requiring only
modest credit (especially seeds, but also fertilizer) could usually be
purchased by relying on own savings or private financing (although capital
improvements requiring longer term repayment, such as tubewells, were more
dependent on official credit). Experience in repayment was also found
discouraging, with an average default rate of 30% for small-farm credit.
The experts also agreed that many subsidized credit programs allegedly for
small farms benefitted larger owners due to the rural political structure,
and that well-intentioned interest ceilings were counterproductive in that
they dried up the flow of both credit to the smaller farmers and savings
from the small farmers to the credit institutions. Existing small-farmer
credit programs were considered to be generally lacking in design conscious
of these economic and social factors and to be characterized by other

inefficiencies such as insistence on unenforceable and economically ques-
tionable prohibitions against use of credit for consumption.[74]

It is undoubtedly true that, as a subsequent A.I.D. policy circular
summarized, "Credit is no panacea for the problems of the small farmer."
Nevertheless, it would be unfortunate to dismiss farm credit as an instrument for improvement of rural equity. There exists difference of opinion
on whether technology justifying borrowing does exist (there are technology
optimists as well as pessimists) and on whether availability of official
credit does stimulate adoption.[75]

In practice it would seem likely both that technological and market
preconditions are met in a sufficiently large number of areas and products
to justify at least existing levels of government inputs into credit programs (although probably requiring reorganization of such programs) and
that governments will proceed to extend similar levels of credit in their
efforts to stimulate agriculture. The relevant question then becomes
whether advantage could not be taken of such credit to spur improvement
in rural equity. This question is especially important where, as is
frequently the case, credit programs continue to be subsidized and carry
low or negative real interest rates, such that an income transfer from
taxpayers to credit recipients is taking place.

One important issue is whether restricted credit will be inefficient.
Since the small-farm sector has little land at its disposal, it might be
argued that credit focused on the sector will have much lower production
impact than that obtainable through an unrestricted flow to agriculture
at large. Evidence from production function estimates in a prior study
by the author suggests that this fear is unfounded.[76] For Northeast Brazil
the study found that in five out of six product sectors the marginal product of "seeds, fertilizer, and insecticides" was higher on small farms
than on large.[77] The small farms appear to compensate for their lack of
land by the heavy application of other factors, especially labor. This
evidence indicates that the production impact of credit for intermediate
inputs is likely to be higher for small farms than for large, rather than
lower.

Thirsk has explored the question of productivity of small-farm credit
using production function estimates applied to data for approximately 3,000
farms in Colombia.[78] His results indicate that in the majority of sectors

examined the marginal product of intermediate inputs is higher on smaller than on larger farms. Making the reasonable argument that credit facilitates purchase of these inputs (buttressed by INCORA credit data for the farm sample). Thirsk concludes that credit to small farmers for intermediate inputs can be an important instrument with favorable output and equity consequences.

A second basis for investigating the question is examination of the resources at the command of the small-farm sector. Data from the 1970 agricultural census indicate that in Northeast Brazil farms under 50 hectares accounted for 80% of total labor, 50% of cropped area, and 38% of cattle, despite possession of only 25% of total land area. These data strongly suggest that the sector of farms below 50 hectares produces as much as half or more of total output, meaning that credit channeled to the sector would have a very substantial output base on which to work. Once again the implication is that policy makers need not fear loss of potential production impact in channeling credit to small farms rather than to large.

An alternative means of channeling credit for equity purposes would be to limit credit availability to a fixed quantity per worker employed. Since the small-farm sector is much more labor-intensive than the large-farm sector, this measure would indirectly focus credit on the small farms. Moreover, it would guarantee that the credit going to large estates would be associated with a large labor force rather than stimulating mechanization for the replacement of labor. More fundamentally, in the developing-country context labor is the factor with a social "shadow price" below its market price. To the extent that farm credit is subsidized, linking credit to the number of workers essentially transfers the subsidy price signal to the labor factor, increasing the tendency to use labor-intensive methods (and produce labor-intensive products) and increasing the overall efficiency of agricultural production.

An alternative policy is to eliminate subsidization of official credit, raising interest rates on loans and, in turn, interest rates paid by institutions and the amount of rural savings mobilized (as emphasized by Adams[79] and others). Such reforms need not be inconsistent with the continued provision of official credit for the stimulus of agriculture; and, in the absence of land reform, channeling official credit to small farms or linking its availability to employment should be a helpful second-best strategy for improving rural equity.

H.   Other measures

Several other policy instruments are available for affecting the rural income distribution. One instrument is agricultural price support. Thirsk has analyzed the distributional impact of farm support prices in Colombia.[80] Disaggregating producers and consumers of agricultural goods by income class, and taking account of foreign exchange scarcity in assessing probable changes in food inputs, Thirsk examines the equity and efficiency impact of changes in support prices. The study finds that increasing support prices leads to more inequitable income distribution and to a decline in social efficiency. Essentially, low-income consumers must pay higher prices for foodstuffs, while high-income food producers benefit from increased farm income due to higher prices.

While specific programs may be analyzed as in the study by Thirsk, generalization about price support policy seems dangerous. One factor which deserves new attention is the apparent increase in instability of world grain markets in recent years, due in part to the entry of socialist countries in purchases at times of poor harvest. This development suggests that price support schemes should have some additional "risk-minimization" benefit attached to them when their costs and benefits are analyzed. Moreover, variations in implementation can change distributional implications. For example, if farm products receive price support for farmers while being subsidized for consumers the distributional impact will be more favorable than in porgrams not subsidizing consumption.

A more general aspect of agricultural pricing concerns the terms of trade between agriculture and industry. Many authors have pointed out that the typical pattern of import-substitution industrialization may cause the income distribution to deteriorate within the country at large by depressing the terms of trade of agriculture (as industrial prices soar behind tariff walls) and in view of the fact that the agricultural mean income is below that in the rest of the economy. Even this general characterization becomes less clearly valid once the battery of subsidies to agriculture (especially subsidized credit) commonly encountered is taken into account. (Pakistan is a case in point. Some authors have emphasized the discrimination against agriculture inherent in its program of industrialization; other authors primarily examining its agricultural sector have criticized excessively high agricultural support prices.)

Other instruments include minimum-wage policy, rent and share-crop
control legislation, colonization, irrigation, farm extension, and rural
education. A recent study on colonization projects in Latin America by
Nelson[81] adds useful compilation of evidence supporting the view that this
painless alternative to land reform is, in most cases, very costly and
incapable of making a major impact in the absorption of rural labor in
the near term.[82] Increasing minimum wages seems likely to encourage the
replacement of agricultural labor by machinery (and various econometric
estimates find high elasticities of substitution between the two for
agriculture); rent or sharecrop control seems likely to encourage owners
to dispel tenants and replace them with temporary hired labor having even
less security (a trend already in progress as a result of the Green Revolution); but more reliable assessment of these policies as well as those of
irrigation, farm extension, and rural education require more detailed
analysis and more specific cases for evaluation than those at the author's
disposal.

I.   Conclusion

Land redistribution is the most powerful instrument for equalizing
rural income distribution, and should permit output gains as well. Land
reforms which benefit only a minority of the rural population, however,
fail to exploit their full potential for improving equity (as may be the
case in the Chilean and Peruvian reforms) and, under certain conditions,
may even worsen the position of the remaining landless labor force. To
increase the political feasibility of land reform, full compensation for
expropriated land deserves consideration as a policy strategy. Despite
full repayment for land, the increase in output following reform leaves
ample room for very significant income gains for beneficiaries. Their
gains will be still larger to the extent that the financial interest
rate at which they repay loans falls short of the capitalist discount
rate, since in this case their annual payments on land value will not
exhaust the pre-reform profits of landlords, leaving over a portion of
pre-reform profit share in addition to labor share for beneficiaries'
net income. Experience in Peru, actual appropriations (but not application)
in Brazil, and reasonable macroeconomic parameters suggest that land reform
with full compensation is financially feasible if implemented over time.

In the absence of land reform, a second-best strategy is to channel credit to small farms, or to link credit access to farm employment (thereby subsidizing the use of labor where credit is on subsidized terms). Evidence on marginal productivity of seeds, fertilizer, and insecticide inputs suggests that credit to small farms would have at least as large a production impact as that obtainable on large farms, and other data suggest the same conclusion since they indicate the "small-farm sector" accounts for a substantial production base despite its small share of land (due to its higher share of labor).

The Green Revolution appears to have concentrated rural income, not because of any scale requirements of the new technology but because of inequality in the distribution of the new inputs involved. To the extent that this inequality is associated with demand based on farmer decision making (rather than supply factors associated with credit and other conditions of access to inputs), the historical pattern of eventual adoption of technology by small producers after initial adoption by larger ones suggests that the concentration may be transitory. The policy implication is clearly that the new varieties and complementary input packages should be disseminated rapidly to smaller farms, rather than curtailed for fear of distributional impact. Most evidence indicates that the new varietal and fertilization technology increases demand for labor per unit of area but reduces labor requirements per unit of output. As long as demand is elastic (as in the replacement of food imports) the new technology should not worsen, and may improve, the absolute position of labor (although reasonable parameters suggest labor's share may decline). Cases where demand is limited pose more serious problems for labor-demand.

Farm mechanization has been exaggerated in many developing countries due to distortions favoring premature use of machinery (subsidized credit, access to foreign exchange at overvalued exchange rates, tariff exemption, low cost finance from foreign aid agencies). Nevertheless, a blanket proscription against further mechanization is inappropriate since there appear to exist circumstances in which it increases output rather than merely replacing labor--although the empirical analysis in support of this proscription remains at a disappointingly undeveloped state. As a minimum, policy should be revised to remove artificial incentives favoring mechanization.

Land taxation is another policy instrument warranting consideration by policy makers concerned about rural equity. Past insensitivity of land use to land tax stems primarily from the very low tax rates usually applied, in conjunction with the initial underevaluation of land for tax purposes and its rapid outdating in the presence of inflation. Especially in Latin American conditions, higher land taxes should stimulate the utilization of underused land on large estates. For this purpose, the variant of applying income tax to "presumed income" which should be generated by available land may be helpful.

Recent literature attempting to demonstrate the efficiency of share-cropping is unconvincing. For practical policy purposes, perhaps the major difficulty with sharecropping is its impediment to the adoption of techno-logical packages requiring higher cost to obtain their much higher benefits. Special attention to adjustment of cost and output share thus appears necessary in credit programs in such circumstances.

Finally, the entire subject of policy instruments for rural equity will require further examination considering the likely impact of higher petroleum prices as well as changes in world grain markets. The fertilizer requirements of high-yielding varieties throw them into jeopardy in view of the impact of petroleum prices on those of fertilizer. Tractor methods would seem even less efficient than before in view of higher fuel prices. The first consideration raises the possibility that the income-equalizing adoption of new technology by smaller farms may be delayed; the second constitutes an additional argu-ment for terminating subsidies to mechanization. Greater scarcity in world grain markets may affect rural equity in opposing directions. By enhancing demand, scarcity would stave off a decline in labor's share which might arise from rising labor productivity (due to new technology) in the face of inelastic demand. At the same time, upward pressure in food prices can hardly have favorable equity implications in macroeconomic terms. Moreover, the "new scarcity" may seriously change the balance against those seeking to weigh equity along with production in policy-making in favor of those proclaiming output maximization alone as the policy objective.

APPENDIX

A MODEL OF LAND REFORM WITH FULL COMPENSATION TO OWNERS

The purpose of the following model is to examine the order of magnitude of improvement in income of the rural workers to be expected from land reform with compensation to owners. The principal policy question is whether, in the attempt to facilitate reform by compensation, the potential for increased income for the rural poor would be sacrificed.

Consider an agricultural region dominated by large farms with aggregate area "A." There are N total workers in the region, of whom N_p are permanent workers on these large farms, and N_o are other workers: the landless labor force plus the labor on very small farms (the aggregate area of which is assumed for convenience to be zero).

As discussed above, in Peru and Chile there has been a tendency to distribute large farm area "A" to existing peranent labor N_p, thereby making them a privileged rural labor class while perhaps reducing the opportunities of the remaining workers N_o. It is assumed here that land reform planners will avoid this mistaken or intended inequity, and will distribute the area among the full rural labor force.

Consider a land redistribution into family farms, each family having "F" workers. There will then be "m" number of post-reform farms, where

(1) $$m = \frac{N}{F} = \frac{N_p + N_o}{F}.$$

The size of each reform parcel (average, with larger size for poorer soil and smaller for better soil) will be:

(2) $$a = A/m.$$

Suppose that prior to reform the relationship of land use to farm size generated a characteristic declining relationship of output per farm area to total farm size,

(3) $q = h(x); \quad h'(x) < 0$

Where: q = output per hectare of total farm area,

         x = total farm area (hectares), and

         h = a function (e.g., $q = e^{\alpha} x^{-\beta}$).

Suppose that prior to reform there were n large farms, each of size s:

(4) $s = A/n.$

Then pre-reform output for the region will have been:

(5) $Q_o = n\,s\,q(s).$

   If post-reform land use follows the patterns found on pre-reform modest-sized farms (but not on the smallest, since they will be expanded by reform due to extra land availability), post-reform total output will be:

(6) $Q^* = m\,a\,q(a),$

since the number of farms times average size must equal the total regional farm area,

(7) $n\,s = m\,a.$

   Therefore the ratio of post-reform output to pre-reform output will be determined solely by the per hectare (of farm area) production characteristic of pre-reform and post-reform average farm sizes,

(8) $Q^*/Q_o = \dfrac{m\,a\,q(a)}{n\,s\,q(s)} = q(a)/q(s).$

This conclusion assumes that labor, capital, and intermediate inputs will be sufficient to reproduce at the full regional level the production features characterizing the reform-parcel-sized farms prior to reform.

Note that in the convenient case of the form $q(x) = e^{\alpha} x^{-\beta}$, equation (8) becomes

(8a) $\qquad Q^*/Q_o = (s/a)^{\beta}$.

For example, suppose $\beta = .1$. Then as farm size rises 10%, per hectare
(of total farm) output falls by 1%. From (8a), a reform which reduced
average farm sizes to 1/100 the original level (e.g., distributing 2,000-
hectare farms into 20-hectare parcels) would raise output by approximately
60% (that is, $\lfloor 100 \rfloor^{.1} = 1.59$).

More generally, let the ratio of post-reform output to pre-reform
output be:

(9) $\qquad \theta = Q^*/Q_o$.

Note that a prior study for the Brazilian case[83] indicates that 25%
increase in output might be a reasonable level to anticipate.

To examine the effect of reform on worker income, consider first
the pre-reform average worker income:

(10) $\qquad \bar{y}_o = \dfrac{wN_p = w(1 - u)N_o}{N}$

where:

$\qquad \bar{y}_o$ = average worker annual income,

$\qquad w$ = wage (annual), and

$\qquad u$ = unemployment rate among the non-permanent laborers.

After reform, gross income per worker (not deducting for payments for land)
will be:

(11) $\qquad y^*_G = Q^*/N = \dfrac{\theta Q_o}{N}$.

The ratio of post-reform gross income per worker to pre-reform average
worker income will therefore be:

(12) $\qquad y^*_G / \bar{y}_o = \left[\dfrac{\theta Q_o}{N} \right] / \left[\dfrac{w\{N_p + (1-u)N_o\}}{N} \right]$.

If we denominate W_o as aggregate wage payments before reform and Π_o as aggregate profits before reform, and abstract from depreciation and intermediate input costs (or, the equivalent, define Q_o and Q^* net of them), then:

(13) $Q_o = \Pi_o + W_o$

and, from (12),

(14) $y^*_G / \bar{y}_o = \dfrac{\theta\left[\Pi_o + W_o\right]}{W_o} = \theta(\Psi_o + 1),$

where:

Ψ_o = the original ratio of profits to wage bill.

Equation (14) tells the proportional rise in average worker income resulting from a land reform with no land payment compensation. The rise can be quite high with reasonable values. For example, if wage and profits shares are equal prior to reform, $\Psi_o = 1$; with $\theta = 1.25$ (as suggested above), $y^*_G/\bar{y}_o = 2.5$, and average labor income hence rises by 150% as the result of reform, in the absence of land repayment. Note that the income rise is greater proportionately for the former landless workers, and smaller proportionately for the former permanent workers, since $y^{LL}_o < \bar{y}_o < w$, where y^{LL}_o is the original average wage for landless workers (equal to $[1-u]\,w$).

Now consider the effect of payment for land by parcel recipients. A crucial question is what value of land is attributed for compensation. By capital theory, this value should be the present discounted value of the future stream of expected profits, or:

(15) $V = \Pi_o / \rho,$

where:

V = aggregate land value, and

ρ = landowners' discount rate.

Let r be the financial interest rate which parcel recipients are charged on the unpaid balance of their land purchases. Because of the standard cleavage between capitalist rate of return and the rate of return paid on financial market instruments (due to the write-up to account for risk in production investment, as well as to capital market imperfections), ρ should be higher than r (for example, ρ will be 15% to 20% rate of return on capital while r is only 6% or 8% interest on bonds and loans).[84]

Note that since a pure transfer from former to new owners is involved, "r" need not equal the opportunity cost of capital for efficiency purposes. More particularly, if the compensation is paid to owners in bonds bearing real interest rate "r" typical in financial markets, there is no reason to charge more than "r" to parcel recipients despite the fact that the social opportunity cost of capital may exceed "r"—since what is involved is a transfer rather than an acquisition of incremental capital beyond that originally held by the landlords.

Defining y_{NI}^{*} as post-reform income per worker net of interest on the land loan, we have in the first year when the full debt on purchased land remains outstanding:

$$(16) \qquad y_{NI}^{*} = y_{G}^{*} - \frac{rV}{N} = y_{G}^{*} - \frac{r\Pi_{o}}{\rho N} \ .$$

That is, total interest payments are rV; there are N workers, so per worker interest payments are $\frac{rV}{N}$. Given (15), the equation yields the final expression on the right. But since

$$(17) \qquad \frac{\Pi_{o}}{N} = \frac{Q_{o}}{N} - \frac{W_{o}}{N} = \frac{Q_{o}}{N} - \overline{y}_{o} \ ,$$

we may write:

$$(18) \qquad y_{NI}^{*} = y_{G}^{*} - \frac{r}{\rho}\left[\frac{Q_{o}}{N} - \overline{y}_{o}\right] = \theta(\Psi_{o} + 1)\overline{y}_{o} - \frac{r}{\rho}\left[\frac{Q_{o}}{N} - \overline{y}_{o}\right] \ ,$$

so that

$$(19) \qquad y_{NI}^{*}/\overline{y}_{o} = \theta(\Psi_{o} + 1) - \frac{r}{\rho}\left[\frac{Q_{o}}{N\overline{y}_{o}} - 1\right] = \theta(\Psi_{o} + 1) - \frac{r}{\rho}\left[\frac{Q_{o} - W_{o}}{W_{o}}\right]$$

$$= \theta(\Psi_{o} + 1) - \frac{r}{\rho}(\Psi_{o}) = \Psi_{o}(\theta - \frac{r}{\rho}) + \theta \ .$$

The final form of equation (19) indicates the proportional rise of average worker income net of interest payments. As the interest rate r falls to zero, the rise approaches that of gross worker income; as r approaches the discount rate used in evaluating land value, the proportional rise in worker income falls by Ψ_o. Thus, in the limiting case of $r = \rho$, average worker income would rise by 50% rather than 150% in the example above.

Note that worker income net of interest would rise over time as outstanding land debt declines. Furthermore, net worker income would rise as a result of any technical progress above pre-reform production characteristics on family farms. Such technological change would have a "leveraged" effect on net income: a given percentage rise in output relative to inputs would allow a larger percentage increase in net income (since net income is a residual between output value, land interest payments, and intermediate costs).

Finally, it is important to consider the fact that net income includes "forced saving" as the land loan is amortized. Thus, the income expressed in equation (18) exceeds the net income available for consumption by the amount of amortization paid during the year. That amortization constitutes income because it represents accumulation of equity, but it is income which must be saved.

If interest and amortization were phased in equal annual installments over z years, as in a home mortgage with declining interest and rising amortization components of a flat annual payment, then "liquid" net income per worker would be:

$$(20) \qquad y^*_{LIQ} = y^*_G - \xi_{r,z} \left[\frac{r}{\rho} \frac{Q_o}{N} - \bar{y}_o \right],$$

where $\xi_{r,z}$ is the ratio of the flat interest-cum-amortization payment to the interest alone on full debt outstanding. (For example, with a 20-year loan with 6% interest, the equal annual installment paid is 8.72% of original principal or $\xi_{6\%}$, 20 years = 8.72%/6% = 1.45).

Following equation (19), the ratio of y_{LIQ} to original worker average income would then be:

$$(21) \qquad y^*_{LIQ} / \bar{y}_o = (\Psi_o)(\theta - \xi_{r,z} \frac{\iota}{\rho}) + \theta.$$

To assess the range of improvement in worker income under capitalistic land reform, the above equations may be examined under reasonable assumptions of parameter values. The results are shown in appendix table 1. It is clear from the table that over the reasonable parameter ranges quite substantial real income increments can be expected for workers even though they must pay for the land. Even liquid income--excluding forced saving through amortization of land debt--shows substantial increases in all cases.

Appendix Table 1.

Effects of "Capitalistic" Land Redistribution on Average Income of Workers

	A	B	C	D	E	F	G	H
Ψ_o	1.0	1.0	1.33	1.33	1.0	1.0	1.33	1.33
θ	1.25	1.50	1.25	1.50	1.25	1.50	1.25	1.50
r	.06	.06	.06	.06	.06	.06	.06	.06
ρ	.15	.15	.15	.15	.10	.10	.10	.10
$\xi_{r,z}$	1.45	1.45	1.45	1.45	1.45	1.45	1.45	1.45
$y^*_G / \bar{y}_o$	2.5	3.0	2.91	3.50	2.5	3.0	2.91	3.5
$y^*_{NI} / \bar{y}_o$	2.1	2.6	2.38	2.96	1.9	2.4	2.11	2.7
$y^*_{LIQ} / \bar{y}_o$	1.92	2.42	2.14	2.72	1.63	2.13	1.76	2.34

In short, compensation to landlords need not rob land reform of its potential for improving income for rural workers and for equalizing the rural income distribution, although this equalization will not be as thorough as would occur in the absence of payment to landlords.

Chapter 8

NOTES

1.   W. Cline, "Interrelationships Between Agricultural Strategy and Rural Income Distribution," Food Research Institute Studies 12 (2) (1973): 139-57.

2.   _____. Economic Consequences of a Land Reform in Brazil (Amsterdam: North-Holland, 1970).

3.   For a detailed treatment of the monopoly influence in agrarian structure, see S. Hunt, "The Economics of Haciendas and Plantations in Latin America," Princeton University Research Program in Economic Development, Discussion paper no. 29, 1972.

4.   Cline, "Economic Consequences."

5.   P. Bardhan, "Size, Productivity, and Returns to Scale: An Analysis of Farm-Level Data in Indian Agriculture," Journal of Political Economy 81 (November-December 1973): 1370-86.

6.   P. Dorner and D. Kanel, "The Economic Case for Land Reform," ed., P. Dorner, Land Reform in Latin America: Issues and Cases (Madison: U. of Wisconsin, 1971).

7.   R.A. Berry, "Land Reform and the Agricultural Income Distribution," Pakistan Development Review 11 (1) (Spring 1971).

8.   J. Sinha, "Agrarian Reforms and Employment in Densely Populated Agrarian Economies: A Dissenting View," International Labour Review 108 (4) (October 1973): 395-421.

9.   B.S. Minhas, "Rural Poverty, Land Redistribution, and Development," Indian Economic Review 5 (1) (April 1970): 97-128.

10.   S. Barraclough and J. Fernandez, Diagnóstico de la Reforma Agraria Chilena (Mexico: Siglo Veintiuno Editores, 1974).

11.   D. Horton, "Land Reform and Reform Enterprises in Peru" (Washington, D.C.: IBRD, 1974), mimeographed.

12.   Furthermore, recent evidence for Colombia indicates that small farms employ more hired labor per hectare than larger farms, suggesting that the land utilization influence would dominate, and reform would boost demand for hired labor. See W. Thirsk, "Some Aspects of Efficiency and Income Distribution in Colombian Land Reform," paper no. 53, Rice University Program of Development Studies (Houston: Summer, 1974).

13.   Sinha, "Agrarian Reforms and Employment."

14.   The author also attempts to disarm the argument that Japan's land reform succeeded on a very small farm, equal distribution basis, maintaining that Japan had irrigation while India's is limited, and that moreover, Japan had a long experience with technological adoption by small tenants prior to the post–World War II land reform whereas India's labor force has a large proportion of landless laborers not similarly trained.

15.   Minhas, "Rural Poverty, Land Redistribution."

16.   Barraclough and Fernandez, Reforma Agraria Chilena.

17.   This pattern of resource misallocation due to private versus collective incentives is not new: in the U.S.S.R. the very small portion of total land allocated to private plots accounts for a disproportionately large share of agricultural output.

18.   This "appropriate" amount equals a fraction of the unemployed rural labor force and a portion of the excess labor on minifundia, consistent with establishing a labor–land ratio on the expropriated area that equals the aggregate rural labor–land ratio (including unemployed labor and adjusting for land quality).

19.   Horton, "Land Reform in Peru."

20.   Note however that there is no evidence that the two reforms worsened the absolute circumstances of rural workers excluded from direct benefits due to replacement of hired labor with family labor in the reform sector.

21.   Suppose the land generates profits of $1,000 yearly. With a discount rate of 15% for risk capital, the market sets a price of $1,000/.15 = $6,670 on the property. After land reform the parcel recipients hold a loan with principal of $6,670 and interest payment of (say) 6% x $6,670 = $400. The remainder of output formerly going to profits ($600) is now free for improvement of labor income. ·

22.   Suppose agriculture provides 30% of GNP. With a capital-(including land) output ratio of 3.3, agricultural capital value equals GNP. Alternatively, suppose non-labor's share in agriculture is 40%, or 12% of total GNP. If the capitalist discount rate is 15%, then the stock value of non-labor's income is 80.4% of GNP (that is, 12%/.15).

23.   R.A. Berry, "Presumptive Income Tax on Agricultural Land: The Case of Colombia," National Tax Journal 25 (2) (June 1972): 169-81.

24.   The argument is that a decline in land price inflicts a wealth loss. If the time preference for consumption is neutral with respect to wealth, there will be no change in the savings rate (and hence, investment)

25.   Behind Berry's concern in this dimension lies an assumption that the structural transformation to small farms would be incomplete: a sector of the rural population would remain landless. Otherwise the concern is irrelevant, as all workers would have employment on their family farms in a "complete" transformation of the ownership structure.

26. The enthusiastic farmers' organization reported by Berry seems to have been thinking of this type of tax.

27. S. Lewis "Agricultural Taxation and Intersectoral Resource Transfers," Food Research Institute Studies in Agricultural Economics, Trade, and Development 12 (2) (1973): 93-114.

28. Note that the classic case of a presumptive income tax on land is that of Meiji Japan, in which taxes were levied on villages on the basis of assumed gross rice production from the land available. See for example Richard M. Bird, Taxing Agricultural Land in Developing Countries (Cambridge, Mass.: Harvard University Press, 1974): 113-16.

29. G. Sazama and H. Davis, "Land Taxation and Land Reform," Economic Development and Cultural Change 21 (4, pt. 1) (July 1973): 642-54.

30. That is, intensively in the neoclassical idiom, extensively in the Ricardian.

31. The issue is related to the dispute over land's "marginal product" in "alternative uses," in neoclassical factor payment analysis, as opposed to land's "rent" as a fixed factor, in Ricardian analysis.

32. Unfortunately, the authors consider "R^2" of .2 to .5 to indicate poor relationships. Robust "t" statistics would be of greater interest, but they are not reported.

33. Recent evidence available to the author for Brazil indicates that the land tax averages only 1/2 of 1% of market value of land in the Northeast and is still lower in the rest of the country. A "high" tax rate of 1.6% of land is reported by Sazama and Davis for Chile in 1965. Such rates are marginal compared with a probable opportunity cost of assets of 15% per annum. They become even less important if the real value of land is rising over time at a substantial rate, and they turn totally inconsequential if the base-year valuation is not updated for inflation. In contrast, Berry suggests approximately 6% of real land value as presumed income; combined with a progressive income tax, the effective rate might reach 3% of land value for large owners. Such a level might begin to influence land use: suppose net income per hectare could double by more intensive land use; then the burden of such a tax would fall from one-fifth to one-tenth of land's earnings.

34. The land reforms of Taiwan and Japan are often cited as owing their success partly to the fact that they involved conversion of pre-existing tenants to owners.

35. The force of this caveat is of course reduced if the agrarian structure is one with a very homogeneous set of tenant farms and with practically no landless labor force.

36. S. Cheung, "Private Property Rights and Sharecropping," Journal of Political Economy 76 (6) (November-December 1968): 1107-22.

37. Where N is labor, w is outside wage, and r is landlord's share.

38.   P.K. Bardhan and T.N. Srinivasan, "Cropsharing Tenancy in Agriculture: A Theoretical and Empirical Analysis," American Economic Review 61 (1) (March 1971): 48-64.

39.   Ibid, p. 49, equation 2.

40.   In addition to the logical point that land's marginal product must be above zero in a context of population density, there exist numerous empirical production function estimates indicating positive marginal product of land.

41.   In a recent critique Newberry has supported Cheung in opposition to Bardhan and Srinivasan. After citing the same problem noted here (the unacceptable requirement of zero marginal product of land), Newberry resurrects the Cheung analysis by emphasizing its feature of landlord specification of minimum acceptable labor applied per hectare in the share-crop contract (and then general equilibrium gurantees that the minimum chosen will be such that labor's marginal product equals the wage). The main value added of the Newberry analysis is a generalization to include the possibility of fixed rent tenure and uncertainty. The debate remains at an unsatisfactory state, with certain key assumptions going unquestioned by both sides (especially, that the alternative of employment at a given outside wage is freely available to the tenant, and that crop shares are sufficiently flexible to reflect changing productivity conditions). Note finally that Bell has provided recent evidence using data for Purnea District, India, supporting the traditional (or "Marshallian") viewpoint of sharecropping's distorting effects on resource allocation. See C. Bell, "Inputs, Outputs and Distribution on Sharecropped Holdings in Purnea District," IBRD (1974), mimeographed; D. Newberry, "Cropsharing Tenancy in Agriculture: Comment," American Economic Review 64 (6) (December 1974): 1060-66.

42.   Z. Ahmad, "The Social and Economic Implications of the Green Revolution in Asia," International Labour Review 105 (1) (January 1972): 9-34.

43.   According to data for 1968-69 from Lahiri, cited in Ahmad, "Social and Economic Implications of the Green Revolution."

44.   W. Bartsch, "Employment Effects of Alternative Technologies and Techniques in Asian Crop Production: A Survey of Evidence" (Geneva: International Labour Office, 1973), mimeographed.

45.   C. Bell, "The Acquisition of Agricultural Technology: Its Determinants and Effects," Journal of Development Studies 9 (1) (October 1972): 123-27.

46.   For wheat, Bell's "typical" or stylized data indicate per-acre increases of 400% for output, 436% for wage bill, and 720% for intermediate input costs. These data are surprising: in general, one would expect the percentage change in labor necessarily to fall short of the percentage change in output, since part of labor should be proportional to unchanged land area while only the remaining part should be proportional to output. Moreover, Bell's data imply a declining labor productivity, contrary to all of the technological or technique improvement results reported by Bartsc "Employment Effects of Alternative Technologies."

47.   J. Bieri, A. de Janvry, and A. Schmitz, "Agricultural Technology and the Distribution of Welfare Gains," American Journal of Agricultural Economics 54 (5) (December 1972): 801-08.

48.   U.K. Srivasta and E.O. Heady, "Technological Change and Relative Factor Shares in Indian Agriculture: An Empirical Analysis," American Journal of Agricultural Economics 55 (3) (August 1973): 509-14.

49.   That is, $(1-\delta)1\delta$ in the production function $Q = \gamma \left[\delta K^{-e} + (1-\delta)L^{-e} \right]^{-1/e}$, where Q, K, and L are output, capital, and labor.

50.   C. Gotsch, "Technical Change and the Distribution of Income in Rural Areas," American Journal of Agricultural Economics 54 (2) (May 1972): 326-40.

51.   D. Dalrymple and W. Jones, "Evaluating the 'Green Revolution,'" paper prepared for joint meeting of American Associaton for the Advancement of Science and Consejo Nacional de Ciencia y Technología, Mexico City, 20 June 1973 (Washington, D.C.:   1973), mimeographed.

52.   It is however true that if demand is inelastic, the S-curve adoption pattern will tend to increase inequality, since by the time the smaller farms have adopted the innovation the product price will have fallen.   Even in this instance the terminal year's output will not show increased inequality, although during the intervening years there will have been an increasing gap between large and small farmers which subsequently reduces again.

53.   W. Thiesenhusen, "Green Revolution in Latin America: Income Effects, Policy Decisions," Monthly Labor Review 95 (3) (March 1972): 20-27.

54.   Bartsch, "Employment Effects of Alternative Technologies."

55.   Ibid.

56.   Bell, "Acquisition of Agricultural Technology."

57.   A. Singh and M. Billings, "The Effect of Technology on Farm Employment in Two Indian States," ed., Ridker and H. Lubell, Employment and Unemployment Problems of the Near East and South Asia, vol. II (Delhi: Vikas, 1971): 502-34.

58.   I. Inukai, "Farm Mechanisation, Output and Labour Input: a Case Study Thailand," International Labour Review 101 (1) (January 1970): 453-73.

59.   R. Lawrence, "Some Economic Aspects of Farm Mechanization in Pakistan" (1970), mimeographed.

60.   H. Kaneda, "Economic Implications of the 'Green Revolution' and the Strategy of Agricultural Development in West Pakistan," Pakistan Development Review (Summer 1969).

61.   S. Bose and E. Clark, "Some Basic Considerations on Agricultural Mechanization in West Pakistan," Pakistan Development Review (August 1969).

62. M. Yudelman, G. Butler, and R. Banerji, <u>Technological Change in Agriculture and Employment in Developing Countries</u> (Paris: O.E.C.D., 1971)

63. Ibid., p. 163.

64. Cline, "Interrelationships Between Agricultural Strategy and Rural Income."

65. C. Gotsch, "Tractor Mechanisation and Rural Development in Pakistan," <u>International Labour Review</u> 107 (1) (January 1973): 133-66.

66. It does not seem, however, that crop prices should influence the choice of technique, except insofar as capital-intensive crops receive relatively more favorable price treatment than labor-intensive crops (or vice versa).

67. Bartsch, "Employment Effects of Alternative Technologies."

68. R. Barker, W. Meyers, C. Crisostomo, and B. Duff, "Employment and Technological Change in Philippine Agriculture," <u>International Labour Revie</u> 106 (2-3) (August-September 1972): 111-39.

69. K. Raj, "Mechanisation of Agriculture in India and Sri Lanka (Ceylon)," <u>International Labour Review</u> 106 (4) (October 1972): 315-34.

70. E. Clayton, "Mechanisation and Employment in East African Agriculture," <u>International Labour Review</u> 105 (4) (April 1972): 309-34.

71. K. Abercrombie, "Agricultural Mechanisation and Employment in Latin America," <u>International Labour Review</u> 106 (1) (July 1972): 11-45.

72. Note that Kilby and Johnston have estimated the industrial labor requirements for production of simple farm implements for bullock tractors. to be much higher than similar indirect labor requirements for tractors. See P. Kilby and B. Johnston, "The Choice of Agricultural Strategy and the Development of Manufacturing," <u>Food Research Institute Studies</u> 11 (2) (1972) 155-75.

73. W. Thirsk, "Income Distribution, Efficiency and the Experience of Colombian Farm Mechanization," Rice University Program of Development Studies, paper no. 33 (Houston: 1972), mimeographed.

74. Agency for International Development, U.S. Department of State, <u>A.I.D. Spring Review of Small Farmer Credit: Small Farmer Credit Summary Papers</u> XX (Washington, D.C.: June 1973).

75. Long reported the finding of Lowdermilk that in Pakistan's Punjab three-fourths of the small farmers considered credit to be inadequate to finance desired amounts of fertilizer; the author cited the opposite finding (that credit was not a constraint on output) by Gotsch for Pakistan, Nesbit for Chile, and both Miller and Tinnermeir for Peru. See M. Long, "Conditions for Success of Public Credit Programs for Small Farmers," <u>A.I.D. Spring Review of Small Farmer Credit</u> XIX (June 1973): 309-23.

76. Cline, "Economic Consequences."

77. The average product of this input was higher on smaller farms (due to more sparse utilization), and hence (with constant output elasticity) so was marginal product.

78. W. Thirsk, "Rural Credit and Income Distribution in Colombia," Rice University Program of Development Studies, paper no. 51 (Houston: Summer, 1974).

79. D. Adams, "The Case for Voluntary Savings Mobilization: Why Rural Capital Markets Flounder," A.I.D. Spring Review of Small Farmer Credit XIX (June 1973): 309-23.

80. W. Thirsk, "Income Distribution Consequences of Agricultural Price Supports in Colombia," Rice University Program of Development Studies (Houston: Summer, 1974).

81. M. Nelson, The Development of Tropical Lands: Policy Issues in Latin America (Baltimore: Johns Hopkins University Press, 1973).

82. The recent Brazilian strategy of meeting rural employment needs through colonization of the Amazon basin already appears to have met serious setbacks. Stretches of the new Trans-Amazonic highway reportedly have washed away; and small-farm colonists are a small fraction of the number anticipated.

83. Cline, "Economic Consequences."

84. It should be noted that landowners who can escape income tax on agricultural income but must pay it on income from financial assets might attribute a lower discount rate (i.e., compensating for lower tax rate) than ρ in their evaluation of land price, reducing the source of income increase for workers after land reform identified on the basis of the excess of ρ over r in this model, and even raising the possibility that this difference is negative (posing an additional burden on worker repayment rather than providing a benefit).

Supplemental Readings

Abdullah, A. "Land Reform and Agrarian Change in Bangladesh." Mimeographed. Dacca: Bangladesh Institute of Development Economics, 1973.

Adelman, I., and Morris, C. Economic Growth and Social Equity in Developing Countries. Stanford: Stanford University Press, 1973.

Barraclough, S. "Agricultural Policy and Land Reform." Journal of Political Economy 78 (4, part 2) (July/August 1970), 906-47.

Griffin, K. The Green Revolution: An Economic Analysis. Geneva: United Nations Research Institute for Social Development, 1972.

Montgomery, J. D. "Allocation of Authority in Land Reform Programs: A Comparative Study of Administrative Processes and Outputs." Administrative Science Quarterly 17 (1) (March 1972), pp. 62-75.

Thirsk, W. "Some Aspects of Efficiency and Income Distribution in Colombian Land Reform." Paper no. 53, Rice University Program of Development Studies (Houston: Summer, 1974).

Thiesenhusen, W. "Chile's Experiments in Agrarian Reform: Four Colonization Projects Revisited." American Journal of Agricultural Economics 56 (2) (May 1974), pp. 323-30.

CHAPTER IX

DESIGNING THE PUBLIC WORKS MODE OF ANTI-POVERTY POLICY

John P. Lewis

A. "Serious" rural public works efforts: the context

For poor countries the idea of undertaking additional labor-intensive
public construction activity, especially in the countryside, as a means both
of mitigating low-end poverty and unemployment and of adding to the stocks
of productive assets of communities certainly is not new. In the modern
literature on development it goes back at least to writings of Ragnar Nurkse
and Arthur Lewis in the early 1950s.[1] Moreover, it is a shopworn idea: on
various occasions and in various modes during the past two decades many developing country governments have experimented with the approach; and in
most cases the results have not appeared particularly successful.

Now in the middle 70s, therefore, when there is redoubled concern
about low-end poverty and underemployment in the poor countries, it is not
likely that expanded rural public works will be the first choice of many
governments as a pro-egalitarian policy instrument. The approach will be
viewed instead, as a fallback, second- or third-best choice for regimes
that, although anxious to increase the incomes and productivity of the
poorest employable segments of their populations, are blocked by political
or other obstacles from launching major land reforms and/or other direct
asset-redistributing attacks on poverty.

The present chapter does not quarrel with this comparative assessment.
Yet its gist is that a "serious" public works effort can have quite powerful redistributive effects--mostly of the intended kind, although the effort may also set certain countervailing forces in motion. Indeed, such a
public works push can, in principle, provide a serviceable vehicle for a
comprehensive program of rural reform. But such a strategy (which, it will
be suggested, almost no poor-country government yet has really tried) would
not be an easy policy option by any means. Its implementation would require adherence to some reasonably difficult economic criteria; it would

pose tough resource requirements, especially in the availability of food; it would be demanding administratively; and it would depend on a special set of political conditions and commitments.

The unorthodox methodology of this chapter--it may appear to some readers as little more than a cookbook manual for some hypothetical government that might "seriously" undertake the rural public works approach--is deliberate. There is a reasonably accessible body of literature on the public works experience of a number of developing countries in recent decades and on the theory of efforts (at least in part distributionally motivated) to mobilize underemployed labor in the creation of productive assets.[2] But, as I shall be suggesting when we get to the matter of scale below, virtually all of these past experiments have been almost trivial compared with the antipoverty needs of countries. Second, the received theory is mainly economic; it says too little about the often dominant role of political and administrative factors. Third, it will be argued below that a number of the critical parameters, including the economic parameters, determining the scope and shape of the public works possibilities in particular countries are especially difficult to establish by antecedent statistical and other analyses--partly because of hard-to-repair data gaps and partly because the parameters themselves seem to keep moving around. Thus even for descriptive and diagnostic purposes the best methodology is policy experimentation--with careful provision that the behavioral data which emerge as the experiment proceeds are fed back into the evolving policy design. Finally, in many countries antipoverty policy needs are perceived to be urgent in the near and medium term. Governments (or indigenous interests anxious to move their governments in pro-egalitarian directions) are impatient to get on with some consequential reforms, however incomplete the social-science mapping of alternative policy courses may be.

Under these circumstances it seems that the best way to sort out both what we may know about the approach and what needs to be determined is to attempt to elaborate a policy design for a hypothetical country where major resort to the public works approach might make sense. Such an analysis should have pertinence for LDC decision makers. It may also be a useful way to encourage students of development to focus on, as it were, the next layer of issues in the public works field--particularly those involving (i) the interpenetration of economic, political, and administrative variables and (ii) the reconciliation of competing policy targets.

The following simulation of a policy design is in two parts. First it will be well to establish the kinds of country conditions--economic, political, and otherwise--in short, the context, in which major resort to the public works approach may be appealing. Then in the rest of the chapter, drawing on this set of context assumptions as well as on past public works experience and relevant theory, a type of policy is suggested that might be attempted under such circumstances. The "design" sketched is not precise or inflexible. But it is sufficiently detailed in its treatment of content, criteria, and procedures to surface most of the salient issues. Finally, implications for assistance agencies and other external actors are examined briefly.

One last preliminary note: This chapter makes the same implicit assumption as the rest of the volume, namely, that analyses of distributionally oriented policy instruments may in some measure be generally applicable to a variety of Third World countries. There is something to this in the public works case. For example, the list of countries which already have experimented fairly strenuously (albeit not massively) with special public works programs includes some very large populous states (India, Indonesia, Bangladesh, Pakistan) as well as some very small insular ones (Mauritius and Trinidad-Tobago). Yet it would be wrong to exaggerate the transferability of the kind of policy analysis that follows. Since the variables that shape and constrain the public works option are so complex and, in many respects, so country-specific, the best way to construct a coherent policy model is to abstract it from a particular regional or country context which the analyst knows well. In the present instance that context is South Asian, especially Indian. My guess is that none of the principal factors or relationships identified below is unique to South Asia and that, therefore, many aspects of the policy design are indeed transferable. But the reader should be warned that this is an hypothesis, not a finding--and remember that the empirical grounding of the paper is mainly South Asian.

1. The context: economic circumstances

Countries for which public works may constitute an interesting vehicle for major reform are poor, predominantly rural, have high ratios of population to arable land, and still have high population growth rates which give them young populations and high dependency ratios. Their rural labor forces are growing faster than the combined labor-absorption capacities of

a modernizing (even if efficiently labor-intensive) agricultural sector
and of the modernizing portions of the industrial, trade, and services
sectors. Moreover, the slackness of employment and earning opportunities
is concentrated in the lower reaches of a highly unequal structure of status, power, and assets as well as income, that is, in the smallest owner-
cultivators, tenant farmers, and especially in the class of unskilled
landless laborers.

The bottom 30% to 50% of these rural populations usually are estimated
to be disadvantaged. Whether or not their marginal products are zero is a
red herring, but, beyond doubt, they are extremely low. In countries of
great overall poverty it is commonly judged that the only feasible way of
increasing the incomes of the rural low-end poor is to increase their output (i.e., pure income redistribution via taxes and transfers will not suffice). But, as noted, opportunities for additional employment either in
agriculture or in industry are limited, especially in the near term.[3]
Hence the interest in supplemental, publicly organized, _productive_ work
opportunities.

Governments drawn to a public works attack on rural poverty tend to
conclude that there are a large number of useful, cost-effective construction jobs in which the rural poor could be employed. This, obviously,
must be a country-specific determination. It depends, among other things,
on the overall development design; on the particular history of infrastructure development and maintenance; on the country's valuation of socia
capital; on its planning, administrative, and technical capacity; and on
the on-going dynamics of other aspects of the development process, includi
agricultural, industrial, and spatial-centering. Yet my own impression is
that there are few developing countries, even few local rural regions with
countries, that cannot identify a substantial array of labor-intensive
rural construction projects with high social returns. The opportunities
tend to be numerous (i) partly because of the fiscal and wage-goods (especially food) restraints that have affected budgetary allocations in the
past and (ii) partly because current agricultural and industrial expansion
keeps generating new construction needs.

The sustained character of the need for well-selected, planned and im
plemented public works means that it is not necessary to think of a labor-
intensive public works program as a temporary palliative. It can indeed b
a bridge to other longer-run (including market-adjustment) answers to the

problem of rural low-end poverty. And in most countries such "bridging" could be productively continued on a large scale for a very long time-- certainly for as long as present planners can sensibly plan.

Furthermore, the technology of public construction, particularly in the countryside, can be quite plastic in its factor proportions. Much of it can be highly labor-intensive (if the construction management is strong and the engineering shrewd) without sacrificing much in construction costs or in the effectiveness and durability of the asset produced. On this point (hasty, make-work relief works aside) the record of comparative experience is fairly clear. It is equally clear that the room for variation in the mix of labor-capital inputs is wide and that, even in the poorest countries, public administrators, interacting with local and foreign business suppliers, will tend to veer toward the capital-intensive end of that range unless they are firmly guided by policies specifically favoring labor-intensity.[4]

Whether and to what extent the low-end, underemployed rural poor constitute an available labor force for additive public works activity has been the subject of great and continuing academic debate. Plainly, in most countries there are no armies of reserve labor standing at the ready, expecially year-around. The slackness of employment is highly seasonal. But plainly also in many rural places there is an available labor supply if the work offers can be fitted to its seasonal shape and other characteristics. The degree and character of labor-supply elasticity in particular locations is best revealed by the response to actual employment offers--a response which (it is apparent from a variety of experience to date) is apt to reflect the nature of the work provided, its location, its perceived reliability over time, the wages paid, modes of organization, the health, nutrition, inhibitions and taboos of potential recruits, and the feasibility of intra-rural migration.

Often it has been assumed that the feasibility of expansion of rural public works crucially depends upon the elasticity of the labor supply. But as soon as income redistribution becomes a principal objective of the program, there is an interesting sense in which the uncertainty about labor-supply elasticity takes on a fail-safe quality. For the more inelastic the labor supply in fact proves to be (and therefore the more constricted the program's direct generation of added low-end employment and income) the more upward pressure additive employment programs place on farm wages,

thereby (unless the effect is fully offset by a parallel tightening
of food demand relative to food supplies) squeezing the margins of farm
proprietors and distributing income more equally within the rural economy.

2.   The context: perceived effects

In the case of countries that share the circumstances just outlined,
it does no great violence to reality (and it provides a useful framework
for our subsequent discussion) to impute to them a common categorization
of the effects or impacts that added labor-intensive public works can be
expected to have.

First, there are those effects that occur <u>while the work is in prog-
ress</u>, before the assets being created or augmented become operative. These
impacts are, or can be, mainly redistributive:

(i) The works programs (if the construction technology is kept
labor-intensive) can generate additional employment and income for the
low-end poor.

(ii) Depending on the elasticity of the labor supply, programs
can bid up the general level of unskilled wages by adding to the demand
for rural labor.

(iii) The construction process can also have these collateral
effects:

- a training function (public works projects often
  provide farm workers with their first encounters
  with the rhythms, patterns, and disciplines of
  organized nonfarm employment);

- improved employment and productivity for the
  educated unemployed (depending on how works
  projects are managed and staffed); and

- changes in the structure of consumer goods
  production which are induced by the changes that
  the works programs effect in the structure of
  incomes.

In the second place, public works programs have <u>asset effects</u>, which
are associated with the kinds of assets they build or renew and the manner
in which the latter are used. Here, of course, the important impacts are
not all distributional, and the distributional outcomes (which will be noted
as we proceed) are a mixed bag which may tend to be perverse but may also
be susceptible to some pro-equity policy guidance:

(i) If the works constructed are indeed productive, they will in some measure increase future output. How much, and whether of private or public goods and services, will depend on the composition of the program and also, of course, on the effectiveness of the on-going activities in which the assets are engaged.

(ii) The effects of the assets on future employment, including work opportunities for the low-end poor, will vary with the assets. Irrigation facilities, for example, while chiefly benefitting landed proprietors may, by increasing multiple cropping, raise the demand for agricultural labor.

(iii) The income-distribution effects of the assets will depend generally on the composition of the projects undertaken and upon who controls the facilities produced. Insofar as the incremental assets tend to complement the unequally distributed array of private assets already existing, longer-run inequality will tend to be aggravated. On the other hand, particular types of new assets, for example, those facilitating the educational and health uplift of the poor, can diminish inequalities.

3.   The assumed scale of the effort—and of needed resources

I would exclude from those to which the chapter's simulated policy design is hypothetically addressed all governments which are disposed merely to dabble in rural public works. To date dabbling has been the norm. Of the 14 most prominent country cases included in the study of the Harvard group for the World Bank, only one is estimated to have claimed a higher fraction of gross domestic product than 1%; five claimed less than 0.5%. Of these countries, only one (Tunisia) generated more than 10 man-days of employment in public works per member of the labor force. The marginal contribution of most others was less than five man-days per member of the labor force.[5] And these are the major ventures. For the most part rural public works initiatives, except for occasional spasms of hastily contrived and quickly abandoned relief works in response to natural disasters, have been exercises in the trivial: dollops of U.S. or FAO food aid to support food-for-work schemes, narrowly circumscribed pilot projects, or "national" programs so thinly sprinkled as to have no discernible impact on aggregate events.

Such initiatives no doubt can continue without triggering many of the political, financial, and management stresses examined below. But small efforts also will continue to accomplish little. There are two reasons for the present insistence on size of effort. One, of course, is the size of the need. The latter has not been adequately measured in any country; obviously it is not uniform across countries; it must be discovered experimentally. But to be responsive to the apparent need, serious experimentation (not the launching level but the initial target toward which a program builds technically and procedurally as quickly as it can) must be comparatively bold. In the second place, there is no way that the public works approach can be sustained as a central plank of antipoverty reform unless it commands the continuing attention and nervous energy of a government's top leadership. The program is unlikely to claim such attention if it does not also levy a very substantial claim on the budget over which the leadership presides.

Fuzzy as they are, the foregoing judgments are inherently quantitative and the reader deserves some idea of what the writer has in mind. Relying on the kind of rough calculation sketched later in subsection B,1 it is my guess that additive public works efforts are unlikely either to represent serious attacks on the low-end poverty need or to be locked into leadership's priority spectrum until they claim (or are rapidly approaching a claim of) 1% to 2% of a jurisdiction's total output and income. This would mean, of course, a correspondingly higher fraction of the jurisdiction's governmental budget, and a higher fraction still of developmental outlays.

Note, however, the word "jurisdiction." It would be a great mistake to think that the same intensity of public works activity must be spread uniformly across whole national countrysides. Regional concentrations of effort within countries may be quite appropriate; indeed they may be necessary. But whether the jurisdiction is national or subnational, it is assumed that "seriousness" will mean using some such fraction of gross jurisdictional product as that suggested.

Quite obviously, this scalar requirement confines resort to "the public works approach" to governments able to muster the necessary resources, both financial and real. As will be indicated in the resources portion of the policy design, virtually every potentially interested government will conclude that it must find some combination of financial offsets that will make noninflationary room for the increased consumption by the employees of the works program. The offsets can consist of increased taxes or of reduced public expenditures in other areas; or of induced expansions in private

saving; or of increased imports financed by more foreign aid or other net
transfers from abroad, or by acceptable drawings on the government's foreign exchange reserves, or by expansions in the government's export earnings (e.g., from oil). But unless governments can accept higher rates of
internal inflation, adequate offsets of some of these kinds must be found,
and typically the finding will not be easy.

Of the needed real resources, the most important is food. Even if sufficient financial offsets are found to maintain overall fiscal balance as
a public works program expands its payrolls, the <u>composition</u> of aggregate
consumption will change, and for those wage goods for which the income elasticity of demand is higher at the low end of the income spectrum, the factor
most likely to be a bottleneck is food. Food claims the biggest share of
incremental purchases by the poor because the substitution possibilities
are limited, because food scarcities are in some sense intrinsically (and,
therefore, politically) more urgent, and because supplies of other low-end
consumer goods are likely--thanks to redundant capacities or to the simplicity of expanding capacity for many commodities in many countries--to
prove more quickly responsive than food to increased demand.

The converse propositions follow: Production breakthroughs in food-
grains production, either underway or genuinely imminent, open up new opportunities for more ambitiously scaled public works ventures. But unless
countries can get major increments of food aid or unless they are falling
heir to enough extra oil or other earnings to place large and reliable incremental claims on a tight international food market, they will need to
regard expanded public works and agricultural production as two symbioti-
cally linked programs. The former, given good project choice and implementation, can promote the latter. But the feasibility of works programs also
is critically dependent upon--and must be scaled to--food production. Moreover, in agriculture itself any pro-egalitarian reforms that would have the
effect of dampening production (some may have a pro-production effect)
would blunt the possibilities for attacking rural inequalities via public
works expansion.

4.   The political context

Of all those circumstances which qualify a government for serious pro-
egalitarian resort to rural public works, the political conditions may be
the most severe. The approach will appeal only to a government with a

special set of purposes and constraints. And it will work only for a government which, despite the constraints, has sufficient strength and determination to prevail in its purposes over entrenched resistances. It must "prevail" at least long enough to extract a substantial passage of short-term redistributive benefits as well as growth benefits from the program, preferably long enough to engender and/or facilitate a basic transformation in the countryside's political structure.

In many developing countries we can posit a government which sits atop a quite highly structured, highly unequal system. The elites are self-interested and there is a rivalry among them for shares of income, assets, and power. They tend to be allergic to major structural changes and indifferent and/or hostile to gains, especially gains of power and assets, by the poorest and weakest classes. At the same time, the elites have a stake in the maintenance of order, including orderly rather than violent processes of change. And the rhetoric and norms of the systems are likely to exalt the concept of popular democratic participation in government. Moreover, the masses are not without latent power. They have some class structuring and subgroup organizations and loyalties; they have internal and external communications networks and are beginning to acquire some of the skills and machinery for power bargaining; and they have begun to listen more and more to egalitarian rhetoric. At least among some of the subgroups of the poor, patience is wearing thin; the inertia of the masses is breaking down.

For its part, government looks like a creature of the elites, but this may be deceptive. Like most reform regimes historically, the government may in some measure be a class renegade. "The" government, of course, is not a monolith; but its topmost leadership plus enough senior political colleagues and enough strategically placed career officials to make the viewpoint influential may have a commitment to the interests of the poor—for a mixture of reasons. The latter may include (i) fear of upheaval if, finally, something substantial is not done for the poor, (ii) a political strategy wherein the leadership, in rivaling with its competing elites, set out to build a constituency among the country's disadvantaged groups, and even (iii) intrinsic compassion for the poor. Social scientists probably dismiss the last too quickly; it may, in fact, have considerable force. In any event our hypothetical government argues all of these reasons and more in seeking to win support for its program among the more sophisticated and/or malleable elites in the parlimentary, journalistic, bureaucratic, intellectual, and other sectors of the public-policy community.

Taking into account the resistance it anticipates to more radical reform as well as its own sense of development priorities, the regime may opt for a labor-intensive employment mode of antipoverty policy. The elites, like others, are interested in additional productive assets. The political calculus of the reformers is that the opposition of the elites to redistributive ventures can be outweighed by their interest in the assets that a public works program will produce. As economic developers, the reformers count this a good social bargain. At any rate, since they share the elites' preference for orderly processes of change (and, indeed, propose to trade heavily on those preferences in promoting their egalitarian purposes), they conclude this bargain is the best that can be had.

Now comes the rub: Such a government launching into a major public works program with serious pro-egalitarian purpose must recognize that much of the life--at least the long early life--of the program will be in some measure an adversary proceeding. It will be a contest between the political leadership and the elites from which it itself has emerged. The elites, especially in the countryside, will persistently try to subvert the egalitarian biases in the program. These tendencies, as will be noted in the section on policy design, are likely to be magnified to the extent that, for resource-raising and/or other reasons, it is decided to decentralize the program and delegate more discretion to local jurisdictions. But in any event the government must be braced to do continuing battle to keep the pro-poor norms of the program high. It will have to strive diligently, not just to keep the operation tolerably honest and efficient but to keep access to employment open to the poor; to keep project wage rates up to minimum standards; to keep some pressure of demand on local labor markets; to keep the unskilled labor content of projects high; and, as far as possible (I shall conclude that the early chances on this score are not good), to encourage a selection of projects that, like the implementation of projects, also has some redistributive benefit.

There are those who, as soon as the underlying political tension in the public works brand of major antipoverty policy is exposed in this fashion, dismiss it as wishful thinking. It is too much, say they, to expect leadership based on elites to sustain as much class schizophrenia as the approach requires. This objection seems to me to be historically naive. Time and

again in many countries, including developing counties, when egalitarian
reforms have been effected within the frame of more-or-less elitist, more-
or-less constitutional power structures, it has been at the instigation of
precisely such semi-declassed leaderships. To be effective in this regard
leaderships do not have to be absolutely consistent, unflagging, or uncom-
promising in their egalitarianism. Nor are the elites either monolithic
or unrelieved in their opposition. In many countries different elites--
e.g., particular parties or factions, the intelligentsia, the press, the
military--differ substantially in their degrees of identification with the
poor; and most elites, even in the traditional countryside, are honey-
combed with individuals and subgroups with such identifications.

Further still, a leadership plotting a course of serious antipoverty
reform by the public works route may be able to reap long-term political
reward. During the first chapters of the venture, as the regime clings to
is pro-poor (antipoverty) norms and thereby does indeed assist in bringing
employment and income benefits to the weakest rural classes, antipoverty
reform by the public works route should quickly win their gratitude. For
the time being, given the existing status structure, such gratitude will
not be very valuable political coin. But as the economic condition of the
rural poor improves, as they acquire a greater variety of nonagricultural
and nontraditional work experiences, as their own organizations strengthen,
and, in particular, as they see more clearly the value of exercising whatever franchise they have in political, especially local political, delibera
tions, their political power will also build. If the commitment of the
old elites to orderly process is strong enough, the traditional status
structure may be substantially transformed without much of an attempt on
the part of the elites, despite their objections, to resort to violent repression. The poor who win power from such a process are likely to emerge
with a considerable allegiance to the instigating reformers.

Nevertheless, such a political scenario will be available only to
leaderships with substantial stocks of egalitarian purpose, courage--and
political capital. At the same time, it would be foolish to exaggerate how
steadfast a regime must be before serious public works undertakings can be
worthwhile. Starting the course strongly and staying it well but staying
it only for a while--long enough to produce some cost-effective assets and
meanwhile win substantial income and employment benefits for the rural poor
but then succumbing to elitist resistance before the transformation of the

traditional status structure is well advanced—should also be counted as success, although of a more limited kind. Most social reform is in fact episodic. Good ventures do some good but then generate backlashes, or simply erode or get tired, and are superseded. There is no reason why the public works approach should be different.

5. The programmatic context: using localized public works as a vehicle for comprehensive rural reform

Finally, as to the setting for which there will be an attempt, in the balance of the chapter, to sketch the rudiments of a policy design, it will be well to make quite explicit something that has been substantially indicated already. I am interpreting the "public works" mode of antipoverty policy in a way, on the one hand, that is ambitiously comprehensive, on the other, that deliberately slights certain organizational and locational varieties of public works activities.

On the first count, "the public works approach" is being taken as shorthand for quite comprehensive rural reform efforts that, besides trying to generate added low-end incomes and employment and create productive assets, are concerned with the reinforcement of agricultural expansion, with the political mobilization of the rural poor, with the rural economy's fiscal and administrative decentralization, and with its pattern of settlements. It does not strain customary usage to suppose that a "major" public works effort would, in fact, embrace some such variety of dimensions. Indeed, otherwise, the very semantics of "public works" as a programmatic concept are anomalous, since our convention is almost always to denominate programs in terms of their functions or outputs (e.g., health, education, defense, public safety). And yet, like any construction (except, possibly, monuments) public works are patently inputs. The linkage between public works and the rest of the rural reform strategy to which they relate is budgetary; most of the other facets require some kinds of physical public investments. Thus it may not be bad shorthand to call the whole complex of such reforms the "public works approach." By the same token, however, a serious public works effort cannot, just because it generates supplemental employment and income, be construed as peripheral to the rest of rural reform. More nearly (although, as we shall see, the reconciliation of input-centered and output-centered activities poses organizational problems) public works become the programmatic vehicle for the rest of the strategy.

So much for the comprehensive aspect of the policy model that will be sketched. The narrow aspect is that, since I am, as it were, interpreting "public works" as a code word for rural reform, attention will be confined to decentralized (i.e., comparatively localized rural varieties of labor-intensive public construction. Much of the same argumentation, and a quite similar policy design, could be applied to urban public works employing unskilled urban labor. Some of the same points could be made about rural projects whose scope or radii are too great (major irrigation schemes inter-city roads, many more) to fit within particular local jurisdictions-- although here the organizational design probably would differ markedly from the decentralized rural case. Finally, one could consider an entirely different mode--namely, the paramilitary or land-army model--for accomplishing essentially the same, essentially local rural, projects that are so differently modeled in the following pages.[6]

As will appear, however, the last of these neglected approaches would sacrifice certain kinds of constructive leverage that locally organized public works can bring to bear on rural reform. And the other two varieties (although they may constitute important links and complements to decentralized rural works) fall outside of that context entirely. Thus in the interests of space the present discussion is confined to the decentralized rural scene.

B. Issues of policy design

Assume that a developing country government judges that its own character and its economic and political context are roughly of the types that have been described; assume, further, that this government opts for a major public-works-centered attack on rural poverty: What kind of program, with what kinds of content, procedures, and organization, might it undertake?

It is well to remember that the logical methodology of such an effort will be experimentation--indeed, since the poverty problems inviting attack probably appear too urgent to wait for much further preliminary research or small-unit pilot projects, it probably will be large-scale experimentation. For a government that wants its new public works venture to escape the blight of triviality, the proper course will be to build, as rapidly as orderly expansion allows, a program that addresses a substantial fraction of the supplemental employment and antipoverty needs indicated by the initially available data and estimates, however imperfect the latter--and whether the program's initial rural target jurisdiction(s) consist of the whole or only of portions of the national countryside. But such boldness will need to be matched by prudence—first, to see that, while pressing the limits of some or all of the political, financial, food, and administrative constraints, the initial scaling of the effort does not overstep them; second, to establish and sustain an abundant feedback of information and analysis, and of consequent program adjustment, as the experiment proceeds.

Although this is a high-risk methodology probably it is not inherently foolhardy in the public works case; most of the processes that need evaluation have long enough gaits to allow the program to be "steered" considerably if the monitoring is ample and alert. Moreover, some of the more likely miscalculations (for example, the offer of too much employment in particular areas) would not be disastrous. It is apparent, however, that such an approach will invite a special symbiosis between a country's public decision making and its applied social science research (whether the latter is conducted within the government itself or by quasi-governmental or non-governmental institutions). The two activities will proceed in parallel; the first, at the beginning, will not wait on the second; but thereafter further actions will become extraordinarily dependent on the cogency, relevance, and timeliness of the research. It will be important for government to support (and use) an adequate research effort. Conversely, the applied social scientists will need to keep their work priorities and rhythms and their modes of analysis responsive to the needs of the policy adjustors.

Large-scale experimentation, moreover, is likely to remain the style of the public works approach. In addition to being inadequately known at the outset, many of the key parameters are apt to keep shifting. Thus a public works reform program will need a persisting capacity to sense and adjust to changes in the behavioral and institutional terrain—to changes, for example, in the shape of labor supply, in the perceived stock of good projects, in the educability of various elites to reform purposes, and in the political responsiveness of the poor to economic uplift (these having been already noted), as well as (yet to be noted) changes in the available or trainable stocks of technical and administrative personnel, in the migratory propensities of labor within the rural sector, and in the feasibility of altering the pattern of rural settlements.

At the same time, this very plasticity that the program will need will
be risk prone. In discussing the political context in which a "serious"
public works program is likely to operate, I have emphasized that one must
expect persisting attempts to subvert the effort's redistributive purposes. For a reformist regime to hold to its pro-egalitarian course against
such cross winds will be all the more difficult if its program parameters
are subject to frequent change. Thus the reformers will need a few sticking points. Along lines suggested below, they must figure out ways to keep
their flexibility appropriately selective.

1. Scaling the program

A national government embarking on a major attack on rural poverty by
means of public works should take an initial, revisable view of what the
aggregate scope of such activity may be. As just indicated, the actual
scaling and design of the effort should be the product of continuing experimentation; and resource or other constraints may well prevent full
adoption, even as revisable targets, of whatever estimates of scope are
first made. Yet to give some order of magnitude to program planning, a
starting estimate of the aggregate requirement should be attempted.

Something as crude as the following might suffice: Imagine a country
of 40 million people with a per capita GNP of $100 annually (GNP = $4 billion). Suppose that the rural population is 80% of the total (32 million),
(i) that some percentage, say 40, have by some means been estimated to be
below "the poverty line" and/or to constitute the "target population"
(13 million) for rural antipoverty policy, (ii) and that, of these, some
percentage--again, for illustrative purposes, say 40--is estimated to belong to the rural labor force (5 million).

With respect to these most disadvantaged rural workers, the formulators
of a starting estimate of the scope for additive rural employment would
judge roughly what fraction of the annual work time of such workers might
be available, on average, for extra work at something in the vicinity of
an unskilled worker's market wage. This guess would take account of whatever evidence and impressions there were of the average slack in rural employment and particularly of farm labor seasonality. In some countries
the estimates might be guided by recent experience with similar programs
and/or by survey research findings concerning rural labor's work preferences.
Either kind of evidence could be untrustworthy. In particular it might not

reflect the wage rates or the kinds, difficulties, and locations of work, or the expectations regarding work continuity that will characterize the new program. Thus the matter of labor availability is, most especially, one that would have to be tested out as the program proceeds. But our crude estimators need a starting number, and let us say they put it at 30%. They guess that in the low end of the rural labor force there is an annual capacity for extra work (if the work is offered at the right times around the calendar, in the right places and forms, and at the right wages) of .3 x 5 million, or 1.5 million man-years.

The next step would be to decide what fraction of this scope for extra work might reasonably be met by an expanded public works program. Quite plainly, particularly at the outset, the whole of the need would not be attacked by this means. Other efforts to raise low-end income and employment would be underway simultaneously; they, together with the works program itself, might bring indirect improvements in the condition of the poor; in particular, the managers of the program would want to watch the impact on general (especially agricultural) unskilled wages in the countryside.

The financial and administrative constraints facing the managers would be such that, while shunning triviality, they would not want to overshoot in the first round. My arbitrary judgment is that a works program that began by targeting to fill one-fifth of the low-end poor's annual capacity for extra work would be appropriately ambitious. In our example the volume of added construction employment to be offered would reduce to 20% of 1.5 million or 300,000 man-years--this being spread, because of the fractional years that most individuals would work, to a number of laborers several times this figure.

To begin to gauge the financial feasibility of such a program, the initial estimators would next need to convert their employment projection into a wage bill and, for that purpose, to estimate the average wage rate the program would pay. Given our assumption at the start of annual per-capita incomes of $100, if the labor-force participation rate for the whole economy were the same as that estimated above for the rural poor (40%), the average GNP per worker in the whole economy would be $250. Program wages would have to be set with a good deal of care with respect to considerations discussed below, which, in the actual case, our estimators could have in mind with some precision even at the outset. But for our present illustrative purposes let us assume authorities decide to pay rural public works employees a daily rate equivalent to 40% of the economy's GNP per worker. Thus the program would pay $100 per full work year, or (if one assumes some 250 work days per year) a daily wage of about 40¢. This would mean a program wage bill of 300,000 x $100 = $30 million.

Finally, there would be the question of what fraction of the total outlays this unskilled labor bill would represent. As discussed below, one would hope for a higher wage share than the following. But for purposes of the illustration let us assume 50%. This implies that the annual cost of the program would be about $60 million, i.e., 1.5% of the GNP.

2.   Financing and decentralization

It has already been suggested that in most developing countries, funding a rural public works program on the scale just hypothesized--one that, if the new venture were nationwide, might equal 5% or more of all current government outlays and perhaps better than 10% of current public development budgets--would not be easy. New windfall oil earnings have now put the strategy within ready financial reach of a few countries. Moreover, in a rational world a number of countries would get some or all of the needed finance by reducing their defense budgets. Most, if they are serious about the public works brand of antipoverty policy, will find some scope for marginal reallocations away from other current-account government spending; or they will effect some reallocations within the existing development budget; or they will achieve some increased yield from the established public reven structure.

Yet I suspect that the following proposition based on South Asia appli more widely: Governments are unlikely to be able to contrive adequate financing for an adequate rural antipoverty program without somehow engineeri the assembly of more (and in some measures "fresh") resources within the countryside itself--especially from the more prosperous farmers in the uppe portions of the rural income distribution.

This circumstance tends to generate a financial case for politico-administrative decentralization. The ability of many central governments t impose greater direct taxes upon, or otherwise to assemble resources from, the relatively affluent in the countryside is severely limited. In some cases (e.g., India) such taxes face formidable legal or constitutional obstacles. The situation depends in part on traditions, on the administrativ structure, particularly that of revenue-gathering, on the feasibility of using central police and/or military power in support of that structure, and on whether there is a history of subjecting farmers to centrally imposed and collected taxes-in-kind. But where there are important barriers to expanded rural taxation by the central government, major public works funding probably will require the passing of greater financial responsibility to lower jurisdictions--in a federal system from central to state, and, in any event (especially within large intermediate jurisdictions like the typical Indian states) to local government units and agencies. Further, in most countries it is unlikely that smaller jurisdictions can be burdened with more responsibility for raising revenues without simultaneously being given a greater share in the decision of what is to be done with public revenues. Further still, if local resource raising is to be adequately stimulated from above, it is likely that some part of the continuing distributions of central resources to local jurisdictions will have to be conditioned on the vigor and quality of local financial performance. The central government will adopt the principle of local self-help and resort extensively to a matching grant format.

The case for decentralizing the governance of expanded rural public works activity is not just financial. Particularly in large countries, decentralization may be administratively necessary: Public construction involves a great deal of detailed, area-specific project choice, design, and implementation that deal in part with inherently localized subject matter. Attempts to manage such activity closely from a central government headquarters may hopelessly congest the decision process. Moreover, in a number of countries presently the problem of "activating the locals," of engaging local energies, initiatives, and leaders, especially in collective efforts, probably is the most evident rural development need. If labor-intensive public works programs are to provide much of the budgetary and decision matrix for rural reform, they will tend to arouse local initiatives only if they are substantially subject to local direction.

Different countries moving in this direction will adopt different patterns for internalizing and broadening participation in decision making at local levels. Some will rely heavily on the promotion of more or less classic, representative, local self-governments which afford broad adult franchise, practice majority rule, and to which all residents of a locally bounded territory are subject and in some sense belong. Others may depend more on party or military or paramilitary cadres, or on such functional

organizations as cooperatives, workers' unions, local development corporations, rural banks, and public enterprises for energizing local efforts.
But in most large countries there are indeed incentives to decentralize
and disperse authority; to organize and finance construction projects that
generate definable private benefits (e.g., minor irrigation works) in ways
that are self-liquidating; and to make projects which are collectively beneficial and whose benefits are largely local heavily dependent on local taxation or other local resource raising.

Decentralization poses some problems. Especially in minds conditioned
to the themes of central development planning, it raises questions of co-
herence and social efficiency. How can one be sure that local decision
makers will pick the right projects, bring to bear sufficient technical
expertise, execute the projects in an effective, reasonably honest manner,
and achieve a systemwide pattern of construction that is internally consistent and serves national goals? Later subsections of the chapter address
these questions. They are, I think, answerable.

But there are some probable distributional consequences of decentralization that are more troublesome. For one thing, greater decentralization
can be expected to aggravate interspatial inequities--between different
rural jurisdictions in the same country. More emphasis on local self-help,
since some localities will help themselves more than others, can scarcely
do otherwise; and greater use of matching grants for resource transfers to
local jurisdictions will only accentuate such inter-area disparities.

It is easy to exaggerate this drawback of rural decentralization.
Geographic disparities are not false issues; but in national policies their
bark often is worse than their bite. They provoke spirited complaints from
representatives of poorer and more backward areas--and significant inter-
area (rich-to-poor) transfers within most national systems. Yet the tolerance for such areal disparities typically is quite high when there is a
general sense within the system that the different degrees of progress between subjurisdictions partly reflect different intensities of local effort
and when the national government preserves fairly ready opportunity for migration between rural areas. Indeed, it is likely that in many larger
countries, the only way that reform led by rural works will have much chanc
of being undertaken on a "serious" scale will be if those provinces, districts, and other localities which are disposed toward serious self-help ar

allowed to run ahead of their neighbors--for one thing, thereby, creating
stimulating examples for laggard jurisdictions.

It is much less easy for an equity-bent analyst to take lightly the
other kind of disparity that decentralization of works programs is likely
to aggravate, namely, that between classes within the same rural areas.
Section A already has identified the elitist resistance that a national
pro-egalitarian public works program is likely to arouse. In general
it is reasonable to guess that these will be worse the more the design
and management of the program lie with lower jurisdictions. Or, more
exactly, such will be the probability in the early phases of a public works
push. The inequalities and subjugations from which egalitarian reform
seeks to rescue the poor all are second nature to most traditional rural
societies. In general it is the rural elites operating in their traditional
village context who are the least disturbed about, have the fewest self-
doubts about, their maintenance and reinforcement of the traditional
inequalities.

The foregoing, obviously, is not an ironclad generalization; as one
gains some familarity with a national countryside one encounters many re-
freshing exceptions in which particular members or small groups of the
privileged classes are not only reasonably generous in the discharge of
their traditional obligations to their inferiors (presumably there always
has been a fair incidence of such behavior) but are busily trying to re-
structure institutions, relations, and rights in behalf of their poor neighbors. Moreover, to point to the decentralization versus equity paradox is
not to suggest that concern for the latter should foreclose the former.
Not only, as just suggested, may decentralization be a necessary means for
generating the resource and growth dividends that serious egalitarian reform requires, but by lowering the level of important decisions to local
jurisdictions it may (as the balance of this section will suggest) bring
them more within reach of potentially effective political participation
by the poor.

Yet if we are talking about the first phases of a major antipoverty
public works effort, there seems little doubt that, on average, choice of
a comparatively decentralized mode of implementation is likely to aggravate
the resistances to the redistributive purposes of the programs. Thus this
issue becomes a theme of the three following subsections, the first dealing
with the choice of public works projects, the second with their

implementation, and the third with the kind of collateral tactics with
which a national regime choosing a public works approach may try to reinforce its pro-egalitarian purposes.

3.   Project choice

For countries adopting a decentralized pattern of rural development
policy in general and of public works activity in particular, it will be
important to get subjects assigned to the right levels in the jurisdictional hierarchy. Under a decentralized regime the "right" level typically
will be the lowest at which projects or activities do not generate major
externalities, either positive or negative, that spill over outside the
jurisdiction. Under this guideline, it will be appropriate for a number
of economic activities, e.g., most electrical power generation and net-
working, to remain subject to direct national management. It will not be
feasible to push responsibility for a number of other activities, e.g.,
inter-city roads and major irrigation projects, below the level of provincial, inter-provincial, or other large intermediate jurisdictions.
Among more local levels, it will be important not to accord to a very small
jurisdiction the yes-or-no decision over whether an integral part of an
important larger system, say a medium-sized irrigation scheme that would
run through the locality, will be implemented. And where an activity with
wider than local benefits is to be taken up in a local area--say soil con-
servation in a particular watershed for the benefit of people and production downstream--the locals should be provided with net compensation as
well as guidance from outside.

In the second place, it will be important for national regimes promoting decentralized patterns of management of works programs to do all they
can to see that minimal supplies of technical expertise are available to lo
cal decision makers. Governments typically will wish to adopt some combina
tion of measures for promoting the local accessibility of needed skills--fo
example, carefully designed and conducted training programs; better linkage
between the local authorities and whatever research and educational institu
tions the area contains; schemes arranging for the redeployment of educated
unemployed from urban areas; national service or other arrangements for assigning university students for periods of rural work; and arrangements for
facilitating access by local authorities to consulting services (private
and/or public) elsewhere in the country. Moreover, government agencies and

or research justification at higher levels should be engaged in studying what are the simplest, most feasible forms of local data gathering that can serve the needs of local public works and other governmental operations—and then in designing, testing, and propagating related local information systems.

One preoccupation of this aspect of decentralization strategy should be progressively to saturate the local decision-making scene, both official and "pluralistic," with the habits and basic tools of project-evaluation and cost-effectiveness thinking. Here as in other aspects of the expertise problem, however, wise decentralizing governments will maintain an insistent emphasis on simplification, spreading the least complicated versions of techniques that will roughly serve the local purpose.

Given such a habitat for local decision, there will (except for the anti-egalitarian bias to which we shall return in a moment) be little risk in giving local authorities substantial discretion in their choice among public works projects of types that have been properly assigned to the local level, i.e., that do not, in fact, have substantial externalities outside the local jurisdiction. A great many possible construction projects that would serve general agricultural, educational, industrial, commercial, and government needs will meet this standard. In these cases: (i) there is no particular reason to think local decision makers will view the appropriate priorities differently from the national decision makers—especially where, under a decentralized financing regime, the locals are being required to invest sizable amounts of their own locally raised resources; and (ii), where local and national perceptions of priorities do diverge, there is no reason to think (again, the equity issue aside) anything but the conceits of national planners will suffer if precedence is given to the local choices.

In terms of the quality of substantive project choice, therefore, national designers of expanded rural public works programs can in most respects safely accept the financial, administrative, and development-dynamics case for greater decentralization. They will wish to take a more systematic view of the needs for decentralized planning (discussed more explicitly below). They will be properly concerned to promote acceptable probity in a decentralized operation. (Actually it can be argued that the fewer the hierarchical clearances upward a decision requires, the fewer are the opportunities for corruption. Beyond this, probity can be served by the requirement of maximum openness in all local budgetary and other transactions.

And beyond this it would be appropriate for national authorities to hold the local authorities and other quasi-official local institutions subject to rigorous financial auditing and to harsh discipline for malfeasance.) Moreover, if a central regime is serious about decentralization it will presumably hold its subjurisdictions strictly accountable to certain procedural norms. They would indeed be expected to generate specified levels of local revenues to trigger the center's matching grants. In view of the resources constraints, they would be required to show that projects generating private benefits are being rendered self-supporting out of charges placed on the beneficiaries. And probably they would be asked in some way to demonstrate that they were availing themselves of the technical and planning services that the central authorities have helped put at their disposal.

But, in principle, a regime can look with favor on the need to decentralize its public works strategy--except for the critically important propensity of local elites to subvert the egalitarian purposes of the program. With regard to the latter problem, the national authorities can in the first place use such suasion as they have together with some matching-grant leverage to influence local authorities to choose projects whose completed, follow-on benefits will be skewed toward the weak and disadvantaged groups. Even at the outset of an expanded works effort, when local decision making can be expected to be dominated by elites, the central government may be able to elicit from the local authorities a mix of projects with more favorable (less unfavorable) redistributive asset effects than would "naturally" emerge. It may encourage the construction of facilities for "human investment" (via training, and so on) in the low-end poor, especially landless laborers being assisted in transferring out of agriculture to the faster-growing nonagricultural local activities that successful farming will help generate. Similarly, the central authorities may argue in behalf of minor irrigation works that will lead to multiple cropping and therefore to increased agricultural employment.

Most particularly, perhaps, the national government may encourage localities to adopt low-cost housing schemes in which members of depressed and landless classes, granted homestead plots, are employed in building their own and/or each other's houses, for which the owners are given institutional loans on (centrally subsidized) favorable terms. (This alternative of building houses for the low-end poor within their self-support capabilities, insofar as it can be sold politically at the local level, deserves special if brief emphasis in the present context. Although it is not usually thought of as "public works," such low-income housing can have the same employment and income effects as more conventional public works; it can, by raising the productivity of the poor, have some positive aftereffect on productive capacity; its distributive aftereffects are by definition tilted positively; and it may importantly assist the local political and social transformation—by reducing the dependence of the landless on the landed even for their living spaces, by entailing the formation of poor people's housing cooperatives or other class-specific organizations, and by building a kind of geographic, albeit ghetto, solidarity among the members of particular disadvantaged groups.)

Yet even with the best efforts of the foregoing kind, the equity-bent but decentralization-committed designers of a national public works policy must face the probability that, as to project choice, theirs will prove to be a second-best strategy initially. In its asset effects, the composite of the projects chosen probably will tend at the outset to reflect the elitist biases of local decision making. To this realization the policy designers can make two further kinds of responses.

4. Project implementation

In the first place, the central government can, by the norms it imposes, make the <u>execution</u> of works projects as positively redistributive as possible. Here the policy designers probably will not be pushing against the grain of local elite preferences as much as will be the case in the selection of projects. If the dominant local interests are getting the types of assets they want, they are apt to be comparatively amenable to national ground rules concerning the implementation of labor-intensive works. Moreover, except in periods of drought or other general deprivation, the better-off rural classes will not be much disposed to compete with the poor for the kinds of work the public works projects offer. They will find such work too hard or distasteful for the wages paid; for many its opportunity costs will be too high.

Nevertheless, there will be some tendency to subvert project execution in elitist directions also, and therefore the central government will need to lay down and enforce some explicit poor-favoring norms. One of these will concern the minimum fraction of project budgets that, if public works

projects are to claim central matching grants, must be allocated to unskilled wages. This should be one of the sticking points; it is a requirement about which, despite the need for general flexibility in the
program, national governments will do well to be comparatively inflexible.
After considering, for their particular economies, the range of constructio
technologies available and the array of project types that local authoritie
are inclined to take up, the central government will need to specify basic
labor-content norms, either for all categories of projects collectively,
or with some (but not much) variance among categories. Few if any of these
basic norms should accept labor shares of less than 50%; some may stipulate
higher fractions.

Requests for relief from these minimum-content standards are sure to
be forthcoming. Local authorities may argue, for example, that even though
a project's direct wages bill would fall short of the general minimum norm,
the project should be accepted for support because it would make extensive
use of a material with high unskilled labor content. The central authorities should be slow to grant such concessions. They should demand convincing proof not only that the material in question has high labor content
but that the work force producing it contains a high proportion of low-end
poor.

A second principal poor-protecting norm would concern project wage
rates. These should be related to market wages for unskilled labor in
the local areas and, therefore, should be allowed to vary among areas.
But the national authorities should retain (again, via matching-grant
leverage) comparatively detailed control over wage rates. On the one hand,
to reinforce the income benefits to the poor, the national government will
need to resist the tendency of local leaders to push down wages and get
their incremental assets on the cheap. Much public construction work is
heavier and harder than most farm work; it may therefore require its participants to eat more; it is likely to involve more local travel; and
higher wages for public works will exert more redistributive pressure on
unskilled wage levels in the general rural labor market. All of these
factors will argue for placing a high, if anything, above-market, floor
under project wages. On the other hand, the central authorities may need
to guard against the inclination of some local bodies to pay wages so high
that the projects begin to attract offers of employment from others than
the low-end poor.

Some governments will find it desirable to protect the interests of the poor in the implementation of the works program with a third norm--one that prohibits or regulates the participation of labor contractors. In some countries conventions concerning the scope of local government functions may be such that these contractors are regarded as indispensible intermediaries for recruiting and managing workers. Where contractors are used, however, invariably they tend to skim project labor budgets. If possible, therefore, local bodies should do their own hiring and bossing of project labor; or they should encourage the formation of labor cooperatives as alternatives to the contractor system; or, if they retain contractors, they should limit and police the fees the contractors are allowed to charge.

Norms of the three kinds just indicated--regarding minimum labor content, wage rates, and labor contracting--should sufficiently fortify the income and employment benefits that the rural poor can gain from a locally managed public works program. One can imagine three other dimensions in which the labor transactions of projects might be regulated, but in each case the intervention would strike me as probably unnecessary, and therefore as undesirable.

First, there could be an effort to establish explicit poverty or disadvantaged-group qualifications for eligibility for project employment; but if the wage rates were appropriately chosen these would be largely redundant.

Second, the central authorities might be disposed to stipulate something about the seasonal pattern of the work that the public works projects could generate. But the local bodies know best the seasonality of labor availability in their own areas. There is no clear conflict between the interests of the local elites and the local poor on the timing of additive work offers. It is to the advantage of both to have such work concentrated in off-seasons. If the work overlaps periods of peak farm employment, it will, on the one hand, tend to push up peak farm wages; but, on the other hand, it will hasten the kind of mechanization of harvesting, threshing, and planting that tends to lop off the same peaks. All the same, if the necessary construction period of a works project cannot be fitted within the slack season, or if the local decision makers are simply too eager for the completed asset to accept the slack-season rhythm, there is no real reason they should be prevented from scheduling it as they wish--

and coping with the consequences, including higher costs and/or the attraction of in-migrant workers.

The third redundant norm would concern this last matter, that of labor
migration. At first it might be thought that locally generated employment
should be reserved for the low-end poor of the home area. Indeed, I would
say that if there is sufficient local underemployment, or enough emerging
political pressure from the local poor, or a sufficient sense of local soli
darity on the part of local leaders so that jurisdictions choose to stipulate such hiring preferences, the national regime probably should go along
with the practice. But certainly it should not be encouraged. The poor
who migrate in, prepared to work on the terms offered, will, from the
national viewpoint, be just as disadvantaged and just as deserving of extra
income and employment as the poor already there. In fact, they may be a
little more disadvantaged and deserving, on average, since they will have
accepted the transfer costs of migration. Moreover, some inter-area mobility within the countryside will be necessary to match differential labor
supplies with different local organizational and financial capacities for
generating additive work. At the same time, it probably is unnecessary
for the central authorities to counter-stipulate against residence qualifications; in areas of greater program vitality, where, relative to local
labor availabilities, there is an excess of public works jobs, the interest
in getting priority projects completed is likely to erode local chauvinism
rather quickly. At least in terms of initial policy design, the migration
question seems to be one that requires neither pro nor con intervention
from above.

Effective project implementation, of course, will not be just a matter
of maximizing the antipoverty benefits generated in the course of project
construction. It also requires that projects be well managed and indeed
succeed, more or less in accordance with local expectations, in creating--on
schedule--the assets in which the localities and central government will
have jointly invested. But I will leave this subsection focused on the
equity dimension of the problem, reserving the management points for a
separate review of the administrative requirements of the public works approach later in the chapter.

5. Pro-egalitarian reinforcements

Along with trying to extract maximum benefit for the poor from the
project construction phase, the second response that pro-egalitarian policy
designers can make to a decentralized public works program's susceptibility
to anti-egalitarian project choices is to adopt a specific collateral strategy for strengthening the rural poor politically.

In general the economic strengthening provided by public works employment and upward pressure on farm wages will tend to build latent political
muscle. But more specifically, the regime can undertake to offer the poor
more supply options and to weaken their dependency mechanisms. As noted
already, it can provide them with homestead sites and assist their attainment of nondependent housing. It can weaken one of the most powerful dependency mechanisms of traditional societies, namely, traditional money lending, by assisting the introduction of accessible institutional lenders into
the countryside. It can make more difficult the traditional capture and
reservation by the elites of modern credit, input-supplying, and trading
institutions by encouraging the entry of a variety of such (at least, partly
competitive) institutions. It can attempt to make educational and training
programs more serviceable and useful to the poor. It can ensure running
room for voluntary service agencies which undertake to act as surrogates
for the poor. In a variety of ways, it can encourage and assist the formation of segregated, autonomous politico-economic organizations of the poor
--farm workers' unions, small producers' (e.g., milk) cooperatives, low-
caste housing societies, associations of tribal voters and the like.

By all of these means a declassed central leadership can help to arm
the rural poor of a nonrevolutionary society for the largely nonviolent
class conflict they must wage to achieve effective participation in the
local polity. In the last analysis, the leadership must rely on the disadvantaged groups to win their own political spurs. In a system of universal franchise the poor will have the right to vote--which typically they
exercise little or at the behest of their local patrons. In other genuinely
participatory modes of governance they have the equivalent. The theory of
decentralized reform is that as the decision-making stakes are raised at
the local level, the value of votes will rise, and the poor will have
greater incentive to organize themselves to use their franchise in a more
self-interested manner--for example, to bargain, in later rounds of choices

of local public works projects, for assortments of projects with a more egalitarian mix of aftereffects.

6. The spatial dimension

Governments choosing expanded rural public works as a principal instrument of rural antipoverty policy are apt to have an increasingly explicit spatial (or centering or settlements) strategy as one of the components of the transformation they are trying to promote. Almost the world over traditional rural societies are village centered; rural populations have lived in a very large number of very small settlements which in turn are served by a comparatively small number of smaller and regional towns intermediate between the villages and the few large cities of the country. During the past decade in many countries there has been not only growing awareness of the changes in settlements patterns that tend to accompany development but growing interest in the possibilities of subjecting these changes to policy guidance.

Most earlier industrializing economies have been rapidly transformed into metropolitan-centered systems. A number of developing countries, particularly in Latin America and Africa, have begun to follow the same path; village leavers no longer employed in agriculture tend to filter quickly through the country's thin intermediate "central places" structure and gather in large metropolitan pools. Increasingly governments are questioning both the desirability and inevitability of such radical population redeployments. Politically they deplore the "dual society" tendencies that the pattern aggravates. They suspect that the centripetal market and services pulls that draw enterprises and populations to metropolitan locations are not so much irresistible as they are (lacking counter policy) uncontested; they suspect that it may not be so difficult to generate competing positive externalities in a larger array of smaller centers--especially for the more labor-intensive industries that the factor endowments of poor countries should be causing them to emphasize. Many governments are persuaded that many of the negative externalities that metropolitan agglomerates impose (mostly on public and consumer, not on enterprise and budgets are larger per capita in very large centers than in small centers. Almost all regimes that in recent years have experienced a resurgent interest in promoting agricultural expansion also are persuaded of the importance that "rural growth centers"--settlements larger than the village but close to the village--can play as engines of agricultural modernization, providing credit, marketing, training, inputs-supplying, and processing services. Finally, in terms of the preoccupation of the present study, many governments probably share the sense--admittedly more impressionistic than documented--that over the long pull a system of dispersed centers is likelier than one of concentrated centers to be conducive to equitable income distribution.

For a variety of reasons, therefore, many governments are committed in principle, in their planning documents and otherwise, to a policy of small-centers building. Fewer of them are yet doing much about it, and in part this is because many of the things that a government actively engaged in building rural growth centers must promote--roads, streets, public buildings, market yards--cost money. Implementation of the policy, in short, requires a local public construction budget.

It would be the height of folly for a regime committed on the one hand to a strategy of rural growth centering, on the other, to a policy of rural public works expansion, not to marry the two. Effecting this marriage will, I should think, require only one major amendment to the policy design already sketched. In most respects growth center building will be more consistent than not with the pattern of decentralized project choice and implementation already discussed. The local authorities certainly will favor the development of more robust local centers. Nor is there reason to think that, in their allocation of locally raised and of nationally supplied resources, their allotments of priorities either between "center-building" and other, say irrigation, projects, or between different types of center-building infra-structure, will need to be second-guessed. Plainly, higher jurisdictions will need to be concerned to see that roads and other networks running out of the local jurisdictions hook up with outside centers, but this is only common sense.

There is one count, however, on which political and administrative decentralization of a public works program, if unchecked, could initially frustrate sensible, discriminatory center building in most rural countrysides. In many countries the present deficits of effectively equipped and operating small supra-village centers are very large. Far more rural centers are needed than, given the resource constraints, can be built quickly. Consequently, if all of the villages of a region that eventually should graduate into being "growth centers" move in parallel, none will advance very fast, none will begin soon to develop much in the way of positive, self-reinforcing externalitites, and none in fact will serve as a growth center in an active, generative way.

The only answer is deliberately to discriminate—for some time to concentrate most of an area's new locations of institutions and facilities with multi-village clienteles in only a few of the potential growth centers. Economically, this is the natural thing to do; left to their own devices, newly entering enterprises will begin to cluster. But politically and administratively such clustering is unnatural, for politico-administrative decision makers can maximize their patronage by sprinkling their distribution of new public-facility locations over as wide a number of aspiring villages as possible.

This tendency toward back-scratching scattering tends to be strongest in the local political context. The local elites can appreciate the advantages of discriminatory, concentrated center building in the abstract. But they are not likely to be able to agree on which of their own particular villages should go first. On this point, therefore, they need (and also are rather likely to accept) direction from above. If a national or provincial government wants its rural works program to have a byproduct of dynamic growth centers, it probably must be prepared to designate which few places in local jurisdiction are, for the time being, to be the preferred growth points. The higher government would stipulate to the local authorities, as well as to the branches of the national and provincial governments themselves, that for a period of time all new discretionary locations of public facilities serving all or much of the area are to be in one of these places. (Ordinarily, to an objective observer moderately familiar with the area, there will be no great mystery about which these places should be. In any event, the choices, once made, will tend to be self-confirming as the favored centers begin to generate positive externalities.)

7. Decentralized planning

We have focused on the antipoverty aspects of the public works approach. This was not so much the case in the very last subsection, where rural centering enters, not mainly because it has direct and reliable pro-egalitarian implications but because it inescapably intersects any public works strategy, and because growth center building can have important arousal effects—under conditions in many countries where rural arousal

is a necessary precondition for any very consequential advance on the
equity front. But otherwise this "policy design" discussion has concentrated on distributive aspects and therefore has not emphasized themes
that any balanced exposition of a viable public works strategy must
include.

One of these other themes, namely, that the assets created by public
works must indeed be productive and satisfying--particularly, under decentralized circumstances, if the program is to continue to command local financing and support--has in fact laced the previous discussion. It was
present especially in the subsection on project choice, which talked about
the importance both of getting subjects assigned to the right levels in
the politico-administrative hierarchy and of improving the access of local
decision makers to some technical expertise. However, we must give more
attention to management issues--to the questions of how locally managed
projects are to be executed efficiently; of what kind of national administrative machinery can best serve a boldly expanded but decentralized program; of how the assets that the program constructs will be operated,
maintained, and otherwise knit into on-going activities in a way that keeps
them productive. And, before that--here, in this subsection--I want to extend the earlier comments that bear on the planning implications of the decentralized rural public works approach.

If "planning" means not simply the thinking ahead that all of us, including the smallest governmental units, in some measure have to do all the
time, but a special staff function manned by personnel specialized and
trained to the task, then in most developing countries the scope for lodging
specialized planning expertise in a large number of little jurisdictions
will be small for a long time to come. Fortunately, however, the needed
scope of such decentralized planning is also smaller than many development
analysts, conditioned by the pervasive role that national planning is expected to play in most national development strategies, are wont to assume.
In particular there is little place for or point in "mini-macro" planning,
i.e., for attempts to provide local authorities with comprehensive, exhaustive, integrated models of the local economic system that are analogous to
those typically attempted at the national level.

Local planning can be far more partial and, in an important sense, less
analytic. The local system is, typically, far more open than the national
system; its internal input-output linkages are less complete; and unexpected

changes in the local system's balance of payments with the economy around
it are much less interesting and significant than are changes in the nation's balance of payments with the world economy around it. Local authorities may wish to take account of but they cannot authoritatively plan most
of the activities of most of the economic actors in their own jurisdic-
tions--neither those of whatever arms and enterprises of the national and
provincial governments happen to be located in the area, nor those of the
quasi-official and nonofficial institutions present, nor those of the
area's own farm and other private enterprises. Nor, in most countries,
would there be anything to be gained from such, as it were, comprehensive
cross-sectional planning. It might well only impede development.

The official planning needed locally will consist mainly of two parts,
first, spatial (i.e., town and country) planning, and second, local government budgeting that summarizes the jurisdiction's allocative choices, both
current and capital, among types of public-expenditure and establishes the
financial plan for funding them. The budgeting need pass only two internal-
consistency tests: first, that outgo not exceed income, and second, that
project choices conform to some rough ranking of their perceived social net
returns. Local budgeting need not treat inter-relations and feedbacks
among expenditure sectors in the explicit, systematic way that is appropriate in national development planning.

So construed, local planning's personnel requirements are not trivial,
but they also are not overwhelming. Planning expertise is an important
part of the technical competence that higher governments, by training programs and other means, should seek to impart to a decentralized system.
But it would be my own prejudice that in most countries the training of local planners should not be allowed to delay decentralization. Much of the
needed planning competence will have to be developed on the ground in any
event. In the public works field as in others a decentralized arousal strategy will get on with the downward delegation--and then help as much as possible to make local planning expertise grow in response to the demands
placed upon it.

8.   Administrative framing

The decentralized scenario for rural public works expansion advanced
in this chapter poses a number of managerial problems with which adopters
of the scenario would have to grapple. For governments which can count on

expandable food supplies, which are limited in the kinds of redistributive measures they can feasibly pursue, which nevertheless have strong commitments to strengthening the poor as well as to rural arousal, and which know that what they are getting into will not be easy politically, the general theory of the strategy should have considerable appeal. But the theory will be useless unless programs launched can in fact be well done.

A common theme of much developing country experience with additive, labor-intensive public works to date has been one of disappointed expectations. Too often public works experiments have not lived up to their advance billing. This propensity to disappoint would be particularly devastating in a decentralized program dependent for its year-to-year support and survival on predominant local satisfaction with the progress and results of the program. Plainly, if more reliance is to be placed on reform through the mode of the public works, the typical gap between expectations and performance must be narrowed.

Much of this narrowing can follow from aspects of the policy design already discussed--from a procedural regime that assures a fairly solid set of project choices; that lodges cells of technical competence at local decision making and implementation levels; in particular, from one that, rather than cramming benefits down the throats of local areas, uses self-help criteria to determine that participating areas are not only interested but prepared to invest in the benefits; and that, therefore, accepts differential degrees and differential patterns of local involvement.

Keeping performance better aligned with expectations will also in part be a matter of not letting early expectations get too high. Ideally an adopting government should make a bold commitment to an antipoverty public works experiment--with comparatively muted fanfare, letting support for the program build more on its accruing results than on its preliminary advertising. Admittedly, for many countries, this is not wholly realistic political counsel. Yet, as discussed in Section A, the approach is likely to be a politically uphill one anyway, with only delayed payoffs for the initiating leadership. A leadership prepared to make this basic political investment may also find it feasible for a time to let the effort remain a big program with a small voice. If so the life expectancy of the venture is likely to increase.

In good part, however, the quality of the program's performance will depend on three administrative issues: the manner in which the central government manages the program from above, the quality of performance of local governments in their project management and funding responsibilities, and the effectiveness with which projects, once their construction is complete, are incorporated into operating activities.

Governments will differ greatly in their answers to the first of these issues. Nevertheless, where a program is genuinely decentralized, i.e., where local authorities are left free or with broad discretion to choose their own substantive projects, there will be an overwhelming case against fragmenting the national management of the program among various substantive ministries such as agriculture, irrigation, education, and health. Likewise, unless one can posit a total transformation of the bureaucratic style and operating norms of most existing, traditional public works departments at the national level, there will be a resounding case in most countries against lodging the guidance of the program there. Whether it is housed in the shell of an established department, is created as an operating appendage to some such central staff agency as the national planning commission, or is set up as a new special-purpose agency, therefore, the managing unit for a new major venture into labor-intensive public works will need to be consolidated. It should have oversight of the whole of the new program. While imbued with concern for the effectiveness and technical validity of the projects promoted, its unifying themes will be public works as such, their labor-intensity, their redistributive benefits, and their efficient administration by decentralized means.

Wherever the agency lies on the organization chart, it will need in fact to be influentially positioned, with ready access to and support from the government's topmost leaders and with the power to command the priority attention of other functional ministries and departments.

The agency will need a substantially different operating style than is common to central-government units dealing with lesser jurisdictions: it will have to cast itself less as a commander of performance, more as a promoter, educator, and facilitator. It will, to be sure, need to be exacting in its enformcement of the limited set of operational norms that it helps establish for local authorities--especially those protecting the income and employment benefits that the low-end poor derive from project implementation. But otherwise much of the agency's concern will be to serve the needs of local operations--for example, to organize and promote needed training, to facilitate the placement of educated unemployed as local technical staff, to encourage the ministry of education to facilitate useful part-time participation by students, and to mobilize as neccessary the energies of the whole government to break whatever materials-supply, transport, and other bottlenecks threaten to impede the program. In view of the highly seasonal character of much of the local work to be done, the central agency will need to have a particularly keen sense of timing, doing all it can to make sure that particular inputs of materials and expertise get to where they are needed when they are needed.

The agency itself should be run by alert, resourceful, innovative managers. They should be stubbornly dedicated to the interests of the rural poor. At the same time, they must be partisans of local self-reliance. When the occasion requires, they must be tough enforcers of their pro-poor norms; yet they should be managers who achieve their greatest satisfaction in accomplishing goals by processes of indirection. Most of all they will need sophisticated and robust political skills.

The second and in a way the most pivotal of the administrative issues --namely, the quality of project management by local authorities--is not one, I think, to which there are any trick answers. The issue is the whole texture of local public administration. Governments embarking on a decentralized reform strategy will be well advised to give more attention to this area than is the present habit in most developing countries. There is much scope for increasing the access of local authorities (part-time and full-time, political and nonpolitical) to information, applied research, training, and advisory services on such matters as local government organization, work scheduling, the supervision of construction labor, the selection, training, and management of foremen, and local public accountability and information mechanisms. Most particularly, perhaps, there is scope for much more research into the problems and possibilities of local public finance. (This last could illuminate a whole side of the present scenario, namely, local resource raising--the bases, incidence, and progressivity of alternative local taxes, the place of users charges, the role of savings and financial institutions--on which this paper is largely silent.)

However, with respect to local management expertise, it probably is reasonable to take the same agnostically optimistic position I have on local planning: typically it will be a mistake to delay decentralization until local managerial capacities are somehow first trained up. There is a good deal of native managerial talent in any local rural population, and there

also is plenty of local capacity to perceive the difference between good
and bad management. As operations proceed, many managers will learn with
practice; others will be replaced. If local regimes value and invest in
the products of the public works program of which they are given charge,
they will tend to set and demand reasonable standards of implementation.

The third administrative issue is critical but also straightforward.
Completed public works, as we have said, are almost never more than inputs.
There must be producing organizations that take responsibility for the
completed assets, use them, and maintain them. In the case of facilities,
such as minor irrigation works, publicly produced for private benefit,
where, under a sensible policy, the costs are recovered from the private
beneficiaries, the transition from the construction phase to the operation
and maintenance phase presents no particular problems. It will be to the
self-interest of the beneficiaries to exploit and preserve the value of the
facilities. But where the assets are public goods the transition requires
specific provision.

In the latter case there are two organizational possibilities: one,
that the using activities are to be those of the local jurisdiction itself,
the other that, although they are conducted in the local jurisdiction, the
activities are ones (e.g., education, health, family planning, industrial
skills training) in large measure directed by the various departments of
higher governments. With respect to the second of these categories, it
will behoove the central public works agency to require that local authorities, in order to insure successful transition from construction to operations, clear their project designs prior to construction with the departments which are to operate the assets and then, upon completion of constru-
tion, formally hand over the facilities to particular departments. (At the
same time, the central agency will have to use some of its tactical energie
to assure that this requirement for departmental clearance does not become
a backdoor means of recentralizing the process of project choice.) In the
case of projects destined for operation by the local jurisdiction, the
central agency may wish to stipulate that the local authorities accompany
their applications for support of new projects with evidence about their
uses of existing facilities and, in particular, with indications of the bud
etary allocations they are making for the maintenance of those facilities.

In this field, however, the central agency's principal role will be
educative. Local authorities clearly have no systematic interest in lettin

their real assets waste for lack of use or upkeep. The depressing record of deterioration and bad maintenance that so many past rural public works programs have accumulated is not because of any deep perversity in public authorities. It is because of failures to insure that particular operating authorities accept responsibility and accountability for newly produced assets, and it is these failures that a new program must avoid.

C. The role of external agencies and transfers

Continuing transnational discussion of an antipoverty policy based on public works is likely and is useful. Some centers of development studies in the rich countries as well as various multilateral and bilateral assistance agencies, may contribute significantly to the further dialogue. Yet the next phase of public works experimentation, especially if it proceeds somewhat along the lines suggested here, would be ill-suited to the process of traditional, didactic, rich-to-poor technical assistance.

The advanced economies have little expertise to provide on this subject that is relevant, is easily transferable, and grows out of their own experience. If the experiments are as large and decentralized as here suggested, it would be nearly impossible for any small cadre of expatriate technicians or advisers to relate to the program's operating level effectively. The program would be peculiarly enmeshed in indigenous institutional complexities, which are hard for expatriates to comprehend and upon which they intrude with little grace. Most especially is this true of the conflicted domestic politics which, if the present analysis is correct, will lie at the core of most redistributive public works strategies.

Hence poor countries adopting the approach are going to have to figure out their own answers to the questions that have been raised in these pages. And the most productive transnational dialogue on the subject will be within the Third World itself--among governments and institutions of countries that opt for serious experimentation. The main contributions that external actors can make to the effort will be the form of concessional transfers either of finance or of food.

There is little of a distinguishing character to be said on the financial assistance side. "Good" aid for public works programs would be much like that which recipients would like to get for other purposes. It should be additive, unless the donor wishes simply to support a recipient's decision to reallocate resources to the works program from other partially aid-financed activity. It should be as concessional, have as high a grant component, as possible. Ideally it would be untied as to country of origin. And almost necessarily (since the public works projects to be assisted would be labor-intensive and have limited direct import content) the recipient of foreign exchange transfers would need to be able to use them for some spectrum of imports, via the formula either of a "program" or non-project loan or of "local cost financing."

In the near and medium term most poor countries may find it nearly impossible, for an additive labor-intensive investment program, to obtain extra external finance with the benign characteristics just recited. Thus (harking back to the emphasis earlier in the chapter on the dependency of the public works strategy on adequate food supplies) the most salient external contribution to major public works experimentation in the years next ahead could be that of expanded, redeployed, and regularized food aid.

Food aid is one form of commodity-tied and country-of-origin-tied assistance that a national public works program can use with considerable efficiency. If it is available to match some or all of the added food demand generated by public works expansion, food aid can tame what otherwise can be, by all odds, the most dangerous and disruptive inflationary effects of such a program. By the same token, if added concessional food imports are indeed coupled with an enlargement of employment and investment that would be dangerously inflationary in their absence, there need be no fear about the food aid's dampening internal agricultural incentives--if, at the same time, the indigenous government's agricultural production priorities are high and are being effectively implemented.

It is not only its usefulness, of course, but its potential availability that makes food aid such an interesting possible input to a rural development strategy centered on public works. The adequacy of world food supplies, to be sure, has become a matter of great concern. Yet, at least for the medium term, the largest but also the worst-lagging O.E.C.D. foreign-aid donor has the same relation to exportable food surpluses as the OPEC countries have to foreign-exchange reserves. The United States is extraordinarily liquid in food. Moreover, even though food aid costs the American government hard budgetary dollars (and no longer can be counted the accidental byproduct of a domestic price-support effort), there is no question that food aid in the United States still is politically a cheaper form of foreign assistance than any other. Thus if American governmental

leaders--a president or a set of congressional leaders or the two together
--became seized in the next few years with genuine determination to change
the trend of American inputs to overseas development, probably the easiest
bold venture they could contrive would be a major restructuring and expansion of food aid. Moreover, if there were serious purpose to make the reliable provision of 10 to 15 million tons of concessional American food-
grains to developmental uses abroad a priority rather than residual claim-
ant on the annual U.S. food budget, there is little reason to think this
could not be phased into the food economy over the space of a very few
years. It probably, for example, would induce some relative price adjustments that in turn would entail putting moderately less feedgrains finish
on some American, Soviet, and other livestock. But a modestly augmented,
stable provision of food aid (with a more developmental, less political,
allocation among recipient countries) would not need to cause any continuing disturbance of either domestic prices or commercial exports.

The foregoing is a summary treatment of a reasonably complex subject.
But it is enough to identify what is probably the most feasible way that
Americans, via their government, could contribute importantly and soon to
the kind of rural redistributive reform we have been examining.

D. Conclusion

There are no easy routes to uplifing the poor in a poor country--none
even that is conceptually easy in a nonrevolutionary context where a middle-
class leadership, blocked from pursuing more radical or surgical redistribution and structural-transformation measures, nevertheless is determined
to maneuver the system into an improved allocation of benefits to the poor.

Clean, reliable redistributive reform is even harder when the pre-
eminent problem of a developing economy, especially a developing countryside, is its lingering stagnation and inertia. Here the dominant need, even
more than for equity, is to arouse greater local participation in the development process. The decentralization of decision and fiscal responsibility
for which this almost inescapably argues, at least in larger countries,
lodges greater discretion with the most localized, least reformed elites.

Major, expanded, labor-intensive public works programs are no simple
or tidy answer for governments which find themselves in this mixture of
circumstances. But such programs can provide a kind of programmatic arena
in which a determined arousal-cum-equity effort can be pursued. They can

serve this purpose for a long time. To do so the programs need to be taken up boldly and, in terms of policy attention, centrally, but also experimentally and, for the most part, flexibly.

Without country-by-country experimentation (especially without more serious attempts to lever local fiscal self-help than virtually any developing country has yet tried), one cannot say what the scale of such programs, and therefore, of their direct and indirect income and employment benefits to the poor, could be. But almost surely the scale could be large. The more interesting question is which initiating regimes would have the perseverance and cunning to make of the public works program a central stratagem, augmented by other tactics, for permanently improving the political condition of the poor.

As for this last, there is no denying that the public works approach is something of a long shot. But for governments facing the hypothesized problems it is hard to think of more promising alternatives. Sensibly designed, the approach can yield a much needed array of productive assets. It can provide income and employment benefits. It can convert desired spatial strategies from theory to practice. It should in most countries be administrable. It can provide the agenda that activates local self-government. Particularly if it does not oversell the approach early on, a determined regime may in fact be able to make public works an enduring instrument of reform.

Chapter 9

NOTES

1. J. R. Nurkse, Problems of Capital Formation in Underdeveloped Countries (Oxford, 1953); W. A. Lewis, "Economic Development with Unlimited Supplies of Labor," Manchester School of Economics and Social Studies (May 1954).

2. See, for example, John Woodward Thomas, "Rural Public Works and East Pakistan's Development," ed., Walter P. Falcon and Gustaf F. Papanek, Development Policy II--The Pakistan Experience (Cambridge, 1971); John Woodward Thomas, Shahid Javed Burki, David G. Davies, Richard M. Hook, An International Comparative Study of the Performance of Employment Creating Public Works Programs, study by the Harvard Institute of International Development for I.B.R.D. (August 1974); International Labour Office, Employment Problems and Policies in the Philippines (Geneva, 1968); Rajaona Andriamanjara, Labor Mobilization and Economic Development: The Moroccan Experience, University of Michigan Center for Research Economic Development, discussion paper no. 15 (Ann Arbor, April 1971); USAID, Rabat, "FY 1969 Promotion Nationale Program," and Tunis, "Task Force Report: The P.L. 480, Title II, 'Food for Work' (LCSD) Program in Tunisia, 1966-69," both unpublished; John P. Lewis, "The Public-Works Approach to Low-end Poverty Problems: The New Potentialities of an Old Answer," Journal of Development Planning, no. 5 (United Nations, 1972); Richard Patten, Belinda Dapice, Walter Falcon, "An Experiment in Rural Employment Creation: Indonesia's Kabupaten Program," Harvard Development Advisory Service, no. 197, 1974; G. B. Rodgers, "Effects of Public Works on Rural Poverty," Economic and Political Weekly (Bombay, February 1973).

3. Factor price adjustments can yield both employment and output gains in most such countries, but there are reasons for questioning the speed with which these can repair the inter-factor misallocations that partly underlie the rural poverty condition. For an elaborated discussion of the several counts on which the public works approach emerges by default as an interesting policy option, see J. Lewis, "The Public-Works Approach to Low-end Poverty Problems," pp. 90-93.

4. Cf. W. Paul Strassmann, "Construction Productivity and Employment in Developing Countries," International Labour Review (June 1970), pp. 503-18

5. Thomas et al., International Comparative Study, p. 10, fn. 1; p. 24, table 3.

6. Cf., for example, W. Graeme Donovan, "Rural Works and Employment: Description and Preliminary Analysis of a Land Army Project in Mysore State, India," Occasional Paper no. 60, Employment and Income Distribution Project, Department of Agricultural Economics, Cornell University (April 1973).

CHAPTER X

EQUITY AND INCOME EFFECTS OF NUTRITION AND HEALTH CARE

Olav T. Oftedal and F. James Levinson

> When the whole property of this universe has been inherited by
> all creatures, how can there be any justification for the sys-
> tem in which someone gets a flow of huge excess, while others
> die for a handful of grains?   S. P. R. Sarkar[1]

> Unfortunately, the tragedy of the poor may be used to justify
> programs which at best provide them small palliatives and at
> worst allocate their benefits to the more well-to-do persons
> who control the economic and political system.   John Mellor[2]

A.   Introduction

Among the strong arguments for redistribution of wealth and income is
the prevalence of malnutrition and ill health among the poor in low-income
countries. Without question, much of the burden and suffering imposed by
disease, hunger, and malnutrition in these countries could be reduced
through the more equitable distribution of resources and services coupled
with a reasonable rate of economic growth. Although the dramatic demonstrations of this proposition have occurred in socialist countries, most
notably Cuba and China, there is no indication that it is inherently limited to these countries. The significant decline in infant mortality in
New York City in the first three decades of this century has been attributed to socio-economic improvement of the poor and developments in the field
of public health, rather than to advances in medical science.[3]

When the process of economic growth bypasses the lowest income groups,
particularly in rural areas, it is not surprising that little improvement
in health and nutrition occurs. The Pan American Health Organization
found that in Argentina, Bolivia, and El Salvador death rates of children
under five years of age in rural areas were nearly twice those of metropolitan areas.[4] Moreover, they note that the rural areas studied are close

to medical centers and thus mortality in the remote rural populations is probably even higher.[5] Yet in these same countries—indeed in almost all low-income countries—one finds a highly skewed distribution of health services, with doctors, nurses, hospitals, and so on, concentrated in urban areas.

This chapter attempts to evaluate the income and equity effects of nutrition and health programs in low-income countries. Unfortunately there is a glaring lack of data upon which to base conclusions. This lack of empiricism on effectiveness, costs, and coverage has made it difficult to consider health and nutrition within the broader economic context. Yet such information is essential if efficient allocation of resources is to occur, and if the growth-promoting and redistributional effects of health and nutrition programs are to be recognized and utilized.

1.   Appeal of nutrition and health policies

In an effort to improve equity, at least in the sense of increasing the income and welfare of the lowest income groups, health and nutrition programs are attractive in principle. Certainly the poor would benefit from more food (especially nutritious food), from improved medical care, and from public health measures. Given estimates that a majority of the rural populace in some areas has a diet inadequate in calories, that nearly half of unmet needs for physician services is due to inaccessibility of treatment places or lack of adequate finances, and that malnutrition and diarrheal disease—interacting manifestations of poverty—are the major underlying causes of death in children under five, this argument takes on particular importance.

To the extent that nutritional supplementation and medical care represent goods and services that otherwise would have to be purchased, they constitute increments in real income. An argument is frequently made that providing food, rather than income, to the poor insures that this increment is appropriately used, the assumption being that food is a more important addition to welfare than, say, a shirt. The fact that the lowest income groups spend 60 to 80 percent of their incomes on food, and that the first income increments usually result in a still higher percentage spent on food, suggests that providing food rather than income is unnecessary. With regard to the poor, income redistribution and nutrition objectives are probably parallel.

From another point of view, health and nutrition policies may be more attractive than other policy instruments, given their humanitarian appeal. Opposition from upper income and politically powerful groups may be less vigorous than in the cases of welfare assistance or a negative income tax. In addition, where the benefits of health and nutrition programs are readily apparent to the recipients, they may be important means of obtaining political support, be it in a democratic country such as India, which proposed an unprecedented eightfold increase in its nutrition budget in the 1974-79 Five Year Plan, or in a socialist country such as China whose rural health system is probably more extensive and more effective than that of any other low-income country.[6]

Conceptually, health and nutrition emerge as likely candidates in the selection of policies aimed at the poor. Indeed, they seem inherently biased toward low-income strata whose needs are greater and who will benefit more from a given nutrition or health increment than those economically better off. Health and nutrition programs may even represent a means of distributing real income in favor of the poor without depending on the redistribution of money income. While attractive in principle, however, it is unclear that they actually do favor the poor, given the nature, location, and magnitude of existing programs in most countries.

2. Income redistribution and the target groups

Nutrition and health policies can only raise the income and welfare levels of the lowest income groups if, in fact, the benefits extend to them. Yet the poor are by no means a homogeneous group and, being widely dispersed, they often prove difficult to reach.

An expenditure rationale which orients itself to improving the nutritional and/or health well-being of the poor must use some definition of poverty. Poverty can be measured by both relative standards, such that economic inequality is emphasized, or by absolute standards which emphasize economic insufficiency. Despite the implications of a relative approach inherent in the notions of income distribution and equity, it is, from the nutrition/health perspective, the absolute poverty--the economic insufficiency--which is of primary concern. One would hope to identify some income level below which malnutrition and illness are especially prevalent as a consequence of insufficient purchasing capacity and substandard environmental conditions. This level would vary from location to location

and would not necessarily be equivalent to the lowest two deciles or the
lowest four deciles of the income distribution. Nor would it need conform
to some arbitrarily selected poverty standard. As the British poverty re-
searcher Peter Townsend has noted, "To establish a minimum income standard
is meaningless unless we also show that there are some families with that
income who do in fact secure a defined level of nutrition. This fundamental criticism could be made of nearly all studies of poverty."[7]

Given the diversity of the lowest income groups in terms of geographical location, environmental context, and ethnic and cultural background,
it is operationally valuable if not essential to determine which subgroup
within an income stratum will derive benefits from a given program. The
urban poor and the rural poor, for example, represent quite different target groups. A health program aimed at urban slum dwellers will face very
different logistical constraints than one directed at scattered peasant
communities in a mountainous area. Whereas the former may be successful in
reaching the low-income groups, the latter may not.

Even if the lowest income groups are not the only beneficiaries of the
programs inplemented, an equity or distributive function may be served if,
relative to alternative policy measures, health and nutrition programs are
more successful in reaching the poor. Spillover to middle-income groups
may, in fact, strengthen the viability of programs by contributing to their
political acceptability. Of course, if this spillover is excessive (as it
sometimes is) the distributive function is aborted.

Where government policies do effectively improve the health and nutritional status of the poor, a series of multiplier or indirect benefits can
be postulated. The benefit most often associated with such improvement is
an increase in the productive capacity of low-income workers. This in turn
may lead to higher productivity per se and hence increased incomes where
worker productivity is a limiting factor in the production process. Whether
this represents a net developmental asset, of course, will depend on the
effect of such increased productivity on total employment. Should productivity and income of the poor increase without exacerbating unemployment
problems, purchasing power would increase, and assuming adequate supply,
nutrition and health status would be further boosted.

The possible external economies produced by higher returns to education
and family planning provide an additional area for speculation. Improved
nutrition of the very young child not only will prevent neurological

damage to the developing brain but is likely to increase the child's access to social and emotional stimulation with consequent effects on learning. Similarly the attentiveness, motivation, and attendance rate of school children may be improved by better nutrition and health. Family planning efforts are likely to be more successful where infant and child mortality is reduced and parents feel less need to overcompensate for expected child losses. In both cases, family income might be increased in the long run by higher earnings of educated offspring and the reduced expenses of fewer children.

B.   A theoretical framework for policy and program determination

Health systems in most low-income countries follow a pattern having their origins in Europe and North America. The system revolves around the physician who in turn has been trained in a perspective inherited from the West: that of viewing ill-health as the outcome of specific diseases of a biologic origin. Medical programs, accordingly, place emphasis on treatment of the biological disorder. Malnutrition is considered a specific disease state resulting from dietary deficiencies; treatment consists of the provision of essential nutrients combined with appropriate medical care.

As valid as this biomedical, bionutritional approach may be in the care of disease, it is unsuited to health and nutrition planning, and to the formulation of policy. From a broader perspective, ill-health and malnutrition are the outcome of a multitude of environmental, socio-economic, cultural, religious, agricultural, demographic, and psychological variables. Providing potable water supply in combination with improved personal hygiene, increasing or reorienting agricultural production, or raising incomes may be more effective means of combatting ill-health and malnutrition than a traditional health center program or a school-based feeding program.

Thus in formulating policy, a socio-medical, socio-nutritional approach is required. An attempt must be made to identify the determinants of the problem, or stated differently, the constraints that inhibit improvements in health and nutrition. Once these constraints are identified, the relative costs and effectiveness of alternative policies and programs designed to alleviate them can be examined.

1.   The constraints model

Detailing the many variables that contribute to malnutrition and ill-
health can as easily lead to confusion and controversy as to concerted
policy. In the nutrition field, for example, some argue in favor of feeding
programs, while others advocate nutrition education or maternal-child
health centers. There has been a tendency for agricultural experts to promote increasing agricultural yields, for clinical nutritionists to promote
rehabilitation centers, for marketing and business professionals to promote
commercially produced nutritious foods--all in response to the same problem:
malnutrition of the population, or, more specifically, of the vulnerable
groups. Yet there have been few systematic studies of the relative importance of the various determinants of malnutrition in specific locales, and
even fewer evaluating the effectiveness of nutrition programs in affecting
these determinants.

The debates of "education versus income," of "medical care versus
feeding programs," and of "health centers versus sanitation" might be better
dealt with if a conceptual model of the limitations or constraints inhibiting the improvement of health and nutrition were devised. While the number
of variables that collectively comprise the "ecology" of malnutrition and
ill-health are numerous, it is possible, for policy purposes at least, to
condense these into four primary categories of constraints:

          (i) Local availability of essential inputs,

          (ii) Adequacy of family income,

          (iii) Socio-cultural factors, and

          (iv) Nutrition-infection interactions.

This constraints model suggests that the pattern and priority of constraints
--and hence of appropriate policy instruments--may differ from country to
country, from community to community, and from one socio-economic group to
another. Yet in analyzing health and nutrition in low-income countries,
certain overall patterns emerge. These are best presented by applying the
model to malnutrition and health separately, although, of course, the fourth
constraint level emphasizes the synergistic interaction between the two.
Health policies which do not take into account nutritional deficiencies will
not be wholly effective, and vice versa.

2.   The model applied to nutrition

The model seeks to identify constraints in the flow of food (calories and nutrients) which result in inadequate consumption, especially by the "vulnerable" groups whose calorie/nutrient requirements may be proportionately elevated. In particular the young child and the pregnant and lactating mother are considered nutritionally at risk.

a)   Local availability of essential inputs

Either the quantity or the quality (in terms of vitamins, minerals, or protein) of food available may be insufficient at the community level. While the aggregate food supply is influenced by import and export policies, as well as agricultural policies, this constraint may also be attributable to underdeveloped marketing, transport, and distribution systems. At the community level in particular, seasonal variations in supply may correlate with nutritional deficiencies. Where seasonal shortages develop, prices increase--a trend which may be accentuated by adverse climatic conditions. The extreme case, of course, is famine. Rural populations being especially dependent on local production are highly vulnerable to seasonal variations in availability.

b)   Adequacy of family income

In an urban monetized community family food consumption may be limited by purchasing capacity, which in turn is a function of income, food commodity prices, and the cost of alternative budgetary demands. In a traditional rural environment, family food supplies will include self-grown crops and foods obtained by barter or purchase. The encroachment of "modernity" is essentially the encroachment of an exchange economy, which is highly monetized, on a traditional economy, which is not. In response to needs for cash, the farming population may (i) offer self-grown foods for sale at the marketplace, (ii) shift to cash crops for sale, (iii) seek rural wage employment, or (iv) migrate to urban areas, perhaps on a seasonal basis, to obtain employment. Thus family income will be a function of such factors as landownership, tenancy arrangements, employment opportunities, wage rates, and credit availability. Where this constraint is limiting, family food supplies will be inadequate, regardless of local food availability.

c)   Socio-cultural factors

Not only are family food purchases in a large degree influenced by cultural preferences, beliefs, and taboos, but intra-family food distribution may be markedly affected.   In some societies, emphasis may be placed on the adult male as household head, to the neglect of pregnant and lactating women and young children.   Even where overall family food access is sufficiently high (due to local availability and adequate income), malnutrition problems often remain,   particularly among the vulnerable groups which usually are the focal point of food taboos and nutrition-related belief patterns.   Migration to urban areas and exposure to mass media need not lead to nutritionally improved patterns: witness the marked decrease in breast feeding in urban areas, with the attendant increase in gastro-intestinal disease and malnutrition among infants and children.

d)   Nutrition-infection interactions

The interrelations of disease and malnutrition have been well documented.[8]   On the one hand, malnutrition increases susceptibility to disease, and on the other, disease--particularly diarrheal disease and intestinal parasites--leads to increased nutrient loss and greater nutrient requirements.   Thus even where adequate food is available one may not be able to utilize it sufficiently due to disease.   Moreover, many cultural dictates (constraint iii) specify that foods be withheld during certain diseases, thereby aggravating the nutritional difficulty.

It should be evident from this model that any policy directed at an inappropriate constraint will be of little benefit.   If local availability is not an important constraint, improved local yields in an agricultural community may not have any nutritional impact unless there are simultaneous increases in the resources of the poor or reduction in food prices. Similarly improved income will not benefit socio-culturally constrained families, nor will nutrition education assist those who are too poor to be able to afford food in sufficient quantity or quality.   Levinson's study on the determinants of malnutrition in the rural Punjab (India) found that while lower-caste landless families were primarily constrained by inadequat income, the upper-caste, landowning families suffered more from socio-cultural constraints (especially nutritionally inappropriate belief patterns). "Most interventions which did not in some way augment real income would have a far greater positive effect on the Jat (upper-caste) child than on

the Ramdasia (lower-caste) and have the ultimate effect of widening existing differentials."[9] With respect to Northeast Tanzania, on the other
hand, Kraut has concluded that differences in nutrition could not be attributed to income or social standing, and that "the supposition that an
increase in income automatically brings about an improvement in nutrition
is inadequate."[10] With increasing opportunity to initiate and evaluate
nutrition intervention, it should be possible to test these conclusions
(obtained from cross-section analysis) with longitudinal observation.

3.   The model applied to health

As in the case with nutrition, four levels of constraints can be specified as limiting improvements to health. To be inclusive, one should
look at all essential inputs that contribute to health: uncontaminated
water, sanitary housing and adequate shelter from the elements, hygienic
food, and so on. Although each of these might be analyzed according to
local availability, family income, socio-cultural factors, and nutrition-
infection interactions, which would permit a broad-based approach to rational health-related resource allocation, the discussion in this chapter
is limited to the provision of health services per se.

a)   Local availability of essential inputs

The extremely skewed distribution of trained health personnel and
health facilities is perhaps the most easily generalized characteristic of
health systems in almost all low-income countries. These health systems
are usually hospital-based and urban-oriented, place major emphasis on the
training of physicians, despite the higher relative cost, and give relatively little attention to auxiliary and preprofessional health personnel.
The distribution of physicians between capital cities and the rest of the
country, indicated in table 1, well reflects the disparities inherent in
such systems. Similar disparities can be observed in hospital bed/popula-
tion ratios. The problem of access in rural areas is exacerbated by poorly
developed transportation systems. It was found in Turkey, for example,
that the combined effect of slower rate of travel and increased distance
resulted in the majority (52%) of rural dwellers taking more than three
hours to reach health facilities, while only 10% of urban dwellers took so
long.[11] This study covered only those persons who actually had access to
health facilities; it can be argued that most of the rural poor do not.

Table 1. Physician Distribution Relative to Population,
Selected Areas, 1964

	Capital City		Rest of Country	
	% of doctors	% of population	% of doctors	% of population
Jamaica	70	26	30	74
Guatemala	82	15	18	85
Senegal	63	15	37	85
Thailand	60	8	40	92
Kenya	54	5	46	95

SOURCE: N. R. E. Fendall, "Medical Care in the Developing Nations," ed.,
John Fry and W. A. J. Farndale, International Medical Care
(Wallingford, Pa.: Washington Square East, 1972), table 7.3,
p. 208.

Oscar Gish has calculated that over 40% of the rural population in many of
the districts in Tanzania live farther than 10 kilometers from any health
facility. "It is important to note that 10 kilometers represent, in practical terms, the catchment area of a dispensary or rural health center, as
well as a substantial part of hospitals."[12] He concludes that receipt of
health care depends on proximity to a health facility, and that the rural
population which has no such access may not receive health care at all.
This, of course, does not take into account the treatment (effective or
otherwise) provided by indigenous health practitioners. In rural Bangladesh, homeopaths, hakims, faith healers and other such personnel were found
to outnumber doctors, nurses, and trained auxiliaries by about 7.5 to 1.[13]
Similar patterns emerge elsewhere, suggesting that it is "modern" medical
care which is unavailable, rather than any treatment at all.

    b)   Adequacy of family income
    The cost of medical services--particularly of private practitioners--
places an inevitable burden on family income. The burden weighs most on
the poor for whom it represents a larger proportion of total income. In
Chile, for example, the unmet need for physician treatment, as assessed in
a large-scale nationwide survey, was found to be inversely related to in-

come, even after correction for urban-rural differentials attributable to accessiblity of services.[14] Moreover, in looking at total cases of unmet need, lack of adequate finances was the reason most frequently given for not obtaining treatment.[15] For the very poor, even the seemingly innocuous fees levied at nonprofit clinics and hospital outpatient services may be significant. In querying mothers in two Tanzanian villages on why more women did not attend an Under Five Clinic, Bornstein and Kreysler discovered a suggestive pattern: in the village where more men had work in a nearby tea estate, thereby earning a cash income, the cost of the clinic (20 cents) was not viewed as an important factor, while in the other villages where this income avenue was not readily available, cost was considered the most inhibiting factor.[16]

c) Socio-cultural factors

The continued use of indigenous practitioners and the reluctance to accept modern medical care have been subjects of much interest in anthropological and sociological circles. As mentioned above, it is a mistake to interpret data on the rural scarcity of health facilities and personnel as indicative of an absence of any treatment. Trained health workers in low-income countries are "not filling a vacuum but rather are offering alternatives and supplements to long-established institutionalized and at least partially efficacious ways of maintaining health and coping with illness."[17] According to one hypothesis, use of modern medical facilities is a measure of relative acculturation. It seems relatively clear that such factors as religious adherence, ethnic origin, familial stability and organization, exposure to formal education, and spatial mobility may contribute to or detract from motivation to use modern health facilities and personnel. Furthermore, "social distance" may exist between medical personnel and patients, given differing educational levels, socio-economic backgrounds, and cultural inclinations. This distance is most pronounced in the case of the lowest income groups. While these class barriers may be most evident in tradition-bound rural areas, they also persist in urban areas as observed by Teller in Honduras.[18] Patterns of "dual use" of medical and traditional "healer" facilities often emerge in cities, particularly among lower socio-economic groups.[19]

d)   Nutrition-infection interactions

The synergistic interaction of nutrition and infection has been noted.
The policy implication is that where malnutrition and poor sanitation prevail, curative medical care may have relatively little community impact.
The work of Scrimshaw, Gordon and others in Guatemala is particularly instructive. A program of relatively expensive preventive medicine and
medical care in one village had no effect on the frequency of illness among
children (though there were fewer deaths), while less expensive supplementa
feeding of the preschool population in a second village, without any other
intervention, gave an appreciable but limited improvement in disease incidence.[20] Since malnutrition is most prevalent among the poor, medical
treatment may be less capable of restoring normal health to low-income
children. Moreover even if the lowest socio-economic groups should receive
health care equivalent to that of higher income levels, this may be insufficient, given their greater needs. Such a situation was indicated in the
health utilization survey in Chile: "Apparently the more affluent found it
possible to satisfy a relatively larger portion of their limited felt need
for care, so that their utilization rates were remarkably similar to those
of other income groups who needed more health care but frequently failed
to satisfy such need."[21]

In conclusion it is apparent that government policies which seek to
promote more equitable health care will be effective only to the extent
that the appropriate constraints are addressed. The health care plight
of the lowest income groups, especially in rural areas, is not due solely
to availability, or to family income, or to socio-cultural constraints,
but rather to a particular mix that will vary from country to country, and
from locale to locale. In attempting to determine whether health policies
effectively allocate "health benefits" to the lowest income groups we are
faced with a complex and heterogeneous situation. Nonetheless, if health
services are not locally available, other constraints remain irrelevant.
A first step, then, must involve the provision of services. Yet care must
be taken not to exacerbate the family income constraint in the process by
excessive fees. An alternative policy measure, probably more relevant in
urban areas of countries with reasonably well-developed administrative
structures, may be the provision of health insurance, particularly to low-
income groups and the unemployed.

C.   Trends in nutrition policy and programs: an evaluation

Interest in nutrition at the governmental level initially took the form of institutional child-feeding programs. Indeed such programs continue to command upward of 95% of all budgets directed to child nutrition in low-income countries.[22] Largely a response to offers of food aid from industrialized countries and multilateral agencies, these programs are attractive for a number of reasons. Primarily they had—and have—political appeal, being direct, highly visible, and generally less sensitive than other forms of foreign aid. Berg estimates that they reach about 125 million children in about 100 countries.[23]

Additional governmental nutrition efforts include food fortification, the encouragement of processed nutritious foods, nutrition education, and support for research efforts on the genetic improvement of the nutritional value of staple food grains. These and other nutrition-related programs are considered in this section as alternative policy instruments of broader policies designed to improve incomes and welfare of the lowest socio-economic strata; yet ironically, although nutrition programs often have been justified as assistance to the poor, only scattered attempts have been made to ascertain their effectiveness in reaching the lowest income groups in a meaningful way.

Ideally, one would hope in evaluation of the equity and income effects of nutrition programs and policies to look in depth into a variety of considerations, most importantly, (i) the extent of coverage of low-income strata, (ii) types of goods and services transferred to the recipients, (iii) evidence that the constraints addressed are appropriate, (iv) probable nutritional and nutrition-related benefits, and (v) projected long-term effects on incomes and equity. In the absence of much quantitative research or systematic evaluation of any of these, it is not possible to specify income and equity implications with any precision. Nonetheless, qualitative trends and hypotheses do emerge from experience to date and are discussed below.

Before analyzing particular programs and policies, a point of clarification is in order, given the focus of the income redistribution project. Nutrition and income redistribution objectives are not always equivalent, although usually interrelated. It is conceivable that certain nutrition programs which do in fact supplement incomes of the poor may have little impact on nutritional status per se. (An example might be investment in labor-intensive fruit and vegetable cultivation.) In such cases, it might be appropriate to conceptualize these as important redistributive tools and only secondarily as nutrition programs. There also are examples of the reverse situation in which effective nutrition programs (some nutrition education activities come to mind) have minimal direct income effects. By emphasizing the broader concept of equity in this chapter an endeavor is made to encompass both possibilities, arguing that either increased incomes or nutritional benefits improve the lot of the poor. An ideal strategy, of course, would integrate both objectives and hence encourage reciprocal exchange whereby increased incomes improve nutrition, and improved nutrition increases income (via greater productivity or reduced population demand for scarce resources).

1. Specific feeding programs

Programs with child feeding as the primary objective include (i) school feeding programs, (ii) preschool feeding programs, and (iii) take-home feeding programs. Those integrated programs which utilize feeding but have additional or alternative objectives such as nutrition or health education are discussed in the section to follow. Adult-feeding programs, while adopted by certain industries, have not received large governmental support, except in famine situations.

Of all these programs school feeding is by far the most prevalent and well established. At least two factors account for this emphasis: (i) when feeding programs were initially developed, particularly in the early post-World War II years, it was not realized that malnutrition exerts its greatest damage on preschool-age children, especially in the range of 6 to 24 months, and on the unborn child of the last trimester of pregnancy; and (ii) that the school system is perhaps the most-widespread institutional vehicle through which feeding programs for children can be channeled. The fact that school attendance and performance may be positively affected offers additional appeal. The development of school feeding in the United States and Europe made this the natural route to go when surplus commodities became available for overseas programs.

Of low-income countries, the most extensive feeding programs are to be found in India, where, prior to the Indian economic crisis of the early and mid-1970s, and cutback of U.S. PL 480 food provision, roughly 17 million people were fed daily.[24] Mid-day meal programs for school children, which alone covered 12 million children daily, were largely supplied by PL 480 (Title II) food donations through CARE and other voluntary agencies. Administratively these programs are operated by state education departments; another Special Nutrition Programme which aims at mothers and preschool children in urban slums and tribal areas, and now covers roughly 3 million children daily, is operated by the central government Department of Social Welfare. Clearly the budgetary expenditures are sizable. The Fifth Five Year Plan calls for a nutrition allocation of slightly over 4 billion rupees ($440 million) of which 3.5 billion is earmarked for feeding programs.[25] And this does not take into account an estimated 2 billion rupees worth of foreign food contributions which are anticipated.

Thus child-feeding programs might represent a significant income transfer--if the lowest income groups are reached. Davidson Gwatkin, in a report to the Ford Foundation, makes a "guesstimate" that in India 10% to 12% of the target recipients are served by the various programs put together.[26] Yet there is little information on the socio-economic groups actually benefiting, or of their urban-rural distribution. Alan Berg observes that "schools in poor, remote villages are the least likely to have feeding programs; and for that matter, the poorest communities--and states and nations--are the least likely to have programs.[27] Moreover, "in most countries the size and location of the programs are planned not only on the basis of need but also on the availability of administrative skills and other resources necessary to carry out the program."[28] There are exceptions of course which prove the rule, such as the school lunch program in the Indian state of Orissa which apparently serves about 70% of schools in predominantly tribal districts, compared with 25% to 30% of schools in non-tribal districts.[29]

As important as the location of school feeding programs is the pattern of school attendance. If children from low-income families do not attend, perhaps because they cannot afford school fees, or because they are needed at home, they will not be reached by the feeding programs. In effect, the less-poor and middle-income groups are likely to be the recipients of the income transfers--not the lowest income and remote rural groups.

A similar situation was found in preschool programs in the Indian state of Tamil Nadu, where coverage of the target preschool population by

all maternal—child feeding centers (including day care centers) operated
or supported by the state. government was about 12% in 1972.[30]   A detailed
study of the balwady (day care) programs revealed that almost all of the
enrolled children lived within a radius of one-quarter to three-eighths of
a mile from the center. "This becomes a critical factor in terms of the
(Government of Tamil Nadu's) stated intention of operating balwadies for
the benefit of the disadvantaged groups. As long as the physical location
(of the) balwady is...dependent on local voluntary effort, the government
(has) no assurance that in fact the (program) is capable of enrolling those
children who are most in need of the services."[31]   In fact, centers were
almost invariably in the main village, while the lowest socio-economic
groups (the scheduled castes) often lived in colonies physically separate
from the village proper. Given the predominant influence of the upper and
landed castes in village decision making, it is not surprising that these
day care programs, with their attendant feeding activities, were located to
the advantage of the more well-to-do.

Take-home feeding represents another distribution design geared to
reach the preschool child: free food is made available at a collection site
on a periodic basis to be "taken home" for child feeding. In many cases the
food is sold in the market or diverted to other members of the family rather
than being consumed by the target group. Although in either case the immediate nutrition objective is thwarted, the food still represents an income transfer to the recipient family. Yet, again, the lowest income families are often the most difficult to reach. At a CARE-sponsored take-home
program in tribal areas of Madhya Pradesh (India) those families who were
"good collectors" (collected food at 75% or more of the total number of
distributions) were compared with "poor collectors" (15% to 20% or less):
a significantly greater proportion of poor collectors was found among families of the landless labor group, and among families with mothers who worked
full time. "Time is precious and is of overriding importance with that income segment which needs to be reached more than any other."[32]   In this
context it is worth noting that to-and-fro walking time to the distribution
point was estimated at more than two hours for 60% of the participating
families. The Tamil Nadu research showed that while only 8% of households
in the study area had monthly incomes of less than 150 rupees ($19), 68%
of the target children who did <u>not</u> participate were from households in this
income range.[33]

Overall then, child-feeding programs to date probably have not been highly successful in effectively reaching the lowest income groups. Interesting and dramatic exceptions were the milk distribution programs under Frei and Allende regimes in Chile.[34] Originating as far back as the 1920s, the milk program saw major expansion in 1959, more than quadrupling in size from the mid-50s, and reaching 20% to 25% of potential beneficiaries (infants, preschool children, and pregnant women). Associated with the system of National Health Care, this distribution probably did reach the urban poor but excluded most of the rural populace. The massive increase of the milk program in the late 1960s and particularly in the early 1970s allowed the inclusion of the rural sector and undoubtedly provided significant additional nutritional and real income benefits to low-income urban groups. By 1967, an estimated 180 million liters of milk were distributed, and coverage of the 0-2-year age group had increased to 70% to 80%; under the Popular Unity government of Allende, children up to the age of 15 were brought under the program, a total of some 420 million liters of milk were distributed, and 60% to 65% of all eligible persons were covered. The milk program was viewed explicitly by the government as an instrument of income redistribution according to Dr. Giorgio Solimano, who headed the country's nutrition program. At the same time, the foreign exchange costs for the program were considerable. Chilean milk imports increased from 6 million kilograms in 1970 to 54 million kilograms in 1971, of which some 25 million kilograms were distributed through the National Health Service. With the military takeover in September 1973, the milk program has been cut by about 40% with elmination of distribution to children over 6 years of age. It continues to be Chile's major nutritional effort and is still a major effort by international standards.

In terms of the constraints model, feeding programs can be viewed as addressing the availability and/or family income constraints: on the one hand previously unavailable food (e.g., milk in sufficient quantity) may be supplied, and on the other the food is a supplement to family resources. In some instances children may be induced to eat what their parents would not otherwise be willing to feed them, thereby addressing a socio-cultural constraint (discussed in more detail in the next section). From a nutritional perspective, the income increment represented by food will be valuable only if the food received by the child supplements, rather than supplants, his normal diet at home. Supplementation is most likely to be the case where parents are unable, due to the income constraint, to feed their child as they wish, while substitution is likely where the parents do not realize that inadequate diet is interfering with the child's health and development. Feeding programs, therefore, will be most effective where malnutrition is primarily a function of poverty. Yet, as shown, due to limitations in the methods of distribution, the poor are the least likely to be reached--except in situations like Cuba and, previously, Chile, where the government has a strong political commitment to assure its success.

In the absence of such a major political commitment (which probably must be part of a broader development program with a high premium on equity), feeding programs can be expected to redistribute income primarily to the middle-income and less-poor groups. The magnitude of the redistribution may not be as great as enrollment figures and budgets suggest, however, due to inefficiencies, wastage, and misrepresentation. In Tamil Nadu attendance at balwadies was found to be, on average, about 75% of enrollment figures.[35] Moreover, food loss resulting from inadequate packaging, infestation, rancidity and blackmarketing can be considerable. For the recipient family, the income supplement and the nutritional benefits will be diminished by irregularities in feeding and irregularities in attendance.

Clearly the priority need in child feeding, aside from the prerequisite need to make it domestically self-sufficient, is a reorientation both toward children who are younger (including their mothers during pregnancy) and those who are economically disadvantaged. Unless those children in greatest need are reached, the program may simply create the erroneous impression that the problem is being addressed. This, in turn, might have the unfortunate effect of diverting attention among political elites and international agencies from basic equity considerations. John Mellor has stated this view succinctly:

> While 30 percent of the population in a low-income country may need major nutritional assistance, a nutrition program is likely to reach only a small proportion of them. It may make the rich feel good that they are doing something for the poor, when what is really needed is for the rich to go along with the kinds of development programs that will expand employment, incomes and consumption of the lower income classes. However, the latter course very often involves much more substantial social, political, and economic change

than the rich are willing to tolerate and certainly much more than is involved in most of the nutritional programs put forward.[36]

In the event of famine, of course, different considerations come into play; mass feeding efforts are perhaps the sole means of addressing the problem of local unavailability of food.

2. Nutrition education and integrated programs

Nutrition education programs address socio-cultural constraints; the basic assumption is that necessary resources are available and that family income is adequate but that these resources are not properly utilized, or not properly allocated within the family. Typically these programs encourage the use of high-protein foods or foods of high vitamin or mineral content, endeavor to educate mothers in nutritionally sound child-feeding and child-care practices, and teach hygiene. To the extent that the last of these instructions is successful, the fourth constraint level (nutrition-infection interaction) may also be affected. In some programs the education is combined with feeding, health care, or both. Hence the reference to integrated programs.

The various programs include: (i) "Applied Nutrition Programs," (ii) nutrition rehabilitation centers, (iii) programs based in maternal-child health (MCH) centers, and (iv) under-five clinics. Of these, the Applied Nutrition Programs (ANPs) are the most widespread and the most numerous, being for the most part the product of concerted United Nations efforts (FAO, WHO, and UNICEF). By 1967 it was reported that ANPs had been initiated in 57 countries,[37] and in the period 1967-70 further programs were formed in 20 countries.[38] In India alone the ANP has been implemented in 833 blocks (1971), with greatest assistance coming from UNICEF (7.24 million dollars in the form of supplies, equipment, and other assistance by December 1969).[39] Nutrition rehabilitation centers (sometimes called mothercraft centers although to some there is a conceptual difference), have been set up in at least a dozen countries, mostly in Latin America: in Colombia, Guatemala, and Haiti they constitute large-scale efforts.[40] Under-five clinics are found in a number of African countries. The incorporation of nutrition education into MCH centers varies considerably, and usually represents good intent rather than established norm.

While each of these programs attempts to incorporate nutrition education objectives, the particular approach varies, not only between the types of program but also within programs themselves. ANPs involve education through demonstration projects, including cooking, gardens, fish ponds, and poultry production, and may include feeding programs; they often are school-based. Nutrition rehabilitation centers provide day care (and in a few cases overnight) facilities for children diagnosed as malnourished; while the health and growth of the children are being restored through feeding and necessary health care, the mothers undergo training in nutrition education. MCH centers attempt to provide nutrition education in addition to regular health treatment. Under-five clinics are child-care centers (sometimes mobile) that provide medical services, nutrition education, and free food.

As an instrument of income redistribution, nutrition education programs cannot be highly significant. Most basically, the programs do not directly address the income constraint which one would expect to be operative among the poor. Moreover, the institutional base of many such programs fails to reach low-income groups. The fact that these programs have not been highly successful in altering community dietary patterns is perhaps indicative. In India, an evaluation of the ANP found no significant difference between villages in which there were ANPs and control villages with respect to consumption of the nutritionally desirable commodities promoted by the program. Nor was any special consideration in ANP villages given to the dietary needs of the vulnerable groups.[41] In part, this was due to limited community impact: "Seventy percent of households in the 30 (studied) ANP villages had neither heard of ANP nor did they know anything about its aims and objectives. Not even one percent knew that it was a coordinated programme of nutrition education, production, and consumption. Instead most of them referred to ANP either in terms of a feeding or health programme."[42] This latter observation in itself may be revealing--almost certainly it is the physical real income transfer (of food or medical care) which is valued most by participants. At an under-five clinic in Tanzania it was found that free distribution of medicines and food were the most appreciated activities. "It is noteworthy that no mother mentioned health education among the most highly appreciated clinic activities."[43] While it would be unfair to accept such valuation as an adequate criterion for the assessment of health education, it is likely that, as in agricultural extension, such perception correlates rather well with actual benefits.

In that nutrition rehabilitation centers feed and offer medical care selectively to the severely malnourished, they do have redistributive potential. Yet in the observations of Warren Berggren, who was instrumental in establishing the program in Haiti, poor families are reluctant to bring their children to the centers, being apparently embarrassed to publicly display their impoverished, poorly clothed condition.[44] This difficulty was overcome by active recruiting of the malnourished and by provision of clothing to the children. Once enrolled, the low-income children had good attendance records, however.

Even so, it is not clear that the nutrition education components will bring about long-term benefits: in an evaluation of nutrition rehabilitation centers in Haiti and Guatemala little improvement was found in the growth of treated children one year after discharge.[45] "Perhaps NRCs should concentrate their educational efforts on families where children have malnutrition because of ignorance of the mother rather than because of the very low economic status of the family.

At least in terms of distributional considerations, it seems relatively clear that programs with nutrition educational objectives should be combined with efforts to address the family income constraint. Thus a recent report to the Indonesian Government emphasized that such programs should be located in areas where employment- and income-generating projects are underway.[46] In and of itself, however, nutrition education cannot be viewed as a means to redistribute income to the poor.

Mention also should be made of the use of mass media for nutrition education, although few if any nationwide efforts have been launched. While the cost per contact made may be significantly reduced by this means, it probably is not an effective way of reaching the poor in those rural areas where literacy is low and radio ownership confined to the more well-to-do. In addition, culturally and linguistically diverse rural populations will be difficult to reach, as the same message may not be appropriate for all; hence, in Zambia a recent mass media effort was concentrated in the urban and more densely populated areas. The potential effectiveness of mass media in reaching those in need almost certainly lies in the development of media which require neither literacy nor the purchase of receivers and which are logistically capable of reaching the rural poor

(mobile movie vans are sometimes attempted). In addition, their effectiveness appears to depend on complementary efforts to disseminate the same
messages in person.

Perhaps the most promising integrated programs are those in which
primary decision making resides in the community. The potential for effective decentralized decision making which can positively affect the poor,
rather than simply reinforcing the power of local ruling elites, surely
varies considerably among low-income countries and relates not only to the
political orientation of the government but also to the prevailing social
dynamics and community cohesiveness. Nonetheless in several socialist
countries, and on a more limited scale in Colombia, Central America, Indonesia, and Pakistan, there have been examples of community-managed nutrition and health programs usually with some referral relationship to the
hierarchical government health system. In the case of nutrition, communities themselves select local personnel who, after a very brief training
period, assume responsibility for home visiting and a monthly or biweekly
weight surveillance program for identification of young children at risk.
For the child who deviates from the growth curve, the worker may provide
information or weaning food, or where complications arise may refer the
family to the appropriate government health service.

3.   Commercial nutritious foods

Since the formation of the Protein Advisory Group at the United Nations in 1955, considerable attention and effort has been directed toward
alleviating the "protein gap." Some of this attention has taken the form
of efforts to develop and commercialize low-cost "protein-rich foods,"
usually through the private sector. In a comprehensive analysis of these
efforts, Elizabeth Orr describes 69 schemes in 36 countries, a number of
which have been discontinued.[47] Aside from 15 schemes in which the responsible enterprise was owned in whole or in part by the government, government aid has, in general, been restricted to purchase of product (often
for use in feeding programs) and to assistance with promotion. The largest volume of production has been achieved by Bal Ahar (26,500 tons in
1969), a product of the government-owned Food Corporation of India.

These foods have been distributed both through institutional feeding
programs and through the commercial market. Given the costs associated

with milling, processing, packaging, transportation, and advertising, the commercially marketed high-protein foods have been more expensive than locally produced traditional foods. They are usually beyond the purchasing capacity of low-income groups but may, if purchased by the poor, displace other food purchases. This need not be nutritionally beneficial. Popkin and Latham have illustrated how "by buying a package of commercial food the poor may pervert in the process their overall food budget. The replacement will all too often result in the availability of less protein, fewer calories, and less other essential nutrients in their overall food budget."[48] This replacement phenomenon will be especially prevalent among the urban poor exposed to the powerful influence of advertising; the rural populace, less in touch with the market mechanism, will be less affected.

Processed nutritious foods cannot be considered equity-promoting unless prices are reduced through government-provided consumption subsidies. At significantly lower prices, these foods may come within the purchasing capacity of the poor; the replacement effect may be transformed to the extent that the overall impact is positive (more nutrients per unit expense than in the traditional diet). Although unlikely to be useful in rural areas, such programs may benefit the urban poor, particularly where the subsidized foods are distributed through existing rationing systems, as is presently being considered in Pakistan.

Unless accompanied by such consumption subsidies, the benefits of commercial protein food distribution will accrue to middle- and upper-income groups. Hence governmental assistance would in effect heighten relative disparities between the poor and the more well-to-do as far as nutritional well-being is concerned. Institutional distribution may in some instances benefit the lowest income groups, though within the limitations discussed with regard to feeding programs.

The fortification concept poses an additional problem in reaching the low-income groups.[49] Fortification is logistically possible only where the vehicle is centrally processed; when cereals are milled in a multitude of village grinding units or when foods consumed are home grown, the fortification approach cannot be used. Yet, certain vehicles such as salt, sugar, and tea, consumed by the population as a whole, may be highly effective carriers where these are centrally processed. Even the rural poor, who are difficult to reach by market distribution, usually consume these

items regularly and hence would benefit directly from their fortification.
The results can be dramatic. In the goiter belt of northern India, a program of salt iodization reduced the prevalence of goiter among those
reached from 38% to 3% in ten years. The Governments of India and Indonesi
are considering the fortification of salt with iron, a measure of enormous
public health potential. In Costa Rica and Guatemala the governments recently passed legislation requiring the fortification of all sugar with
vitamin A, and in Pakistan, the government is considering nationwide fortification of tea with vitamin A.

For rather minimal cost, the magnitude of benefits may be substantial.
Reduction in the incidence of blindness due to vitamin A deficiency, increased physical capacity (and possibly productivity) with a reduction of
iron deficiency anemia, and prevention of goiter (and in extreme cases,
deaf-mutism and cretinism) by overcoming iodine deficiency, are cases in
point. Unfortunately, the fortification of unconventional carriers (sugar,
salt, and tea) is still very much the exception rather than the rule.
There also has been some reluctance by governments to subsidize the cost of
the fortification, although the expense involved usually is not high relative to other health-related expenditures. If the lowest income groups are
to benefit, such additional costs will have to be assumed by the government
--or, in some cases, absorbed by the processor. These subsidies can be
considered redistributive measures, in that they overcome price
disincentives for the poor to purchase fortified foods. In some cases it
is possible to go even further, in a distributional sense, by fortifying
only items or grades of commodities consumed by the poor. The fortification of "flour mill atta," a low-grade form of wheat shunned by middle-
and upper-income groups in South Asian cities (actually much of this wheat
is imported from the United States), is such an example.

Another potentially attractive instrument is the genetic manipulation
of the nutritional content of cereal strains. As in the case of fortification programs, the constraints themselves are minimally addressed (unless
one argues that nutrient availability is increased). Yet unlike fortification, the effort and expense is not recurring once an improved strain
has been successfully introduced. Most of the work to date has concentrated on corn (Opaque 2), sorghum, and wheat, and has attempted to increase
their protein content or improve their amino acid profiles (i.e., improve
protein quality). Where protein deficiencies exist independent of caloric

needs (a question of raging international controversy among nutritional scientists, but surely one with no universal answer), and where these staples are consumed by the poor and the vulnerable groups, the plant breeding approach should be pursued.

While conceptually attractive in benefiting the rural poor who are difficult to reach through most commercially distributed fortified foods, large-scale utilization of cereal strains with high nutritive value is still many years off. Important problems of yield reduction, disease susceptibility, and consumer acceptability still have to be overcome. If they can be, they offer major promise for nutritional improvement, and a means of addressing at least part of the malnutrition problem of the poor.

4. Nutrition-related policy areas

That family income is a limiting constraint to improvements in nutrition for the poorest groups in many if not all low-income countries has been observed repeatedly in this presentation. Obviously, then, any government policy which increases the incomes or wealth of the poor may be nutritionally beneficial; conversely, policies which undermine their economic base may be nutritionally detrimental. Such measures as employment generation, wage increases, improved tenancy relations, redistribution of land, increases in small-farm yields, extension of credit to smaller farmers--in fact all policies and programs that redistribute income in favor of the poor, as discussed in other presentations at the Research Program in Economic Development Conference at Princeton, may lead to improvements in nutrition and thereby well-being.

Government price policies are of particular nutritional significance. Many less developed countries have used positive price policies as an incentive to producers: higher food prices serve to redistribute income from the nonagricultural to the agricultural sector. Yet the greatest increases in income will be to those who sell more of their produce; the rural subsistence farmers who sell little will not benefit equally from such a price policy. At the same time, low-income food purchasers--i.e., the cash-dependent rural poor, the urban poor and, to the extent that they purchase from the market, landless farm laborers--will have to pay higher prices and hence may have to decrease their food consumption. "A rise in agricultural prices redistributes income away from low-income urban consumers and towards high-income agricultural producers."[50]

In the case of cash crops, the effect is different. Price increases lead to higher incomes for the small cash-crop farmers, while the urban poor and rural poor are not hurt since these goods usually are beyond their purchasing capacity. This is true also of high priced food commodities produced by farmers for sale. At the same time, excessive zeal for higher production of such crops has had the effect, in an increasing number of countries, of luring land away from the production of domestically consumed staples, thus decreasing their availability and increasing their price to the low-income consumer (who also benefits least, if at all, from the benefits of any foreign exchange earnings from the cash crops).

Negative price policies which artificially depress prices favor consumers. But unless small farmers are able to increase ouput enough to compensate for the lower price, they lose income. Urban and rural cash-dependent poor would benefit, unless scarcity conditions arise (due to unmet demand): "What is produced would probably end up in the hands of the well-to-do, who are usually better able to procure scarce commodities, unless a rigid program of distribution to low income groups were implemented."[51]

A final consideration must be given to relative yields and prices. One detrimental impact of the Green Revolution may have been a decrease in pulse production as farmers turn to more profitable cereal strains. Again the losers are the poor whose income elasticity of demand for pulses considerably exceeds that of the wealthier groups. Today with higher pulse prices (up 40% in two years in Pakistan) and less fertilizer on which the new cereal strains are dependent, this imbalance may be redressed. The development of higher yielding strains of pulses, however, would help considerably in this regard with benefits skewed to the poor.

Call and Levinson suggest that discriminatory prices, by which the consumption of low-income groups would be subsidized by the government, could improve the nutrition of the poor.[52] In spite of high costs (the Government of Pakistan spent $100 million on a two-tier consumer pricing policy for wheat in 1973) and major administrative expense and commitment, such policies, which assure adequate amounts of essential commodities at subsidized prices, may represent the only effective means of translating production increases into improved consumption for the poor. In Pakistan, this subsidized consumption system has increased the real income of the lowest income group by roughly 10 percent and the caloric intake of this group by between 9 and 14 percent. Without the subsidy their nutritional needs, only a small portion of which constitute effective demand and hence are taken into account in agricultural supply projections, will continue to be largely neglected.

Trade policies can have a significant effect on nutrition, particularly where a large portion of food needs are imported, or where land use is oriented around export crops. Cash crops may be encouraged for export, to the detriment (or benefit) of nutritional considerations. Food imports influence domestic food prices and thereby consumption. Conversely, nutrition programs can influence trade: witness the milk powder imports required for government distribution programs in Chile.

It goes without saying that education can influence the social and cultural factors which in turn influence food habits and child-feeding practices. It also, at least conceptually, can affect productivity and future earnings, thereby addressing the family income constraint in the future.

The development of transportation networks--roads, railroads, or water transport--may also have significant impact on nutrition, not only by allowing greater access to markets (both for sale and purchase) but by enabling food to be transported into areas of scarcity. As Alan Berg notes, "the major contribution to the solution of regional famines in India appears to have been construction of the railroads."[53] Likewise, improved food storage can help balance out the seasonal fluctuations in supply.

Disaster relief measures themselves may bring not only short run relief but long-term nutrition policy gains. Thus the Bihar famine of 1967 and the emergency relief program dramatized to the Indian Government the importance of nutrition: "The famine led to interest and in some cases emotional commitment, which in turn led to a variety of programs, a nutrition policy, and a chapter on nutrition for the first time in the Five Year Plan."[54]

The importance of public health efforts--improved water supply, sanitation, waste removal, infectious disease control, anti-parasite programs --to name but a few, all impinge upon the nutrition-infection constraint and may bring marked improvement in the nutritional well-being of the malnourished.

Lastly, family planning efforts are interrelated with nutritional considerations. To the extent that family size is reduced, the availability per person within the family may be increased. It is also possible that the success of family planning may depend on improved nutrition—as long as infant and child mortality rates are high, a result of the interaction of malnutrition and disease, there may be little motivation for low-income parents to limit family size, given that children, especially sons, are important investments as future income earners. In fact parents often over-compensate for expected mortality to assure the desired number of sons. Needless to say, the initial impact of improved nutrition may be an increase in family size (due to increased survivorship), but this, it is assumed, would merely represent a transitional phenomenon. Operationally there is increasing evidence of the value of integrating family planning and nutrition efforts, where both are being delivered through community-based centers or extension agents.[55] Where health and nutrition services are also provided, there usually is greater receptivity to the family planning message.

From this brief summary of related policy fields it is evident that nutrition planning must be an integral part of overall development planning. Indeed, the fact that the lowest deciles in the income distribution are often bypassed by the development process could argue in favor of nutrition considerations that could inject a greater concern for the poor. Evidence from areas which have witnessed rapid growth rates suggests that socio-economic growth without explicit attention to the malnutrition problems of the poor and the vulnerable population groups may well leave these groups marginally affected. At the same time, it is unlikely that nutrition policies alone provide viable long-term benefits to the lowest income groups in the absence of related socio-economic improvements. The two are complementary and must be addressed in tandem if desirable results are to be achieved.

D.   The distributive impact of health programs

The skewed distribution of health care services can be viewed along at least two component axes: the urban-rural dimension, and the income dimension. Both the urban poor and the rural peasant tend to be by-passed by health delivery systems in low-income countries. Yet in terms of numbers of persons affected, there can be little doubt that physical inaccessibility of modern medical services is the first limiting factor. In Ghana, for example, "health facilities are so distributed that they cannot offer any kind of service to more than, at most, 20% of the population."[56] The rural health center system in Thailand reaches at most 6% of the rural population, although an additional 15% to 20% are able to use district hospital services.[57] Even where more effective rural health programs have been launched, as in Iran, only half the rural population may gain access to outpatient care.[58]

The emphasis of this section, accordingly, will be on the extent to which government health policies overcome urban-rural inequities. This is probably a more pressing concern and certainly a more decipherable situation than that of differential use of health services by income groups. Virtually the only studies of differential use by socio-economic levels are a few utilization surveys (e.g., Chile,[59] Colombia,[60] and scattered pieces of sociological research; as a whole the medical profession has been remarkably unconcerned with the need to collect information on the nature of its coverage. While Charles Teller may be accurate in his doubt that "a more equitable geographic distribution of health personnel and resources (alone) would be sufficient to make a noticeable improvement in the medical care of the lower classes in most Latin American countries,"[61] given powerful social class barriers, equitable distribution is almost certainly a necessary, even if not a sufficient, condition for health improvement of the poor.

In the following pages, then, the problem of health facilities and personnel distribution, i.e., the "local availability" constraint, will be addressed primarily.

1. Organization of the health sector

Patterns of health care delivery have varied widely from one low-income country to another as a result of differing historical--and particularly colonial--experiences. While health care in some countries is organized and coordinated at the national level under an encompassing national health service, there is, in other countries, fragmentation and duplication of delivery systems, such that effective governmental control is minimal. Thus the mere observation that health resources are highly concentrated in urban areas does not, in itself, indicate whether this is due to governmental policies, or to a lack thereof. It is therefore useful to look at the organization of the health sector in discussing the distributive impact of governmental health policies.

The degree to which a government is able to direct the allocation of health resources is dependent on the extent of governmental coordination

of health-related delivery systems, and on the relative strength of the
public versus the private health services. Experience has shown that the
private sector usually represents particular interests rather than the
needs of society as a whole. When the private services are particularly
dominant in a country, they often dominate the public services, rather
than vice versa.

The public and private sectors can be further broken down into various
types of services, according to the pattern of ownership and the particular
recipients serviced. While the organization of services in no two countries is likely to be the same, the following broad categories can be
defined: ministry of health services, special government services, social
insurance schemes, mission and charity services, industrial and agricultural enterprise services, private practitioners, and indigenous health
practitioners. Each category will be discussed briefly, with special
reference to the population group being served.

a) Ministry of health services

Although some countries, such as Cuba, have developed strong centralized national health services, ministries of health often have relatively
little control over the delivery and distribution of services: "Although
responsible for health planning, ministries of health in Latin America
have had very little authority over medical care."[62] This may be due to
the development of other governmental services, such as social insurance
schemes in Latin America, or due to the predominance of mission and charity
institutions (especially in Africa), or due to the strength of the private
sector (as in Pakistan). Even more decisive, the ministry of health may
suffer from severe budgetary constraints. Yet for redistributional purposes, ministry of health services generally need both expansion and reorientation, even if the ultimate goal may be community-based, decentralized control and decision making. Instead, all too often, resources are
channeled into politically attractive (and also expensive) urban hospitals
and clinics.

b) Special government services

In low-income countries, these usually include special services for
the military and the civil service. In Latin America, for example, the
military, and subsequently the police forces, regarded as important for

the maintenance of political and social stability, have enjoyed preferential access to health services from early colonial times to the present.[63] Thus in Peru the armed forces and police own and operate 7 hospitals, thereby utilizing about 7% of the nation's hospital beds, 10% of the medical personnel, and 17% of the professional nursing personnel--although the number served is less than 3% of the population.[64] The extent of coverage by such systems usually is limited, and biased away from the lowest income groups who are less likely to be employed in these services.

c) Social insurance schemes

A variety of social insurance schemes have been established, differing in extent of coverage and provision of services. Given the overall shortage of health resources, these schemes often own and operate their own facilities with their own personnel. In addition to direct patterns of health care provision, some schemes may also allow the purchase of services from the private sector. Social insurance schemes, however, usually are limited to wage earners and salaried employees, and sometimes to the self-employed in urban areas. The programs for white-collar salaried employees may be distinct from those established for wage earners, as is the case in Peru.[65] Social insurance schemes are most prevalent in Latin America,[66] but are relatively rare in Africa--over 30 of the independent countries of Africa are without them.[67] The few that exist in Asia usually are confined to the industrial and commercial sectors, and sometimes to only part of these. Thus the Employees' State Insurance Corporation in India is limited to employees in nonseasonal establishments of 20 or more persons in which a manufacturing process is under power.[68] In no case is the rural agricultural population significantly covered: "In many cases the law excludes the farming population; in others the coverage provided is restricted to wage earners; in others again the protection provided for by law remains a dead letter because the necessary administrative services are lacking."[69]

d) Mission and charity services

Religious and humanitarian organizations have contributed significantly to the development of medical care in many low-income countries. The Catholic Church, for example, assumed responsibility for the sick among the poor in many Latin American countries, and a system of charity hospi-

tals was established. By 1961, charity hospitals accounted for 40% of
hospital beds in Peru and provided the only readily accessible facilities
for many communities.[70] Of prime importance, the religious hospitals often
were constructed in rural areas, where the need was greatest; as they are
unable to be fully self-supporting, these rural hospitals are dependent
on government grants and foreign support for their continuance. In Africa,
where overall health services are generally less developed, the mission
hospitals are particularly significant: in Malawi they provide 2,027
hospital beds out of a total of 8,074; in Kenya, 2,207 out of 10,368; and
in Ghana, 1,622 out of 7,037.[71]

e) Industrial and agricultural enterprise services

In many countries the largest employers have established some medical
facilities for the care of their workers. The Ivory Coast, for example,
requires an employer with more than 20 employees to make a nurse permanently available, and an employer with more than 100, to provide a first-
aid post and a dispensary.[72] In Tanzania, enterprises employing more than
100 workers must provide regular medical care, and in Cameroon any plantation having more than 1,000 workers must appoint a full-time doctor. "In
practice, however, although the situation may be satisfactory in the larger
undertakings, it is very difficult to ensure that the small and medium-
sized plantations comply with these standards."[73] Nonetheless a substantial portion of privately owned hospitals may belong to industrial and
agricultural enterprises: in Peru 42% of private-sector hospital beds
are in this category.[74] Their coverage is limited, of course, to employees, and eligibility is retained only as long as they continue to
work.

f) Private practitioners

Private practitioners usually engage in a fee-for-service practice
and hence cater to the upper-income groups, although some doctors also
offer limited services to poor patients without charge. In general, the
forces of effective demand—coupled, of course, with prestige and other
benefits—attract the private practitioner to the larger cities: in Turkey over two-thirds of full-time private physicians are located in Istanbul
and eight other large cities.[75] The rural areas are generally avoided.
The proportion of physicians in private practice varies widely from country

to country; moreover physicians in public service often augment their incomes through private practice. Oscar Gish has emphasized the importance of the private medical sector in determining utilization of public facilities:

> Where the private sector is dominant,...the public sector
> becomes more an instrument of private medicine than anything
> else. The misdirection of public sector hospital beds,
> services and drugs toward private patients is a commmonplace
> in all the countries of the Indian sub-continent. However,
> it is where the private sector is most dominant that these
> phenomena are most common; it is not unusual in such countries
> for the resources of publicly owned hospitals to be very
> substantially at the disposal of the senior hospital doctors'
> private patients.[76]

g) Indigenous health practitioners

In most rural areas, indigenous health practitioners outnumber modern health personnel to a considerable extent and are the primary source of health care. While the quality of these practitioners undoubtedly varies considerably, not all are ineffective. Thus in China and India, there are "many traditional doctors who practice an empirical medicine and who are certainly not sorcerers or magicians; the Ayurvedic and Chinese arts of healing, for example, are effective against many symptoms and the drugs are very cheap."[77] In addition to traditional doctors, there are traditional specialists such as midwives, wound dressers, and bone-setters, as well as supernatural healers. While at the present virtually all such personnel (except in China) are outside of organized health delivery systems, there is increased interest in the question of using them to reach rural communities with more effective health care. The former Director of Medical Services of Ghana has observed that "this resource, which has yet to be tapped, is likely (when properly harnessed) to help bring more of health as we understand it to the people of Ghana than can any orthodox medical practitioners."

From this overview it should be apparent that a diversity of health care services exists in low-income countries. It also is evident that the health care offered by government services, by social insurance schemes,

by industrial and agricultural enterprise services, and by private practitioners are largely biased toward the urban-dwelling, employed, and the
more well-to-do.

In that these systems concentrate services in urban areas and generally bypass the lowest income groups, they actually augment income disparities between the participants and nonparticipants. With regard to
social insurance schemes, Robert Savy observes:

> It is even more obvious (in Africa) than in Latin America
> that the benefit of social security is enjoyed by the
> privileged few. A minority of workers, in industry and
> occasionally in agriculture, are lucky enough to receive
> a regular income far higher than that of the African
> peasant, and social security has assumed responsibility
> for guaranteeing this income against the ordinary contin-
> gencies of life, thereby emphasizing, rather than reduc-
> ing, the disparities between the two groups. It is only
> now that we are beginning to realize that, paradoxically,
> progress in the social security field may be an obstacle
> to the achievement of greater social justice in the devel-
> oping countries, and the implications will have to be
> clearly understood before adequate policies to eliminate
> the danger can be framed.[78]

2. Patterns of health facility development

Inasmuch as health priorities in low-income countries have been patterned after those in industrialized countries, it is no surprise that
much emphasis and expenditure has gone into the construction and operation
of hospitals in preference to health centers, whether in the private or
public sector. In evaluating this trend, a few salient points are worth
considering:

(i) Hospitals are best suited to high population densities. In
the rapidly expanding capital cities, there may be advantages in concentrating and centralizing limited resources in one or a few multistoried
buildings. Yet in rural areas where the population is widely dispersed
and transportation facilities poor, the net effect of concentrating resources is to isolate them, making health care unavailable to the majority.

(ii) <u>The catchment area of any health facility is limited</u>. In rural areas, distance from a health facility is a major determinant of utilization. In Kenya it was found that 75% of admissions to hospitals and 95% of outpatients come from within a 25-mile radius.[79] Two surveys in Tanzania revealed that about half of rural health center outpatients came from within 7 or 8 kilometers and a full 80% from within 15 kilometers. Moreover, when hospitals or health centers are located in cities or towns, a very large proportion of admissions and outpatients will come from that city or town.

(iii) <u>The cost of hospital construction and operation is very high</u>, <u>relative to utilization</u>. Oscar Gish estimates that for the same volume of expenditure that is required to build and equip a modest 200-bed regional hospital in Tanzania, it would be possible to build 15 fully equipped rural health centers, including staff housing:

With 15 such centers it would be possible to meet most of the curative health care needs of approximately 300,000 to 0.5 million people, and to launch a wide variety of preventive health care activities. In Tanzania today at 15 such centers there are close to 15,000 admissioned and 1 million outpatient visits per annum. At the regional hospital, by contrast, it would be possible to admit about 9,000 inpatients, a great majority of whom—at least potentially—could be treated as well at a health center (15 centers would contain more beds than a regional hospital), and a total of close to 400,000 outpatients, virtually all of whom could be provided for as well at a health center. The running costs for 15 RHCs in Tanzania are virtually the same as for one 200-bed regional hospital.

A consultant hospital, furthermore, might cost twice as much per hospital bed as a regional hospital. It is not unusual for the capital expenditures on a large capital city teaching hospital in Africa to be greater than the entire annual health budget of the country.[80] In Senegal 40% of the annual health budget is allocated to the large teaching hospital in Dakar, while in Guatemala 73% of hospital expenditures are devoted to hospitals in the capital city which represents only 15% of the national population.

(iv) <u>Large city hospitals are more prevalent than smaller rural hospitals</u>. Table 2 indicates that the number of general hospital beds may be as much as ten times the number of rural or local hospital beds, especially in Latin American countries, which have relatively more total hospital facilities than most African or Asian countries. The figures for total beds are somewhat deceptive when compared with government-administered beds, however. Thus in Peru, although 87% of all hospital beds are in the public sector, only 35% are under the Ministry of Health;[81] in Ghana, 23% of all hospital beds are in mission hospitals[82] and another fraction is in hospitals operated by various industrial concerns.[83]

(v) <u>Large hospitals are more suited to the requirements of medical specialists</u>. The larger hospitals are apt to be better equipped, more specialized (either as a whole or in terms of internal divisions), and more teaching/research-oriented. With the growing numbers of highly trained medical specialists, the pressure for costly facilities increases. F. T. Sai, the former Director of Medical Services in Ghana, notes that in his country, doctors as a group "have actively misinformed the political leadership on the importance of hospital specialists and hospital equipment in relation to the total health needs of the people. This kind of misinformation, added to the politician's own desire to be identified overtly in the short term with visible results, has impeded reorientation of the health system.[84]

(vi) <u>Health facility priorities are essentially political decisions</u>. "The major influence on health-service policy in Ghana, up till now, has been political. This is true of all developing countries, and will probably remain true for the next ten or twenty years."[85] Hospitals are highly visible and likely to attract the backing of urban and governmental elites. A rural health center, on the other hand, is less visible and less politically attractive, although much more in accord with the needs of the majority of the population. In low-income countries experiencing socialist transformations, however, the emphasis on rural areas is part of the political platform--be it in China, Cuba, or Tanzania. In Chile, emphasis shifted toward health centers with the election of Salvador Allende's Popular Unidad government but, apparently, reverted to hospital-orientation following the change of government.[86]

Table 2. Number of Hospital Beds in Medical Establishments
(per 10,000 total population)

	All Types	General Hospitals	Local or Rural Hospitals	Medical and Maternity Centers
Chad	12.1[a]	4.1[a]	2.2[a]	2.3[a]
Dahomey	9.5[a]	3.9[a]	0.8[a]	4.5[a]
Egypt	17.6[a]	8.3[a]	2.5[a]	0.1[a]
Ghana	10.4	3.0[a]	5.8	0.3[a]
Nigeria	5.2	3.7	0.1[a]	0.5
Senegal	13.5[a]	7.4[a]	2.0[a]	4.1[a]
Tunisia	24.7[a]	15.0[a]	4.3[a]	0.2[a]
Uganda	18.6	11.7	b	5.8
Argentina	55.8	38.3	b	2.2
Cuba	50.0[a]	19.2[a]	1.2[a]	7.8[a]
El Salvador	21.0	11.9	1.0	1.8[a]
Mexico (1966)	19.5	15.1	b	0.6
Panama	32.5	22.2	b	0.9[a]
Peru (1968)	23.9	18.5	1.2	0.3
Venezuela	31.7	16.5	1.5	1.8[a]
Hong Kong	38.9	27.1	0.0[a]	2.3
Indonesia	6.8	5.1	0.6	b
Iran	12.9	6.1	0.2	2.3
Pakistan	6.0	4.3	0.1	0.6
Thailand	10.3	2.0	4.5	0.7[a]
Turkey	20.2	11.8	b	1.1[a]

[a]Figures are for government establishments; otherwise, they indicate the total number in the country.

[b]Not known.

SOURCE: World Health Organization, World Health Statistics 1969 (Geneva: WHO, 1973).

From these considerations it is evident that emphasis on "quality care"--the highly equipped modern hospital--serves to further concentrate health resources in urban areas where they are of limited value to the rural poor. The much discussed referral system, that allows the referral of patients with difficult or demanding health problems to successively higher and more specialized levels of care, has not proven effective in most low-income countries, given the neglect of rural health centers.

3.   Health personnel: supply and distribution

The medical graduate, as presently trained in most low-income countries, is poorly prepared to tackle the pressing health problems of rural areas. If not actually a graduate of a foreign medical program, the young doctor has been schooled in a medical education system patterned after a European model. In particular, the medical student is trained in such subjects as anatomy, physiology, and biochemistry, and accordingly views disease from a biomedical perspective. His public health exposure is minimal. Medicine becomes, for many, a field of scientific and intellectual interest, with higher status accorded to those who specialize and produce original research. In pursuit of these interests, and to obtain further specialty training, many medical doctors travel to Europe or the United States--often not to return. Those who do return are likely to pursue specialty practice, often in specialties largely irrelevant to the poverty-embedded populations of their countries. Thus of 80 Ceylonese doctors who returned to Ceylon from study in Britain, there were only two specializing in nutrition or public health, while ten specialized in anaesthesia, ten in general surgery, ten in obstetrics and gynecology, eight in psychiatry, and six in eye surgery.[87] Many of these persons will insist upon sophisticated hospital facilities to continue in their specialty, while few will be willing to engage in rural work (see table 1).

The extensive training of medical doctors, requiring clinical experience in teaching hospitals, is a costly business for countries with limited budgetary resources. The substantial loss of medical graduates from low-income countries to the wealthier nations can represent a major economic drain. The loss from the Philippines is especially severe but not unique among low-income countries: in 1968, the number of Filipino medical graduates who took the examinations required for full medical registration in the United States (i.e., who planned to practice full time in that country) was equivalent to more than half the output of the Philippine medical schools in the same year.[88]

An educational system which is geared to produce doctors best suited for practice in the industrialized nations is certainly contrary to the health needs of the majority of the population in a low-income country. Hence doctors must be coerced to engage in rural health work: in a number of countries medical graduates face compulsory rural service under ministry of health jurisdiction for one or a few years. In Tunisia new medical graduates are required to spend two years at a rural assignment;[89] in Iran medical graduates are drafted into the rural health corps rather than into regular military service. While such steps certainly help to redistribute health resources to rural areas, they are an inadequate solution, since the doctors almost always return to the cities at the end of the compulsory period.

An approach sometimes advocated is to increase the output of medical graduates so that doctors in the cities will become surplus and will have to seek employment in rural areas. The most basic faults with this notion are (i) that medical graduates may prefer emigration to rural work, given their training and (ii) that the process of filtering out to the country-side may occur so gradually (first large cities, then small cities, towns, large villages, and so on) as to be insignificant relative to the pressing needs of the rural populace; the gains might not even match the rate of population growth. In countries where physicians are particularly scarce, as in many African countries, and which must depend on foreign nationals to provide medical care this argument seems especially out of place; while expansion of highly trained health personnel may be desired for other reasons, it is no solution to the problem of maldistribution. Mere expansion of medical schools in a low-income country is unlikely to have any redistributive benefit to the rural population.

Table 3 compares the ratios of physicians and other health personnel to population in a number of countries. The table reflects both the inadequate number of health personnel and the opposition of physicians to larger numbers of (and greater delegation of responsibility to) auxiliaries.

The alternative strategy is to train a select group of rural persons in some basic health skills and to delegate to them major responsibility for primary care in rural areas. The most massive and successful example of this approach has been implemented in the People's Republic of China,

Table 3. Population per One Member of Professional
Health Personnel Category

	Per Physician	Per Nursing and Midwifery Personnel	Per Medical Assistant
Algeria	7,680	2,460	134,850
Ethiopia	71,800	a	164,040
Ghana	15,200[b]	1,050[b]	46,000
Kenya	12,140	3,140	12,120
Senegal	15,120	2,200	39,790
Tanzania (Tanganyika)	24,680	3,410	53,450
Tunisia	5,780	760[c]	a
Uganda	12,920	1,370	22,720
Zambia	13,580	a	4,450
Brazil	1,950	3,080[d]	a
Chile	2,440[c]	4,330[c]	a
Guatemala	4,860	5,220	a
Haiti	13,210	7,340	a
Peru	1,920	2,580	a
Venezuela	1,100	460	28,120
Bangladesh	7,600[b]	43,160[b]	a
Ceylon	3,690	1,460	9,560[c]
India	5,240	5,650	a
Indonesia (1967)	27,560	5,740[c]	a
Iran	3,330	2,850	293,580
Pakistan	4,020	7,400[c]	a
Thailand	8,410	2,360	330,860
Turkey	2,260	1,240	a

[a]Not known.

[b]Number on register; not all working in the country.

[c]Personnel in government services.

[d]Hospital personnel.

SOURCE: World Health Organization, World Health Statistics 1969 (Geneva: WHO, 1973).

where rural medical services were dramatically expanded beginning with the "Cultural Revolution" in 1965. Rural workers were (and are) trained in sanitation, health education, immunization, first aid, and some aspects of primary care and post-illness follow-up; in the villages they serve as "barefoot doctors," able to deal with the majority of rural health prob- lems.[90] There are now said to be over a million of these rural health workers. This professional approach, when combined with other social and economic benefits to the poor, and in the context of mass participation and effective governmental authority, has led to convincing evidence of improved health. Perhaps most dramatic are the estimates of infant mortal- ity which range from 40 or 50 deaths per 1,000 live births down to 15 and even lower--this in comparison with a reported rate of 150 in Shanghai in 1948.[91]

Without detailed discussion of alternative schemes for the use of auxiliary personnel,[92] a few basic generalizations are possible;

(i) Auxiliaries can be trained much more rapidly and at lower cost than professionals (or, for that matter, for paraprofessionals such as nurses): in Guatemala the estimated training cost (total) for a rural health technician (20 months of training) is $1,920, while training for a registered nurse (3 years) costs $4.320, and for a physician (7 years) $19,150.[93]

(ii) Auxiliaries are also less expensive to employ: in Malaysia auxiliaries cost 75% to 85% less than a doctor per working day.[94]

(iii) Auxiliaries provide primary care and simple treatment for which they have practical training, a much more efficient utilization of resources than employing highly trained physicians for such work. In fact, the bulk of disease in rural areas does not require specialty or advanced medical care. A problem faced in the rural health-corps stations in Iran is that health-corps physicians are excessively overloaded: "The aides are not allowed to screen patients, but the physicians feel that 30% of the complaints they see do not require a physician but could be handled by an auxiliary."[95]

(iv) As auxiliaries are drawn from rural areas for training, the phenomenon of "social distance" between health personnel and patients is substantially reduced. Auxiliaries also are less likely to harbor the expectations and ambitions of the medical graduates, enabling them to accept rural life with equanimity.

(v) A primary difficulty in launching auxiliary-based programs has been the opposition from the medical establishment. In many cases auxiliaries have been assigned to remote and isolated areas but have received virtually no support or further training thereafter. In some countries the licentiate (a category of doctor with a shorter period of training, though more than that of an auxiliary) used to fill the many vacant posts in government rural services but now is being abolished so that the "quality" of medical care may not be diminished.[96] To avoid posing such a threat to the medical establishment and its professional and economic interests, the rural health technician in Guatemala can, by law, only work in rural areas.[97]

In terms of distributional effects, the physician-dominated, urban-oriented health system clearly is skewed toward middle- and upper-income groups and has the overall effect of widening differentials in health care, and in turn, in real income. Auxiliary-based systems, particularly those utilizing local personnel responsible to the community, have the opposite effect by providing services inherently biased toward the poor, who being more in need, will benefit most from them.

4. Country programs

Although brief generalizations can be dangerous and misleading (and run the risk of being quickly outdated), there is some value in examining the directions actually being pursued in a range of low-income countries. First Asia: where the private sector is particularly strong, as in Thailand, Indonesia, and even Iran, the public health sector is generally short of resources and dependent on physicians who engage in part-time practice to supplement their incomes. It is no surprise, then, that in such circumstances public sector physicians are geographically distributed in a fashion similar to that of the private sector. In Turkey, for example, "the symmetry of the geographical distribution of physicians in both sectors is contrary to the general impression that the public sector allocates its roster of physicians differently from the spontaneous market control of the private sector."[98] In both sectors only about 16% were found to practice in towns and rural areas.

Ceylon, on the other hand, is an example of a low-income country with a reasonably effective public sector: the private sector is relatively small, inexpensive to the user, and supportive of the more equitable distribution of resources of the public health sector. Oscar Gish observes that in terms of equity Ceylon has one of the best health care systems in all of Asia:

> To begin with, the rural areas of Ceylon are more accessible, better developed and more attractive than those of India and Pakistan. In addition, the fact of a relatively small private health sector coupled with reasonable public sector expenditures had made it possible for government employment to become sufficiently attractive, particularly in the rural areas, so as to be more appealing to the young medical graduates than the vagaries of private practice.[99]

In black Africa, the recent colonial experience and the overall shortage of modern health personnel have produced a somewhat different picture. Here, the private sector is less developed (although highly skewed) and the public sector seems, at least in some countries, better able to pursue independent priorities. Native-born doctors practice predominantly in the large cities, while rural areas have depended in large part on foreign nationals and immigrants from Europe and Asia. (With recent trends toward Africanization, many of these doctors have emigrated, especially from East Africa.) Meanwhile, an extensive proportion of the population may have no access to health care at all.

A diversity of government policies emerges. In Tunisia, new medical graduates are required to spend two years in rural service, and an attempt has been made (without much success) to prohibit private medical practitioners from settling in the capital.[100] In Ethiopia, most of the rural medical care which does exist is supplied by auxiliaries, as in the commonwealth countries of East Africa (especially Kenya), but these auxiliaries are generally isolated from the medical system as a whole.[101] In Ghana, the government has attempted to provide all health services without substantial charge, although this probably has discriminated in favor of urban residents with easy access to facilities.[102] In Tanzania, the socialist-oriented government has placed high priority on the rapid expansion of rural health services through health center construction and the training of all types of health auxiliaries.[103] Thus, while great

disparities exist between urban and rural populations, several governments
have been making efforts to alleviate them.

Latin America, finally, is in a peculiar position: although the
public sector exerts significant influence in many countries, this influence is fragmented into separate delivery systems which to some extent
are replicative. Ministries of health generally lack substantial authority
over medical care, and the health services often are poorly coordinated
(reform measures have been taken to address this problem in Colombia and
Argentina). The more influential interest group, i.e., the military and
the white-collar employees, are able to corner the best resources: in
Colombia, for example, "the expenditures for social security health coverage (some 30 to 40 percent of government health spending) primarily benefit
employees of government and modern private enterprise, who represent only
about 10 percent of the total population."[104] As elsewhere, the private
sector is highly skewed in distribution, being concentrated in urban areas
and largely catering to upper-income groups.

An exception to this pattern is Cuba. Following the socialist revolution in 1959, a strong, centrally administered national health service
developed which put much emphasis on the rural health system.[105] Of the
more than 200 rural health centers constructed, a majority are in areas
not previously covered by the health system. A program of rural service
for new medical graduates has been initiated, and almost all physicians
are required to devote some time to the health centers and rural areas
in the course of each year. Equally important, the health services have
had the cooperation of mass organizations in public health campaigns.
Although urban-rural differentials continue to exist, they are minor
compared to those of other Latin American countries, or to Cuba prior to
the change of government.

5. Other health measures

While the above overview has been largely confined to health care
services per se, it is important to recall that other measures, while
commanding but a small and perhaps erratic portion of the health budget,
can have significant distributive consequences.

In particular, programs aimed at the control or eradication of
vector-mediated or infectious disease have contributed substantially to
the reduction of mortality rates. The discovery of particular weapons

against disease--first the vaccines, then specific prophylactic drugs, and more recently the residual insecticides--have enabled nationwide efforts which have been universal in target. Unlike health care services, which can be manipulated to benefit the upper-income and urban groups, the mass disease-prevention efforts promote the welfare of rural and low-income strata as well--although, of course, coverage may extend to the more accessible and more influential first. The antimalarial programs in India, for example, have been viewed as a means toward greater equity, given their broad benefit incidence:

> Especially in poor countries with severe resource constraints
> such as India, preventive public health measures, such as
> antimalarial programs, may be one of the cheapest and quickest
> ways of generating widespread improvement in human well-being,
> and especially of extending significant tangible benefits to
> the poorest third or half of the population.[106]

A further beneficial spin-off has been the encouragement of local health service development by these programs: in Latin America early campaigns against yellow fever, hookworm, and leprosy stimulated the development of rural services.[107]

As environmental conditions are closely associated with morbidity and mortality, environmental sanitation and improved water supply may be as vital to health improvement as access to health care. Yet rural areas lag seriously behind the cities: in a Colombian survey, although virtually all urban houses and apartments had inside toilets and water supply, over half of all dwellings in rural areas had no water supply, and three-fourths no toilets (inside or outside).[108]

Health education is a third area in which benefits could be extended to low-income groups: instruction in hygiene and sanitation might be particularly valuable in child-rearing and in combination with the provision of potable water, for example. Yet given the marginal environmental conditions in which the poor live, it is not likely that health education alone could bring about marked changes in morbidity or mortality incidence. As with nutrition education, health education is most appropriate where the family has adequate income to implement the messages received. Mass media health education programs suffer from the same limitation.

Finally, nutritional improvement is crucial to infant and young child health and their ability to cope with disease. Yet, as discussed earlier, nutrition programs to date usually have bypassed those most in need.

E.   Some concluding comments

Nutrition traditionally has been subsumed under the heading of health, and nutrition programs relegated to doctors and clinical nutritionists. Yet with the advent of a broader nutrition perspective, this fledgling policy field has gained a respectability of its own, and today has the audacity to analyze and criticize the health sector from which it emerged.

In both the nutrition and health fields, more careful thought and study must be given to the redistributive potentialities and shortcomings of programs. All too often it has been assumed that additional outlays for health and nutrition reflect governmental concern for those most in nee --the lowest income groups. Yet in countries where there are major disparities both in economic and in political power, there is little assurance that benefits will accrue to the poor.

At the same time, in countries characterized by such political and economic disparities, and where these are taken as given, it probably is unrealistic to expect acceptance of a health system actually skewed toward the poor. Health innovators should be glad to settle for an even distribution of services, which, in terms of redistribution, would be victory indeed.

The problems encountered in attempting to increase benefits to the lowest income and rural groups differ substantially in the two areas of nutrition and health. In the health sector, where maldistribution of facilities and personnel seems to be the overriding constraint, considerabl opposition can be expected from medical professionals--who are largely drawn from and represent the interests of the upper-income, urban elite-- to major attempts at reallocation of resources. The example of Cuba is instructive in this regard. Prior to the revolution in 1959, the public health sector was weak and poorly coordinated, although the quality (by professional standards) of the Havana-based private practitioners was high. With the change of government, however, a strong national health service was created with broader responsibility to the population as a whole; private practice was discouraged; and facility construction and

expenditure was oriented toward rural areas. In the course of three
years, half of the medical doctors emigrated to the United States. They
were quickly replaced, however, and the total number of physicians increased shortly thereafter.[109]

Nutrition programs are at an advantage, in this regard, with less
potent vested-interest groups to tackle. Nonetheless, the political
orientation and power base of the government may limit the extent to which
nutrition programs aimed at the poor are acceptable. After all, with
nutrition problems concentrated among the poor, nutrition programs often
represent a form of income redistribution, sometimes well camouflaged,
sometimes not. The primary need, again, is to evaluate in more detail
the extent to which programs do reach the poorest, and to devise delivery
mechanisms which have a greater redistributive impact. As a corollary
to this, nutrition programs should be integrated with income-generating
efforts for the lowest income groups; unless the family income constraint
is addressed, the benefits of nutrition programs to the poor may be
minimal.

The identification and development of health and nutrition delivery
systems which do reach the poor cannot be considered a substitute for more
basic changes in patterns of economic growth. Instead, the injection of
health and nutrition considerations into development planning should help
refocus such planning on the problems of equity, and stimulate the development of patterns of growth which include as active participants those
who, in the past, have been largely forgotten.

Chapter 10

NOTES

1. Shrii Prabhat R. Sarkar, Problem of the Day (Purulia, India: Ananda Marga Pracaraka Samgha, 1968), p. 3.

2. John Mellor, "Nutrition and Economic Growth," ed., Alan Berg, Nevin Scrimshaw, and David Call, Nutrition, National Development and Planning (MIT Press, 1973), p. 72.

3. Oscar Gish, "Health Planning in Developing Countries," Journal of Development Studies, vol. 6 (July 1970), pp. 67-76.

4. Ruth R. Puffer and Carlos V. Serrano, "Patterns of Mortality in Childhood," Scientific Publication 262 (Pan American Health Organization, 1973), p. 61.

5. Ibid., p. 65.

6. Victor W. Sidel and Ruth Sidel, "The Delivery of Medical Care in China," Scientific American, vol. 230 (April 1974), pp. 19-27.

7. Quoted in Samuel Mencher, "The Problem of Measuring Poverty," ed., Jack Roach and Janet Roach, Poverty (Penguin Books, 1972).

8. Nevin S. Scrimshaw, Carl E. Taylor, and John E. Gordon, "Interactions of Nutrition and Infection," World Health Organization Monograph Series 57 (Geneva: WHO, 1968).

9. J. F. Levinson, "Morinda: An Economic Analysis of Malnutrition Among Young Children in Rural India," Cornell/MIT, International Nutrition Policy Series (MIT, 1974), p. 62.

10. H. Kraut, "Investigations in North East Tanzania (I): Introduction and General Survey," ed., H. Kraut and A. D. Cremer, Investigations into Health and Nutrition in East Africa (Munchen, West Germany: Weltform Verlag 1969), p. 21.

11. Carl E. Taylor, Rahmi Dirican, and Kurt W. Deuschle, Health Manpower Planning in Turkey (The Johns Hopkins Press, 1968), p. 73.

12. Oscar Gish, "Resource Allocation, Equality of Access, and Health," International Journal of Health Services, vol. 3 (August 1973), p. 404.

13. Robert S. Northrup, "Health, Manpower and Organization," ed., Linco C. Chen, Disaster in Bangladesh (New York: Oxford University Press, 1973), p. 97.

14. William A. Reinke, "Analysis and Projection of Physician and Dental Services Utilization and Need in Chile," in process.

15. _____. Factors Affecting Non-Response, p. 11.

16. Annika Bornstein and Joachim Kreysler, "Social Factors Influencing the Attendance in 'Under Fives' Clinics'," Journal of Tropical Pediatrics and Environmental Child Health, vol. 18 (June 1972), pp. 150-57.

17. Anthony C. Colson, "The Differential Use of Medical Resources in Developing Countries," Journal of Health and Social Behavior, vol. 12 (September 1971), p. 227.

18. Charles H. Teller, "Access to Medical Care of Migrants in a Honduran City," Journal of Health and Social Behavior, vol. 14 (September 1973), pp. 214-26.

19. Irwin Press, "Urban Illness: Physicians, Curers and Dual Use in Bogota," Journal of Health and Social Behavior, vol. 10 (September 1969), pp. 209-18.

20. Nevin S. Scrimshaw et al., "Nutrition and Infection Field Study in Guatemalan Villages, 1959-1964. Part V: Disease Incidence Among Preschool Children Under Natural Village Conditions, With Improved Diet and With Medical and Public Health Services," Archives of Environmental Health, vol. 16 (February 1968), pp. 223-34.

21. Reinke, "Analysis and Projection," pp. 8-9.

22. Alan Berg, The Nutrition Factor (The Brookings Institution, 1973), p. 160.

23. Ibid., p. 160.

24. Reported in Davidson R. Gwatkin, Health and Nutrition in India, (report to Ford Foundation, January 1974), p. 40.

25. Ibid., p. 39.

26. Ibid., p. 42.

27. Berg, The Nutrition Factor, p. 170.

28. Ibid.

29. Prodipto Roy and Radha Nath Rath, ed., Evaluation of School Lunch Programme, Orissa (New Delhi: Council for Social Development, 1970), p. 95.

30. Sidney M. Cantor Associates Inc., Tamil Nadu Nutrition Study, vol. II, sec. D., pt. II, A Study of Feeding Programs in Tamil Nadu (Haverford, 1973), p. 19.

31. Ibid., p. 20.

32. T. Gopaldas et al., Rural Ecology of Tribal India in a 'Take Home' Food Delivery System for Preschool Children (paper presented at the 9th International Congress on Nutrition, Mexico City, September 1972), p. 6.

33. Sidney M. Cantor Associates Inc., The Tamil Nadu Nutrition Study, vol. II, sec. C, pt. II, Nutrition Intervention: A Study of Take Home Dry Food As a Distribution System, Exhibits and Tables (Haverford, 1973), tables 13, 25.

34. Data on Chile have been provided by Giorgio Solimano and Peter Hakim, presently associated with the M.I.T. International Nutrition Planning Program and preparing a book analyzing the Chilean nutrition experience.

35. Cantor, Study of Feeding Programs, p. 26.

36. John Mellor, "Nutrition and Economic Growth," p. 73.

37. Jean A. Ritchie, Learning Better Nutrition: A Second Study of Approaches and Techniques (Rome: Food and Agriculture Organization of the United Nations, 1967), p. 75.

38. Joint FAO/WHO Expert Committee on Nutrition, Eighth Report (Rome: Food and Agriculture Organization of the United Nations, 1971), pp. 81-83.

39. Gunvant M. Desai and V. R. Gaikwad, Applied Nutrition Programme. An Evaluation Study (Ahmedabad, India: Centre for Management in Agriculture, Indian Institute of Management, 1971), pp. 21, 32.

40. Research Corporation, A Practical Guide to Combatting Malnutrition in the Preschool Child (Appleton Century Crofts, 1969), p. 4.

41. Desai and Gaikwad, Applied Nutrition Programme, pp. 191-92.

42. Ibid., pp. 189-90.

43. Bornstein and Kreysler, "Social Factors," p. 154.

44. Warren Berggren, personal communication, April 1974.

45. Micheline Beaudry-Darisme and Michael C. Latham, Nutrition Rehabilitation Centers - An Evaluation of Their Performance, report to the Protein Advisory Group of the United Nations, December 1971.

46. International Nutrition Planning Program, M.I.T., Nutrition Program Development in Indonesia, report prepared for the World Health Organization, May 1974.

47. Elizabeth Orr, The Use of Protein-Rich Foods for the Relief of Malnutrition in Developing Countries: An Analysis of Experience (London: Tropical Products Institute, 1972).

48. Barry M. Popkin and Michael C. Latham, "The Limitations and Dangers of Commerciogenic Nutritious Foods," The American Journal of Clinical Nutrition, vol. 26 (September 1973), p. 1018.

49. F. James Levinson, "Food Fortification in Low Income Countries – A New Approach to an Old Standby," American Journal of Public Health, vol. 62 (May 1972), pp. 715-18.

50. John Mellor, "The Functions of Agricultural Prices in Economic Development," Indian Journal of Agricultural Economics, vol. 23, no. 1 (1968), p. 25.

51. David Call and F. James Levinson, "A Systematic Approach to Nutrition Intervention Programs," ed., Alan Berg, Nevin S. Scrimshaw, and David Call, Nutrition, National Development and Planning, p. 181.

52. Ibid., p. 182.

53. Berg, The Nutrition Factor, p. 201.

54. Ibid., p. 217.

55. James E. Austin and F. James Levinson, "Population and Nutrition: A Case for Integration," Milbank Memorial Quarterly (Spring 1974).

56. Fred T. Sai, "Ghana," ed., I. Douglas-Wilson and Gordon McLachlan, Health Service Prospects, An International Survey (Little, Brown & Co., 1973).

57. Oscar Gish, Doctor Migration and World Health, Occasional Papers on Social Administration 43 (London: G. Bell and Sons, 1971), p. 95.

58. Ibid., p. 100.

59. Reinke, "Analysis and Projection"; also, Emanuel de Kadt, "Distribucion de la Salud en Chile," Center for the Study of National Planning, Catholic University of Chile, document no. 29 (Santiago, October 1973).

60. Ministry of Public Health of Colombia and Colombian Association of Medical Schools, Study of Health Manpower and Medical Education in Colombia, presented at International Conference on Health, Manpower and Medical Education, Maracay, Venezuela, June 1967.

61. Teller, "Access to Medical Care of Migrants," p. 224.

62. Dieter K. Zschock, "Health Planning in Latin America," Development Digest, vol. 9 (July 1971).

63. Thomas L. Hall, Health Manpower in Peru (The Johns Hopkins Press, 1969), p. 22.

64. Ibid., p. 23.

65. Ibid., pp. 25-28.

66. Robert Savy, Social Security in Agriculture, International Labour Office (Geneva, 1972), p. 57.

67. Ibid., p. 87.

68. R. V. Rajan, Monograph on the Organization of Medical Care Within the Framework of Social Security in India, International Labour Office (Geneva, 1972), p. 7.

69. Savy, Social Security in Agriculture, p. 131.

70. Hall, Health Manpower in Peru, p. 21.

71. N. R. E. Fendall, "Medical Care in the Developing Countries," ed., John Fry and W. A. J. Farndale, International Medical Care (Wallingford, Pa.: Washington Square East, 1972), pp. 231-32.

72. Savy, Social Security in Agriculture, p. 87.

73. Ibid., p. 87.

74. Hall, Health Manpower in Peru, p. 30.

75. Taylor, Dirican, and Deuschle, Health Manpower Planning, p. 67.

76. Gish, Doctor Migration, pp. 85-86.

77. R. F. Bridgman, "International Trends in Medical Care Organization and Research," ed., Fry and Farndale, International Medical Care, p. 16.

78. Savy, Social Security in Agriculture, p. 110.

79. Fendall, "Medical Care," p. 234.

80. Gish, "Health Planning," p. 68.

81. Hall, Health Manpower in Peru, p. 30.

82. Fendall, "Medical Care," p. 232.

83. Sai, "Ghana," p. 134.

84. Ibid., p. 142.

85. Ibid., p. 149.

86. Vicente Navarro, What Does Chile Mean? An Analysis of Events in the Health Sector Before, During, and After Allende's Administration, paper based on a presentation in the International Health Seminar, Harvard University, January 1974.

87. Gish, Doctor Migration, p. 84.

88. Ibid., p. 93.

89. Ahmed Balma, Monograph on the Organization of Medical Care within the Framework of Social Security in Tunisia, International Labour Office (Geneva, 1968).

90. Victor W. Sidel, "The Barefoot Doctors of the People's Republic of China," The New England Journal of Medicine, vol. 286 (15 June 1972), pp. 1292-1300.

91. Reports containing these figures are referred to in Joe D. Wray, "Health and Nutritional Factors in Early Childhood Development in the People's Republic of China" (Bangkok, Thailand, February 1974).

92. See N. R. E. Fendall, Auxiliaries in Health Care, Programs in Developing Countries (The Johns Hopkins Press, 1972).

93. E. Croft Long and Alberto Viau, "Health Care Extension Using Medical Auxiliaries in Guatemala," The Lancet (26 January 1974), pp. 127-30.

94. Paul C. Chen, "The Medical Auxiliary in Rural Malaysia," The Lancet (5 May 1973), pp. 983-85.

95. Ronaghy and Solter, "Auxiliary Health Worker," p. 427.

96. Gish, Doctor Migration, p. 81.

97. Long and Viau, "Health Care Extension," p. 128.

98. Taylor, Dirican, and Deuschle, Health Manpower Planning in Turkey, p. 66.

99. Gish, Doctor Migration, p. 81.

100. Milton I. Roemer, The Organization of Medical Care Under Social Security, International Labour Office (Geneva, 1969), p. 173.

101. Gish, Doctor Migration, pp. 103-08.

102. Sai, "Ghana," p. 138.

103. Oscar Gish, "Doctor Auxiliaries in Tanzania," The Lancet (1 December 1973), pp. 1251-54.

104. Zschock, "Health Planning in Latin America," p. 84.

105. Vicente Navarro, "Health Services in Cuba - An Initial Appraisal," New England Journal of Medicine, vol. 287 (9 November 1972), pp. 954-59.

106. Edwin A. Cohn, "Assessing the Costs and Benefits of Anti-Malaria Programs: The Indian Experience," American Journal of Public Health, vol. 63 (December 1973), p. 1096.

107. Fendall, "Medical Care," p. 236.

108. Zschock, "Health Planning in Latin America," p. 83.

109. Navarro, "Health Services in Cuba," p. 957.

CHAPTER XI

URBAN LAND POLICY, INCOME DISTRIBUTION AND THE URBAN POOR

Rakesh Mohan

This chapter is an attempt to bring together various aspects of the problem of urban land allocation in less developed countries. It surveys a diverse literature on urban problems and particularly as they relate to the urban poor. In so doing various broad generalizations are made from the available evidence, inadequate though it often is. They are made, partly with the hope that further research will be stimulated to test such generalizations and to offer some theory in an area which is particularly lacking in theory.

A.   Rapid urbanization: a challenge to urban land policy

As a prelude to discussing urban land policy, it is necessary to clarify the role of cities in development and to recognize certain patterns in their growth. The first fact to accept is that the last two decades have seen an explosive growth in the size of cities in almost all LDCs.

NOTE:

I am indebted to the IBRD Urban and Regional Economics Division in the Development Economics Department for providing me with research facilities and access to their documents which contain a wealth of information in an area where information is hard to come by. In particular, I am indebted to Orville F. Grimes, Jr., for making this possible. He also helped greatly in introducing me to various aspects of the literature and in providing detailed comments on the first draft.

I am also grateful to: Professor John P. Lewis, for initiating my interest in the subject; Eleanor Oxman for drawing all the diagrams; Charles Frank and Michael Cohen for comments on the first draft; Marcelo Selowsky, Sudhir Anand, and John Carson for useful discussions; Edwin Mills and Arnold Harberger for ordering my thinking; and Amanda Paiz, Jerri Kavanagh, and Ann DeMarchi for the typing. All views are my own and no agency or individual should therefore be held responsible for them.

Table 1 illustrates this for selected cities in Asia, Africa, and Latin
America. This growth can in large measure be attributed to rural-urban
migration in reaction to poor conditions in the countryside or to expectation of higher incomes in the city. There is, in general, no sign that
the growth of these cities is slowing down, although in some of the
largest it is, perhaps, tapering off. So land policy has to recognize
that one of its primary aims is to provide space and services for a population that is increasing quickly. There has to be an expansion of the
supply of urban land and further crowding. While the supply of <u>land</u> is
obviously inelastic (except for reclamation), the supply of <u>urban</u> land is
not. Conversion of rural land to urban use provides space as does the
release of undeveloped lands in urban areas.

The converse of the above is that city size should be contained by
some means and that urban land policy should be such as to discourage
growth. Indeed, this is the view of many policy makers and the result is
that attempts are made to find measures discouraging the growth of cities.
The growth of cities, however, proceeds unabated and the result of such
attitudes is only an exacerbation of the situation through failure to provide for growth. That the form, nature, and structure of cities in poor
countries is an area neglected in research as well as action is one aspect
of this failure.

Since large cities are here to stay anyway, and their growth cannot be
slowed, the position adopted in this chapter is that urban land policy must
accept these facts and respond accordingly. We hold this position because
we believe that the opposite view (of containing cities) is erroneous (or
dubious at best) in the context of development and income distribution concerns. The containment view is usually based on two beliefs popularly held

(i) That the poor in cities are particularly disadvantaged and that
they would be better off elsewhere, and

(ii) That cities beyond a certain size involve diseconomies of scale
in the provision of services. After examining the available evidence, we
call into question both of these beliefs.

First, it seems that large city per capita incomes are usually about
twice those of rural areas. Table 2 gives urban and rural mean incomes
for various countries for which data are available. Although the sources
are varied (as are the definitions), the differential between urban and

Table 1. Population and Growth Rates of Selected Cities

City	Estimated 1970 Population (in millions)	Growth Rates (% per year)	
		1950–60	1960–70
Africa			
Casablanca	1.5	4.1	4.2
Cairo	5.6	4.1	4.1
Lagos	.8	4.6	6.7
Nairobi	.5	7.4	6.2
Latin America			
Mexico City	3.5	2.4	2.3
Rio de Janeiro	7.2	4.4	4.4
Sao Paulo	8.2	6.4	6.4
Bogota	2.5	7.4	7.3
Lima	2.5	4.8	5.1
Buenos Aires	9.4	5.0	3.0
Santiago	2.6	4.1	3.1
Asia			
Hong Kong	4.1	7.0	2.9
Seoul	4.7	5.2	6.7
Manila	4.1	4.3	4.3
Ankara	1.3	3.4	6.8
Bombay	5.9	2.1	3.2
Delhi	3.1	2.9	3.0

SOURCE: Kingsley Davis, World Urbanization 1950–1970, vol. 1, table E, Institute of International Studies, University of California, Berkeley, 1969.

Table 2. Urban and Rural Mean Incomes in Selected Countries

Country	Type of Population[a]	Urban	Rural	Year
Brazil	Economically active population	3,300 new cruz. (.46)	1,450 new cruz. (.41)	1960
		4,650 new cruz. (.53)	1,650 new cruz. (.43)	1970
Colombia	Income recipients	16,270 pesos (.52)	1,730 pesos (.45)	1970
India	Household	Rs2,700 (.45)	Rs1,360 (.35)	
Malaysia[b]	Household per capita	M$744 (.46)	M$456 (.45)	1970
Philippines[c]	Household	7,785 pesos	3,736 pesos	1971
Thailand	Household	21,600 baht (.43)	8,800 baht (.37)	1970
Tunisia	Per capita	U.S.$160 (.46)	U.S.$75 (.44)	1961
Uganda	Adult male employees	3,120 sh (.38)	1,780 sh (.25)	1970

NOTE: Figures in parentheses are Gini coefficients.

[a]Type of population refers to the different units reported in various studies: Income recipient - Individuals who receive income of any kind. Economically active population - Individuals who are able to work, both employed and unemployed.

[b]Malaysia - Sudhir Anand (1973), p. 40.

[c]Philippines - IBRD Manila Urban Sector Survey, July 1974. Section 2, p. (mimeo).

MAIN SOURCES: Shail Jain and Arthur Tiemann, Size Distribution of Income: Compilation of Data; and IBRD Development Research Center Discussion Paper 4 (August 1973).

rural incomes is clearly very large. We also observe that according to the Gini ratios, inequality is higher in urban areas. Understatement of rural incomes because of nontraded goods and overstatement of urban incomes because of higher prices in cities also increase the observed urban-rural difference. Nonetheless, there is such a large difference in the means that we can say, with some justification, that the average level of well-being is higher in urban areas.

The belief about diseconomies of scale is also not well supported. U.S. evidence[2] indicates that there may be _economies_ of scale for at least part of social overhead cost expenditures; that per capita expenditures for sewage and water decline precipitously for cities over 1 million. For LDCs Alonso[3] and Mera[4] demonstrate that per capita income rises much faster than per capita local government expenditure. Even if social overhead costs do rise for large cities, their productivity rises even faster.

We therefore see that policies aimed at containing city size have, at best, dubious underpinnings. Plans encouraging new towns around an existing city (e.g., Delhi Master Plan, 1961) or completely new towns in the hinterland (e.g., Ciudad Guyana in Venezuela) are examples of policies encouraging urban decentralization. Clearing of slum and squatter areas is another. That such plans often fail is, perhaps, because they go against the pressure of basic economic forces.

For all these reasons our orientation in this chapter is that urban land policy should not be geared to containing city size but should rather be aimed at providing the best structure possible for the growing city. In terms of income distribution, the argument above does pose a dilemma. On the one hand large cities tend to help along economic growth in general, while on the other, regional inequality is increased. The high urban immigration rates are a response to this imbalance and constitute one solution to the problem. Despite their importance, this paper does not consider such problems further and is limited to the effect of urban land policy on the intra-city distribution of income.

B. The redistributive effects of land policy: some simple analytics

1. The problem in perspective

Here we are primarily concerned with issues of urban land policy as they relate to income distribution. We touch mainly on intra-city distribution and neglect inter-regional and other related problems. Questions concerning the measurement of income distribution are not being addressed here. There are two reasons for this neglect. First, such questions are too technical in nature to be merely mentioned. They must be discussed in depth if discussed at all, as has been done in specialized papers at the Research Program in Economic Development conference. Second, the level of analysis in this chapter does not warrant fine calculations of the effects on income distribution. Rough evaluations of the degree of effects only will be made.

We do, however, need to make clear the process by which land policy can affect the distribution of income and be aware of its limitations. While distribution of landownership may be a major determinant of income distribution in rural areas it is not likely to be so in urban areas. Land is primarily a productive resource in agriculture, while it is a heterogeneous commodity in urban areas, as is discussed later. It is a productive resource, i.e., an asset, as well as a consumption good. The determinants of its price are complex and their analysis, correspondingly difficult. The problem is compounded by the fact that demand for urban land is really derived from the demand for housing, recreation, space for manufacturing, commercial and administrative activities, and for assets. It is therefore a demand for various characteristics of the land rather than for land itself as a commodity. The economic theory of land price and rent is, as a consequence, not well developed. The theory we have is mainly derived from experience in Western cities and may therefore not be universal in application.

Urban economists have recognized the difficulty that durability of structures causes in applying competitive equilibrium analysis to urban phenomena, but they have concluded that long-term trends and adjustments can be so analyzed[5] as long as these limitations are kept in mind. The rapid change in LDC cities makes this problem much more serious. The change in land price is particularly fast and appears to be consistently ahead of the general price index in most countries. Segmented markets and extensive public intervention also make market analysis suspect. This, however, must not be overstated. Land markets do work and the resulting price and rent of land provide some indication of its social value. The message here is that the market is not efficient enough to make all proper allocations, yet any public land allocation must observe and obey the signals it has to offer.

2. Spatial settlement patterns in cities

In designing urban land policy which favors the poor we need to know the existing structure of cities. We are particularly interested in finding out patterns of residential location and why people live where they live.

While evidence is scanty, it is generally true in LDCs that both population density and land rents decline with distance from the city center, as is true of most Western cities.[6] As one descends from this level of generalization, significant and systematic differences are found within LDCs and between LDCs and Western cities. First, geographically each continent has significant differences from the others. Latin American, African, and Asian cities can each be classed as a group. Latin America is more urbanized than either Asia or Africa; the cities tend to be large (i.e., many with over 1 million inhabitants) and have high growth rates. Their distinguishing feature is that they are expanding in area faster than in population.[7] African cities tend to be small (few with population over 1 million) but also with high growth rates. They are almost all colonial cities and as such have residential areas highly segregated by income as well as by race. They are also characterized by low population densities except for some cities in West Africa. Asia's cities are very densely populated and are not growing as fast as African or Latin American ones. Land supply is a major problem and land use in these cities is very mixed, i.e., residential, commercial, and industrial activities are often contiguous.

It is now received urban economic theory that the poorest live in the center of cities and richest the farthest out, with various gradations in the middle. Systematic evidence for this statement is very scanty for LDC cities and such a generalization may not be possible. Various maps (Seoul, Bombay, Calcutta, Bogota, Singapore, Hong Kong, Mexico City, and Lima) and written descriptions of these cities coupled with impressionistic observation yield the following patterns:

(i) Income classes are much more integrated spatially in LDC cities. A poor slum is quite likely to be adjacent to a rich neighborhood.

(ii) Residential areas nearest the city center are likely to have high-income residents interspersed with the poor.

(iii) The next area is that of the middle class, usually very densely packed.

(iv) The rich are again the next area in their equivalent of suburb-
anization but still not very far from workplaces.

(v) The farthest out are squatter settlements which house the next
to poorest groups but not the poorest.

(vi) The poorest are interspersed in slums all over or sleep on the
streets, as in Calcutta.

Figure 1 gives a stylized representation. It must be emphasized
that these representations are conjectures based on scanty information.
In an LDC city, the pattern can be represented as the "poor are everywhere."

The rich occupy the areas with the highest amenities--good scenic
areas, locations with good views, and so on.[8] The poor are relegated to
the most inhospitable terrain, such as steep slopes and marshes. This
suggests that amenities are highly valued, and if we are not careful, the
best land will always go to the rich.

We can now begin to analyze how urban land policy affects income
distribution. Urban land policy may be defined as those public decisions
(usually governmental) whose effects influence the allocation of urban land
between different uses and among different people. We will first look at
land as an asset and then as a consumption good--a classification not
strictly justified since land can also be regarded as a productive factor,
say, in the production of housing. Such use here is regarded as a characteristic of shelter and therefore a consumption good. The distinction is
made because the demand for land as an asset is in some sense pure demand:
the one demanding land is not per se interested in the particular characteristics of the land but only its value. The demand for land as a consumption good is, on the other hand, a demand for its characteristics
summed largely in the word "location."

3.   Land as an asset

In the absence of well-developed capital markets, land is seen as
an important asset in LDCs and is often a major component of people's
portfolios. As ownership of land, however, is limited to a relatively
small percentage of the population, so is its distribution clearly more
unequal than that of income. Thus any policy which reduces the concentration of ownership clearly improves income distribution, e.g., a policy
which removes market imperfections which make access to land markets
difficult for people with lower incomes. Such policies would include

Figure 1. Residential location by income classes

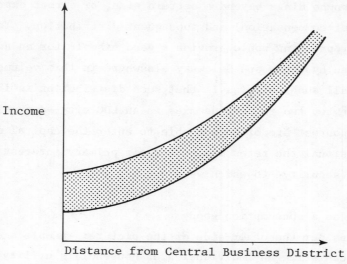

Income

Distance from Central Business District

Figure 1a. Received Western urban pattern

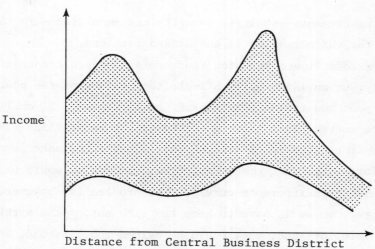

Income

Distance from Central Business District

Figure 1b. Stylized pattern for an LDC city

creation of appropriate financial credit mechanisms for poorer people
or high taxes on holdings beyond a certain size, or direct expropriation
(with or without compensation) and subsequent distribution. The case of
government expropriation would provide a good example for an analysis of
the type offered by Cauas and Selowsky elsewhere in this volume. The
limitation to all such policies is that such distribution is likely to
affect only the top two to five deciles in an LDC city--depending on the
country. The poorest are often not able to enter the capital markets
however concessional the rates may be. Their primary interest is in land
as shelter and security--to which we now turn.

4. Land as a consumption good

Now we consider the other side of the picture: people's consumption
patterns. We can write an individual's or household's utility function as

$$U = U \text{ (shelter, security, amenities; other things).}$$

The three requirements--shelter, security and amenities--are those services
the demand for which results in the demand for land.[9]

Now consider figure 2a which represents standard consumer theory.
Conceptually, urban land policy affects the welfare of the poor only if it
raises the poor household from point P_1 on I_2, to say, P_2 on I_3, a higher
indifference curve. This happens either if the budget line itself moves
up to CD or it rotates to AE (figure 2b). Thus if we make land availability easier, i.e., make the price of land lower, we would be raising
people to higher indifference curves. The problem is, however, not so
simple. First, we would have to keep the rich out of the market, for unless
land is an inferior good, they would be helped too. Second, we have to
look into the preference structures of different groups to be really certain
of what we are doing. There is a reasonable amount of evidence from surveys of squatter populations, slums, and so on,[10] that the preference
structure of the poorest is rather like that indicated in figure 2c.
The diagram shows that _paying_ for land is low on their priority list.
This is not to claim that the poor would not undergo a certain amount of
inconvenience to get better shelter. We _are_ suggesting that they are not
willing to pay for land in monetary terms because other subsistence necessities, mainly food, have higher priority for monetary expenses. Land

Figure 2. The choice between land and other goods

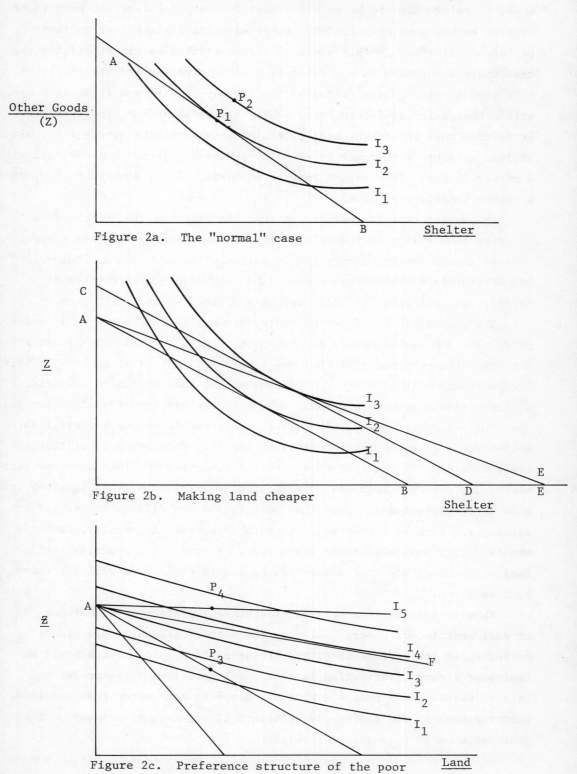

Figure 2a. The "normal" case

Figure 2b. Making land cheaper

Figure 2c. Preference structure of the poor

would therefore have to be made drastically cheap (AF) for the poor to be willing to pay something for it. Other essentials are higher on their preference list and in this stylized representation we are describing the case where a squatter is occupying land without paying for it: he is at P_4. Thus a policy which relocates him, in say, a site and services project with a charge for it is, in fact, making him worse off--P_3 in figure 2c. It is then easy to see why many relocated squatters give up their new piece of land as soon as they get it--usually subleasing it to an individual with a higher income. They return to free squatting, i.e., move back to P_4 at a higher indifference level.

The upshot of this analysis is that the determination of the impact of urban land policy on income distribution necessarily involves a knowledge of the preference structures of different income groups. Turner[11] has hypothesized that people demand land because of three functional priorities: (i) location, (ii) security of tenure, and (iii) amenity.

The poorest (e.g., fresh migrants) are mainly interested in location. Being near job markets saves on transport costs. In their highly uncertain situation the only security they are interested in is job security. Their meager income only allows for food consumption and other bare essentials in a kind of lexicographic ordering. The only amenity they need is space for sleeping. The next group, with a reasonably stable income but still not well-off, is interested in security of tenure. This group is willing to trade location for security of tenure. A temporary job loss or other econom misfortune does not then mean displacement of residence as well. They are also more interested in space than amenity and are willing to pay for it. Finally the richest income group is more interested in amenity, having a stable income and subsistence essentials. Electricity, plumbing, well-designed houses, and recreation then become important and will be demanded by this group.

This is one stylized version of different preference structures of different income groups. Clearly the number of such income groups can be increased to, say, deciles, and the urban land policy which would be improving income distribution is that which operates on the preference of the lowest income groups. What has happened more often than not is that the high-income preference structure of planners is imposed on the poor, of whom we have little knowledge.

5. Urban land markets and the price of land

We do not, in this chapter, wish to deal in any detail with the theory of urban land price determination and of land rents. The essentials are, however, necessary since much of urban land policy is concerned with altering the price of land (implicitly or explicitly). Here we will highlight the features special to LDCs and for income distribution.

Whether land is viewed as an asset or a consumption good its price can be regarded as the discounted sum of the income stream yielded by it over time

$$P_{LO} = \sum_{t=0}^{T} \frac{R_t}{(1 + r_t)t} .$$

where:

P_{LO} is the price at time t (marginal product as an asset, proportional to marginal utility as a consumption good).

R_t is rent at time t (yield of an asset, service of a consumption good) and r is the relevant discount rate.

This formulation is deceptively simple since both R_t and r_t themselves are determined by a host of other variables. The role of expectations in both these variables is the key to understanding the land market. Future rent depends on the attractiveness of the location in the future, which is determined by factors outside the control of the suppliers and demanders. In LDCs there is a considerable amount of uncertainty surrounding both of these expectations, and speculation is the natural result. Here we use the word "speculation" in a neutral manner, merely describing the uncertainty component in the actions of suppliers and demanders.

Figure 3 illustrates various possible time patterns of trends in the price of a piece of urban land. The owner who holds land wants to maximize the present worth of his asset. He would sell it at the time its present worth is maximum. Thus the supply of urban land depends crucially on the expectations of the land suppliers. If the expectations correspond to figure 3a, where the PV lines are constant present value lines and P_t represents the expectations of the land suppliers, the land would appear in the market at time t_1. If the expectations are as in figure 3b it is ambiguous because there may be another point of tangency in the future.

Figure 3. Speculation in the urban land market

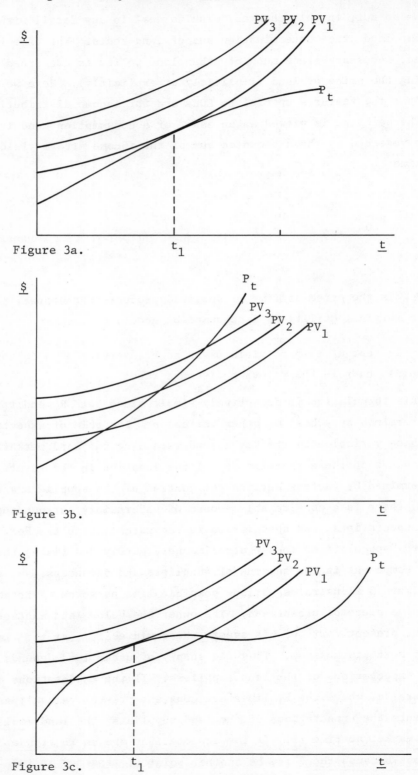

Figure 3a.

Figure 3b.

Figure 3c.

We can expect different people to have different expectations and these vary with each location. Furthermore, the PV lines themselves shift around depending on the pattern of discount rates.

Speculation is generic to the operation of the land market. Most policy documents and pronouncements concerning urban land reveal the popular belief that speculation is rife and is <u>instrumental in raising prices to undesirable levels</u>. Various policy instruments are then prescribed to control such "speculation."

To evaluate these policies we need to examine the validity of this belief. Speculation, viewed neutrally, is merely the maximization of present worth in a situation of uncertainty. For the activity itself to affect the price we would expect that either:

(i) The situation is as in figure 3a and there is a monopoly so that one person's expectations or a small group's expectations dictate constricting supply, to raise the P_t curve; or

(ii) The situation is as in figure 3b so that all sellers' expectations are such that land would be held back from the market.

There is little evidence of the first situation. While landownership <u>is</u> concentrated it is dispersed over a reasonably large number of people so that a monopoly situation does not exist in most LDC cities--<u>unless the monopolist is a public authority</u>, itself. We can expect different people's expectations to be different <u>and</u> their discount rates to be different so that we should observe a range of t_1s (in figure 3a) in the market.

Case (ii) is more realistic and is probably the nub of the problem confronting most land policy. Past trends <u>would</u> predict such a price trend and the landowner <u>is</u> faced with a decision-making problem. Behind the price trend is the expected income stream from the asset. If the asset is held from the market indefinitely there is no income stream, although the asset can be used as collateral to secure bank loans. The landowner must, therefore, allow development at some point or sell it to get any return or to pay back the bank loan. It is in his interest to sell the land <u>only</u> if he perceives the trend to be as in figure 3a. How is speculation then affecting price? In the short run, when sellers want to reap capital gains from price rises, restriction of supply itself feeds back into the price, which increases further as a result. <u>It is this price rise that should be called an undesirable speculative price rise and which needs to be controlled</u>. We have to be clear about the following:

(i) That speculation arises <u>initially</u> because of expected real price increases reflecting rising productivity of the land; and

(ii) That if price rise expectation is not widespread, different people will be releasing land at different times and speculation will be performing the useful function of "land husbandry." Speculation will be holding out of development that land which is needed for later higher density purposes.

The short-run nature of the speculative price effect has to be considered. Much of the demand for urban land is for housing or shelter and such demand is met by the renting of land. Furthermore, we can expect peripheral lands to come into the urban market if current urban land is kept from it. This would have a price-depressing effect, and the uniform price expectations would be belied. Thus the speculative component of the price rise would be curbed by expanding supply in the rental market and in peripheral lands. In the long run, therefore, "undesirable" speculation is likely to be self-corrective.

6.   Increase in land prices and distributional implications

To the extent that the land market works well and supplies and demands adjust in the "normal" way we should not be concerned with the price level. In equilibrium, the price would reflect the land's marginal productivity, present and future, and the land would be in its best use. As mentioned earlier the problem is that, in fact, the urban land market in LDCs is in characteristic disequilibrium and, therefore, considerable uncertainty surrounds its operation. Not only is there uncertainty about the future but information is imperfect about the present. Efficient operation of a market requires quick responses to changing conditions. The supply responses in the land market are sluggish. Some of the land is built up and therefore cannot change use quickly while some is undeveloped and therefore is not amenable to quick urban use. Zoning also hampers the speed of response since use is restricted to certain activities in the zoned areas.[12] On the demand side, where the demand is as a consumption good, it has a high price tag as a proportion to total expenditure. It is this lumpiness that engenders caution and retards market clearance.

Fast-rising price of land is an income distribution issue because:

(i) If income growth is lagging land price growth, then the access to land is getting more and more restricted and we can expect further concentration of wealth; and

(ii) The rise in productivity is not due to any action of the owners while they reap the benefit. The rise is due to general economic trends and specific activity by the government concerning urban services. Part of the price rise is due to expenditure from tax revenues and therefore that part should accrue to public account.

These concerns issue from land seen as an asset. In addition, price rise has distributional implications for consumption-good demanders:

(i) Again, if income growth is lagging land price rise, people either spend higher and higher proportions of their income on housing or live in more and more crowded buildings, or both. Figure 4a illustrates this. With slower income growth, the demand curve rises more slowly than the supply curve. Thus $Q_3 < Q_2 < Q_1$ and $P_3 > P_2 > P_1$, i.e., there is less and less land consumed per capita. The precise results depend on the magnitude of the relevant demand and supply elasticities. Nonetheless, the likely effects will strike different income groups disproportionately. The expenditures of lower income groups on shelter are constrained by expenditures on other essentials, mainly food. Health is affected by lower expenditures on food and by higher overcrowding. Schorr[13] documents instances of such overcrowding that people have to sleep in shifts, so that children only get five hours of sleep a night, with severe effects on health. The important point is that the rich are not similarly affected. They also have to live in more crowded conditions and pay more for housing but there is no effect on nutrition and health.

(ii) Figure 4b illustrates an extension of the above argument. Deriving from figure 2c, say, for the next to lowest income group, members of which consume Q_1 of land with the price line at P_2A, we find that a rise in price to P_2B pushes them to P_2, i.e., reduces their land consumption to zero and to the lower indifference curve I_2. The result is that a higher proportion of people can be expected to be squatters, outside the housing market, with rising land prices.

(iii) A corollary of the above is that the poor look for cheaper land. As noted earlier, rents decline with distance from the central business district and according to the quality of amenities. The result is that with rising land prices the poor locate:

(a) further and further away, and

in marginal locations like steep hill slopes and marches. This accounts for the "urban sprawl" that so disturbs planners and the phenomenon of the poor living on peripheral lands.[14]

Figure 4. The rising price of land

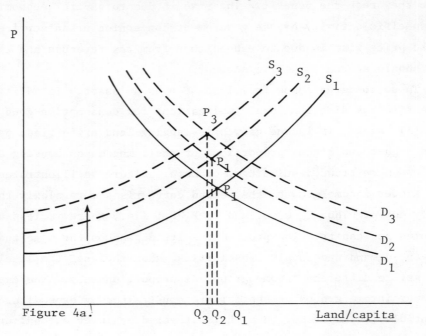

Figure 4a.

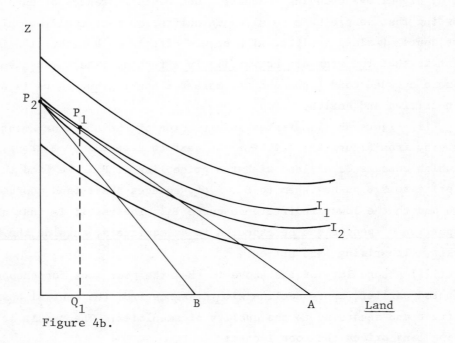

Figure 4b.

The analysis above indicates that, even if we believe that land prices reflect true productivity (however measured), we have reason to be disturbed about its distributional implications and need policy measures to alleviate the problems.

C.   Issues in land use and the urban poor

1.   Land use planning and the market: need for a symbiotic relationship

We need urban land policy to help the market overcome these difficulties and to do those things that the market cannot do. To paraphrase Andrews,[15] we need land policy to establish conditions conducive to land-use cooperation and controlled competition. Unless the whole economy is planned, and prices, in general, are not seen as important information signals about relative scarcity, urban planning must take into account the land market and people's preferences. Most LDCs fall into the category of mixed economies, so this structure can be regarded as a general one. The attempt to do comprehensive urban planning has met with failure in most cities where it has been tried. The reason for this is not difficult to understand. As has been emphasized, the characteristic state of LDC cities is that of flux. Planning must, of necessity, be done by a small group of individuals, whose attempts to predict the future contain a large element of their own sets of preferences which are not shared by everyone else. New political systems are not able to transmit the wants of people very successfully to planners. Planning methods themselves are not adequate for the needs of cities. The process of planning itself takes a finite amount of time during which the base conditions change and the plan becomes somewhat outdated as soon as it comes out. The problem is further complicated as the market responds to an enunciated plan. Services like roads, drainage, sewerage, water supply, and electricity are supplied by a public authority. Their planned provision has a crucial effect on the expected values of land. Speculators, developers, and others quickly alter their activities in response to a declared plan, sometimes constructively and sometimes perversely. These decisions cannot be predicted with any precision, so an exercise in urban planning can easily have unintended results inimical to its objectives. Yet we must have some planning for decisions that cannot be made on a small scale (the analogy is of finding the global optimum rather than a local one): the general form of a city needs to be guided; services need to be provided; recreation areas and parklands have to be protected or provided; long-term investments have to be coordinated (e.g., construction of a major connecting bridge); and a watch has to be kept on the distribution of welfare. The market does not do these things well. We therefore need a dynamic, symbiotic relationship between urban planning and the urban land and housing market. Planning should use private energies which are being offered and not usurp their functions.

2.   Synthesis of policy prescriptions

We can now classify land policy instruments according to their operation through the market or as direct measures allocating land to different groups. Within the group of instruments operating through the market we can distinguish those which are specifically aimed at curbing undesirable speculation, since this is an issue that receives prominence in land policy. In addition to efficient allocation of land we can regard the objective of land policy as the curbing of price rise because of the concerns outlined in the earlier section. Mere control of price is really a control of productivity if we assume that price reflects productivity. Policy which curbs price rise through the market can really be regarded as an exercise which pushes the supply curve. With the constant tendency of the supply curve of land per capita to be pushed upward with the fast growth of urban population, the task of land policy is to push it down. It can do this by expanding supply or by facilitating market clearance activities. We consider each policy instrument in such a context.

a)   Facilitating information exchange

The problem of information is an important one in LDC land markets. We have emphasized uncertainty as the main cause of speculative activities. Although we have been talking about _the_ urban land market, in reality one should talk about _many_ urban land markets. It has been mentioned earlier that the demand for urban land is a derived demand from that for various characteristics. Each location has different characteristics, thus the market is highly segmented. This segmentation, though, is partly caused by a lack of information on alternatives and partly by an uncertainty about future characteristics of various locations. Market clearance is helped along if such information increases.

(i) <u>Planning notification</u>. Since a public authority must provide various services, of which roads, transportation, electricity, and water

are the most important, uncertainty about the future is decreased if plans
for these services are announced considerably in advance. Both buyers
and sellers then have better information on which to base their actions.
As far as the price of land is concerned this is a two-edged instrument.
Recall that

$$P_{LO} = \sum_{t=0}^{T} \frac{R_t}{(1 + r_t)t} \ .$$

Planning notification makes the expectation of R_t more determinate. The
result is that it can <u>decrease</u> or <u>increase</u>, and some owners gain while
others lose. Tracts of land that are expected to increase in value (because
of, say, provision of a new road) may be kept out of the supply because of
higher expectations for some time. In such a case we have to be clear that
the price rise is a reflection of a true value increase. The question to
debate is Who should benefit from this increase? Various tax and other
measures can be devised to deal with that question. Efficiency of land
use is likely to increase assuming that the planning decisions are good.
The distributional implications are ambiguous because there are classes
of both gainers and losers through increased determinacy of R_t and smaller
variance around r_t. These classes also depend on the particular taxation
provisions.

As mentioned earlier, planning is a difficult process because conditions
are always changing. In this case the mere announcement of a plan causes
land prices to change and therefore the assumptions of the plan. In an
LDC context we also have to remember that planning skills are in short
supply and, characteristically, planners are not economists, and even if
they are economists their training does not help in predicting the devious
workings of a land market.

(ii) <u>Informing demanders</u>. The land market is often lopsided since
suppliers are often developers or "professional" landowners while demanders
are merely demanders of consumption goods. The suppliers, therefore, have
better information (an element of monopoly) and can set the price. Two
kinds of measures can be effective here. First, within the market, intermediaries specializing in advising consumers can improve the information
gap. There are, for example, real estate brokers (<u>pokdokpang</u>) in Korea
who perform this function. Second, the government can run such an advisory

service. The government can supplement this by monitoring prices in various
areas and publishing fair prices for each location in a city. Both have
their drawbacks. The private intermediaries could be in collusion with
suppliers since their commissions would normally depend on the price. Price
announcements would be based on some kind of assessment practices, which are
notoriously difficult to standardize. Both Tokyo and Stockholm have variant
of such price announcements and monitoring which are generally regarded as
successful.[16] We should expect beneficial effects on integration of segmented markets and on market clearance. Since demanders are helped and
some monopoly elements are undercut, the distributional effects are positive.

(iii) Land as a hedge against inflation. Land is often held as an
asset for the want of better assets in the face of considerable uncertainty
surrounding inflation. This is important in LDCs and in particular in Latin
America. The problem is again the absence of information about the future,
which leads to speculation. Not much can be done to improve prediction,
but measures can be taken to (i) reduce losses due to inflation, and (ii) to
provide alternative forms of assets.

If monetary indexing is introduced, losses due to inflation are reduced considerably and interest-bearing assets become viable alternatives.
Interest rates can then be real interest rates rather than nominal rates
incorporating uncertainty about inflation. The indirect effect of this
is that demand for land as an asset decreases and therefore more land is
available for development as a consumption good: the demand and supply
curves both tend to shift downward and land price is therefore controlled.
This is really a wider monetary policy issue and we are only concerned with
unlinking the demand for land and the uncertainty about inflation rates.

b) Expanding the supply of land

Measures to expand the supply of land are both direct and indirect.

(i) Municipal land banks. Sweden and the Netherlands provide prime
examples of the device of using municipal land banks to control the price
of land as well as to control the form of a city. If a public authority
owns tracts of land in various parts of a city and in the periphery it can
use them in much the way that buffer food stocks are used. First, such
lands can be bought before development so that they are bought at undeveloped prices. They should, for example, be bought before a planning
notification is issued. The public authority then makes gains from later

price rises. Second, when private owners are holding back land, such lands can be released to have a depressing effect on prices. The expectations could then be changed from the pattern in figure 3b (rising continuously) to figure 3a (logistic trend) or figure 3c (uncertain): in either case, more land would then come on the market and the price rise would be slowed. Such a policy is not easy in an LDC because:

(a) Public funds are sunk as "unproductive" capital until a gain is actually made. They are justified if the capital gain and effect on prices are large enough to be competitive with alternative public investment possibilities.

(b) The administration of such policies needs a considerable amount of skill and lack of corruption. In present LDC conditions both these requirements are difficult to fulfill.

If price of land is kept stable (as it has been until very recently in Sweden and the Netherlands) by such a policy, the access of lower-income groups is clearly improved and the tendency of people to be shut out of the housing market because of land price is arrested. Some method has to be found, however, to restrict access by the rich, since a curb in price helps them as well. One other distributional effect of such policies is usually ignored. Acquiring or buying undeveloped land prior to urban development deprives the original owners of gains that would otherwise occur. It can be argued that these gains should not accrue to them in any case, but the fact is that such lands on the periphery of a city are often owned by relatively poor agriculturists. The gainers (those who eventually get the developed land and urban people in general through the income effect of lower prices) are usually richer than the agriculturists. The results depend on the income levels of the particular owners in each case. Such concerns are important in densely populated Asian cities while not so important in African and Latin American cities.

(ii) Government participation in land market. This is distinguished from the above in the scale of operation. A municipal land bank operation can be seen as a benign monopoly. A public authority or a multiplicity of public agencies can deal in the land market much as any other private developer. The idea would be to make gains from land price increases for public account and to provide competition to private developers. We refer back to figure 3b where a great amount of land is being held back from the market. In such a situation a public agency can reduce the speculation by supplying land that <u>it</u> owns. The idea is to reduce the feedback effect of speculation by initiating a supply of land in conditions of speculative restriction of supply. This can also be done by joint partnerships with private developers. The advantage of a multiplicity of public or joint agencies over one public authority is in the reduction of monopoly effects. When there is one public authority dealing in the land market, private developers and owners watch its actions closely and respond in a volatile fashion, which itself feeds back into the price. The actions of each of many agencies would not be viewed in a similar fashion. Stockholm has even used decoy agents for the public authority to perform the same function, as have some LDCs.

c) Taxation measures to control price

(i) <u>Capital gains taxation</u>. That owners of land should not reap all the benefits from price rise has been alluded to often enough. However, as long as one is operating in a market economy there is no reason to discriminate against land as an asset in comparison with other assets. Landowners bear the risk of holding land for future use. They should then be permitted to gain an adequate return on their investment which, in the case of undeveloped land, is only through capital gains. Thus taxes on capital gains from land should take account of an adequate return and then tax the rest. In that case, the attractiveness of land as an asset compared with other assets will be reduced and the speculative element in price removed.

(ii) <u>Taxation of vacant holdings</u>. Taxation of vacant holdings is considered here because it is another device to control land price. It is often suggested that vacant holdings should be taxed at penal rates so that "speculation" would then be decreased. If this were done, all land would be available at the same time and none left for future use. Such a measure has few equity effects—only distortions of efficiency. The role of speculation in the maintenance of land inventory has already been discussed. As long as there is a sensible capital gains tax, an additional tax on vacant holdings is unnecessary except to encourage selective development at a particular time. At the same time, there should not be any special exemption from the prevailing property taxes.

(iii) <u>Tax on land transfer</u>. Most countries have a registration tax at the point of sale, which is usually based on the sale price. Its effects are limited except in increasing costs of transactions and therefore

slowing down market clearance. Its distributive impact is uncertain unless we assume that those who transact property are relatively rich and
that the tax revenues are used for general welfare. It must be mentioned,
though, that part of the costs of transactions are in bureaucratic delays
which do weigh more heavily on the poor. It does give an incentive to understate transaction prices which then affect all taxes based on property value.
It cannot be seen to have any effect on speculative price rise except a
negative one of slowing down market clearance by discouraging supply.

d)   Direct price controls

(i) Price freezing. Price freezing can only be justified if prices
are seen to be "unduly high" for some reason. Unless this is so, price
freezing is tantamount to restricting productivity. With low frozen prices
the land is then underdeveloped and allocation is clearly inefficient. One
of the natural consequences is the development of a black market so that
official prices remain frozen while actual transaction prices follow the
market. The government loses on all taxes based on property, and again
the cause of equity is not served. If, of course, price is frozen and land
is bought by a government agency for redistribution to the relatively poor,
income distribution is clearly improved. If price is expected to be frozen
for a long time, we should also expect landowners to be supplying more land.
This is really expropriation and should be seen as such. Because of political uncertainties price is seldom expected to be frozen for a very long time.

(ii) Rent controls. Rent controls are merely another form of frozen
prices but are discussed separately since they are so widely practiced.
Almost every country has had some form of rent controls since the end of
World War II, and such controls have been consistently criticized by
economists. It is not always the case that tenants are poorer than landlords. If we are really interested in subsidizing the poor at the expense
of capital owners, why should landlords be singled out? Old settlers are
protected at the cost of recent migrants, the young and mobile tenants.
Maintenance of old buildings is discouraged, thereby causing unnecessary
depletion of housing stock. In terms of economic efficiency it is inefficient because it is a tied subsidy; the tenant might wish to use the
subsidy for other purposes were he given the choice. The analysis in
early sections suggests that the really poor do not value housing very
highly anyway.

The deterioration of central cities, e.g., Mexico City, has been caused by rent controls to a large extent.[16] Indeed, one is hard pressed to find a good word for rent controls anywhere except from those who occupy such properties. It is a genuine puzzle that they have persisted for more than 25 years in the face of such widespread condemnation.

One other deleterious effect on the distribution of income is that property taxes suffer because of rent controls. Assuming that tax expenditures on urban services benefit everyone and that properties are only owned by the higher-income groups (which is largely true), income distribution is clearly worsened. In the case of Mexico City, Jane Cowan Brown[17] does suggest that the relatively poor live in the rent controlled areas and that they have benefited. The resulting distortions in land use are difficult to weigh against these beneficial effects.

All of the preceding discussions has been concerned with land policies attempting to keep the price of land down. It can be summarized by the following:

(i) "Artificially" controlling the price of land (as of any other commodity) is a short-run policy with short-run distributional effects but long-run allocational effects.

(ii) Supply-expanding policies "naturally" control the price and are therefore preferred. Allocation of land is not distorted while distributional effects, if any, are long term through the distribution of wealth.

(iii) If the rising trend of land price _is_ arrested, distribution is improved because the access of lower income groups to the market is improved. This effect is greater if higher-income groups are somehow restricted from the market.

(iv) We recall the distinction of land as an asset and as a consumption good. It has to be reemphasized that the really poor are usually more interested in land as a consumption good and, in particular, as a free consumption good. All these price controlling measures then do not affect the lowest group, except in that they keep this group from expanding.

We now discuss land policies that can be regarded as direct or physical measures. They would affect land prices also but that is not their aim.

e) Restrictions on land use

(i) _Zoning_. Conceptually zoning has the effect of expropriating part of the property rights of owners. To that extent the value of zoned land is depressed since the set of possible uses is restricted. That, however, is not the whole story. It has been mentioned earlier that zoning is not very important in LDCs. The reason is that LDC cities characteristically have very mixed land use and therefore attempts to segregate uses do not meet with much success. Not much can be said about the distributional effects of zoning on an a priori basis. What can be said is that where there is zoning it usually goes against the poor. In the United States it has usually been used to "protect property values" by keeping high-income people at low densities. This keeps low-income, often black, people out. Zoning tends to freeze land use and is therefore likely to have harmful effects in the context of fast-changing LDC cities.

(ii) Building codes. Urban planners and local administrators often recommend building codes to maintain high standards in housing quality and to "protect" tenants from shoddy houses. The problem is that such codes are usually too high for LDC standards and are derived from preference structures of administrators. The result is that legal residental land use gets restricted to relatively expensive housing, thereby shutting out the poor to extra-legal options.

f)   Restrictions on landownership

(i) Ceilings on land holdings. Imposing a ceiling on land holdings essentially limits the use of land as an asset. The negotiability of land would then be limited since no one would be able to hold more than a certain amount. The distributional effects of such a measure are difficult to work out. People holding more than the ceiling would sell the excess and convert it to other forms of wealth. In static terms we merely expect the composition of portfolios to change while the distribution of wealth remains constant. Since land rises in value over time, the dynamic effects are more problematical. What is clear is that concentration of landownership is reduced and thereby monopoly power in the land market. The access of slightly lower income groups to the land market is made easier. If these income groups get a higher return from land than from other assets previously held, then we expect an improvement in the distribution of wealth. There are, however, other problems. We have noted the function of holding land for inventory purposes. Individuals (usually rich) bear the risk of holding land for future higher land use. Where there are land ceilings, who will perform this function? If the government does it we have to consider the problem of sunk capital and the government then has to bear the risk. Further, there is loss of tax revenue which is also a consideration.

In the case of built-up properties which are over the ceiling, there are severe administrative problems on their subdivision. This is so regardless of whether the ceiling is in physical terms or in value terms. There is the further problem of the ownership of large commercial and industrial properties.

In sum, imposing land ceilings, while possibly theoretically attractive for distributional purposes, poses insuperable practical problems.

(ii) Expropriation of vacant lands. Expropriation of vacant lands is often suggested as a measure to combat speculation in the land market. Expropriation is clearly justified where there is extreme concentration of landownership, causing monopoly power over the market. The distributive effects depend on what is done after expropriation and the terms of expropriation. The price effects of the reduction of monopoly power through expansion of land supply have already been discussed. The expropriating authority will have to exercise a great amount of judgment on which lands to expropriate. To curb uncertainty, reasonably clear guidelines will have to be issued. Indeed, the threat of expropriation could be instrumental in keeping vacant lands to a minimum. The question of use after expropriation is discussed in a later section.

(iii) Nationalization of land. Those who believe (i) that the urban land market does not work at all, and (ii) that land is a special commodity in some sense too valuable to be privately owned, suggest that land should be nationalized. If the economic analysis of nationalization of industry is difficult so is it of land. Cauas and Selowsky suggest avenues of analysis for industry that is owned by local nationals. Their approach has been criticized because industry in LDCs is often owned by foreign nationals. In the case of urban land, their analysis is particularly relevant since most urban land is locally owned. Complication in analysis is caused by the fact that the value of land characteristically rises over time, and copensation formulae are difficult to arrive at. The pricing of nationalized land services is rather more problematical than that of industrial products. Redistributive effects depend on past nationalization policies. If land is acquired with less-than-value compensation and is made available for use by a larger subset of the total population

than the nationalized owners, there are certain to be beneficial
distributive results.

In the absence of a totally controlled economy we have also to consider the effects of land nationalization on other sectors. Investment
might be retarded because of uncertainty concerning possible future
nationalization of other sectors. The unpredictability of city growth and
the difficulties of comprehensive land planning have been emphasized earlier.
The nationalization of land clearly involves detailed comprehensive planning
since the allocation functions of the market have been usurped. Those who
believe that the land market does not work propose nationalization for
precisely this reason. I consider comprehensive land planning to be particularly untenable in a mixed economy but not if the whole economy is planned.[18]

As a compromise between those two poles there is a continuum of
possibilities of the degree of property rights that can be allowed subsequent
to land nationalization. The mechanism of limited time leases gives control
of the leased property to the leasee within constraints imposed by the lease.
These constraints include:

(i) Time of lease--the shorter the operation of the lease, the more
restricted are property rights;

(ii) Restrictions on land use; and

(iii) Restrictions on land transfer.

All these can be of varying degrees but the more flexible the better
for dynamic land use planning. The market can be allowed to optimize
within the constraints imposed by the lease conditions. The public authority is then relieved of making detailed decisions while guiding overall
land use. The device of limited time lease provides a useful way of
preventing the freezing of land use where this is deemed to be harmful.
Capital investment on the land is crucially affected by the length of lease
since the lease has to be at least long enough to make the capital worth
investing. Additionally, the duration of the lease must not be too long
for then its very purpose of introducing flexibility in land use will be
thwarted.

3.   Provision of shelter for the poor

We have emphasized the different preference structures of different
income groups. Policies directed at the consumer therefore have to be
group-specific. Much of the preceding discussion has been concerned with

smoothing out the rough edges of the urban land market, but mostly from the supply side. From the demand side we mainly consider land as a consumption good required for shelter purposes. Demand for land for industrial and commercial purposes is neglected because land policy mainly affects its location and not many general comments can be made in the context of income distribution. It is relevant only from the viewpoint of job accessibility, access to markets, and so on, and that is covered under residential location.

Land demanded for shelter is not a trivial commodity so we expect consumers to be particularly thoughtful in their land consumption decisions. For this reason the revealed preference of different income groups should be deemed as particularly important by policy makers. We can divide land consumers into three operational income groups: the highest who do not need any help from policy makers; the middle-income group, who participate in the land market but have access difficulties; and last, the lowest-income groups who are effectively shut out of the urban land market. The first group can be left to its own devices except that it should be taxed. Here we only consider the second and third groups. The second group only needs marginal help to participate more effectively in the land market. In LDCs the main problem that such groups face is limited access to capital markets as mentioned by Oldman et al.[19] The thrust of land policy for this group is provision of adequate financial institutions to provide mortgages, and so on, and provision of information of the kind suggested in an earlier section.

Here we are mainly concerned with the third group. Most land policies considered until now do not affect this group. The reason for this was illustrated in figure 2c where it was shown that the preference structure of the poor is such that prevailing land prices cannot allow them any expenditure on land. The market produces a corner solution that is being found unacceptable by policy makers. It must be made clear here that the correct solution is an increase in the dispensable income of the poor. This has to be stated even at the risk of sounding trite. When we are trying to raise the income of the poor through urban land policy we are either saying that direct income increments are too difficult to provide or that provision of shelter is particularly important when compared with other things.

People shut out of the land market are generally called squatters although each country has its own descriptive word, e.g., colonias proletarias in Mexico, <u>poblaciones callampas</u> in Chile, <u>villas miseria</u> in Argentina, <u>favelas</u> in Brazil, <u>jhuggis</u> and <u>bastis</u> in India. The exact implications of each term vary according to local circumstances. The order of magnitude of the problem is indicated by the following rough estimates of proportion of squatters to toal population for various cities around the world: Ankara, 45%; Istanbul, 21%; Manila, 20%; Singapore, 15%; Lusaka, 37%; Caracas, 38%; Santiago, 25%; and Lima, 25%. These estimates should only be seen as indicative since they are for different years and are based on different definitions (which sometimes are unclear).

The phenomenon of squatters is usually associated with high migration rates, although it is not clear that they, in fact, are the most recent rural-urban migrants. Their problem has received most attention in Latin America where a vast social science literature has developed on characteristics of squatter populations and settlements. There is, however, little in the economics literature about them.

We seek to increase the income of squatters by providing more land as a consumption good to raise them to higher indifference curves. The analysis of figure 2c has shown that the poorest become worse off if they are moved from the land that they are occupying free to a site where they have to pay for it in monetary terms. This is so even if the new site has superior services. As mentioned by Vernez,[20] the poor are price-oriented while the rich are location-oriented. This is consistent with the analysis offered in section B.4. One further problem in the relocation of the poor is distance from job opportunities. Once again, they cannot afford to pay for transportation but they <u>are</u> willing to walk. There is some indication that people are willing to walk 2 to 3 miles (40 minutes to 1 hour) but not much more.[21] People slightly better off can afford bicycles and can therefore live farther away. Land policy for shelter of the poor has to take such considerations into account to be realistic and to be effective. For the very poorest we may <u>have</u> to provide land at zero money cost or they will find such land anyway. We use Anthony Leeds' terminology[22] to discuss policies aimed specifically at the poor.

a) Producer orientation

Policies which place essential programming, construction, designing, planning, financing, and administration of residence building in the hands of a small number of large enterprises which specialize in such building may be called producer-oriented. Such policies have the following pattern:[2]

(i) Slum or squatter eradication by force;

(ii) Development of high-density housing of high construction quality but low environmental quality on the fringe of the city.

(iii) Relocation of removed slum dwellers and squatters in these new estates at subsidized rates.

The reaction of the relocated people is usually

(i) To disappear between the time of removal and relocation and reappe in some other slum or squatter area or,

(ii) To take possession of the new dwelling and then to sublease it at the earliest opportunity to a member of a higher-income group. They then return to the most convenient location near their previous one.

In the latter reaction, income distribution of the direct kind is the end result and may well be efficient although not intended by the scheme. The reasons for these reactions are summarized by figure 2c but in addition we conjecture

(i) That such housing developments are usually way out on the periph- ery of the city while economic opportunities are not similarly located and a long commute is necessary. It is in the nature of such developments that they are built on the cheapest land available, so this is a logical conse- quence.

(ii) The preference of the poor is for space. Such housing development are usually very cramped--again dictated by economic requirements. LDCs are generally in warm climates. A great part of the lives of the poor is conducted outdoors. It is simply too uncomfortable indoors without some kind of cooling or air circulation, which they cannot afford. Slums and squatter areas are usually low-rise developments, though very tightly packed in. Outdoor life becomes very restricted in the new developments.

In sum, the preference structure of planners is imposed which, even if it is imaginative, imposes uniformity. Housing built in such a manner minimizes the social and cultural meanings and roles of housing, curtails values and interest expression of users, and generally restricts adaptabilit for the varied needs of users.

This critical approach to "producer orientation" must not be regarded as a questioning of the motivation of those who initiate the housing. It is, rather, a logical consequence of this orientation. Large-scale public projects require capital as well as managerial and coordination activities and labor. All of these have to be paid for from public funds, so economies have to be made at all opportunities. The result, however, is that a great amount of money is spent with little increase in utility to those for whom it is intended.

With the magnitudes indicated above it is not surprising that such an orientation can only touch a few of the squatters, given normal governmental budget constraints in an LDC. Indeed, all the evidence[24] points to the fact that public housing goes to lower-middle and upper-lower classes, never to the poorest. Even in Singapore, where public housing expenditure amounted to 43% of the total development plan, the housing did not go to the lowest income groups.[25] The Singapore housing program, basically producer-oriented, does seem to be approaching success otherwise. Only about 40% of the population is not in public housing.

We note, however, that Singapore is a city state where the form of the city is very important and the urban land supply is inelastic, so that detailed planning is necessary. Furthermore, per capita income of Singapore is higher than in most LDCs (about U.S. $900), so that the government budget is more easily able to include a really large-scale program.

b)   Consumer orientation

Following John Turner it is increasingly being accepted that squatter settlements form the most viable solution for providing shelter to the poor. Squatter settlement implies the occupation of land without payment. No higher redistribution can take place as far as urban land is concerned. Figure 5 illustrates this. The act of occupying a site moves the consumer from P_1 (consuming no land) on I_1 to P_2 (consuming L_1) on I_2, a higher indifference curve. He can do better only if he is actually paid to occupy a site (i.e., pay a negative price for the land).

The sequence of the formation of squatter settlements are well established now for Latin America.[26] Squatters are not the most recent migrants, nor the poorest. They are those who have been in the city for some time and have reasonably stable incomes. It is only then that they think of the amenities provided by dwelling units of their own. Settlements are occupied by the very organized invasion which is planned in secret months in advance. Plots are laid out, allocations are made, and legal work is done prior to occupation. Then a slow additive transformation takes place as houses begin to go up with progressive improvement of materials from, say, mats

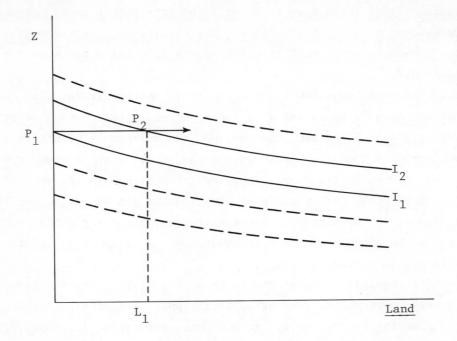

Figure 5. Redistribution through squatter settlements

and tin sheets to brick and reinforced concrete. In parallel, the settlement's urbanistic infrastructure unfolds. Street systems develop by self-
help and self-financing but generally with some collectivity, such as a
group of neighbors. The accent is on providing maximum quality and flexibility with minimum cost.

Owner-builders entirely avoid formal capital markets; consciously
speculate about rising realty value; cut out cost of management and coordination and labor; eliminate cost of transport and storage; build according
to their own task and style of household; and change progressively with
their domestic life cycle. The result is that the living space is substantially cheaper than mass housing (50% to 60% for similar quality?) and
consumers are following their own preferences. This process has been call-
incremental development.[27] Part of the reason for this preference is that
the poor do not like to enter into long-term loan or mortgage contracts[28]
because of greater uncertainty about the future. They prefer to build
incrementally as their income increases. Vernez provides evidence for
Bogota which shows that the higher the income the higher the amount of
contracted labor that goes into house building. That capital markets are

not totally closed to squatters is seen from the fact that they are observed to have all kinds of consumer durables like TV sets, radios, and refrigerators in various Latin American cities. On can surmise that

(i) The squatters are willing to invest in such items since they are easily movable, and

(ii) Traders are willing to provide credit for these goods since they can be taken back readily in the event of default.

In the case of land for shelter, neither of the above is true as both sides are reluctant to enter into loan agreements.

Lest this picture look too rosy it must be pointed out that these settlements are not such as to pass any urban planner's approval. They are ramshackle, very densely populated, dirty, and "badly" laid out. Furthermore, the description above is mainly of Latin American conditions. There is, however, evidence of dynamic self-help by squatters and slum dwellers in Africa as well. Muench[29] describes slums in Ibadan and how they have adapted to the rapidly changing world. Werlin[30] describes the indigenous housing market and self-help by squatters in Nairobi. Indian slum dwellers help themselves according to Clinard.[31] Asian cities have a more difficult problem than those in Africa and Latin America since the extent of public land (preferred by squatters) is limited, whereas it is not as critical in the other two poor continents. One is hard pressed to find such partial solutions for the Asian cities with high populations. The indication from Singapore is that rising income _can_ solve shelter problems.

Having described the pattern of self-help, the relevant question here is about the role of land policy. It is tempting to say that squatter settlements should be legalized readily and governmental help offered as technical assistance and for infrastructure. But the problem is not quite so simple. We want to maximize asset creation by self-help since that creates physical capital as well as human capital through learning-by-doing with beneficial long-term distributional effects. There is some evidence that this is forthcoming individually and collectively most readily when then there is an adversary like a public authority. (The analogy is of a nation in wartime.) That would suggest the maintenance of some tension between the government and squatters. On the other hand, there is conflicting evidence[32] that encouragement from the government activates slum dwellers for self-help projects. So the conclusion is uncertain. One thing that _can_ be stated unambiguously is that government must not substitute for private energies under any circumstances. We can look at this problem from the economist's viewpoint. Refer to figure 5. The price line is horizontal depiciting free land. The question of optimization is begged in the diagram. Somehow L_1 is allotted to the consumer. The maintenance of some tension between the squatters and the authorities is like a price, albeit nonmonetary. We can then conceptually tilt the price line somewhat and consequently optimize and find land allocations. In that sense the maintenance of some tension is good. We can tentatively conclude that the government should legalize squatter settlements and provide technical assistance and other infrastructural help but not too readily

We can summarize the contrast between the consumer and producer orientations by quoting Michael Koll:

> It is waste to concentrate the scarce manpower and capital
> on the planning and constructing of a few housing projects;
> it is waste to allow uncontrolled city growth which leads
> to chaotic city structure; and it is waste not to improve
> by an input of technical assistance the people's own way of
> building houses. It is economical, on the other hand, to
> use the few available planners for the most important tasks--
> the allocation and control of land use. Government can
> never hope to solve the problem of housing by unilateral
> effort; the alternative is to mobilize the savings and
> initiative of the common people and to guide orderly
> city growth.

D. Directions for policy and research

This chapter has emphasized repeatedly that urban land policy has to be made in the presence of great uncertainty about the future. Cities in poor countries are expanding in both area and population at unprecedented rates, so the task of policy making is not simple. It has been suggested that we are more likely to help the urban poor if we accept their presence and try to understand their preferences and wants. We do not know enough about the urban poor. We need to find out how poor the poor really are to design effective land policy. This search should involve both (i) household surveys to determine income and consumption patterns, and (ii) attitudinal surveys to investigate preference structures. It might seem an extravagance to gather such comprehensive information for designing urban land policy but it is justified on two counts. First, such surveys are necessary for understanding rural-urban migration and for understanding the urban economy in general. Second, land policy for the poor simply cannot be evaluated without additional knowledge about the expenditure patterns and preference structures of the poor. In this search for information, well-conducted case studies are particularly valuable. They give us a better appreciation of the behavior patterns of the urban poor and how they interact with the urban economy. When this kind of specific information is available, more comparative information about land markets in a variety of LDCs can be sought.

When we look at land as an asset, we regard it as one of a set of assets that an individual can hold in his portfolio. When treated in this way, it should be taxed as any other asset. Yet, it is common to find that it is treated as a special asset, and a host of special taxes are put on it. For equity purposes, the capture of increased land values to public account is suggested most often. The effectiveness of such measures needs to be examined critically. Specific studies are needed to measure the effect, say, of a betterment tax on land on people's portfolio decisions. That people make windfall gains from land investments is undeniable. What we need to know is the distribution of these gains among different income groups, as well as their effects on the development of the city. An often neglected aspect of discussions in this realm is the relative probabilities of gains and losses in land speculation. If speculators bear a great amount of risk, this must be taken into account in designing taxes. This kind of information can only be gained through detailed studies at the micro level. To obtain good information on speculators' activities and their actual gains and losses, research has to employ enrepreneurial methods.[33] If we know the methods, aspirations, and objectives of developers and speculators, policy could better use their particular talents in conjunction with formal planning methods. This is one aspect of what is meant by a symbiotic relationship between planning and the market. Each can inform the other. Each also acts as a balance to the excesses of the other. The market does this automatically while planning needs to do it explicitly.

An understanding of the dynamics of land price in urban areas is very important for policies designed to help the poor. This can only come with the parallel development of theory as well as detailed information on the workings of land markets. If there is, indeed, a particular effect of speculation on price, this should be determined. The extent to which the government should participate in the urban land market will then be clearer. We also need cost-benefit studies of municipal land bank operations. Would it, for example, be better for the poor if the rich bear the risk of land-holding rather than government? If a land bank effort is instrumental in controlling prices, we need to weigh the benefits of this against, for example, losses in property tax revenues. Does the control of price, for example, really benefit the rich? For the purposes of distribution of income, such benefits and losses should be assigned to different income groups. If distributional weights are to be applied at all, we should know the preference structures of each income group; otherwise we end up with the preferences of the researchers. In the latter case it would be better not to have any weights at all.

We also need to know much more about the effects of public service installations on land values, and the extent of cost recovery possible by the public. By focussing on different income groups, a system of cross-subsidies could be designed in the provision of public services. There is virtually no information on the impacts of water supply and transport improvements on land price in LDCs.

It has been suggested in this chapter that the poorest should be provided shelter free of money cost. This prescription obviously varies with the level of income in the country concerned. In India, for example, where the very poorest have money incomes which are almost zero, such a prescription cannot be questioned if we are really interested in helping them through land policy. On the other hand, the poorest in the relatively richer LDCs may well be able to pay at least partially for their shelter. In such a case, the "free land" prescription should obviously not be taken literally. Whatever the degree of relative poverty, the full cost of land to the poor is never quite zero. Nonpecuniary costs like waiting times and paper work and other transactions costs have to be considered. There may well be a tradeoff between money costs and other costs that a consumer faces. He may trade a saving in walking time for slightly higher money costs or, perhaps, risk of eviction from an illegally occupied plot. Here again we need more specific information on the decision-making patterns of the poor. In land policy, as in all other policies designed to help the poor, the fundamental consideration is that the most direct way to relieve poverty is to increase the incomes of those who have very little. The challenge is to decide among alternative methods of increasing the real income of the poor.

Lastly, we need to mention that even if policies to help the poor are well-known, their implementation may not be possible because of political and administrative constraints. Neither should be neglected relative to the other. But as these constraints change, so should land policy. Above all, urban land planning must incorporate a great amount o flexibility to cope with uncertainty about the future.

Chapter 11

NOTES

1. Such attitudes are found, for example, in Brazil (James A. Gardner, 1973); Argentina (Carlos Tobar, 1972); Morocco (Katherine Marshall Johnson, 1970, 1973); Kenya (Herbert H. Werlin, 1974); Chile (John P. Robin and Frederick Terzo, 1973); and Indian Plan Documents.

2. John M. Carson et al., 1973.

3. W. Alonso (1968c).

4. K. Mera (1973).

5. E.S. Mills (1972).

6. Confirmation for this pattern is found for Hong Kong (D.J. Dwyer, 1971 and Yue-man Yeung, 1973); Nairobi (S.M. Kimani, 1972); Bogota, Lima, Quito, Santiago (P. Amato, 1969, 1970a); Indian cities (John Brush, 1974); Kinshasa (Orville Grimes, 1974).

7. Peter Amato (1970a).

8. For example, Nairobi (personal observation; Herbert H. Werlin, 1974; Oscar Ornati, 1968); Bogota, Lima, Quito, Santiago (P. Amato, 1970b); Kinshasa (Orville Grimes, 1974); Kano (Oscar Ornati, 1968).

9. John Turner (1967, 1968).

10. See John Turner (1967, 1968); William Mangin (1968); Jane Cowan Brown (1972).

11. John Turner (1967, 1968).

12. This is not so important in LDCs since zoning is not very strict and where it exists it is popularly disregarded.

13. Alvin Schorr (1968).

14. James A. Gardner (1973).

15. Richard B. Andrews (1971).

16. O. Oldman et al. (1967).

17. Jane Cowan Brown (1972).

18. When an economy is fully planned, priorities are either imposed or arrived at by the methods other than prices. The same can be done for land.

19. O. Oldman et al. (1967).

20. Georges Vernez (1973).

21. Muench, in Michael Koll, ed. African Urban Development, 1972.

22. Anthony Leeds (1973).

23. This pattern has been distilled from: Lagos (Akin L. Mabogunje, 1968, ch. 10); Nairobi (Herbert H. Werlin, 1974); Rio de Janeiro (James A. Gardner, 1973); Buenos Aires (Carlos Tobar, 1972); Singapore (Yeu-man Yeung, 1973); Hong Kong (D.J. Dwyer, 1971); Delhi (Delhi Development Authority, 1961; Ashish Bose, 1972); Bogota (Roberto Pineda, 1972).

24. For example, Mexico City (Wayne A. Cornelius, 1973); Bogota (Georges Vernez, 1973); Singapore (Yue-man Yeung, 1973).

25. Yue-man Yeung (1973).

26. This section draws from John Turner (1967, 1968); William Mangin (1968); Jane Cowan Brown (1972); David Collier (1971); Ford Foundation Surveys; Anthony Leeds (1973); Sara Michl (1973); Janice E. Perlman (1973); T.F. Ray (1969); Alvin Schorr (1968); Herbert H. Werlin (1974).

27. Georges Vernez (1973).

28. Sara Michl (1973).

29. Meunch, in Michael Koll, ed. African Urban Development, 1972.

30. Herbert H. Werlin (1974).

31. Marshall B. Clinard (1966).

32. Marshall B. Clinard, 1966, on India.

33. Ashish Bose (1972).

SELECTED BIBLIOGRAPHY

There is relatively little economics research work on the form of cities in LDCs and on urban land policy as related to income distribution. So this is a rather wide-ranging bibliography drawn from various disciplines. The abbreviations used are:

Journals

A.E.R.	American Economic Review
A.J.S.	American Journal of Sociology
E.D.C.C.	Economic Development and Cultural Change
E.J.	Economic Journal
E.P.W.	Economic and Political Weekly
J.A.I.P.	Journal of the American Institute of Planners
J.E.L.	Journal of Economic Literature
J.P.E.	Journal of Political Economy
Q.J.E.	Quarterly Journal of Economics
R.E. Stud.	Review of Economic Studies

Others

C.I.D.C.O.	City and Industrial Development Corporation, Bombay
IBRD	International Bank for Reconstruction and Development
I.C.S.S.R.	Indian Council for Social Science Research
IURD	Institute of Urban Research and Development

Abrams, Charles. Man's Struggle for Shelter in an Urbanizing World. Cambridge, Mass.: MIT Press, 1964.

Abu-Lughod, J.L. "Urbanization in Egypt: Present State and Future Prospects." E.D.C.C. (April 1965).

_____. "Cities Blend the Past to Face the Future." African Report (June 1971).

Acosta, Maruja, and Hardoy, Jorge E. "Urbanization Policies in Revolutionary Cuba." In Geisse and Hardoy, eds. Latin American Urban Research, 1972.

Akinola, R.A. "The Industrial Structure of Ibadan." Nigerian Geographical Journal (December 1964).

Alonso, W. Location and Land Use. Cambridge, Mass.: Harvard University Press, 1964.

_____. (1968a) "Equity and its Relation to Efficiency in Urbanization." Working paper 78, University of California, Berkeley, 1968.

_____. (1968b) "The Form of Cities in Developing Countries." Papers and Proceedings of the Regional Science Association (1968).

_____. (1968c) "Urban and Regional Imbalances in Economic Development." E.D.C.C. (October 1968).

_____. "The Economics of Urban Size." Papers and Proceedings of the Regional Science Association 26 (1971).

Alonso, W., and Fajans, M. "Cost of Living and Income by Urban Size." Working paper 128, University of California, 1970.

Amato, Peter. "Population Densities, Land Values and Socioeconomic Class in Bogota, Columbia." Land Economics (February 1969).

_____. (1970a) "A Comparison: Population Densities, Land Values and Socioeconomic Class in Four Latin American Cities." Land Economics (November 1970).

_____. (1970b) "Elitism and Settlement Patterns in the Latin American City." J.A.I.P. (March 1970).

Anand, Sudhir. "Size Distribution of Income in Malaysia." Mimeographed. Washington, D.C.: IBRD, 1973.

Anderson, Nels, ed. Urbanism and Urbanization. Leiden: Brill, 1964.

Andrews, Richard B. Urban Land Economics and Public Policy. London: Collier-Macmillan, 1971.

Archer, R.W. "Urban Planning and the Property Market: Notes for a Course of Lectures on Urban Land Economics Policy." University College, London (n.d.).

Armstrong, W.R., and McGee, T.G. "Revolutionary Change and the Third World City: A Theory of Urban Involution." Civilisations 18, no. 3 (1968), pp. 353-78.

Atkinson, A.B. "Capital Taxes, Redistribution of Wealth and Individual Savings." R.E. Stud. 38 (1971), pp. 209-27.

Baker, P.H. Urbanization and Political Change; The Politics of Lagos, 1917-67. Berkeley, Calif.: University of California Press, 1974.

Balakrishna, K. A Portrait of Bombay's Underworld. Bombay: Manaktala, 1966.

Bannister, Jerry B. Urban Development and Housing the Urban Poor. Mimeographed. New Delhi: Agency for International Development, 1971.

Barr, J.L. "City Size, Land Rent and Supply of Public Goods." Regional and Urban Economics 2 (1972), pp. 67-103.

Baumol, W.J. "Macroeconomics of Unbalanced Growth: The Anatomy of Urban Crisis." A.E.R. (September 1967).

Beckmann, M.J. "City Hierarchies and the Distribution of City Sizes." E.D.C.C. (April 1958).

Berry, B.J.L. "City Size Distributions and Economic Development." E.D.C.C. (July 1961).

Bjeren, Gunilla. Some Theoretical and Methodological Aspects of the Study of African Urbanization. Uppsala: Scandinavian Institute of African Studies, 1971.

Bloomberg, Lawrence, and Abrams, Charles. Report of the U.N. Housing Mission to Kenya. Nairobi, 1965.

Bloomberg, Warner, and Schmandt, Henry, eds. Power, Poverty and Urban Policy. Urban Affairs Annual Review 2. Beverly Hills, Calif.: Sage Publications, 1968.

Bose, Ashish. Urbanization in India: An Inventory of Source Materials. Bombay: Academic Books, 1970.

_____. Studies in India's Urbanization 1901-71. New Delhi: Tata McGraw Hill, 1972.

_____. "Administration of Urban Areas." I.C.S.S.R. (1973).

Breese, G. Urbanization in Newly Developing Countries. Englewood Cliffs: Prentice-Hall, 1966.

Breese, G., ed. The City in Newly Developing Countries. Englewood Cliffs: Prentice-Hall, 1969.

Brewer, Michael. "Local Government Assessment: Its Impact on Land and Water Use." Land Economics (August 1961).

Brown, H.G. "Tax Policy and the Modern City." A.J. of Economics and Sociology 17 (1958).

_____. "Land Value Taxation and the Rights of Property." A.J. of Economics and Sociology 18 (1959).

Brown, Jane Cowan. Patterns of Intra-Urban Settlement in Mexico City: An Examination of the Turner Theory. M.A. dissertation, Cornell University, 1972.

Brunn, Stanley D. "Urbanization in Developing Countries: An International Bibliography." Latin American Studies Center, Michigan State University, 1971.

Brush, John. "Spatial Patterns of Population in Indian Cities." In D.J. Dwyer, ed. The City in the Third World, 1974.

Bryant, R.G.W. Land: Private Property, Public Control. Montreal: Harvest House, 1972.

Burns, Leland S., and Mittelbach, Frank G. "Location--Fourth Determinant of Residential Value." Appraisal Journal (April 1964).

Burroughs, Roy J. "Should Urban Land be Publicly Owned?" Land Economics 42 (February 1966).

Calcutta Metropolitan Planning Organization (CMPO). Basic Development Plan--Calcutta Metropolitan District - 1966-86. Calcutta, 1966.

Carson, John M.; Rivkin, Goldie W.; and Rivkin, Malcolm D. Community Growth and Water Resources Policy. New York: Praeger, 1973.

Cauas, Jorge, and Selowsky, Marcelo. "Potential Distributive Effects of Nationalization Policies: the Economic Aspects." Working paper 178, IBRD, Washington, D.C.; 1974.

Caufriez, Antonio Labadia. "Operacion Sitio: A Housing Solution for Progressive Growth." In Geisse and Hardoy, eds. Latin American Urban Research, 1972.

Chenery, H.B.; Ahluwalia, M.S.; Bell, C.L.G.; Duloy, J.H.; and Jolly, R. Redistribution with Growth. London: Oxford University Press, 1974.

Chinitz, B. City and Suburb. Englewood Cliffs: Prentice-Hall, 1967.

C.I.D.C.O. New Bombay Draft Development Plan. Bombay, 1973.

Clark, C. "The Economic Functions of a City in Relation to its Size." Econometrica 13 (1945).

_____. "Land Taxation: Lessons from International Experience." In P. Hall, ed. Land Values, 1965.

Clawson, Marion. "Urban Sprawl and Speculation in Urban Land." Land Economics (May 1962).

Clawson, Marion; Harris, M.; and Ackerman, J., eds. Land Economics Research. Baltimore: Johns Hopkins Press, 1962.

Clinard, Marshall B. Slums and Community Development: Experiments in Self-Help. New York: Free Press, 1966.

Collier, David. "Squatter Settlement Formation and the Politics of Cooptation in Peru." Paper presented at the Annual Meeting of the American Political Science Association, 1971.

Cornelius, Wayne A. "The Impact of Government Performance on Political Attitudes and Behaviour: A Case of the Urban Poor in Mexico City." In Rabinovitz and Trueblood, eds. Latin American Urban Research, 1973.

Crane, R.I. "Urbanization in India." A.J.S. (March 1961).

Czamanski, Stanislaw. "Effects of Public Investments on Urban Land Values." J.A.I.P. (July 1966).

Davis, Kingsley, and Golden, Hilda H. "Urbanization and the Development of Pre-Industrial Areas." E.D.C.C. (October 1954).

Davis, Otto. "Economic Elements in Municipal Zoning Decisions." Land Economics (November 1963).

Delhi Development Authority (D.D.A.). Delhi Master Plan. Delhi, 1961.

Dwyer, D.J. "The Problem of In-Migration and Squatter Settlement in Asian Cities: Manila and Victoria-Kowloon." Asian Studies 2 (1964).

Dwyer, D.J., ed. Asian Urbanization: A Hong Kong Casebook. Hong Kong: Hong Kong University Press, 1971.

_____. The City in the Third World. London: Harper, 1974.

Edgeworth, F.Y. "Recent Schemes for Rating Urban Land Values." E.J. 1906.

Elias, T.O. Nigerian Land Law and Custom. London: Routledge, 1962.

El-Shakhs, S., and Obudho, R., eds. Urbanization, Theories and Regional Planning in Africa. New York: Praeger, 1974.

Ely, R.J., and Wehrwein, G.J. Land Economics. Madison: University of Wisconsin Press, 1940, chapter 4.

Fisher, E.M. et al. "Land: A Special Income." House and Home (August 1960).

Ford Foundation. International Urbanization Survey. New York, 1973.
   Jamaica: Trowbridge
   Brazil: Gardner
   Colombia, Venezuela, Peru, Chile: Robin and Terzo
   Tropical Africa: Colin Rosser
   Nigeria: Green and Milone
   Kenya: Laurenti, Gerhart

Zambia: Simmance
Morocco: K. Johnson, 1973
Turkey: Keles
India: Rosser
Thailand: Romm
Infrastructure: Koenigsberger
Race: Tinker

Frankenhoff, C.A. "Elements of an Economic Model for Slums in a Developing Economy." E.D.C.C. (October 1967).

Friedmann, John. "Planning as Innovation: The Chilean Case." J.A.I.P.
(July 1966).

_____. Regional Development Policy: A Case Study of Venezuela.
Cambridge, Mass.: MIT Press, 1966.

_____. Urbanization, Planning and National Development. Beverly
Hills, Calif.: Sage Publications, 1973.

Furnbotn, Eirik, and Pejovich, Svetozar. "Property Rights and Economic
Theory: Survey of Literature." J.E.L. 10 (December 1972).

Gaffney, Mason. "Land and Rent in Welfare Economics." In M. Clawson,
et al., eds. Land Economics Research. Baltimore: Johns Hopkins
Press, 1962.

_____. "Land Rent, Taxation and Public Policy." American Journal of
Economics and Sociology (January 1973).

Gamer, Robert. The Politics of Urban Development in Singapore. Ithaca,
N.Y.: Cornell University Press, 1972.

Gardner, James A. Urbanization in Brazil. New York: Ford Foundation,
1973.

Geiger, Theodore, and Geiger, Frances. Tales of Two City States: the
Development Progress of Hong Kong and Singapore. Washington, D.C.:
National Planning Association, 1973.

Geisse, Guillermo, and Hardoy, Jorge E., eds. Latin American Urban
Research, vol. 2. Regional and Urban Development Policies: A Latin
American Perspective. Beverly Hills, Calif.: Sage Publications, 1972.

George, Henry. Progress and Poverty. Book (IV), Ch. 2. New York:
Doubleday, 1914.

Gerhart, John. Urbanization in Kenya: Rural Development and Urban
Growth. New York: Ford Foundation, 1973.

Ghana, Government of, Town and Country Planning Division. "A Plan for
the Town." Accra, 1957.

Golds, J.M. "African Urbanization in Kenya." Journal of African
Administration (January 1961).

Green, Leslie, and Milone, Vincent. Urbanization in Nigeria: A Planning Commentary. New York: Ford Foundation, 1973.

Grimes, Orville. "Land Prices in Kinshasa: An Empirical Overview." Washington, D.C.: IBRD, 1973.

_____. "Urban Land and Public Policy: Social Appropriation of Betterment." Working paper 179, Washington, D.C.: IBRD, 1974.

Gulick, John. "Baghdad: Portrait of a City in Physical and Cultural Change." J.A.I.P. (May 1967).

Gutkind, E.A. International History of City Development. Vols. 1-5. Glencoe, Ill.: Free Press, 1964-70.

Gutkind, Peter C.W. "The Poor in Urban Africa." In Bloomberg and Schmandt, Power, Poverty and Urban Policy, 1968.

Hägerstrand, T. Innovation Diffusion as a Spatial Process. Chicago: University of Chicago Press, 1967.

Hall, Peter. Land Values. London: Sweet, 1965.

_____. The World Cities. London: Weidenfeld, 1966.

Hance, William A. Population, Migration and Urbanization in Africa. New York: Columbia University Press, 1970.

Hanna, J.L., and Hanna, W.J. Urban Dynamics in Black Africa: An Interdisciplinary Approach. Chicago: Aldine, 1971.

Hardoy, Jorge E. "Urbanization Policies and Urban Reform in Latin America." In Geisse and Hardoy, Latin American Urban Research, 1972.

Hauser, Philip, and Schnore, Leo, eds. The Study of Urbanization. New York: Wiley, 1965.

Haworth, Lawrence. "Deprivation and the Good City." In Bloomberg and Schmandt, Power, Poverty and Urban Policy, 1968.

Hayes, H.G. "The Capitalization of the Land Tax." Q.J.E. (1919-20), pp. 373-80.

Heilbrun, James. Real Estate Taxes and Urban Housing. New York: Columbia University Press, 1966.

Heimburger, Peter. The Use of Municipal Land Ownership as an Instrument in Influencing the Structure of Urban Development: Sweden's Experience. Paris: OECD, 1973.

Herbert, John D., and Van Huyck, Alfred, eds. Urban Planning in Developing Countries. New York: Praeger, 1968.

Herrick, Bruce. Urban Migration and Economic Development in Chile. Cambridge, Mass.: MIT Press, 1966.

Hicks, John, and Hicks, Ursula. Report on Finance and Taxation in Jamaica. Kingston: Government Printer, 1955.

Holland, Daniel. "The Taxation of Unimproved Value in Jamaica." Proceedings of National Tax Association, 1965.

Hoover, E.M. The Location of Economic Activity. New York: McGraw, 1963.

Hoselitz, Bert (1955a) "Generative and Parasitic Cities." E.D.C.C. (April 1955).

_____. (1955b) "The City, Factory and Economic Growth." A.E.R. (May 1955).

_____. "Urbanization and Economic Growth in Asia." E.D.C.C. (October 1957).

Howe, C.W. "Lower and Middle Income African Consumer Behaviour in Nairobi." Discussion paper 7, Institute of Development Studies, University of Nairobi, 1965.

Hoyt, Homer. One Hundred Years of Land Values in Chicago. Chicago: University of Chicago Press, 1933.

Hulton, John, ed. Urban Challenge in East Africa. Nairobi, 1972.

Indian Council for Social Science Research (I.C.S.S.R.) A Survey of Research in Public Administration. Vol. 1, New Delhi, 1973.

IBRD. Peru Economic Mission Urban and Regional Aspects. Mimeographed. Washington, D.C., 1972.

_____. Urbanization Sector Working Paper. Washington, D.C., 1972.

Jakobsen, Leo, and Prakash, Ved. Urbanization and National Development. Beverly Hills, Calif.: Sage Publications, 1971.

Jensen, Jens P. Property Taxes in the United States. Chicago: University of Chicago Press, 1931.

Johnson, E.A.J. The Organization of Space in Developing Countries. Cambridge, Mass.: Harvard University Press, 1970.

Johnson, Katherine Marshall. Urban Government for the Prefecture of Casablanca. New York: Praeger, 1970.

_____. Urbanization in Morocco. New York: Ford Foundation, 1973.

Johnson, V., and Barbwe, R. Land Problems and Policies. New York, 1954.

Juppenplatz, Morris. Cities in Transformation: The Urban Squatter Problem in the Developing World. Queensland, Australia: University of Queensland Press, 1970.

Kamerschen, David R. "Further Analysis of Overurbanization." E.D.C.C. (January 1969).

Keare, Douglas H. Urban Land Policy - Supply, Use and Values. Mimeo-
    graphed. Washington, D.C.: IBRD, 1971.

Keiper, Joseph; Kurnow, E.; Clark, Clifford; Gegal, H. Theory and
    Measurement of Rent. Philadelphia: Chilton, 1961.

Keles, Rusen. Urbanization in Turkey. New York: Ford Foundation,
    1973.

Khusro, A.M. "Ceiling in Urban Poverty." Mimeographed. Delhi:
    Institute of Economic Growth, 1973.

Kimani, S.M. "Spatial Structure of Land Values in Nairobi, Kenya."
    Tijdschrift voor Economische en Sociale Geographie (March/April 1972).

Knight, Frank H. "The Fallacies in the Single Tax." The Freeman
    (10 August, 1953), pp. 809-11.

Koenigsberger, Otto H. et al. Infrastructure Problems of the Cities
    of Developing Countries. New York: Ford Foundation, 1973.

Koh, T.T.B. "Rent Control in Singapore." Malaya Law Review 8 (1966),
    pp. 32-45, 176-232.

Koll, Michael, ed. African Urban Development: Four Political Approaches.
    Dusseldorf: Bertelsmann Universitätsverlag, 1972.

Kutty, M.G. "Planning for Municipal Lands." Nagarlok (January-March 1971).

Lampard, Eric E. "The History of Cities in the Economically Advanced
    Areas." E.D.C.C. (January 1955).

Larsson, Yngre. "Building a City and a Metropolis: The Planned
    Development of Stockholm." J.A.I.P. (November 1962).

Laurenti, Luigi. Urbanization in Kenya: Urbanization Trends and
    Prospects. New York: Ford Foundation, 1973.

Leeds, Anthony. "Political, Economic and Social Effects of Producer
    and Consumer Orientation Toward Housing in Brazil and Peru: A
    Systems Analysis." In Rabinovitz and Trueblood, eds. Latin American
    Urban Research, 1973.

Lichfield, Nathaniel. "Economics in Town Planning: A Basis for
    Decision-Making." The Town Planning Review (April 1968).

Lindholm, R. "Land Taxation and Economic Development." Land Economics
    41 (1965), pp. 121-30.

_____. Property Taxation. Madison: University of Wisconsin Press,
    1967.

Little, Kenneth. West African Urbanization. Cambridge University
    Press, 1965.

Lowry, Ira S. Rental Housing in New York City. New York, N.Y.: Rand Institute, 1970.

Mabogunje, Akin L. Urbanization in Nigeria. London: Oxford University Press, 1968.

McBride, G.A.; and Clawson, Marion. "Negotiation and Land Conversion." J.A.I.P. (January 1970).

McGee, T.G. The Urbanization Process: Western Theory and South East Asian Experience. New York: SEADAG Papers, 1969.

_____. The Urbanization Process in the Third World: Explorations in Search of a Theory. London: G. Bell, 1971.

McLoughlin, Peter F.M. "The Sudan's Three Towns: A Demographic and Economic Profile of an African Urban Complex." E.D.C.C. (October 1963, January 1964).

Madhab, Jayanta. "Controlling Urban Land Values." E.P.W. (July 1969).

Maini, K.M. Land Law in East Africa. Nairobi: Oxford University Press, 1967.

Mangin, William. "Poverty and Politics in Cities in Latin America." In Bloomberg and Schmandt, eds. Power, Poverty and Urban Policy, 1968.

Margolis, Julius. "The Variation of Property Tax Rates within a Metropolitan Region." National Tax Journal 9 (1965).

Marriot, Mckim. "The Social Structure and Functions of Cities." E.D.C.C. (October 1954).

Marris, Peter. Family and Social Change in an African City. Chicago: Northwestern University Press, 1962.

Massel, B.F., and Heyer, J. "Household Expenditure in Nairobi: A Statistical Analysis of Consumer Behaviour." E.D.C.C. (January 1969).

Maunder, W.F. Hong Kong Urban Rents and Housing. Hong Kong: University of Hong Kong Press, 1969.

Meek, C.K. Land Law and Construction in the Colonies. London: Frank Cass, 1968.

Meier, R.L. "Developmental Features of Great Cities of Asia II." Working paper 124, College of Environmental Design, University of California, Berkeley, 1970.

Mera, K. "Regional Production Functions and Redistribution Policies: The Case of Japan." Discussion paper 45, Program on Regional and Urban Economics, Harvard University, 1969.

_____. "On the Urban Agglomeration and Economic Efficiency." E.D.C.C. (January 1973).

Michl, Sara. "Urban Squatter Organization as a National Government Tool: The Case of Lima, Peru." In Rabinovitz and Trueblood, Latin American Urban Research, 1973.

Mieszkowski, Peter. "On the Theory of Tax Incidence." J.P.E. 75 (June 1967).

_____. "Tax Incidence Theory: Effects of Taxes on Distribution of Income." J.E.L. (December 1969).

Miller, John, and Gakenheimer, Ralph, eds. Latin American Urban Policies and the Social Sciences. Beverly Hills, Calif., 1971.

Mills, E.S. "The Value of Urban Land." In H.S. Perloff, ed. The Quality of the Urban Environment. Washington, D.C.: Resources for the Future, 1969.

_____. Urban Economics. Glenview, Ill.: Scott Foresman, 1972.

Miner, Horace, ed. The City in Modern Africa. New York: Praeger, 1968.

Mishan, E.J. "Rent as a Measure of Welfare Change." A.E.R. (May 1959).

Mohan, Rakesh. "Indian Thinking and Practice Concerning Urban Property Taxation and Land Policies." Discussion paper 47. Research Program in Economic Development, Princeton University, 1974.

Morcillo, Pedro Pablo. "Urban Reform in Colombia." In Geisse and Hardoy, eds. Latin American Urban Research, 1972.

National Swedish Insitute of Building Research. Municipal Land Policy in Sweden. Document D5. Stockholm, 1970.

Nelson, J.M. "Migrants, Urban Poverty, and Instability in Developing Nations." Working paper 22, Center for International Affairs, Harvard University, 1969.

Neutze, G. Max. The Price of Land and Land Use Planning Policy Instrument in the Urban Land Market. Paris: OECD, 1973.

Nevitt, A.A. Housing, Taxation and Subsidies; A Study of Housing in the United Kingdom. London: Nelson, 1966.

Odman, Ella, and Dahlberg, Gun-Britt. Urbanization in Sweden. Stockholm: Government Publishing House, 1970.

Oldman, O.; Aaron, H.; Bird, R.M.; Kass, S. Financing Urban Development in Mexico City. Cambridge, Mass.: Harvard University Press, 1967.

Ollenu, N.A. ed. Principles of Customary Land Law in Ghana. London: Sweet, 1962.

Ornati, Oscar. "The Spatial Distribution of Urban Poverty." In Bloomberg and Schmandt, eds. Power, Poverty and Urban Policy, 1968.

Oshima, Harry T. "Food Consumption, Nutrition and Economic Development in Asian Countries." E.D.C.C. (July 1967).

_____. "Income Inequality and Economic Growth: the Postwar Experience of Asian Countries." Malayan Economic Review (October 1970).

Passow, Shirley S. "Land Reserves and Teamwork in Planning Stockholm." J.A.I.P. (May 1970).

Perlman, Janice E. "Rio's Favelados and the Myths of Marginality." Working paper 223. Institute of Urban Research and Development, University of California, Berkeley, 1973.

Perloff, H.S., and Wingo, L., eds. Issues in Urban Economics. Baltimore: Resources for the Future, 1968.

Pickard, Jerome P. "Changing Urban Land Uses as Affected by Taxation." Research monograph 6. Washington, D.C.: Urban Land Institute, 1962.

Pineda, Roberto. "The Colombian Instituto de Credito Territorial: Housing for Low Income Families." In Geisse and Hardoy, eds. Latin American Urban Research, 1972.

Pitts, Forest R., ed. "Urban Systems and Economic Development." Oregon, 1962.

Portes, Alejandro. "The Urban Slum in Chile. Types and Correlations." Land Economics (August 1971).

Rabinovitz, Francine F., and Trueblood, Felicity M., eds. Latin American Urban Research, vol. 1. Beverly Hills, Calif.: Sage Publications, 1971.

_____. Latin American Urban Research, vol. 3. National-Local Linkages: the Interrelationship of Urban and National Politics in Latin America. Beverly Hills, Calif.: Sage Publications, 1973.

Rajadhyaksha, N.D. A Study of the Adverse Effects of Rent Control Act on the Assessment of Properties in Bombay. All India Institute of Local Self-Government, Bombay, 1973.

Ramusubramanian, K.A. "Steep Rise in Values of Urban Land." Yojana (26 January 1966).

Rawson, Mary. "Property Taxation and Urban Development." Research monograph 6. Washington, D.C.: Urban Land Institute, 1961.

Ray, T.F. The Politics of the Barrios of Venezuela. Berkeley, Calif.: University of California Press, 1969.

Redfield, Robert, and Singer, Milton B. "The Cultural Role of Cities." E.D.C.C. (October 1954).

Richardson, H.W. Urban Economics. Baltimore: Penguin, 1971.

_____. The Economics of Urban Size. Farnborough: Saxon House, 1973.

Reissman, L. The Urban Process: Cities in Industrial Societies. Glencoe, Ill.: Free Press, 1964.

Robin, John P., and Terzo, Frederick. Urbanization in Colombia. New York: Ford Foundation, 1973.

_____. Urbanization in Venezuela. New York: Ford Foundation, 1973.

_____. Urbanization in Peru. New York: Ford Foundation, 1973.

_____. Urbanization in Chile. New York: Ford Foundation, 1973.

Rodwin, Lloyd. Nations and Cities: A Comparison of Strategies for Urban Growth. Boston: Houghton Mifflin, 1970.

Rojas Calvimontes, Carlos. "Urban Land Reform in Bolivia during the Victor Paz Estenssoro Administration." In Geisse and Hardoy, eds. Latin American Urban Research, 1972.

Romm, Jeff. Urbanization in Thailand. New York: Ford Foundation, 1973.

Rosser, Colin. Urbanization in India. New York: Ford Foundation, 1973.

_____. Urbanization in Tropical Africa: A Demographic Introduction. New York: Ford Foundation, 1973.

Schachar, Arie. "Israel's Development Towns Evaluation of National Urbanization Policy." J.A.I.P. (November 1971).

Schmid. A. Allan. Converting Land from Rural to Urban Uses. Washington, D.C.: Resources for the Future, 1968.

Schorr, Alvin. "Housing the Poor." In Bloomberg and Schmandt, eds. Power, Poverty and Urban Policy, 1968.

Shoup, Donald C. "Advance Land Acquisitions by Local Governments: A Cost Benefit Study." Yale Economic Essays (1969), pp. 147-207.

Sibert, E. G. "Town Planning and Land Values." Town Planning Institute Journal. (January 1952).

Simmance, Alan. Urbanization in Zambia. New York: Ford Foundation, 1973.

Simon, Herbert. "The Incidence of a Tax on Urban Real Property." In R. Musgrave and C. Shoup, Readings in the Economics of Taxation. Homewood, Ill.: Richard D. Irwin, 1959, pp. 416-35.

Sjoberg, Gideon. The Preindustrial City: Past and Present. New York: Free Press, 1960.

Sovani, N.V. "The Urban Social Situation in India." Artha Vijnana (June-September 1961).

_____. "The Analysis of Overurbanization." E.D.C.C. (January 1964).

_____. Urbanization and Urban India. London: Asia Publishing House, 1966

Stokes, Charles J. "A Theory of Slums." Land Economics (August 1962).

Stone, P.A. "Economics of Housing and Urban Development." Journal of Royal Statistical Soc. (1959), pp. 417-60.

Taira, Koji. "Urban Poverty, Ragpickers, and the Ants Villa in Tokyo." E.D.C.C. (January 1969).

Tamilnadu, Government of. Madras Metropolitan Plan. 1971-91. Madras, 1971.

Tinker, Hugh. Race and the Third World City. New York: Ford Foundation, 1973.

Tobar, Carlos. "The Argentine National Plan for Eradicating Villas de Emergencia." In Geisse and Hardoy, eds. Latin American Urban Research, 1972.

Trowbridge, James W. Urbanization in Jamaica. New York: Ford Foundation, 1973.

Turner, John et al. "Dwelling Resources in South America: Conclusions." Architectural Design (August 1963).

_____. "Barriers and Channels for Housing Development in Modernizing Countries." J.A.I.P. (May 1967).

_____. "Uncontrolled Urban Settlement Problems and Policies." U.N. International Social Development Review. New York, 1968.

Turner, Roy. India's Urban Future. Bombay, 1962.

Turvey, R. Economics of Real Property. London: George Allen & Unwin, 1957.

United Nations. Urban Land Use Policies and Land Use Conrol Measures.
Vol. I   Africa
Vol. II   Asia and the Far East
Vol. III   Western Europe
Vol. IV   Latin America
Vol. V   Middle East
Vol. VI   Northern America
Vol. VII   Global Review

University of Michigan. African Urban Notes 1-3 (1966-1968).

Vernez, Georges. "Bogota's Pirate Settlements: An Opportunity for Metropolitan Settlement." Ph.D. dissertation, University of California, Berkeley, 1973.

Vining, Rutledge. "A Description of Certain Spatial Aspects of an Economic System." E.D.C.C. (January 1955).

Werlin, Herbert H. Governing an African City: A Study of Nairobi. New York: Africana Publishing Corporation, 1974.

Williamson, J.G. "Regional Inequality and the Process of National Development: A Description of Patterns." E.D.C.C. (July 1965).

Winger, Alan. "How Important is Distance from the Center of the City as a Determinant of Urban Residential Land Values?" Appraisal Journal (October 1973).

Woodruff, A.M., and Brown, J.R. Land for the Cities of Asia. Hartford, Conn.: Lincoln Institute, 1971.

Yeung, Yue-man. "National Development Policy and Urban Transformation in Singapore." Research paper 149. Department of Geography, University of Chicago, 1973.

APPENDIX I

MEASURING INCOME INEQUALITY

Richard Szal and Sherman Robinson

A. Introduction

Discussions of income distribution have occupied a place in the economic literature for a long period of time.[1] Empirical studies are of more
recent vintage, being a function of the availability of statistical data.
From the time of the landmark study by Pareto, published in 1897, the
availability and accuracy of statistical data on income distribution in
the developed countries have improved continuously. Empirical studies of
the size distribution have proliferated accordingly. The situation with
respect to data in less-developed countries is much worse and there is currently a great deal of work being done to generate and evaluate income distribution data from a number of these countries.

The development of measures reflecting the distribution of income has
progressed in parallel both (i) with the development of data and (ii) with
theorizing about the significance and determinants of the distribution.
Any economic statistics or measures, by definition, embody economic theory
about the characteristics or effects being measured and are useful only in
terms of the theories which underlie them. Historically, new theories have
almost always generated new measures, and distribution theory is no
exception.

This chapter has three purposes. First, there is a brief discussion
of the theoretical framework which has ordered how economists have viewed
and measured the distribution of income. It will be argued that the traditional static economic framework, both positive and normative, within
which economists have studied and measured income distribution is too narrow and restrictive. Second, a survey is made of the existing measures of
income inequality, classifying them and discussing their properties. Finally, some new measures are proposed which reflect a wider, dynamic

approach to the determination and welfare implications of changes in the distribution over time.

B. The traditional framework

Economists have traditionally approached the question of income distribution from two vantage points: normative and positive. Income distribution has always been a major preoccupation of welfare economics. The problem of how to deal with normative judgments about equity in welfare economics has divided the profession. The positive analysis of income distribution has historically been based on marginal productivity theory and comparative statics. This traditional framework, as well as traditional welfare economics, has ordered the way in which economists have approached questions of income inequality and have analyzed the relationships between income distribution and economic development.

1. Normative framework

Traditional welfare economics (i.e., post-Pigou) has been concerned with separating questions of equity from those of efficiency. Under various assumptions about the workings of the economy, one can show that the economic system will reach an equilibrium at a Pareto optimal point; that is, at a position from which the economy cannot move without making someone worse off. If the economy is not at a Pareto optimal point, then it is possible to make a move so that at least one person is made better off and no one is made worse off. Welfare economists assume that moving to a Pareto optimal point from a nonoptimal point always makes society "better off." More efficiency (defined as moving to a Pareto optimal point) is always desirable, so one can treat questions of equity separately.

Of course, the economy may be at equilibrium at an infinite number of Pareto optimal points (corresponding to different distributions of assets), and there is no way to choose among them on the basis of efficiency. Welfare economists have postulated an externally supplied social welfare function which can be used to evaluate all efficient points and so choose that Pareto optimum (and the corresponding income distribution) which maximizes social welfare. There has been a lively debate concerning the conditions under which one can and cannot derive such a social welfare function,[2] but the main point is that the notion of Pareto optimality has been used to separate equity questions and judge them by normative criteria that are

completely independent of criteria of economic efficiency. Since any
normative judgements about income inequality must necessarily involve
making interpersonal comparisons of utility--anathema to post-Robbins welfare economists--it is very convenient to relegate them to some externally
supplied social welfare function.

In the past, the separation of equity and efficiency criteria in welfare judgments has, in practice, resulted in economists simply ignoring
equity. A Pareto optimal point is preferred and one can let distribution
take care of itself. More recently, there have been some attempts to deny
the separability of equity and efficiency criteria. For example, one might
assume that the income distribution affects people directly and so enters
as an argument in their utility function. In this case, the distribution
becomes a pure public good and can no longer be treated separately in a
social welfare function.[3] A current debate revolves around whether or not
one should try to include equity criteria directly in benefit-cost analysis
by giving distributional weights to benefits, depending on who gets them.[4]
One side argues that this practice unnecessarily mixes separable criteria,
causing only confusion. The other side sees it as an attempt to incorporate
knowledge of the social welfare function directly in project analysis--
knowledge which would otherwise be ignored.

In formulating welfare criteria, welfare economists have sought criteria which are "widely acceptable." The value judgment that moving from
an inefficient point to some efficient (Pareto optimal) point always increases social welfare is appealing precisely because it seems reasonable
and widely accepted. It is, however, merely a value judgment and many
might argue that making the rich richer while leaving the poor alone decreases social welfare. When considering equity judgments, wide agreement seems unattainable, and one can understand why welfare economists have
sought to avoid them. Welfare economists notwithstanding, most discussions
of economic policy have necessarily involved questions of income distribution. From such discussions, one can identify some normative judgments
which, if not widely acceptable, are at least often proposed.

(i) More equality of income distribution is preferable to less, given
the initial situation. This is not usually carried so far as to imply that
perfect equality is best but simply that a decrease in inequality is better.
How "equality" is defined and measured is, of course, very important.

(ii) The existence of a group of people living in poverty is, in itself, a bad thing. The major problem inherent in this judgment is the proper definition of "poverty." There seems to be no widely accepted definition that can be applied even within one country, let alone across countries.

(iii) The existence of a group of very rich people--a power elite--is a bad thing. This judgment is clearly more controversial and also depends on how one defines "very rich." While proverty is usually defined in absolute terms with respect to some set of minimun needs, "very rich" is usually defined relatively. The rich might be considered "too rich" if the top decile of the population controlled, say 50 percent of total income instead of the more usual 25 percent to 40 percent.

(iv) The existence of a group of chronically poor or chronically rich people is a bad thing. "Chronic poverty" is defined as a situation in which the same individuals (or, alternatively, their children) remain in poverty period after period. The case where not only the same individuals but also their children remain in poverty--that is, chronic intergenerational poverty--is perhaps the most distasteful to egalitarians. "Chronic wealth" is defined analogously.

Judgment (i) represents the usual normative view of income distribution: any decrease in inequality is a good thing regardless of who gets what from whom. This approach is completely static, and the evaluation of a change in inequality is normally accomplished through comparative statics.

Judgments (ii) and (iii) are also widely proposed. Judgment (ii), the problem of poverty, underlies much of the recent policy discussions both in the developed and less-developed countries. The problem of excessive wealth seems to be of much less concern to established governments and international agencies.

Judgment (iv) reflects the notion that more equality of opportunity is a good thing. Society is better off when people can easily change their position in the distribution over time, regardless of the distribution at any point in time. There are possible tradeoffs, in welfare terms, between the various judgments. One might consider, for example, a highly unequal static distribution as acceptable, or even desirable, if there were great mobility over time within the distribution.

It is only very recently that considerations of social and economic mobility have begun to assume a role in economic models.[5] The existing models, however, are framed in terms of the experience of developed countries and, although relevant, they do not explicitly integrate the analysis of inequality into the framework.

Questions of mobility, judgment (iv), are very difficult to analyze within a completely static framework. When analyzing and evaluating income distribution over time, economists usually use a comparative statics framework and consider the distribution of wealth. It is obvious that if there were a great deal of economic mobility--that is, if individuals readily re-ranked in the distribution of income from period to period--the distribution of average (or permanent) income would be more equal than the distribution of marginal (or one-period) income. In this situation, one need not worry about current-period income inequality.

The comparative statics framework is not adequate, however, for the analysis of long-run chronic poverty or chronic wealth. One would need to define some notion of inter-generational permanent income and its determinants, which seems a bit much. Even in the short and medium run, one is interested in how the distribution changes from period to period, and thus an explicitly dynamic approach is required.

2. Positive framework

Since the time of Smith and Ricardo, the positive analysis of income distribution has concentrated on the determinants of the functional distribution. The usual approach has been to start from the marginal productivity theory of factor renumeration and examine the effect various economic variables have on wages, profits, and rents. There has been continuing controversy regarding the adequacy of the neoclassical approach to the functional distribution, and the whole problem has received a great deal of attention.[6]

On the other hand, the theoretical analysis of the size distribution (the distribution by households or individuals) is much less developed and is clearly inadequate.[7] The earliest models were overly mechanistic. With little or no economic justification, they assumed some stochastic income generation mechanism and derived the frequency function for the overall distribution (usually lognormal or Pareto). This approach has been extended by assuming that earnings depend on ability and that ability (however defined) follows some known distribution. One can then derive the resulting frequency function for the overall distribution--again, lognormal or Pareto.

The human capital theorists have further extended this approach by assuming that earning ability is a function of human capital, an asset for which there is a market and which therefore can be considered within the realm of usual economic analysis. The nagging problem with the latter approach is the virtually unsolvable problem of defining a unit of human capital.

The relative lack of interest in the size distribution by economic theorists in the past is somewhat surprising considering that it is the size distribution rather than the functional distribution that is important to welfare economics. In any case, both approaches have emphasized explaining the distribution of income at a point in time and so have not had a dynamic focus.

Traditionally, the analysis of income distribution (either size or functional) has been restricted to narrowly defined economic variables. The social, cultural, and political institutions are assumed to be exogenous or unchanging. Many would argue that such assumptions are wrong for a developed country. They are, in any event, clearly inadequate for analyzing the determinants of income distribution over time in a developing country. Some examples of non-economic factors that seem inextricably linked to economic variables in the determination of income distribution are the distribution of political power, the role of social and economic institutions (e.g., capitalism versus socialism), and the form of government. If one wishes to widen the analysis to include social and political factors, then one is naturally interested in the distribution of income and wealth by social classes or other politically and socially relevant groups. The traditional approach which concentrates on the distribution either by size or by functional group becomes too narrow and restrictive and needs to be expanded.

3.   Measuring inequality

The measures surveyed in the next section all reflect the traditional positive and normative frameworks and share their shortcomings. All the measures are static in the sense that no account is taken of individual mobility. In section E a dynamic framework is proposed and some measures are based on it. All the measures relate to households or individuals rather than to social classes, regions, or other interesting groupings. In section D there is a discussion of how the measures can be decomposed into between-group and within-group measures.

A majority of the measures are concerned only with relative inequality in the sense that a proportionate change in all incomes does not change the measure. To a neoclassical welfare economist, a relative measure is appealing because it enables one to separate changes in distribution (considerations of equity) from changes in absolute income (considerations of efficiency). Many feel that this separation is illusory and that measures should reflect the absolute level of income since the importance (in some sense) of inequality may depend on income levels.[8] The issues clearly cannot be resolved simply, and it is important to note how the various measures depend on income levels.

Any measure of inequality should embody a sensible notion of "inequality." Perhaps the simplest definition is to state that there is inequality whenever one person has more income than some other person. Given this definition, a reasonable minimum standard to set for any measure of inequality would be that a transfer of income from a poorer person to a richer person should increase the measure. A. K. Sen cites this property as the Pigou-Dalton condition.[9] Since the standard against which inequality is measured is perfect equality, the Pigou-Dalton condition by itself provides no way to judge the validity of comparisons of different degrees of inequality. It is a very limited standard.

If measures are to be comparable across countries or over time, there are some general properties that are desirable for them to have. First, they should be unit free. This criterion is self-evident and is satisfied by almost all the measures surveyed. Second, they should be unaffected by the number of units (people, households, and so one) summarized in the measure. A number of inequality measures are subject to this problem, and many ingenious techniques have been developed to cope with problems of incomplete or badly grouped data. Related literature tends to be both specific and technical and will not be surveyed here. Third, a measure should be bounded. This last property is not as important as the first two but is clearly convenient, especially when one has no benchmark against which to make comparisons.

Recently, there has been much discussion in the literature about the social welfare function, or classes of them, implied by various measures of income inequality. It is clearly very important to understand the properties of different measures so that one can understand how they define "inequality." One can then assess measures in terms of how useful their definition of "inequality" is in making normative equity judgments. However, it seems unfair to criticize a given descriptive measure because it is difficult to determine the analytic form of the social welfare function on which it is implicitly based. Furthermore, for many purposes the welfare implications of a given measure may not be as important as its descriptive properties.

C. Static measures of inequality

Pictorially, the income distribution has usually been presented in two ways. The first is simply to graph the frequency function of the distribution. On the horizontal axis is income in money units and on the vertical axis is the percent frequency of the population with that income. As with all frequency functions, the area under the curve must equal one. A typical income distribution frequency is graphed in figure 1.

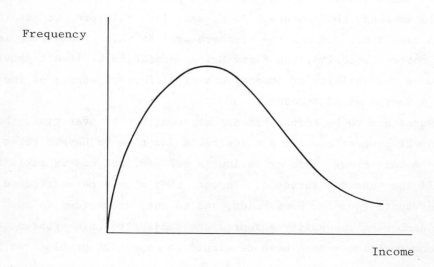

Figure 1

The second common way to represent income distribution data is to graph the Lorenz curve. Assume one had income data for a sample of households. The data are first arranged in ascending order of income and then cumulated. They are then expressed as shares and plotted. The result is a Lorenz curve. A given point indicates what percentage of the total aggregate income of the group (on the vertical axis) is held by a specified percentage of the total population (on the horizontal axis). An example of a Lorenz curve is shown in figure 2.

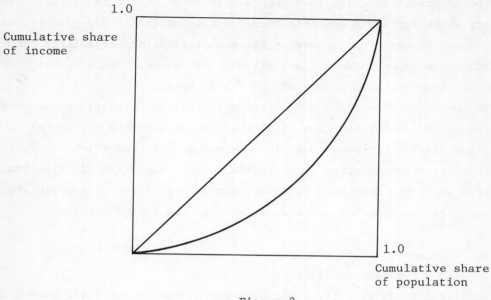

Cumulative share
of income

1.0

1.0

Cumulative share
of population

Figure 2

If everyone had the same income, then the Lorenz curve would be a
straight 45 degree line (the first 10 percent of the population receives
10 percent of aggregate income, and so on). The more unequal is the distribution, the further is the Lorenz curve from the diagonal 45 degree
line.

Almost all of the summary measures of inequality are based either on
figure 1 or figure 2 and attempt to summarize in a single statistic the
information contained in one picture or the other. Considering the extensive literature on inequality measures, a picture is worth thousands and
thousands of words!

The two graphs obviously contain the same information in the sense
that one can be derived from the other. At least one can go from the frequency function to the Lorenz curve by integrating both over people and income. To go the other way requires, in addition, data on income levels.
Intuitively, however, the notion of inequality is more easily defined in
terms of the Lorenz curve. Equality is defined as equal shares of aggregate income accruing to equal shares of the population. In figure 2, any
deviation from the 45 degree line indicates the presence of inequality. In
terms of the frequency function (figure 1), perfect equality implies a de-
generate distribution concentrated at the point of mean income--hardly a
very satisfying diagram.

The frequency function is of special interest if one is concerned with a theory which implies a specific form for the function. For example, as noted above, theories that assume a certain distribution of ability can generate a Pareto or lognormal distribution of income. The parameters of these distributions then become of special interest.

In the discussion below, we divide the measures into: (i) those which describe the frequency function, (ii) those which describe the Lorenz curve, and (iii) other measures. In some cases, the classification is a bit arbitrary since measures which relate to the cumulative distribution (the area under the frequency function) can be considered as descriptive of the frequency function but are also related to the Lorenz curve.

1. Frequency function measures

    a) Pareto α coefficient

According to Pareto, the upper brackets of the income distribution can be described by a frequency function called the Pareto-Levy function. Let Y be a level of income (above the mode) and let X be the proportion of income receivers with income equal to or greater than Y. Then the distribution is given by:

(1) $X = AY^{\alpha}$,

where A is a constant. When plotted on double log paper, the Pareto distribution is linear. The more equal is the distribution of income, the greater is the value of α. Pareto's empirical estimates of α for various countries tended to cluster between 1.5 and 1.7. He felt that he had discovered something akin to Newtonian physics and he built a "magical constant" theory on this clustering. Others have gone so far as to relate social revolutions to certain values of the coefficient. Subsequent research has questioned the stability of the parameter.

    b) Variance of the logs of income

The variance of the logarithms of income has long been used as a measure of income inequality. Letting Y denote income and n the sample size, the log variance is

(2)
$$\text{Var (log Y)} = (1/n) \sum_{i}^{n} (\log Y_i - \overline{\log Y})^2 ,$$

where $\overline{\log Y}$ is the mean of the logarithms of incomes.

This measure is attractive for a number of reasons. First, if one assumes that income is distributed according to the lognormal distribution, the log variance is the maximum likelihood estimate of the variance of the distribution. In the statistical literature, the log variance is defined around the geometric mean (as in the formula above) rather than around the arithmetic mean. This is not always the case in the income distribution literature.

The log variance measure is attractive to welfare theorists because relatively greater weight is given to lower incomes when logs are used. A given amount of money given to an individual with a small income will result in a larger decrease in the measure than an equal subtraction from the income of an individual with a large income. If one assumes a social welfare function which exhibits increasing marginal social welfare from increments of income to each individual, then money given to a poor person increases social welfare more than the same amount of money given to a rich person. Although this is true of other measures (e.g., the Gini concentration coefficient), the degree of greater weight given to the lower incomes is larger with the log variance than it is for such arithmetically calculated measures as the Gini coefficient.

According to the human capital theory of income determination, the log variance is an interesting measure because it can be shown under certain assumptions to be related to the variances in training and in the rate of return to training, to the levels of training and of the rate of return, and to the covariance between the two.[10]

Finally, note that the log variance is a relative measure and is not affected by proportional changes in all incomes. It is thus independent of mean income and is unit free. It has one drawback, however, that Sen has noted: it can violate the Pigou-Dalton condition.[11] Comparing two distributions, it is possible that one with a higher Lorenz curve (a curve everywhere closer to the 45 degree line of perfect equality) will be judged more unequal in terms of its log variance.

c) Coefficient of variation

The variance of a frequency distribution measures the spread of observations and can be used as a measure of inequality. It is, however, a
function of the units in which the variable is measured, so comparisons
are usually difficult. The coefficient of variation is defined as the
standard deviation divided by the mean and is unit free. It is a measure
of relative dispersion.

While often used in statistics, there seems no particular justification for using it as a measure of inequality. It certainly satisfies the
Pigou-Dalton condition, but there is no special positive or normative justification for using the squared deviations from the mean rather than absolute values or some other even power. For that matter, there is no strong
reason to use deviations from the mean rather than from some other value.
Unlike log variance, the coefficient of variation is equally sensitive to
transfers at all income levels.

d) Pearsonian skew coefficient

The frequency distribution for an income distribution is usually not
symmetric but has relatively more observations at low incomes. Such a
distribution is skewed to the right with the majority of observations to
the left of the mean. For a right-skewed distribution, it can be shown
that the mean is greater than the median which, in turn, is greater than
the mode. For a left-skewed distribution, the inequalities run the opposite
way. Karl Pearson developed what has become the standard measure of skewness based on this inequality.[12] It is given by:

(3)
$$S_k = \frac{3(\text{mean} - \text{median})}{\text{standard deviation}} .$$

This measure is unit free and is higher (in absolute value) the more skewed
is the distribution.

The skew coefficient is not, in itself, a measure of inequality. A
distribution with a very low variance is very equal, regardless of the
degree of skewness. However, the variance and skewness coefficient, taken
together, provide a good description of the frequency function.

e) Poverty measures

There are a number of measures designed to reflect only part of the income distribution, usually the lower tail or poverty population. These measures are usually very simple and only two examples will be given here. The second example does not really describe the shape of the frequency function but is included here as an interesting poverty measure.

The proportion of the population in relative poverty (PRP) is defined as the fraction of the total population that has incomes which are less than half of the median income.[13] The PRP measure defines poverty in relative terms and so guarantees that the poor shall always be with us. If individuals care about their relative position in the overall income distribution, the specification of poverty as a percent of a measure of central tendency, such as the median, may be quite reasonable.

Albert Fishlow has developed a measure of inequality based on a specified level of income Y_p which defines the boundary of absolute poverty.[14] Those with incomes less that Y_p are classified as in poverty and those with incomes above are not. Fishlow's measure is the share of total aggregate income which must be transferred from those above the poverty level to those below so that everyone in the poverty population receives Y_p. It is closely related to the maximum equalization percentage measure discussed in the next section.

Fishlow's measure is both simple to compute and simple to interpret. A major drawback, however, is that the measure is unaffected by transfers on the same side of the poverty line. One might find that after a set of transfers to the poor, Fishlow's measure decreased while another inequality index increased if the transfers came from those just above the poverty line.

The above measures, in common with all poverty measures, suffer from the difficulty of agreeing on a definition of poverty. In countries where an official definition of the absolute level of poverty has been set (such as the United States and India), there has been constant and considerable disagreement over it.[15] Furthermore, what is considered to be poverty has changed over time, not only with general price increases but also with general changes in the standard of living. If one defines poverty in relative terms as in the PRP measure, then the question arises: Relative to what? Clearly, comparisons over time or across countries are extremely difficult.

2. Lorenz curve measures

    a) Gini coefficient

The Gini coefficient is undoubtedly the most commonly used summary measure of the Lorenz curve. It is defined as the ratio of the area between the Lorenz curve and the diagonal to the total area under the diagonal.[16] It is an increasing function of inequality and equals zero when the distribution is perfectly equal (the Lorenz curve is the diagonal line). For a set of income data, the Gini coefficient is defined numerically as:[17]

$$(4) \qquad G = \frac{(1/n^2) \sum_i \sum_j |Y_i - Y_j|}{2\overline{Y}} \ .$$

Figure 3 is a simple example of a Lorenz curve. The line OC is the diagonal and OPC is the Lorenz curve. The Gini concentration coefficient is the ratio of the areas OPC and OZC:

$$G = \text{area (OPC)/area (OZC)} \ .$$

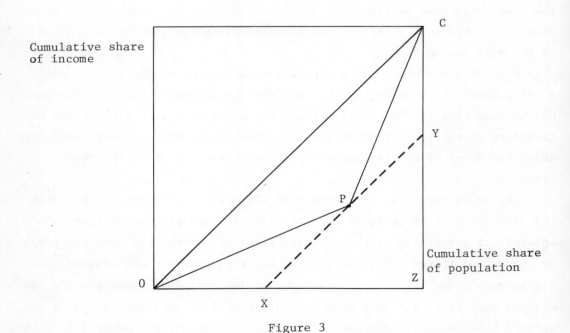

Figure 3

Because of its wide usage, the theoretical aspects of the Gini coefficient have been investigated thoroughly. The coefficient is insensitive to changes near the center of the distribution.[18]   Figure 3 can be used to illustrate this graphically. The broken line XY is drawn parallel to the diagonal and tangent to the Lorenz curve at point P. It is obvious geometrically that any distribution giving rise to a Lorenz curve tangent to XY at any point along XY will result in the same Gini coefficient.[19]   That is, P can be shifted anywhere along XY without affecting the value of the Gini coefficient. Clearly, very different distributions give rise to Lorenz curves with the same Gini coefficient.

The Gini coefficient has come under attack recently because the ranking of income distributions it gives is not consistent with the ranking given by a social welfare function with certain desirable properties.[20] It is however true that the Gini coefficient satisfies the Pigou-Dalton condition. It is not clear that problems with its implicit social welfare function need disqualify the Gini coefficient as a useful summary measure of the Lorenz curve. One need only keep in mind the inherent ambivalence of the measure.

b)   Elteto-Frigyes inequality indices

Elteto and Frigyes have presented three indices of inequality that are based on the Lorenz curve.[21]   The three measures are:

(5) $u = \overline{Y}/\overline{Y}_1$,

           $v = \overline{Y}_2/\overline{Y}_1$,

           $w = \overline{Y}_2/\overline{Y}$,

where:

$\overline{Y}$ is the mean income of the entire distribution,

$\overline{Y}_1$ is the mean income of those people with incomes less than $\overline{Y}$, and

$\overline{Y}_2$ is the mean income of those people with incomes more than $\overline{Y}$.

The measure v reflects inequality in the entire distribution, while u and w measure inequality in the respective lower and upper parts of the distribution.

Note that:

$$(6) \qquad v = (\overline{Y}/\overline{Y}_1) \cdot (\overline{Y}_2/\overline{Y}) = u \cdot w ,$$

so that the three measures are not independent.

The range of all three measures is one to infinity, but they can be normalized to have a range of zero to one. The standardized measures are:

$$(7) \qquad u^* = (\overline{Y} - \overline{Y}_1)/\overline{Y} ,$$

$$v^* = (\overline{Y}_2 - \overline{Y})/\overline{Y}_2 , \text{ and}$$

$$w^* = (\overline{Y}_2 - \overline{Y}_1)/\overline{Y}_2 .$$

These measures are easily calculated and readily interpreted. Further more, they are closely related to the Gini coefficient and it is possible to estimate the value of the Gini coefficient within reasonable and known limits from the three measures.[22] They are actually more descriptive of the Lorenz curve than is the Gini coefficient since, given $\overline{Y}_1$ and $\overline{Y}_2$, one can easily identify the points where the Lorenz curve bulges.[23]

c) The maximum equalization percentage

To summarize the inequality of a distribution of income simply, many economists have presented the shares of income received by arbitrarily defined percentiles.[24] The percentiles can be deciles, quintiles, quartiles, and so on. The difference between the percentage of the population and the share of income received is a measure of inequality since, with perfect equality, the two percentages are equal. The maximum equalization percentage is based on the Lorenz curve and is defined as the share of aggregate income that would need to be redistributed in order that the distribution be perfectly equal. Algebraically, it is equal to one-half the sum of the absolute differences in the percent shares of population and income.[25] That is:

$$(8) \qquad MEP = \tfrac{1}{2} \sum_i \left| p_i - y_i \right| .$$

The measure is very similar to the Gini coefficient and shares both its advantages and disadvantages. Furthermore, it is quite sensitive to the type of percentile grouping chosen and is unaffected by redistributions within a given group.

d) The Kuznets ratio

The Kuznets ratio is a weighted measure of inequality of sectoral levels of per worker product. Kuznets found empirically that the average product per worker in the agricultural sector was generally much below the countrywide average in developing countries, while it was close to the average in countries with higher per capita income. In the nonagricultural sectors—that is, manufacturing and services—the product per worker was closest to the countrywide average in countries with high per capita income, and further above the countrywide average in developing countries. It follows that the relative disparity in sectoral levels of product per worker is inversely related to the level of economic development.

Kuznets created a measure to summarize the sectoral disparities based upon the sectoral percentage distributions of total product and of total labor force.[26] The sum of the absolute value of the differences between sectoral product and sectoral labor force is a measure of the relative inequality among sectoral average products, weighted by the share of each sector in the labor force. For example, if the agricultural sector produces 40 percent of total output and employs 70 percent of the total labor force, the difference (30 percent) is really the difference between relative per worker product and the countrywide average, weighted by the share of agriculture in the total labor force. In this example, the Kuznets ratio is:

$$K = \left[70 \left| \frac{40}{70} - 1.0 \right| \right] = 30 .$$

The Kuznets ratio varies from zero, in the case where all sectoral average products are equal to the countrywide average, to close to 200, in the case where the total product is assigned to one sector, and when the share of this sector in the labor force is infinitesimally small.

The Kuznets ratio is much like the Gini coefficient, being based on a type of Lorenz curve distribution classified by sectors. It provides a convenient descriptive measure of the functional distribution of income for countries where no data on personal or household incomes exist. Furthermore,

measuring the distribution by sectors rather than by households may well
be more useful for some purposes.

3. Other measures

    a) Theil information measure

Theil has proposed an inequality measure based on information theory.[27]
It is given by:

$$(9) \qquad T = \log (n) - \sum_{i=1}^{n} y_i \log (1/y_i) ,$$

where y_i is the share of aggregate income going to person i, and n is the
total number of people.

The measure clearly satisfies the Pigou-Dalton condition and is a
relative measure (i.e., unaffected by proportional changes in all incomes).
It is bounded from above by log (n), so the larger is n the greater is the
amount of possible inequality. This, Theil feels, is quite natural. If a
society is made up of two people and one receives all income while the
other receives nothing, the value of the measure is log (2). When a society is made up of 2 million people and one person receives all income,
there are 1,999,999 people who receive nothing. The latter situation, he
reasons, is clearly more unequal. In the second case, the value of T will
equal log (2) when half of the 2 million people receive all income, and
each receives an equal share, while the other half receive nothing. This
characteristic of the measure, however desirable one wishes to view it,
makes comparisons difficult unless sample sizes are equal. One could, of
course, normalize the measure by dividing it by log (n). This makes it independent of population size but somewhat alters the notion of inequality
being measured.

No matter how well grounded in information theory, the Theil measure
is nonetheless an arbitrarily defined measure of income inequality. For
example, transformations other than the logarithm would be equally satisfactory in the definition of T as far as information theory is concerned,
and there is no real reason to choose one such transformation over another.

    b) Atkinson measure

In a recent article, Atkinson has criticized some of the better known
measures of inequality on the grounds that the social welfare functions

which underlie them are either difficult to define or unrealistic theoretically.[28] Atkinson defines a measure based on what he terms "the equally distributed equivalent income," Y^e. He defines it as the level of per capita income which if equally distributed would yield the same level of social welfare as the present distribution. Atkinson's inequality measure is defined as:

$$(10) \qquad A = 1 - \frac{Y^e}{\overline{Y}} \, ,$$

where $\overline{Y}$ is the current mean income. If income is equally distributed, then $Y^e = \overline{Y}$ and $A = 0$. For any distribution, A will be between zero and one.

The measure depends crucially on the social welfare function with which Y^e is defined. Atkinson suggests one such function which contains an inequality aversion parameter, epsilon. If one chooses an epsilon equal to zero, the social welfare function is linear in incomes, and distribution does not matter. As epsilon increases, the measure is more sensitive to transfers to the lowest income group. For the welfare function he suggests, the measure reflects only relative inequality.

Atkinson's measure is explicitly normative and defines inequality in a way that may not be descriptive of the distribution. A given value of the measure will correspond to an infinite number of different distributions which may, depending on the social welfare function, have dramatically different shapes. Of all the measures surveyed, the Atkinson measure probably has the most welfare content and requires the user to specify exactly how he "values" inequality.

D.   Decomposition of static measures

All the measures surveyed in section C refer to the distribution of income by households or individuals, except for the Kuznets ratio which refers to the distribution by workers in different producing sectors. In analyzing the determinants and significance of a given distribution, or of changes in it, one often wants to deal with different aggregations of the population. For example, the distribution by social class, region, ethnic group, or even age class may be of special interest for different countries at different times. If the entire population is classified into a mutually exclusive set of such groups, then it is interesting to determine how much of the total inequality in the population is due to within-group inequality and how much is due to between-group inequality.

There are other notions of decomposability that one might use. For example, one might try to decompose a measure by causal factors rather than by subgroups. For example, Fei and Ranis have devised a decomposition of the Gini coefficient based on a decomposition by income sources.[29] They derive the contributions to total inequality (as measured by the Gini coefficient) from inequality in the various factor components of income (e.g., wage, property, and transfer income). Elteto and Frigyes have derived a causal decomposition of their inequality measure into contributions due to factors such as the wage rate, the participation rate, the unemployment rate, and the share of wages in total income.[30]

Of all the measures, only five are really susceptible to decomposition of the aggregate measure into within- and between-group inequality. The five are: (i) the log variance, (ii) the coefficient of variation, (iii) the Gini coefficient, (iv) the Theil measure, and (v) the Atkinson measure. The measures vary in the ease and intuitive reasonableness of their decompositions. The properties of the various decompositions are discussed below. The detailed algebra is presented in an appendix.

In most cases, the decomposition defines the total measure as a sum of two terms. The first term is the measure defined between the groups (treating each group mean income as a single observation) and the second term is a weighted sum of the within-group measures. Perhaps the simplest and best known is the log variance which simply follows the statistical decomposition of variance formula. The total log variance equals the between-group log variance plus a weighted average of the within-group log variances. The Theil measure also decomposes easily into a simple weighted sum of between- and within-group measures.[31]

The coefficient of variation decomposes easily, but in terms of its squared value.[32] The numerator squared is the variance, and the decomposition follows from the simple decomposition of variance formula. The coefficient squared decomposes into the sum of the square of the between-group coefficient of variation and the weighted sum of the squared within-group coefficients. The weights in the weighted sum do not add to one but instead sum to the square of the between-group coefficient--the terms of the decomposition are not independent, a drawback that is not shared by the other measures.

The decomposition of the Gini coefficient is not nearly so straight-forward. Mangahas defines a decomposition of the total coefficient into the sum of two terms.[33] The first term is the weighted average (weights add to one) of the within-group Gini coefficients. The second term is a weighted sum (weights add to zero) of all possible Gini coefficients between paired groups. The weights are functions of group size, population size, group mean income, and total mean income. The calculation of the between-group Gini coefficients requires comparable data on the income frequency functions for each subgroup. It is not enough to have data on only group mean incomes, group sizes, and within-group Gini coefficients.

It is possible to decompose the Atkinson measure, but not as the weighted sum of within- and between-group measures. Given Atkinson's social welfare function, the decomposition involves the weighted sum of the within-group measures. The between-group measure does not appear explicitly, although it is related to the sum of the weights. The decomposition is not easily interpretable.

Of the five readily decomposable measures, the log variance and the Theil measure seem best in terms of their decomposition properties. For both of them, one can easily determine the independent contribution of within- and between-group inequality to total inequality, and the decomposition is simple to calculate. The Gini coefficient can also be decomposed into independent within- and between-group contributions, but the decomposition requires that one has distribution data for each subgroup. These data may often not be available.

E.   Dynamic mobility framework

All the measures discussed so far have been static in that they characterize a distribution at a point in time. Such measures cannot reflect the degree of income mobility in a society. Even comparing inequality measures at two different points of time in no way indicates how many people have moved in the distribution or by how much. Static measures cannot indicate the presence of chronic poverty as defined in section A.

A dynamic framework which has been suggested for the analysis of economic mobility is based on transition-probability matrices of finite Markov processes. For this discussion, such a transition matrix will be called a mobility matrix, M.

Each cell M_{ij} in the mobility matrix is the percent of people in group i who move to group j in the period t to t + 1. We shall define the groups by income classes, although this is by no means the only way they can be (or have been) defined.[34] It is also convenient to order the groups by the level of mean income, from highest to lowest. Since everyone in each group must be accounted for in the next period, it follows that the rows of the mobility matrix must sum to one. An example of a mobility matrix is given below. Measures based on it are given in the appendix.

(11)
$$M = \begin{bmatrix} .7 & .2 & .1 \\ .3 & .6 & .1 \\ .1 & .1 & .8 \end{bmatrix}.$$

Looking at the first row of M, one can see that 70 percent of the richest group maintains its mean income, 20 percent of that group moves to the group with the next lower mean income, and 10 percent loses enough so that they move to the group with the lowest mean income. The matrix M thus defines how people change position in the distribution of income over time--an inherently dynamic process--and allows the identification of individual movement through income classes.

Define the variable $f_{t,i}$ as the relative size of group i in period t. It is a distribution giving the shares of the population in each income class. One is interested in how the population shares of the various income classes change over time. The changes in relative group sizes can be calculated using the M matrix. For example, the product $M_{1,1} f_{t,1}$ represents the relative number of people who will remain in group 1. $M_{2,1} f_{t,2}$ represents the relative number of people who will move to group 1 from group 2 during the period. Summing, one can see that:

(12)
$$f_{t+1, i} = \sum_{j} M_{ji} f_{t,j} \quad \text{for each i.}$$

The size of a given income class i in period t + 1 is found by summing the number of people who stay in the class during the period and the number of people who move into the class from other classes.

By repeated application of equation (12) one can obtain the distribution at any time in the future. Assuming a constant mobility matrix, it can be shown that the frequency function will converge over time to a stable distribution with constant relative group sizes.[35] This distribution is called the ergodic distribution and depends only on the mobility matrix. It does not depend at all on the initial distribution.

The ergodic distribution can be calculated given only the mobility matrix. It can be used to answer the counterfactual question: With a given mobility matrix, what will be the eventual distribution? It is of course interesting to compare the present and ergodic distributions. It is also interesting to note that in actual empirical application, the ergodic distribution is reached in only a few periods.[36] Of course, it is not necessary, especially in applications to developing countries, to assume a constant mobility matrix. The ergodic distribution is then of less interest, but the other mobility measures are still useful.

If there is no mobility in the society, the M matrix will equal the identity matrix (ones on the diagonal and zeroes everywhere else) and no one will move from his initial class from period to period. The larger the off-diagonal elements (and the further away they are from the diagonal), the greater is the mobility (both up and down) in the society. Measures of mobility which take perfect immobility as their point of comparison will attempt to measure the amount and degree of "off-diagonalness" in the mobility matrix.[37]

All measures summarizing the mobility matrix are relative measures in the sense that they take no account of changes in the level of mean income. It is of course possible to calculate the change in the overall mean income due to movements of people among the various income classes as a function of the original distribution and the mobility matrix.

There are two general ways in which one can summarize the mobility matrix: (i) cell-related mobility measures, and (ii) overall mobility measures. Cell-related measures seek to associate a statistic to more than one cell of the matrix, i.e., they are multivalued measures. Overall measures attempt to summarize the entire mobility matrix in a single number.

1. Cell-related mobility measures

Cell-related measures of the mobility matrix have long been used. They are the generally accepted statistics for summarizing the elements of a transition matrix.[38] We will discuss two well-known measures: (i) average time spent in a class, and (ii) mean first passage times. More detailed algebraic derivations are given in an appendix.

a)   Average time spent in a class

One cell-related summary measure of the mobility matrix is the average time spent in a class. If there is perfect immobility (M is an identity matrix), then each person would remain in his initial income class for an infinite period of time. The greater the mobility in a society, the shorter the period a particular person can expect to remain in a given income class. The expected value of the amount of time spent in a class is a measure of the mobility of a given society.

Note that the average time spent in class is determined only by the size of the diagonal element of the mobility matrix. The measure does not reflect how far one moves in terms of income, but only that one leaves one's current class. It measures the existence of mobility, not the extremeness of it.

b)   Mean first passage times

The mean first passage times are the only mobility measures which generate a separate value for each cell of the original M matrix. The measure is defined as the expected value of the length of time required to go from class i to class j for the first time.

It is interesting to compare the absolute and relative sizes of the different mean first passage times. For example, one might be interested not only in the expected number of periods to go from the lower to the higher income class but also in the relative size of this compared to the mean time to go from higher to lower. One would expect the former to be larger than the latter, and one might relate such figures to economic variables such as the growth rate of GNP.

2.   Overall mobility measures

Obviously, some information is lost when a single valued statistic is used to summarize a multivalued matrix such as M. Such statistics, however, can prove beneficial for quick evaluations of the structure of the matrix if they are carefully constructed. In this section we present two such summary measures: (i) the determinant of M and (ii) the aggregate mobility measure.

a)   Determinant of M

Given that each element of M is less than or equal to one and that the rows of M sum to one, it can be shown that the determinant of M, |M|, must lie between -1 and +1.[39]

(13) $-1 \leq |M| \leq 1$.

The value of |M| will be 1 when M is an identity matrix. Since M = 1 signifies no mobility, so does |M| = 1. When M is such that it completely reverses the frequency distribution from t to t + 1, the value of |M| is -1. For example, if M is a 3 x 3 mobility matrix of the form

$$(14) \qquad M = \begin{bmatrix} 0 & 0 & 1 \\ 0 & 1 & 0 \\ 1 & 0 & 0 \end{bmatrix},$$

then:

$$|M| = -1.$$

There is one shortcoming to the use of the value of the determinant as a summary measure. The value of M will be zero whenever linear dependence is present in M. Since M can be expected to be a dominant diagonal matrix in the short run, this should not usually be a problem.

b)   Aggregate mobility measure

In summarizing mobility, both the value of the off-diagonal elements and their distance from the diagonal are important. The first determines how many people move and the second determines how far they move. A summary measure can be constructed that weights the value of the off-diagonal elements by their distance from the diagonal. Since the difference between the row and column subscripts is a measure of the distance from the diagonal, a summary mobility measure can be used on the statistic:[40]

$$\sum_{i} \sum_{j} (i - j)^2 M_{ij} .$$

The problem with using this statistic as an aggregate mobility measure is that its maximum possible value is a function of the number of classes in the mobility matrix. Define an aggregate mobility measure, then, as the above statistic divided by its maximum attainable value (which is easily calculated):[41]

$$(15) \quad \mu = \frac{\underset{ij}{\Sigma\Sigma} (i - j)^2 M_{ij}}{\text{maximum value}} .$$

The measure μ ranges from zero to one and equals zero only when M is the identity matrix (perfect immobility).

F. Conclusion

Studies of income distribution are normally framed in terms of comparative statics, narrowly defined economic variables, and individual or functional distributions. This is an inadequate framework for analyzing dynamic aspects of the long-run distribution of income. The static framework does not approach the question of the income experience of individuals or groups over time. The fact that most studies are narrowly economic means that interactions between the social, political, and economic variables are not taken into account. The use of individual or household data alone means that socio-economic, regional, or class differences in income tend to be neglected.

A survey of the better known measures of income inequality indicates that they all reflect the traditional approach. The measures are all static and, with the exception of the Kuznets ratio, concentrate on the distribution of income by individuals or households. None of them measures the dynamic aspects of economic and social mobility.

A framework for analyzing mobility has been presented based on the transition-probability matrix of a finite Markov process. The mobility matrix describes a dynamic process of income distribution and the approach can be adapted to the study of various other dynamic processes (for example, inter-sectoral labor migration, the education process, and social class mobility). A number of measures reflecting the mobility framework have been presented.

The concern with income distribution in the developing countries emanates from the high and increasing degree of inequality observed in studies done to date.[42] This work implies that significant proportions of the populations of developing countries are not sharing in the benefits of the high growth rates of income experienced in the recent past. How chronic is the poverty implied by the increase in static inequality measures is an open question, and one that cannot really be approached within a static framework. Dynamic analysis using the mobility framework and the measures based on it should be useful both in the identification of the chronically poor and in the structuring of policies so that their effects reach the intended recipients.

Appendix 1

NOTES

1. In sections of <u>The Republic</u>, Plato discusses the question of equity. See Hugh Dalton (1920).

2. Kenneth Arrow (1951) and Amartya K. Sen (1970).

3. Lester Thurow (1971) and Robinson (1975).

4. H. Chenery et al. (1974) and A. Harberger (1971).

5. See, for example, Christopher Jencks et al. (1972) or J. Conlisk (1974).

6. G. C. Harcourt (1972).

7. For an excellent review of size-distribution theories, see Alan S. Blinder (1973). See also Martin Bronfenbrenner (1971).

8. Amartya K. Sen (1973), especially pp. 36-37. Also A. O. Hirschman and M. Rothschild (1973).

9. Amartya K. Sen (1973), p. 27. See D. G. Champernowne (1974) for an interesting discussion of desirable properties of inequality measures and an empirical comparison of some measures.

10. Barry R. Chiswick (1968).

11. Amartya K. Sen (1973), p. 32. Also Anthony B. Atkinson (1970). A proof is given in P. Dasgupta, Amartya K. Sen, and D. Starrett (1973).

12. See F. E. Croxton, D. J. Cowden, and S. Klein (1967), pp. 202-03.

13. Victor R. Fuchs (1965).

14. Albert Fishlow (1973).

15. Parnab K. Bardhan (1973), especially pp. 27-35.

16. M. G. Kendall and A. Stuart (1963), pp. 48-49. Also see Corrado Gini (1914).

17. The numerator of the Gini coefficient is an interesting statistic in itself and can be used as an inequality measure. It represents the

expected value of the difference between two individuals selected at random from the total population.

18. David Newberry (1970).

19. The altitude of the triangle OPC with base OC does not change, and so its area is constant.

20. Namely, a social welfare function which is strictly quasi-concave on individual incomes. See Amartya K. Sen (1973), pp. 33-34, for a review.

21. O. Elteto and E. Frigyes (1968).

22. The Gini coefficient can be written in terms of any two of the measures:

$$G = \frac{U^*W^*}{U^* + W^* - U^*W^*} - \frac{(V^* - W^*)U^*}{(1 - W^*)V^*} \ .$$

23. Patricia Wilson (1973).

24. P. C. Mahalanobis (1960).

25. For an application of this measure, see Felix Paukert (1973).

26. Simon Kuznets (1957).

27. Henri Theil (1967).

28. Anthony B. Atkinson (1970) and Amartya K. Sen (1973).

29. J. C. H. Fei and G. Ranis (1974).

30. O. Elteto and E. Frigyes (1968).

31. Henri Theil (1967), pp. 91-96.

32. Ibid., pp. 124-25.

33. Mahar Mangahas (1974). For other decompositions, see G. Pyatt (1976) and J. C. H. Fei and G. Ranis (1974).

34. For example, see Isadore Blumen, Marvin Kogen, and Phillip McCarthy (1955); Nathan Keyfitz (1968); E. O. Laumann (1970); and S. J. Prais (1955). S. Robinson and K. Dervis (1977) use socio-economic groups and explicitly derive the overall distribution of income from group distribution.

35. John G. Kemeny and J. Laurie Snell (1960), pp. 69-70. An example is given in the appendix.

36. Richard J. Szal (1973).

37. Sociologists have generally used perfect mobility (all elements of M equal) as their point of comparison. See Laumann (1970).

38. John G. Kemeny and J. Laurie Snell (1960).

39. The value of the determinant for input-output matrices has been investigated as a summary measure for the complexity of an input-output system. See Y. K. Wong (1954).

40. One could just as well take the absolute value of (i - j) as the weight. This would yield an arithmetically weighted mobility measure, whereas squaring (i - j) yields a weighting scheme that allocates exponentially greater weight to movements farther from the original class. The choice is arbitrary.

41. The maximum value is given by:

$$2 \sum_{i=1}^{n/2} (i - n)^2 \quad \text{for even } n,$$

and

$$2 \sum_{i=1}^{n/2} (i - n)^2 + \frac{(n - 1)}{2} \quad \text{for odd } n,$$

where n is the number of income classes.

42. I. Adelman and C. T. Morris (1973); Felix Paukert (1973); and Chenery et al. (1974).

Appendix A

DECOMPOSITION OF STATIC MEASURES

Five of the static measures of inequality discussed in the text are susceptible to decomposition into within- and between-group inequality. These measures are: (i) the variance of the logs of income, (ii) the coefficient of variation, (iii) the Gini coefficient, (iv) the Theil measure, and (v) Atkinson's measure. In all cases but that of Atkinson's measure, the detailed algebra of the decompositions have been presented elsewhere and will not be duplicated here.

Several symbols will be utilized repreatedly throughout the following discussion. They are defined here so as to minimize redundancy:

n = total sample size,

n_g = sample size of the gth group,

G = number of subgroups of total sample,

Y_i = income of the ith individual or household,

$\overline{Y}_g$ = mean income of the gth group,

$\overline{Y}$ = sample mean income,

v = variance of the logs of income,

C = coefficient of variation,

R = Gini coefficient of concentration,

T = Theil measure of inequality, and

I = Atkinson measure of inequality.

A. ## Variance of the logs of income

Decomposition of the variance of the logs of income follows the usual decomposition of variance formula. The variance of the logs is defined as

$$V = (1/n) \sum_{i=1}^{n} (\log Y_i - \overline{\log Y})^2 ,$$

which can also be written as

$$V = (1/n) \sum_{i=1}^{n} \left[\log\left(\frac{Y_i}{\overline{Y}}\right) \right]^2 ,$$

where $\overline{Y}$ is defined as the geometric mean income. Straightforward decomposition of the log variance yields

$$V = \sum_{g=1}^{G} \frac{n_g}{n} \left[\log\left(\frac{\overline{Y}_g}{\overline{Y}}\right) \right]^2 + \sum_{g=1}^{G} \left(\frac{n_g}{n}\right) \left(\frac{1}{n_g}\right) \sum_{i=1}^{n_g} \log\left(\frac{Y_i}{\overline{Y}_g}\right)^2 ,$$

or more conveniently

$$(A1) \qquad V = V_b + \sum_{g=1}^{G} \left(\frac{n_g}{n}\right) V_g ,$$

where V_b is the between-group log variance and the second term is a weighted average of the within-group log variances, the weights being equal to the population shares of each group.

B. Coefficient of variation

The coefficient of variation is defined as

$$C = \frac{s}{\overline{Y}} ,$$

where s is the standard deviation of the distribution. The decomposition of this measure is accomplished through squaring the numerator and the denominator and decomposing the squared numerator which is, of course, the variance. The decomposition[1] results in

$$C^2 = \frac{\displaystyle\sum_{g=1}^{G} \left(\frac{n_g}{n}\right) \left(\overline{Y}_g - \overline{Y}\right)^2}{\overline{Y}^2} + \sum_{g=1}^{G} \left(\frac{n_g}{n}\right) \left(\frac{\overline{Y}_g^2}{\overline{Y}^2}\right) \left[\frac{\left(\frac{1}{n_g}\right) \displaystyle\sum_{i=1}^{n_g} \left(Y_i - Y_g\right)^2}{\overline{Y}_g^2} \right] ,$$

or

$$(A2) \qquad C^2 = C_b^2 = \sum_{g=1}^{G} \left(\frac{n_g}{n}\right) \left(\frac{\overline{Y}_g^2}{\overline{Y}^2}\right) C_g^2 .$$

c_b^2 is the square of the between-group coefficient of variation and the second term is a weighted sum of the squared within-group coefficients of variation. Note that the second term is not a weighted _average_, since the weights do not sum to one. The sum of the weights is

$$\sum_{g=1}^{G} \left(\frac{n_g}{n}\right)\left(\frac{\overline{Y}_g^2}{\overline{Y}^2}\right) = \frac{\overline{Y}_2 + \sum_{g=1}^{G}\left(\frac{n_g}{n}\right)\left(\overline{Y}_g - \overline{Y}\right)^2}{\overline{Y}^2} = 1 + \frac{\sum_{g=1}^{G}\left(\frac{n_g}{n}\right)\left(\overline{Y}_g - \overline{Y}\right)^2}{\overline{Y}^2},$$

which equals one plus the square of the between-group coefficient of variation. The sum of the weights is thus related to the size of the between-group coefficient of variation and, to this extent, the between- and within-group measures are not independent.

C. The Gini coefficient

Decomposition of the Gini coefficient is complicated because it is defined in terms of absolute values. A decomposition, however, has been derived by Mangahas.[2] Defining

R_g = Gini coefficient for the size distribution of the gth population group, and

R_{ij} = Gini difference coefficient computed on the difference between the size distributions of groups i and j,

the total Gini coefficient can be decomposed into two terms:

$$(A3) \qquad R = \sum_{g=1}^{G} \left(\frac{n_g}{n}\right)\left(\frac{\overline{Y}_g}{\overline{Y}}\right) R_g + \sum_{i=2}^{G} \sum_{j=1}^{G-1} \left(\frac{n_i \, n_j}{n^2}\right)\left[\frac{\overline{Y}_i - \overline{Y}_j}{\overline{Y}}\right] R_{ij} ,$$

where $i \neq j,\ \overline{Y}_i > \overline{Y}_j$.

The term $R_{ij} = 1 - \left[\left(\frac{1}{\overline{Y}_i - \overline{Y}_j}\right)(f_i - f_j)' \, HX \, (f_i - f_j)\right]$,

where:

$f_i,\ f_j$ = column vectors of the size distributions of income in the ith and jth groups,

H = an L x L matrix, where L is the number of income classes defined for each group, with 2's below the diagonal, 1's on the diagonal, and zeroes above it, and

X = an L x L diagonal matrix whose kth diagonal element is the mean income of the kth income class.

Equation (A3) is a decomposition of the total Gini coefficient into a weighted average (weights summing to one) of the within-group Gini co-efficients and a weighted sum (weights summing to zero) of all possible Gini difference coefficients between paired groups. Graphically, the Gini difference coefficients are derived from differences in the Lorenz curves of paired groups. The decomposition of the Gini coefficient requires comparable, detailed data on the frequency distribution of income in each of the groups (in order to calculate the between-group coefficients R_{ij}).

D.   The Theil measure

The Theil measure is defined in terms of income shares rather than absolute incomes. Denote these shares by y_i. Defining y_g as the share of the gth group in total income, Theil's measure can be decomposed to:

$$(A5) \qquad T = \sum_{g=1}^{G} y_g \log\left[\frac{y_g}{\left(n_g/n\right)}\right] + \sum_{g=1}^{G} y_g \left\{ \sum_{i=1}^{n_g} \left(\frac{y_i}{y_g}\right) \log\left[\frac{\left(y_i/y_g\right)}{\left(1/n_g\right)}\right] \right\}$$

or

$$(A6) \qquad T = T_b + \sum_{g=1}^{G} y_g T_g \ .$$

The first term, T_b, is a measure of the inequality between group incomes. When each group's share of income is equal to its population share, T_b equals zero. Note that:

$$(A7) \qquad y_g = \frac{\text{income of } g}{\text{total income}} = \frac{n_g \cdot \text{per capita income of } g}{n \cdot \text{total per capita income}} \ .$$

In the event that total per capita income and the per capita income of group g are equal, (A7) reduces to $\left(n_g/n\right)$. The first term of (A6) then vanishes, since

$$= y_g \log\left[\frac{n_g/n}{n_g/n}\right] = y_g \log(1) = 0$$

for all G groups.

The second term in (A6) deals with within-group inequality. It is weighted average (weights summing to one) of the within-group measures of inequality. In each separate within-group expression on the right, (y_i/y_g) and $(1/n_g)$ are, respectively, the income share and the population share for the ith individual in the kth group. As with the between-group expression, this term vanishes for groups in which each individual income is equal to the per capita income of the group.[3]

E.   Atkinson's measure

Of all measures discussed in this appendix, Atkinson's measure of inequality is the least straightforward and most difficult to interpret in terms of its decomposability. The measure is defined as

$$(A8) \qquad I = 1 - \left[\sum_{i=1}^{n} \left(\frac{Y_i}{\mu}\right)^{1-\varepsilon} f(Y_i) \right]^{1/(1-\varepsilon)}.$$

When one is dealing with individual incomes,

$$f(Y_i) = 1/n$$

so that (A8) can be rewritten as

$$(A9) \qquad I = 1 - \left[\sum_{i=1}^{n} \left(\frac{Y_i}{\mu}\right)^{1-\varepsilon} \left(\frac{1}{n}\right) \right]^{1/(1-\varepsilon)}.$$

Adding group-specific terms to (A9) yields

$$(A10) \qquad I = 1 - \left\{ \sum_{g=1}^{G} \sum_{i=1}^{n_g} \left[\left(\frac{Y_i}{\overline{Y}_g}\right)\left(\frac{\overline{Y}_g}{\mu}\right) \right]^{1-\varepsilon} \left(\frac{1}{n_g}\right) \left(\frac{n_g}{n}\right) \right\}^{1/(1-\varepsilon)}.$$

For each of the G components that make up the rightmost term of (A10), the terms $\left(\frac{\overline{Y}_g}{\mu}\right)^{1-\varepsilon}$ and $\left(\frac{n_g}{n}\right)$ are constant so that

$$1 - I = \left[\sum_{g=1}^{G} \left(\frac{\overline{Y}_g}{\mu}\right)^{1-\varepsilon} \left(\frac{n_g}{n}\right) \sum_{i=1}^{n_g} \left(\frac{Y_i}{\overline{Y}_g}\right)^{1-\varepsilon} \left(\frac{1}{n_g}\right) \right]^{-1/(1-\varepsilon)}$$

The first set of terms within brackets can be written as:

$$(A11) \qquad 1 - I_b = \left[\sum_{g=1}^{G} \left(\frac{\overline{Y}_g}{\mu} \right)^{1-\epsilon} \left(\frac{n_g}{n} \right) \right]^{1/(1-\epsilon)} ,$$

where I_b is the Atkinson measure for between-group differences in income. They also form a set of weights that are applied to the within-group terms to obtain the total measure. One can arrive at the between- and within-group components of total inequality by calculating I_b from group means and group sample sizes and treating within-group inequality as a residual. That is,

$$(A12) \qquad I_w = I - I_b .$$

This treatment is analogous to one suggested by Meesook. She defines the quantity I_w as

$$I_w \approx \sum_{g=1}^{G} \left(\frac{n_g}{n} \right) \left\{ 1 - \left[\sum_{i=1}^{n_g} \left(\frac{Y_i}{\overline{Y}_g} \right)^{1-\epsilon} \left(\frac{1}{n_g} \right) \right]^{1/(1-\epsilon)} \right\}$$

or,

$$(A13) \qquad I_w \approx \sum_{g=1}^{G} \left(\frac{n_g}{n} \right) \left(1 - I_g \right) ,$$

which is simply a weighted average (weights sum to one) of the within-group measures of inequality.[4]

Appendix A

NOTES

1. Henri Theil (1967), pp. 123-25.

2. Mangahas (1974).

3. Henri Theil (1967), pp. 91-96.

4. The decomposition suggested here can be termed an intuitive one, since the sum of the terms of I_w do not exactly sum to the residual value of I_w suggested in the previous paragraph. The definition of I_w was suggested in correspondence with Oey Astra Meesook.

Appendix B

MEASURES OF MOBILITY

This appendix presents some of the algebra underlying the measures of mobility discussed in the text. A numerical example is also given.

A. Ergodic distribution

Defining F_t as the row vector distribution of observations in time t and M_t as the mobility matrix in time t, the finite Markov process is defined as

(A14) $F_t M_t = F_{t+1}$.

If each element of M_t is assumed invariant with respect to time, then (A14) can be written

$$F_t M^P = F_{t+p} ,$$

where M^P is M raised to the power P. When p is sufficiently large M^P approaches idempotency.[1] That is,

$$\lim_{p \to \infty} M^P = A ,$$

where A is referred to as the limiting matrix of M. The fact that M^P approaches idempotency means that F_{t+p} approaches stability. The stable vector, which we will refer to as ϕ, is called the ergodic distribution of M. There is one and only one ϕ associated with a given M and it is independent of the initial F.

It is straightforward to solve for ϕ. Assuming M is a 3 x 3 mobility matrix, the following set of simultaneous equations will yield a solution for ϕ:

$$1 = \phi_1 + \phi_2 + \phi_3$$

$$\phi_1 = m_{11}\phi_1 + m_{21}\phi_2 + m_{31}\phi_3$$

$$\phi_2 = m_{12}\phi_1 + m_{22}\phi_2 + m_{32}\phi_3$$

$$\phi_3 = m_{13}\phi_1 + m_{23}\phi_2 + m_{33}\phi_3$$

An interesting aspect of the limiting matrix of A, and one that permits its identification once ϕ is known, is the fact that each row of A is equal to ϕ. That is,

$$A = \gamma\phi$$

where γ is a column vector with each element equal to 1. The fact that each row is equal to every other row in A means that each element of a given column of M is the same value.[2]

B. Average time spent in a class

Assume that there are f_i individuals or families currently in the ith income class. Of these, $f_i m_{ii}$ will be there next period, $f_i m_{ii}^2$ will remain after two periods have elapsed, and so on. The total time spent in the ith class by the f_i original members of the class is

$$T_i = f_i + f_i m_{ii} + f_i m_{ii}^2 + \ldots$$

The average time spent in the ith class is then obtained by dividing T_i by f_i. Thus,

$$t_i = T_i/f_i = 1 + m_{ii} + m_{ii}^2 + \ldots$$

or, taking the limit,

(A15) $t_i = 1/(1 - m_{ii})$.

The variance of the average time spent in a class is

(A16) $\sigma t_i^2 = m_{ii}/(1 - m_{ii})$.

Since the rows of M must sum to one, the average time spent in a class can be considered a summary measure of the "off-diagonalness" of M. However, the relative magnitudes of the off-diagonal elements have no effect on the value of the measure.

C. Mean first passage times

The matrix of mean first passage times is defined as[3]

(A17) $Q = (I - Z + EZ_{dg}) D$

where:

$Z = (I - M + A)^{-1}$,

Z_{dg} = matrix agreeing with Z on the main diagonal with zeroes elsewhere,

E = square matrix with all elements equal to 1,

D = diagonal matrix with the jth element equal to $1/\phi_j$, and

ϕ_j = jth element of the ergodic distribution associated with M.

The variances of the elements of Q are given by $W - Q_{sq}$ where:

$W = Q (2Z_{dg} D - I) + 2 [ZQ - E(ZQ)_{dg}]$, and

Q_{sq} = matrix resulting from Q by squaring each entry.

D. An example

Let us assume that we have the following mobility matrix:

$$M = \begin{matrix} & & U & M & L \\ U & & & & \\ M & & & & \\ L & & & & \end{matrix} \begin{bmatrix} .7 & .2 & .1 \\ .3 & .6 & .1 \\ .1 & .1 & .8 \end{bmatrix}$$

The measures of mobility associated with this matrix are:

(i) Ergodic distribution

U = .40

M = .27

L = .33

(ii) Average time spent in a class

	Average Time	Variance
U	3.33	1.373
M	2.50	.938
L	5.00	2.222

(iii) Mean first passage times

$$\text{MFPT} = \begin{bmatrix} 2.5 & 6.2 & 10.0 \\ 4.2 & 3.7 & 10.0 \\ 7.0 & 4.2 & 3.0 \end{bmatrix}.$$

$$\text{Var(MFPT)} = \begin{bmatrix} 13.2 & 40.7 & 90.8 \\ 20.7 & 28.6 & 90.8 \\ 33.8 & 28.5 & 34.3 \end{bmatrix}.$$

(iv) Value of the determinant = .280.

(v) Aggregate mobility measure = .167.

Appendix B

NOTES

1. This result obtains for all regular Markov chains. A chain is termed regular if, for some power of p, the matrix M^p has no zero entries. See John G. Kemeny and J. Laurie Snell (1960), pp. 60-70.

2. As a practical matter, the rate of convergence of M^p to A is exponential. Nathan Keyfitz (1968) has pointed out that the elements of M^5 are sufficiently stable for results correct to four decimal places.

3. For the derivations of the man first passage times and their variances, see John G. Kemeny and J. Laurie Snell (1960), pp. 78-89.

4. John G. Kemeny and J. Laurie Snell (1960) also give a number of examples in chapter 7.

SELECTED BIBLIOGRAPHY

Adelman, I., and Morris, C. T. Economic Growth and Social Equity in Developing Countries. Stanford: Stanford University Press, 1973.

Arrow, Kenneth. Social Choice and Individual Values. New York: Wiley, 1951.

Atkinson, Anthony B. "On the Measurement of Inequality." Journal of Economic Theory 2 (September 1970).

Bardhan, Parnab K. "The Pattern of Income Distribution in India: A Review." Unpublished paper. Washington, D.C.: IBRD, 1973.

Blinder, Alan S. Towards an Economic Theory of Income Distribution. Cambridge, Mass.: M.I.T. Press, 1975.

Blumen, Isadore; Kogen, Marvin; and McCarthy, Phillip. The Industrial Mobility of Labor As A Probability Process. Ithaca: Cornell University Press, 1955.

Bronfenbrenner, Martin. Income Distribution Theory. Chicago: Aldine-Atherton, 1971.

Champernowne, D. G. "A Comparison of Measures of Inequality of Income Distribution." Economic Journal, vol. 84, no. 336 (December 1974).

Chenery, H.; Ahluwalia, M. S.; Bell, C. L. G.; Duloy, J. H.; Jolly, R. Redistribution With Growth. Oxford: Oxford University Press, 1974.

Chiswick, Barry R. "The Average Level of Schooling and the Intra-Regional Inequality of Income: A Clarification." American Economic Review 58 (June 1968).

Conlisk, J. "Can Equalization of Opportunity Reduce Social Mobility?" American Economic Review (March 1974).

Croxton, F. E.; Cowden, D. J.; and Klein, S. Applied General Statistics. Englewood Cliffs, N.J.: Prentice-Hall, 1967.

Dalton, Hugh. Some Aspects of the Inequality of Incomes in Modern Communities. New York: Dutton, 1920.

Dasgupta, P.; Sen, A.; and Starrett, D. "Notes on the Measurement of Inequality." Journal of Economic Theory 5 (April 1973).

Elteto, O., and Frigyes, E. "New Income Inequality Measures as Efficient Tools for Causal Analysis." Econometrica (April 1968).

Fei, J. C. H., and Ranis, G. "Income Inequality by Additive Factor Components." Discussion Paper 207, Economic Growth Center, Yale University, June 1974.

Fishlow, Albert. "Brazilian Income Size Distribution." Unpublished paper. Berkeley: University of California, 1973.

Fuchs, Victor R. "Toward a Theory of Poverty." In Task Force on Economic Growth and Opportunity, Chamber of Commerce of the United States, The Concept of Poverty. Washington: United States Government Printing Office, 1965.

Gibrat, Robert. Les Inegalites Economique. Paris: Librarie du Recueil Sirey, 1937.

Gini, Corrado. "Sulla misera della concentrasione e della variabilita dei caratteri." Transactions of the Real Instituto Veneto di Scienze, Lettre e Arti, vol. LIII, pt. ii. Venice, 1914.

Harberger, A. "Three Basic Postulates for Applied Welfare Economics." Journal of Economic Literature 9 (September 1971).

Harcourt, G. C. Some Cambridge Controversies in the Theory of Capital. Cambridge: Cambridge University Press, 1972.

Hirschman, A. O., and Rothschild, M. "Changing Tolerance for Inequality in Development." Quarterly Journal of Economics (November 1973).

Hotelling, Harold, and Solomons, Leonard M. "The Limits of a Measure of Skewness." Annals of Mathematical Statistics (May 1932)

Jencks, Christopher et al. Inequality: A Reassessment of the Effect of Family and Schooling in America. New York: Basic Books, 1972.

Kaldor, Nicholas. "Alternative Theories of Distribution." Essays in Value and Distribution. New York: Free Press, 1960.

Kemeny, John G., and Snell, J. Laurie. Finite Markov Chains. Princeton: D. Van Nostrand, 1960.

Kendall, M. G., and Stuart, A. The Advanced Theory of Statistics, vol. I, 2nd edition. New York: Hafner, 1963.

Keyfitz, Nathan. Introduction to the Mathematics of Population. Reading, Mass.: Addison-Wesley, 1968.

Kuznets, Simon. "Quantitative Aspects of the Economic Growth of Nations, II, Industrial Distribution of National Product and Labor Force." Economic Development and Cultural Change. Supplement (July 1957).

Laumann, E. O., ed. Social Stratification. New York: Bobbs-Merrill, 1970.

Mahalanobis, P. C. "A Method of Fractile Graphical Analysis." Econometrica 28 (April 1960).

Mangahas, Mahar. "A Note On Decomposition of the Gini Ratio Across Regions." Revised. Research Discussion Paper 74-2. Institute of Economic Development and Research, School of Economics, University of Philippines, 1974.

Newberry, David. "A Theorem On The Measurement of Inequality." Journal of Economic Theory 2 (September 1970).

Paukert, Felix. "Income Distribution At Different Levels of Development." International Labour Review 108 (August–September 1973).

Prais, S. J. "Measuring Social Mobility." Journal of the Royal Statistical Society 118 (1955).

Pyatt, G. "On the Interpretation and Disaggregation of Gini Coefficients." The Economic Journal, vol. 86, no. 342 (June 1976), pp. 243-55.

Robinson, S. "Income Distribution and the Social Welfare Function." Discussion Paper 52, Woodrow Wilson School, Princeton University, Research Program in Development Studies (February 1975).

Robinson, S., and Dervis, K. "Income Distribution and Socioeconomic Mobility: A Framework for Analysis and Planning." Journal of Development Studies, forthcoming, 1977.

Roy, A. D. "The Distribution of Earnings and of Industrial Output." Economic Journal (1950).

Sen, Amartya K. Collective Choice and Individual Welfare. San Francisco: Holden-Day, 1970.

_____. On Economic Inequality. New York: Norton, 1973.

Sheshinski, Eytan. "The Relation Between A Social Welfare Function and the Gini Index of Income Inequality." Journal of Economic Theory (February 1972).

Szal, Richard J. Dynamic Aspects of the Long Run Distribution of Income: A Cohort Analysis. Unpublished Ph.D. thesis (July 1973).

Taussig, Michael K. Alternative Measures of the Distribution of Economic Welfare. Princeton: Princeton University Press, 1973.

Theil, Henri. Economics and Information Theory. Amsterdam: North-Holland, 1967.

Thurow, Lester. "The Income Distribution as a Pure Public Good." Quarterly Journal of Economics 85 (1971).

Weintraub, Sidney. An Approach To The Theory of Income Distribution. Philadelphia: Chilton, 1958.

Wilson, Patricia. "The Relationship Between the Gini Index of Inequality and the Elteto Measures of Inequality." Unpublished paper, Cornell University, 1973.

Wong, Y. K. "Some Mathematical Concepts for Linear Economic Models." In Oskar Morgenstern, ed., Economic Activity Analysis. New York: Wiley, 1954.

APPENDIX II

POTENTIAL DISTRIBUTIVE EFFECTS OF NATIONALIZATION POLICIES: THE ECONOMIC ASPECTS

Jorge Cauas and Marcelo Selowsky

A. <u>Introduction, summary, and conclusions</u>

1. Introduction and summary

Arguments for nationalization policies--here defined as the transfer of existing privately owned sectors of the economy into government owner-ship--have become increasingly popular in the literature concerning growth strategies in developing countries. These arguments run from purely politi-cal ones (i.e., an increase in political control, particularly in cases of foreign-owned sectors of the economy) to purely economic arguments (i.e., the need to control monopoly power, nationalization as a means of raising aggregate investment, and so on).

Arguments for nationalization as a means of improving the distribution of income have become increasingly popular in the development literature. The purpose of this chapter is to explore that particular aspect, inquiring specifically into the determinants of the potential redistributive effects of a nationalization policy. What we have in mind is the type of ex ante exercise a Planning Office ought to carry out in order to identify the main parameters determining the distributive effects of such a policy.

Section B of this chapter first explores the determinants of the mag-nitude of the net transfer implicit in a nationalization policy; second, it attempts to derive some figures for such a transfer with orders of mag-nitude that appear plausible for the case of Latin America. Section C discusses the different channels by which such a transfer can be distribu-ted to different sectors of the economy. Section D explores the probable net redistributive effect of using particular channels for distributing

NOTE:
The views expressed in this chapter are those of the authors and should not be ascribed to the World Bank or to its affiliated institutions.

such a transfer. Section E derives some conclusions and suggests additional lines of research.

In order to narrow the scope of analysis we have focused on a particular scenario underlying a nationalization policy; it is characterized as follows:

(i) We will analyze the effect of nationalizing a subset of the corporate sector of the economy owned by the nationals of the country in question. We will leave out foreign-owned enterprises as well as the banking sector, either owned by foreigners or nationals.

(ii) Nationalization will be defined as the purchase by the government of the privately owned capital stock of the sector at a price representing a certain fraction of the market price of that capital.

(iii) After nationalization, the institutional setup will be characterized by state ownership of the nationalized industries.

The first part of the chapter explores the choices open to a government facing such a program of nationalization when the objective is to raise a fiscal tranfer equivalent to the one that could have been obtained through additional taxation.

Two parameters--for which there is usually a sharp difference between ex ante or intended values and the post-nationalization or effective values --appear to be important in determining the size (and sign) of the transfer: the capacity of the government to maintain the previous reinvestment rate in the now-nationalized industries and, second, the extent to which the nationalization program induces changes in the investment behavior of other sectors due to expectation of further nationalization.

In analyzing the magnitude of the transfer as a function of the two policy instruments (the expropriation factor and the post-nationalization reinvestment rate), it was found that under a full expropriation a (permanent) transfer of 0.5 percent of the GNP requires a post-nationalization reinvestment rate at least equal to one-quarter of the rate prior to nationalization. A permanent transfer of 1 percent of GNP requires a new reinvestment rate equal to at least four-fifths of the pre-nationalization rate.

On the other hand, if the pre-nationalization rate is maintained, the government can raise a (permanent) transfer of 1 percent of the GNP only if the implicit expropriation factor is at least three-quarters, i.e., the compensation paid is, at the most, equal to one-quarter of the (present

value of the) net private personal income from the ownership of the expropriated enterprises.

The redistributive effect of such a policy (analyzed in sections C
and D) will depend on the channels being used to distribute the transfer
and on the relative income brackets of the beneficiaries of those particular channels. Two broad categories of channels can be defined, those that
distribute the transfer to the labor input employed in the now-nationalized
industries and those that distribute the transfer to the rest of the
economy.

The first category includes those cases where the transfer is used to
finance additional wages of already employed labor in the sector, and (or)
additional employment over and above the level where the market wage equals
the productivity of labor. The second includes those cases where the
transfer is used to finance a price policy in the nationalized industries
by which the goods produced are sold at a lower price than the previous
(clearing) price. Perhaps most important, it also includes those cases
where the transfer is used to finance public programs via the budget in
other sectors of the economy.

In discussing the net redistributive effects of the nationalization
policy it is useful to distinguish between two situations. The first situation is where the government has the ability to control the surplus in the
now-nationalized enterprises (in other words it can finance the foregone
taxation as well as the compensation payments out of the surplus of those
enterprises and not through the general budget). Basically this means
that the mechanisms by which the net transfer is generated are internal to
the sector to be nationalized and do not induce transfers from other sectors in the economy; under this case the only groups losing from the policy
are the expropriated stockholders in the nationalized sectors.

A second, and different, situation arises when the government is unable
to control such a surplus. A specific case is the one where the workers in
the now-nationalized industries do not allow the enterprise surplus to be
taxed in order to finance the compensation payments as well as the previous
(foregone) taxation. Under this case the losers are not only the expropriated stockholders but also those sectors affected by a decline in public
programs financed by the central budget.

2. Conclusions

In this exercise an attempt has been made to organize a framework in which the main parameters determining the magnitude of the net transfer could be identified. As such the most important conclusions are perhaps related implications for further research.

Two aspects appear important in determining the net transfer: first, the reinvestment policy to be followed by the government vis-a-vis the policy that otherwise would have been undertaken by the private sector; second, the effect of the nationalization policy on the investment behavior of other sectors of the economy.

The effect of nationalization policies in one sector on the investment behavior of other sectors will depend (i) on the amount of uncertainty created by such policy on these sectors and (ii) on the effect of uncertainty on investment behavior. As economists, how much can we say about (i)? What are the ways of implementing a nationalization policy to minimize the amount and therefore the cost of the uncertainty created in other sectors?

With respect to the net redistributive effect of such a transfer it appears to depend crucially on the ability of the government to maintain a constant level of expenditure in other sectors; otherwise the net transfer from the expropriated stockholders can easily be accompanied by perhaps much bigger transfers from income groups affected by a decline in public programs that are not related to the sector in question.

The above considerations lead us to conclude that the redistributive effect will depend crucially on the ability of the government to choose the channels of distribution. If this ability changes as a result of new pressure groups—associated with the nationalization policy—the effective redistributive effects can be quite different from those anticipated. These considerations are reinforced in the case of a negative transfer.

B. Framework

1. The potential behavior of the corporate sector; potential present value of government revenues

The following notation characterizes the corporate sector in question:

K = Capital stock of the sector,

ρ = Net of depreciation rate of return to capital,

$\pi = \rho \cdot K$ = Profits (net-of-depreciation),

τ = Corporate income tax,

$(1 - \tau)\Pi$ = Net profits,

β = Fraction of net profits being distributed as dividends,

$(1 - \beta)$ = Reinvestment rate, and

$t = \sum_i t_i\left(\dfrac{D_i}{D}\right)$ = Weighted personal income tax rate on dividends,

where t_i is the marginal personal income tax applicable to the ith stockholder and (D_i/D) is the share of total distributed dividends perceived by that stockholder.

The above parameters define the distribution of profits between reinvestment, taxation, and net private personal income:

$$
\Pi \Big\langle
\begin{array}{l}
\tau\Pi \text{ (corporate taxes)} \\[4pt]
(1 - \tau)\Pi \text{ (net profits)}
\end{array}
\Big\langle
\begin{array}{l}
(1 - \tau)\beta\Pi \text{ (distrib. profits)} \Big\langle
\begin{array}{l}
(1 - \tau)\beta t\Pi \\ \text{(personal taxation)} \\[4pt]
(1 - \tau)\beta (1 - t)\Pi \\ \text{(net personal income)}
\end{array} \\[14pt]
(1 - \tau)(1 - \beta)\Pi \\ \text{(reinvestment)}
\end{array}
$$

If the above parameters remain constant over time—and we assume all investment consists of reinvested profits—the profits at any year T will be:

(1) $\qquad \Pi = \Pi_0 e^{gT}$,

where g is the rate of growth of profits,

(2) $\qquad g = \dfrac{1}{\Pi}\cdot\dfrac{d\Pi}{dT} = \dfrac{1}{K}\cdot\dfrac{dK}{dT} = (1 - \tau)(1 - \beta)\rho$.

At any year T, the revenue of the government—out of corporate and personal income taxation—becomes equal to:

(3) $\qquad \Pi_0 e^{gT} [\tau + (1 - \tau)\beta t]$.

The present value of government revenues, expressed as a proportion of Π_0, can be written as:

(4) $\qquad R = \dfrac{\tau + (1 - \tau)\beta t}{r - g}$

where r is the discount rate relevant to the government.[1] The condition for convergence is $r > g$ which implies $r > \rho (1 - \tau)(1 - \beta)$.

2. Potential value of government revenues after nationalization

    a) General relation

After nationalization the <u>potential</u> yearly profits (or now "surplus") out of the sector is equal to $1 - \ell(1 - \tau)(1 - \beta)$, profits minus reinvestment, and where the reinvestment rate is defined as a proportion ℓ of the rate before nationalization.

The post-nationalization growth rate of the surplus can now be written as $g_N = \ell(1 - \tau)(1 - \beta)\rho_N$, where ρ_N is the post-nationalization rate of return to capital; ρ_N can be different from ρ reflecting changes in efficiency as a result of the nationalization policy. The <u>present value</u> of such "surplus" is:[2]

$$(5) \qquad S = \frac{1 - \ell(1 - \tau)(1 - \beta)}{r - g_N} \; .$$

Assume the government decides to pay a compensation equal to a proportion k of the present value--as seen by the private sector--of the net personal income out of the ownership of the capital to be nationalized, V. The value of this compensation becomes therefore kV, where V can be defined as:

$$(6) \qquad V = \frac{(1 - \tau)\beta(1 - t)}{i - g} \; ,$$

where i represents the discount rate as seen by the private sector.[3]

The present value of the <u>change</u> in government revenues due to the nationalization policy, which we will define as N, is:

$$(7) \qquad N = S - R - kV,$$

$$(8) \qquad N = \frac{1 - \ell(1 - \tau)(1 - \beta)}{r - g_N} - \frac{\tau + (1 - \tau)\beta t}{r - g} - \frac{k(1 - \tau)\beta(1 - t)}{i - g} \; .$$

Assuming for simplicity that $\rho_N = \rho$, that is there is no change in productivity after nationalization, we can write $g_N = \ell g$ and we have:

$$(9) \qquad N = \frac{1 - \ell(1 - \tau)(1 - \beta)}{r - \ell g} - \frac{\tau + (1 - \tau)\beta t}{r - g} - \frac{k(1 - \tau)\beta(1 - t)}{i - g} \; .$$

Given the values of β, τ, t, ρ, r, and i, N will be a function of ℓ and k, the post-nationalization reinvestment policy and the compensation policy. We can analyze two special cases: first, maintaining the reinvestment policy ($\ell = 1$) and second, a situation where reinvestment becomes zero after nationalization ($\ell = 0$).[4]

b) Maintaining the reinvestment policy

In this case, with $\ell = 1$, expression (9) becomes:

$$(10) \qquad N_1 = \frac{1 - (1 - \tau)(1 - \beta)}{r - g} - \frac{\tau + (1 - \tau)\beta t}{r - g} - \frac{k(1 - \tau)\beta(1 - t)}{i - g} \;.$$

Defining as V_G the present value of the personal income as seen by the government (where r is now used in discounting the future flows), we have:

$$(11) \qquad V_G = \frac{(1 - \tau)\beta(1 - t)}{r - g} \;.$$

Defining $\sigma = \dfrac{i - g}{r - g}$ we can write:

$$(12) \qquad V_G = \sigma V \;.$$

Expression (10) can now be written as:

$$(13) \qquad N_1 = (\sigma - k)V \;.$$

The term $(\sigma - k)$ can be interpreted as the expropriation factor as seen by the government; if $i = r$, this factor becomes $(1 - k)$ equal to the expropriation factor as seen by the private sector; if $r > i$ ($\sigma < 1$), the expropriation factor, as seen by the government, is smaller than the one perceived by the private sector; the reverse is true when $\sigma > 1$.

The value of k that makes the potential transfer--as seen by the government--equal to zero is $k_1^* = \sigma$; if $\sigma = 1$ ($r = i$) the value of k_1^* becomes one.

c) No reinvestment

Assuming the government does not undertake any (net) reinvestment after nationalization, ($\ell = 0$), expression (9) becomes:

$$(14) \qquad N_2 = \frac{1}{r} - \frac{\tau + (1 - \tau)\beta t}{r - g} - \frac{k(1 - \tau)\beta(1 - t)}{i - g} \, .$$

After some manipulation we can write:

$$(15) \qquad N_2 = (\sigma - k)V + \frac{(1 - \tau)(1 - \beta)}{r - g} \left(1 - \frac{\rho}{r}\right) ,$$

$$(16) \qquad N_2 = N_1 + \frac{(1 - \tau)(1 - \beta)}{r - g} \left(1 - \frac{\rho}{r}\right) .$$

From (16) it is clear that:

$$N_2 < N_1 \text{ if } \rho > r,$$
$$N_2 = N_1 \text{ if } \rho = r.$$

Expression (16) shows that N_2 can be written as N_1 plus a correction factor whose sign depends on the sign of $\rho - r$. If $\rho > r$, the present value of one dollar invested is larger than one: in this case the transfer out of the nationalization is a positive function of the post-reinvestment rate. If $\rho = r$, the present value of one dollar invested is equal to one dollar's worth of consumption: in this case the transfer is invariant to the reinvestment policy to be followed by the government after nationalization.[5]

The value of k that makes the transfer equal to zero (k_2*) becomes now:

$$(17) \qquad k_2* = k_1* + \frac{\sigma(1 - \beta)}{\beta(1 - t)} \left(1 - \frac{\rho}{r}\right) .$$

Expression (17) is a direct reflection of the relationships between N_2 and N_1 (under different values of ρ/r) just discussed. If $\rho = r$, the compensation factor (k*) that makes the transfer equal to zero is invariant to the reinvestment policy of the government. If $\rho > r$, the value of k* becomes smaller ($k_2* < k_1*$) for the no reinvestment case.

3.   Some extensions
     a)   Side effects of the nationalization policy on the rest of
          the industrial sector

What are the effects of the nationalization policy on the investment behavior and therefore on the growth of the rest of the industrial sector?

How does this affect the present value of tax revenues out of the income of capital from this sector? This section attempts to explore such questions.

To the extent that today's nationalization policies generate uncertainty about the possibility of future nationalization policies in other sectors, the reinvestment policies of such sectors will be affected. It is hard to specify a functional form for such a change in investment behavior.

We can only speculate on the determinants of uncertainty induced by a given nationalization policy in the present. It will depend on the extent to which "rules of the game" concerning other sectors can be institutionalized; on the other hand, the "degree of uncertainty" will be itself a function of time, where such a "degree" is revised over time according to how consistently the government behaves concerning such rules of the game.

In order to derive some orders of magnitude we will simply assume that the reinvestment rate in other sectors changes forever by a certain amount as a result of today's nationalization policies in the corporate sector.[6]

The present value of tax revenues out of capital income in the industrial sector not to be nationalized—in terms of the base-year profits of that sector—can be written as:

$$(18) \qquad R_s = \frac{\tau_s + (1 - \tau_s)\beta_s t_s}{r - \rho_s(1 - \tau_s)(1 - \beta_s)} .$$

Expression (18) is equivalent to expression (4); we have simply added a subscript s to the parameters; these parameters are therefore specific to the other industrial sectors not to be nationalized. Although we are referring to the noncorporate sectors, we have left the parameter τ in the formula: it is simply a convenient way of taking into account other taxes on capital at the level of the firm or the fact that the government has decided to nationalize a subset of the corporate sector; in this case τ will reflect the corporate tax weighted by the fraction of corporate profits in the total profits of the sectors not to be nationalized.

The effect on such revenue of a once and for all change in β or the "non-reinvestment" rate is:

$$(19) \qquad dR_s = \frac{(1 - r_s)}{(1 - g_s)^2} \left\{ t_s \left[r - \rho_s (1 - \tau_s) \right] - \rho_s \tau_s \right\} d\beta_s .$$

Given the convergence condition $r > g_s$ and if $\rho_s \geq r$, it can be shown that the coefficient of $d\beta_s$ in (19) is always negative. This means that the present value of tax revenues on the capital income of the other sector declines when the reinvestment rate in these sectors, $(1 - \beta_s)$, goes down.[7]

After this extension we need to define a new concept of transfer, the one that takes into account this decline in tax revenues out of other sectors; we will define therefore:

$$(20) \qquad \Omega = N + \gamma dR_s \ ,$$

where Ω is the <u>net transfer</u> out of the nationalization policy and where γ is the ratio between the base-year profits of those other sectors over the profits of the corporate sector to be nationalized.

For the two alternative values of ℓ, $\ell = 0$ and $\ell = 1$, we can define:

$$(21) \qquad \Omega_1 = N_1 + \gamma dR_s \ ,$$

$$(22) \qquad \Omega_2 = N_2 + \gamma dR_s \ .$$

b)   Tax policy as a substitute

What is the magnitude of an additional tax on distributed dividends-- over and above the existing personal income tax--yielding an increase in tax revenues equal to the net transfer out of nationalization.[8]

Differentiating expression (4) and solving for dt we get:

$$(23) \qquad dt = \frac{(r - g)}{(1 - \tau)\beta} \ dR \ .$$

If the policy is to obtain a value of dR which will be a substitute of a nationalization policy aiming at a given net transfer $\hat{\Omega}$, we have:

$$(24) \qquad dR = \hat{\Omega} = \Omega(\hat{k}) \ .$$

Where $\hat{k}$ is the implicit value of k that, given the values of all other parameters, determines a net transfer equal to $\hat{\Omega}$.

The tax change required to yield a value of dR $= \hat{\Omega}$ can also be expressed in terms of $\hat{k}$:

(25) $\hat{dt} = f(\hat{k})$.

The above relationships are shown graphically in figure 1.

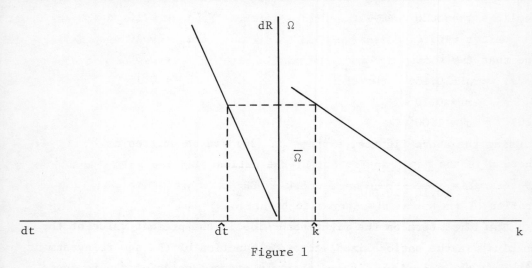

Figure 1

4.   Some orders of magnitude

(i) We attempt here to evaluate some of the earlier equations in order to derive some orders of magnitude. The main expressions required for such an evaluation are:

N = Present value of the transfer due to nationalization,

dR_s = Change in the present value of taxation from other sectors induced by the nationalization policy,

$\gamma = \dfrac{\Pi_s}{\Pi_0}$ = Initial profits in (other) sectors whose investment behavior is affected by the policy over the initial profits of the sector to be nationalized, and

$\Omega = N + \gamma dR_s$ = Present value of the <u>net</u> transfer.

Given that N is expressed in terms of the base-year profits of the sector to be nationalized and dR_s is expressed in terms of the base-year profits of the other (relevant) sectors, we need γ to add up N and dR_s. In this way Ω can also be expressed in terms of the initial profits of the sector to be nationalized (Π_0).

For given values of the other parameters Ω can be written in terms of k, ℓ, and γ.

$$(26) \qquad \Omega(k, \ell, \gamma) = S(\ell) - R - kV + \gamma dR_s \ .$$

We will use the following values for those other parameters:

$\tau = 0.20$	$\tau_s = 0.10$
$t = 0.20$	$t_s = 0.10$
$\beta = 0.50$	$\beta_s = 0.50$
$\rho = 0.15$	$\rho_s = 0.15$
$r = 0.10$	
$\sigma = 1.00$[9]	

By using the above figures, expression (26) can be written as:

$$(27) \qquad \Omega = \frac{1 - 0.4\ell}{0.10 - 0.06\ell} - 7 - 8.k + \gamma dR_s \ .$$

The first term on the right-hand side is the present value of the "surplus" in the nationalized sector, a function of the new reinvestment policy ℓ; the second term shows that the present value of the foregone taxation out of the sector to be nationalized amounts to seven times the base-year profits of the sector; the third term shows that the present value of net personal income of that sector is equal to eight times the base-year profits of the sector.

Table 1 shows that the value of N_1 ranges from 0 to 8, while that of N_2 lies between -5 and 3 for values of k between 1 and 0. The difference between these two ranges reflects the fact that, independent of the value of k, nationalization policies that maintain the previous reinvestment rate will yield an additional transfer of five times the base-year profits of the sector in relation to a situation where the reinvestment rate becomes zero.

The value of dR_s has been obtained by assuming that the reinvestment rate in the other sectors falls by 20%, as a result of the nationalization policy, from a value of $1 - \beta_s = 0.5$ to a value of $1 - \beta_s = 0.4$.[10] This implies a value of $dR_s = -1.1$.[11]

For γ we have chosen two alternative values, one and two; in other words we assume the sectors whose investment behavior is negatively affected by the nationalization policy have (in the base year) profits which are at most twice the profits of the sectors to be nationalized.

Table 1. Present Value of the Net Transfer (Ω) in Terms of the Base
Year Profits of the Sector to be Nationalized

Reinvestment Policy Followed	k (1)	S(ℓ) (2)	R (3)	kV (4)	N (5)=(2)-(3)-(4)	γdR_s $\gamma=1$ (6)	$\gamma=2$ (7)	Ω $\gamma=1$ (8)=(5)-(6)	$\gamma=2$ (9)=(5)-(7)	$\hat{d}t$ $\gamma=1$	$\gamma=2$
Constant ($\ell=1$)	0	15.0	7	0	8	-1.1	-2.2	6.9	5.8	0.69	0.58
	0.3	15.0	7	2.4	5.6	-1.1	-2.2	4.5	3.4	0.45	0.34
	0.5	15.0	7	4.0	4.0	-1.1	-2.2	2.9	1.8	0.29	0.18
	0.8	15.0	7	6.4	1.6	-1.1	-2.2	0.5	-0.6	0.05	
	1.0	15.0	7	8.0	0	-1.1	-2.2	-1.1	-2.2		
Zero net reinvestment ($\ell=0$)	0	10.0	7	0	3	-1.1	-2.2	1.9	0.8	0.19	0.08
	0.3	10.0	7	2.4	0.6	-1.1	-2.2	-0.5	-1.6		
	0.5	10.0	7	4.0	-1.0	-1.1	-2.2	-2.1	-3.2		
	0.8	10.0	7	6.4	-3.4	-1.1	-2.2	-4.5	-5.6		
	1.0	10.0	7	8.0	-5.0	-1.1	-2.2	-6.1	-7.2		

Perhaps the most important message of table 1 is:

(a) It shows the importance of the post-nationalization reinvestment policy to be undertaken by the government. The value of N(k) appears very sensitive to this policy, even reaching negative values; this means Ω could be negative in those cases, even disregarding the effect of the nationalization policy on other sectors of the economy ($\gamma dR_s = 0$).

(b) It shows the large magnitudes that the (negative) value of γdR_s can achieve vis-a-vis the value of N(k). In other words it shows the importance--on the value of Ω--of the negative effect that the nationalization policy can have on the investment behavior of the rest of the economy.[12]

Figure 2 summarizes the information concerning Ω that appears in table 1; it shows the value of Ω as a function of k for alternative values of γ.

From figure 2 it is clear that if the nationalization policy is characterized by zero net investment, only extremely low figures of k are able to generate positive values of Ω ($k \leq 0.10$ for $\gamma = 1$ and $k \leq 0.25$ for $\gamma = 2$). On the other hand, in the best of all situations--a constant reinvestment policy and a value of $\gamma = 1$--the government can pay at the most a compensation equal to k = .85 if a positive net transfer wants to be achieved.

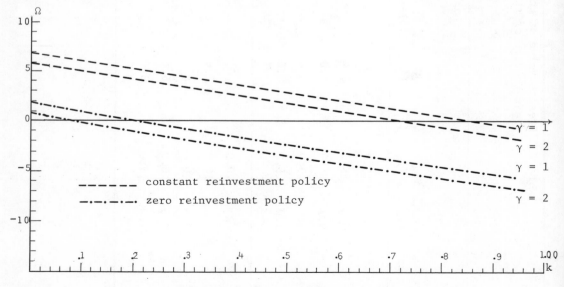

Figure 2. Present value of the net transfer in terms
of the yearly profits of the base year
of the sector to be nationalized

Table 2 shows the annual equivalent of the net transfer as a fraction of GNP and government expenditure. We have assumed that the government decides to spread the use of the net transfer over an infinite period of time and as a constant fraction f_Y of that year's gross national product Y_T:

$$(28) \qquad \Omega . \Pi_0 = {}_0\int^{\infty} f_Y Y_T dT .$$

Expression (28) shows that the present value of the annual equivalent $f_Y . Y_T$ must be equal to the present value of the transfer. Denoting g_Y as the exponential growth rate of the GNP we get:

$$(29) \qquad \Omega \cdot \Pi_0 = \frac{f_Y Y_0}{r - g_Y} ,$$

$$(30) \qquad f_Y = \frac{\Pi_0}{Y_0} \Omega (r - g_Y) .$$

Table 2. Annual Equivalent of the Net Transfer as a Proportion of GNP and Government Expenditure, E

Reinvestment Policy Followed	k	As a percentage of GNP		As a percentage of E	
		$\gamma = 1$	$\gamma = 2$	$\gamma = 1$	$\gamma = 2$
Constant	0	1.38	1.16	6.90	5.80
	0.3	0.90	0.68	4.50	3.40
	0.5	0.58	0.36	2.90	1.80
	0.8	0.10	−0.12	0.50	−0.60
	1.0	−0.22	−0.44	−1.10	−2.20
No reinvestment	0	0.38	0.16	1.90	0.80
	0.3	−0.10	−0.32	−0.50	−1.60
	0.5	−0.42	−0.64	−2.10	−3.20
	0.8	−0.90	−1.12	−4.50	−5.60
	1.0	−1.22	−1.44	−6.10	−7.20

If government expenditure represents a constant fraction ε of GNP, the annual equivalent of the net transfer as a function of that expenditure becomes:

(31) $$f_E = \frac{1}{\varepsilon} \cdot f_Y .$$

In order to compute f_Y and f_E we have used the following values:

$\frac{\Pi_0}{Y_0} =$ "Declared" profits of the sector to be nationalized as a fraction of GNP at the base year = 0.05,

$\varepsilon = 0.20$,

$g_Y = 0.06$.

Table 2 shows that the annual equivalent of the net transfer--as described above--can range between -1.4% and +1.4% of GNP and between -7% and +7% of government expenditure, according to the value of k and γ being used.[13]

(ii) Assume that the government decides to undertake a nationalization policy in order to obtain an annual equivalent of the transfer equal to, let's say, 0.5 and 1.0 percent of GNP ($f_Y = 0.005$ and $f_Y = 0.010$). What are the choices open to the government concerning the two policy variables, (1 - k) and ℓ, the expropriation factor and the reinvestment policy, consistent with those magnitudes of the transfer?

Solving for Ω from expression (29) and substituting into (27) we obtain, for given values of γ, the combination of (1 - k) and ℓ able to generate a value of f_Y equal to 0.005 and 0.010, respectively. These combinations are shown in the "isotransfer" lines presented in figure 3.

From the figure it becomes clear that, in the best of situations (γ = 1), a transfer of 0.5 percent of GNP cannot be achieved if the post-nationalization reinvestment rate is less than one quarter of the previous rate. Similarly, a transfer of 1 percent of GNP cannot be achieved if ℓ becomes smaller than 0.8.

On the other hand, by choosing a relatively high expropriation factor, equal to three-quarters, the value of ℓ cannot be lower than 0.725 and 1.0 if the target transfer is 0.5 and 1.0 percent of GNP, respectively; in other words by maintaining the reinvestment rate (ℓ = 1) the government can raise

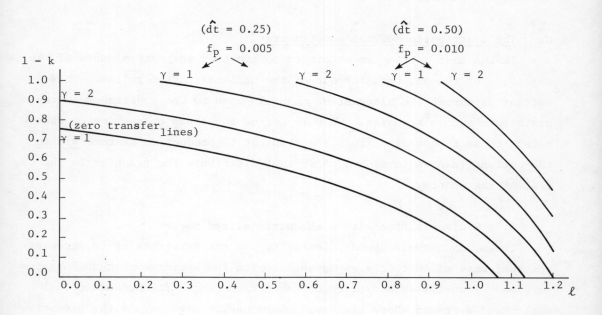

Figure 3. "Isotransfers"

(as a function of the expropriation factor and the
post-nationalization reinvestment policy)

1 − k: Expropriation factor

ℓ: Post-nationalization reinvestment factor

γ: Relative dimension of the sectors subject to uncertainty

f_p: Transfer as a proportion of GNP

$\widehat{dt}$: Additional tax rate on dividends equivalent to the
nationalization policy.

---

a transfer equal to 1 percent of GNP only be expropriating 75 percent of
the private personal income of the sector.

(iii) What is the additional tax on dividends that can be considered
as a substitute for the nationalization policy in the sense of yielding an
equivalent magnitude of the net transfer? Those values of $\widehat{dt}$--obtained
through expression (20)--are shown (for positive values of the net transfer)
in the last two columns of table 1. For example, that a nationalization
policy characterized by $\ell = 1$ and k = 0.5 will yield, under $\gamma = 2$, the
same net transfer as an additional tax on dividends of 18%.

Figure 3 shows those values of $\hat{dt}$ for an annual transfer amounting to 0.5 and 1.0 percent of GNP; the values of $\hat{dt}$ are 25% and 50%, respectively.

C. The distribution of the net transfer

In the last section we attempted to identify the determinants of the magnitude of the net transfer out of the nationalization policy. This section discusses the alternative channels open to the government to redistribute such a transfer. We will define two broad categories of channels: those that redistribute the transfer to productive factors within the nationalized sectors, and those that distribute the transfer to the rest of the economy.

1. Redistribution within the nationalized sector

Two main channels appear clear: to use the net transfer to increase the real wage of currently employed labor in the sector over and above its marginal productivity and/or to use such transfer to finance additional employment over and above the level where market wage equals the productivity of labor. These alternatives can be seen in figure 4.

For any year the volume of employment--if, as we have assumed before, the nationalized firms attempt to maximize their yearly surplus or profits --will be determined where the market wage is equal to the marginal productivity of labor. The annual equivalent of the net transfer can now be used either to increase the real wage over the initial wage and/or finance additional employment over and above the initial value of L.

If the transfer is used to finance a combination of changes in real wages and employment it can be shown as the shaded area in figure 4. Defining $a(T) = f_Y \cdot Y_T$ and linearizing the demand for labor, that area can be written as:

$$(32) \qquad a(T) = \Delta w \cdot (L + \Delta L) + \tfrac{1}{2} (\Delta F_L \cdot \Delta L) \ ,$$

and where F_L represents the marginal productivity of labor; after manipulating the last term in order to express it in terms of the elasticity of the demand for labor and dividing by W or the initial wage bill we get:

$$(33) \qquad \frac{a(T)}{W} = \frac{\Delta w}{w} + \frac{\Delta L}{L} \left[\frac{\Delta w}{w} + 1/2 \ \frac{1}{\eta} \ \frac{\Delta L}{L} \right] \ ,$$

where η is the elasticity of demand for labor (here defined as $\eta > 0$).

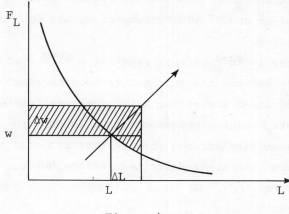

Figure 4

Expression (33) shows the combinations of increases in real wages (over the marginal productivity of labor) and changes in employment (over the one determined under maximization conditions) able to be financed by the net transfer $\frac{a(T)}{W}$. These combinations are also shown in figure 5.[14]

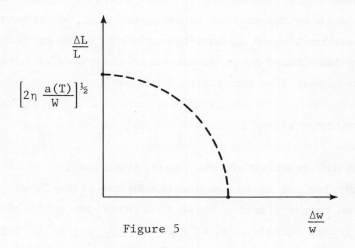

Figure 5

The higher the elasticity of demand for labor the larger the change in employment that can be financed given the values of $\frac{a(T)}{W}$ and $\frac{\Delta w}{w}$; the reason is that larger elasticities imply a smaller decline in the marginal productivity of labor as employment increases: this means a smaller gap between the wage rate and the marginal productivity of labor to be financed by the net transfer. On the other hand, given the value of $a(T)$, the initial wage bill W is crucial in determining the values of $\frac{\Delta w}{w}$ and $\frac{\Delta L}{L}$.

Given that the ratio $\frac{a(T)}{W}$ is a function of the ratio $\frac{\pi}{W}$, it is clear that the magnitudes of $\frac{\Delta w}{w}$ and $\frac{\Delta L}{L}$ will depend crucially on the (ex ante) shares of capital and labor.[15]

At this stage it is important again to notice that a(T) is a function of the difference between the yearly net-of-reinvestment surplus generated in the now-nationalized enterprise minus foregone taxation and minus compensation payments, which are assumed to be taken care of adequately. This is not without some significance for the institutional arrangements required to implement the above-described redistribution; we will come to this point later on.

2. Redistribution to the rest of the economy

The net transfer a(T) can be redistributed to the rest of the economy through two mechanisms:

(i) An increase in the government budget that now can be used to finance public programs not directly related to the nationalized sectors.

(ii) By following a price policy by which the goods produced by the nationalized sector are sold at a lower price than the "real" or clearing price implicit in the earlier evaluations of π; in other words the net transfer can be seen as an implicit subsidy to the price that otherwise would have been faced by consumers in that particular market.

For any year T we can write:

$$(34) \qquad Q \cdot \Delta P = a(T) \ ,$$

where Q is the quantity produced under maximization of the (ex ante distribution) surplus and ΔP is the decline in the price faced by the consumers in relation to the clearing price that otherwise would have prevailed in that particular market. Notice that Q <u>is invariant to the way the government distributes the transfer</u> and therefore is not "revised" according to the price policy followed by the government

$$(35) \qquad \frac{\Delta P}{P} = \frac{a(T)}{Q \cdot P} = f_Y \cdot \frac{Y_T}{Q \cdot P} \ .$$

Expression (35) shows that the "implicit" percentage subsidy that can be financed is equal to f_Y divided by the ratio of total sales (valued at the ex ante clearing price) to GNP. This is also shown in figure 6.

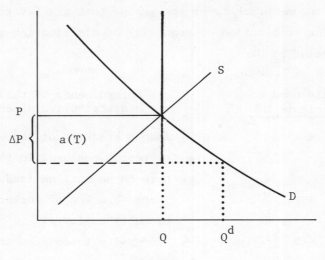

Figure 6

It is important to notice that the real redistributive effect of this policy will depend heavily on how the government rations the quantity Q, given that at the new price the quantity demanded is large (Q^d). If that rationing is exactly equal to the structure of the pre-nationalization consumption pattern, then the implicit subsidy will be proportional to how much of that good was originally consumed by different income groups. Otherwise it will depend completely on the new criteria followed by the government concerning how to ration the quantity Q.

D.   The net redistributive effect and further considerations

    1.   The net redistributive effect

In discussing the redistributive effect among different income groups out of the nationalization policy it is useful to distinguish between two situations.

    (i) A situation where the government can control the (net of reinvestment) surplus generated in the nationalized sectors in such a way it can finance kV, R, and γdR_s <u>out</u> of that surplus and not through the use of the government budget. In other words the <u>mechanisms by which Ω is generated are internal to the sector to be nationalized</u> and do not induce transfers from other sectors of the economy. This is the implitict framework used in the preceding section.

If this is the case, the net redistributive effect will depend on the relative income brackets of the stockholders of the nationalized industries

vis-a-vis the income brackets of the groups that are favored by the particular channel (or combination of channels) of distribution being used to
transfer the value of Ω.

Channels used to distribute Ω		Determinants of the net redistributive effect
(1)	$+\Delta w$	Income brackets of the workers currently employed in the sectors to be nationalized.
(2)	$+\Delta L$	Income bracket of workers additionally employed.
(3)	$-\Delta P$	Propensity to consume the goods of the sector to be nationalized by different income groups. Rationing criteria to be used.
(4)	$+$ Budget	Income brackets of the groups favored by public programs that now can be financed by an increased government budget.

Even if the government can control the value of Ω as described above,
the question arises to what extent it can in practice control the channel
to be used to distribute it. In other words, is it realistic to assume
that the channel used to distribute Ω is independent of the mechanism by
which Ω is generated?

This is obviously an empirical question. At this stage and given the
empirical evidence, it would seem channel (1) has the highest chance and
channel (4) the lowest.

(ii) A somehow more complicated situation, but perhaps a more realistic
one, arises when the government is unable to generate Ω without inducing
some transfers _from_ other sectors of the economy; in other words Ω is
raised by mechanisms that are not completely internal to the sector to be
nationalized.

The most relevant example is a situation where the value of the compensation, or perhaps more importantly the decline in general government revenues due to R and dR_s, cannot be replenished from the surplus generated
in the enterprises now nationalized. In this case not only does the

government not have any control of the mechanism by which Ω is generated, almost surely it also will not have control of the channel to be used to distribute it.

Assume a situation where the workers of the now-nationalized industries do not allow the enterprise surplus to be taxed in order to pay for kV and the replenishment of the government budget due to -R and $-\gamma dR_s$. In this situation we observe the following effects for the case where the reinvestment rate is being maintained ($\ell = 1$):

Income of Workers in the Nationalized Sector	Previous Stockholders	Government Budget
$+ V(1 - k)$	$-V(1 - k)$	
$+ Vk$		$-kV$
$+ R$		$-R$
		$-\gamma dR_s$
Total $\quad V + R = S$	$-V(1 - k)$	$-kV - R - \gamma dR_s$

The total transfer to the workers, equal to $V + R = S$ or present value of the net of reinvestment surplus of the sector, is obviously larger than Ω; part of the transfer, $V(1 - k)$ or the expropriation component, is financed by the previous stockholders; the compensation factor kV and the previous taxation R are implicitly being financed by the income groups affected by a reduction of government spending in the rest of the economy. The value of γdR_s, although it does not represent a gain in income for the workers in the nationalized industries, is nonetheless a cost for the income groups affected by that reduction in government spending.

It is perhaps interesting to obtain some orders of magnitude for the ratio kV + R/V + R, or the fraction of the present value of the increased income of already employed workers in the sector that is financed under this scenario by the rest of the economy via a decline in government expenditure in other sectors.

This ratio ranges from 46,6% to 100% for the extreme values of k; for a value of k = 0.5 the ratio is 73,3%. In this case almost three-quarters of the higher wages that now can be financed in the sector will come at the expense of the income groups affected by the decline in public funds available for other programs in the rest of the economy. This is without taking

	V	kV	R	$kV + R\big/V + R$
k = 0	8	0	7	46,6%
k = 0.3	8	2.4	7	62,7%
k = 0.5	8	4.0	7	73,3%
k = 0.8	8	6.4	7	89,3%
k = 1.0	8	8.0	7	100,0%

into account the effect of $-\gamma dR_s$ which also must be borne by these income groups.[16]

2.   What happens if Ω is negative?

As we saw in table 1 there is a possibility of a negative Ω, particularly in the cases where net reinvestment becomes zero after the nationalization. What are the net redistributive effects of a negative Ω?

An easy way of interpreting a negative Ω is the following: after the government has taxed the surplus in the now-nationalized industries in order to finance compensation payments as well as induced declines in government revenues (R and γdR_s)--therefore holding constant the level of real expenditure in other sectors--the end result is that those enterprises run into a deficit.

To the extent that deficit--as defined above--is financed by a subsidy out of the government budget the channel by which the (now-negative) value of Ω is being distributed is clear: again it will be at the expense of the income groups affected by a decline in government spending in other sectors of the economy.

From the above it would appear that under a negative Ω the government has very little choice concerning the channel by which that negative value can be "distributed"; it is hardly conceivable that labor in the now-nationalized sector would accept a decline in their real income vis-a-vis the pre-nationalization situation.

3.   Adjustments for tax evasion at the level of the enterprise

Up to now we have used the same concept of Π, namely the declared profits as they appear in the national accounts, in computing the present value of the surplus after nationalization, the value of the compensation, and the foregone taxation out of the sector.

To the extent there is a difference between effective and declared profits (to which the legal rate τ is applied), an adjustment must be made to the present value of the surplus after nationalization. This obviously will increase the present value of the net transfer Ω.

We can define:

$$\Pi \text{ effective} = (1 + \lambda)\Pi$$

where λ is the implicit rate of evasion and where Π represents the declared profits to which the legal rate τ is applied. The value of Ω will increase by an amount that will depend on the investment policy followed after nationalizaton:

$$\text{Constant reinvestment:} \quad \frac{\lambda}{r - g} = 25\lambda$$

$$\text{Zero reinvestment:} \quad \frac{\lambda}{r} = 10\lambda$$

If we assume $\lambda = 0.10$, the value of Ω increases in an amount equal to 2.5 and 1.0 for the alternative investment policies.

Table 3. Value of the Net Transfer Corrected by Tax Evasion

	Ω		Annual equivalent			
			As Percentage of GNP		As Percentage of Government Expenditure	
	$\lambda = 0$	$\lambda = 0.10$	$\lambda = 0$	$\lambda = 0.10$	$\lambda = 0$	$\lambda = 0.10$
Max	6.9	9.4	1.38	1.88	6.90	9.40
Min	-7.2	-6.2	-1.44	-1.24	-7.20	-6.2

Table 3 shows the effect of correcting the extreme values of the net transfer by a rate of tax evasion at the level of the enterprise equal to 10% ($\lambda = 0.10$).

4. Adjustments for changes in productivity

In the earlier exercises we have implicitly assumed that the productivity of capital ρ is maintained after the nationalization takes place; to the extent that there are changes in efficiency in the use of resources in the sector, that productivity ought to be adjusted and, correspondingly, the value of the net transfer Ω.

Appendix 2

NOTES

1.
$$\int_{o}^{\infty} e^{(g - r)T} dT = \frac{1}{r - g}$$

$$g - r < 0$$

2. This analysis assumes the same ex post market behavior concerning the "degree of use of monopoly power" on the part of the government; otherwise expression (5) must be corrected by a factor reflecting a change in the degree of competitive behavior of the enterprise. This correction factor is basically a function of the elasticities of supply and demand of the firm.

3. It is possible to identify some values of k corresponding to particular compensation criteria:

   (i) The government decides to pay the present value of the base year net personal income out of the firm

$$k' = \frac{(1 - \tau)\beta(1 - t)}{i} \bigg/ V = \frac{i - g}{i} \ .$$

   (ii) The government decides to pay the present value of the base year net personal income _assuming_ all future net profits will be distributed. We can now define:

$$k'' = \frac{(1 - \tau)(1 - t)}{i} \bigg/ V = \frac{i - g}{i\beta} \ .$$

4. The choice of investment policy can be treated in more sophisticated terms, assuming a choice through intertemporal optimization. Nevertheless, this treatment would not add substantially to the problem addressed specifically in this chapter, and would substantially complicate the treatment.

5. The case of $\rho < r$ means that the productivity of the enterprise is lower than the government's discount rate. In this case, reinvestment has a negative contribution to the present value of the transfer.

6. We could specify a more complex behavior of the reinvestment rate of the other sectors over time. Denoting the reinvestment rate as ϕ_T (where $\phi_T = 1 - \beta_{sT}$ and β_{sT} is the fraction of profits not reinvested in

such other sectors), we could assume a behavior similar to the one shown in the following figure.

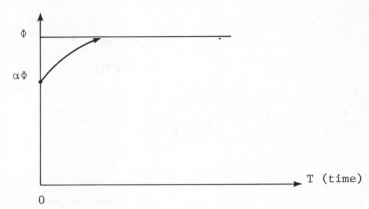

ϕ_T (reinvestment rate)

Without nationalization policies, the long-run (no uncertainty) reinvestment rate is equal to ϕ; the year of nationalization (T = 0) that that rate drops to a fraction α of the long-run rate. However that rate can be "revised" over time according to the "consistency" of the government concerning "the rules of the game." That revision of ϕ_T can be proportional to the differences between the current value and the long-run no-uncertaint value ϕ. We can therefore write:

$$\frac{d\phi_T}{dT} = \mu(\phi - \phi_T) \ .$$

Solving the differential equation we obtain

$$\phi_T = \phi \left[1 - (1 - \alpha)e^{-\mu T} \right] \ .$$

At time T after the nationalization policy, the reinvestment rate will depend on: (i) the long-run no-uncertainty rate ϕ; (ii) the short-run drop in that rate due to the nationalization, $1 - \alpha$; (iii) the value of μ, or the speed of "recovery."

The value of α probably depends on the "short-run credibility gap" of the government as seen by the sectors not to be nationalized; the value of μ probably depends on "how consistent" is the future behavior of the government concerning such sectors.

7. The general value for dR_s, when β_s follows the behavior assumed in the previous footnote, has to be calculated as the present value of the differences in each moment of time of the value of R_s after and before the change in β_s.

8. For simplicity we assume the value of β is invariant to this additional tax.

9. A value of $\sigma = 1$ implies $r = i$, the discount rate of the private sector to be equal to the discount rate relevant to the government. Notice however that we do allow for a difference between such a discount rate and the marginal productivity of capital.

The assumption of $\sigma = 1$ tends, if anything, to bias our results in favor of nationalization policies in the sense that the use of $\sigma < 1$ would reduce the value of the transfer as seen by the government.

It is likely that the typical rate of social yield on government investments would be higher than the <u>after-tax</u> (though not necessarily higher than the <u>before-tax</u>) rate of return on private investments. The theoretical basis for considering the social rate of discount--in a mixed economy--to be a weighted average of the before-tax and after-tax rates of return on private-sector investments can be found in A. C. Harberger, "On Measuring the Social Opportunity Cost of Public Funds," in <u>Project Evaluation</u> (Chicago: Markham, 1973) and A. Sandmo and J. Dreze, "Discount Rates for Public Investments in Closed and Open Economies," <u>Econometrica</u> (November 1971) also reprinted in Niskanen et al., ed., <u>Benefit Cost and Policy Analysis 1972</u> (Aldine, 1973).

Our assumption that $r = i$ thus selects from this range the extreme which produces results most favorable to a nationalization policy.

10. We are again assuming here that most of the investment undertaken in these other sectors is financed internally.

11. This figure was obtained as $R_S(\beta_S + \Delta\beta_S) - R_S(\beta_S)$ and not through formula (19). The reason is that the coefficient of $d\beta_S$ in (19) is highly sensitive to the value of β_S.

12. We have attempted to compute the value of dR_S according to the change in investment behavior outlined in footnote 6. For such an exercise we have used $\alpha = 0.5$ (investment drops down by 50% in the year of nationalization) and an adjustment factor of $\mu = 0.23$; that adjustment factor implies approximately half of a "recovery" in three years and 95% of "recovery" in 10 years. The value of dR_S derived under these conditions was -0.8.

13. If the government decides to pay a compensation based on a static firm we can use the values of k' and k'' (as defined in footnote 3 to derive the value of the transfer in tables 1 and 2. These values are $k' = 0.4$ and $k'' = 0.8$.

14. The concavity or convexity of the function will depend on the relative magnitudes of $a(T)/W$ and $1/2\eta$. In the case of the figure, $a(T)/W > 1/2\eta$.

15. The <u>change</u> in income of the additionally employed labor can be larger or smaller than the volume of the transfer ABDC; if their wage in alternative activities $(\hat{w})$ was smaller than their productivity in the corporate sector (F_L) the change in their income becomes equal to ABFE, a magnitude larger than ABDC.

On the other hand the employment of
ΔL can have a net effect on GNP if the
productivity of that labor in other sectors ($\hat{F}_L$) was smaller than the productivity in the corporate sector F_L. This net
increment in GNP becomes CDHG in this
particular case. Notice that if $\hat{F}_L = \hat{w}$
this increment in GNP is exactly equal to
the difference between the change in the
income of that labor and the volume of
the transfer.

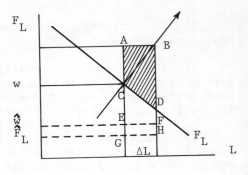

16. We are not considering here other short-run adjustment mechanisms,
particularly deficit financing of the budget; deficit financing through an
increased indebtedness with the Central Bank can be particularly important
for some countries.

APPENDIX III

MATHEMATICAL APPENDIX

Henry Bruton and Charles R. Frank, Jr.

In this appendix we specify formally a model of a developing economy which has three main sectors: (i) a modern sector, (ii) a rural traditional or informal sector, and (iii) an urban traditional sector.

Modern-sector output Q_m is a function of capital K invested in the modern sector, and employment in the modern sector, L_m

$$(1) \qquad Q_m = F(\alpha K, \beta L_m).$$

The parameters α and β represent capital- and labor-augmenting technical change, respectively. Both α and β are functions of time.

The modern-sector wage rate W is a function of the marginal productivity of labor in the modern sector.

$$(2) \qquad W = F_L.$$

We assume that traditional-sector output for urban and rural sectors Q_u and Q_r, respectively, are each composed of two parts, the first of which is output of the traditional sector consumed by the traditional sector Q_{ut} and Q_{rt}, respectively, and the second of which is output of the traditional sector which is sold to the modern sector or Q_{um} and Q_{rm}, respectively. Thus, for the urban traditional sector, we have

$$(3) \qquad Q_u = Q_{ut} + Q_{um},$$

and for the rural traditional sector,

$$(4) \qquad Q_r = Q_{rt} + Q_{rm}.$$

We also assume that traditional-sector ouput consumed by the traditional sector is a constant amount per worker in the urban or rural traditional sector. That is,

$$(5) \qquad Q_{ut} = L_u \cdot S_u,$$

and

$$(6) \qquad Q_{rt} = L_r \cdot S_r,$$

where L_u and L_r are the labor force employed in the urban and rural traditional sectors, respectively, and S_u and S_r are constants. Traditional sector output produced for consumption by the modern sector, however, is assumed to be a function of the level of modern sector output. That is,

$$(7) \qquad Q_{um} = g_u(Q_m)$$

and

$$(8) \qquad Q_{rm} = g_r(Q_m).$$

The urban labor force is affected by migration from the countryside. As in Todaro,[1] we assume that the urban labor force, $L_m + L_u$, depends on the expected wage E_w which can be achieved in the urban areas. The expected wage is a weighted average of the modern sector wage rate W and per capita income in the urban traditional sector Q_u/L_u

$$(9) \qquad E_w = (L_m W + Q_u)/(L_m + L_u).$$

The urban labor force is a function then of the difference between the wage in the urban areas and per capita income in the rural areas.

$$(10) \qquad L_m + L_u = h(E_w - Q_r/L_r).$$

A.   The rate of labor absorption

In this model, we assume that the rate of labor absorption into the modern sector is a function of the rate of capital accumulation in the modern sector, the rate of technological change, and the rate of change of the wage rate. The labor absorption function can be derived as follows:

First, let us assume that the production function F in (1) is homogeneous of degree γ. That is, we may have non-constant returns to scale but the production function is still homogeneous. With homogeneity, we may write (1) as

(11) $Q_m = (\beta L_m)^\gamma f(k)$

where

(12) $f(k) = F(k,1)$

and

(13) $k = \alpha K/\beta L.$

Differentiating (11) with respect to L_m, we obtain

(14) $\dfrac{\partial Q_m}{\partial L_m} = \beta(\beta L)^{\gamma-1}[\gamma f(k) - f^\prime(k) \cdot k] = W.$

Multiply (14) through by L_m to obtain

(15) $\gamma Q_m - (\beta L)^\gamma f^\prime(k) \cdot k = WL_m .$

Differentiate (15) with respect to time and divide through by Q_m

(16) $\dfrac{\gamma \dot{Q}_m}{Q_m} = \dfrac{\gamma \dot{\beta}}{\beta} \dfrac{f'k}{f} + \dfrac{\gamma \dot{L}_m}{L_m} \dfrac{f'k}{f} + \dfrac{f''}{f} \dot{k}k + \dfrac{f'}{f}\dot{k} + \dfrac{\dot{W}}{\beta^\gamma L_m^{\gamma-1} f} + \dfrac{\dot{L}}{\beta^\gamma L^{\gamma-1} f L_m} .$

Differentiate (11) with respect to time and divide through by Q_m

(17) $\dfrac{\dot{Q}_m}{Q_m} = \dfrac{\gamma \dot{\beta}}{\beta} + \dfrac{\gamma \dot{L}_m}{L_m} + \dfrac{f'k}{f} .$

Differentiate (13) with respect to time and divide through by k

$$(18) \qquad \frac{\dot{k}}{k} = \frac{\dot{k}}{k} + \frac{\dot{\alpha}}{\alpha} - \frac{\dot{L}_m}{L_m} - \frac{\dot{\beta}}{\beta} \, .$$

Divide (15) by W and Q_m as given by (11). The result is

$$(19) \qquad \frac{1}{\beta^\gamma L_m^{\gamma-1} f} = \frac{\gamma}{W} - \frac{f'k}{fW} \, .$$

Substitute (17), (18), and (19) into (16) and collect terms

$$(20) \qquad \left[(\gamma - 1)(\gamma - 2\frac{f'k}{f}) + \frac{f''k^2}{f} \right] \frac{\dot{L}_m}{L_m} = \left[(\gamma - 1)\frac{f'k}{f} + \gamma(\frac{f'k}{f} - \gamma) - \frac{f''k^2}{f} \right] \frac{\dot{\beta}}{\beta}$$

$$+ \ (\gamma - \frac{f'k}{f}) \, \frac{\dot{W}}{W} + \left[\frac{f''k^2}{f} - (\gamma - 1)\frac{f'k}{f} \right] (\dot{K}/K + \dot{\alpha}/\alpha).$$

One can show that the elasticity of substitution σ can be expressed as [2]

$$(21) \qquad \sigma = \frac{f'f'k^2 - f'fk}{f''k^2} \, .$$

We may rearrange terms as follows:

$$(22) \qquad \frac{f}{f''k^2} = \frac{-\sigma}{\frac{f'}{f}k(1 - \frac{f}{f}k)} \, .$$

From (15) and (11), we may write

$$(23) \qquad \frac{f'k}{f} = \frac{\gamma Y - WL_m}{(\beta L)^\gamma f} = \gamma - \frac{WL_m}{Y} \, .$$

If we let WL_m/Y be denoted by μ, the share of labor in total output, the result is

$$(24) \qquad \frac{f'k}{f} = \gamma - \mu \, .$$

Substitute (22) and (24) into equation (20). The result is

$$(25) \qquad \frac{\dot{L}_m}{L_m} = \frac{(\gamma - \mu)}{\phi} [(\gamma - 1)(\sigma - 1) + \mu] (\dot{K}/K + \dot{\alpha}/\alpha - \dot{\beta}/\beta)$$

$$- \frac{\mu\sigma}{\phi} (\dot{W}/W - \gamma \dot{\beta}/\beta) ,$$

where

$$(26) \qquad \phi = (\gamma - \mu)[(\gamma - 1)(\sigma - 1) + \mu] - \mu(\gamma - 1)\sigma .$$

Equation (25) is the labor absorption function. It gives the rate of labor absorption into the modern sector as a function of the rate of capital accumulation, the rate of capital- and labor-augmenting technological change and the rate of growth in the wage rate. A couple of special cases are of interest. If there are no economies of scale ($\gamma = 1$), then the labor absorption function reduces to the following:

$$(27) \qquad \frac{\dot{L}_m}{L_m} = \frac{\dot{K}}{K} + \frac{\dot{\alpha}}{\alpha} - \frac{\dot{\beta}}{\beta} - \frac{\sigma}{(1 - \mu)} (\dot{W}/W - \dot{\beta}/\beta) .$$

In this case the coefficient of the rate of change of modern-sector wages is a simple function of the elasticity of substitution σ and the labor share μ. Even if the elasticity of substitution is less than unity, the wage elasticity of employment may be greater than unity. For example, if the wage share of output is one-half, then employment is wage elastic if the elasticity of substitution is greater than one-half. If the wage share is 80 percent, employment is wage elastic if the elasticity of substitution is greater than 0.2.

Another special case arises when the elasticity of substitution is equal to unity (a Cobb-Douglas production function). Equation (25), the labor absorption function, reduces to

$$(28) \qquad \frac{\dot{L}_m}{L_m} = \frac{(\gamma - \mu)}{(1 - \mu)} (\dot{K}/K + \dot{\alpha}/\alpha) + \frac{\mu}{(1 - \mu)} \frac{\dot{\beta}}{\beta} + \frac{1}{(1 - \mu)} \frac{\dot{W}}{W} .$$

The elasticity of employment with respect to both capital accumulation and capital-augmenting technological change is greater than unity if there are economies of scale and less than unity if there are decreasing returns to scale. The elasticity with respect to labor-augmenting technological change is always positive and greater than unity if the labor share is greater than 50 percent, but less than unity if the labor share is less than 50 percent. Finally, with the Cobb-Douglas function, the wage elasticity of employment is always greater than unity and varies directly with the wage share of output.

B. Wage changes in the modern sector and effects on per capita incomes in the traditional sector

In this section we analyze the effect of wage changes in the modern sector on per capita incomes in the traditional sectors. If the modern-sector wage rate rises, then modern-sector workers receive more income. There are a number of adverse effects, however. First, there will be fewer modern-sector workers at high wage levels. Second, per capita income in either the urban or rural traditional sectors is likely to decline when wages are raised in the modern sector.

To determine the effect of a wage change, first differentiate the labor supply function (10):

$$(29) \qquad dL_m + dL_u = \frac{dh}{dD} (dE_w - dP_{rt}) \, ,$$

where

$$(30) \qquad P_{rt} = Q_r / L_r$$

is the per capita income in the rural traditional sector and

$$(31) \qquad D = E_w - P_{rt}$$

is the difference between the expected urban wage and per capita incomes in the rural traditional sector. We can also rewrite (29) in terms of the elasticity of supply of urban labor with respect to the urban-rural wage differential

$$(33) \qquad dL_m + dL_u = e_D \frac{(L_m + L_u)}{(E_w - P_{rt})} (dE_w - dP_{rt}) \; ,$$

where e_D is the elasticity of urban sector labor force.

In order to determine dE_w and dP_{rt}, we may rewrite (9) and (30) as follows:

$$(34) \qquad (L_m + L_u) \; E_w = (L_m W + Q_u)$$

and

$$(35) \qquad L_r P_{rt} = Q_r \; ,$$

and differentiate each implicitly. We obtain [note that $dl_r = -(dL_m + dL_u)$]:

$$(36) \qquad dE_w = [WdL_m + L_m dW + dQ_u - (dL_m + dL_u) \; E_w]/(L_m + L_u)$$

and

$$(37) \qquad dP_{rt} = [dQ_r + (dL_m + dL_u) \; P_{rt}]/L_r \; .$$

Note, also, by substituting (5) and (6) into (3) and (4) and differentiating, we get

$$(38) \qquad dQ_u = S_u dL_u = dQ_{um}$$

and

$$(39) \qquad dQ_r = S_r dL_r + dQ_{rm} = -S_r (dL_m + dL_u) + dQ_{rm}.$$

Furthermore, from (7) and (8), we have

$$(40) \qquad dQ_{um} = e_{um} \frac{Q_{um}}{Q_m} dQ_m$$

and

(41) $dQ_{rm} = e_{rm} \dfrac{Q_{rm}}{Q_m} dQ_m$,

where e_{um} is the elasticity of output of the urban traditional sector and e_{rm} is the elasticity of output of the rural traditional sector with respect to modern-sector output. From equations (1) and (2), we have

(42) $dQ_m = F_L dL_m = WdL_m$.

Finally, from (27), we can deduce the change in employment in the modern sector given a change in the modern-sector wage rate (holding capital stock and technical change constant)

(43) $dL_m/L_m = -(\mu\sigma/\phi)(dW/W)$.

Combining equations (36) and (43), substituting into (33), and rearranging terms, we obtain [assuming constant returns to scale in which case $\gamma = 1$ and $\phi = \mu(1 - \mu)$]:

(44) $(dL_m + dL_u) = \dfrac{e_D L_m}{\eta(1 - \mu)}\Big\{ W(1 - \mu) - \sigma[W(1 + \xi) - S_u] \Big\} \dfrac{dW}{W}$

where

(45) $\eta = (E_W - P_{rt}) + e_D(E_W - S_u) + e_D\dfrac{(L_m + L_u)}{L_r}(Q_{rm}/L_r)$

and

(46) $\xi = [e_{um} L_r Q_{um} - (L_m + L_u)e_{rm} Q_{rm}]/L_r Q_m$.

Equation (44) gives an expression for the change in the total urban labor force, both modern sector and traditional sector, as a function of the change in the modern-sector wage rate. The change in the rural traditional-sector labor force is simply the same expression with the opposite sign.

It is not clear whether the urban labor force will increase or decrease (i.e., whether there will be net migration from urban to rural areas) if there is an increase in the modern-sector wage rate. Note that the term η in (45) would be expected to be positive in that the expected wage is likely to exceed the per capita income in the rural traditional sector (P_{rt}) and per capita subsistence income in the urban traditional sector. Thus the sign of the expression in (44) depends on the sign of the terms in brackets and this sign is ambiguous. The term ξ is a weighted difference of derived demand elasticities, e_{rm}, and e_{um}, and may be positive or negative. Some of the other terms in brackets are positive and others are negative. The ambiguity arises because, on the one hand, the increase in the wage rate raises the expected urban wage. The induced reduction in modern-sector employment, however, throws more urban workers into the urban traditional sector which pays less than the modern sector. This latter effect tends to depress the expected wage. If the expected wage increases, there is migration from the rural to urban area, the amount depending on the elasticity of labor supply e_D with respect to the urban-rural wage differential.

The percentage change in per capita income in the rural traditional sector is the difference between the percentage change in output and the percentage change in the rural-sector labor force. That is,

$$(47) \qquad \frac{dP_{rt}}{P_{rt}} = \frac{dQ_r}{Q_r} - \frac{dL_r}{L_r} \, .$$

From (39), we have

$$(48) \qquad \frac{dP_{rt}}{P_{rt}} = \frac{S_r \, dL_r}{Q_r} + \frac{dQ_{rm}}{Q_r} - \frac{dL_r}{L_r} \, .$$

From (41), (42), (43), and (44), we may write

$$(49) \qquad \frac{dP_{rt}}{P_{rt}} = \frac{L_m Q_{rm}}{L_r Q_r \eta (1 - \mu)} \left\{ e_D W(1 - \mu) - \sigma[W(1 + \xi) - S_u]e_D \right.$$

$$\left. - \sigma \eta e \frac{WL_r}{rm_{Q_m}} \right\} \frac{dW}{W}$$

The sign of the expression in (49) can be presumed generally to be negative; that is, an increase in the modern-sector wage rate reduces per capita income in the rural traditional sector. This results from the fact that there is a reduction in modern-sector output due to higher wages and reduced derived demand for modern-sector output; at the same time the work force of the rural traditional sector is unlikely to change by much. The derived demand effect is represented by the last term in brackets in equation (49) and the labor force effect by the other terms in the brackets. If there is no net migration (all terms in the brackets in (49) except the last term equal to zero), then per capita income is certain to fall. If there is enough net migration to urban areas, per capita incomes in the traditional rural sector may not fall.

The expression for the percentage change in per capita income of the urban traditional sector can be derived in a similar fashion. First, we solve (44) for dL_u, substituting the expression (43) for dL_m. After collecting terms we obtain:

$$(50) \qquad \frac{dP_{ut}}{P_{ut}} = \frac{L_m Q_{um}}{L_u O_u''(1 - \mu)} \left\{ -e_D W(1 - \mu) + \sigma[W(1 + \xi) - S_u]e_D \right.$$

$$\left. -\sigma\eta(1 + e_{um} WL_u/Q_m)\right\} \frac{dW}{W} .$$

Here, again, the most likely sign for the expression in (50) is negative; i.e., the result of an increase in the modern-sector wage rate is a reduction in the per capita income in the urban traditional sector. But the likelihood of a reduction in the urban sector is even greater than in the rural sector. The increased wage reduces employment in the modern sector and adds to the pool of workers in the urban area which must seek a livelihood in the traditional sector. At the same time there may be migration from rural to urban areas, further adding to the labor pool. Finally, the reduction in modern-sector output reduces demand for products of the urban traditional sector. The combined effect of reduced demand for output and increased supply of workers tends to reduce per capita incomes in the urban traditional sector.

The only case in which per capita output might rise is if the expected urban wage is reduced and the supply of workers to urban areas is elastic enough that there is substantial net outmigration to rural areas. In this case per capita incomes in the urban traditional sector might not fall, but they will certainly be reduced in rural areas. In any case, the tendency is for per capita incomes to fall in both urban and rural traditional sectors and certainly in one or the other of the two sectors.

Appendix 3

NOTES

1.   M. P. Todaro, "A Model of Labor Migration and Urban Unemployment in Less Developed Countries," American Economic Review 59 (March 1969).

2. See Roy G. B. Allen, Macro-Economic Theory (St. Martin's Press, 1968), p. 48.

SELECTIVE BIBLIOGRAPHY ON INCOME DISTRIBUTION

(With Special Reference to
Developing Countries)

Prepared by Gerald Epstein and Jean-Louis Terrier.

A More Complete Bibliography Has Been Prepared For
U.S. Agency for International Development
Reference Center, Bibliography Series
(forthcoming)

CONTENTS

BIBLIOGRAPHY

BIBLIOGRAPHY

PART I: INCOME DISTRIBUTION: ETHICS
THEORY, DATA, AND MEASUREMENT

I_1 - Ethical, Social and Political Variables

1. Abernethy, G. L., ed. The Idea of Equality--An Anthology. Richmond, Va.:
   John Knox Press, 1959.

2. American Academy of Political and Social Science. "Income Inequality."
   The Annals 409 (September 1973).

3. Arrow, K. Social Choice and Individual Values. New York: John Wiley,
   1951.

4. Barlow, R. et al. Economic Behavior of the Affluent. Washington, D.C.:
   The Brookings Institution, 1966.

5. Bedau, H. A. "Egalitarianism and the Idea of Equality." In J. R. Pennock
   and J. W. Chapman, eds. Nomos IX: Equality. New York: Atherton, 1967.

6. Bell, C. L. G. "The Political Framework." In H. Chenery et al. Redistribution with Growth. London: Oxford University Press, 1974.

7. Bell, D. "Meritocracy and Equality." Public Interest 29 (Fall 1972).

8. Berlin, I. "Equality as an Ideal." In F. A. Olafson, ed. Society, Law
   and Morality. Englewood Cliffs: Prentice-Hall, 1961.

9. Bottomore, T. B. Elites and Society. Baltimore: Penguin Books, 1966.

10. Boulding, K. E. Beyond Economics: Essays on Society, Religion and
    Ethics. Ann Arbor: University of Michigan Press, 1968.

11. _____. "Social Justice in Social Dynamics." In R. Brandt, ed. Social
    Justice. Englewood Cliffs: Prentice Hall, 1973.

12. Bowen, I. Acceptable Inequalities. London: George Allen and Unwin, 1970.

13. De Jouvenel, B. The Ethics of Redistribution. Cambridge: Cambridge
    University Press, 1951.

14. Fried, A., and Sanders, R., eds. Socialist Thought. New York: Doubleday,
    1964.

15. Friedman, M. Capitalism and Freedom. Chicago: University of Chicago
    Press, 1962.

16. Galbraith, J. K. The Affluent Society. Boston: Houghton Mifflin, 1958.

17. Gibrat, R. "On Economic Inequality." International Economic Papers (1957).

18. Hirschman, A. O. Journeys Toward Progress. New York: Twentieth Century Fund, 1963.

19. Kyrk, H. "The Income Distribution as a Measure of Economic Welfare." American Economic Review 40 (May 1950).

20. Lampman, R. J. "Recent Thought on Egalitarianism." Quarterly Journal of Economics 71 (May 1957).

21. Laumann, E. O., ed. Social Stratification. New York: Bobbs-Merrill, 1970.

22. Lerner, A. P. Economics of Control. New York: Macmillan, 1944.

23. Nozick, R. "Distributive Justice." Philosophy and Public Affairs 3 (Fall 1972).

24. Phelps, E. S., ed. Private Wants and Public Needs. New York: Norton, 1965.

25. Pigou, A. C. Socialism versus Capitalism. London: Macmillan, 1937.

26. Rawls, J. A Theory of Justice. Cambridge, Mass.: Belknap Press of Harvard University Press, 1971.

27. Sen, A. K. Collective Choice and Individual Welfare. San Francisco: Holden-Day, 1970.

28. Spengler, J. J. "Hierarchy versus Equality: Persisting Conflict." Kyklos 21, Fasc. 2 (1968).

29. Tawney, R. H. Equality. New York: Capricorn Books, 1961.

30. Titmuss, R. H. Income Distribution and Social Change. London: George Allen and Unwin, 1962.

I_2 - Income Distribution Theories

A.   General Readings

31. Ahluwalia, M. "Income Inequality: Some Dimensions of the Problem." In H. Chenery et al. Redistribution with Growth. London: Oxford University Press, 1974.

32. Atkinson, A. B., ed. Wealth, Income, and Inequality: Selected Readings. New York: Penguin Modern Economics Readings, 1968.

33. Blaug, M. Economic Theory in Retrospect. Homewood, Ill.: Richard D. Irwin, 1968.

34. Blinder, A. S. Towards an Economic Theory of Income Distribution. Cambridge, Mass.: MIT Press, 1975.

35. Clark, C., and Stuvel, G., eds. Income Redistribution and the Statistical Foundations of Economic Policy. London: Bowes and Bowes, 1964.

36. Cline, W. R. Distribution and Development: A Survey of Literature. Washington, D.C.: The Brookings Institution, 1973.

37. Fellner, W. "Significance and Limitations of Contemporary Distribution Theory." American Economic Review 43 (May 1953).

38. Ferguson, C. E., and Nell, E. J. "Two Review Articles on Two Books on the Theory of Income Distribution." Journal of Economic Literature 10 (June 1972).

39. Garvy, G. "Functional and Size Distributions of Income and Their Meaning." American Economic Review 44 (May 1954).

40. Harberger, A. C. "Reflections on the Problem of Income Distribution in Less Developed Countries." Mimeographed. Report prepared for the Agency for International Development, February 1973.

41. Kennedy, C. "A Static Interpretation of Some Recent Theories of Growth and Distribution." Oxford Economic Papers 12 (June 1960).

42. Lydall, H. F. The Structure of Earnings. London: Oxford University Press, 1968.

43. Marchal, J., and Ducros, B., eds. The Distribution of National Income. New York: St. Martin's Press, 1968.

44. Marsh, W. "Distribution of Gains, Wealth and Income from Economic and Political Development." Paper no. 24, Program of Development Studies, Rice University, 1972.

45. Meade, J. Efficiency, Equality and the Ownership of Property. Cambridge, Mass.: Harvard University Press, 1965.

46. Nelson, R.; Schultz, P.; and Slighton, R. Structural Change in a Developing Economy. Princeton: Princeton University Press, 1971.

47. Papanek, G. F. "Distribution of Income, Wealth and Power." Economic Development Report no. 236, Center for Economic Affairs, Harvard University, 1973.

48. Pen, J. Income Distribution: Facts, Theories and Policies. New York: Praeger, 1971.

49. Pigou, A. C. The Economics of Welfare. London: Macmillan, 1960.

50. Preiser, E. "Property, Power and Distribution of Income." In Rothschild, K., ed. Power in Economics. New York: Penguin Books, 1971.

51. Rothschild, K. W. "Some Recent Contributions to a Macro-Economic Theory of Income Distribution." Scottish Journal of Political Economy 8 (October 1961).

52. Ruggles, R. "Income Distribution Theory." Income and Wealth Series 16 (September 1970).

53. Scitovsky, T. "A Survey of Some Theories of Income Distribution." In National Bureau of Economic Research, The Behavior of Income Shares. Princeton: Princeton University Press, 1964.

54. Soltow, L., ed. Six Papers on the Size Distribution of Wealth and Income. New York: Columbia University Press, 1965.

55. Taussig, M. K. "Distribution Issues: Trends and Policies." American Economic Review 60 (May 1970).

56. Thurow, L. C. "The Income Distribution as a Pure Public Good." Quarterly Journal of Economics 85 (May 1971).

See also 3, 17, 19, 28, 61, 70, 72, 76, 81, 126, 127, 157, 336, 352, 393, 394, 402, 407.

B. Theories

a. Neo-Classical Approach

57. Adams, F. G. "The Size of Individual Incomes: Socio-Economic Variables and Chance Variation." Review of Economics and Statistics 40 (November 1958).

58. Blinder, A. S. "A Model of Inherited Wealth." Quarterly Journal of Economics 87 (March 1974).

59. Bowen, H. R. et al. "Income Distribution: Discussion." American Economic Review 47 (May 1957).

60. Brittain, J. "Research on the Transmission of Material Wealth." American Economic Review 63 (May 1973).

61. Bronfenbrenner, M. Income Distribution Theory. Chicago: Aldine-Atherton, 1971.

62. Champernowne, D. "A Model of Income Distribution." Economic Journal 68 (June 1953).

63. Conlisk, J. "An Approach to the Theory of Inequality in the Size Distribution of Income." Western Economic Journal 7 (June 1969).

64. Corrmea, H. "Wealth and Income Distribution, Investment, and Economic Development." Southern Economic Journal 34 (October 1967).

65. Friedman, M. "Choice, Change, and the Distribution of Personal Income." Journal of Political Economy 61 (August 1953).

66. _____. A Theory of the Consumption Function. Princeton: Princeton
    University Press, 1957.

67. Harcourt, G. C. "A Critique of Mr. Kaldor's Model of Income Distribu-
    tion and Economic Growth." Australian Economic Papers 2 (June 1963).

68. _____. "A Two-Sector Model of the Distribution of Income and the
    Level of Employment in the Short Run." Economic Record 41 (March
    1965).

69. Harris, D. J. "On Marx's Scheme of Reproduction and Accumulation."
    Journal of Political Economy 80 (May-June 1972).

70. Johnson, H. G. The Theory of Income Distribution. London: Gray-Mills,
    1973.

71. Keesing, D. B. "Causes and Implications of Growing Inequalities of
    Income Within Developing Countries." Memorandum no. 127, Research
    Center in Economic Growth, Stanford University, 1972.

72. Lydall, H. F. "The Theory of Distribution and Growth with Economies
    of Scale." Economic Journal 81 (March 1971).

73. Metcalf, C. An Econometric Model of the Income Distribution. Chicago:
    Markham, 1972.

74. Michaelson, S. "The Economics of Real Income Distribution." Review of
    Radical Political Economy 2 (Spring 1970).

75. Morgan, J. N. "The Anatomy of Income Distribution." Review of Economics
    and Statistics 44 (August 1962).

76. Nuti, D. M. "Vulgar Economy in the Theory of Income Distribution." De
    Economist 118 (1970).

77. Samuelson, P. A. "A Fallacy in the Introduction of Pareto's Law of
    Alleged Constancy of Income Distribution." Rivista Internazionale
    Di Scienze Economiche e Commerciali 12 (May 1965).

78. Sato, K. "The Neo Classical Theorem and Distribution of Income and
    Wealth." Review of Economic Studies 33 (October 1966).

79. Schelling, T. "Discrimination Without Prejudice: Some Innocuous
    Models." John F. Kennedy School of Government, Harvard University,
    1972.

80. Smolensky, E. "An Interrelationship Among Income Distributions."
    Review of Economics and Statistics 45 (May 1963).

81. Varian, M. R. "Equity, Envy, and Efficiency." Journal of Economic
    Theory 9 (September 1974).

See also Part I, I₂B(d); and 20, 33, 34, 40, 41, 42, 43, 45, 54, 55, 94,
    189, 604, 605, 615, 639, 640, 659, 752.

b.   Neo-Marxian Approach

82. Arswui, H. and Vikaido, H. "Income Distribution and Growth in a Mono-
    polistic Economy." Zeitschrift für Nationalökonomie 28 (December
    1968).

83. Bowles, S. "Understanding Unequal Economic Opportunity." American Econ-
    omic Review 63 (May 1973).

84. Bowles, S., and Gintis, H. "The Problem with Human Capital Theory--A
    Marxian Critique." American Economic Association, Papers and Pro-
    ceedings (May 1975).

85. Hilbrast, J. G. M. Monopolistic Competition, Technical Progress, and
    Income Distribution. Rotterdam: Rotterdam University Press, 1965.

86. Kalecki, M. "The Distribution of the National Income." In American
    Economic Association, Readings in the Theory of Income Distribution.
    Homewood, Ill.: Richard D. Irwin, 1951.

87. _____. Theory of Economic Dynamics: An Essay on Cyclical and Long
    Run Changes in Capitalistic Economy. London: George Allen and Unwin,
    1954.

88. _____. "Class Struggle and the Distribution of National Income."
    Kyklos 24 (1971).

89. Krueger, A. O. "The Political Economy of the Rent-Seeking Society."
    American Economic Review 64 (June 1974).

90. Marx, K., and Engels, F. Value, Price and Profit. Moscow: Foreign Pub-
    lishing House, 1962.

91. Winston, G. C. "Overinvoicing Underutilization and Distorted Industrial
    Growth." Pakistan Development Review 10 (Winter 1970).

See also 69, 123, 183, 185, 745.

c.   Neo-Keynesian Approach

92. Furtado, C. "Development and Stagnation in Latin America: A Structur-
    alist Approach." Studies in Comparative International Development 1
    (1965).

93. Kaldor, N. "Alternative Theories of Distribution." Review of Economic
    Studies 23 (1956).

94. Seer, A. K. "Neo-Classical and Neo-Keynesian Theories of Distribution."
    Economic Record 39 (1963).

95. Tobin, J. "Towards a General Kaldorian Theory of Distribution." Review
    of Economic Studies 27 (February 1960).

96. Weintraub, S. A Keynesian Theory of Employment Growth and Income Distribution. Philadelphia: Chilton, 1966.

See also 67 and 72.

d.   Human Capital Approach

97. Becker, G. Human Capital. New York: Columbia University Press, 1970.

98. Becker, G. S. "Investment in Human Capital: A Theoretical Analysis." Journal of Political Economy 78 (1970 Supplement).

99. Ben-Porath, Y. "The Production of Human Capital and the Cycle of Earnings." Journal of Political Economy 75 (August 1967).

100. Conlisk, J. "A Bit of Evidence on the Income-Education-Ability Interrelation." Journal of Human Resources 6 (Summer 1971).

101. _____. "Can Equalization of Opportunity Reduce Social Mobility?" American Economic Review 64 (March 1974).

102. Grant, J. P. "Equal Access and Participation vs. Trickle Down and Redistribution: The Welfare Issue for Low-Income Societies." Mimeographed. Washington, D.C.: Overseas Development Council, February 1973.

103. Haley, W. "Human Capital: The Choice Between Investment and Income." American Economic Review 63 (December 1973).

104. Hansen, W. L. "Income Distribution Effects of Higher Education." American Economic Review 60 (May 1970).

105. Harbison, F. H. Human Resources as the Wealth of Nations. New York: Oxford University Press, 1973.

106. Juster, F. T., ed. Education, Income and Human Behavior. New York: Columbia University Press, 1975.

107. Miller, H. P. "Annual and Lifetime Income in Relation to Education." American Economic Review 56 (November 1966).

108. Morgan, J., and David, M. "Education and Income." Quarterly Journal of Economics 77 (August 1963).

109. Pscharapoulos, G. "Marginal Contribution of Education to Economic Growth." Economic Development and Cultural Change 20 (July 1972).

110. Soltow, L. "The Distribution of Income Related to Changes in the Distribution of Education, Age and Occupation." Review of Economics and Statistics 42 (November 1960).

111. Stiglitz, J. E. "The Theory of 'Screening,' Education and the Distribution of Income." American Economic Review 65 (June 1975).

112. Weisbrod. B. A. "Expenditures on Human Resources: Investment Income Redistribution, or What?" In Joint Economics Committee, United States Congress, Federal Program for the Development of Human Resources. Washington, D.C.: U.S. Government Printing Office, 1968.

113. Welch, F. "Human Capital Theory: Education Discrimination, and Life Cycles." American Economic Association, Papers and Proceedings (May 1975).

See also Part I, $I_2B(f)$; Part I, $I_3C(c)$, and 84, 755.

   e.   Neo-Paretian Approach

114. Fair, R. C. "The Optimal Distribution of Income." Quarterly Journal of Economics 85 (November 1971).

115. Fisher, F. M., and Rothenberg, J. "How Income Ought to be Distributed: Paradox Lost." Journal of Political Economy 69 (April 1961); and "Paradox Now" 70 (February 1962).

116. Hamada, K. "On the Optimal Transfer and Income Distribution in a Growing Economy." Review of Economic Studies 34 (July 1967).

117. Hochman, H., and Rogers, J. D. "Pareto Optimal Redistribution." American Economic Review 59 (September 1969).

118. Houthakker, H. S. "The Pareto Distribution and the Cobb-Douglas Production Function in Activity Analysis." Review of Economic Studies 23 (December 1955-January 1956).

119. Mandelbrot, B. "The Pareto-Levy Law and the Distribution of Income." International Economic Review 1 (May 1960).

120. _____. "Paretian Distributions and Income Maximization." Quarterly Journal of Economics 76 (February 1962).

121. Rhodes, E. C. "The Pareto Distribution of Incomes." Economia New Series 11 (February 1944).

122. Von Fustenberg, G., and Mueller, D. C. "The Pareto Optimal Approach to Income Redistribution: A Fiscal Application." American Economic Review 61 (September 1971).

See also 62, 77, 405.

   f.   Welfare Economics

123. Dobb, M. Welfare Economics and the Elements of Socialism. New York: Cambridge University Press, 1969.

124. Hicks, Sir John. "The Foundations of Welfare Economics." Economic Journal 49 (December 1939).

125. Tinbergen, J. "Welfare Economics and Income Distribution." American Economic Review 47 (May 1957).

126. _____. "A Positive and a Normative Theory of Income Distribution." Review of Income and Wealth 16 (September 1970).

127. _____. "An Interdisciplinary Approach to the Measurement of Utility or Welfare." Mimeographed. Rotterdam: Economic and Social Research Institute, 1973.

See also 49, 199, 200, 320, 447.

I₃ - Growth and Income Distribution

A.   Inequality in Developing Countries: A New Concern

128. Haq, M. Ul. "A New Perspective on Development." In Society for International Development. Development Targets for the 70's: Jobs and Justice, 12th World Conference of the S.I.D. held in Ottawa, Canada, 16-19 May 1971.

129. Hirschman, A. O. "Changing Tolerance for Income Inequality in the Course of Economic Development." Quarterly Journal of Economics 87 (November 1973).

130. McNamara, R. "Development in the Developing World, A Maldistribution of Income." Vital Speeches 38 (June 1972).

131. Robinson, J. "The Second Crisis of Economic Theory." American Economic Review 62 (May 1972).

See also 71.

B.   Inequality in the Process of Economic Development

132. Adelman, I., and Morris, C. T. "An Anatomy of Patterns of Income Distribution in Developing Nations." Mimeographed. Paper prepared for Agency for International Development, 1971.

133. _____. "Who Benefits from Economic Development?" Mimeographed. Paper prepared for the International Bank for Reconstruction and Development, 1972.

134. _____. Economic Growth and Social Equity in Developing Countries. Stanford: Stanford University Press, 1973.

135. Adler, J. H. "Development and Income Distribution." Weltwirtschafliches Archiv 108 (1972).

136. Anderson, W. H. "Trickling Down; The Relationship Between Economic Growth and the Extent of Poverty Among American Families." Quarterly Journal of Economics 78 (November 1964).

137. Bardhan, P. K., and Srinivasan, T. N. "Income Distribution: Patterns, Trends and Policies." Economic and Political Weekly, 24 April 1971.

138. Baster, N. Distribution of Income and Economic Growth. New York: United Nations Research Institute for Social Development, 1970.

139. Berry, R. A. "Income and Wealth Distribution in the Development Process and Their Relationship to Output Growth." Discussion Paper no. 89, Economic Growth Center, Yale University, 1970.

140. Branson, W. H. "Dynamics of Income Distribution: Poverty and Progress: Discussion." American Economic Review 60 (May 1970).

141. Eltis, W. A. Growth and Distribution. London: Macmillan, 1973.

142. Ewusi, K. "Notes on the Relative Distribution of Income in Developing Countries." Review of Income and Wealth 17 (December 1971).

143. Goldsmith, S. F. "Changes in the Size Distribution of Income." American Economic Association, Papers and Proceedings (1956).

144. Kooros, A. "Economic Growth and Income Inequality in the Developing Countries." Bank Markasi Iran Bulletin 12 (July-September 1973)

145. Kravis, I. G. "International Differences in the Distribution of Income." Review of Economics and Statistics 42 (November 1960).

146. Krelle, W. "The Laws of Income Distribution in the Short Run: An Aggregate Model." In J. Marchal and B. Ducros, eds. The Distribution of National Income. New York: St. Martin's Press, 1968.

147. Kuznets, S. "Economic Growth and Income Inequality." American Economic Review 45 (March 1955).

148. _____. "Quantitative Aspects of the Economic Growth of Nations: Distribution of National Income by Factors Shares." Economic Development and Cultural Change 6 (April 1958).

149. _____. "Quantitative Aspects of Economic Growth of Nations: VIII, Distribution of Income by Size." Economic Development and Cultural Change 11 (January 1963).

150. Morgan, T. "Income Distribution in Developed and Underdeveloped Countries: A Rejoinder." Economic Journal 66 (March 1956).

151. Oshima, H. T. "A Note on Income Distribution in Developed and Underdeveloped Countries." Economic Journal 66 (March 1956).

152. _____. "The International Comparison of Size Distribution of Family Incomes with Specific Reference to Asia." Review of Economics and Statistics 44 (November 1962).

153. _____. "Income Inequality and Economic Growth--The Postwar Experience of Asian Countries." Malayan Economic Review (October 1970).

154. Pasinetti, L. L. "The Role of Profit and Income Distribution in Relation to the Role of Economic Growth." Review of Economic Studies 2 (October 1962).

155. Paukert, F. "Income Distribution at Different Levels of Development: A Survey of Evidence." International Labour Review 108 (August-September 1973).

156. Rao, V. K. R. V. "Redistribution of Income and Economic Growth in Underdeveloped Countries." In C. Clark and G. Stuvel, eds. Income Redistribution and the Statistical Foundations of Economic Policy. London: Bowes and Bowes, 1964.

157. Reder, M. W. "A Partial Survey of the Theory of Income Size Distribution." In L. Soltow, ed. Six Papers on the Size Distribution of Wealth and Income. New York: Columbia University Press, 1965.

158. Schultz, T. P. "Long-Term Changes in Personal Income Distribution: Mythologies, Facts and Explanations." Mimeographed. Rand Corporation, November 1971.

159. Strassman, P. "Economic Growth and Income Distribution." Quarterly Journal of Economics 70 (August 1956).

160. Streissler, E. "Long-term Structural Changes in the Distribution of Income." Zeitschrift für Nationalökonomie 29 (January 1969).

161. Swamy, S. "Structural Changes and the Distribution of Income by Size: The Case of India." Review of Income and Wealth 13 (June 1967).

162. Thweatt, W. O. "The Inevitability and Irrelevancy of the Increasing Income Gap." Journal of Economic Issues 4 (June-September 1970).

163. Tyler, W. "Income Distribution and Economic Development: A Macro Interpretation." Mimeographed. Paper prepared for the 1973 Meeting of the Latin American Studies Association.

164. Ward, R. J. "Aspects of the Income Inequality Problem in the Less Developed Countries." Economia Internazionale (February 1972).

165. Youngson, A. J., ed. Economic Development in the Long Run. New York: St. Martin's Press, 1972.

See also Part I, $I_2B(a)$; I_5B; and 31, 42, 44, 46, 61, 62, 64, 65, 71, 72, 80, 82, 85, 169, 172, 180, 197, 253, 352, 389, 402, 601, 672, 703, 704, 705, 735.

C. Factors Affecting Income Distribution: The Static Approach

a. General Models

166. Adelman, I., and Robinson, S. "A Non-Linear, Dynamic Microeconomic Model of Korea -- Factors Affecting the Distribution of Income in the Short Run." Discussion Paper no. 36, Research Program in Economic Development, Woodrow Wilson School, Princeton University, 1973.

167. Adelman, I., and Tyson, L. D. "A Regional Micro-economic Model of Yugoslavia: Factors Affecting the Distribution of Income in the Short Run." Mimeographed. Development Research Center, International Bank for Reconstruction and Development, April 1973.

168. Metcalf, C. E. "The Size-Distribution of Personal Income During the Business Cycle." <u>American Economic Review</u> 53 (September 1969).

169. Mirer, T. "The Effects of Macroeconomic Fluctuation on the Distribution of Income." <u>Review of Income and Wealth</u> 18 (December 1973).

170. Pryor, F. L. "Simulation of the Impact of Social and Economic Institutions on the Size Distribution of Income and Wealth." <u>American Economic Review</u> 63 (March 1973).

See also 73, 85, 146, 164, 287, 352.

b. Sectoral and Regional Differences in Income

171. Abercrombie, K. C. "Incomes and Their Distribution in Agriculture and the Rest of the Economy." <u>FAO Monthly Bulletin of Agricultural Economics and Statistics</u> (June 1967).

172. Bauer, P. T., and Yancey, B. S. "Economic Progress and Occupational Distribution." <u>Economic Journal</u> 61 (December 1951); and "Further Notes," 64 (March 1954).

173. Chaudhry, M. D. "Economic Distance Among Regions: A Statistical Analysis." <u>Economic Development and Cultural Change</u> 19 (July 1971).

174. Hanushek. Eric A. "Regional Differences in the Structure of Earnings." <u>Review of Economics and Statistics</u> 55 (May 1973).

175. Hughes, R. B., Jr. "Interregional Income Difference--Self-Perpetuation." <u>The Southern Economic Journal</u> 28 (July 1961).

176. Leff, N. H. "Economic Development and Regional Inequality: Origins of the Brazilian Case." <u>Quarterly Journal of Economics</u> 86 (May 1972).

177. Lewis, S. "Agricultural Taxations and Intersectoral Resource Transfers." <u>Food Research Institute Studies in Agricultural Economics, Trade and Development</u> 12 (1973).

178. Papola, T. S. "Inter-Regional Variations in Manufacturing Wages in India, Industrial Structure and Region Effects." <u>Indian Journal of Industrial Relations</u> (January 1972).

179. Roussel, L. "Measuring Rural-Urban Drift in Developing Countries: A Suggested Method." <u>International Labour Review</u> 101 (March 1970).

180. Williamson, J. G. "Regional Inequality and the Process of National Development: A Description of Patterns." <u>Economic Development and Cultural Change</u> 13 (July 1965).

See also 110, 187, 324, 346, 612, 617, 618, 659, 769.

c. The Educational Variable

181. Arrow, K. J. "Higher Education as a Filter." <u>Journal of Public Economics</u> 2 (1973).

182. Becker, G. S., and Chiswick, B. R. "Education and the Distribution of Earnings." American Economic Review 56 (May 1966).

183. Bhagwati, J. "Education, Class Structure and Income Inequality." World Development 1 (May 1973).

184. Boudon, R. "Educational Growth and Economic Equality." Quality and Quantity 8 (1974)

185. Bowles, S. "Schooling and Inequality from Generation to Generation." Journal of Political Economy 80 (March-April 1972).

186. Chiswick, B. R. "The Average Level of Schooling and the Intra-Regional Inequality of Income: A Clarification." American Economic Review 58 (June 1968).

187. _____. "An Interregional Analysis of Schooling and the Skewness of Income." In L. Hansen, ed. Education, Income and Human Capital. New York: Columbia University Press, 1970.

188. Dasgupta, A. K. "Income Distribution, Education and Capital Accumulation." Mimeographed. Paper prepared for the Development Economics Department, International Bank for Reconstruction and Development, May 1974.

189. Griliches, Z. and Mason, M. "Education, Income and Ability." Journal of Political Economy 80 (March-April 1972).

190. Hoerr, O. D. "Education, Income and Equity in Malaysia." Economic Development and Cultural Change 21 (January 1973).

191. Hollister, R. "Education and Distribution of Income: Some Exploratory Forays." In Education and Distribution of Income. Paris: OECD, 1971.

192. Jencks, C. Inequality: A Reassessment of the Effect of Family and Schooling in America. New York: Basic Books, 1972.

193. Mayer, T. "The Distribution of Ability and Earnings." The Review of Economics and Statistics 43 (May 1960).

194. Mincer, J. "The Distribution of Labor Incomes: A Survey." Journal of Economic Literature 8 (March 1970).

195. Rado, E. "The Explosive Model." In McGill University, Montreal, Manpower and Unemployment Research in Africa. Special issue of Centre for Developing Area Studies 6 (November 1973).

196. Riweh, T. "Problem of Equal Opportunity: A Review Article." Journal of Human Resources 7 (Fall 1972).

197. Stiglitz, J. "Distribution of Income and Wealth Among Individuals." Econometrica 37 (July 1969).

198. Thurow, L., and Lucas, R. The American Distribution of Income: A Structural Problem. Joint Economic Committee, United States Congress. Washington, D.C.: U.S. Government Printing Office, 1972.

199. Tinbergen, J. "The Impact of Education on Income Distribution." Review of Income and Wealth 18 (September 1972).

200. Tinbergen, J. et al. "Econometric Models for Education." In M. Blaug, ed. Economics of Education. Baltimore: Penguin Books, 1969.

See also, Part I, $I_2B(d)$; Part II, II_3.

d.   Absolute Poverty: Determination, Causes and Effects

201. Allen, V. L., ed. Psychological Factors in Poverty. Chicago: Markham, 1970.

202. Bardhan, P. K. "On the Minimum Level of Living and the Rural Poor." Indian Economic Review 5 (April 1970).

203. _____. "On the Incidence of Poverty in Rural India in the Sixties." Economic and Political Weekly 8, special number (February 1973).

204. Beckford, G. L. Persistent Poverty. New York: Oxford University Press, 1972.

205. Budd, E., ed. Inequality and Poverty. New York: Norton, 1967.

206. Dandekar, V. M., and Rath, M. R. "Poverty in India." Economic and Political Weekly 6 (2 January and 9 January 1971).

207. Fuchs, V. R. "Toward a Theory of Poverty." In Task Force on Economic Growth and Opportunity. The Concept of Poverty. Washington, D.C.: U.S. Government Printing Office, 1965.

208. Gordon, D. M., ed. Conference on Poverty in America. San Francisco: Chandler, 1965.

209. Gordon, D. M. Theories of Poverty and Underemployment. Lexington, Mass.: Lexington Books, 1972.

210. Myrdal, G. Asian Drama: An Inquiry into the Poverty of Nations. New York: Twentieth Century Fund, 1968.

211. Orshansky, M. "The Shape of Poverty in 1966." Social Security Bulletin 31 (March 1968).

212. Rajaraman, I. "Poverty, Inequality and Economic Growth: Rural Punjab 1960-61 - 1970-71." Discussion Paper no. 45, Research Program in Economic Development, Princeton University, 1974.

213. Roach, J., and Roach, J., eds. Poverty. Baltimore: Penguin Books, 1972.

214. Thurow, L. C. "The Causes of Poverty." Quarterly Journal of Economics 81 (February 1967).

See also Part II, II_6A; and 31, 234, 687, 689, 751, 758.

e. Demographic Factors of Inequality

215. Aluko, S. A. "Population Growth and the Level of Income: A Survey." *Journal of Modern African Studies* (December 1971).

216. Bilsborrow, R. "Fertility, Savings Rates and Economic Development in Less Developed Countries." International Union for the Scientific Study of Population, *International Population Conference*, vol. 1. Liege, Belgium, 1973.

217. Blandy, R. "Population and Employment Growth: An Introductory Empirical Exploration." *International Labour Review* 106 (October 1972); with a supplement 107 (May 1973).

218. Cassen, R. H. "Economic-Demographic Interrelationships in Developing Countries." Paper read to the Conference on Population Size and Its Determinants, Oxford, March 1973.

219. Coale, A. J., and Hoover, E. M. *Population Growth and Economic Development in Low Income Countries*. Princeton: Princeton University Press, 1958.

220. Johnston, B. F. "Consequences of Rapid Population Growth: Unemployment and Underemployment." Paper prepared for California Institute of Technology Conference on Technological Change and Population Growth, Pasadena, 6-8 May 1970.

221. Kelley, A. C. "Demographic Changes and American Economic Development: Past, Present. and Future." U.S. Population Commission Reports, vol. II. In *Economic Aspects of Population Change*. Washington, D.C.: U.S. Government Printing Office, 1972.

222. _____. "Population Growth, the Dependency Rate, and the Pace of Economic Development." *Population Studies* 27 (November 1973).

223. National Academy of Sciences. *Rapid Population Growth*. Vol. II. Baltimore: Johns Hopkins Press, 1971.

224. Robinson, E. A. G., ed. *Economic Factors in Population Growth*. London: Macmillan, forthcoming.

225. Sadie, J. L. "Demographic Aspects of Labour Supply and Employment." Background paper presented at the World Population Conference, Belgrade, 1965.

See also Part II, II$_4$.

f. Rural Underemployment

226. Cline, W. "Interrelationships between Agricultural Strategy and Rural Income Distribution." *Food Research Institute Studies in Agricultural Economics, Trade and Development* 12 (1973).

227. Falcon, W. P. "Agriculture Employment in Less Developed Countries: General Situation, Research Approaches, and Policy Palliatives." Economic Staff Working Paper no. 113, International Bank for Reconstruction and Development, 1971.

228. Hendrix, W. E. "Size and Distribution of the Income of Farm People in Relation to the Low Income Problem." Journal of Farm Economics 36 (December 1954).

229. Paglin, M. "Surplus Agricultural Labor and Development: Facts and Theories." American Economic Review 55 (September 1965).

See also 209, 217, 220, 225, 235, 258, 266, 678, 784.

g.   Land Tenure Problem

230. Bardhan, P. K., and Srinivasan, T. M. "Cropsharing Tenancy in Agriculture: A Theoretical and Empirical Analysis," American Economic Review 61 (March 1971); with a "Comment" by D. Newberry 64 (December 1974).

231. Barkin, D. "Agricultural Development in Mexico -- A Case Study of Income Concentration." Social Research 37 (Summer 1970).

232. Barraclough, S. L., and Danike, A. L. "Agrarian Structure in Seven Latin American Countries." In R. Stavenhager, ed. Agrarian and Peasant Movements in Latin America. New York: Doubleday, 1970.

233. Enke, S. "Labor Supply, Total Land Rents, and Agricultural Output in Backward Countries." Southern Economic Journal 23 (October 1962).

234. Minhas, B. S. "Rural Poverty, Land Redistribution and Economic Strategy." Indian Economic Review 5 (April 1970).

See also Part II, II$_7$A; and 675, 772.

h.   Rural/Urban Migration: Causes and Effects

235. Byerlee, D., and Eicher, C. "Rural Employment, Migration and Economic Development: Theoretical Issues and Empirical Evidence from Africa." Conference of the International Economic Association on the Place of Agriculture in the Development of the Developing Countries, Bad Godesburg, West Germany, August 1974.

236. Gaude, J. "Agricultural Employment and Rural Migration in a Dual Economy." International Labour Review 106 (November 1972).

237. Harris, J. R., and Todaro, M. P. "Migration, Unemployment and Development: A Two Sector Analysis." American Economic Review 60 (March 1970).

238. Porter, R. G. "Labor Migration and Urban Unemployment in Less Developed Countries." Discussion Paper no. 25, Center for Research on Economic Development, University of Michigan, 1973.

239. Todaro, M. P. "A Model of Labor Migration and Urban Unemployment in Less Developed Countries." <u>American Economic Review</u> 59 (March 1969).

240. _____. "Income Expectations, Rural-Urban Migration and Employment in Africa." <u>International Labour Review</u> 104 (November 1971).

See also, Part I, $I_3C(i)$; Part II, II_7 and II_8; and 179, 740.

i.   Urban Unemployment and Underemployment: Industrialization and Labor Absorption, the "Labor-Surplus Model"

241. Baer, W., and Herve, M. "Employment and Industrialization in Developing Counties." <u>Quarterly Journal of Economics</u> 80 (February 1966).

242. Bairoch, P. <u>Urban Unemployment in Developing Countries</u>. Geneva: International Labour Organization, 1973.

243. Berry, R. A. "Unemployment as a Social Problem in Urban Colombia." Discussion Paper no. 145, Economic Growth Center, Yale University, 1972.

244. Bruton, H. J. "Employment, Productivity, and Import Substitution." Research Memorandum no. 44, Center for Development Economics, Williams College, 1972.

245. Doctor, K. C., and Gallis, H. "Modern Sector Employment in Asian Countries: Some Empirical Estimates." <u>International Labour Review</u>, 90 (December 1964); and a similar study for Africa, 93 (February 1966).

246. Edwards, E. O., ed. <u>Employment in Developing Nations</u>. New York: Columbia University Press, 1974.

247. Fei, J. C. H., and Ranis, G. <u>Development of the Labour-Surplus Economy: Theory and Policy</u>. Homewood, Ill.: Richard D. Irwin, 1964.

248. _____. "Income Inequality by Additive Factors Components." Discussion Paper no. 207, Economic Growth Center, Yale University, 1974.

249. Hofmeister, R. "Growth With Unemployment in Latin America: Some Implications for Asia." In R. G. Ridker and H. Lubell, eds. <u>Employment and Unemployment Problems in the Near East and South Asia</u>. New Delhi: Vikas, 1971.

250. Kim, K. S. "Labour Force Structure in a Dual Economy: A Case Study of South Korea." <u>International Labour Review</u> 101 (January 1970).

251. Lal, D. "Employment, Income Distribution and a Poverty Redressal Index." <u>World Development</u> 1 (March-April 1973).

252. Land, J., and Soligo, R. "Income Distribution and Employment in Labor Redundant Economies." Discussion Paper no. 3, Program of Development Studies, Rice University, 1971.

253. Lewis, W. A. "Economic Development with Unlimited Supplies of Labor." Manchester School of Economic and Social Studies 22 (May 1954).

254. McCabe, J. L., and Lele, M. M. "Income Distribution and Optimal Growth: The Case of Open Unemployment." Discussion Paper no. 141, Economic Growth Center, Yale University, 1972.

255. Mazumdar, D. "Theory of Urban Underemployment in LDC's. Mimeographed. Paper prepared for the International Bank for Reconstruction and Development, 1973.

256. Miller, R. U. "The Relevance of Surplus Labour Theory to the Urban Labour Markets of Latin America." International Institute for Labour Studies Bulletin (1971).

257. Morawetz, D. "Employment Implications of Industrialization in Developing Countries: A Survey." Mimeographed. Staff Working Paper no. 170, International Bank for Reconstruction and Development, 1974.

258. Mouly, G. "Some Remarks On the Concepts of Employment, Underemployment and Unemployment." International Labour Review 105 (February 1972).

259. Oshima, H. T. "Labor-Force 'Explosion' and the Labor-Intensive Sector in Asian Growth." Economic Development and Cultural Change 19 (January 1971).

260. _____. "Labour Absorption in East and Southeast Asia." Malayan Economic Review (October 1971).

261. Perrakis, S. "The Labor-Surplus Model and Wage Behavior in Mexico." Industrial Relations 11 (February 1972).

262. Piore, M. "The Dual Labor Market: Theory and Implications." In D. M. Gordon, ed. Problems in Political Economy. London: Heath, 1971.

263. Ranis, G. "Industrial Sector Labor Absorption." Economic Development and Cultural Change 21 (April 1973).

264. Rees, A. "An Overview of the Labor Supply Results." Journal of Human Resources 9 (Spring 1974).

265. Reynolds, L. G. "Economic Development With Labor Surplus: Some Complications." Oxford Economic Papers 21 (March 1969).

266. Ridker, R., and Lubell, H. Employment and Unemployment Problems of Near East and South East. Bombay: Vikas, 1971.

267. Rosen, S., and Welch, F. "Labor Supply and Income Redistribution." Review of Economics and Statistics 53 (September 1971).

268. Strassman, W. P. "Construction Productivity and Employment in Developing Countries." International Labour Review 101 (June 1970).

269. Thorbecke, E. "The Employment Problem: A Critical Evaluation of Four ILO Comprehensive Country Reports." International Labour Review 107 (May 1973).

270. Turnham, D., and Jaeger, I. The Employment Problem in Less Developed Countries: A Review of Evidence. Paris: OECD, 1971.

See also Part II, II$_8$A(b); and 68, 209, 217, 220, 225, 229, 456, 647, 656, 681, 696, 730, 731, 733.

j.   Effects of Inflation on Income Distribution

271. Alchian, A. A. "Inflation and the Distribution of Income and Wealth." In J. Marchal and B. Ducros, eds. The Distribution of National Income. New York: St. Martin's Press, 1968.

272. Bach, G. L., and Ando, A. K. "The Redistributional Effects of Inflation." Review of Economics and Statistics 39 (February 1957).

273. Bombach, G. "Price Stability, Economic Growth and Income Distribution." International Economic Papers 10 (1960).

274. Brownlee, O. H., and Conrad, A. "Effects Upon the Distribution of Income of a Tight Money Policy." American Economic Review 51 (May 1961).

275. Budd, E. C. "The Impact of Inflation on the Distribution of Income and Wealth." American Economic Review 61 (May 1971).

276. Huddle, D. L. "Distribution Equity, Inflation and Efficiency in the Brazilian Fluctuating Exchange Rate System." Discussion Paper no. 30, Program of Development Studies, Rice University, 1972.

277. _____. "Inflation, Government Financing of Industrialization and the Gains from Development in Brazil." Paper presented at the Workshop on Income Distribution and Its Role in Development, Houston, Texas, Rice University, 25 April 1974.

278. Pesek, B. "Distribution Effects of Inflation and Taxation." American Economic Review 50 (March 1960).

279. Sherf, H. "Inflation and Income Distribution," Weltwirtschaftliches Archiv 100 (June 1968).

280. Williamson, J. G. "Relative Price Changes, Adjustment Dynamics, and Productivity Growth: The Case of Philippine Manufacturing." Economic Development and Cultural Change 19 (July 1971).

See also 341.

D.   Income Distribution and Growth: The Dynamic Approach

(See also Part I, I$_4$A and I$_5$B)

a. Effect on the Structure of Demand and on Employment Through Factor Usages

281. Bacha, E., and Taylor, L. "The Unequalizing Spiral: A First Growth Model for Belindia." Discussion Paper no. 15, Universidade de Brasilia, 1973.

282. Ballentine, J. G., and Soligo, R. "Consumption and Earnings Patterns and Income Redistribution." Paper presented at the Workshop on Income Distribution and Its Role in Development, Houston, Texas, Rice University, 25 April 1974.

283. Bilkey, W. J. "Equality of Income Distribution and Consumption Expenditures." Review of Economics and Statistics 38 (February 1956).

284. Borch, K. "Effects on Demand of Changes in the Situation of Income." Econometrica 21 (April 1953).

285. Brady, D. S. "Individual Incomes and the Structure of Consumer Units." American Economic Review 68 (May 1958).

286. Chinn, D. "Potential Effects of Income Redistribution on Economic Growth Constraints: Evidence from Taiwan and South Korea." Ph.D. dissertation, University of California, 1973.

287. Cline, W. R. Potential Effects of Income Redistribution on Economic Growth: Latin American Cases. New York: Praeger, 1972.

288. Desai, B. M. "Analysis of Consumption Expenditure Patterns in India." Paper no. 54, Department of Agricultural Economics, Cornell University, 1972.

289. Duesenberry, J. S. "Income-Consumption Relations and Their Implications." In L. A. Metzler et al., eds. Income, Employment and Public Policy: Essays in Honour of Alvin H. Hansen. New York: Norton, 1964.

290. _____. Income, Saving and the Theory of Consumer Behavior. Cambridge, Mass.: Harvard University Press, 1943.

291. Food and Agriculture Organization. "The Impact on Demand of Change in Income Distribution: A Case Study of Eleven Latin American Countries." Monthly Bulletin of Agricultural Economics and Statistics (March 1972).

292. Fortune, J. N. "Income Distribution as a Determinant of Imports of Manufactured Consumer Commodities." The Canadian Journal of Economics 5 (May 1972).

293. Jarvis, S. F., and Beckerman, W. "Interdependence of Consumer Preferences in the Theory of Income Redistribution." Economic Journal 63 (March 1953).

294. Land, J., and Soligo, R. "Consumption Patterns, Factor Usage, and the Distribution of Income: A Review of Some Findings." Paper presented at the Workshop on Income Distribution and Its Role in Development, Houston, Texas, Rice University, 25 April 1974.

295. Laumas, P. S. "Income Redistribution, Interdependent Consumers' Preferences and Aggregate Consumption." Weltwirtschaftliches Archiv (1971).

296. Lubell, H. "Effects of Redistribution of Income on Consumers' Expenditures." In M. Mueller, ed. Readings in Macroeconomics. New York: Holt, Rinehart, and Winston, 1966.

297. Modigliani, F., and Brumberg, R. "Utility Analysis and the Consumption Function." In K. Kurihara, ed. Poor-Keynesian Economics. New Brunswick: Rutgers University Press, 1954.

298. Morley, S. A., and Smith, G. W. "The Effect of Changes in the Distribution of Income on Labor, Foreign Investment and Growth in Brazil." In A. Stepan, ed. Authoritarian Brazil. New Haven: Yale University Press, 1973.

299. Ojha, P. D., and Bhatt, V. V. "Pattern of Income Distribution in an Underdeveloped Economy: A Case Study in India." American Economic Review 54 (September 1964).

300. Paukert, F.; Skolka, J.; and Maton, J. "Redistribution of Income, Patterns of Consumption and Employment -- A Case Study for the Philippines." Working Paper, International Labour Office, May 1974.

301. Soligo, R. "Factor Intensity of Consumption Patterns, Income Distribution and Employment Growth in Pakistan." Discussion Paper no. 44, Program in Development Studies, Rice University, 1973.

302. Sunman, T. M. "Short-Run Effects of Income Distribution on Some Macro Economic Variables: The Case of Turkey." Discussion Paper no. 46, Program in Development Studies, Rice University, 1973.

303. Thorbecke, E., and Sengupta, J. K. "A Consistency Framework for Employment Output and Income Distribution: Projections Applied to Colombia." Mimeographed. Paper prepared for Development Research Center, International Bank for Reconstruction and Development, 1972.

304. Weisskoff, R. "Demand Elasticities for a Developing Economy: An International Comparison of Consumption Patterns." In H. Chenery, ed. Studies in Developmental Planning. Cambridge, Mass.: Harvard University Press, 1971.

305. _____. "A Multi-Sector Simulation Model of Employment, Growth, and Income Distribution in Puerto Rico: A Re-evaluation of 'Successful' Development Strategy." Mimeographed. Economic Growth Center, Yale University, 1973.

See also Part II, II_1B and II_8A; and 61, 66, 67, 68, 79, 85, 93, 159, 175, 252, 399, $630_1^{}$, 780.

b.   Income Distribution and the Savings Constraint

306. Friend, I., and Kravis, I. "Entrepreneurial Income, Saving and Investment." American Economic Review 47 (June 1957).

307. Gupta, K. L. "Dependency Rates and Savings Rates: A Comment." American Economic Review 61 (June 1971).

308. Houthakker, H. S. "On Some Determinants of Saving in Developed and Underdeveloped Countries." In E. A. G. Robinson, ed. Problems in Economic Development. London: Macmillan, 1966.

309. Leff, N. "Dependency Rates and Savings Rates." American Economic Review 59 (December 1969).

310. Mamalakis, M. J. "Forced Saving in Underdeveloped Countries: A Rediscovery or a Misapplication of a Concept?" Economia Internazionale 17 (August 1964).

311. Meade, J. E. "Life Cycle Savings, Inheritance and Economic Growth." Review of Economic Studies 33 (January 1966).

312. Mikesell, R. F., and Zinser, J. E. "The Nature of the Savings Function in Developing Countries: A Survey of the Theoretical and Empirical Literature." Journal of Economic Literature 11 (March 1973).

313. Reynolds. C. "The Recent Evolution of Savings and the Financial System in Mexico in Relation to the Distribution of Income and Wealth." Paper presented at the Workshop on Income Distribution and Its Role in Development, Houston, Texas, Rice University, 25 April 1974.

See also Part II, II_2A; and 61, 64, 156, 216, 287, 290, 297, 302, 366, 479, 774.

I_4 – Income Distribution Measurement

A.   Types of Income: Annual versus Lifetime Income

314. Denison, E. F. "Income Types and the Size Distribution." American Economic Review 44 (May 1954).

315. Ranadive, K. R. "Concept of Personal Income in Underdeveloped Countries." Indian Economic Journal 13 (April-June 1966).

316. Summers, R. "An Econometric Investigation of the Size Distribution of Lifetime Average Annual Income." Technical Reprint no. 31, Department of Economics, Stanford University, 1956.

317. Szal, R. J. "Dynamic Aspects of the Long Run Distribution of Income: A Cohort Analysis." Ph.D. dissertation, Duke University, 1973.

318. Taubman, P. "Annual and Lifetime Earnings Distributions: Information and Tests of Some Theories." Mimeographed. National Bureau of Economic Research, 1973.

319. Yung, K. H. "Optimum Life-time Distribution of Consumption Expenditures." American Economic Review 60 (1970).

See also, Part I, I_5B; and 58, 61, 62, 107, 108, 113, 754.

B.   Problems and Solutions in Measurement

320. Aigner, D. J., and Heins, A. J. A. "A Social Welfare View of the Measurement of Income Inequality." Review of Income and Wealth 13 (March 1967).

321. Aitchison, J., and Brown, J. A. C. The Lognormal Distribution With Special Reference to Its Uses in Economics. Cambridge: Cambridge University Press, 1957.

322. Alker, H., and Russett, B. "Indices for Comparing Inequality." In R. Merritt and S. Rokkan, eds. Comparing Nations, The Use of Qualitative Data in Cross-National Research. New Haven: Yale University Press, 1966.

323. Atkinson, A. B. "On the Measurement of Inequality." Journal of Economic Theory 2 (September 1970).

324. Bachmura, F. T. "An Application of the Lorenz Curve to the Study of Regional Income Disparity." Review of Economics and Statistics 41 (February 1959).

325. Benson, R. A. "Gini Ratios: Some Considerations Affecting Their Interpretation." American Journal of Agricultural Economics 52 (August 1970).

326. Bentzel, R. "The Social Significance of Income Distribution Statistics." Review of Income and Wealth 16 (September 1970).

327. Bose, A. C., and Ray, S. B. "Application of the Pareto Formula to the Distribution of Personal Income in India." Indian Economic Review 3 (August 1956).

328. Champernowne, D. G. "A Comparison of Measures of Inequality of Income Distribution." Economic Journal 84 (December 1974).

329. Clark, E., and Fishman, L. "Appraisal of Methods of Estimating the Size Distribution of a Given Aggregate Income." Review of Economics and Statistics 20 (February 1947); and "Further Remarks" 32 (February 1950).

330. Clyman, B. "The Effect of Aggregate Versus Per Capita Income per Unit Ranking or Personal Income Size Distributions." Review of Economics and Statistics 38 (May 1956).

331. Dasgupta, P.; Sen, A.; and Starett, D. "Notes on the Measurement of Inequality." Journal of Economic Theory 5 (April 1973).

332. Dich, J. S. "On the Possibility of Measuring the Distribution of Personal Income." Review of Income and Wealth 16 (September 1970).

333. Dobb, M. H. "A Note on Income Distribution and the Measurement of National Income at Market Prices." Economic Journal 66 (June 1956).

334. Durand, M. H. "A Simple Method for Estimating the Size Distribution of a Given Aggregate Income." Review of Economics and Statistics 25 (August 1953).

335. Elteto, O., and Frigyes, E. "New Income Inequality Measures As Efficient Tools for Causal Analysis and Planning." Econometrica 36 (April 1968).

336. Garvy, G. "Inequality of Income: Causes and Measurement." Studies in Income and Wealth 15 (1952).

337. Gastwirth, J. L. "A General Definition of the Lorenz Curve." Econometrica 39 (November 1971).

338. _____. "The Estimation of the Lorenz Curve and Gini Index." Review of Economics and Statistics 54 (August 1972).

339. Gini, C. "Measurement of Inequality of Income." Economic Journal 31 (March 1921).

340. Goldsmith, S. "Appraisal of Basic Data Available for Constructing Income Size Distribution," Studies in Income and Wealth 13 (1951).

341. Iyengar, N.; Sreehivasa, N.; and Bhattacharya, N. "On the Effect of Differentials in Consumer Price Index on Measures of Inequality," Sankhya (1965).

342. Knowles, K. G., and Hill, T. P. "On the Difficulties of Measuring Wage Differentials." Oxford University Institute of Statistics 16 (November–December 1954).

343. Kondor, Y. "An Old-New Measure of Income Inequality." Econometrica 39 (November 1971).

344. Lorenz, M. O. "Methods of Measuring the Concentration of Wealth." Journal of the American Statistical Association 3 (1905).

345. Mahalanobis, P. C. "A Method of Fractile Graphical Analysis." Econometrica 28 (April 1960).

346. Mangahas, M. "A Note on Decomposition of the Gini Ratio Across Regions." Research Discussion Paper no. 74(2), Institute of Economic Development, University of the Philippines, 1974.

347. Martic, L. "A Geometric Note on New Income Inequality Measures." Econometrica 38 (November 1970).

348. Mencher, S. "The Problem of Measuring Poverty." In J. and J. Roach, eds. Poverty. Baltimore: Penguin Books, 1972.

349. Morrison, C. "Note on a Methodology for Estimating Income Distribution." Mimeographed. International Bank for Reconstruction and Development, 1973.

350. Newberry, D. "A Theorem in the Measurement of Inequality." Journal of Economic Theory 2 (September 1970).

351. Prais, S. J. "Measuring Social Mobility." Journal of the Royal Statistical Society 118 (1955).

352. Sen, A. K. On Economic Inequality. New York: Norton, 1973.

353. Szal, R. J. "A Methodology for the Evaluation of Income Distribution Data." Discussion Paper no. 54, Research Program in Economic Development, Princeton University.

354. Taussig, M. K. Alternative Measures of the Distribution of Economic Welfare. Princeton: Princeton University Press, 1971.

355. Theil, H. Economics and Information Theory. Amsterdam: North-Holland, 1967.

356. United Nations. Sources and Methods of Estimating the Data of Income Consumption and Accumulation of the Household Sector (E/CN.14/NAC/52), 1972.

357. Yntema, D. "Measures of the Inequality in the Personal Distribution of Wealth or Income." Journal of the American Statistical Association 28 (December 1933).

358. Young, A. A. "Do the Statics of Concentration of Wealth Mean What They are Commonly Assumed to Mean?" Journal of the American Statistical Association 15 (March 1917).

I_5 - Income Distribution Data and Sources

A.   International Comparisons

359. Adelman, I., and Morris, C. T. "An Anatomy of Patterns of Income Distribution in Developing Nations." Mimeographed. Agency for International Development, 1971.

360. Andic, S., and Peacock, A. T. "The International Distribution of Income 1949 and 1957." Journal of the Royal Statistical Society 124 Series A, Part II (1961).

361. Beckerman, W., and Bacon, R. "The International Distribution of Income." In P. Streeten, ed. Unfashionable Economics: Essays in Honour of Lord Balogh. London: Weidenfeld and Nicholson, 1970.

362. Figueroa, A., and Weisskoff, R. "Viewing Social Pyramids: Income Distribution in Latin America." Paper read to the Second Latin American Conference of the International Association for Research in Income and Wealth, Rio de Janeiro, 10 July 1974.

363. Gannage, E. "Distribution of Income in Underdeveloped Countries." In J. Marchal and B. Ducros, eds. The Distribution of National Income. New York: St. Martin's Press, 1968.

364. Haley, B. F. "Changes in the Distribution of Income in the United States." In J. Marchal and B. Ducros, eds. The Distribution of National Income. New York: St. Martin's Press, 1968.

365. Kothari, U. N. "Disparities in Relative Earnings Among Different Countries." Economic Journal 80 (September 1970).

366. Lluch, C., and Powel, A. "International Comparison of Expenditure and Saving Patterns." Paper prepared for the Center of Economic Research, International Bank for Reconstruction and Development, 1973.

367. Okogbo, P. "The Distribution of National Income in African Countries." In J. Marchal and B. Ducros, eds. The Distribution of National Income. New York: St. Martin's Press, 1968.

368. United Nations Economic Commission for Asia and the Far East. Distribution of Income and Wealth in the Philippines. Bangkok: ECAFE Secretariat, November 1971.

369. _____. Distribution of Income and Wealth in Thailand. Bangkok: ECAFE Secretariat, January 1972.

370. _____. Distribution of Income and Wealth in India. Bangkok: ECAFE Secretariat, October 1971.

371. United Nations Economic Commission for Europe. Incomes in Postwar Europe: A Study of Policies, Growth, and Distribution. Part II of Economic Survey of Europe in 1965. Geneva: United Nations, 1967.

372. United Nations Economic Commission for Latin America. Income Distribution in Latin America. New York: United Nations, 1971.

373. United Nations. Economic Development and Income Distribution in Argentina. New York: United Nations, 1969.

374. Weisskoff, R. "Income Distribution and Economic Growth in Puerto Rico, Argentina and Mexico." Review of Income and Wealth 16 (December 1970).

See also Part I, I_3B; and 31, 180, 308, 322, 464, 468, 471, 508, 536, 616, 620, 647.

B.   Intertemporal Comparisons

375. Allen, R. G. D. "Changes in the Distribution of Higher Incomes." Economica 24 (May 1957).

See also Part I, I_4A, and I_3B; and 58, 80, 155.

C.   Data Availability and Sources

376. Agency for International Development. "Developing Country Policies on Popular Participation in Development, with Particular Regard to Income Distribution and Employment: A Source Book." Mimeographed. Agency for International Development, June 1972.

377. Chenery, H. et al. Redistribution with Growth. London: Oxford University Press, 1974.

378. Choo, H. "Review of Income Distribution Data: Korea, the Philippines and Taiwan." Discussion Paper no. 55, Research Program in Economic Development, Princeton University, 1975.

379. International Labour Organization. Household Income and Expenditures Statistics. Geneva: ILO 1967.

380. Jain, S., and Tiemann, A. "Size Distribution of Income: A Compilation of Data." Discussion Paper no. 4, Development Research Center, International Bank for Reconstruction and Development, 1973.

381. Langoni, C. G. "Review of Income Distribution Data: Brazil." Discussion Paper no. 60, Research Program in Economic Development, Princeton University, 1975.

382. Meesook, O. A. "Review of Income Distribution Data: Thailand, Malaysia, and Indonesia." Discussion Paper no. 56, Research Program in Economic Development, Princeton University, 1975.

383. Morgan, T. "Distribution of Income in Ceylon, Puerto Rico, the United States and the United Kingdom." Economic Journal 63 (December 1953).

384. Phillips. A. O. "Review of Income Distribution Data: Ghana, Kenya, Tanzania and Nigeria." Discussion Paper no. 58, Research Program in Economic Development, Princeton University, 1975.

385. Rajaraman, I. "Review of Income Distribution Data: Pakistan, India, Bangladesh and Sri Lanka." Discussion Paper no. 57, Research Program in Economic Development, Princeton University, 1975.

386. United Nations. Statistics of the Distribution of Income Consumption and Wealth (E/CN.3/426), 1972.

387. _____. Household Economic Surveys in Africa (E/CN.14/NAC/53), 1972.

388. Urrutia, M. "Review of Income Distribution Data: Colombia, Mexico, and Venezuela." Discussion Paper no. 59, Research Program in Economic Development, Princeton University, 1975.

PART II.   INCOME DISTRIBUTION POLICIES

II$_1$ - General Issues

A.   General Readings

389. Adelman, I. "Reflections on Strategies for Distribution Oriented Growth." International Bank for Reconstruction and Development, 1974.

390. Ahluwalia, M. "The Scope for Policy Intervention." In H. Chenery et al. Redistribution With Growth. London: Oxford University Press, 1974.

391. Bell, C. L. G., and Duloy, J. H. "Formulating a Strategy." In H. Chenery et al. Redistribution With Growth. London: Oxford University Press, 1974.

392. Bentzel, R. "Some Aspects of the Economic Integration of Changes in the Inequality of Income Distribution." Income and Wealth Series 6 (1957).

393. Boulding, K., and Pfaff, M., eds. Redistribution to the Rich and Poor. Belmont, Calif.: Wadsworth Publishers, 1972.

394. Chenery, H. et al. Redistribution With Growth. London: Oxford University Press, 1974.

395. Fisher, A. G. B. "Alternative Techniques for Promoting Equality in Capitalist Society." American Economic Review 40 (May 1950).

396. Klappholz, K. "What Redistribution May Economists Discuss?" Economica 35 (May 1968).

397. Kumagai, H. "How Should Income Be Distributed?" Osaka Economic Papers 15 (November 1966).

398. Lampman, R. J. "Transfer Approaches to Distribution Policy." American Economic Review 60 (May 1970).

399. Land, J., and Soligo, R. "Models of Development Incorporating Distribution Aspects." Discussion Paper no. 22, Program in Development Studies, Rice University, 1972.

400. Marsden, K. "Towards a Synthesis of Economic Growth and Social Justice." International Labour Review 100 (November 1969).

401. Mishan, E. J. "Redistribution in Money and in Kind: Some Notes." Economica 35 (May 1968).

402. Nicholson, J. L. "Redistribution of Income - Notes on Some Problems and Puzzles." Review of Income and Wealth 16 (September 1970).

403. Peacock, A. T., ed. Income Redistribution and Social Policy. London: Jonathan Cape, 1954.

404. Rivlin, A. "Income Distribution--Can Economists Help?" American Economic Association, Papers and Proceedings (May 1975).

405. Strotz, R. H. "How Income Ought to be Distributed: A Paradox in Distributive Ethics." Journal of Political Economy 66 (June 1958); with a discussion by F. M. Fisher and J. Rothenberg, 69 (April 1961); and response by the author, 69 (June 1961).

406. Thurow, L. C. "Cash Versus In-Kind Transfers." American Economic Review 64 (May 1974).

407. United Nations Department of Economic and Social Affairs. Social Policy and the Distribution of Income in the Nation. New York: United Nations, 1969.

See also Part I , I$_2$B(è); and 6, 12, 13, 18, 27, 30, 46, 55, 61, 64, 170, 287, 447, 460, 467, 470, 485, 495, 514, 528, 534, 587, 600, 607, 613, 614, 620, 626, 627, 628, 635, 636, 642, 644, 647, 651, 663, 666, 742, 759.

B.   Income Distribution and Model of Development

   a.   Capitalism versus Socialism

408. Bergson, A. "Capitalism and Equality of Income: Discussion." American Economic Review 60 (May 1970).

409. Chenery, H. B., and Eckstein, P. "Development Alternatives for Latin America." Journal of Political Economy 78 (July-August 1970).

410. Pryor, F. L. "Economic System and the Size Distribution of Income and Wealth." Working Paper no. 1, International Developments Research Center, University of Indiana, 1971.

411. Wiles, P. J. D., and Markowski, S. "Income Distributes under Communism and Capitalism." Soviet Studies 22 (January 1971).

See also 14, 15, 16, 22, 25, 74, 82, 85, 87, 123, 128, 395, 610, 786, 791, 796.

   b.   Some Case Studies--The Chinese Model, Tanzania's "Ujamaa," Cuba, etc.

412. Green, R. H. "Toward Ujamaa and Kujiregemea: Notes on Income and Employment Policy in Tanzania." Dar es Salaam: The Tanzanian Treasury, 1973.

413. Hernandez, R. E., and Mesa-Lago, C. "Labor Organization and Wages." In C. Mesa-Lago, ed. Revolutionary Change in Cuba. Pittsburgh: University of Pittsburgh Press, 1971.

414. Perkins, D. H. "Growth and Changing Structures of China's Twentieth Century Economy." Discussion Paper no. 339, Institute of Economic Research, Harvard University, 1974.

415. Prybyla, J. The Political Economy of Communist China. New York: Intext Educational Publications, 1970.

416. Weisskopf, T. E. "China and India: A Comparative Survey of Economic Development Performance." Discussion Paper no. 41, Center for Research in Economic Development, University of Michigan, 1974.

417. Zala, J. "Major Factors Determining the Distribution of the National Income in a Centrally Planned Economy." In J. Marchal and B. Ducros, eds. The Distribution of National Income. New York: St. Martin's Press, 1968.

See also 475, 512, 522, 523, 638, 809, 810, 811, 813, 814.

II_2 - Fiscal Policy

A.   Tax Incidence

418. Ahmed, M. "Taxation and the Changes in Income Distribution." Indian Economic Journal 12 (April-June 1965).

419. Atkinson, A. B. "Capital Taxes, the Redistribution of Wealth and Individual Savings." Review of Economic Studies 38 (April 1971).

420. Bird, R., and De Wulf, L. "Taxation and Income Distribution in Latin America: A Critical Review of Empirical Studies." International Monetary Fund Staff Papers 20 (November 1973).

421. _____. "Fiscal Incidence Studies in Developing Countries - Survey and Critique." Mimeographed. Fiscal Affairs Department, International Monetary Fund, 15 February 1974.

422. Break, G. "The Effects of Taxation on Work Incentives." In E. Phelps, ed. Private Wants and Public Needs. New York: Norton, 1965.

423. Chelliah, R. "Trends in Taxation in Developing Countries." International Monetary Fund Staff Papers 18 (July 1971).

424. Due, J. Indirect Taxation in Developing Countries. Baltimore: Johns Hopkins Press, 1970.

425. Gandhi, V. "Indirect Taxes and Personal Income Distribution." Mimeographed. New Delhi, April 1972.

426. Gordon, D. "Taxation of the Poor and the Normative Theory of Tax Incidence." American Economic Review 62 (May 1972).

427. Harberger, A. C. "The Incidence of the Corporation Income Tax." Journal of Political Economy 70 (June 1962).

428. Harberger, A. C., ed. Taxation and Welfare. Boston: Little, Brown, 1974.

429. Hart, A. G. "Fiscal Policy in Latin America." Journal of Political Economy 78 (July-August 1970).

430. Herschel, F. J. "Estimating the Distribution of the Tax Burden: Comment." In R. A. Musgrave, ed. Problems of Tax Administration in Latin America. Baltimore: Johns Hopkins Press, 1965.

431. McLure, C. E. "The Proper Use of Indirect Taxation in Latin America: The Practice of Economic Marksmanship." Paper no. 29, Program of Development Studies, Rice University, 1972.

432. _____. "The Incidence of Colombian Taxes, 1970." Paper no. 41, Program of Development Studies, Rice University, 1973.

433. McLure, C. E., and Thirsk, W. R. "A Numerical Exposition of the Harberger Model of Tax and Expenditure Incidence." Paper no. 48, Program of Development Studies, Rice University, 1973.

434. Meerman, J. "Fiscal Incidence in Empirical Studies of Income Distribution in Poor Countries." Discussion Paper, Agency for International Development, 1972.

435. Mieszkowski, P. "Tax Incidence Theory: Effects of Taxes on Distribution of Income." Journal of Economic Literature 7 (December 1969).

436. Musgrave, R. A. The Theory of Public Finance: A Study in Public Economy. New York: McGraw Hill, 1959.

437. Musgrave, R. A., and Musgrave, P. B. Public Finance in Theory and Practice. New York: McGraw Hill, 1973.

438. Pechman, J. A., and Okner, B. A. Who Bears the Tax Burden? Washington, D.C.: The Brookings Institution, 1974.

439. Phelps, E. S. "The Taxation of Wage Income for Economic Justice." Quarterly Journal of Economics 87 (August 1973).

440. Rangarajan, C. "Taxation As a Tool of Distribution in Developing Economics." Economic Development and Cultural Change 19 (January 1971).

441. Rao, V., and Rao, K. S. H. "The Incidence of the Corporate Income Tax in the Short Run: The Case of Indian Corporations." Public Finance 26 (1971).

442. Recktenwald, H. C. Tax Incidence and Income Redistribution. Detroit: Wayne State University Press, 1971.

443. Rolph, E. R. The Theory of Fiscal Economics. Berkeley: University of California Press, 1954.

See also 122, 278, 444, 756.

B.   Expenditures Incidence

444. Clark, C., and Peters, G. H. "Income Redistribution Through Taxation and Social Sciences: Some International Comparisons." Income and Wealth Series 10 (1964).

445. Gillespie, I. "Effect of Public Expenditures on the Distribution of Income." In R. A. Musgrave, ed. Essays in Fiscal Federalism. Washinton, D.C.: The Brookings Institution, 1965.

446. Harberger, A. C. "On Measuring the Social Opportunity Cost of Public Funds." In Project Evaluation: Collected Papers. Chicago: Markham, 1971.

447. _____. "Three Basic Postulates for Applied Welfare Economics." Journal of Economic Literature 9 (September 1971).

448. McLure, C. E., Jr. "Public Goods and Income Distribution: An Explanatory Comment." Paper no. 49, Program of Development Studies, Rice University, 1974.

449. _____. "The Theory of Expenditure Incidence." Finanz Archiv 30 (1972).

450. _____. "On the Theory and Methodology of Estimating Benefit and Expenditure Incidence." Paper presented at the Workshop on Income Distribution and Its Role in Development, Houston, Texas, Rice University, 25 April 1974.

451. Weisbrod, B. A., and Hansen, W. L. "Distributional Effects of Public Expenditure Programs." Public Finance 27 (Fall 1972).

See also 461, 467, 474, 477, 501, 743.

II_3 - Educational Policies

452. Blaug, M. The Economics of Education: An Annotated Bibliography. Oxford: Pergamon, 1970.

453. Bowles, S. Planning Educational Systems for Economic Growth. Harvard Economic Studies, vol. 133. Cambridge, Mass.: Harvard University Press, 1969.

454. Carmoy, M. "Rates of Return to Schooling in Latin America." Journal of Human Resources 2 (Summer 1967).

455. Eckaus, R. Estimating the Returns to Education. New York: McGraw Hill, 1973.

456. Fields, G. "Private and Social Returns to Education in Labor Surplus Economies." Eastern Africa Economic Review 4 (June 1972).

457. Haller, T. "Education and Rural Development in Colombia." Ph.D. dissertation, Purdue University, 1972.

458. Hansen, W. L. "Total and Private Rates of Return to Investment in Schooling." Journal of Political Economy 71 (April 1963).

459. _____. "Patterns of Rates of Return to Investment in Education: Some International Comparisons." Paris: OECD, 1971.

460. Illich, I. De-Schooling Society. New York: Harper and Row, 1971.

461. Jallade, J. P. Public Expenditure on Education and Income Distribution in Colombia. Baltimore: Johns Hopkins Press, 1974.

462. Maton, J. "Experience on the Job or Formal Training as Alternative Means of Skill Acquisition: An Empirical Study." International Labour Review 100 (September 1969).

463. Mincer, J. "Investment in Human Capital and Personal Income Distribution." Journal of Political Economy 66 (August 1958).

464. Pscharapoulos, G. The Economic Return to Education: International Comparison. Amsterdam: Elsevier, 1972.

465. Selowsky, M. "Investment in Education in Developing Countries: A Critical Review of Some Issues." Mimeographed. Washington, D.C.: International Bank for Reconstruction and Development, 1973.

466. Shultz, T. W. "Rate of Return in Allocating Investment Resources to Education." Journal of Human Resources 2 (Summer 1967).

467. Thurow, L. C. Investment in Human Capital. Belmont, Calif.: Wadsworth, 1970.

See also Part I, $I_2D(d)$, and $I_3C(c)$; and 535, 736, 781, 793.

II_4 - Population Planning

468. Behrman, S. J. et al., eds. Fertility and Family Planning: A World View. Ann Arbor: University of Michigan Press, 1970.

469. Berelson, B. "An Evaluation of the Effects of Population Control Programs." Studies in Family Planning 5 (January 1974).

470. _____. "Beyond Family Planning." Studies in Family Planning Supplement (March 1969).

471. _____. "World Population: Status Report 1974." Reports on Population and Family Planning, no. 15 (January 1974).

472. Blandy, R. "The Welfare Analysis of Fertility Reduction." Economic Journal 84 (March 1974).

473. Boulier, B. "Mortality and the Returns to Investment in Human Capital." Unpublished manuscript. Princeton University, 1974.

474. Cassen, R. H. "Population Growth and Public Expentiture in Developing Countries." International Union for the Scientific Study of Population, International Population Conference, vol. I, Liege, Belgium, 1973.

475. Chen, Pi Chao. "China's Birth Control Action Programme, 1956–1964." Population Studies 24 (July 1970).

476. Davis, K. "Population Policy: Will Current Programs Succeed?" Science 158, 10 November 1967.

477. Demeny, P. "Investment Allocation and Population Growth." Demography 2 (1965).

478. Heer, D., and Smith, D. O. "Mortality Level, Desired Family Size: Further Variations on a Basic Model." Demography 6 (1969).

479. Isbister, J. "Birth Control, Income Redistribution, and Saving." Demography 10 (February 1973).

480. Isbister, J., and Lee, B. M. "The Impact on Birth Control Programs on Fertility." In B. Berelson et al., eds. Family Planning and Population. Chicago: University of Chicago Press, 1966.

481. Moore-Cavar, E. C. International Inventory of Information on Induced Abortion. New York: International Institute for the Study of Human Reproduction, Columbia University, 1974.

482. Mueller, E. "Economic Motives for Family Limitation." Population Studies 26 (November 1972).

483. Nortman, D. Population and Family Planning Programs: A Fact Book. Reports on Population/Family Planning (September 1973).

484. Office of Population Research, Princeton University. "Bibliography." In Population Index 41 (January 1975).

485. Rich, W. Smaller Families through Social and Economic Progress. Monograph Series no. 7, Overseas Development Council, 1973.

486. Ridker, R. "Synopsis of a Proposal for a Family Planning Bond." Studies in Family Planning 43 (June 1969).

487. Ridley, J. C. et al. "The Effects of Changing Mortality on Natality: Some Estimates from a Simulation Model." Milbank Memorial Fund Quarterly 45 (January 1967).

488. Ross, J. A. et al. "Findings From Family Planning Research." Reports on Population/Family Planning no. 12 (October 1972).

489. Schultz, T. P. "Explanation of Birth Rate Changes over Space and Time: A Study of Taiwan." Journal of Political Economy 82 (March–April 1973).

490. _____. "Determinants of Fertility: A Microeconomic Model of Choice." In E. A. G. Robinson, ed. Economic Factors in Population Growth. London: Macmillan, forthcoming.

491. Simmons, G. B. The Indian Investment in Family Planning. New York: The Population Council, 1971.

492. Trussel, T. J. "Cost versus Effectiveness of Different Birth Control Methods." Population Studies 28 (1974).

493. Wolfers, D. "The Demographic Effects of a Contraceptive Programme." Population Studies 23 (1969).

See also Part I, I$_3$C(e); and 434, 528.

II$_5$ - Health and Nutrition

494. Austin, J. E., and Levinson, J. F. "Population and Nutrition: A Case for Integration." Milbank Memorial Quarterly (Spring 1974).

495. Berg, A. The Nutrition Factor. Washington, D.C.: The Brookings Institution, 1973.

496. Berg, A.; Scrimshaw, N.; and Call, D., eds. Nutrition, National Development and Planning. Cambridge, Mass.: MIT Press, 1973.

497. Colson, A. C. "The Differential Use of Medical Resources in Developing Countries." Journal of Health and Social Behavior 12 (September 1971).

498. Fendall, N. R. E. "Medical Care in the Developing Countries." In J. Frey and W. A. J. Farndale, eds. International Medical Care. Wallingford, Pa.: Washington Square East, 1972.

499. _____. Auxiliaries in Health Care; Programs in Developing Countries. Baltimore: Johns Hopkins Press, 1972.

500. Gish, O. "Health Planning in Developing Countries." Journal of Development Studies 6 (July 1970).

501. _____. "Resource Allocation, Equality of Access, and Health." International Journal of Health Services 3 (August 1973).

502. Gwatkin, D. R. "Health and Nutrition in India." Report to the Ford Foundation, January 1974.

503. International Nutrition Planning Program. "Nutrition Program Development in Indonesia." Report prepared for the MIT-WHO project on Nutrition, Massachusetts Institute of Technology, May 1974.

504. Kraut, H., and Cremer, A. D., eds. Investigations into Health and Nutrition in East Africa. Munich: Weltforum Verlag, 1969.

505. Lele, U. J. "'The Green Revolution; Income Distribution and Nutrition." In P. L. White, ed. Proceedings - Western Hemisphere Nutrition Congress, III. Mount Kisco, N.Y.: Futura, 1972.

506. Levinson, F. J. "Food Fortification in Low Income Countries - A New Approach to an Old Standby." American Journal of Public Health 62 (May 1972).

507. _____. "Morinda: An Economic Analysis of Malnutrition Among Young Children in Rural India." Cornell/MIT, International Nutrition Policies Series, 1974.

508. McLachlan, G., and Douglas-Wilson, I., eds. Health Service Prospects, An International Survey. Boston: Little, Brown, 1973.

509. Malenbaum, W. "Health and Productivity in Poor Areas." In H.E. Klarman, ed. Empirical Studies in Health Economics: Proceedings. Baltimore: Johns Hopkins Press, 1970.

510. _____. "Health and Economic Expansion in Poor Lands." International Journal of Health Services 3 (1973).

511. Mellor, J. W. "Nutrition and Economic Growth." In A. Berg et al., eds. Nutrition, National Development and Planning. Cambridge, Mass.: MIT Press, 1973.

512. Navarro, V. "Health, Health Service and Health Planning in Cuba." International Journal of Health Services 2 (August 1972).

513. _____. "What Does Chile Mean? An Analysis of Events in the Health Sector Before, During and After Allende's Administration." Paper presented at the International Health Seminar, Harvard University, January 1974.

514. _____. "The Underdevelopment of Health or the Health of Underdevelopment." Paper presented at the Pan American Conference on Health Manpower Planning, Ottawa, September 1973.

515. Orr, E. The Use of Protein-Rich Foods for the Relief of Malnutrition in Developing Countries: An Analysis of Experience. London: Tropical Products Institute, 1972.

516. Oshima, H. T. "Food Consumption, Nutrition and Economic Development in Asian Countries." Economic Development and Cultural Change 15 (July 1967).

517. Ritchie, J. A. Learning Better Nutrition: A Second Study of Approaches and Techniques. Rome: Food and Agriculture Organization, 1967.

518. Roemer, M. I. The Organization of Medical Care Under Social Security. Geneva: International Labour Office, 1969.

519. Scrimshaw, N. S.; Taylor, C. E.; and Gordon, J. E. "Interactions of Nutrition and Infection." Monograph Series no. 57, World Health Organization, 1968.

520. Selowsky, M. "An Attempt to Estimate Rates of Return to Investment in Infant Nutrition." In W. Niskanen et al., eds. Benefit-Cost and Policy Analysis. Chicago: Aldine, 1973.

521. Selowsky, M., and Taylor, L. "The Economics of Malnourished Children: An Example of Disinvestment in Human Capital." Economic Development and Cultural Change 22 (October 1973).

522. Sidel, V. W. "The Barefoot Doctors of the People's Republic of China." The New England Journal of Medicine 286 (15 June 1972).

523. Sidel, V. W., and Sidel, R. "The Delivery of Medical Care in China." Scientific American 230 (April 1974).

524. Zshock, D. K. "Health Planning in Latin America." Development Digest 9 (July 1971).

II$_6$ - Policies Aimed at Eradicating Poverty

A. General Issues

525. Coombs, P. H., and Ahmed, M. Attacking Rural Poverty: How Nonformal Education Can Help. Baltimore: Johns Hopkins Press, 1974.

526. International Bank for Reconstruction and Development. "Rural Development." Sector Policy Paper, IBRD, 1975.

527. Jodha, N. S. "Special Programmes for the Rural Poor: The Constraining Framework." Economic and Political Weekly 8 (31 March 1973).

528. Kocher, J. E. Rural Development, Income Distribution and Fertility Decline. New York: Population Council, 1973.

529. Lampman, R. J. Ends and Means of Reducing Income Poverty. Chicago: Markham, 1971.

530. Lele, U. J. "Phase I Report of the African Rural Development Study (Parts I and II)." Mimeographed. Paper prepared for the Development Economics Department, International Bank for Reconstruction and Development, 1974.

531. Minhas, B. S. "Mass Poverty and The Strategy of Rural Development." Mimeographed. International Bank for Reconstruction, 1971.

532. Theobald, R., ed. The Guaranteed Income. New York: Doubleday, 1966.

See also Part I, I$_3$C(d); Part II, II$_7$A, B, C, and D; and 251, 457, 505, 653, 758.

B. How Public Works May Help

533. Donovan, W. G. "Rural Works and Employment: Description and Preliminary Analysis of a Land Army Project in Mysore State, India." Occasional Paper no. 60, Employment and Income Distribution Project, Department of Agricultural Economics, Cornell University, 1973.

534. Lewis, J. P. "The Public Works Approach to Low-End Poverty Problems: The New Potentialities of an Old Answer." Journal of Development Planning 5 (1972).

535. Rodgers, G. B. "Effects of Public Works on Rural Poverty." Economic and Political Weekly 8 (February 1973).

536. Thomas, J. W. et al. "An International Comparative Study of the Performance of Employment Creating Public Works Programs." Prepared for the International Bank for Reconstruction and Development by the Institute of International Development, Harvard University, August 1974.

II$_7$ - Redistribution in the Rural Sector

A. Agrarian Reform

537. Agency for International Development. Bibliography: Land Reform. AID Bibliography Series, 1 May 1970.

538. Berry, R. A. "Land Reform and Agricultural Income Distribution." Pakistan Development Review 11 (Spring 1971).

539. _____. "Presumptive Income Tax on Agricultural Land: The Case of Colombia." National Tax Journal 25 (June 1972).

540. Dorner, P. Land Reform and Economic Development. Baltimore: Johns Hopkins Press, 1972.

541. Dorner, P., and Felstehausen, H. "Agrarian Reform and Employment: The Colombian Case." International Labour Review 102 (September 1970).

542. Flores, E. "Issues of Land Reforms." Journal of Political Economy 78 (July-August 1970).

543. International Bank for Reconstruction and Development. "Land Reform." World Bank Paper, Rural Development Series, July 1974.

544. Lehmann, A. D., ed. Agrarian Reform and Agrarian Reformism. London: Faber & Faber, 1974.

545. Lindholm, R. "Land Taxation and Economic Development." Land Economics 41 (1965).

546. Lipton, M. "Towards a Theory of Land Reform." In A. D. Lehman, ed. Agrarian Reform and Agrarian Reformism. London: Faber & Faber, 1974.

547. Platt, K. B. et al. "Land Reform in Iran, Iraq, Pakistan, Turkey, Indonesia." Agency for International Development, Spring Review of Land Reform (June 1970).

548. Sazama, G., and Davis, H. "Land Taxation and Land Reform." Economic Development and Cultural Change 21 (July 1973).

549. Sinka, J. "Agrarian Reforms and Employment in Densely Populated Agrarian Economics: A Dissenting View." International Labour Review 108 (October 1973).

550. Sternberg, M. J. "Agrarian Reform and Employment, with Special Reference to Latin America." International Labour Review 96 (January-February 1967).

551. _____. "Agrarian Reform and Employment: Potential and Problems." International Labour Review 103 (May 1971).

552. Thirsk, W. "Some Aspects of Efficiency and Income Distribution in Colombia Land Reform." Paper no. 53, Program of Development Studies, Rice University, 1974.

See also Part I, $I_3C(g)$; and 177, 226, 227, 674, 677, 714, 716, 717, 718, 725, 727, 734, 771, 776, 787, 790, 792, 812.

B.   "Green Revolution"

553. Ahmad, Z. "The Social and Economic Implications of the Green Revolution in Asia." International Labour Review 105 (January 1972).

554. Byres, T. J. "The Dialectic of India's Green Revolution." South Asian Review 5 (January 1972).

555. Cepede, M. "Green Revolution and Employment." International Labour Review 105 (January 1972).

556. Dalrymple, D., and Jones, W. "Evaluating the 'Green Revolution'." Paper prepared for Joint Meeting of American Association for the Advancement of Science and Consejo Nacional de Ciencia y Technologia, Mexico, 20 June 1973.

557. Falcon, W. P. "The Green Revolution: Generations of Problems." American Journal of Agricultural Economics 52 (December 1970).

558. Griffin, K. The Political Economy of Agrarian Change--An Essay on the "Green Revolution". Cambridge, Mass.: Harvard University Press, 1974.

559. Johnston, B. F., and Cownie, J. "The Seed-Fertilizer Revolution and Labor Force Absorption." American Economic Review 59 (September 1969).

560. Ladejinsky, W. "Ironies of India's Green Revolution." Foreign Affairs 48 (July 1970).

561. Lele, U. J., and Mellor, J. W. "Jobs, Poverty and the 'Green Revolution'." International Affairs 48 (January 1972).

562. Tiesenhusen, W. "Green Revolution in Latin America: Income Effects, Policy Decisions." Monthly Labor Review 95 (March 1972).

563. Wharton, C. R., Jr. "The Green Revolution: Cornucopia or Pandora's Box?" Foreign Affairs 47 (April 1969).

See also 226, 227, 505, 573, 693.

C.   The Technological Problems--Factors Substitutability, Mechanization, etc.

564. Abercrombie, K. C. "Agricultural Mechanization and Employment in Latin America." _International Labour Review_ 106 (July 1972).

565. Banerji, R.; Butler, G.; and Yudelman, M. _Technological Change in Agriculture and Employment in Developing Countries_. Paris: OECD, 1971.

566. Bartsch, W. "Employment Effects of Alternative Technologies and Techniques in Asian Crop Production: A Survey of Evidence." Mimeographed. Geneva, International Labour Office, 1973.

567. Bell, C. "The Acquisition of Agricultural Technology: Its Determinants and Effects." _Journal of Development Studies_ 9 (October 1972).

568. Bieri, J.; Janvry, A. de; and Schmitz, A. "Agricultural Technology and the Distribution of Welfare Gains." _American Journal of Agricultural Economics_ 54 (December 1972).

569. Billings, M. H., and Singh, A. "Mechanization and Rural Employment: With Some Implications for Rural Income Distribution." _Economic and Political Weekly_ (June 1970).

570. Chaudri, D. P. "New Technologies and Income Distribution in Agriculture." In A. D. Lehmann, ed. _Agrarian Reform and Agrarian Reformism_. London: Faber & Faber, 1974.

571. Clayton, E. "Mechanization and Employment in East African Agriculture." _International Labour Review_ 105 (April 1972).

572. Gotsch, C. "Technical Change and the Distribution of Income in Rural Areas." _American Journal of Agricultural Economics_ 54 (May 1972).

573. Herdt, R. W., and Baker, E. A. "Agricultural Wages, Production and the High-Yielding Varieties." _Economic and Political Weekly_ 7 (25 March 1972).

574. Thirsk, W. "Income Distribution, Efficiency and the Experience of Colombian Farm Mechanization." Paper no. 33, Program of Development Studies, Rice University, 1972.

575. _____. "Ease of Factor Substitution in Agriculture." Paper no. 34, Program of Development Studies, Rice University, 1972.

See also Part II, II.7B; and 226, 227, 673, 688.

D.   Agricultural Prices and Credit, Wages and Social Security

576. Agency for International Development. _Bibliography: Agricultural Credit and Rural Savings_. AID Bibliography Series, December 1972.

577. Agency for International Development. _Spring Review on Small Farmer Credit_ (June 1973).

578. Echeverria, R. "A Note on the Distribution Effects of Chilean Agricultural Price Policies." Paper no. 15, Department of Agricultural Economics, Cornell University, 1959.

579. _____. "The Effect of Agricultural Price Policies on Intersectoral Income Transfers." Paper no. 30, Department of Agricultural Economics, Cornell University, 1970.

580. Mabro, R. "Employment and Wages in Dual Agriculture." Oxford Economic Papers 23 (November 1971).

581. Mellor, J. W. "The Functions of Agricultural Prices in Economic Development." Indian Journal of Agricultural Economics 23 (1968).

582. _____. "The Basis for Agricultural Price Policy." Paper no. 51, Department of Agricultural Economics, Cornell University, 1970.

583. Newberry, D. M. G. "The Choice of Contract in Peasant Agriculture." Paper presented at the Conference on Agriculture in Development Theory, Bellagio, May 1973.

584. Patten, R.; Dapice, B.; and Falcon, W. "An Experiment in Rural Employment Creation: Indonesia's Kabupaten Program." Development Advisory Service, no. 197, Harvard University, 1974.

585. Savy, R. "Social Security in Agriculture." Geneva, International Labour Office, 1972.

586. Thirsk, W. "Rural Credit and Income Distribution in Colombia." Paper no. 51, Program of Development Studies, Rice University, 1974.

See also 518, 671.

II$_8$ - Redistribution in the Urban Sector

A. Fostering Employment

a. General

587. International Labour Organization, Economic Research for the World Employment Programme. In A Collection of Papers by J. Tinbergen et al. International Labour Review 101 (May 1970).

588. International Labour Organization. Matching Employment Opportunities and Expectations: A Program of Action for Ceylon. Geneva: ILO, 1971.

589. _____. Employment, Incomes and Equality: A Strategy for Increasing Productive Employment in Kenya. Geneva: ILO, 1972.

590. _____. Towards Full Employment: A Programme for Colombia. Geneva: ILO, 1970.

591. _____. Employment and Income Policies for Iran. Geneva: ILO, 1973.

592. _____. Sharing in Development: A Programme of Development, Equity and Growth for the Philippines. Geneva: ILO, 1973.

593. _____. "Projection Model for a Full Employment Strategy." Technical Paper no. 3. Geneva: ILO, 1971.

594. Organization of American States. Guidelines for Achieving Maximum Employment and Growth in Latin-America. Washington, D.C.: Inter-American Economic and Social Council, OAS, 1973.

595. Seers, D. "New Approaches Suggested by the Colombian Employment Program." International Labour Review 102 (October 1970).

See also 241, 244, 246, 247, 254, 255, 257, 263, 268, 269, 270.

b.   The Wage Policy Issue

596. Berg, E. "Wages, Policy and Employment in Less Developed Countries." Paper presented to the Conference on Prospects for Employment Opportunities in the Nineteen Seventies, University of Cambridge, 1970.

597. Bjerke, K. "Some Income and Wage Distribution Theories: Summary and Comments." Weltwirtschaftliches Archiv 86 (1961).

598. _____. "Income and Wage Distribution. Part I: A Survey of the Literature." Review of Income and Wealth 16 (September 1970).

599. Cassidy, H. J. "The Rate of Change in the Size Distribution of Wages as a Vector." Review of Income and Wealth 15 (December 1969).

600. Dayal, S. "Wage Policy in India; A Critical Evaluation." Indian Journal of Industrial Relations (October 1970).

601. Edgren, G.; Faxier, K. O.; and Odhner, C. E. "Wages, Growth and the Distribution of Income." Swedish Journal of Economics 71 (September 1969).

602. Ericksson, J. "Wage Change and Employment Growth in Latin American Industry." Research Memorandum no. 36, Center for Developmental Economics, Williams College, 1970.

603. Harberger, A. "On Measuring the Social Opportunity Cost of Labor." International Labour Review 106 (June 1971).

604. Harcourt, G. "Some Cambridge Controversies in the Theory of Capital." Journal of Economic Literature 7 (June 1969).

605. Hicks, J. R. Theory of Wages. New York: St. Martin's Press, 1963.

606. Isbister, J. "Urban Wages and Employment in a Developing Economy: The Case of Mexico." Economic Development and Cultural Change 20 (October 1971).

607. Jackson, D., and Turner, H. A. "How to Provide More Employment in a Labor-Surplus Economy." International Labour Review 107 (June 1973).

608. Kilby, P. "Industrial Relations and Wage Determination: Failure of the Anglo-Saxon Model." Journal of Developing Areas 1 (July 1967).

609. Knight, J. B. "Wages and Employment in Developed and Underdeveloped Economies." Oxford Economic Papers 23 (March 1971).

610. Levinson, H. M. "Collective Bargaining and Income Distribution." American Economic Review 44 (May 1954).

611. Peterson, J.M., and Stewart, C. T., Jr. Employment Effects of Minimum Wages. Washington, D.C.: American Enterprise Institute for Public Policy Research, 1969.

612. Reder, M. W. "A Theory of Occupational Wage Differentials." American Economic Review 45 (1955).

613. Reynolds, L. "Wages and Employment in a Labor-Surplus Economy." American Economic Review 55 (March 1965).

614. Smith, A. D., ed. Wages Policy Issues in Economic Development. London: Macmillan, 1969.

615. Stiglitz, J. "Alternative Theories of Wage Determination and Unemployment in LDC's." Discussion Paper no. 335, Cowles Foundation , Yale University, 1973.

616. Taira, K. "Wages Differentials, in Developing Countries: A Survey of Findings." International Labour Review 99 (March 1966).

617. Taylor, S. D. "Discrimination and Occupational Wage Differences in the Market for Unskilled Labor." Industrial and Labor Relations Review 21 (April 1968).

618. Thormann, P. H. "The Rural-Urban Income Differential and Minimum Wage Fixing Criteria." International Labour Review 107 (August 1970).

619. Tidrick, G. M. "Wage Spillover and Unemployment in a Wage Gap Economy: The Jamaican Case." Research Memorandum no. 47, Center for Development Economics, Williams College, 1972.

620. Turner, H. A., and Jackson, D. A. S. "On the Determination of the General Wage Level: A World Analysis; or Unlimited Labour Forever." Economic Journal 80 (December 1970); criticized by Knight, J. B. and Mabro, R. In "A Comment" Economic Journal 82 (June 1972).

621. Wachtel, H. M., and Betsey, C. "Employment at Low Wages." Review of Economics and Statistics 54 (May 1972).

622. Weintraub, S. Some Aspects of Wage Theory and Policy. Philadelphia: Chilton, 1963.

See also Part I, $I_3C(i)$; and 178, 679, 680, 685, 695, 764, 788.

c. Fiscal Incentives

623. Ahluwalia, M. S. "Taxes, Subsidies and Employment." Quarterly Journal of Economics 88 (August 1973).

624. Ericksson, J. R. "Employment and Development: The Problem and Some Policy Alternatives." Mimeographed. Agency for International Development (October 1971).

625. International Labour Organization. "Fiscal Measures For Employment Promotion in Developing Countries." International Labour Review 106 (July 1972).

626. Lent, G. "Tax Incentives for the Promotion of Industrial Employment in Developing Countries." International Monetary Fund Staff Papers (1971).

627. Peacock, A., and Shaw, G. K. "Fiscal Policy and the Employment Problem in Less Developed Countries." Paris: OECD, 1971.

See also Part II, II$_2$A.

d. Capital/Labor Substitution

628. Arrow, K. et al. "Capital-Labor Substitution and Economic Efficiency." Review of Economics and Statistics 43 (August 1961).

629. Behrman, J. R. "Sectoral Elasticities of Substitution between Capital and Labor in a Developing Economy: Time Series Analysis in the Case of Postwar Chile." Econometrica 40 (March 1972).

630. Brown, M., and DeCany, J. S. "Technological Change and the Distribution of Income." International Economic Review 4 (September 1963).

631. Davison, J. P. et al. Productivity and Economic Incentives. London: George Allen and Unwin, 1958.

632. Dougherty, C. R. S. "Substitution and Structure of the Labor Force." Economic Journal 82 (March 1972).

633. Galenson, W., and Leibenstein, H. "Investment Criteria, Productivity, and Economic Development." Quarterly Journal of Economics 69 (August 1955).

634. Pack, H., and Todaro., M. "Technological Transfer, Labor Absorption and Economic Development." Oxford Economic Papers 21 (November 1969).

635. Robinson, J. "The Production Function and the Theory of Capital." Review of Economic Studies 21 (1953-54).

636. Salter, W. E. G. Productivity and Technical Change. London: Cambridge University Press, 1960.

637. Sen, A. K. Employment Policy and Technological Choice. Geneva: International Labour Office, 1973.

638. Sigurdson, J. "Technology and Employment in China." <u>World Development</u> 3 (March 1974).

639. Winston, G. C. "Capital Utilization, Investment and Employment: A Neo-Classical Model of Optimal Shift Work." Research Memorandum no. 51, Center for Development Economics, Williams College, 1972.

See also Part I, $I_3C(i)$.

e.   Trade

640. Aukrust, O. "Prim I - A Model of the Price and Income Distribution Mechanism of an Open Economy." <u>Income and Wealth</u> Series 16 (March 1970).

641. Berry, R. A. "International Trade Fluctuations and the Income and Wealth Fluctuations of Economic Groups." Discussion Paper no. 100, Economic Growth Center, Yale University, 1970.

642. Diaz-Alejandro, C. "Trade Policies and Economic Development." Discussion Paper no. 180, Economic Growth Center, Yale University, 1973.

643. Fei, J. C. H., and Ranis, G. "A Model of Growth and Employment in the Open Dualistic Economy: The Cases of Korea and Taiwan." Yale University.

644. Hsieh, C. "Measuring the Effects of Trade Expansion on Employment: A Review of Some Research." <u>International Labour Review</u> 107 (January 1973).

645. Keesing, D. B. "Income Distribution from Outward Looking Development Policies." Mimeographed. Center for Development Economics, Williams College, 1974.

646. Kemp, M. C. "Tariff, Income and Distribution." <u>Quarterly Journal of Economics</u> 70 (February 1956).

647. Little, I. M. D.; Scitovsky, T.; and Scott, M. <u>Industry and Trade in Some Developing Countries: A Comparative Study</u>. London: Oxford University Press, 1970.

648. Singer, H. W. et al. "Trade Liberalization, Employment and Income Distribution: A First Approach." Discussion Paper no. 31, Institute of Development Studies, University of Sussex.

649. Streeten, P. ed. <u>Trade Strategies for Development</u>. London: Macmillan, 1973.

650. Watanabe, S. "Exports and Employment: The Case of the Republic of Korea." <u>International Labour Review</u> 106 (December 1972).

B.   The Problem of Urbanization

651. Aaron, H., and Von Furstenberg, G. "The Inefficiency of Transfers In-Kind: The Case of Housing Assistance." <u>Western Economic Journal</u> 9 (June 1971).

652. Alonso, W. "Equity and Its Relation to Efficiency in Urbanization." Working Paper no. 78, University of California, 1968.

653. Bannister, J. B. "Urban Development and Housing the Urban Poor." Mimeographed. New Delhi: Agency for International Development, 1971.

654. Bloomberg, W., and Schmandt, H., eds. Power, Poverty and Urban Policy. Beverly Hills, Calif.: Urban Affairs Annual Reviews, 1968.

655. Brunn, S. D. "Urbanization in Developing Countries: An International Bibliography." Latin American Studies Center, Michigan State University, 1971.

656. Dalton, H. Some Aspects of the Inequality of Incomes in Modern Communities. New York: Dutton, 1920.

657. Ford Foundation. International Urbanization Surveys, including: "Jamaica" by J. W. Trowbridge; "Brazil" by J. A. Gardner; "Colombia, Venezuela, Peru, Chile" by J. Robin and F. Terzo; "Tropical Africa" by L. Rosser; "Nigeria" by L. Green and V. Milone; "Kenya" by L. Laurenti; "Zambia" by A. Simmance; "Morocco" by K. Johnson; "Turkey" by R. Keles; "India" by L. Rosser; "Thailand" by J. Romm. New York, 1973.

658. Herbert, J. D., and Van Huyck, A., eds. Urban Planning in Developing Countries. New York: Praeger, 1968.

659. Johnson, H. G., and Nuiskowski, P. "The Effects of Urbanization on the Distribution of Income: A General Equilibrium Approach." Quarterly Journal of Economics 84 (November 1970).

660. Nelson, J. "Public Housing, Illegal Settlements and the Growth of Colombian Cities." Report to the Urban and Regional Development Division of Agency for International Development, Bogota.

661. Nelson, J. N. "Sojourners vs. New Urbanites." In J. R. Harris and M. Weiner, eds. Cityward Migration in Developing Countries: Determinants and Consequences. Cambridge, Mass.: MIT Press, 1973.

662. Sovani, N. V. "The Analysis of Overurbanization." Economic Development as Cultural Change 12 (January 1964).

See also 342, 518, 721, 722.

II$_9$ - Some Implications for Development Planning and Projects Evaluation

663. Chenery, H. B. et al., eds. Studies in Development Planning. Cambridge, Mass." Harvard University Press. 1971.

664. Cohn, E. J., and Eriksson, J. R. "Employment and Income Distribution Objectives for A.I.D. Programs and Policies." Mimeographed. Policy Background Paper, Agency for International Development, October 1972.

665. Lal, D. "On Estimating Income Distribution Weights for Project Analysis." Occasional Paper no. 130, International Bank for Reconstruction and Development, 1972.

666. Lopes, F. L. "Inequality Planning in the Developing Economy." Ph.D. dissertation, Harvard University, 1972.

667. Mehmet, O. "Benefit-Cost Analysis of Alternative Techniques of Production for Employment Creation." International Labour Review 104 (July-August 1971).

668. Ranis, G.; Peck, M. J.; and Warner, J. S. "Growth, Employment and the Size Distribution of Income--Research Proposal to the International Bank for Reconstruction and Development." Economic Growth Center, Yale University, April 1973.

669. Rosenstein, R. P. "The Role of Income Distribution in Development Programs." Rivista Internazionale di Scienze Economiche e Commerciali 12 (May 1965).

See also 446, 453, 455, 456, 459, 461, 462, 464, 465, 466, 467, 468, 469, 477, 480, 492, 496, 500, 517, 520, 521, 526, 528, 530, 531, 534, 536, 543, 584, 587, 593, 594, 595, 603, 607, 613, 614, 620, 621, 623, 626, 627, 629, 637, 649, 658, 663, 697, 698.

PART III: COUNTRY STUDIES

III$_1$ - Asia

A.   India--A Case Study

670. Ahmed, M., and Bhattacharya, N. "Size Distribution of Per Capita Personal Income in India." Economica and Political Weekly, Special Number (August 1972).

671. Bardhan, P. K. "Variations in Agricultural Wages." Economic and Political Weekly 8 (26 May 1973).

672. _____. "Size Productivity and Returns to Scale: An Analysis of Farm Level Data in Indian Agriculture." Journal of Political Economy 81 (November-December 1973).

673. _____. "The Pattern of Income Distribution in India: A Review." Paper prepared for the Development Research Center, International Bank for Reconstruction and Development, 1973.

674. Bell, C. "Ideology and Economic Interests in Indian Land Reform." In A. D. Lehmann, ed. Agrarian Reform and Agrarian Reformism. London: Faber & Faber, 1974.

675. _____. "Inputs, Outputs and Distribution on Share Cropped Holdings in Purnea District, India." Mimeographed. International Bank for Reconstruction and Development, 1974.

676. Blaug, M.; Lydall, R.; and Woodhall, M. The Causes of Graduate Unemployment in India. London: Penguin Books, 1969.

677. Byres, T. "Land Reform, Industrialization and the Marketed Surplus in India: An Essay on the Power of Rural Bias." In A. D. Lehmann, ed. Agrarian Reform and Agrarian Reformism. London: Faber & Faber, 1974.

678. Evenson, R. "Employment in Indian Agriculture." Mimeographed. New Haven, 1973.

679. Jackson, D. "Wage Policy and Industrial Relations in India." Economic Journal 82 (March 1972).

680. Johr, C. K. Issues in Indian Labour Policy. New Delhi: Shri Ram Center for Industrial Relations, New India Press, 1969.

681. Krishna, R. "Unemployment in India." Indian Journal of Agricultural Economics 28 (January-March 1973).

682. Krishnamurthy, J. "Changes in Wages, Employment and Occupational Structure in India since 1951: A Partial and Preliminary Analysis." Paper presented at the Seminar on Income Distribution, Indian Statistical Institute, New Delhi, February 1971.

683. Ranadive, K. R. "The Equality of Income in India." Bulletin of the Oxford University Institute of Economics and Statistics 27 (May 1965).

684. _____. "Distribution of Income: Trends Since Planning." Paper presented at the Seminar on Income Distribution, Indian Statistical Institute, New Delhi, February 1971.

685. Sandesara, J. C., and Deshpande, L. K. Wage Policy and Wage Determination in India. Economic Series no. 20, University of Bombay, 1970.

686. Suisha, R. P. "An Analysis of Food Expenditures in India." Journal of Farm Economics 48 (February 1966).

687. Vaidyanathan, A. "Some Aspects of Inequalities in Living Standards in Rural India." Paper presented at the Seminar on Income Distribution, Indian Statistical Institute, New Delhi, February 1973.

688. Visaria, P., and Visaria, L. "Employment Planning for the Weaker Sections in Rural India." Economic and Political Weekly 8 (February 1973).

689. Zagoria, D. S. "A Note on Landlessness, Literacy and Agrarian Communism in India." Archives Europeemies oe Sociologie 13 (1972).

See also 137, 161, 173, 178, 202, 203, 206, 210, 212, 230, 288, 299, 327, 341, 370, 384, 416, 418, 440, 441, 491, 502, 507, 527, 531, 533, 540, 549, 554, 560, 581, 657, 671.

B.   Other Countries of South Asia

690. Azfar, J. "The Distribution of Income in Pakistan, 1966-1967." Pakistan Economic and Social Review (Spring 1973).

691. Bergan, A. "Personal Income Distribution and Personal Savings in Pakistan: 1963-1969." Pakistan Development Review 7 (Summer 1967)

692. Bose, S. R. "Trend of Real Income of the Rural Poor in East Pakistan, 1965-66." Pakistan Development Review (Autumn 1968).

693. Chaudhry, G. M. "Rural Income Distribution in Pakistan in the Green Revolution Perspective." Pakistan Development Review 13 (Autumn 1973).

694. Chen, L. C., ed. Disaster in Bangladesh. New York: Oxford University Press, 1973.

695. Khan, A. R. "What Has Been Happening to Real Wages in Pakistan?" Pakistan Development Review 7 (Autumn 1967).

696. Lewis, S. R., Jr. "Notes on Industrialization and Income Distribution in Pakistan." Research Memorandum no. 37, Center for Development Economics, Williams College, 1970.

697. MacEwan, A. Development Alternatives in Pakistan: A Multisectoral and Regional Analysis of Planning Problems. Harvard Economic Studies, Vol. 136. Cambridge, Mass.: Harvard University Press, 1971.

698. Papanek, G. F., and Falcon, W. P., eds. Development Policy: The Pakistan Experience. Cambridge, Mass.: Harvard University Press, 1971.

699. United Nations, Economic Commission for Asia and the Far East. The Distribution of Income in the ECAFE Region: Causal Factors and Remedial Policies. Bangkok: ECAFE Secretariat, December 1972.

700. _____. Distribution of Income in Wealth in Ceylon. Bangkok: ECAFE Secretariat, October 1971.

See also 210, 301, 382, 384, 588.

C. Southeast Asia.

701. Anand, S. "The Size Distribution of Income in Malaysia." Paper prepared for the Development Research Center, International Bank for Reconstruction and Development, 1974.

702. Encarnación, J. "Income Distribution in the Philippines: The Employed and the Self-Employed." Working Paper, International Labour Office, October 1974.

703. Lean, L. L. "The Pattern of Income Distribution in West Malaysia, 1957–1970." Working Paper, International Labour Office, July 1974.

704. McCleary, W. A. "Sources of Change in Distribution of Income in Thailand, 1962–63 and 1968–69." Discussion Paper Series, Faculty of Economics, Thammasar University (Thailand), August 1972.

705. Mijares, T. A., and Belarmino, L. C. "Some Notes on the Sources of Income Disparities Among Philippine Families." Journal of Philippine Statistics 24 (Fall 1973).

706. Parel, C. P. "The Distribution of Family Income in the Philippines." The Philippine Statistician 18 (1969).

707. Snodgrass, D. R. Bibliography on Income Distribution and Development in Malaysia and Elsewhere. Economic Planning, University of Kuala Lumpur (February 1971).

708. Stroup, R. H., and Marcis, R. G. "Analysis of Income and Expenditure Patterns in Rural South Vietnam." Western Economic Journal 6 (December 1967).

709. Sundrum. R. M. "Consumer Expenditures Patterns: An Analysis of the Socio Economic Surveys." Bulletin of Indonesian Economic Studies 9 (March 1973).

710. _____. "Household Income Patterns." Bulletin of Indonesian Economic Studies 10 (March 1974).

711. Vonder Mehden, F. R. "Communalism, Industrial Policy and Income Distribution in Malaysia." Paper presented at the Workshop on Income Distribution and Its Role in Development, Houston, Texas, Rice University, 25 April 1974.

See also 190, 210, 260, 280, 300, 368, 369, 377, 381, 503, 547, 584, 592, 657.

D.   China--A Case Study

712. Mizoguchi, T. "A Comparision of Levels of Consumption of Urban Households in Japan and in Mainland China - A Summary." Income and Wealth Series 15 (June 1969).

See also Part II, II$_1$B(b); and 475, 522, 523, 638.

E.   Other Asian Countries (including Taiwan)

713. Chang, K. "Distribution of Personal Income in Taiwan in 1953 and 1964." In K. Chang, ed. Economic Development in Taiwan. Taipei: Cheng Chung, 1968.

714. Dore, R. P. Land Reform in Japan. London: Oxford University Press, 1959.

715. Institute of Social Science, Chung-Ang University. Income Distribution and Consumption Structure in Korea. Seoul: 1966.

716. Koo, A. Y. C. "Agrarian Reform, Production and Employment in Taiwan." International Labour Review 104 (July-August 1971).

717. Misawa, T. "Agrarian Reform, Employment and Rural Incomes in Japan." International Labour Review 103 (April 1971).

718. Nakamura, J. I. "Meiji Land Reform, Redistribution of Income and Saving from Agriculture." Economic Development and Cultural Change 14 (July 1966).

719. Nose, N. "On the Structure of the National Income Distribution in Japan." Kobe Economic and Business Review 2 (1957); with a Supplement, "More on the Structure" 4 (1959).

720. Ohkawa, K. "Changes in National Income Distribution by Factor Share in Japan." In J. Marchal and B. Ducros, eds. The Distribution of National Income. New York: St. Martin's Press, 1968.

721. Paine, S. H. "Wage Differentials in the Japanese Manufacturing Sector." Oxford Economic Papers 23 (July 1971).

722. Taira, K. The Dynamics of Japanese Wage Differentials, 1881-1959. New York: Columbia University Press, 1961.

723. Wada, R. O. "Changes in the Size Distribution of Income in Postwar Japan." Working Paper, International Labour Office, October 1974.

See also 153, 165, 210, 245, 249, 250, 259, 260, 263, 266, 286, 377, 489, 516, 542, 553, 566, 643, 650, 712.

III$_2$ - Middle East

724. Ben-Shahar, H., and Sandberg, M. "Economic and Institutional Effects on Income Distribution: The Case of Israel." Public Finance 22 (1967).

725. Foster, P.; Simmons, J. G.; and Platt, K. B. "Land Reform in Algeria, Tunisia, the United Arab Republic." Agency for International Development, Spring Review of Land Reform, June 1970.

726. Hansen, B., and Marzouk, G. Development and Economic Policy in the UAR (Egypt). Amsterdam: North-Holland, 1965.

727. Warriner, D. "Employment and Income Aspects of Recent Agrarian Reforms in the Middle East." International Labour Review 101 (June 1970).

See also 266, 302, 547, 591, 657.

III$_3$ - Africa

728. Ellman, A. O. "Progress, Problems and Prospects in Ujamad Development in Tanzania." Paper no. 72.18, Economic Research Bureau, University of Dar es Salaam, 1972.

729. Ewusi, K. "The Distribution of Monetary Incomes in Ghana." Technical Publication no. 14, Institute of Statistical, Social and Economic Research, University of Ghana, 1971.

730. Frank, C., Jr. "Urban Unemployment and Economic Growth in Africa." Discussion Paper no. 120, Economic Growth Center, Yale University, 1968.

731. _____. "The Problem of Unemployment in Africa." In R. C. Ridker and H. Lubell, eds. Employment and Unemployment Problems of the Near East and South Asia. New Delhi: Vikas, 1971.

732. Chai, D. "Incomes Policy in Kenya: Need, Criteria, and Machinery." East African Economic Review (June 1967).

733. Hart, K. "Informal Income Opportunities and the Structure of Urban Employment in Ghana." Journal of Modern African Studies 11 (March 1973).

734. Herz, B. K., and Parsons, K. H. "Land Reform in Kenya: The Land Tenure Problem in Nigeria." Agency for International Development, Spring Review of Land Reform (June 1970).

735. Jackson, D. "Economic Development and Income Distribution in Eastern Africa." The Journal of Modern African Studies (1971).

736. Knight, J. B. "Earnings, Employment, Education and Income Distribution in Uganda." Bulletin of the Oxford University Institute of Economics and Statistics 30 (November 1968).

737. _____. "A Theory of Income Distribution in South Africa." Bulletin of the Oxford University Institute of Economics and Statistics 26 (November 1964).

738. Medholm, C. "Research on Employment in the Rural Non-Farm Sector in Africa." Africa Research Employment Paper no. 4, Michigan State University, 1973.

739. Phillips, A. O., and Teriba, O. "Income Distribution and National Integration." Michigan Journal of Economic and Social Studies 15 (March 1971).

740. Sabot, R. H. "Education, Income Distribution and Rates of Urban Migration in Tanzania." Paper no. 72.6 Economic Research Bureau, University of Dar es Salaam, 1972.

741. Singer, H. W., and Reynolds, S. "Aspects of the Distribution of Income and Wealth in Kenya." Paper presented at UNESCO Conference on the Social Science Project on Human Resources Indicators, University of Sussex, November 1973.

See also 235, 240, 367, 383, 386, 504, 561, 571, 589, 608, 657.

III$_4$ - Americas

A. The United States--A Case Study

742. Aaron, H. Why is Welfare So Hard To Reform? Washington, D.C.: The Brookings Institution, 1973.

743. Aaron, H., and McGuire, M. "Public Goods and Income Redistribution." Econometrica 38 (November 1970).

744. Ackerman, F. et al. "Income Distribution in the United States." Review of Radical Political Economy 3 (Summer 1971).

745. _____. "The Extent of Income Inequality in the United States." In T. E. Weiskopf et al., eds. The Capitalist System. Englewood Cliffs: Prentice-Hall, 1972.

746. Bowman, M. J. "A Graphical Analysis of Personal Income Distribution in the United States." American Economic Review 35 (September 1965).

747. Brady, D. S. "Age and Income Distribution." Research report no. 8, U.S. Department of Health Education and Welfare Social Security Administration, 1965.

748. Budd, E. C. "Postwar Changes in the Size Distribution of Income in the United States." American Economic Review 60 (May 1970).

749. Duncan, O. D. "Inheritance of Poverty or Inheritance of Race?" In D. P. Moynihan, ed. On Understanding Poverty. New York: Basic Books, 1968.

750. Farbman, M. "An Econometric Analysis of Variations in the Size Distribution of Family Incomes in U.S. Cities, 1960." Ph.D. dissertation, Cornell University, 1973.

751. Harrington, M. The Other America. New York: Penguin Books, 1962.

752. Johnson, D. G. "The Functional Distribution of Income in the United States, 1850-1952." Review of Economics and Statistics 36 (May 1954).

753. Miller, H. P. "Income Distribution in the United States." Washington, D.C.: Bureau of the Census With Social Science Research Council, 1966.

754. _____. "Lifetime Income and Economic Growth." American Economic Review 55 (September 1965).

755. Mincer, J., and Chiswick, B. R. "Time Series Changes in Personal Income Inequality in the United States from 1939, with Projections to 1985." Journal of Political Economy 81 (1973).

756. Pechman. J. A. "Distribution of Federal and State Income Taxes by Income Classes." Journal of Finance 27 (May 1972).

757. Solow, R. M. "Income Inequality Since the War." In E. Budd, ed. Inequality and Poverty. New York: Norton, 1968.

758. Tumin, M. M. Social Stratification: The Forms and Functions of Inequality. Englewood Cliffs: Prentice-Hall, 1967.

759. Weisbrod, B. A. "Collective Action and the Distribution of Income: A Conceptual Approach." In Joint Economic Committee, United States Congress. The Analysis and Evaluation of Public Expenditure: The PPB System. Washington, D.C.: U.S. Government Printing Office, 1966.

See also 20, 75, 83, 86, 87, 101, 104, 107, 111, 112, 136, 168, 174, 181, 182, 185, 186, 187, 192, 194, 196, 198, 201, 207, 208, 211, 214, 221, 222, 314, 318, 348, 364, 382, 404, 406, 426, 436, 437, 438, 439, 445, 453, 529, 532, 651.

B. Central America and the Caribbean

760. Ahiram, E. "Distribution of Income in Trinidad-Tobago and Comparison with Distribution Income in Jamaica." Social and Economic Studies 15 (June 1966).

761. Andic, F. M. "Distribution of Family Incomes in Puerto Rico." Caribbean Monograph Series no. 1, University of Puerto Rico, 1964.

762. Bernardo, R. The Theory of Moral Incentives in Cuba. University, Ala.: University of Alabama Press, 1971.

763. Cole, W. E., and Sanders, R. D. "Income Distribution, Profits and Savings in the Recent Economic Experience of Mexico." Inter-American Economic Affairs 24 (Autumn 1970).

764. Everett, M. "The Evolution of the Mexican Wage Structure." Mimeographed. El Colegio de Mexico, 1967.

765. Hansen, R. D. The Politics of Mexican Development. Baltimore: Johns Hopkins Press, 1971.

766. Navarette, I. "La Distribución del Ingreso en Mexico." In El Perfil de Mexico en 198C. Mexico: Siglo XXI, 1970.

767. Seers, D., ed. Cuba: The Economic and Social Revolution. Chapel Hill: University of North Carolina Press, 1964.

768. Singer, M. Growth, Equality and the Mexican Experience. Austin: University of Texas Press, 1969.

769. Van Ginneken, W. "Mexican Income Distribution Within and Between Rural and Urban Areas." Working Paper, International Labour Office, July 1974.

See also 204, 231, 261, 287, 291, 305, 313, 374, 382, 387, 512, 542, 556, 606, 619, 657.

C. South America

a. General

770. Cordova, E. "Labor Legislation and Latin American Development: A Preliminary Review." International Labour Review 106 (November 1972).

771. Dorner, P., ed. "Land Reform in Latin America: Issues and Cases." Land Economics Monograph no. 3, University of Wisconsin, 1971.

772. Feder, E. The Rape of the Peasantry: Latin America's Landholding System. New York: Doubleday, Anchor Books, 1971.

773. Higgins, B. "Social Aspects of Economic Development in Latin America." Paris: UNESCO, 1963.

774. Landau, L. "Determinants of Savings in Latin American." In H. B. Chenery, ed. Studies in Development Planning. Cambridge, Mass.: Harvard University Press, 1971.

775. Ramos, J. Labor and Development in Latin America. New York: Columbia University Press, 1970.

See also 92, 204, 232, 249, 256, 288, 291, 362, 372, 409, 420, 429, 432, 454, 524, 544, 550, 562, 564, 602, 641, 657.

b. Brazil--A Case Study

776. Cline, W. Economic Consequences of a Land Reform in Brazil. Amsterdam: North-Holland, 1970.

777. Fishlow, A. "Brazilian Size Distribution of Income." American Economic Association, Papers and Proceedings (1971)

778. _____. "Brazilian Income Size Distribution: Another Look." Mimeographed. 1973.

779. Langoni, C. G. "Income Distribution and Economic Development in Brazil." Conjuntura Economica 27 (September 1973). (Translated by BNH Information Office, Rio de Janeiro, 1974).

780. Morley, S. A., and Williamson, J. G. "The Impact of Demand on Labor Absorption and the Distribution of Earnings: The Case of Brazil." Discussion Paper no. 39, Program of Development Studies, Rice University, 1973.

781. Patrick, F., and Kehrberg, E. "Costs and Returns of Education in the Agricultural Areas of Eastern Brazil." American Journal of Agricultural Economics 55 (May 1973).

782. Sahota, G. "The Distribution of Tax Burden Among Different Education Classes in Brazil." Economic Development and Cultural Change 19 (April 1971).

783. Serra, J., and Tawares, M. C. "Beyond Stagnation: A Discussion on the Nature of Recent Development in Brazil." In J. Petras, ed. Latin America: From Dependence to Revolution. New York: John Wiley, 1973.

784. Silva, J. H. G. "Disguised Unemployment in a Subsistence Economy." Discussion Paper no. 23, Program of Development Studies, Rice University, 1972.

785. Wells, J. "Distribution of Earnings, Growth and Structure of Demand in Brazil, 1959-1971." Working Paper no. 11, Center of Latin American Studies, University of Cambridge, 1972.

See also 21, 92, 176, 232, 256, 276, 277, 281, 287, 291, 298, 309, 362, 380, 788.

c. Other Countries in South America

786. Berry, R. A., and Urrutia, M. Income Distribution and Government Policy in Colombia. New Haven: Yale University Press, forthcoming.

787. Clark, R. J. "Land Reform in Bolivia, Ecuador, Peru." Agency for International Development, Spring Review of Land Reform (June 1970).

788. Erickson, K. P.; Peppe, P.; and Spalding, H. "Research on the Urban Working Class and Organized Labor in Argentina, Brazil and Chile: What is Left to be Done?" Latin American Research Review 9 (Summer 1974).

789. Hirschman, A.O. "Land Use and Land Reform in Colombia." In A. O. Hirschman, Ed. Journeys Towards Progress. New York: Twentieth Century Fund, 1963.

790. Horton, D. "Land Reform and Reform Enterprises in Peru." Mimeographed. International Bank for Reconstruction and Development, 1974.

791. Hunt, S. "Distribution, Growth and Government Economic Behavior in Peru." In G. Ranis, ed. Government and Economic Development. New Haven: Yale University Press, 1971.

792. Lehmann, A. D. "Political Incorporation Versus Political Stability: The Case of the Chilean Agrarian Reform, 1965-1970." Journal of Development Studies 7 (July 1971).

793. Shultz, T. W. "Returns to Education in Bogota, Colombia." RM-5645-AID, Rand Corporation, 1973.

794. Urrutia, M. The Development of the Colombian Labor Movement. New Haven: Yale University Press, 1969.

795. Webb, R. "Trends in Real Income in Peru, 1950-1966." Discussion Paper no. 41, Research Program in Economic Development, Princeton University, 1974.

796. _____. Government Policy and the Distribution of Income in Peru, 1963-1973. Cambridge, Mass.: Harvard University Press, 1977.

See also 232, 243, 287, 291, 303, 373, 374, 387, 453, 457, 461, 462, 513, 520, 521, 539, 541, 542, 552, 574, 578, 579, 586, 590, 595, 623, 657, 660.

III$_5$ - Europe

A. Western Europe

797. Aukrust, O. "Trends and Cycles in Norwegian Income Shares." Income and Wealth Series 6 (1957).

798. Bjerke, K. "Redistribution of Income in Denmark Before and After the War." Income and Wealth Series 10 (1964).

799. Comens, C. A., and Palthe, T. H. "The Distribution of Income Between Socio Economic Groups in the Netherlands." Review of Income and Wealth 16 (December 1970).

800. Feinstein, C. H. "Changes in the Distribution of the National Income in the United Kingdom since 1860." In J. Marchal and B. Ducros, eds. The Distribution of National Income. New York: St. Martin's Press, 1968.

801. Lecaillon, J. "Changes in the Distribution of Income in the French Economy." In J. Marchal and B. Ducros, eds. The Distribution of National Income. New York: St. Martin's Press, 1968.

802. Mitchell, D. J. B. "Income Policy and the Labor Market in France." Industrial and Labor Relations Review 25 (April 1972).

803. Prest, A. R., and Stark, T. "Some Aspects of Income Distribution in the United Kingdom since World War II." Manchester School of Economic and Social Studies (September 1967).

804. Rothschild, K. W. Development of Income Distribution by Factor Shares in Western Europe. Paris: OECD, 1971.

805. Soltow, L. Towards Income Equality in Norway. Madison: University of Wisconsin Press, 1965.

806. _____. "Long-Run Changes in British Income Inequality." Economic History Review 21 (April 1968).

807. Thatcher, A. R. "The Distribution of Earnings of Employees in Great Britain." Journal of the Royal Statistical Society 131, pt. 2 (1968).

808. Ulizzi, A. "Income, Saving and Structure of Wealth in Italian Households in 1967." Review of Economic Conditions in Italy (July 1969).

See also 371 and 382.

B.   USSR and Eastern Europe

809. Adam, J. "Wage Differentials in Czechoslovakia." Industrial Relations 11 (May 1972).

810. Apel, H. "Income and Its Distribution in East Germany." Challenge 8 (February 1965).

811. Bruzek, A. "The Main Factors and Methods of the Income Distribution in the Czechoslovak Socialist Republic." In J. Marchal and B. Ducros, eds. The Distribution of National Income. New York: St. Martin's Press, 1968.

812. Dovring, F., and McEntire, D. "Land Reform in Hungary, Italy, Yugoslavia." Agency for International Development, Spring Review of Land Reform (June 1970).

813. Kabaj, M. "Evolution of the Incentives System in USSR Industry." International Labour Review 94 (July 1966).

814. Sefer, B. "Income Distribution in Yugoslavia." International Labour Review 97 (April 1968).

See also 167 and 417.

III$_6$ - Oceania (Australia)

815. Podder, N. "Distribution of Household Income in Australia." Economic Record 48 (June 1972).

PART IV: BIBLIOGRAPHIES ON INCOME DISTRIBUTION
AND RELATED SUBJECTS

816. Agency for International Development. Bibliography: Social Indicators.
AID Bibliography Series, 15 December 1972.

817. Groupo de Trabajo sobre Estadisticas de la Distribución del Ingresso,
el Consumno y la Riqueza. Bibliografia. Santiajo, Chile: Documento
de Referencia no. 10 (November 1971).

818. Gruber, J. "A Bibliography on Income Distribution." Institute for
Social and Policy Studies, Yale University, December 1974.

819. International Labour Office, World Employment Programme. "Bibliography
on Income Distribution." Geneva: ILO, September 1973.

See also on related subjects--36, 421, 452, 459, 468, 481, 483, 484, 537,
576, 655, 707.